Children of the Revolution

The Glam Rock Story 1970–75

DAVE THOMPSON

First published in Great Britain in 2010 by Cherry Red Books (a division of Cherry Red Records Ltd), Power Road Studios, 114 Power Road, Chiswick, London W4 5PY

ISBN: 978 1 901447 47 7

Designed by: Dave Johnson
Printed in the UK by Ashford Colour Press

Children of the Revolution

The Glam Rock Story 1970–75

DAVE THOMPSON

PREFACE

Legend has it that David Bowie and Ronnie Wood were once overheard in a Los Angeles hotel, discussing David's role as the King of Glam Rock.

'I'm very proud of that tag, 'the Thin White one said. 'That's what the public made me, and that's what I am.'

Wood laughed. 'Yeah, the reigning king.'

He handed Bowie a slip of paper. 'I don't like giving people tags, but here.'

Bowie glanced down. It was a $15 price tag with 'The King of Glam Rock' scrawled on the back. He was horrified.

'Fifteen dollars?' And then he smiled. 'Well, I guess Glam Rock was always pretty cheap.'

What's included?

Not everything, that's for certain. Nobody has, because nobody could, ever catalogue every Glam record released in the UK between 1970 and 1975, simply because nobody can ever agree on what a Glam record is. Websites such as Robin Wills' redoubtable http://purepop1.uk/blogspot and the leviathan http://www.45cat.com both serve up startling overviews of the sheer wealth of material being thrown into the marketplace during this period and it is for readers and collectors alone to decide what is and isn't Glam.

Or bubblegum, or pub rock, or belated psych-pop, or proto-punk, or any of the myriad other genres we now declare were burgeoning then. And which will also have slipped into these pages.

I certainly make no distinction between what might be called 'High' Glam (Bowie, Cockney Rebel, the Doctors of Madness, Be Bop Deluxe etc) and 'Low' Glam (Slade, Chinnichap, the Glitters etc…with Marc Bolan walking the thin line between the two). Rather, I agree with Virginia Scott, Mellotron Queen of Beggars Opera (yes, they're in here too) when she told me, 'Glam Rock was fashion. I am not so sure that what is now called *glam* was any different from a lot of the progressive rock at the time except that the songs were shorter/more accessible and ultimately more banal and Dadaistic.'

It is, she reminds us, simply 'a question of stylistic tectonics' whose plates were noisily siding into punk.

Instead, *Glam Rock: The Definitive Chronology* attempts to delineate the widest boundaries within which Glam could be found, both musically, visually and, for readers of a certain age, culturally. Several of the groups and many of the records referenced here really can't be described as 'true' Glam Rock. Some of the artists themselves would furiously deny any association whatsoever with the genre. But they are guilty by association, chronologically caged within a genre that may not have been of their own making, but which allowed them to make something of themselves all the same.

The layout of the book is simple. It can be used as a straightforward A-Z: go to the index at the front of the book, find the band you wish to look up and then follow the month-by-month references from there. It can be left in the bathroom, to be randomly dipped in and out of as and when nature calls.

Or, and this would be my preference, you could start at the beginning, read through to the end and emerge with an understanding of the era *not* as a piece of ancient pop history, littered with theories, condemnations and thoughts; not as an encyclopaedia in which every band has its own nice, neat entry but as it actually unfurled, with bands reacting to one another's releases, with flops and follow-ups falling into place in the context of the other acts they were all competing against.

Read it like that, and it's one helluva story.

At the end of each month, additional listings are compiled under the titles On The Radio, On The Box and On The Shelves. The first notes 'live' radio sessions recorded by the bands in the book for and broadcast by the BBC, the second notes their television appearances broadcast during that month and the third is concerned with other record releases of interest. These listings are not inclusive or complete; other artists played sessions, other artists appeared on the listed shows and other artists released records. But they weren't Glam.

Another point to bear in mind is that this book is only concerned with British Glam in Britain. There was a wealth of bands springing up on the continent and beyond, usually in response to the UK example and another entire book could be devoted to their activities and histories. Likewise the United States, where Glam scenes flourished in both the New York and Los Angeles undergrounds and burbled elsewhere too.

Of course, these restrictions are abandoned when it suits me, but that in turn requires the band in question to have made some sort of impact on British shores – Jobriath being advertised on the back of a London bus, the New York Dolls on the *Old Grey Whistle Test*, Arrows' Alan Merrill trailing Japanese stardom and so on.

For the most part, though, I refer you back to that immortal *Times* headline from 1909 (or so). 'Fog in channel, continent cut off.'

I hope that you have as much fun reading this book as I did writing it and, maybe, if we all wish *real* hard, the last 40 or so years will roll back right now and we can relive it.

Are you ready, Steve?

Contents

Dates below band names correspond to entries in the main text.

ELECTRIC DOLLS
September 1973

ENO, BRIAN
January 1974
February 1974
March 1974
June 1974
November 1974
July 1975
See also ROXY MUSIC, WINKIES

ESSEX, DAVID
April 1973
August 1973
November 1973
May 1974
October 1974
December 1974
July 1975
September 1975
November 1975
See also THAT'LL BE THE DAY

FANCY
June 1974
October 1974
January 1975
March 1975
November 1975

FANTASY
September 1973

FARM
February 1974

FARNHAM, JOHNNY
June 1973

FELIX, JULIE
April 1970

FERRY, BRYAN
September 1973
October 1973
May 1974
July 1974
August 1974
See also ROXY MUSIC

FINNIUS FOGG
March 1975

FLAME
May 1975
September 1975

FLASCHER, WILLY
March 1974

FLOATING OPERA
August 1974

FOX
February 1975
May 1975
October 1975

FRENZY
December 1975

FUZZ
June 1974

GEORDIE
September 1972
March 1973
June 1973
August 1973
November 1973
August 1974
October 1974
February 1975
July 1975

GIDIAN'S LEAGUE
January 1972

GIGGLES
April 1974
September 1974
November 1974

GILLESPIE, DANA
February 1974
March 1974
January 1975

GLEN
July 1973

GLITTER, GARY
March 1972
June 1972
August 1972
September 1972
October 1972
January 1973
March 1973
June 1973
July 1973
November 1973
March 1974
June 1974
November 1974
April 1975
June 1975
October 1975
November 1975
See also GLITTER BAND

GLITTER BAND
November 1972
March 1974
July 1974
September 1974
October 1974
January 1975
April 1975
August 1975
September 1975
December 1975
See also GARY GLITTER, JOHN ROSSALL

GO GO THUNDER
January 1975

GODZILLA & YELLOW GYPSY
December 1972
July 1973
See also ALAN MERRILL, ARROWS, VODKA COLLINS

GRANNY
January 1974

GREY, MAL & FLIGHT 56
April 1975

GRUDGE
April 1973
See also PAUL ST JOHN, SPIV

GRUMBLE
June 1973

GRUNT FUTTOCK
January 1972

HAMMERHEAD
April 1973

HAMMERSMITH GORILLAS
September 1974

HARLEY, STEVE
See also COCKNEY REBEL

HARLEY QUINNE
October 1972
November 1973

HEAVEN
See also HEAVY METAL KIDS

HEAVY METAL KIDS
August 1974
July 1974
June 1975
October 1975
November 1975
See also BIGGLES

HECTOR
November 1973
June 1974

HELLO
April 1972
June 1972
October 1972
November 1972
September 1973
October 1974
February 1975
May 1975
August 1975
See also GLITTER BAND

HELTER SKELTER
See also HAMMERSMITH GORILLAS

HENN, PETER
September 1973

HOBOKIN
July 1973

HODGE, CHRIS
March 1974

HOLLYWOOD BRATS
September 1973

HOT CHOCOLATE
August 1970

HOT ROCKS
September 1973

HOT ROD
May 1973

HOTLEGS
July 1970
January 1971
March 1971
September 1971
See also 10cc

HUNTER, IAN
March 1975
April 1975
July 1975
See also MICK RONSON, MOTT THE HOOPLE

MIKE HURST
See also FANCY, NEW WORLD, SHOWADDYWADDY

IGGY AND THE STOOGES
July 1972
May 1973

IRON CROSS
July 1972

IRON VIRGIN
February 1974
June 1974

JACK AND THE GIANTKILLERS
July 1974

JACKSON FIVE
January 1970

JAMES, SALLY
October 1974

JET
August 1974
March 1975
May 1975
See also JOOK, ROXY MUSIC, SPARKS

JETS
October 1973

JOBRIATH
December 1973
May 1974
August 1974
September 1974
October 1975

JOHN, ELTON
March 1970
December 1970
April 1972
August 1972
October 1972
January 1973
June 1973
December 1973

JOOK
October 1972
March 1973
July 1973
November 1973
April 1974
May 1974

JUMPING BEAN BAG
November 1975

KENNY
November 1974
February 1975

KENNY cont.
May 1975
August 1975

KENTON, RIK
November 1974
See also ROXY MUSIC

KID DYNAMITE
September 1973

KIDROCK
September 1973

KINDNESS
October 1974
See also SMOKEY

KINKS
June 1970
See also PERCY

KISS
February 1974
March 1974
October 1974
March 1975
September 1975

KRISTINE SPARKLE
September 1973

MIKE LEANDER
See also GARY GLITTER, GLITTER BAND, HELLO, JET

LIGHT FANTASTIC
February 1973
November 1973
See also SWEET

LIEUTENANT PIGEON
February 1972
August 1972
February 1973
See also STAVELY MAKEPEACE

LIFT OFF WITH AYSHEA
See also AYSHEA BROUGH

LONDON ROCK AND ROLL REVIVAL SHOW
August 1972
See also GARY GLITTER, WIZZARD

LULU
January 1974
See also DAVID BOWIE

LUREX, LARRY
June 1973
See also QUEEN

MACKAY, ANDY
August 1974
See also ROXY MUSIC

MAINMAN
See also CHERRY VANILLA, DANA GILLESPIE, IGGY POP, LOU REED, LULU, MOTT THE HOOPLE, PORK, MICK RONSON, SPIDERS FROM MARS, WAYNE COUNTY

MANSFIELD, MIKE
See also SUPERSONIC

MEDICINE HEAD
January 1971

MEN
April 1973

MERRILL, ALAN
November 1971
See also ARROWS, GODZILLA & YELLOW GYPSY, STREAK, VODKA COLLINS

MIGHTY 'EM
September 1973

MILK'N'COOKIES
February 1975
July 1974

MICKIE MOST
See also ARROWS, JULIE FELIX, MUD, NEW WORLD, PETER NOONE, COZY POWELL, RAK RECORDS, CHRIS SPEDDING, SMOKEY

MOTT
August 1975
October 1975
See also MOTT THE HOOPLE

MOTT THE HOOPLE
July 1972
August 1972
October 1972
November 1972
May 1973
July 1973
August 1973
November 1973
March 1974
April 1974
June 1974
November 1974
See also DAVID BOWIE, IAN HUNTER, MICK RONSON, MOTT

MOUNTAIN CHILD
May 1975

MR BIG
July 1974
November 1974
March 1975
November 1975

MUD
August 1970
November 1970
January 1973
June 1973
October 1973
January 1974
April 1974
July 1974
September 1974
November 1974
February 1975
April 1975
June 1975
August 1975
September 1975
October 1975
November 1975
December 1975

SLADE cont.
February 1975
April 1975
May 1975
November 1975

SLEAZE
June 1975

SLIK
October 1974
March 1975
November 1975

SLOPLY BELLYWELL
January 1975

SMALL WONDER
January 1975

SMILEY
December 1973

SMILEY, BRETT
September 1974

SMOKE
January 1974

SMOKEY/SMOKIE
October 1974
April 1975
See also KINDNESS

SMOOTH LOSER
August 1972

SOHO JETS
January 1975
June 1975

SPARKS
November 1972
April 1974
May 1974
June 1974
July 1974
October 1974
November 1974
January 1975

SPARKS cont.
July 1975
September 1975
October 1975

SPEDDING, CHRIS
August 1975
December 1975

SPIDERS FROM MARS
November 1975
See also DAVID BOWIE

SPIV
October 1973
See also PAUL ST JOHN, GRUDGE

SPUNKY SPIDER
October 1973

STARDUST
December 1974
See also DAVID ESSEX

ST CECILIA
June 1971
January 1972
April 1972

ST CLEMENT WELLS
June 1973

ST JOHN, PAUL
October 1972
See also GRUDGE, SPIV

STARBUCK
April 1973
October 1973
April 1974
July 1974
See also SHAMBLES, TRUE ADVENTURE

ALVIN STARDUST
October 1973
February 1974
March 1974
April 1974
August 1974

ALVIN STARDUST cont.
November 1974
February 1975
June 1975
August 1975
See also ALVIN'S HEARTBEATS

STAVELY MAKEPEACE
December 1970
March 1972
April 1972
October 1972
January 1973
April 1973
November 1974
See also LIEUTENANT PIGEON

STEPHEN
November 1974

STREAK
March 1973
See also ARROWS

STREAKERS
April 1974

STUMPY
August 1973

SUGAR CANDY
April 1975

SUPERSONIC
March 1975

SWEET
December 1970
January 1971
April 1971
May 1971
August 1971
October 1971
November 1971
February 1972
March 1972
June 1972
July 1972
September 1972
November 1972

VILLAIN
Octobcr 1975

VODKA COLLINS
November 1972
November 1973
See also ALAN MERRILL, GODZILLA & YELLOW GYPSY, ARROWS

WARWICK
July 1975

WASHINGTON FLYERS
July 1974

WELLS, BRIAN
October 1972

WHISTLE
April 1973

WIG WAM
July 1972

WILD ANGELS
October 1973

WILDE, MARTY
June 1974
See also RICKY WILDE, ZAPPO

WILDE, RICKY
November 1972
February 1973
February 1974
March 1974
July 1974

WILDFIRE
January 1975

WINKIES
January 1974
February 1974
March 1974
September 1974
February 1975
See also BRIAN ENO

WINSTON
September 1973

WIZZARD
August 1972
November 1972
March 1973
April 1973
July 1973
December 1973
March 1974

WORTH
January 1972
See also TIGER

X CERTIFICATE
September 1973

YELLOW BIRD
October 1974

YOUNG, MURIEL
See also AYSHEA BROUGH, SHANG-A-LANG, ARROWS

ZAKATEK
March 1973
October 1973
See also LYNSEY DE PAUL

ZAPPO
October 1973
See also MARTY WILDE

ZIG ZAG
October 1974

ZIPPERS
June 1974

INTRODUCTION

It was Marc Bolan who set the glitter ball rolling. Five years out from his debut single ('The Wizard' in 1965), two years on from his first mini-hit as the leader of the Tyrannosaurus Rex duo ('Debora' in 1968), Bolan's transition from underground anti-hero to superstar demi-god completely shattered all predictions and preoccupations for the mewling newborn decade.

In an age when Rock was serious and Fun was for the bubblegum babies, Marc flounced on stage in sequins and satin, blasting out a joyous celebration of youth and potency. He dragged rock'n'roll out of the grave, at the same time as screwing down the coffin lid on pretension and reserve.

And with just one flick of his corkscrew curls, he ushered in the most invigorating high that British Pop had or would ever experience.

How did he do it?

It has, over the years, been suggested that Glam Rock, or a close approximation thereof, would have happened anyway, that Bolan was simply the lucky first contestant. And it's true that there are antecedents galore.

Flamboyant Fifties rocker Little Richard was Glam, 15 years before Bolan even dreamed of donning glitter. The Rolling Stones dressed up as girls while Marc was still wearing short hair. Screamin' Jay Hawkins took the stage dragged up as a ghoul. The Kinks sang of transvestites, and there's a small forest's worth of tabloid newsprint that insists that the early Beatles, Stones and Beat-boom bands were all a bunch of lady-boy cissies.

All of this is true, and if Glam had been purely a visual confection that would be an end to it. But it was also a blending of a variety of other cultural currents.

The extravagances of the psychedelic era, though dead and buried as a musical force by the end of 1969, clung on as a sartorial statement into the new decade, and they continued evolving as well. But the velvets, lace and dandyism of the original London underground had shifted their focus away from the disgraced statements of political and social liberation towards sexual liberation, an awareness that the moral currents that had survived unchanged through the 20th century-so-far were finally getting the facelift they required.

Homosexuality was decriminalised in 1967; but just as significant was the following year's decision to strip the Lord Chamberlain's office of its 231-year-old right to vet and censor any play or production destined for a public stage – itself the culmination of a decade-long campaign that began in 1958 with the banning of Tennessee Williams' *Cat On A Hot Tin Roof* on the grounds that it mentioned homosexuality.

British theatre exploded with new plays celebrating the ensuing freedom; on 27 September 1968, 24 hours after the Theatres Act became law, the American hippy musical *Hair* opened at the Shaftesbury Theatre, the first stage show ever to openly present nudity, sexuality, blasphemy and bad language on a London stage.

More would follow. For months before Kenneth Tynan's latest play, the similarly nude *Oh! Calcutta!*, arrived, rumour flew that it would include a scene featuring actual sexual intercourse; at the same time as similar scuttlebutt revolved around the much-delayed release of Mick Jagger's first movie, *Performance*.

In the event, neither was true (or, at least, proven). But hand-in-hand with the on-stage revolution that had nonetheless taken place, other arts moved towards centre stage that might otherwise have remained the preserve of artists.

'Mime was one of the key breakthrough movements,' says Michael Des Barres, one of the young actors and artists on the London arts scene at that time. 'Lindsay Kemp was a huge influence on everyone who was taking notice of everything. That silent exhibition with white face was very intoxicating because it looked so removed, and it looked so glamorous, and you didn't have to learn anything. You just had to move.'

The young David Bowie had already worked with Kemp, on stage and on television, had even opened for Tyrannosaurus Rex as a mime act, and he and Bolan were friends. But they did not circulate in the same circles. For Bowie, home was the arts-lab scene he was creating in the London suburb of Beckenham where the lights of local hippydom would all come out to play.

For Bolan, particularly in the years when the deeply psilocybic Steve Peregrin Took was his bandmate, home was in the velvet and satin world of the true underground, a nation whose boundaries were drawn between the Speakeasy nightclub and the Biba boutique on Kensington Church Street, and which was populated by the likes of Des Barres and the similarly unknown Gary Holton, drama students with a rock'n'roll eye.

By sundry members present and future of bands like the Deviants and the Pink Fairies.

By the cast of crazies who undertook the publication each month of the *International Times*.

By a high-rolling handful of industry mavericks: Move manager Tony Secunda, with his enterprising fingers in any entrepreneurial pie he thought might stir up a hornet's nest. His wife Chelita, elfin dark and beautiful, a muse to whoever needed her. BP Fallon, a publicist whose career stretched back from Jimi Hendrix to the Beatles, the man journalist Nick Kent once described as a Glam-Rock leprechaun and the mastermind of so much of the intellectual ferment that this select band imbibed.

It was a world, Des Barres continues, 'where hashish was smoked and clothes were exchanged between sexes. And there was a very specific bunch of guys who were androgynous, and who were into that debauchery, but – and this is where a lot of people miss the point – they *weren't* gay. A lot of people talking and writing about this period focus on boys fucking boys, when in fact it was boys who *looked* like girls *fucking* girls.'

Of course homosexuality existed in this world, and so did bisexuality. But they were merely single acts within the entire play. Hedonism in *all* its guises was what these searchers truly sought and, just as Rimbaud employed it as the battering ram to rewrite the poetry of a century before, so now the point was to use it to completely rewrite rock'n'roll.

Bolan moved with these people; he was moved by them and they were moved by him in return. BP Fallon would become Bolan's publicist once things started to happen. Tony Secunda would become his manager; Chelita was the one who dabbed the first drops of glitter beneath his eye.

'Marc was really an anomaly at the time,' Des Barres remembers. 'He was an extraordinary figure, a real influence on all of us, just his sensitivity and his cuteness and his brilliance. His poetry. He *was* poetry.'

Tony Secunda agreed. 'Marc was constantly watching, always learning, almost taking notes. He was silent far more than he talked, but when he took the lead everybody followed him.'

First within his own circle, and then around the world. No, Marc was not the first person to play with all of the different elements that rock historians can cite as his antecedents. But he was the first to take all of those elements – sexual ambiguity, sartorial sensuality, literary art and theatrical cinema – and blend them into a cohesive whole.

Musically, Glam might well have been little more than an hysterical reaction to the musical and cultural stagnation of the previous couple of years. But it was also a social revolution, a cultural uprising, an erotic explosion and a moral reassessment. Glam Rock was Sex Rock, Art Rock, Poetry Rock, Mime Rock, West End Musical Rock, Edgy Art-house Cinema Rock and more, and none of those components would be the same again.

So far, so intellectual. But Glam was also a commercial force, one that was destined to reign supreme for close to five years – which it certainly couldn't have done if the only people to whom it appealed were a bunch of self-styled deviants who liked wearing each other's clothes. And that is where Bolan truly stepped out alone.

Music had grown serious. Back in the early-mid Sixties, an artist was only ever as good as his, her or their last single. The Beatles, Stones, Who, Kinks, the lot; they lived and died according to their most recent Top Thirty placing.

But the purity of the British Beat boom that spawned those bands had mutated wildly since then, twisted in the gutters of San Francisco's Haight-Ashbury district to emerge a frenzied confection that required no more stimulus than a few tabs of acid and a cosmic lightshow to raise it above its peers. But just as the musical liberation ignited by that enlightenment would uncork some stellar careers and fabulous records, it would also swiftly degenerate into a slough of intense introspection and 40-minute solos.

Now it was the LP that reigned supreme, targeted at an audience of mature listeners who would readily appreciate all the hours of work that went into creating every second of sound. Suddenly the leading lights of the Sixties' scene were abandoning the custom-built singles that originally made their career to concentrate instead on album length masterpieces. Singles were simply songs pulled off the latest LP as and when the marketing man demanded.

By the end of the decade, rock'n'roll was essentially split between two extremes. Either you were Prog (or some variation thereof) or you were Pop. No prizes for guessing which one 'serious' musicians despised.

The problem was, there was no viable alternative. Eight year-olds were catered for by the bubblegum boom, 18 year-olds by the longhairs playing the colleges. But for the generation that hung in-between those extremes, too old to be boppers but too young to be heads, there was nothing to sing to, nothing to dance to and nothing whatsoever make out to. The Cufflinks and Atomic Rooster might have been opposites in every imaginable way, but they were both non-starters in the teenage libido stakes.

And that was the opening Marc Bolan had been waiting for.

In electrifying fashion, he relaunched the single as a work of art, shrugging aside the belief that it was impossible to have a revolution at 45 rpm and letting rip in a surge of sequins and sex. It took him one hit to make it, one hit to consolidate it, and after that he could do what he wanted.

Even after Glitter exploded like acne across the teenage scene, Bolan's initial impact was still so great that he both encapsulated and transcended the rest of the pack. Gary Glitter, Slade, the Sweet, even the recently revitalised David Bowie, could do nothing more than stand on the outside gazing enviously in on the universe Bolan had constructed around himself – a universe wherein the performer, the performance and all the peripheral little things that mattered so much were suddenly joined as one.

Nothing else mattered – nothing else could matter. There was not one possible physical, emotional or critical response that could even dent the bubble. Marc Bolan was invincible.

The genre Bolan so effortlessly created was essentially one of pure narcissism, nothing more or less. Other pop stars seemed larger than life; the Glam-Rock pack was even larger than that. Aided by British television's recent conversion to colour (*Top Of The Pops* switched in 1970, not at all coincidentally the year of Bolan's breakthrough), and a massive resurgence in the power and sales of the pin-up press (*Music Star, Popswop*, even the monthly lyric mag *Disco 45*), it revolved around looking good, sounding good and being good. Bolan could do all three.

It meant projecting glamour, *not* as the nebulous property of some Hollywood screen goddess (although that was a part of it) but as something tangible, something that could be encapsulated in a word, a gesture, a chord. And most important of all, something which could be emulated. Like Monroe's beauty spot or Harlow's platinum blondeness, Bolan's image was a series of carefully calculated visual hooks; his mane of curling hair, the glittering eye paint, the elfin smile, the metallic green and electric blue in which he dressed. Everything was designed to catch the eye. Bolan might have been short but he would stand out in any crowd.

The magic was delivered on every level. Even a simple photograph captured it; Bolan was absurdly photogenic, a trait above all others that was to be aspired to by the bands who grew up in his wake. And that in itself was a breakthrough. Music had often been seen as a poor second to the packaging, but in the past only a privileged few could get away with it.

Bolan, however, liberated the halt, the lame, the ugly and the hopeless. Suddenly a sprinkling of glitter and a pair of platform boots were all that was required to bring a hint of glamour to the most disparate of careers.

When the Strawbs went on *Top Of The Pops* with false cheekbones, they created Glitterfolk, prompting a disbelieving Martin Gordon to quip: 'The glam Strawbs hadn't quite figured it out, I remember seeing a pic in some teeny mag with the singer [Dave Cousins] gleaming red lipsticked lips peering moistly out from his bushy beard. A truly horrible sight.'

When Edgar and Johnny Winter took to smothering themselves in rhinestones, they were no longer Bluesmen, they were Glitterbluesmen. Jenny Haan packed a suitcase of costumes that transformed Babe Ruth's prog into Glamprog. There was

Glittersoul (Labelle, silver spaceship divas asking very rude questions in French), Glittertrash (the New York Dolls), Glitterfunk from George Clinton's family tree and, in the subterranean realms that we today call Junkshop Glam, who knows what other curious hybrids await?

Not every instance was mercenary. In fact, the American ones certainly weren't, simply because Glam didn't mean enough over there to merit the expense of a new wardrobe. Even at home, some of these artists truly did believe in what they were doing. But it didn't matter either way. To both the saddest cynic and the most dedicated progenitor, Glam functioned on a level so transparent that you could indulge it to whatever level you liked: lifestyle, image or just a pair of neat trousers to beef up and beautify an otherwise rotting carcass.

There was Rod Stewart, another Sixties club veteran for whom the spangles had no other purpose than to keep our minds off the fact that it had been people like Rod who made Glam Rock so necessary in the first place. An old gold lamé jockstrap will never let you down, especially if everybody else is wearing one.

There was Mungo Jerry, pounding out a winning combination of jugband jollity and old Vince Taylor, maintaining a constant commentary on the singles chart for the entire duration of Glam.

And there was Elton John, a short balladeer with medium paunch and severe myopia, suddenly emerging in extravagant glasses, extravagant boots and, when the mood took him, an ostrich-feather headdress that simply defied you to say he was going bald. It was cabaret, Liberace with a jungle beat and, when you combine that with his costuming, the recipe for an overall vision that might actually have been quite horrifying had the mood of the times been a little less flippant.

But it *was* a flippant time. Even the darkest of fantasies could be defused without the slightest effort. It was only later that Glam Rock historians began to draw the dividing line between Good and Bad Clean Fun, and even then it was clear that the process was little more than a safety valve by which an ego could justify appreciating something so ultimately facile.

But Glam was not facile, any more than it was ultimately rock. Glam was an attitude, a feeling, a shift in societal tempo and an upsurge in cultural awareness.

It let you know that it was okay to be strange, or different or weird. It taught you that sexuality is not defined by who you fuck, but by why you fuck them.

It lined up its targets:

The crushing conformity of class and education (it is no coincidence that one of the biggest cult movies of the immediately pre-Glam era was Lindsay Anderson's *If...*).

The dull repetition of work and suburbia (Punk Rock, the musical movement that followed Glam with such indecent haste, was simply the sound of Glam's audience showing what they'd learned).

The ponderous burden of tradition and history...

And it picked them off one by one.

Alice Cooper told us school was out, and Slade taught us how not to spell.

T Rex told us love was hot and Bowie showed us how to dance.

Gary Glitter was the leader and Alvin Stardust stood alone.

Mud were crazy, the Sweet blocked buster and the Glitter Band gave us all the face of an angel.

What more could any generation have asked for?

CHAPTER ONE

1970

The Beginning of Doves

The pot was empty in 1970. The biggest records of the year were almost uniformly ghastly. Ireland's Eurovision winner 'All Kinds Of Everything'; the England World Cup Squad's monotone 'Back Home'; Cliff Richard's cloying 'Goodbye Sam, Hello Samantha'. The Beatles drifted away with 'Let It Be', the Stones were nowhere in sight. And Rolf Harris' 'Two Little Boys', the final Number 1 of 1969, continued shifting so many copies that it was the eighth biggest-selling single of 1970 as well...

But there were a few glimmers of hope. Mungo Jerry, all wild hair and washboard bluegrass, went to Number 1 in the summertime *with* 'In The Summertime'. Norman Greenbaum's 'Spirit in The Sky' unleashed a riff that would shape the next decade's worth of hits ('My Coo Ca Choo' for starters), and is still a reliable fallback today. The Kinks' 'Lola' pushed transvestism to the top of the chart and Hotlegs gave us 'Neanderthal Man'. Oh, and there was this little chap named Elton John coming up as well.

That was more or less it, though, and when we look back on 1970 from today a lot of its highlights are in hindsight alone. Unknown bands that burbled on the back burners of the BBC; odd gestures and gyrations from names that meant nothing; here and there, little hints of hope that would make the next five years stand out so loudly.

For now, though, the Sixties were over and, with them, a lot of the optimism that had infected what the newspapers still called the Younger Generation. Less than six months had passed since the Woodstock festival consolidated a utopia of love, peace and flowers, but those six months had been busy.

The Manson murders, the nightmare of Altamont and, coming soon, the Ohio State Massacre, all these things shattered the humour. The Vietnam War was still raging and, no matter how much hope the kids had for the future, the governments of the world ensured that the present would just grind on.

And then you heard the Jackson Five...

January 1970 – The Jackson Five: I Want You Back/Who's Loving Who? (Tamla Motown TMG 724)

Suddenly things didn't look quite so grim. At least they looked like they were having fun. And, before anybody else had broken free of the previous decade's chains, the Jacksons were poised and ready to breed a musical movement that looked set to dominate the west for the foreseeable future.

It was called Teenybop, and the three acts that would come to personify it – the Jackson Five, the Osmonds and the Partridge Family – remain as much a part of the early-Seventies landscape as anything that would emerge from the Glam-Rock closet. Not because *they* were a part of *it*, though, but because *we* were all a part of *them*. They truly were inescapable.

Berry Gordy, the head of the Motown label, was first alerted to the all-singing, all-dancing family by singer Gladys Knight, even if it is

Diana Ross who is remembered as the group's cheerleader.

Either way, not one of them could count, for the Five, in reality, were actually nine; stage performers Michael, Tito, Jermaine, Jackie and Marlon, a younger brother, Randy, who was already being groomed to step into Michael's pre-pubescent shoes the moment the older boy's voice started to break, cousins Ronnie Ransom and Johnny Jackson, who pumped out the actual music; and Joe Jackson, an ex-R&B guitarist who had started pushing his brood into showbiz almost from the moment they opened their eyes.

With born mimic Michael leading the way with his note-perfect James Brown routines, the family would pile into a van and hit clubs as far apart as New York and Phoenix and, by the time Knight came across them, the troupe had already been sighted by Sam Moore of Sam and Dave fame.

But it was Gordy who swooped first, intuitively aware of the family's inevitable stardom, instinctively knowing that, just as the Supremes' name had once been hearty enough to package white bread, so the Jacksons were so hale and wholesome, cute and cuddly that Middle America would be powerless to resist.

Black militancy was at its peak, but the Jackson Five were as divorced from all that as if they'd been Martians. And when the ABC network gifted Diana Ross a television special, it was her little guests who stole the show, especially Michael. In one segment he was Frank Sinatra, in another he whirled like a dervish. He was so damned sweet.

In December 1969, 'I Want You Back' gave the Jacksons their first American hit. 'ABC' followed it to the top of the chart in the New Year and, by the end of 1970, the Five had notched up two more Number 1s, a top-ranked television special and a Saturday morning cartoon series. And if the latter was little more than *A Hard Day's Animated Monkee Bizness*, with the Five having nothing more to do with it than stand still long enough for the artists to come up with passable likenesses, that didn't matter a jot.

The Jackson Five were all-powerful in a way that past pubescent idols like the Archies, the Monkees and the Cowsills never were. The teen press adored them, the serious press respected them. Blithely, they would cover a Bobby Day song with one single, a Jackson Browne number with another, and both would assimilate the best parts of their victim into an easily recognisable Jackson sound.

The Jacksons were stars and Michael was a supernova. Even at the age of 11 or 12 he was a phenomenal talent; the cream of the family group, the hero of American youth, and any number of outside concerns would have paid any amount of money to get their hands on him. They couldn't, so they set about creating their own substitutes.

January 1970 – It's Number 1, it's Top Of The Pops

Great Britain's longest-running music television programme went colour at the beginning of 1970. Six years after it first burst onto the screens in monochrome, *Top Of The Pops* made the switch as part of the BBC's service-wide changeover...the same technological advance that was simultaneously extended to the news, Alan Whicker and (oxymoronically, it was said), the *Black And White Minstrel Show*.

And colour made all the difference. Bands had always competed to look good, but now they could look better. A show that had once rendered every one of its guests in egalitarian shades of grey was now a battleground of hues. It would be a year before music truly embraced all of the possibilities colour television opened up to its performers. But it was coming.

29 January 1970 – The earliest surviving full Seventies episode of Top Of The Pops

Arrival – 'Friends'
Badfinger – 'Come And Get It'
Chicago – 'I'm A Man'
Blodwyn Pig – 'Same Old Story'
Brotherhood of Man – 'United We Stand'
Canned Heat – 'Let's Work Together' (video)
Edison Lighthouse – 'Love Grows'
Jethro Tull – 'The Witch's Promise'
Mary Hopkin – 'Temma Harbour' (dance)
Rare Bird – 'Sympathy'
Shocking Blue – 'Venus'

Yuk.

January 1970 – Pan's People: First Ladies of Glam Rock

The face of *Top Of The Pops* throughout the Glam era, and on either side of it too, was Pan's People, a six-piece troupe put together by American choreographer/dancer Felicity 'Flick' Colby in December 1967.

Ruth Pearson, Patricia 'Dee Dee' Wilde, Barbara 'Babs' Lord. Louise Clarke and Andrea 'Andi' Rutherford completed a line-up Colby originally intended calling Dionysus' Darlings. But Pan's People slipped more easily off the tongue.

It was hard work breaking into the business. When Colby first arrived in London in 1966, 'dancing girls had big hair and small dogs, and they all looked exactly alike.' In addition, television was very much a closed shop when it came to hiring dancers; producers would have their favourites and it was hard for anybody new to break into things. But Babs Lord and Ruth Pearson had both been members of *Beat Room*'s Beat Girls troupe and *Top Of The Pops*' Go-Jos, and finally *Top Of The Pops* director Colin Charman agreed to watch the troupe rehearse.

He clearly liked what he saw. Pan's People made their debut on the show in July 1968, dancing to Tommy James and the Shondells' bubblegum classic 'Mony Mony'. (That same month, they were special guests on Bobbie Gentry's BBC TV show; they would also appear on *Happening For Lulu* later in 1968.) They were back again the following month and, although never intended to become a weekly feature, gradually found themselves being called upon more frequently. Finally, Wilde recalled, 'it became apparent that Pan's People were an integral part of the show.'

'Pan's People hit *Top Of The Pops* like a large steamhammer' – Jimmy Savile.

Their purpose was twofold – to entertain the audience, of course, but more importantly, Pan's People were there to allow the show to feature records by artists who weren't available to perform in the studio. 'It was globular lights or us,' Colby explained. 'And we were much more fun.'

It was a harsh routine, all the same. At best, the group would have four days notice of the song they were expected to dance to – a provisional running order for the show would be drawn up on the Friday preceding the following Wednesday's taping. But a final decision could not be taken until the new week's charts were

published on the Tuesday. If the selected (and rehearsed) record had fallen down the charts, then that was the end of it. Pan's People would have to routine another song just 24 hours before filming.

For that reason, Colby conceded, not all of their routines were as brilliant as they could have been. Indeed, Pan's People were frequently ridiculed for their often literal interpretations of the songs they were dancing to ('Monster Mash' dressed as monsters; 'Get Down' sung to a pack of dogs). But they became a pop institution regardless, better known (and certainly better loved) than many of the records that they exploring.

Colby left the public face of Pan's People shortly after the group became established. As the choreographer as well as a dancer, she found herself spending too much time worrying about the technical side of the group's routines and not enough concentrating on her own dancing. She remained the power behind the throne, however, and she also took the decision not to replace herself. Pan's People remained a quintet for much of the remainder of their career.

Among the conditions of the dancers' contracts with the BBC was a stipulation that they could not marry while they remained a part of Pan's People. When Rutherford announced that she *was* marrying, she was out; in late 1972, open auditions were held for a replacement before Cherry Gillespie was unveiled – literally. She appeared for the first time on the 1972 Christmas *Top Of The Pops*, gift-wrapped for the rest of the group to open. The new-look group's first routine was Nilsson's 'Without You'.

For the next three years, Pan's People ruled supreme, not only dominating *Top Of The Pops* but also starring in their own edition of the popular *In Concert* programme (17 April 1974) and incurring the wrath of TV clean-up fiend Mary Whitehouse, after they appeared – seated and almost perfectly immobile – on Jimmy Savile's *Clunk Click* show. They were wearing the same low cut, high-split black dresses they had worn on a recent *Top Of The Pops*, dancing to the Three Degrees' 'When Will I See You Again'. The difference was the outfits proved to be a lot more revealing when the girls weren't moving.

Clarke was the next to leave in late 1974 and was replaced by Sue Menhenick (the group danced as a sextet in the weeks before Louise's departure), and business appeared to continue as usual. It was becoming clear to the others, though, that their day was finally ending. 'We were all getting on,' Lord confessed. 'I was almost 30.' By late 1975, she had gone, to be replaced by Mary Corpe. In February 1976, *Blue Peter* hostess Lesley Judd became the latest recruit (albeit for just one routine, dancing to Manuel and the Music of the Mountains), and then Dee Dee, too, was gone. Lee Ward took her place and with Pearson the only surviving original member, the troupe was all but unrecognisable.

But still it was a sad day when Pan's People gave their final performance, on 29 April 1976. Their final dance was to Andrea True Connection's 'More More More'.

Pan's People were replaced on *Top Of The Pops* by another Colby creation (co-managed with Pearson), the mixed-sex Ruby Flipper – Cherry and Sue, plus Floyd, Gavin, Lulu and Patti. Six months later, a third Colby troupe, the all-girl Legs and Co (Sue, Lulu and Patti, plus Gill, Pauline and Rosemary) supplanted them. And Pan's People themselves would be reborn in 1979, albeit without a return to *Top Of The Pops*.

And they were okay. But they weren't Pan's People.

POSTSCRIPT: Pan's People were the subject of a BBC documentary, *Digging The Dancing Queens*, as part of *Top Of The Pops'* 30th anniversary celebrations. Somewhat less complimentary, but very amusing, was their inclusion in a round of the BBC quiz programme *Never Mind The Buzzcocks* in which contestants were shown a minute or so of silent footage and asked to guess which song was being interpreted.

March 1970 – Tyrannosaurus Rex: A Beard Of Stars (Regal Zonophone SLRZ1013)

In late 1970, singer Andy Ellison attended a Marc Bolan and T Rex concert, anxious to see how his old bandmate (the pair had been members of Sixties' mod hooligans John's Children) was coping with the fame and fortune that had suddenly ridden a white swan to his doorstep.

'It was pandemonium, and Marc was

milking it for everything. He came out on stage, held his guitar in the air and said, "I am Jimi Hendrix and I have taken over." I was so embarrassed I walked out.'

For Ellison, and for many others who watched while Bolan wandered the British underground of the late Sixties, with nothing more than his monstrous self-belief to sustain him, the singer's elevation to God, or at least substitute Beatlehood, was a phenomenon that defied either belief or tolerance.

Yet Ellison should not really have been surprised by the ease with which Bolan slipped into the electric groove that would make him a star, or by the grace with which he grasped that star once it came in sight.

True, when the 19 year-old Bolan first appeared at a John's Children rehearsal in February 1967, there was little to suggest he was anything more than the teenage Donovan clone whom two UK record labels, Decca and Parlophone, had spent the last year (and three flop singles) grooming, and who fled the studio at 10.30pm insisting, 'Look, I've got to go now, otherwise my parents will be really mad at me.'

But once he'd learned to swap his acoustic guitar for electric, the possibilities of noise seemed endless. And what were his first words to Simon Napier-Bell, the manager who he and John's Children shared with the Yardbirds?

'Hi, I'm a singer and I'm going to be the biggest British rock star ever, so I need a good manager to make all the arrangements.'

Napier-Bell told him to mail a tape over. Bolan turned up on his doorstep instead and played a 45-minute concert in the living room. From all accounts, it was an astonishing performance.

Bolan's earliest recordings, the now much-circulated demos of Dion's 'The Road I'm On' and Dylan's 'Blowin' In The Wind', and the singles 'The Wizard'/'Beyond The Rising Sun' (Decca F12288); 'The Third Degree'/'San Francisco Poet' (Decca F12413) and 'Hippy Gumbo'/'Misfit' (Parlophone R5539), all cut during 1965-1966, are usually described as little more than the average folkie fodder, either blessed or cursed by Marc's warbling voice. One reviewer dismissed an early Bolan 45 for sounding like Larry the Lamb, and he wasn't far off the mark.

But listen again.

Mike Hurst, who produced the first two Bolan singles, recalls those early sessions. 'In 1965, when I finished with my band, the Methods, because we couldn't get anywhere, I became a record producer and I went to work for a mad Californian called Jim Economides, who'd set up in London. He'd been a recording engineer at Capitol in Los Angeles, and came over. And Jim said he'd found this kid called Marc Bolan.

'Well, Jim the recording engineer was really not Jim the producer, so he asked if I would go into the studio with Marc and cut a couple of tracks. We went to Decca in Broadhurst Gardens, and did "The Wizard". Marc was so spaced out. I asked him to explain what "The Wizard" was all about, and he says, "Man, he's there". I said "Where?" and he said "Outside the window in that tree." I hadn't realised he'd read Tolkien, he loved it, whereas me, I hadn't read Tolkien so I thought he was on another planet.

'Then I did the next one, which was "The Third Degree", and the interesting thing is, when you listen to that, that really *is* T Rex. You can hear it coming. He had a Bo Diddley type of beat and he threw me completely when he played it because no-one could say Marc was the greatest guitarist in the world, but he had all the front that was necessary. He put all the feeling into that chord progression, and it was great. It's very basic, but I wouldn't have changed that for the world. It would have been easy for me to say, "Let's get another guitarist in to play this," but why? It was very simple and very basic, but it worked.'

That was the energy that Napier-Bell heard during the living-room concert, and that is the power he intended to tap. He agreed to represent Bolan on just two conditions. He should go electric, and he should confine his voice to backing vocals alone. The public needed time to grow accustomed to his sound.

Bolan agreed and, having been accepted into John's Children, he was handed his first electric guitar, 'a really stodgy old Gibson SG' previously belonging to local musician Trevor White of the A-Jaes (White would later resurface in Sparks). 'And Marc played it incredibly loudly,' recalled drummer Chris Townson. 'His first rehearsal with us was deafening, even by our normal standards.

'I think the band actually got worse when Marc first joined because all he did was stand there and make this muddy blurge,' Townson continued. 'It really was a horrible noise, so bad that I used to sneak round before a gig and retune his guitar to how I thought it should sound. He could never be bothered to do it properly, he seemed to think that it didn't matter. In a way, I suppose he was right.'

Andy Ellison agreed. 'He was a great songwriter, even if he wasn't a particularly good guitarist. He moved well, and made lots of strange noises. I remember we turned up for one gig, and he'd had some special metal foil screens made, quite big ones, which folded out behind the amps. He said they reflected the sound so you could get feedback in different places. I was never quite sure if they really did do that, but Marc seemed quite happy with them and they looked good.'

Bolan's first live appearance with John's Children was in Watford. Backstage, he'd drunk his way through two bottles of red wine to combat his nerves and, with the rest of the band feeling obliged to accompany him on the road to inebriation, it was a very drunken John's Children that staggered on stage to greet its audience – a solitary leather-clad rocker girl who stood at the back chewing gum, then walked out midway through the first song.

Optimistically presuming she had raced out to tell her friends what a phenomenal band they were missing, John's Children continued playing and had just finished their second number when the club manager came in and told them to stop. 'Marc ended the evening in tears,' remembered Townson, 'which was quite a usual reaction for him. If we did a bad gig, he'd really take it to heart, but if we did a good one he'd be really bubbly for about half an hour afterwards. The rest of us never used to care how a gig went, we'd just get on with whatever was happening afterwards, a party or something. But Marc used to get really upset.'

Bolan also set himself apart from his bandmates when John's Children were on the road. 'He wouldn't even hang around after gigs,' Townson continued, 'which we all thought was the most important part; get the gig out of the way and start looning around, having outrageous parties and being obnoxious little pop stars. But that sort of thing never used to interest him. He'd go and sit quietly in the corner and write strings of words on little bits of paper.'

At the beginning of April 1967, John's Children were dispatched to Germany for a seven-date tour with the Who, to whose newly founded Track Records label they had just signed. It was a volatile combination. The Who were well established as the masters of the auto-destruct button, but John's Children did not so much blow them offstage as blow the stage away from beneath them.

In Nuremberg, vocalist Ellison encouraged the audience to completely destroy the venue's wooden seating. In Dusseldorf, he took two kilos of feathers on stage with him which he then released into the draughty, sweaty air. In Ludwigshafen, a full-scale riot broke out which brought the police and fire brigade down to the hall and forced the Who's set to be cancelled. John's Children were thrown off the tour the next day. The band returned home via the cross-channel ferry, but all Napier-Bell remembers of that journey was coming across a drunken Bolan sitting cross-legged on a table in the restaurant area, reciting pornographic poetry to the munching multitude.

John's Children would release just two singles during Bolan's tenure with the group, 'Desdemona' and 'Midsummer Night's Scene'. Both were Bolan compositions, drawn from the veritable mountain of material that the group was now recording, but which would leak out only piecemeal over the next three decades. 'Desdemona', Bolan boasted, was 'a song I wrote in about 25 seconds. It's about a girl named Desdemona, a rich girl, and a fellow who works by the River Swine, all rather complicated and difficult to explain.'

Released in May 1967, 'Desdemona' was well received in the press, but a BBC radio ban swiftly quelled its hopes of actually becoming a hit. The lyric 'lift up your skirt and fly' was deemed offensive, prompting Ellison to return to the studio to obscure the original obscenity with a new line – 'why do you have to lie?' Unfortunately, the record remained unplayed and sank soon after.

Unperturbed, John's Children's next contribution to the Summer of Love was 'Midsummer's Night's Scene', a song that Bolan and Ellison co-wrote over a plate of mushrooms at Bolan's parent's house in Summertown, south London. A slab of fine psychedelic surrealism, 'Midsummer Night's Scene' was nevertheless doomed. Somewhere between 50 and 100 copies of the record were pressed before the release was cancelled and, today, 'Midsummer's Night's Scene' is officially recognised among the Top Ten rarest singles in British record-collecting history. Bolan left the band just weeks later.

It would be another three years before Bolan again found himself in a position where the press would go looking for him, as they had during John's Children's tempestuous months on the verge of success, rather than the other way around. But once that happened, Bolan quickly rediscovered its advantages and promptly applied them to his personal legend.

Just as, for example, he could turn a night spent in Paris in the arms of a gay conjuror into a mystical experience involving wizards and the invocation of evil spirits, so six months in a band from which he faded gracefully could be transformed into two tempestuous weeks with an equally stormy conclusion.

'Marc really knew how to treat journalists,' Simon Napier-Bell laughed. Bolan himself would later claim that it was the band's arrangement of 'Midsummer Night's Scene' that not only prompted its withdrawal, but also forced him to quit. He hated the record, the band hated him. No-one tried to stop him leaving, and he wouldn't have listened if they had.

According to his bandmates, however, Bolan never voiced a single objection to their treatment of his music. 'Maybe he thought we were prostituting his songs,' Ellison suggested. 'I think he envisaged them as being much lighter weight; a lot of the stuff that turned up on the first Tyrannosaurus Rex albums were things John's Children had been doing as a heavy metal type thing. But he never complained about it to us. I think John's Children was a period that he didn't like to remember too much. He was really kinda annoyed that he'd had to join a group to get any kind of recognition, so he just blotted out that whole period. But I think he did enjoy himself despite everything.'

Simon Napier-Bell believes Bolan 'had his own ideas of what he wanted to do, and he suddenly realised that John's Children were heading towards exactly the same thing. He resented that because it wasn't happening under his own name or under his guidance. He wanted to be the leader of it when it happened, not just the lead guitarist, and getting his own band together was his way of kind of stealing a march on the others.'

Bolan had, in fact, told Napier-Bell several months earlier that he wanted to start a second band he could work with when John's Children were off the road. 'But that side of him that was so determined to succeed wouldn't let him burn his bridges just like that.'

Bolan wasted little time in putting John's Children behind him. Napier-Bell recalled. 'He got a gig at the Electric Garden, then put an ad in *Melody Maker* to get the musicians. The paper came out on Wednesday, the day of the gig. At three o'clock he was interviewing musicians, at five he was getting ready to go on stage. And that was all there was to it. He didn't audition anybody, he just picked people who looked good or who had nice names. Marc thought he could just magic it all together. His theory was that you just went on stage, told the audience what you were going to do, then you did it, simple as that. And he genuinely believed that it would all come together, and that he would wake up in the morning as a superstar.'

Instead, 'It was a disaster. He just got booed off the stage, it really was the worst thing that had ever happened to him.'

The experience, Napier-Bell believes, not only put Bolan off the idea of having his own band, it put him off electric instruments as well. 'He didn't think he'd done anything wrong, it was the musicians who had been incompatible. The fact they hadn't rehearsed or anything had nothing to do with it. But he didn't have the courage to try it again, it really had been a blow to his ego. So he just went out, bought himself a rug and a joss stick, and then he and Steve Took went out as a duo. Later he told everyone he'd been forced into going acoustic because Track Records had repossessed all his gear. In fact he'd been forced into going acoustic because he was too scared to do anything else.'

At 19, a year younger than Bolan, Steve Peregrin Took was one of the musicians on stage at the Electric Garden that fateful night, the only one with whom Bolan felt any camaraderie whatsoever. The pair, after all, looked great together, Took with flowing silks, bongos and the name he borrowed from *Lord Of The Rings*, a Shakespearean elf-child with the broadest smile ever; Bolan, with corkscrew curls and acoustic guitar, was elf-like too, with a quavering voice which scarcely even sounded English and lyrics which sometimes weren't. Set adrift within the psychedelic potpourri of Aquarius, with their pixiephones and one-stringed fiddles, Tyrannosaurus Rex flourished from the start.

'And Marc hated it, hated every single minute of it,' insists Napier-Bell. 'He'd do a gig and the promoter would say, "Oh sorry, we can't pay you. Have a couple of joints instead, or a couple of sugar lumps." Marc would have to say "Oh yeah, cool man," but inside he'd be really seething. And the more it went on, the more he hated it because he was trapped in this horrible hippy thing...he'd gone out of his way to attract an anti-commercial hippy audience.'

It was that, Napier-Bell affirmed, which prompted him to stop managing the duo. 'He'd never be able to get the right image if he had a pushy, conventional manager behind him, pushing for an extra £10 a gig. And then Marc went off and signed to Blackhill, who were just as conventional as I was, but I suppose they had the right credentials, Pink Floyd and all that. And Marc was still trapped in it. He was desperate to break out, go electric again, but he just didn't dare in case he lost his audience.'

In fact, Bolan never really lost sight of his electric destiny, even as Tyrannosaurus Rex sawed away on their acoustic toys, for they did so within a rock'n'roll framework that had hitherto been lacking in his solo work. Of course he was not alone in fashioning the unique blend that would be spread over three successive Tyrannosaurus Rex albums. Steve Took was vastly instrumental in the creation of the Tyrannosaurus Rex sound, but of equal importance was producer Tony Visconti, with whom he was to continue working until 1974.

He and Bolan met in 1967, just months after

Visconti arrived in London from his native New York. 'Marc was playing at the UFO Club, sitting cross-legged on stage playing his strange little songs in a wobbly voice, while Steve Took was banging on his bongos. At that point, I hadn't really produced anyone because I was holding out for something really different and unusual. I thought Marc was perhaps that.'

Uncertain whether or not Bolan could even speak English ('I couldn't understand a word he said on stage'), Visconti first approached Took. Assured that the singer wasn't some strange breed of eastern European gypsy, the American pushed through the crowd and introduced himself.

Bolan was on top form that night, as Visconti recalled. 'He told me how there were all these people who were interested in him and Steve, that John Lennon had been down wanting to produce them. He had all these tall stories, and I thought I didn't have a chance. But I gave him my phone number, telling him to call me if it all fell through. He rang at 10.30 the following morning.'

Tyrannosaurus Rex signed to Regal Zonophone, an all but moribund EMI subsidiary best known for its Salvation Army output, but which had recently been reactivated by the latest *wunderkind* to erupt onto the mid-Sixties' pop scene, the Straight Ahead management and production team of Tony Secunda and Denny Cordell.

Already renowned for its work with the Move, Procol Harum and Joe Cocker, the Straight Ahead set-up offered Tyrannosaurus Rex an ideal environment, combining Secunda and Cordell's own talents with the music publishing skills of the veteran David Platz and, of course, the enthusiastic vision of Cordell's assistant, Tony Visconti.

That said, Secunda acknowledged that he would have little to do with Bolan throughout this period. 'Tyrannosaurus Rex was Visconti's toy, we were busy with everything else. In fact, it wasn't until Marc called me up three years later, looking for someone to get him out from Platz's clutches, that we really got to know each other.'

Tyrannosaurus Rex's first album, 'My People Were Fair and Had Sky in Their Hair, But Now They're Content to Wear Stars On Their Brows' (Regal Zonophone SLRZ1003) emphasised the qualities that Visconti spotted that night at UFO. It approaches the listener from a totally unique angle; the Bolan voice, hardened from the slight warble which carried through his early solo material (and is still noticeable on the back-ups he performed for John's Children), remains uncompromising, but blends with the bizarre, almost eastern-sounding instrumentation to create the impression of a medieval caravansary whose demented Bedouin cast has suddenly been let loose in a recording studio.

Neither was it all as outlandish as it sounded. Although it would be close to three years more before T Rextasy was ignited across Europe and the east, Bolan scored his first hit single as early as May 1968 when the driving, percussive folk of 'Debora' (c/w 'Child Star', Regal Zonophone RZ3008) reached Number 34.

The duo's first ever single, the hit version was recorded amid the sessions for 'My People Were Fair' but omitted from the album; following its success, a new version was cut for inclusion on their sophomore set, 'Prophets Seers And Sages, The Angels Of The Ages' (Regal Zonophone SLRZ1005). Opening the album, 'Debora' follows its familiar course for 1 minute 40, then repeats in its entirety backwards (hence the cut's full title 'Deboraarobed'. It's a dislocating listen, although Bolan's trademark otherworldly warble and partner Took's manic bongo-playing are both well served by the effects.

Subsequent singles 'One Inch Rock'/'Salamanda Palaganda' (Regal Zonophone RZ3011), 'Pewter Suitor'/'Warlord Of The Royal Crocodiles' (Regal Zonophone RZ3016) and 'King Of The Rumbling Spires'/'Do You Remember' (Regal Zonophone RZ3022) kept Tyrannosaurus Rex in touch with the charts – the first reached Number 28, the third Number 44, while the band continued enlarging upon and experimenting with their audience's limitations.

Bolan's apparent plunge into electric rock on the fourth Tyrannosaurus Rex album, 1970's 'Beard Of Stars' album (Regal Zonophone SLRZ1013), for instance, had already been hinted at over the course of its three predecessors, while the duo's first US tour, in the wake of their third LP, 'Unicorn' (Regal

Zonophone SLRZ1007), not only caught him utilising electric guitar, it also saw Steve Took exchange his bongos for a full drum kit.

But there was one final, protracted, drama to be played out before Bolan could embrace his destiny. The disharmony that America would draw out of Tyrannosaurus Rex's once closely bonded ranks had a number of flashpoints. Took, for example, was a prolific songwriter, as unique in his own way as Bolan.

But Tyrannosaurus Rex never recorded one of his songs and, to hear Bolan talk, one would never have known they existed. But they did, and when Took donated two of them ('Three Little Piggies' and 'The Sparrow Is The Sign') to 'Think Pink', the work-in-progress solo debut by Pretty Things drummer Twink, Bolan was furious.

He was also growing increasingly unhappy with Took's drug intake. The two musicians hung with very different crowds, Bolan living quietly with wife-to-be June Child, Took plying his body with chemicals and spending his time with like-minded fellows. Even when the pair visited the office together, they would immediately separate. Tony Secunda remembered Bolan heading into an office to talk money and percentages, while Took disappeared onto the roof for a joint he'd roll from the stash he kept in a bag around his waist.

Staunchly anti-drug himself, Bolan only barely tolerated Took's proclivities. According to Tony Secunda, that was to change the night somebody spiked his drink with acid.

Bolan freaked out completely, a night-long trip culminating in June driving him around a darkened Hampstead Heath while Bolan tried to eat his own hand. And though no-one knew for sure who exactly did the deed, Bolan himself had no doubts. Took had long since rejoiced in the nickname of the Phantom Spiker. Well, this time, the Phantom had spiked the wrong person.

Against this festering backdrop, the duo's American tour, which kicked off in San Francisco on 6 August 1969, was ill-starred from the outset. And it only got worse. Took almost missed the flight out of London, while the duo's New York debut, at the Club Au Go Go, coincided with the Woodstock festival and was very sparsely attended. Tyrannosaurus Rex's US label Blue Thumb was equally underwhelmed by their presence, contributing nothing more than a handful of ill-matched support slots to the itinerary – in Seattle, the duo opened for It's A Beautiful Day; in Detroit, the Turtles.

But according to Bolan, the biggest obstacle was Took. Several shows were marked by his penchant for stripping naked on stage; at others, he indulged in what Bolan described as 'musical sabotage', playing one song midway through another, missing cues, fluffing breaks. Finally, with the last date behind them, Bolan and June Child flew home alone. By the time Took returned to England, he was already history.

It was Took's departure that gave Bolan the final push he needed to 'go heavy', as he called it. Promptly recruiting a new percussionist, Mickey Finn, Tyrannosaurus Rex now recorded what would become their crowning achievement, January 1970's 'By The Light Of A Magical Moon'/'Find A Little Wood' (Regal Zonophone RZ3025) single, and the truly monumental 'Beard Of Stars' album. From there, of course, it would be but a small step into the full-blown rock'n'roll of 'Electric Warrior' and 'The Slider'.

'Marc always knew what he wanted to do,' Finn said a decade after his bandmate's 1977 death. 'One of the first things he told me after I joined was that he was going to be enormous, and I laughed because he said that to everybody. But once we started talking, and he outlined what he intended to do, then I started believing. And everything happened just as he said it would.'

'Beard Of Stars" closing track, 'Elemental Child', remains particularly impressive, an all-out electric assault course that would only grow in intensity every time Bolan played it in concert. Until soon, the Hendrix-inspired boast that so embarrassed Andy Ellison seemed little more than a statement of fact. On that evidence, he *was* Jimi Hendrix, and he *had* taken over.

March 1970 – David Bowie: The Prettiest Star/Conversation Piece (Mercury 1135)
25 March 1970 – Andy Ferris Show: David Bowie

Bolan's next opportunity to unveil his electric guitar-playing talents came not on one of his own records, but on the latest single by another of producer Tony Visconti's clients, David Bowie.

Like Bolan, Bowie had been struggling through the confines of cult obscurity for much of the Sixties; unlike Bolan, for whom chart success was still a minor ripple (three out of Tyrannosaurus Rex's five singles made the lower leagues of the chart), Bowie had just scored a major hit with 'Space Oddity'. Now he was thinking about the follow-up and, in early January 1970, he got to work, a moving love song for his bride to be, Angela Barnett, titled 'The Prettiest Star'. Bolan would supply the haunting lead guitar line that soars through the song.

Tony Visconti remembers the occasion vividly. 'That was the only time they could have worked together, the only time their egos would have allowed it. But you could tell the rivalry between them was there. Marc was okay about it. He loved the fact he'd been asked to play electric guitar on that record, because he'd only just got out of his acoustic days on his own releases. But his girlfriend, June Child, sat through the playback, announced that the best thing about the record was Marc's playing and walked out of the room.'

Three weeks later, she and Marc would themselves be married.

As for Bowie, he's been a part of the furniture for so long that it's easy to forget that he was once a one-hit wonder. 'Space Oddity' charted in late summer 1969, but 'The Prettiest Star' was a resounding flop and it would be another two years before the erstwhile David Robert Jones came up with a single the record-buying public deemed a worthy follow-up to the tale of Major Tom

Like Bolan, Bowie was already something of a veteran. His first single ('Liza Jane'/'Louie Louie Go Home' – Vocalion V9221), recorded with the King Bees, appeared in 1964.

Other bands and names followed in a series of increasingly desperate solo attempts to raise himself out of obscurity: 'I Pity The Fool'/'Take My Tip' with the Mannish Boys (Parlophone R5250); 'You've Got A Habit Of Leaving'/'Baby Loves That Way' as Davy Jones (Parlophone R5315) were both released in 1965, as Bowie came into the orbit of producer Shel Talmy, then at the top of his game with the Who and the Kinks.

'David was...one of those people who impressed me immediately,' Talmy remembers. 'I thought he was really bright and very talented, I liked him enormously.'

Their work, together, was destined for obscurity, and Talmy has no doubts as to why. 'I did the records with him and, generally speaking, what we were doing was six years ahead of the market because the stuff we were doing didn't sell then, but it did sell six years later. It was fun to do and I just wish we had a market because there was no question in my mind he was going to make it. It just took a long time for the buyers to come round.'

Tony Hatch was the next big-name producer to try his luck with the singer: 'Can't Help Thinking About Me'/'And I Say To Myself' as David Bowie and the Lower Third (Pye 7N 17020); 'Do Anything You Say'/'Good Morning Girl' (Pye 7N 17079) and 'I Dig Everything'/'I'm Not Losing Sleep' (Pye 7N 17157) were released during 1966, but again, they did nothing.

He moved to producer Mike Vernon for 'Rubber Band'/'The London Boys' (Deram DM 107); 'The Laughing Gnome'/'The Gospel According To Tony Day' (Deram DM 123); 'Love You Till Tuesday'/'Did You Ever Have A Dream' (Deram DM 135) and the LP 'David Bowie' (Deram DML 1007). Nothing. He was passed on to the young Tony Visconti, and they cut some tracks that would later become staples of countless Bowie compilations. But they weren't released at the time, and when Bowie did seem at last to have a chance of success Visconti declined to produce it. Gus Dudgeon took the honours instead.

Space Oddity'/'Wild Eyed Boy From

Freecloud' (Phillips BF 1801) was released to coincide with the summer 1969 moon landing, and did very well out of it too. But if Bowie thought for a moment that it was his music, and not its subject matter, that caught the public imagination, he was swiftly disabused. 'The Prettiest Star' was joined in oblivion by an album, 'Man Of Words, Man Of Music'.

He had a record deal, and he had his admirers, both in the music press and at the BBC (this was his second session there that year). What he didn't have was any idea of what he wanted to do next.

Or did he? It was three years since Bowie first heard Lou Reed and the Velvet Underground, when his then-manager, Kenneth Pitt, returned home from a trip to New York with a copy of the Velvets' debut LP. One song from the record, 'I'm Waiting For The Man', immediately leaped into Bowie's live set; another, 'Venus In Furs', would be plundered for a new Bowie composition, 'Little Toy Soldier'.

Now, he was returning to the Velvets songbook, rewiring 'I'm Waiting For The Man' as a duet for voice and harmonica, alongside one cut from the lost 'Man Of Words' album and two from its gestating follow-up. Between them, those songs would delineate his musical plans for the next 18 months – and beyond.

The crucial difference was, he was no longer visualising his future alone. Six weeks earlier, on Radio 1's *Sunday Show* (5 February 1970), Bowie appeared for the first time alongside his new guitarist, Hull-born Mick Ronson, a man destined to become both his musical and visual foil as the future unspooled.

A little over a fortnight later, on 22 February, the pair fronted a new band, David Bowie and the Hype, at the London Roundhouse, resplendent in flashy superhero style costumes run up by Angie and bassist Tony Visconti's girlfriend Liz Hartley, to run the band up a set of extravagant costumes, each one representing a superhero-style cartoon character.

The group – which also included drummer John Cambridge – was horrified. Bowie laughed, 'When I first heard [Ronson] play I thought, "That's my Jeff Beck! He is fantastic! This kid is great!" And so I hoodwinked him into working with me. I didn't quite have to tell him in the beginning that he would have to wear make-up and all that... Mick came from Hull. Very down to earth. "What do you mean, make up?"

'I reverted to things like "You looked very green tonight on stage... I think if you wore make up you'd look a little more natural-looking," lies like this, and gradually got them into areas of costume and theatre. Actually, when they realised how many girls they could pull when they looked so sort of outlandish, they took to it like a fish to water.'

Bowie, in stripy tights and blue cape, was Rainbowman, Ronson harked back to Thirties Chicago to become Gangsterman, Cambridge in a ten-gallon hat became Cowboyman and Visconti, resplendent in a Superman-style outfit with a giant 'H' on the chest, was Hypeman. But the audience scoffed and when the band resurfaced at the same venue a couple of weeks later (the unknown Genesis supported them) they were back in their daily clothes again.

But Bowie was convinced that his instincts for dressing up were correct, a conviction that was only amplified after he was introduced to Tony Defries, a brilliant legal strategist who would become Bowie's new manager. Alongside wife Angela – Angie to the world at large – it was Defries who would encourage the butterfly ferment of Bowie's imagination to finally take flight.

March 1970 – Alternate Realities I – the Elton John Band, featuring Mick Ronson

A former member of the (then unknown) Hull-based blues band the Rats, Ronson was freshly installed in David Bowie's band, but he was also still working with folkie Michael Chapman, with whom he had recently recorded the 'Fully Qualified Survivor' LP. And when producer Gus Dudgeon invited Chapman along to the Trident Studios sessions to play on Elton John's upcoming second LP, 'Tumbleweed Connection', Ronson accompanied him.

Chapman later recalled recording as many as five tracks before label head Dick James called a halt on the session, complaining it was 'too psychedelic'. Gudgeon, too, spoke highly of the recordings, and while he could not recall how many other songs were attempted, he too was disappointed when the plug was pulled. He even recommended that Elton consider offering

Ronson full-time employment, but again Dick James nixed the notion.

Just one of the tracks has ever been released (on Elton's 1992 'Rare Masters' compilation), an eight-minute version of 'Madman Across The Water' which, even allowing for all that the guitarist would subsequently accomplish, is quintessential Ronson, wildly inventive over a wash of piano and sundry acoustics. And all a very far cry from the sparse piano-slinger that Dick James, head of Elton's DJM label, thought he had signed.

Ronson returned to Bowie, and Elton (though he would later augment his approach with a full band and a great guitarist, Davey Johnstone) returned to basics. And it's unlikely that either had any complaints about how the next few years panned out. But, for one glorious moment, the entire course of Glam-Rock history could have been altered.

March 1970 – Slade: Shape Of Things To Come/C'mon C'mon (Fontana TF 1079)

Nobody doubted that the Next Big Thing was just around the corner; it invariably is, after all. And four lads from Wolverhampton thought they knew exactly what it was.

Anybody who had spent the last few months studying the UK chart would have seen them, an army of crop-headed bovver boys who danced their way into tabloid infamy on the back of a string of reggae singles. Major hits by Harry J and the All Stars ('The Liquidator'), the Upsetters ('Return Of Django'), Boris Gardner ('Elizabethan Reggae') and Bob & Marcia ('Young, Gifted And Black') make a mockery of the English media's later insistence that it was Bob Marley, in 1975, who brought Jamaican music to mainstream prominence. It was already there in 1969-1970, soundtracking the rise and rise of the original Skinhead movement.

But reggae music needed to be imported before the Skins could even hear it. What, our Wolverhampton boys were wondering, would happen if a British band arose from the same working-class environment the Skins themselves hailed from, dressing and dancing in the same way as its audience and playing high octane rock'n'roll to boot?

There was only one way to find out.

The roots of Slade lay in an October 1965 meeting on a ferry bound for Germany between vocalist Noddy Holder, a member of Steve Brett and the Mavericks, and Don Powell and Dave Hill of the N'Betweens.

Neither party had any success behind them, although both had released singles. The N'Betweens were responsible for 'Take A Heart'/'Little Nightingale' (Barclay 70985) in 1965, while Steve Brett and the Mavericks had cut 'Wishing'/'Anything That's Part Of You' (Columbia DB7470), 'Sad Lonely And Blue'/'Candy' (Columbia DB 7581) and 'Chains On My Heart'/'Sugar Shack' (Columbia DB 7794).

Even earlier than that, in 1964, Hill and Powell recorded a four-track EP as the Vendors, although this got no further than acetate stage. (This would subsequently be released on the 'Genesis Of Slade' compilation.)

Talking, the trio readily discussed their growing disillusion with their current bands and when they met again, back home in Wolverhampton in the New Year, they agreed to team up.

The N'Betweens had just recruited a new bassist, Jim Lea, who was unhappy to learn his new band was about to shatter before he'd even had a chance to play with them. But he was enthusiastic about the others' plans, particularly their notion of layering the front line with two lead guitars, and when the N'Betweens were relaunched Lea remained on board. So, for a short time, did fellow N'Betweens Mickey Marson (guitar) and Johnny Howells (vocals). But the first time the core quartet played alone together, Hill recalled, 'It was really exciting.'

The expanded version of the band made its live debut at Walsall Town Hall on 1 April 1966. But Marson dropped out and, two months later in Plymouth in June, Howells excused himself for the duration of a gig ('He had this bird coming round to his caravan,' explained Holder) and the N'Betweens were a foursome at last.

It was not an easy transition – as the band's established frontman, Howells had a vociferous following. But Holder swiftly developed his own public persona, a wildman crossed with a vaudevillian comic who thought nothing of dressing up as a vicar for gigs while the band pounded out their standard repertoire of Motown and R&B covers. That (or something like it) was the sight that greeted visiting American producer Kim Fowley, one evening at Tiles in Oxford Street, London. Instantly intrigued, he took the N'Betweens under his wing, arranged a one-off deal with Columbia and produced the band's next single, the Young Rascals cover 'You Better Run'/'Evil Witchman' (Columbia DB 8080).

It was a brief relationship. The single topped the chart in Wolverhampton but did nothing anywhere else. Fowley moved on and the N'Betweens continued grinding around the club circuit. There was a brief respite with a four-month booking at the Tropicana Club in the Bahamas in summer 1968, but then it was back to the midlands rain.

In February 1969, acting on a tip from the N'Betweens' booking agency, Fontana Records A&R man Jack Baverstock invited the band to audition for him in London. They passed and, having agreed to Baverstock's insistence that they change their name to Ambrose Slade, set about reinventing themselves.

They found a manager in Chas Chandler, the ex-Animal who had spent much of the past three years handling the Jimi Hendrix Experience. He saw them for the first time at the nightclub Rasputin's and, within 48 hours, he had bought out all the band's existing contracts. He declared himself to be their exclusive producer, then set to work convincing the band to begin writing their own material. It was his idea, too, to reinvent the band as Skinheads.

The band members themselves were not keen. But they went along with the notion regardless, buzzcut their hair and turned up their jeans and picked up the boots and braces. When Ambrose Slade's first single, 'Genesis'/'Roach Daddy' (Fontana TF 1015), appeared that May, the photos that accompanied the press kit revealed all four looking as menacing as they could muster.

More of the same followed in October 1969, with the release of 'Wild Winds Are Blowing'/'One Way Hotel' (Fontana TF 1056) – so much so that the producer of *Top Of The Pops* took one look and refused to even consider Slade (the newly truncated name was another Chandler innovation) for the show. His son had recently been beaten up by real Skinheads and that was the end of that.

Chandler wasn't discouraged. The Skinhead look was still generating plenty of press, both positive and negative, and a new single, the Barry Mann/Cynthia Weill-composed 'Shape Of Things To Come', was lined up for March 1970.

Again the portents were good. On 2 April they made their *Top Of The* Pops debut alongside an earnest young Elton John and appeared on BBC TV's *Disco Two* music show twice in the space of a month on 21 March and 25 April. Three days after that, they guested on Radio 1's *Mike Harding Show*. But again the single stubbornly failed to move – a fate that also awaited their next release, October 1970's 'Know Who You Are'/'Dapple Rose' (Polydor 2058 054) despite both a switch to the larger Polydor label, and yet another appearance on *Disco Two*.

Second album 'Play It Loud' followed in November (Polydor 2382026), and it, too, was dumper-bound. At last, Chandler was ready to admit that the Skinhead look just wasn't taking off. It was time for a change.

Because the Next Big Thing was just around the corner...

April 1970 – The birth of RAK Records

The first release on producer Mickie Most's RAK label, folkie Julie Felix's 'If I Could (El Condor Pasa)'/'Alone' (RAK101), saw the company begin as it would continue, with a hit. Indeed, Most himself expected nothing less. Between 1963, when he returned to the UK after four years of superstardom in South Africa, and the early Eighties, when he launched Kim Wilde onto the international scene, Most was responsible for some of the most distinctive hits of the age, beginning with the Animals' reinvention of 'House Of The Rising Sun', the record that single-handedly put the rock into folk rock and then made sure it stayed there.

But his death, from cancer on 30 May 2003, did not merely rob us of a very successful producer. It also took one of the few men who can truly claim to have influenced and directed the very course of Glam Rock, and that despite being surprisingly late to board the bandwagon. It would be 1973 before RAK enjoyed its first

Glam hits (Mud's 'Crazy' and Suzi Quatro's 'Can The Can' were released within weeks of one another), although Most himself shrugged off any accusation that his legendary radar had let him down on that account.

'I never made records for the sake of making them, and I never signed bands for the sake of signing them. I could have signed the Sweet and I could have signed David Bowie. They weren't ready. But I gave Bowie a hit, and I did sign Suzi Quatro and Mud, and all that happened before anybody had even heard of Glam Rock. So what was your question?'

RAK was just eight singles (and seven hits) old when Most turned down the Sweet. But his brother David picked up their publishing, and Most himself was sufficiently entranced with songwriters Nicky Chinn and Mike Chapman that he began feeding their songs to another RAK act, New World; the hits duly followed. Weeks later, RAK released former Herman's Hermits frontman Peter Noone's version of David Bowie's then-unreleased 'Oh You Pretty Things' and gave Bowie his first taste of chart glory since 'Space Oddity'.

As Chris Spedding said following Most's death, 'Mickie had a tremendous positive effect upon my own life and the lives of many other people. He was quite unique and I feel honoured to have known him.'

Born Michael Peter Hayes in Aldershot, England, in June 1938, Most's own singing career commenced amid the same Big Bang of talent that ignited British rock'n'roll in general in 1957, and his recollections, within Andrew Loog Oldham's *Stoned* autobiography, capture all the youthful excitement present at that Creation. 'I carried my recording contract with me in my pocket for at least a year, because it was really something,' Most remembered. 'There were only about 12 people in England who had a recording contract.' He never even knew what the royalty rate was, he laughed. 'I didn't care. I made records.'

In fact he made three, as one half (with Alex Murray) of the Most Brothers. In 1958, however, he left Britain for South Africa, to be with his girlfriend (and future wife) Christina, and it was there that Most's singing career went into overdrive. A string of hits between 1959-63 included two, 'Think It Over' in 1959 and a cover of Cliff Richard's British hit 'D In Love' in 1961, which ranked among their year's Top 10 best sellers.

Equally remarkably, all were self-produced and when Most returned to beat-crazed Britain in 1963, he did so as a producer. The Animals' 'House Of The Rising Sun' was only his second UK production (after the same band's debut 'Baby, Let Me Take You Home'), but its success established him in the vanguard of the new generation of young, hungry producers and managers who were tearing up the record-industry rule book at that time. Hits for Brenda Lee and the Nashville Teens followed, alongside a slew of further Animals classics.

His longest lasting-success, however, came with Herman's Hermits. Describing Most as 'the dashing prince in the record biz,' Peter 'Herman' Noone remembers, 'The first time I saw him was on a bill with the Everly Brothers and, I think, the Rolling Stones. After the show my friends and I were trying to be cool when Mickie came out chatting to Phil Everly. Phil got on a tour bus and Mickie got in a 1963 Porsche. I was pretty impressed!'

Indeed, when Herman's Hermits began their search for a producer, 'One of the reasons we approached him was because he played the guitar, he had a Porsche, he didn't get on the tour bus and he didn't play golf. All the other producers in England played golf.'

By 1967, Most's stable had expanded to include Donovan, the Yardbirds, Terry

Reid, the Jeff Beck Group and Lulu. 'I had so many hits with Mickie I can't remember,' says the latter. 'I've such a lot to be grateful for. He was an absolute hitmaker, he didn't try to be over-intelligent. That's why he had so many hits.'

And still Most's greatest triumphs were to come, as he shrugged away even the loose constraints that past employers EMI and Columbia had placed on his work and brought RAK into being. Before the end of 1970, the label had already scored hits with Julie Felix, Herman's Hermits, R&B legend Alexis Korner's CCS and singing comedian John Paul Joans (whose 'Man From Nazareth' was cut with the still-fledgling 10cc); better was to come.

By the mid Seventies, RAK was averaging one hit for every two or three singles released – the most successful label, independent or otherwise, of the era. 'Mickie was a perfectionist in the studio,' Arrows' Alan Merrill remembers. 'He prided himself on his work. In the studio he was like a strict uncle, never letting a duff pass by his aural radar. And he got the results.' Or, as Peter Noone puts it, 'He was the lazy manipulator who knew how to get performances to sound "real".'

June 1970 – David Bowie: Memory Of A Free Festival Parts 1 and 2 (Mercury 6052 026)

An electrified version of a highlight from Bowie's already-moribund 'Man Of Words, Man Of Music' LP, 'Memory Of A Free Festival' marks the vinyl debut for one of the partnerships that would come to epitomise Glam Rock, David Bowie and Mick Ronson.

An idealised commentary of an afternoon festival staged by Bowie's Beckenham Arts Lab – idealised because the aliens didn't show up – the song packed a lot of the same elements that Joni Mitchell had incorporated into her recently released 'Woodstock', and more that Melanie would feature in 'Lay Down (Candles In The Rain)' (also about Woodstock), not least of all the mass singalong that almost bullies the listener to join in.

Whereas those songs were as phenomenally successful as the event that they praised, however, Bowie's caused no more than a modest ripple – much like the festival that he celebrated. In other words, another flop.

June 1970 – The Kinks: Lola/Berkeley Mews (Pye 7N 17961)

The Kinks final UK chart-topper, 'Lola' may not have been a musical influence on the gender-bending joys to come, but it became a cultural touchstone regardless, the first (and, for many years, the most overt) ever hit record to admit that girls and boys aren't always what they seem.

Ray Davies wrote 'Lola' after a night out clubbing with manager Robert Wace. 'I remembered an incident in a club. Robert Wace had been dancing with this black woman, and he said, "I'm really on to a thing here." And it was okay until we left at six in the morning, and then I said, "Have you seen the stubble?" He said "Yeah", but he was too pissed [drunk] to care, I think.'

Unsurprisingly, given the song's subject matter, 'Lola' ran into immediate opposition from the BBC. But it was not this that alarmed dear Auntie. It was the use of the phrase 'Coca-Cola', a contravention of the Corporation's strict policy against advertising. Davies returned to the studio and sung a new line, 'cherry cola', and 'Lola' was on her merry way.

July 1970 – Hotlegs: Neanderthal Man/You Didn't Like It Because You Didn't Think Of It (Phillips 6007 019)

Take one red-hot axeman, steeped in the stew of the British beat boom, and armed with a chart-topping US hit single; add the best British songwriter this side of the Beatles; sprinkle on a couple of eccentric art students and lock them all away in a studio of their own. God knows what you'd get from such a combination today, and nobody was really sure what would happen at the very end of the Sixties, either.

But, between 1970 and 1976, the team of ex-Wayne Fontana and the Mindbenders guitarist Eric Stewart; 'Bus Stop'/'No Milk Today' (etc, etc) songsmith Graham Gouldman and an odd singing duo that Giorgio Gomelsky once christened Frabjoy and Runcible Spoon – Kevin Godley and Lol Creme – combined to create some of the most startling music of the era.

Strawberry Studios was their playground, the brainchild of Stewart, once the Mindbenders melted, and Peter Tattershall, a former roadie for Billy J Kramer's Dakotas; Gouldman later became a third partner.

Their first venture was Inter City Studios, a dilapidated concern situated over a hi-fi shop in Stockport which, Tattershall recalled, 'was lined with egg boxes 'cause we couldn't really afford acoustic tiles, and that was the nearest thing. It was very basic. But, believe it or not we did some quite good things in there. We even had the original Syd Lawrence Orchestra. But then we had to move because the studio was next to a listed building and we were classed as a fire hazard.'

When the lease ran out, Stewart continued, 'they kicked us out. So we had to make a big decision, whether we were going to build a real studio or just give the whole thing up. And, fortunately, this building came up in Stockport at a very low rent but a really, really good size. So we leased the building and got some money together to buy some more equipment, went to the bank to get some money, and we renamed it Strawberry Studios after "Strawberry Fields Forever".'

From these humble beginnings, Strawberry would rise to become one of the best, and best-appointed studios in Britain, staffed by one of the most courageous quartets in the country. And, at that point, one of the closest-knit. Godley and Creme had been friends since the early Sixties; Gouldman since not long after.

According to Godley, 'We both hung out at the local youth club in our teens. I ran the "Art group" on Tuesday nights, and Graham was a rung further up the music ladder in a slick, bow-tied cabaret group called the Whirlwinds. They did jokes, dance moves and the drummer played a timbale solo, but Graham played a red Stratocaster so his future was, therefore, assured. They also had almost exclusive use of the bigger rehearsal space at the club.'

In spite of his later fame, Gouldman had barely dreamed of writing songs at this point. In fact, when the Whirlwinds landed a one-off single deal with the HMV label, it was to the 16-year old Creme that he turned for the B-side, 'Baby, Not Like Me'. The A-side was a Buddy Holly song, 'Look At Me' ((HMV POP 1301))

Recorded at Abbey Road Studios, neither side broke new ground, 'probably because we were in Studio Two,' laughs Gouldman. 'The Beatles got Studio Three.' 'Look At Me' adhered closely to Holly's prototype, with a casual nod to the Stones, who had just made the Top Three with another Holly song, 'Not Fade Away'; Creme's effort, despite a great Gouldman guitar solo, was very much in the mould of countless Beatles-influenced lightweight R&B numbers. It didn't chart, and the Whirlwinds broke up shortly after.

By late 1964, however, Gouldman had begun writing his own material, and was soon looking to put together another band to play it, the Mockingbirds. Retaining bassist Bernard Basso and guitarist Steve Jacobsen from the Whirlwinds, he then headhunted Godley, drummer in a dirty R&B combo called the Sabres (for whom Creme played occasional guest guitar). Although, 'actually, we weren't that dirty. Our singer played the trumpet and the band played retirement homes and ice-skating rinks.'

Perhaps the greatest Should-Have-But-Didn't band of the mid-Sixties', the Mockingbirds signed to Columbia and announced their debut single would be 'For Your Love', a song Gouldman wrote in the changing-room of the men's clothing shop where he worked. Columbia promptly rejected it in favour of another Gouldman original, taped on the same day, 'That's How It's Gonna Stay', only for the discarded song to resurface, on the same label, two months later, courtesy of the Yardbirds.

It was the first in a still unbeatable (not to mention unbelievable) string of hits and classics that Gouldman would write throughout the Sixties' for – deep breath – the Hollies, Herman's Hermits, Cher, Dave Berry, the Shadows, Wayne Fontana, Jeff Beck...everyone, in fact, but himself. Neither the Mockingbirds nor the solo Gouldman so much as smelt a hit.

The Mockingbirds, shudders Godley, were cursed. 'We had one of the top songwriters in the country in the band and we couldn't get a bloody hit. No idea why. Maybe we didn't look right, maybe we didn't sound right, maybe because were tucked away in Manchester and weren't accessible.

'We weren't professional; we were an amateur band or a semi-pro band. I remember a choice I had to make when I was in my second year at art college; I was hauled over the coals by the principal of the college. "What do you want to do? Do you want to be a musician, or do you want to be a commercial artist, because you're spending too much time on music. You're going to a gig till three in the afternoon when you should be here at nine in the morning..."

'I used to skive off to do a gig, so it wasn't ideal. But we never turned pro, in inverted commas. It was local gigs, a little club in Stoke called the Place, a club in Manchester called the Oasis, small clubs or ice rinks – not "concerts", because people didn't do concerts in those days.

'I think the most interesting thing we did was the warm ups at *Top Of The Pops*, when it was being filmed in Manchester. We met the Who there a few times and got a real taste of it. We were young, everything was an experience. We had no idea where any of this stuff would lead, we were doing it because it was a hoot. Driving from one place to the other, stuck in the back of a van with a bunch of blokes, falling asleep in a bass bin – that was kinda cool. We were doing it because it was fun and it was enjoyable. We never had a huge amount of ambition because it wasn't too serious. We were in a band, and that was enough.'

So they made their little records – 'That's How It's Gonna Stay'/'I Never Should Have Kissed You' (Columbia DB7480); I Can Feel We're Parting'/'Flight Of The Mockingbird' (Columbia DB7565); 'You Stole My Love'/'Skit Skat' (Immediate IM 015); One By One'/'Lovingly Yours' (Decca F12434); How To Find A Lover'/'My Story' (Decca F12510 – scrabbled around the circuit and, all the while, Gouldman's songs continued to conquer the world.

Peter Noone: 'Graham was just a phenomenal songsmith. Everything he played to me, I loved. And it's the construction. We turned down Carole King songs and Neil Diamond songs, but we never, ever turned down a Graham Gouldman song. I, still to this day, say, "Why didn't I get him in Herman's Hermits?"'

Instead, when Gouldman did join another band, following the demise of the Mockingbirds and a stillborn solo career that included an entire album's worth of his finest songs, 'The Graham Gouldman Thing' (RCA LPM 3954) that did no better than the Mockingbirds' output, he fell into the final days of the Mindbenders.

Hitmakers supreme in their prime, racking up six Top Fifty hits with original frontman Wayne Fontana and another four once he left, the Mindbenders had now fallen on hard times. Their last hit, a cover of the Box Tops' 'The Letter', had been creamed by the simultaneous release of the original and Gouldman knew his time in the band would be brief.

'I wasn't an official member,' he explains. 'I only joined right at the end when Eric [Stewart, guitarist and lead vocalist] was the only original member left. I'd known him for a while; it was just Eric doing the clubs. He said do you fancy coming on the road with us, so I did.'

Nevertheless, both he and Stewart still recoil from the memory of the group's final release, 1968's 'Uncle Joe, The Ice Cream Man'. 'We were recording that at Olympic Studios,' Stewart remembered, 'and the Stones were next door working on ['Beggar's Banquet']. Mick Jagger popped his head round while I was doing the vocal and said, "Why are you singing this shit?" It was the final nail in the coffin.'

The Mindbenders broke up almost before the record was in the racks, calling it a day at the Liverpool Empire on 20 November 1968, the last night of a UK tour with the Who, Arthur Brown, Joe Cocker and the Small Faces.

Freed from the band, and the need to play 'A Groovy Kind Of Love' every night until he died, Stewart threw himself into his newly purchased studio dream. Gouldman, meanwhile, returned to his maverick wanderings, playing some sessions for Giorgio Gomelsky's newly founded Marmalade label.

'We recorded a few tracks,' he says, 'although it wasn't like we were going to do a Graham Gouldman album. I think it was just the odd track. It's a bit vague that period. What was I doing? I dunno.'

Nevertheless, it was through these auspices

that Kevin Godley and Lol Creme finally found themselves preparing to hit 'the big time'. The pair had spent the past several years studying for diplomas in graphic design; together, they designed the promotional cardboard models that went out with such movies as *The Railway Children* and *Cromwell*. 'Altogether, I think I must have spent about 11 years at art college,' Godley later recollected. 'I just dug being a student. About that time, I was working with Lol on various projects that were vaguely to do with music and getting further away from painting and drawing all the time.

'We were writing shows and ideas for shows, and crazy sort-of-multimedia things which at that time was pretty avant-garde. So it was more a matter of deciding whether to go into that properly, or whether to do art or whatever.'

The decision was finally made for them when a commission, painting a mural on an office wall, introduced them to Kennedy Street Enterprises, the Manchester-based management structure that already handled Gouldman and sundry former Mindbenders.

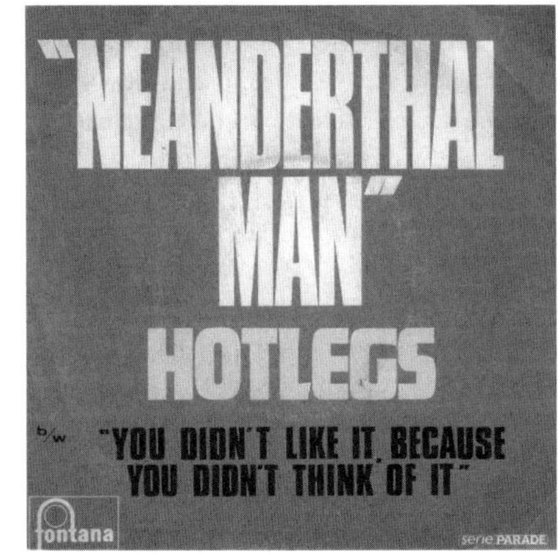

Under their guidance, the duo started recording the songs they were already composing. 'We were both at art college,' Godley continues. 'Lol was in Birmingham and I was in Stoke, and we used to meet at weekends and write and record stuff. We liked to get together at Graham's house and record stuff on his Revox. That was our first experience of the recording process. Seminal Godley and Creme stuff.'

He recalls the songs that poured onto those tapes, but have never seen the light of day since then. '"Seeing Things Green", "Cowboys and Indians", "Over And Above My Head" and "One And One Make Love" were recorded with Whirlwinds singers Phil Cohen and Malcolm Wagner on backing vocals. All done on a reel-to-reel Revox. Heady times. I wish I could unearth the tapes. But then again...'

One day in 1968, Gouldman asked Godley to join him at a Marmalade session. The moment Godley opened his mouth to unleash his ethereal falsetto, Gomelsky offered him a record deal. It was, Godley laughs, the prelude to a nightmare.

'More than anything, I remember the life change. The scene is still vivid in my head. A three-hour drive, in a howling gale, from one life to another, leaving behind three years at Stoke on Trent College of Art and heading for London, and a totally unknown future. I remember crying and trying not to show it as Lol drove my MG Midget out of the college car park. I was missing everybody there before we even hit the road. I also remember the hood of the car flying up and smacking into the windshield and nearly killing us, then operating the wipers by hand through a crack in the soft top.'

Things were calmer in the studio, but only just. 'Cut to Eddy Offord behind the control desk at Advision Studios. A small, dark space smelling of last night's session. A whiff of weed and Afghan coats. Very London. Very hip. There was an old Mellotron in one corner, Giorgio, big and rumbling, coming on like a hip Rasputin and me singing in a real studio. Intimidating, impossible, the beginning of everything. When he decided to call us Frabjoy and Runcible Spoon, it was almost the end of everything.'

The song they were recording was a gentle little number called 'To Fly Away'. 'It was quite a challenging session,' Godley continues, 'as it was the first time I'd stepped up to the microphone. We were more confident for "I Am Beside Myself", which had brass arranged by Tony Meehan, late of the Shadows. Graham may have played on these sessions. Not one hundred per cent sure, but I do remember Keith Tippett being vaguely involved.'

Gomelsky apparently saw the duo as the English Simon and Garfunkel, a notion with which Godley finds himself agreeing. 'Yeah, I can see that. The songs we were writing back then were kinda acoustic, rural-sounding stuff. When you're that kind of age, you are consciously copying someone, and we were probably consciously copying Simon and Garfunkel. It was only later in our careers, when we didn't really have too much time to think, that we started recording stuff that sounded like ourselves.'

As Frabjoy and Runcible Spoon, the duo began work on an album in September 1969. Basic tracks were recorded at Strawberry Studios, with Eric Stewart on guitar and Gouldman on bass, and things were progressing so wonderfully that, by the end of the month, Frabjoy and Runcible Spoon's debut single, 'I Am Beside Myself'/'Animal Song' (Marmalade 598 019) was on the shelves.

'To Fly Away' appeared on Marmalade's '100% Proof' sampler (Marmalade 643 314), where it was mistakenly credited to Godley and Gouldman, while the same team also convened for a Graham Gouldman cut on that album, the whimsical 'The Late Mr Late', about a gent whose timekeeping was so slipshod that he missed his own funeral. 'We were one of many new artists on a very cool label,' Godley recalls. 'We were obviously thrilled when both records were released, but learned a valuable lesson when they promptly disappeared. The rest is more haze than history...'

Marmalade folded shortly after this pair of releases, and the Frabjoy album was abandoned. Hopes that Marmalade's parent label, Polydor, might pick up the option were briefly raised when 'I'm Beside Myself' found its way onto a Polydor compilation, but nothing came of it.

'Giorgio certainly had the right attitude,' says Godley. 'I'm not sure anyone really knew what they were doing, but I think his overriding concern was to document the music that was around; he didn't really think the rest of it through. Full marks to him for being around, though, because nobody else was doing it. He got a lot of bands recorded that no-one else would touch.'

Godley and Creme faded from view for a time; Gouldman, meanwhile, landed on his feet by taking up an offer to fly to New York to join Kasenetz-Katz. The major purveyors of 'bubblegum' music, K-K owned dozens of hit name bands (all made up of session men), and an equally large roster of staff writers who, in true Brill Building tradition, were allocated a desk and expected to simply keep the songs coming.

'Kasenetz-Katz decided they wanted to get legit,' Gouldman explains, 'so they wanted someone a little more valid in their factory. Artistically, it was not a good move on my part, but there's always good comes out of things like that. Actually they did contribute to 10cc coming together, because I was working in New York and I said, "Look, I'm fed up here. I've got involved in this studio back in Manchester, I want to take all the stuff we're recording here, and do it with my own guys back in England." So Strawberry got a tremendous amount of business. Those records, the early ones, were Kevin, Lol and myself, and Eric was engineering them.'

In fact, the first Kasenetz-Katz sessions took place in London, while Strawberry Studios were being properly equipped; together, the Gouldman-Stewart-Godley-Creme team wrote and played on a host of Super K Productions records, released under varying names around the world.

Godley: 'We briefly and uncomfortably became Crazy Elephant, Ohio Express, Silver Fleet, Fighter Squadron, Festival and fuck knows who else under the production tutelage of the late Richie Cordell, brought in from NY to keep the crazy Brits in check. Crazy Brits. This was a guy who ate pickled onions straight from the jar and nothing else. I think Richie introduced spliff into our lives. Thank you, Ritchie.'

The hits kept coming. Gouldman's 'Have You Ever Been To Georgia' was a smash for many artists, including Tony Christie, another Kennedy Street act. He was also responsible for two Ohio Express hits, 'Sausalito' and 'Tampa Florida', while Freddie and the Dreamers sold a million copies of 'Susan's Tuba' in France, with Gouldman writing and singing.

'Graham was still residing in New York at the time,' Godley continues, 'but he was out of energy and wanted to come home and work with us. [So] it was me, Lol and Eric, and a blank canvas. Eric had the ears and technical know-how and, while waiting for Graham to return, we started playing around.'

It was now early 1970, and Godley laughingly remembers the trio 'strumming, wailing and banging anything in sight' to test the new equipment coming into the studio.

'The first musical noises that had any cohesion...started life as an unorthodox drum test featuring full kit overdubbed onto all four tracks, with Lol singing this spooky, retarded nursery rhyme that got mixed in via the bass drum mike. Like all the early work, it was driven by applied ignorance and adrenalin but we knew it had something. Unfortunately the track got erased but we liked the vibe so much we started again adding recorders, tone generator, anvil, backwards echo until it sounded like nothing else on earth.'

Stewart picked up the thread. 'Dick Leahy, from Philips, came in and he said, "What the hell's that you're playing?" I said, "It's a studio experiment; a percussive experiment." He says, "It sounds like a hit record to me – can we release it?" And we said, "Yeah, okay. What should we call it?"'

'Neanderthal Man.'

And what shall we call ourselves?

Hotlegs. 'We had a girl at the studio,' Stewart continued. 'Kathy Gill, who had very, very nice legs and she used to wear these incredible hotpants. Green, leather hotpants. So we called the group, ah, Hotlegs.'

'Neanderthal Man' reached Number 22 in the US, Number 2 in Britain (Hotlegs debuted on *Top Of The Pops* on 16 July), Number 1 in Italy and ultimately sold over two million worldwide.

The record was enormous. The Idle Race, heading towards the end of their brief but glorious career, wrestled one final hit from the jaws of oblivion when they covered the song for German and Argentine consumption. Elton John, eking out a pre-fame career as a jobbing sessioneer, recorded his own distinctive version for a budget-priced collection of soundalike hits. 'We thought we had it made,' laughs Godley. 'We were on our way, baby!'

August 1970 – Alternate Histories II – Hot Muddy Chocolate

Making it three hits out of three releases for RAK with August 1970's 'Love Is Life' (c/w 'Pretty Girls', RAK 103), Hot Chocolate developed out of the songwriting partnership of Errol Brown and Tony Wilson.

In 1969, the pair were approached to reggae-fy various hits of the day, one of which was John Lennon and the Plastic Ono Band's 'Give Peace A Chance'. Having submitted their version to Lennon, so that he might approve some lyric changes they'd made, the pair were rewarded not only with the wise walrus's blessing, they were also handed a one-off record deal with Apple and a band name. Riffing on Wilson and Brown's West Indian heritage, Lennon christened them Hot Chocolate.

'Give Peace A Chance', backed by Wilson/Brown's own 'Living Without Tomorrow' (Apple 18) was released that October and, while it didn't chart, it did attract the attention of Mickie Most. By the new year, Wilson and Brown had been adopted as in-house songwriters at RAK, and quickly scored when Peter Noone and Herman's Hermits' version of their 'Bet Yer Life I Do' (RAK 102) reached Number 22.

The duo also brought the Hot Chocolate name with them, albeit without a band, and the search was now on to find one. Which Most duly did, one night at the Speakeasy. They were called Mud.

Mud had already been around the block a few times. The band formed in Mitcham, south London, in 1967, from the nuclei of two local bands, the Mourners, featuring brothers Les (vocals) and Pete Gray (drums), guitarist Rob Davis and bassist Nigel Munt, and the Remains: Ray Stiles (bass), Dave Mount (drums) and that same Rob Davis on guitar. That situation ended when the Remains suggested he throw his all into their band ('We were the better group,' explains Stiles), only for Davis to throw in with the Mourners instead.

The Remains petered out soon after, as Munt quit the Mourners and was replaced by Stiles, around the same time as the group changed its name to Mud. 'I've no idea why we chose the name Mud,' Les Gray confessed. 'There have been many stories. One said it was because [we] got stuck in the mud in a field...' Stiles adds another one, that they renamed themselves after hearing Davis say of a passing fringed jacket, 'it looks like mud'. But the most likely explanation, as they both agreed, was 'it was chosen because it was short. If you stuck "Mud" on a poster, you got a huge billing, because it was only three letters.'

Mud turned professional on 1 April 1968, on the eve of a Swedish tour; Dave Mount joined the band at the same time, after Pete Gray announced he didn't want to make the trip. 'We went, and we had a great time,' Stiles recalls mysteriously.

Home again, most of Mud's time, according to Les Gray, was spent 'living in the back of our Transit van, 'with the band's energies primarily devoted to the northern circuit of discotheques, rock clubs, cabaret and working men's clubs. Anywhere they could get a booking. They developed different acts for each one as well, knowing instinctively what kind of performance would work best with the evening's audience and seldom getting it wrong.

'Each one of us did a different job,' Stiles explains. 'I looked after the equipment and made sure the van was always serviced. Rob looked after the money although there wasn't much of that; Les was very much a socialiser, and would put the name of the band around, and Dave looked after the bookings, dealing with agents.'

It was Mount who brought the band to the attention of the SLA agency in Manchester, 'and they got us working up there. We did all the clubs around the north and north-east, and we did so much work there that people thought we were a northern band. We'd go up to Newcastle and do two or three weeks solid, six shows a week, plus a couple of lunchtime shows backing strippers. We were always working.'

Mud's debut single, 'Flower Power'/'You're My Mother' (CBS 203002) appeared that same year. 'We were all into wearing kaftans, beads and bells,' Gray shuddered. 'Up The Airy Mountain' ('us trying to be avant-garde')/'Latter Days' (CBS 3355) followed, before a switch to Philips brought 1969's 'Shangri-La'/'House On The Hill' (Phillips BF1775). None really sold, but Mud were having fun regardless, and another night at the Speakeasy was just one more engagement until they were told, as they set up their gear, that they'd have to make do with less space than usual, because another group was coming in to audition for Mickie Most.

Stiles: 'In those years when we were just milling around doing the northern clubs, we did used to work in London. We used to play the trendy clubs, we were the little band in the corner, we took the mickey out of all the flash people, we just had a good time,' So they obediently sat out the 'other' group's set, then took the stage for their own.

'And afterwards, one of the lads from the office came backstage and said 'Mickie Most was out there after the other lot cleared off. He stayed in there and he couldn't take his eyes off you lot'.'

The 'office' was Mud's publisher, Feldman's; the 'lad' was Ian Kimmet, soon to be forming a band of his own, Jook. Right now, though, his eyes were on Most and, when the Great Man returned to the Speakeasy the following evening to see Mud perform once again, Kimmet grasped the opportunity to introduce them. The following morning, Mud made the short trip to the RAK offices in the West End, settled on Most's large leather couch and listened as the producer outlined their destiny.

First he introduced them to his label, and his intentions to establish it as the most successful hitmaker in the industry.

Stiles: 'He said, "It's called RAK Records. You wanna be on RAK Records, don't you?" "Yes we would, please." Then he told us how he had these two songwriters, and they'd be writing our songs, and they had a band name that John Lennon had given them...they were Errol Brown and Tony Wilson, and the name of the band was Hot Chocolate. And that's who we were going to be.

'But then Mickie found out we were with Feldman's, and a couple of years earlier he'd had a falling-out with them and lost the court case. So we were called back in, and he told us, "When you get freed from Feldman's, come back to me." And the next thing we know, Hot Chocolate have "Love Is Life" out, and we thought "Bloody hell, that could have been us."'

August 1970 – Dib Cochran and the Earwigs: Oh Baby/Universal Love (Bell 1121)

With Marc Bolan now balancing precariously on the brink of a major musical shift, David Bowie loaned guitarist Mick Ronson and drummer John Cambridge to Dib Cochran and the Earwigs, a one-off project with which Bolan and Finn intended again testing the electric waters – at the same time, says producer Tony Visconti, as competing with the lightweight pop sounds of Edison Lighthouse and Christie then clogging up the chart. Visconti even arranged a one-off deal with Bell Records, the chief perpetrators of such music, to further boost this bizarre effort's chances.

As meaningless slices of bubblegum buoyancy go, 'Oh Baby' was certainly up there with such current pop nuggets as 'Love Grows', 'Yellow River' and 'My Baby Loves Lovin'', and was vastly superior. But it received little if any airplay, and with the music press treating it with the disdain they presumably felt another passing piece of pap deserved the whole project fizzled away unnoticed.

Bolan, though, was satisfied and, as the sessions progressed for his next album, 'T Rex', his ambition only gained momentum.

Of course, it still remained essential to Bolan's game plan that he establish himself with a hit single, but even that was around the corner. Former manager Simon Napier-Bell explains, 'Kit Lambert [co-founder of Bolan's new label, Fly] and Tony Visconti...spent hours working on him, trying to convince him that it was now or never as far as his electric ambitions went. Marc finally took the plunge.'

September 1970 – The only Performance that matters...

It's been praised so often that it seems impossible there was ever a time when director Nic Roeg's *Performance* was not a part of the rock mythos. Or a time when its vision of the darkness at the end of pop was not seen as the ultimate quest for any young rocker, raised on rock's mythos of violence, drugs and ultra-sex.

Within weeks of it appearing in the cinemas – before that even, with just the ads in the imported American press, and a glimpse of Jagger's face on the cover of the soundtrack LP – *Performance* hit home. Michael Des Barres recalls a time, long before Glam Rock, months before Bolan, when life itself seemed to have become 'A competition to see who could be most like Turner from *Performance*. It was, and it remains, a key seminal image.'

It is also the ultimate rock'n'roll movie, and that despite having very little to say on the subject beyond its lead character, the singularly named Turner the archetypal post-psychedelic burnout, struggling to revitalise his career at the same time as tacitly acknowledging he didn't have a clue where to start.

It's a dark film, possibly Roeg's darkest, and a disturbing one. The intersection of pop decadence and gangster hedonism was not new, even when *Performance* was being planned; London gangland figureheads Ronnie and Reggie Kray had cavorted with showbiz heroes a decade before, and when Morrissey wrote 'Last Of The Famous International Playboys' in 1989 he was tapping into precisely that same mythology.

The difference was, that when Morrissey sang a love song to his 'dear hero in prison', that's all he did. He sang. When Mick Jagger arose at the peak of his own supposedly blackest hour, stepping out of a world of sympathetic devils, banqueting beggars and stray-cat blues, and into the even more stygian universe of Turner and *Performance*, many critics complained he wasn't actually acting. He was simply playing himself.

Performance was that good.

Performance was the creation of writer Donald Cammell, who originally conceived it as *The Performers*, a light-hearted romp through the Swinging Sixties with Marlon Brando cast as an American gangster hiding out in London at the pad of a pop star.

Slowly, however, the mood shifted, and by the time the script drifted into Mick Jagger's orbit, with James Fox stepping into the role once meant for Brando, it was a very different creation – one which supplanted its basic premise with a series of questions relating to identity crisis, madness and murder. Indeed, we are still awaiting more than a glimpse of Jagger when Fox, in the role of gangster Chas, murders his childhood friend and rival Joey in a scene all the more intense for the homoerotic gun-and-whip play that precedes the actual shooting.

Chas goes on the run, not from the law but from his own former gangster allies, a mob headed up by 'respectable' London 'businessman' Harry Flowers, himself a role model for every Cockney mob boss Guy Ritchie has ever imagined.

Rightfully fearing for his life, the hard man Chas dyes his hair with red paint and heads underground. Or, at least, to the grubby café where he overhears a very Hendrix-like musician

MICK JAGGER in
PERFORMANCE
William Hughes
A story of violence and
sadism... a sensational film

conveniently discussing the plight in which he'd just left his landlord, complete with names, addresses, outstanding rent, the works.

It's the one false note in the entire movie, but it's also the pivot around which the rest of the film revolves, for it's the scene that ensures Chas' immediate destiny, fetching up at a once-glorious but now somewhat seedy address in London's traditionally bohemian Notting Hill district on the corner of Powys Square.

Aware that his would-be host is in the entertainment business, but sufficiently square that he has no real clue who he is calling upon, Chas introduces himself as a fellow performer – a juggler. It is not an introduction guaranteed to thrill his hosts, Turner, and his assistants/lovers Pherber (Anita Pallenberg) and Lucy (Michele Breton), and there's some doubt whether they will even allow him into the house. But Chas forces the rent into Pherber's hand, pushes his way into the hallway and, before anybody can do anything about it, Turner has a new lodger.

Still, their early relationship is shaped by dislike and distrust. Turner may have enjoyed a string of hits in the past. But he has 'lost his demon' in the years since then and is now a virtual recluse, amusing himself by purchasing art, spray-painting his walls, strumming Robert Johnson and having sex with the girls.

Which doesn't sound that bad a life, but Chas is openly contemptuous. 'Funny little geezer,' he spits in one scene. 'You'll look funny when you're 50.'

But there's a bond forming as well, one which Pherber, in particular, is intent on furthering, and as Chas realises that his only chance of escape is to flee the country, Turner comes close to begging him to stay. But then a twist of underworld betrayal is added to the plot, and on the day that Chas is preparing to leave, Harry Flowers and his men come calling. And somebody gets shot and killed. But is it Turner by Chas, as it originally appears? Or Chas by Turner?

The filming of *Performance* began in October 1967, with Jagger and Fox joined by a very impressive array of talent. Early hopes that Jagger's girlfriend, Marianne Faithfull, would be cast as Pherber were dashed when Faithfull discovered she was pregnant. Keith Richard's girlfriend, Pallenberg, was cast in her stead, and hindsight reckons it was the right decision. Faithfull was too English to truly play the role; the German-born Pallenberg, on the other hand, adds both an exotic twist and a cruel sexuality to the role, and the scenes when she and Chas interact become all the more powerful for her natural strength, a quality Chas never seems previously to have encountered in a woman.

Established character actors Stanley Meadows, Allan Cuthbertson, Anthony Morton and Johnny Shannon, and the fast-rising Anthony Valentine were all recruited, and so was John Bindon, a real-life gangster turned actor who was something of a society darling during the mid-Sixties despite (or, perhaps, because of) his criminal past.

And then Roeg screened the film for its backers. Believing themselves secure in the knowledge that Roeg and Cammell were hatching the Rolling Stones' riotous answer to the Beatles' *A Hard Days Night*, Warner Brothers paid little attention to the film as it came together. Their £1.8 million, they believed, was in safe hands. Only when Roeg and Cammell delivered their creation did the executives realise just how wrong their initial assumptions had been.

'In a sense, most of the people in *Performance* weren't acting at all,' Marianne Faithfull recalled. 'They were exhibiting themselves. Real gangsters, real rock stars, real drug addicts, real sirens. The film was truly our *Picture Of Dorian Gray* – an allegory of libertine Chelsea life in the late Sixties with its baronial rock stars, wayward *jeunesse dorée*, drugs, sex and decadence. It preserves the whole era under glass.'

And the picture wasn't pretty. According to legend, the wife of one Warners executive was physically sick during one test screening as bloody beating after beating rolled out of the gangland sequences; as an innocent chauffeur is cruelly shaved and then forced to watch while his employers' car is drenched in acid; as Chas is held down and beaten with a switch; and so on.

Other corporate reactions were less extreme, but Warners was taking no chances. They had asked for *A Hard Day's Night* and they received an atrocity. The film was canned; worse than that, there were moves afoot within the company to have the negative destroyed, as if to purge the world for good of this malignant slice of celluloid garbage.

It would be two years, and a new decade, before the film was finally cleared for release, years during which the original print was cut and recut, impenetrable Cockney accents redubbed by other actors (for the American release only) and Warners itself underwent a major change in administration and outlook. Finally, *Performance* was in the cinemas, but still the film raised hackles.

Respected movie critic John Simon wrote it off as 'the most loathsome film of all time.' Historian David Thomson called it 'a load of rubbish'. Another critic, Richard Schickel, described it as 'the most completely worthless film I have seen since I began reviewing.'

The underground press was more forgiving, of course, and more than one hip young thing found his or herself laughing aloud at the in-jokes that permeated the movie – the delivery of Mars Bars that waits outside Turner's front door, for example. Yet even the most avid admirers of *Performance* will admit that, by the standards of the day, the film pushed buttons.

Buttons the assembled hordes of Glam Rock – Bowie, Ferry, Harley and Strange – would soon be nailing into place.

Viewed today, the sex and drug scenes in *Performance* seem strong, even when compared to some of what is currently splashed over our screens. At the time, they were widely regarded as being tantamount to pornography, especially after rumours began insisting that Jagger and Pallenberg were not acting during one of their on-screen sexual romps. Yet, whereas such a reputation might have been expected to send the prurient punters flocking to see the sex, it appears to have had the opposite effect.

Performance fared poorly in the cinemas, and the spin-off industry scarcely set the world on fire either. A monetisation of the movie, by author William Hughes, came and went all but unnoticed. The soundtrack album, released worldwide through Warner Brothers followed suit.

Through all of these tempests, however, *Performance* marched on, a midnight cinema staple that had, by the mid-Seventies, established itself not as merely one of the greatest rock movies of all time but also as one of the masterpieces of British cinema in general.

Certainly its influence not only on movies but also across the entire audio-visual palette is undeniable. From a technical standpoint, it was the first feature film ever to use the cut-up technique of filming; from a censorial angle, it opened new doors of permissiveness, at least among directors, and the likes of *Midnight Cowboy* owe it a terrific debt.

Yet, no matter how pernicious its influence might be, no matter how many fingers and toes one employs to count the number of would-be rock'n'roll outlaws who have tried to take Turner's natural magic for their own, no more than a handful – the same quartet that has already been mentioned – ever grasped the single most important truth that gives *Performance* its most solid grounding.

'The only performance that really matters,' Turner tells Chas during a discourse on juggling, 'is the one that achieves madness.'

Performance achieves madness.

October 1970 – T Rex: Ride A White Swan/Is It Love/Summertime Blues (Fly BUG 1)

It all seems so simple now, but even Marc Bolan was worried as the release of 'Ride A White Swan' drew closer. According to Simon Napier-Bell. 'He was so scared of it bombing out that he was going around telling everybody that he disowned the record. What he really meant was that he disowned it if it was a flop. When it was a hit, though, it simply wasn't worth the bother of trying to explain all that crap to people who said he'd sold out. Because now he was God, and whoever heard of God selling out?'

Besides, T Rex had one thing that John's Children didn't. Flo and Eddie.

Howard Kaylan and Mark Volman, the Fluorescent Leech and Eddie to their friends, were the American singer-songwriters behind the Turtles, who in turn were the power behind three of the most memorable singles of the last few years, 'Elenore', 'Happy Together' and 'She'd Rather Be With Me'. More recently, they'd been performing with the Mothers of Invention and were, in fact, in London with Zappa as Bolan was preparing for the crucial recording session.

He'd met the pair when Tyrannosaurus Rex opened for the Turtles during that fractious American tour; with some time to spare one afternoon, he decided to visit them at their hotel, and ask if they'd like to sing on the record.

Kaylan alone was home.

Kaylan: 'Mark [Volman] had gone out, he was off kicking around Kings Road or something, so I said "Shit, I'll do it, and the worst that can happen is you'll put me on twice." So I went into the studio with Marc and Tony Visconti, did "Ride A White Swan" and we really didn't need more voices than that, it was just that simple little high "ooh and ah" stuff and we double-tracked it.'

Bolan was on the road as the single came out, touring behind some heavily advertised reduced-rate ticket prices – ten shillings, or 50p in the forthcoming decimal currency. Audiences swooped and, buoyed by their enthusiasm, 'Ride A White Swan' entered the chart on 24 October.

Its progress was convoluted. A *Top Gear* BBC radio session helped the single to Number 30 on 14 November. One week, and another session (Bob Harris on 16 November) later, it had leaped to Number 15, and it was Number 7 by the end of the month.

Top Of The Pops came calling. T Rex's maiden appearance on the show, on 12 November, saw the group lining up alongside Dave Edmunds, Don Fardon, McGuinness Flint, the Move and the Bee Gees. Matthews Southern Comfort were Number 1, soon to be replaced by the recently deceased Jimi Hendrix.

Would any of them see such glory days again?

T Rex were back on Britain's best-loved pop show a fortnight later, and again two weeks after that, on 10 December. By 12 December, the single was Number 6 and then commenced its descent; down to Number 12 on 19 December. Bolan had finally scored his first major hit.

But 'Ride A White Swan' wasn't finished yet. That same week, T Rex appeared on DJ Dave Lee Travis' show, gifting the self-styled Hairy Cornflake tremendous versions of 'Ride A White Swan', its B-side 'Summertime Blues', and a new song, 'Hot Love'. And seven days later, the single soared again, back up to Number 10 for Christmas. And now it seemed unstoppable: Number 4 for two weeks in January and finally, on 23 January, it was Number 2, butting up against actor Clive Dunn's surprise chart-topper 'Grandad'.

Elsewhere, McGuinness Flint's 'Malt And Barley Blues', Glen Campbell's 'It's Only Make Believe' and the Jackson Five's 'I'll Be There' jousted for supremacy. But 'Ride A White Swan' held firm. T Rexstasy was on the move.

'I wasn't really surprised when he made it,' Andy Ellison admits, 'because he had always been a very shrewd and well-organised young man. I was in France when all that T Rex stuff got going, and I must admit I was feeling pretty envious. In fact, I was feeling a *lot* envious because, although he really deserved that success, I often wondered what would have happened if...'

October 1970 – Alternate Histories III: Medicine Headmania

Marc Bolan was not the only person experimenting with acoustics and electrification at the end of 1970. A pair of midlands art students, John Fiddler and Peter Hope-Evans, too, were toying with the limits of their chosen sound, and the fact that they were also a duo lazy ears might have pigeonholed as 'folky' was as coincidental as the fact that, months before Bolan donned his first dash of glitter, Medicine Head were already renowned for splashing body paint and make-up over themselves.

The similarities between the two acts at this time were both manifold and, with hindsight, startling.

Like Marc, Medicine Head were loudly championed by DJ John Peel. He signed them to his newly formed Dandelion label and once claimed with a self-deprecating smile that he'd been considering signing Tyrannosaurus Rex too. But 'I didn't want two bands that people might say sounded the same.' Bolan went to another start-up company, Fly Records, instead.

Like Marc, they looked the part – the angelic Peter Hope-Evans was the Bolanic beauty that could (and did) set the teenyboppers' hearts a-flutter; John Fiddler was the intellectual giant who promised substance to match his style.

And like Marc, they sounded right. A largely acoustic duo in the same spirit as Tyrannosaurus Rex and the Incredible String Band, their array of esoteric instrumentation may not have included anything as twee as glockenspiel and pixiephone, but Hope-Evans' deployment of the Jew's Harp pledged an atmosphere far removed from basic bass and guitar, probably inspiring the Who, too, to break out the instrument on the following year's 'Join Together'.

Where the two acts separate is what they did with that esotericism – Bolan dumped it altogether, and only the bongos remained to remind us of it. Medicine Head continued exploring. And while T Rex built from a base of classic rock'n'roll, Medicine Head employed a template drawn from Delta blues, Cajun atmospheres and deep south Americana in general – a notion that Fiddler believes neither Bolan, nor any of his successors, would truly grasp. 'I didn't ever feel any connection between David Bowie and the Blues, or Marc Bolan and the Blues, in the way that Peter Hope-Evans and I connected with the Blues.'

But still, caught up in that delicious moment where 'Ride A White Swan' was imminent, and Medicine Head's 'Coast To Coast'/'All For Tomorrow' (Dandelion 5075) was still warm, there lurks the temptation to wonder what might have happened had Dandelion only had the financial and promotional resources to match Fly's?

Both records 'rock up' an earlier, more eclectic sound; both have a punch and drive far beyond expectations. And both have a percussive edge that was born to boogie. The difference was, Bolan's release had muscle behind it. Medicine Head's didn't.

In the event, it would be six months *after* Marc's first hit that Medicine Head made their chart debut, when '(And The) Pictures In The Sky' reached Number 22, by which time T Rexstasy was already in bloom, Bolan had hallmarked the boogie and the music had already spun off in a direction that Medicine Head had no intention of following.

And yet, of all the bands that *weren't* Glam Rock, but who have made more than one list of the genre's greatest exponents, Medicine Head are the one act who sit so firmly on the fence that their omission from these pages would be the cause of as much dispute as their inclusion.

'I honestly don't think Medicine Head had much at all in common with Glam Rock,' confirms Fiddler, while acknowledging that 'Peter obviously enjoyed dressing up in some rather interesting outfits. But such sartorial experiments began way before Glam Rock' – way before Medicine Head itself, in fact. 'Coming from an Art background, our use of make-up, body paint etc began way back in the Sixties, before Glam Rock had become a marketing siren.'

But when Medicine Head re-emerged on the chart in spring 1973, after three further singles had failed to capitalise on that first hit, glimpses of what they could have been were never hard to discern. 'One And One Is One', 'Rising Sun' (both 1973) and 'Slip And Slide' (1974) remain Glam-era mix-tape favourites, the latter positively lascivious in its conjuring-up of teenage currents.

Fiddler: 'Sexuality, and sexual awareness are massively important in an adolescents life. "Slip And Slide" is filled to the hilt with sex; the title leads and the song follows. Of course my influence for this song was the sound of Slim Harpo – sleazy, sexual, forbidden, dangerous, but undeniably drenched in the hot sweat of sexual engagement.'

Lick that.

---

4 November 1970: Lift Off with Mud

Granada TV's teatime children's music spectacular *Lift Off* started life in December 1968 under the less distinctive title *Discotheque*. A succession of co-hosts included Merseybeat survivor Billy J Kramer, actress Diane Greaves and singer Graham Bonney before singer, model and actress Ayshea Brough arrived (replacing Greaves and working alongside Bonney) in March 1969, just weeks before her debut (12 May) as Lieutenant Ayshea Johnson in the Gerry Anderson sci-fi show *UFO*.

Discotheque became *Lift Off* that November, and *Lift Off* in turn would become a key prime time vehicle both for the visiting artists and for the lovely Ayshea. Although her recording career would prove sporadic she regularly performed on the show, in the process building up a public persona that made her as instantly identifiable as any of her popstar guests.

Few of the early shows were memorable. Children's TV tended to attract lightweight performers, many of whose names are forgotten even by hardened vinyl sleuths. But nestling in among them were the likes of John Walker, White Plains, Maggie Brown and Baskin and Copperfield (featuring future Rubettes Alan Williams and John Richardson – small world!); and on tonight's instalment, Mud – the band that didn't become Hot Chocolate.

Their fourth single, 'Jumping Jehosophat'/ 'Won't Let It Go' (Philips 6006 022) was new on the racks (but not the RAK) and, for a while, it looked like it was going to place the Most disappointment firmly in the past.

Ray Stiles: 'We did "Jehosophat" with Mitch Murray and Pete Callendar, and it looked like it was going to take off. We did *Lift Off*, and that would have been one of our first TV performances. We did *Basil Brush* around that time, as well. And we did *Opportunity Knocks*, which went appallingly terrible. I did this thing where I was doing cheek-slapping for a rhythmic thing, and they messed up our sound. It sounded absolutely dreadful.

'Rather than get work, we lost it – but for years afterwards, after we became successful, Hughie Green would go on there and talk about the show's big successes. Mary Hopkin, New World, Lena Zavaroni, Mud... "Hey, don't put us in there, your programme nearly finished us off."'

December 1970 – T Rex: T Rex (Fly HIFLY 2)

The fifth Tyrannosaurus Rex album was also the first T Rex set, as Bolan abbreviated the band name at the same time as enlarging everything else – most notably the group's sound. Transitional through and through, 'T Rex' is the obvious successor to 'A Beard Of Stars', but it's clearly looking towards 'Electric Warrior' too, a point proven when the band hit the tour and TV circuits early in 1971.

'Jewel', 'Beltane Walk' and a reprise of the 1968 single 'One Inch Rock' are all bona fide Bolan classics and, if 'T Rex' was to be overshadowed by the simultaneous success of the 'Ride A White Swan' single (pointedly not included on the album), then that only allowed Bolan more time in which to plan his next move.

In fact, in many ways, this is the quintessential Bolan album, the last to be made before his entire life was swallowed up by superstardom, but the first to begin imagining what that might feel like. Certainly he has fun revisiting his first ever single, 'The Wizard', while his ambition is writ large throughout the opening and closing snippets of 'The Children Of Rarn', excerpts from a fully fledged concept album that he was then contemplating.

Also on board: 'Is It Love', one of his most contagiously under-rated compositions ever; 'Sun Eye', with its grim portent of tyrannosaurus rex, the eater of cars; and the poignant 'Seagull Woman', with guitar to melt your heart. But really, there's not a sour note to be found all album long. And it's the last Bolan album that you could say that about.

16 December 1970 – Lift Off with Stavely (Granada TV)

Another of those episodes that hindsight raises its eyebrows at... Julie Felix and Herman's Hermits celebrating RAK's first Christmas, an appearance from somebody named Jeff Collins and – making the first of several showings on *Lift Off* – Stavely Makepeace.

Perched at one of the furthest extremes of Glam, both in intent and delivery, Stavely Makepeace was the union of long-time friends Nigel Fletcher and sometime pop hero Rob Woodward – aka Shel Naylor, purveyor of a brace of classy Decca singles in 1963.

As with so many uniquely titled talents of the age, Naylor was named by his manager, in this case, impresario Larry Page. 'This was early in the spring of 1963,' explains Woodward, 'when Larry was the manager of a ballroom in Coventry called the Orchid. He was hosting a talent competition, the prize being a recording contract with Decca Records – tracks were to be produced by Shel Talmy and Mike Stone from the US. I sang and played two Jerry Lee Lewis numbers, and I believe the fact that Page was a big Lewis fan more than helped him take great interest in me.

'He asked me to go to London with him, and introduced me to a fair contingent of top brass involved in recording, TV and music publishing. Not long after this – along with local singer Johnny B Great (John Goodison) and a schoolgirl singing trio called the Orchids – I secured a contract with Decca Records and Larry decided to christen me Shel Naylor. The Shel was inspired by Shel Talmy and the Naylor seemed to complement (it) as a surname.'

Released the same November day that JFK was assassinated, Naylor's debut single was 'a bizarre musically corrupted version of the Irving Berlin classic 'How Deep Is The Ocean'; the B-side, a somewhat more orthodox concoction of the Richie Valens track 'La Bamba' – not exactly critically acclaimed by the music press!' Nor on *Juke Box Jury*, where the record was proclaimed a miss. (Decca F11776).

A second Decca release in March 1964 coupled an early Ray Davies composition, 'One Fine Day', with 'It's Gonna Happen Soon', and featured a stunning lead guitar break from an 18 year-old Jimmy Page. (Decca F11856). (Naylor also recorded a fifth song, 'Stomping Joe', with Talmy in early 1964, but it remains unreleased.)

Apart from securing a summer season at Great Yarmouth in 1964, this final release was the last act in the short-lived existence of Shel Naylor. The Larry Page association and Decca were amicably wound up, and Woodward reverted to his own name and launched onto the Northern club and cabaret circuit, an ideal training ground 'and an invaluable apprenticeship'.

Nigel Fletcher, meanwhile, was in the merchant navy; he returned to dry land in 1967, and the pair set about building a recording studio in Woodward's parents' living room in Coventry.

'It gave us unlimited time for creative projects and product, as opposed to the pay by the hour recording studios which, at that time, proved to be an expensive route to travel. The front room was already flourishing as a music room for many years, as my mother was teaching pupils to learn to play piano, and it was large enough to house a basic recording set-up. The centrepiece of the studio was a two-track analogue domestic tape machine (Sony TC 200) and was hooked up to a very crude basic mono system – light years away from today's digital technology!

There, the pair sought out and developed a rough-hewn potpourri of electronics, tape effects, and so-called found sounds. If it could be banged, they banged it – and, years before sampling brought the sounds of the kitchen sink into the studio, Stavely were playing the thing for real.

Woodward: 'The "Stavely" scrap-iron sound emerged from literally hours of recording experimentation through from the 1967 to 1972 period. In fact the phrase "scrap iron" was coined by one of our musician friends who, on listening to the Stavely track "Edna" exclaimed, "the whole thing sounds like a load of scrap iron!"'

With bassist Pete Fisher and guitarist Don Ker completing the line-up, Stavely Makepeace signed with Pyramid Records – an odd and oddly prescient move. Pyramid was renowned at the time as a reggae label, pumping out a solid stream of Jamaican gems; a decade later, Stavely's Coventry hometown would become the centre of the 2 Tone ska revival.

At the time, however, it made less sense. 'Both Nigel and myself were already signed to music publishers Campbell Connelly as songwriters,' Woodward explains. 'Campbells had their own label called Concord, but it was in the initial stages of development back in 1969, so manager John AB Read farmed us out to Pyramid, which was run by an Australian friend of his, Graeme Goodall.

'Goodall's main charges were Desmond Dekker and his band the Aces and the label's image *was* pretty much exclusively reggae-orientated. But Goodall, having a flexible and pragmatic approach to the industry, relaxed this restriction and fixed up a release for us.'

Sales-wise, 'I Wanna Love You Like A Mad Dog'/'Greasy Haired Woman' (Pyramid PYR 6072) failed to scratch the surface but did interest Goodall in issuing a follow-up single, 'Tarzan Harvey' and 'Reggae Denny', recorded with reggae band the Pyramids. The latter worked out so well that Goodall decided to release the single as a double A-side (Pyramid PYR 6082), shortly before Christmas 1969.

The Pyramids had just recorded what would become their only hit 'Skinhead Reggae', under the almost-anagrammatical name of Symarip. 'The day we recorded "Reggae Denny" with them,' Nigel Fletcher recalls, 'they did a rendition of "Skinhead Moonstomp" in the studio. They put four empty bottles on the floor and the singer danced round them as he was singing, a fast and complicated move without kicking any of the bottles over. It was quite impressive. They were a fun bunch of musicians, always laughing and larking about.'

Sadly, the fruits of their labours went unreleased. 'We can only surmise that there was a considerable amount of "Mad Dog" singles pressed up and not sold, and Pyramid were reluctant to shell out further money on future product.'

By this time, the Concord label was up and running, around the same time as Steve Johnson replaced Pete Fisher on bass and multi-instrumentalist Steve Tayton was added to the Stavely line-up. 'Edna'/'Tarzan Harvey' followed, a much-loved 45 that earned the band what Woodward recalls as a 'nerve-wracking and exciting at the same time' appearance on *Top Of The Pops* on 30 July 1970. Though it failed to chart, 'it was the track that really started the ball rolling for Stavely Makepeace and for that matter Lieutenant Pigeon!'

Radio 1 played it a lot, and its failure to chart was probably a marked problem with distribution. 'However, it certainly heralded the Makepeace/Pigeon sound and put us on the map!'

A new single, 'Smokey Mountain Rhythm Revue' (Concord 013), and the band's debut on *Lift Off* followed, after Granada TV producer Muriel Young became the next personality to fall in love with the band's unique sound. But it was the instrumental B-side, 'Rampant On The Rage', that truly prompted Woodward and Fletcher into forming a side project, with Woodward's mother, Hilda, on piano. Lieutenant Pigeon was born.

The irony, Woodward concedes, is that 'in our opinion, "Smokey Mountain" symbolises the route we would have liked to take had Lieutenant Pigeon not happened. It is gutsy *joie de vivre* hoedown rock'n'roll, and one of the best Stavely recordings up to that date. Unfortunately once again distribution problems reared their head which meant most of the pressings failed to reach the essential record shops.'

30 December 1970 – Lift Off with the Sweet

The final episode of the year, but the birth of a band destined to become a televisual phenomenon – the Sweet. And few people could have been more surprised by what the future held in store for them than the Sweet themselves. Performing their newly released fifth single, 'Funny Funny', the Sweet were as sweet as their name and sound suggested. Nobody, watching them make their UK television debut, could have guessed that, of all the bands who would be thrown up by the Glam explosion, not one would lead so torturously schizophrenic an existence as this lot.

Or maybe they could? 'We had bought clothes for the show that were quite unusual,' bassist Steve Priest recalled. 'The trousers had one red leg, and one black. We all had some sort of black top. I bought mine with the buttons on from a girl's clothes shop. One of the dancers on the show could see we were nervous, and took pity on us. She gave me good advice to smile and show plenty of confidence and teeth. When the camera did pan onto me for a fleeting moment, I grinned like a demented ape and looked completely stupid.'

If only he'd known what the future had in store.

Famously, the Sweet spent the vast majority of their chart career bucking against the nursery-rhyme pop that self-styled songwriting Svengalis Nicky Chinn and Mike Chapman foisted upon them and, classic 45s though those old hits might be today, at the time they were as welcome as bubblegum in a denture factory – for bubblegum is what most right-thinking rock fans thought they were.

Behind the scenes, however, there pulsed a furious hard-rock band that threw every trick they could think of into the mix in a bid to raise themselves above the level that their puppetmasters seemed to think they should maintain. The result, running from late 1970 into mid 1975, stands among the most essential runs of 45s that any band of the era could have dreamed of releasing, a mix of pure commercial genius and seditious rocking revolution. Quite simply, the Sweet were sensational.

But even rock'n'roll rebels have to start out somewhere and, for three years before 'Funny Funny' gave the Sweet a silly silly hit in early 1971, across a clutch of singles that went absolutely nowhere at all, the Sweet would have sold their grannies for a hit. On stage, on air, and on their B-sides, they were one of the most inventive vocal harmony bands Britain has ever produced. But give them a day in the studio, and they'd give you whatever you wanted. No matter how hard they needed to grit their teeth.

'We wanted a hit, it's as simple as that,' said the band's vocalist, the late Brian Connolly in 1986. 'And we didn't care what it took.'

It was Connolly who formed the band in summer 1967. Vocalist at the time with Wainwright's Gentlemen, a sprawling seven-piece revue that could turn its hand to most things, but rarely got thanked for doing so, he had sparked a powerful friendship with that band's drummer, Mick Tucker; so powerful that, when Tucker was fired for allegedly being 'too flamboyant', Connolly promptly called him up to ask if he fancied forming a new band.

Another Wainwright's reject, guitarist Frank Torpey, followed and bassist Steve Priest became the final piece of the jigsaw after Tucker caught him playing in another band, the Army. Before that, Priest had been the mainstay behind the Countdowns, a west London band best remembered for having spent most of their career under Joe Meek's tutelage without ever actually getting a record of their own released.

They have one cut, 'You Stole My Heart Away', on the late-Nineties compilation 'The Joe Meek Collection: Hidden Gems Volume One', and there are probably others to be found in the fabled Meek tea chests. But that was it for them, so it was no surprise to find Priest moonlighting at Southern Music studios on Denmark Street, where he made his presence felt on a couple more of the decade's swingingest legends – the Roaring Sixties' 'We Love The Pirate Stations' and the Ministry of Sound's 'White Collar Worker'.

This new band was a far cry from any of those concerns. Exquisitely designed around the stunning vocal harmonies the quartet quickly developed, the Sweetshop, as they named themselves, quickly worked out a remarkable repertoire. Torpey and Connolly had written at least one song together, a faintly progressive rocker called 'Too Late Early In The Morning', but the bulk of the menu was borrowed.

They mastered the Byrds' 'Eight Miles High', the blues classic 'Stormy Monday', the Supremes' 'Stop! In The Name Of Love' and Eddie Cochran's 'Summertime Blues'. 'We wouldn't try anything,' Connolly recalled, 'unless we thought we could bring something different to it, something of our own. So while you could look at our set list and call us a covers band, we were a lot more creative than a lot of people would give us credit for. I always thought of us in the same way as people like Scott Walker, who didn't write his own material either – but you always knew it was him.'

An image began moving into view, albeit one that Priest insists 'ranged from the sublime to the ridiculous. I wore a kaftan with beads and no shoes. Frank wore jeans and looked like a builder. He didn't like the idea of stage clothes. Mick and Brian wore frilly shirts with chiffon scarves. They both looked like a couple of tarts. Later, we decided that we should have some sort of common stage attire, but we couldn't afford that yet. I was unable to buy a decent pair of boots.'

The Sweetshop debuted live at the Hemel Hempstead Pavilion on 4 March 1968. It was a venue all four members had played in the past and they hoped that might serve them in good stead with the audience. What they didn't consider was that they only had sufficient material for a 20-minute performances – barely enough for one full set, let alone the two that the contract demanded.

Nevertheless 'we seemed to go down well,' recalled Priest and, with the venue's management confirming that they would happily rebook the band, so long as they could double their repertoire, the Sweetshop were off and running. Indeed, a month or so later, a brief moment of at least reflected glory arrived in the form of a three-week residency at the Dolce Vita cabaret club in Birmingham, opening for all-girl trio the Paper Dolls and returning to the stage to accompany the ladies. The Dolls' single 'Something Here In My Heart (Keeps Telling Me No)' was knocking on the Top Ten door at the time, and Priest recalled, 'I had seen them on the TV, and they looked like go-go dancers with short skirts and obvious, curly wigs.'

The two groups met up at a rehearsal studio in London, to run through the set, and Priest admitted 'this whole thing was a completely new experience for me. I thought that showbusiness was putting on a guitar and playing in front of a load of drunks. Here we were in a professional rehearsal studio with three young ladies who had a record in the charts. It was frightening.'

Connolly played little part in the show; occasionally he would be handed an unplugged guitar and invited to strum along – one particularly dark night, he was handed one that had inadvertently been plugged in and drowned out the show with his wild twanging. The Sweetshop were dismissed from the tour soon after.

They also engaged a manager, surprisingly turning not towards a hard-bitten industry maven but a fellow singer. Paul Beuselinck was the former pianist of Screaming Lord Sutch's Savages, and the son of Oscar Beuselinck, a music-business lawyer whose clients included the Who. As Paul Nicholas, he had already released a few singles through Robert Stigwood's Reaction label, and would go onto release many more. Right now, however, he was toying with management and publishing, working at Robert Mellin Publishing, which is where he ran into a young go-getter named Phil Wainman.

Wainman, a seasoned drummer on the military base circuit, a former member of pre-Procol Harum band the Paramounts and co-writer of the Yardbirds' 'Little Games', Wainman was now looking to break into production. So, when Nicholas buttonholed him in the office one day, and mentioned that he was considering taking on a band called the Sweetshop, Wainman agreed to come down with him to watch them play.

The group auditioned for Wainman in a church hall in Stanmore, running through a set that was largely Motown-based, but impressing him with their harmonies. He suggested they record together and then, with a sure-fire hit in hand, seek out a suitable record label.

Glancing across to his friendship with Stigwood, Paul Nicholas suggested a Bee Gees' song – Stigwood managed and produced the brothers Gibb, and the 18 months since they arrived in the UK had seen the band chalk up a string of hits, both as performers and songwriters. Connolly recalled, 'He wanted us to cover "Down To Earth" [from the Bee Gees' recently released "Idea" album], which was all right but it wasn't one of their strongest songs.'

Wainman, on the other hand, was leaning towards 'Baby Come Back', a classy pop nugget that had just been released in Germany by the multi-racial Equals; that plan, however, was scuppered by the song's phenomenal success – it topped the German chart, landed a UK release immediately after and went to Number 1 there as well. The Equals were off and running, and the Sweetshop were still searching for their first single.

'Paul was still keen for us to do the Bee Gees song,' Connolly continued, 'but we were siding with Phil, that we'd be better off doing something that people didn't already know.' Finally he came up with 'Slow Motion', a song he picked up while visiting the publishers Valley Music. Written by David Watkins, pianist with Wolverhampton band the Magicians, 'Slow Motion' had already been pencilled in as that band's next B-side, behind another Watkins composition, 'Painting On Wood'.

Wainman didn't care, if he was even aware of the fact. Taking an instant liking to 'Slow Motion', he cut a demo with pianist Alan Benson, then played that to Jack Baverstock at the Fontana label. The A&R colossus declared that he wouldn't turn it down if he was offered it as a new band's first single and, with Robert Mellin agreeing to finance the session in return for the Sweetshop cutting a couple of the songs he published, 'Down To Earth' and the eventual B-side, 'It's Lonely Out There', the Sweetshop decamped to Jackson's Studios in Rickmansworth.

A fourth song, the insistent Nicholas' Bee Gees pick, was also recorded during the session, although the session did not necessarily go smoothly. Rumour has spent the past 40 years insisting that Phil Wainman and yet another Wainwright's Gentlemen mainstay, Gordon Fairminer, played on the ensuing recordings in place of Mick Tucker and Frank Torpey respectively, pulling off a sleight of hand that would become all too familiar to the band in the future. Steve Priest, however, is adamant that neither substitution was made. 'I know what they're talking about, but it wasn't "Slow Motion".'

Whoever performed on it, Jack Baverstock's enthusiasm for Wainman's initial demo did not wane when he heard the finished record. The man who had brought fame to so many artists, giving Fontana hits with Wayne Fontana and the Mindbenders, the Pretty Things, Scott Walker, Dave Dee and so many more, placed 'Slow Motion' on the release schedule for 19 July 1968, three months ahead of the Magicians' version. The Sweetshop were open for business.

The Sweetshop were gigging now, not as regularly as they would have liked, perhaps, but sufficient for them to hone their repertoire and abilities even tighter. The majority of gigs tended towards hotels and social clubs, any place that was willing to hand them £20 for their troubles, while they also landed a week long tour of Scotland in June. Then it was back to London, gigging around the outer suburbs in a series of shows that Connolly later groaned 'really do blur into one another.' There was just one show that he still recalled almost 20 years later.

3 August 1968 saw the Sweetshop coax their battered red van up to the northern town of Warrington, where they discovered that the support act was a band whose name had been pilloried all over the music press just days before. Deep Purple was a new progressive rock act whose all-important UK debut, opening for the Byrds at the Roundhouse earlier in the month, had loudly been declared one of the most disappointing showings that fabled venue had ever witnessed. Purple were off for the United States in a matter of weeks, where the Tetragrammaton label had already declared them superstars in waiting. Britain, however, had no time for their convoluted organ and guitar-led meanderings around sundry pop classics – Vanilla Fudge were bad enough, for heaven's sake – and the handful of British warm-up shows Purple were playing were killing time more than anything else.

'I remember that show,' Connolly laughed years later. The Red Lion 'wasn't a big pub, more like a cosy local with a little stage at one end. And Purple came sauntering on with their American hit single, their purple amps, their flashy clothes...they were a great band, lovely people, but they were so out of place that you really felt sorry for them.'

The Sweetshop, too, were feeling a little hard done by. 'Slow Motion' was about to hit the Fontana pressing plants when the news came through that another band had beaten them to the name the Sweetshop – and, just to make matters worse, not only was it helmed by Mark Wirtz, with whom Wainwright's Gentlemen had recorded some demos the previous year, it was also released by Fontana! 'Barefoot And Tiptoe' did nothing sales or chartwise, but there was no way a second Sweetshop single could be released by the same label just weeks after the first. With no time to even give the matter any serious consideration, the Sweetshop dropped the Shop. They were now the Sweet.

'That was Brian and Mick with their big mouths,' laughs Priest. 'They knew Mark Wirtz and they were going "Oh, we've got a band together and it's called the Sweetshop," and Mark already had the song together and went "Okay, we're the Sweetshop as well." And Fontana didn't give a flying shit, because all they cared about was making some money. So we had to change our name...'

Not that it mattered. 'Slow Motion'/'It's Lonely Out There' (Fontana TF 958) fared no better than 'Barefoot And Tiptoe'; there was a handful of radio plays, if that, and a clutch more live shows staggered around the record's release 'all blur into one' as Connolly put it. 'One long dreadful mess.' Paul Nicholas pulled some strings with Robert Stigwood and arranged for his agency to book a handful of Sweet gigs; Mick Tucker also believed Stigwood's influence lay behind the Sweetshop making their first ever session appearance on the BBC's now year-old Radio 1, for DJ Dave Symonds.

'Fontana really weren't pulling their weight with us,' the drummer complained. 'They released so many singles every week and they couldn't work them all even if they'd wanted to. Anyway, what can you say about a label that has two acts with the same name and doesn't even realise that? So Paul was pulling in favours wherever he could, and Stigwood had some influence at the BBC, probably through the Bee Gees or Cream [who he also managed] or whoever, and that's how we got in there. He sent us back up to Scotland as well, and we had a residency at some little place in Cornwall [a fortnight in Newquay] although I don't think he really knew who we were.'

The band recorded three songs for the BBC, both sides of the single plus 'Too Late Early In The Morning', and later dismissed the session as desultory, badly performed and scarcely heralded by Symonds himself. Nevertheless, the BBC retained a degree of faith in them and, the following month, they were invited back to record a similar selection of songs for DJ Stuart Henry.

The group's frontiers were expanding gently. Early 1969 saw Connolly, Priest, Torpey and Tucker go into the studio with Wainwright's Gentleman's old vocalist Ian Gillan, and his new band Episode 6's bassist Roger Glover, to record a demo for a song they'd written called 'Questions'. All six were close friends now; Glover and Connolly even shared a flat for a time, and Glover recalled 'for a couple of years in the Sixties we were inseparable friends.

'I liked him because he had a car and drove me places. He liked hanging around my flat in Uxbridge, just around the corner from our local pub – the Gardeners Arms. We were both in struggling bands and shared the same lack of funds and dreams of success...' And his fondest memory of this period? 'He was a man who most of all wanted to be a great singer in the tradition of Sinatra or Bennett (as he told me once in the pub) but he achieved no mean feat by his work in the Sweet.'

The band were also in demand at Mellin Music, being called in to demo any number of songs for the publisher, usually with Phil Wainman overseeing the sessions. Later years would see some confusion over this material, with Connolly usually insisting that he alone appeared on the best known of these tracks...one of Mellin's own co-compositions, 'I'm On My Way.' In fact, the whole band cut that track; he did, however, appear alone on a brace of recordings by an Italian band called the Closed, 'My Little Girl From Kentucky' and 'Spider', laying down a guide vocal the band's own vocalist would follow at the final recording session.

Five years later, two of these songs found their way out as a single in Europe ('I'm On My Way'/'My Little Girl From Kentucky' – RednWhite 40140, France) and onto a dubious compilation album in the United States. Only now they were credited to the Sweet. The Sweet were finally forced to resort to legal action to close the operation down.

Sessions such as these kept the musicians busy, but they were scarcely rewarding; the money was poor and was, in any case, largely swallowed up by the band members' on-the-road needs... food, petrol, lodgings, cigarettes, drink and any other highs that might be on offer. Nobody was getting rich, nobody was really happy, and in March 1969 Frank Torpey announced he was leaving 'to buy a house'.

The band immediately offered the vacant spot to Gordon Fairminer. He turned them down, and it would be a few weeks more before a full-time replacement, Mick Stewart, was brought in by Mick Tucker. Stewart was most recently a member of the last ever line-up of Johnny Kidd and the Pirates, formed in the mid Sixties to try and resurrect the old rock'n'roller's career, but doomed to a tragic end following Kidd's death in a car accident. Bassist in that same line-up was Nick Simper, a founder member of Purple in 1968, and it was Simper who recommended him to Tucker.

Paul Nicholas had drifted away by now, as had a lot of the Sweet's other contacts. Their Fontana deal was only ever intended as a one-off, the label opting for nothing more than an option on retaining the group's services in the future. They passed and, with that, Phil Wainman too faded from their lives. It would be mid 1969 before a new manager hove into view; Roger Easterby was managing the pop group Vanity Fair at the time, and saw the Sweet as being cut in a similar mould. His enthusiasm was certainly enough to intrigue legendary producer George Martin, who signed the Sweet to his AIR London production company. This funnelled releases onto EMI's Parlophone label, where their labelmates would include...Deep Purple.

One of Stewart's first tasks as a member of the Sweet was to join them at Abbey Road to begin work on the band's next single, 'Lollipop Man'/'Time' (Parlophone R5803). Composed by Albert Hammond and Mike Hazelwood, members of the band Family Dogg, it was a fairly inconsequential song despite a squeak of Hendrix-shaped guitar percolating over the intro. By the time it reached its chorus, however, it was unquestionably a slab of what the rock cognoscenti had already written off as 'bubblegum' music – and Connolly admitted he hated it.

Talking to DJ Brian Matthew, he pushed 'Lollipop Man' with as much dedication as the record label would have demanded, even reminding listeners that it was written by the same team that gave Leapy Lee a hit with 'Little

Arrows'. But, behind the scenes and years later, he growled, '"Lollipop Man" was shit. Everything they gave us to record was shit.'

The Sweet continued gigging, up and down the UK as their bookers demanded; a trip across to the Channel Islands for a short residency at a club on Jersey and, shortly before Christmas 1969, a three-week residency at the Piper Club in Rome – an adventure in itself as Priest, Tucker and Stewart manhandled the band's temperamental van across Europe and through the Alps (Connolly, sensibly, flew). But the band continued to struggle.

The Sweet's new single, 'All You'll Ever Get From Me'/'The Juicer' (Parlophone R5826) had been recorded by now, taking the band back to Abbey Road this time to cut a song written by the hottest songwriting duo of the era, Roger Cook and Roger Greenaway – both stars in their own right as members of, respectively, television novelty band the Pipkins and the multi-racial Blue Mink and, before that, as the pop duo David and Jonathan.

But radio play was sparse, proving the old adage that it's not what you do that counts, it's who you know...and the Sweet really didn't know anybody. "That would have been a big hit if we had done something like *Top Of The Pops*,' Connolly reasoned. 'But we were playing abroad at the time and couldn't get back to promote it properly.'

In fact, it probably wouldn't have helped. The occasional BBC session would offer the Sweet a flash of hope but, after three 45s, they knew that any number of bands were invited in to cut sessions for the various DJs and only a handful would ever get more action than that. The week after the Sweet's latest airing, on Dave Cash's show in mid-January, for instance, the same DJ plugged another band of struggling unknowns, Tangerine Peel, featuring an Australian singer songwriter named Mike Chapman. Nothing happened for them, either.

'It was strange,' Priest said of 'All You'll Ever Get From Me'. 'Because to listen to it, it did sound like a hit, but it just didn't happen.' It also sold a lot better than its predecessor, and the handful of people who did buy it were treated to one of their best ever songs on the B-side, a band-built rocker called 'The Juicer'. But the plaudits of a few fans were barely enough to sustain the group and, by the time the Sweet came to cut their next 45, 'Get On The Line'/'Mr McGallacher' (Parlophone R5848), it was clear that something had to give.

The last six months had seen the group's finances hitting new depths, and their confidence racing to join them. Now they took a new blow as they arrived at the studio to find themselves being expected to cut an excruciating piece of pop flotsam called 'Get On The Line' – written, to the accountants' delight if nobody else's, by the same team that had been responsible for 'Sugar Sugar' the previous year, songwriters Jeff Barry and Andy Kim.

In fact, the Archies themselves had already recorded the song; but whereas Jonathan King completely restructured 'Sugar Sugar' as a brooding slab of fuzzy psychedelia when he took on the cartoon caperers, the Sweet's cover was to be all but identical to the original. And, to make certain that they didn't deviate from the plan, they were presented with a pre-recorded backing track and told that Connolly alone was required at the session. Everything else had already been cut.

'They wouldn't even let us sing the background vocals,' snarled a furious Priest. 'Instead it was done, of all things, by the Ladybirds, who were a trio of women that would sing on shows like *Benny Hill*, or basically any show they could.'

Again, the band was allowed to stretch its wings on the B-side with another group composition, 'Mr McGallacher'. But 'Get On The Line' was doomed to be as great a failure as its predecessors, and again, the only bright spot was the now inevitable invitation down to the BBC, to record a fresh version of the single for the *Jimmy Young Show*. It would be broadcast during the week of 15-19 June, but nobody expected it to make an iota of difference. If the Sweet had split up there and then, it is unlikely that anybody would have even noticed.

Instead they hung around – literally. Their own session complete, Connolly and Tucker were idling some time away at the Beeb's Aeolian Hall studios when they caught sight of a familiar figure coming into, or leaving, one of the studios. It was Phil Wainman and, when they fell into conversation with him, he had some rather exciting news to pass on. About a pair of songwriters he'd just become involved with, Nicky Chinn and Mike Chapman. About a song they'd just written he thought the Sweet might like, called 'Funny Funny'. And about the plans the threesome had already hatched to create the biggest pop sensation of the early Seventies.

The Sweet were round at his flat the following morning.

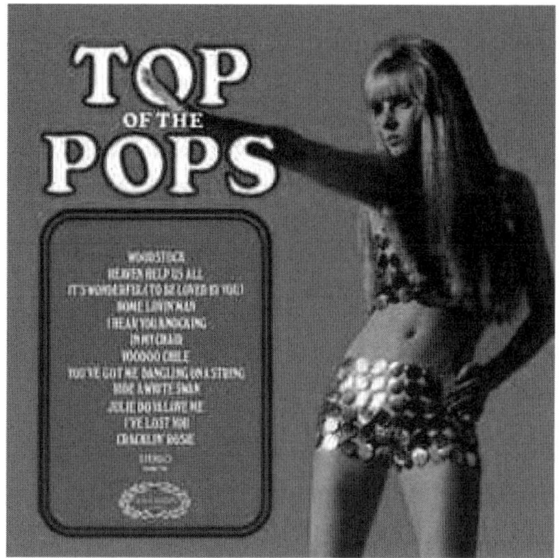

December 1970 – Various Artists: Top Of The Pops Vol 14 (Hallmark SHM 710)

It's Number 1...it's the *other* Top Of The Pops...

'Imagine', mused a mid-Nineties issue of American magazine *Goldmine*, 'a time when a trip out to buy the latest hot pop hits did not involve holding up your taste in music to the ridicule of the lethally hip young gunslinger at the local branch of Indie-trash R Us.

'Imagine, too, a time when you could pick up a sizeable chunk of the latest Top Forty, plus a handful of hopeful-but-helpless first timers, and get an eyeful of a tastefully clad young dollybird, and still have change out of a crisp pound note.

'And imagine, finally, that you are legally deaf, which means you don't even notice that the groovy stash you now place on the turntable doesn't sound anywhere near the same as when it turns up on the radio.

'Congratulations! You are now the proud owner of...'

There can be few institutions in rock history as reviled as the Hallmark budget label's Top Of The Pops series. Even today, almost 30 years after the final edition (and more than 40 years after the first), the 'kitsch' value the series holds for certain collectors is balanced by unease, and a self-conscious smirk that insists 'they're so bad, they're good.'

But a quarter-million or so purchasers cannot be wrong. And for the five or six years that were dominated by Glam Rock, Top Of The Pops on vinyl was as vital and vibrant a record of the movement's pulse as *Top Of The Pops* on TV.

The two were wholly separate from one another. Conceived in 1968 by the Hallmark subsidiary of Pickwick Records, themselves already leaders in the world of cheapo compilations, the Top Of The Pops series took its name from the BBC television music show of the same name, but did so not through any kind of linkage but because the Beeb had rather foolishly forgotten to trademark the title. A rival series, the Music For Pleasure label's Hot Hits, debuted soon after, while a handful of others (most notably Marble Arch's Chartbusters) surfaced for an album or two. But Top Of The Pops was the benchmark and, while the others passed into oblivion, it became a tradition.

The concept was simplicity itself. While the design department worked on the sleeve, and invariably wound up with a pretty, pouting, dollybird wearing hotpants and a tank top, a team of crack sessionmen were given approximately five days in which to turn out an album's worth of soundalike smash hits, torn from the top of the chart.

There was a regular team of musicians, responsible for almost every song on the album. Across the full spectrum of releases, vocalists like Tony Rivers, Martha Smith, John Perry and Danny Street can be heard aping everyone from Donny Osmond to Johnny Rotten. Miller Anderson/Kenny Young sidekick Bob Falloon lashed out a decade's worth of incredible licks and there was even a singing pianist rejoicing under the marvellous name of Reginald Dwight.

Hold it right there!

Would that be *the* Reginald Dwight, the little fat one who went on to become Elton John?

It would indeed. Even future superstars have to eat, after all, and if you've ever wanted to find out what a piano-playing balladeer would make of 'Neanderthal Man' or 'Spirit In The Sky', the CD 'Reg Dwight's Piano Goes Pop' (RPM 142) tells the rest of the story,

Who bought these records? At their peak, the Top Of The Pops series was topping 300,000 copies per volume. There were 92 volumes. Retailing at little more than the price of a single 45, these collections weren't simply out-performing full-price records by a considerable margin, they were also outselling many of the original singles as well. And, while that was great for the music publishers, who got their money whoever performed the song, the poor labels were left to starve. Not for the first (and certainly not the last) time in history, the cry went up – it's the death of the music industry as we know it.

It would be another year before that particular saga played out. In the meantime, Top Of The Pops Volume 14 marks the moment when the series met the music that would confirm both its future and its success. The birth of Glam Rock. 'Ride A White Swan' was a shoo-in for this edition and, though the vocals are weak, the spirit is strong.

CHAPTER TWO

1971

Getting it On

January 1971 – David Bowie: Holy Holy/ Black Country Rock (Mercury 6052 049)
January 1971 – Ronno: Powers of Darkness/ 4th Hour Of My Sleep (Vertigo 6059 029)
January 20 1971 – Granada TV: David Bowie

Bowie's third album, recorded with Mick Ronson, drummer Mick 'Woody' Woodmansey, keyboard-player Ralph Mace and bassist/producer Tony Visconti, was originally to be titled 'Holy Holy'.

Mercury Records nixed that, presumably on some kind of peculiar religious grounds, but were happy to release the abandoned title track as a single around the same time as Bowie removed it from the album.

It probably wouldn't have mattered either way. Nobody heard the tight spiralling riff that highlighted the A-side; nobody cared for the sharp Bolanisms with which Bowie inflected his vocal on the flip. The single was ignored, but it was not a wholly wasted effort. On 20 January, Bowie and the band appeared at the Granada TV studios to record their one and only television performance of 'Holy Holy', under the aegis of director Roger Price.

Talking in the canteen afterwards, Price mentioned a new children's' TV series that he was in the process of developing, *The Tomorrow People* – revolving around the adventures of the so-called Homo Superior (themselves a variant on the Marvel Comics' X-Men concept…the next step in human evolution).

According to Price, Bowie was the first person he'd spoken to who truly grasped the notion. And while the singer's input apparently proved invaluable to the continuing development of the show, the show would prove equally useful to Bowie. He took the term 'homo superior' and wrote it into a new song, 'Oh! You Pretty Things'. (*The Tomorrow People* debuted on screen on 30 April 1973.)

January 1971 – Hotlegs but cool temperaments

A follow-up to 'Neanderthal Man' was not forthcoming.

'We hit an unexpected nerve with 'Neanderthal Man",' says Godley. 'It was one of those lucky accidents than turn into something both interesting and successful, without knowing how or why. When you go back and try to recreate the same circumstances it just doesn't work.'

Nevertheless, Hotlegs returned to the chart, albeit anonymously, at the end of the 1970. Kennedy Street's Harvey Lisburg had recently discovered a new talent named John Paul Jones; not the pop arranger turned Led Zeppelin bassist, explains Gouldman, 'but a comedian who had the most wonderful rich voice.'

Aware, though he was, that Zeppelin's Jones already had some claim on the name, Lisburg went ahead with launching his new client's career. 'I still don't know why he used it,' Gouldman marvels. 'It was such a bizarre thing to do! But Harvey always liked the name.'

All four of the Strawberry team played on Jones' 'Man From Nazareth'/'Got To Get Together Now' (RAK 107), a single which was well on its

simply
POP
could you pass
'O' level or C.S.E. in POP?
see inside
by tony jasper

way to being a Christmas 1970 hit when the other John Paul succeeded in getting a court injunction, forcing the artist to respell his surname Joans. The single had already reached Number 41 on the British chart; in the ensuing chaos, while RAK Records reprinted the label, 'Man From Nazareth' dropped from the charts but reappeared in the new year when it rose to Number 25. (In the US, the name was truncated to John.)

Meanwhile, the Hotlegs project continued to grow. Adopting a new guise, the New Wave Band, the trio (augmented by former Hermit Derek Leckenby) vainly pursued another hit with a percussion-heavy cover of Paul Simon's 'Cecilia' (c/w 'Free Free Free', Major Minor MM 694).

Another was called Doctor Father. 'There Ain't No Umbopo' (c/w 'Roll On' – Pye 7N17977), Godley recalls, 'was one of those runt songs that hung around looking for a home for a long time. Everybody liked it, but couldn't work out where it belonged. I remember Lol coming up with this cool open guitar tuning and two hypnotic chords and us writing the song at my parents' house...forever. It was a long song, about six minutes or thereabouts and it was eventually released under the name Doctor Father.' (It was also released as part of the Kasenetz-Katz package under the Crazy Elephant brand name.)

January 1971 – The Sweet: Funny Funny/ You're Not Wrong For Loving Me (RCA 2051)

Former car salesman Nicky Chinn and sometime singing waiter Mike Chapman met at Jermyn Street nightclub Tramp, one of the London music business' most exclusive watering holes. Chinn was hanging out, and trying to impress people with a test pressing of the first songs he'd ever had recorded, co-writing Mike d'Abo's latest single 'Miss Me In The Morning' and 'Arabella Cinderella'; Chapman, who had just abandoned his own dreams of success by quitting the band Tangerine Peel, was working as a waiter.

Chinn had just passed the record to the evening's DJ when Chapman approached him. 'He asked the DJ who I was and we started chatting. We became fairly pally over the next two or three months and, one evening, he said to me, "How do you fancy writing together?"

'We were both very pop. We were very aware of current songwriters, people like Roger Cook and Roger Greenaway and Tony Macaulay and what they were doing.'

They were also aware of current trends. The Archies' 'Sugar Sugar' was a year old now, but its spectre still hung over the pop scene, still encouraged writer after writer to try and emulate its simplicity. Nor was it alone. Although all were largely the work of the same stable of songwriters and sessionmen, bands like Edison Lighthouse, Blue Mink, White Plains and the Brotherhood of Man were all assaulting the chart with their brand of lightweight pop, sweetly singable songs about love and happiness.

It was a market that Cook and Greenaway, in particular, seemed to have sewn up, as they simply racked up the hits, effortlessly peeling off such pop anthems as 'You've Got Your Troubles', 'Banner Man', 'I've Got You On My Mind' and 'I'd Like To Teach The World To Sing'. But there was always room for competition and, very quickly after they started writing together, both Chinn and Chapman sensed they were poised to strike.

Chinn explained, 'Mike played guitar and I didn't, but I have always felt I had a very good head for melody and a good ear for a tune. So I think it was pretty much of a co-write. But if there was a strength, Mike's was certainly melody, 'cause I don't make up original melody, and mine was lyrics. I think we both had commercial ears and we both were pretty good on structure. We often started with a title and would take it from there. Get a bit of melody, some words, then bit by bit piece it together.'

Mike Chapman and Nicky Chinn had already tried their hand at writing a few songs together, which they played to Wainman. He wasn't impressed; they were 'a bit lightweight'. But the two young would-be writers intrigued him, because they really did seem to understand his, Wainman's, own musical theories and ambitions.

They were keen learners, too. All Wainman had to do was tell them the sort of songs that he wanted and the chances were they'd be able to deliver them. So when he mentioned 'Sugar Sugar' and the outlandish quantity of records it had sold – seven or eight million copies worldwide – he knew that they would take the thought and run with it. 'We talked about the charts, and we talked about why hit records were hits, and I thought "Wouldn't it be great to tap into that pop bubblegum market?"'

The next time Wainman saw Chinn and Chapman, they played him a brand new song they'd written. It was called 'Funny Funny'.

Recorded with Wainman's stock crew of studio session men, with only Connolly appearing on the record itself, 'Funny Funny' was ready for release by early summer. In fact it took another six months before Wainman was finally able to secure a deal for the record, with RCA, and it would be another four months before they finally started to see any action.

A lot can change in four months.

ON THE RADIO
4 January 1971 – Terry Wogan Show: The Sweet
12 January 1971 – Mike Harding Show: Slade
ON THE BOX
7 January 1971 – Top Of The Pops: T Rex

February 1971 – T Rex: Hot Love/Woodland Rock/King Of The Mountain Cometh (Fly BUG 6).
13 February 1971 – T Rex and Comus, North-East London Polytechnic, Barking

'Ride A White Swan' was still on the chart when Bolan unleashed the follow-up, a song previewed on the radio back in December but now revealed as an orchestrated masterpiece. With newly acquired bassist Steve Currie and drummer Bill Legend making their recording debut, and Turtle Howard Kaylan joined by his partner Mark Volman, 'Hot Love' set in stone all that would become universally renowned as the T Rex sound, much imitated but never recreated.

'There's a certain intrinsic whining quality to that kind of backing vocal,' Kaylan explains, 'that I believe came largely from our time with [Zappa]. We were singing those notes all our lives, but there was a certain nasal-ness, a whininess to it, that came from singing those parts with a little tongue-in-cheekness. "Hot Love", in particular, has a swaggering, fake sass; it's us pretending to be chicks, with every bit of the gris-gris-gumbo-ya-ya that we could muster. It's almost mocking and it should be, because it's guys. It sounds like two 300lb guys in tutus, daring you to lift their skirts.'

'Hot Love' entered the chart on 27 February; the following week it was Number 17; a fortnight later, it was Number 1. It remained at the top for the next six weeks.

But that, it would transpire, was only the first of its achievements.

Meanwhile, a glimpse into how swiftly things took off for T Rex is provided by the billing for their North-East London Polytechnic show. When the two groups, T Rex and Comus, were booked the previous autumn, nobody thought anything about them sharing an audience because they already did. (They would also share a fuzzbox – Bolan borrowed one from Comus bassist Andy Hellaby for the evening.)

Now, however, Comus took the stage to play their twisted folk to be confronted by what frontman Roger Wootton recalls as 'lots of teenyboppers shouting throughout our set for T Rex,' Bandmate Rob Young promptly started to shout back at them. 'I liked that.'

February 1971 – Percy

Any one of the myriad movies released in the UK in the early Seventies could be singled out as being somehow especially evocative of all the era would pertain to, from the obvious charms of *Confessions Of A Pop Performer* on down.

But *Percy* seems especially appropriate, not least because its subject matter was just askew enough to raise it (in theory, anyway) above the run-of-the mill sex romps of the day and into a realm of more surreal suggestion. A key element, of course, in what would become Glam.

But it was also a strangely thoughtful and, in turn, thought-provoking film.

There was a lot going on in the medical world in 1971, after all. The newspapers were still marvelling over Dr Christiaan Barnard's pioneering perfection of the heart transplant in 1967, and the announcement the following June that British doctors had made a similar breakthrough. But 1968 saw the country's first successful liver transplant, while April 1969 saw American surgeons swap somebody's eye out for the first time. Kidneys and cornea switches were commonplace already. What other broken-down bodily parts might we be able, at some as yet unforeseen point in time, to simply trade in for a better model?

Well, a Cleveland surgeon, Robert White, had just finished transplanting a monkey's head, and the Soviet propaganda machine was alleging all manner of fabulous breakthroughs, primarily to annoy the Americans. But the greatest advance of all, if we are to believe a word of *Percy*, the one that gave hope to sufferers and 16 year-olds the entire world over, was being undertaken at a small hospital in London where the brilliant Doctor Emmanuel Whitbread announced, after years of research, that he had perfected the penis transplant.

The headlines howled, some with mirth, some with delight and some, because this was England in 1971, in horror. When Whitbread appeared on a live TV chat show, shortly after his announcement, he actually walked off the set in disgust after the word 'penis' was bleeped from his conversation once too often. Only as he made his way out of the studio did anybody think to tell him the word he should have employed in its place. 'In my home,' a technician told him, 'we called it a percy.'

Percy. There's probably not a movie history in existence that would actually call it a good movie, let alone a great one. Even the booklet accompanying the film's American DVD release in 2000 could muster no higher praise than to call it 'about as good as you can get for a film like this' – meaning that run of mildly smutty, if not downright indecent sex comedies the British movie industry churned out through the Sixties and beyond. That, in itself, is a remarkable lineage and we could debate all night long the relative merits of *Not Tonight, Darling, Sweet And Sexy* and, best of all, *Virgin Witch* before we even get into the *Carry On* series.

The plot. The doctor has perfected his surgery, but only in theory. He needs a patient – two, in fact, a donor and a recipient – and what are the chances of that? Pretty good, as it turns out. Antique dealer Edwin Anthony (Hywel Bennett) is on his way to deliver a pricey cut-glass chandelier to an obnoxious American customer. Several storeys above him, a young man is disturbed *in flagrante delicto* with a married woman. He has just one escape route – onto her balcony. 'But darling,' his paramour murmurs as he clambers out of the window. 'We don't have a balcony.'

The two, the luckless lover and his unexpected soft landing, are rushed to the hospital; one is dead, the other, gasps a bystander, will probably wish he was. But the doctor is delighted. He has his patients. He has his opportunity. He has his Percy. And young Edwin awakens to discover that, while he might not be the man he used to be, thanks to his donor he's probably twice as much.

It's a curse as much as a blessing, however. On the one hand he's famous, and a couple of fantasy sequences find him on stage with the Stones (using footage from the 1969 Hyde Park show) and on the field with Manchester United (George Best has a cameo). On the other, he's the laughing stock of every two-bit comedian and taxi driver in town. There is just one thing for him to do. Try to grasp some meaning from the entire situation and seek out his Percy's previous owner – a litany of the recently bereaved, all of whom he must interview.

The jokes come thick and fast now, and are utterly symptomatic of the time – one of the bereaved is a black woman, so we know without words that it wasn't her mate. Another sounds like a genuine possibility until the wife pulls out a picture of an Orthodox Jew. And a third is the special young friend of a very cultivated middle-aged gent who might still be grieving but still offers Edwin the dead man's old bedroom.

Finally he finds the woman he was seeking, the lovely Cyd Hayman – and the temptation to bring Percy home is a hard one to resist. So hard, in fact, that he promptly sets out on a second quest, to reacquaint his new friend with all the other women it had known, and maybe the essential premise of the film does start to droop as it thrusts on and on.

But with its well-honed digs at censorial Britain, as the last gasp of Victorian prudishness struggled to stay afloat in a sea of new permissiveness, it had points to make far beyond the most obvious ones; while students of irony surely saw the humour inherent in its disapproving examination of the already pernicious tabloid press. *The Sun* published its first Page Three girl in November 1970, more or less around the same time as the still unreleased

Percy received its first 'must we fling this filth'-style lambasting in the gutter press.

More than any of that, though, *Percy* is funny, it is clever, it is saucy and it has one of the most sobering soundtracks ever grafted to a comedy film. Ray Davies and the Kinks rolled out 'All God's Children' to run over the credits (one of four songs specially composed for the soundtrack) and leave us all with something really profound to think about. Man's done all this really clever stuff, Davies sings, skyscrapers and cars and aeroplanes and all. But 'he didn't make the flowers and he didn't make the trees...and he's got no right to turn us into machines.'

Yeah, well this film's gonna be a real bundle of laughs. Let's go home and have sex.

February 1971 – The Partridge Family: I Think I Love You/Somebody Wants To Love You (Bell 1130)

In September 1970, American television received its first glimpse of *The Partridge Family*, a 30-minute sitcom revolving around the activities of a singing, dancing, one-parent family growing up in middle-class America.

It was based, very loosely indeed, on the lives of past pop sensations the Cowsills, but was aimed at a considerably older audience than either its role models or, bearing in mind the undoubted influence of the Jacksons, its contemporaries.

Whereas the Jacksons' cartoon show went out on Saturday mornings, *The Partridge Family* had its own peak-time evening slot, smack in the middle of Family Viewing Hour. Similarly, while both the Jacksons and later, the Osmonds, took for their focal point the youngest members of the crew, *The Partridge Family* revolved around the growing pains of the painfully good-looking, decidedly post-adolescent Keith Partridge, played by David Cassidy.

The son of Broadway stars Jack Cassidy and Evelyn Ward, David was partnered in the series' star billing by his real-life stepmother, Shirley Jones. It was her performance as the long-suffering mother trying to keep the kids on an even keel that lent the show its most powerful images. Jones, alone of the cast, was an accomplished player; David, for all his thespian ambition and heritage, had developed only an endearing self-consciousness while his screen sister Laurie (Susan Dey) was required to do nothing more than look pretty, represent the spirit of socially conscious youth and pour scorn on David's crasser on-screen antics.

Of the three younger members of the cast, Danny (Danny Bonaduce, today a radio jock with a less than wholesome reputation) wavered between an under-aged prototype for the Michael J Fox role in *Family Ties* a decade later and a precocious Beaver Cleaver. Tracy (Suzanne Crough) seemed to play less of a part in the action with every passing show and Chris (Jeremy Gelbwaks and, later, Brian Forster) simply stood around twiddling his thumbs and looking totally bewildered.

Throughout its three-year run, *The Partridge Family* profited immeasurably from its intended older adolescent catchment area. Some surprisingly mature or, at least, innovative storylines were introduced; Danny masquerading as a Jew so that he might date the daughter of a local Rabbi; Keith using a problem page edited by Laurie to win an introduction to a new girl in the neighbourhood; Laurie entering the Homecoming Queen competition so that she might use her acceptance speech as the platform for her feminist views.

In-jokes, too, proliferated. A show which revolves around Laurie's disdain of Keith as the idol of every girl in America closes with the Family performing before an audience whose average age has to be in the upper forties. In another, the family dissuade Keith from pursuing a career in classical music by convincing him that his own songs are valid enough, then close by performing a Herman's Hermits cover.

The Partridge Family had been on the air in America for little more than a month before the family scored their first US Number 1; it was released in the UK soon after and, once again, the choice of material and the way in which it was delivered indicated just how much more sophisticated a market they were aiming to tap.

'I Think I Love You' boasted an up-beat maturity, both musically and lyrically, to which the Jacksons seemed utterly oblivious. 'I Want You Back' aside, too much of their earliest material now seemed endearing only through

Michael's precociousness and their occasionally profound choice of subject-matter. And while the Osmonds, too, were destined to make one very valiant stab at redressing the balance with the socio-pomp of 'Crazy Horses', in musical terms the Partridge kids were way out ahead.

Simply by virtue of the competition, David Cassidy was always regarded with a little more sympathy, too, than his teenybop peers. For a start, he was hopelessly outnumbered – but, more importantly, he never seemed to take his role seriously.

On stage, he would pepper his repertoire with material by artists he respected as musicians and writers, not because they wrote simple, singalong melodies; off, he viewed the maelstrom in which he was caught with an amused, almost bemused attachment. Yet, at the same time, he was occasionally persuaded to go along with the most ridiculous publicity stunts, not the least of which was living on a boat moored in the middle of the River Thames during one London visit. 'We were fishing them out of the water all week,' a local policeman said of the fans.

Perhaps more than any other teen idol, Cassidy's career was a constant battle between his own love of privacy, and his advisors' love of publicity. In an interview with *Rolling Stone* in 1972, he spoke openly about drink, drugs and sex. Weeks later he was denying it and claiming he'd been misquoted, only to repeat highlights from the original interview when *The Sun* caught up with him a few weeks later.

His looks, and genuine musical abilities aside, Cassidy's greatest asset was his manager, former table-tennis champion Ruth Aarons. He inherited her from his father, whose theatrical agent she had been – and, while she knew precious little about rock'n'roll, she did understand the laws of supply and demand.

At the end of the show's second series, Cassidy publicly 'retired' from acting to concentrate on his music. The studio was stunned, the fanclub outraged. 'I got letters from fans asking if I'd stopped loving them,' an incredulous Cassidy said. 'They thought I was giving up the *Partridge* show because I'd stopped loving my fans.' No, he'd given up as a way of getting a new contract from the studio, one that would apparently make him a very rich man, regardless of whether he ever worked again.

Fairly early into his career as Keith Partridge, David took to working outside of the family group, turning the show's success into his own by persuading Bell Records (who distributed the group product) that he was talented enough – or adored enough, it didn't matter which – to be launched as a performer in his own right. Together with Shirley Jones, he was the only member of the TV family who did actually sing on the group's records; Susan Dey, it was said, had a curious atonal voice, while the kids simply stood about looking bored every time the adults got down to the heavy stuff.

Indeed, even as a beginner, David evinced enough potential as a vocalist for Wes Farrell, the show's musical director, to abandon his original plan of bringing in some well-tried session singer to dub Keith's lines and give the kid a break of his own.

Both Cassidy's voice and what was to become the established Partridge sound were thus both firmly in place very early in the first series. But soon he was to step out absolutely alone.

Cassidy's first solo single, April 1972's 'Cherish', was excellent even by the standards the Partridges had set, and the description also fits his first album, likewise titled 'Cherish'. Indeed, Cassidy's mature choice of material made the set a far more enduring selection than any of the Family's long-playing offerings, if only because Cassidy, for the most part, was free of the constraints under which the Family laboured. He even admits that musically, the most satisfying of all the Partridge albums were the last couple – 'Bulletin Board' and 'Crossword Puzzle'.

'Wes had lost interest, Shirley had lost interest, so I just went in and went through the songbook, picked out the songs I wanted to cover and did them. There was no pressure, no hassles and (laughingly) no sales. I don't even remember those records!'

And while it was to be another three years before he was ever to be truly on his own, quitting Bell for RCA and releasing the prophetically titled 'The Higher They Climb, The Harder They Fall' album, Cassidy seldom let events stray far from his grasp.

The exception to this – indeed, the event which persuaded him that it was finally time to take his leave of the teeny market – was the 1974 White City, London, concert where a young girl was fatally crushed. Cassidy was devastated, all the more so because he had already warned his advisors that such a tragedy was inevitable, given the hysteria whipped up by his every public appearance.

With thousands of people so obviously out of control, it was simply a matter of time before someone got hurt. Within weeks of the concert, he had quit *The Partridge Family*; within 18 months he was forgotten. He later confessed he had never felt so happy in his life.

ON THE RADIO
February 1971 – Jimmy Young: The Sweet

---

25 March 1971 – Top Of The Pops: The birth of Glitter Rock
March 1971 – T Rex: Flyback – The Best Of T Rex (Fly TON 2)
March 1971 – Disco 45: T Rex Special
'Hot Love' was already firmly ensconced at Number 1, and T Rex were on the box again. Just another night plugging another hit single. Until Chelita Secunda halted Marc as he prepared to step out onto the stage and splashed some glitter

on his face to match the silver lamé top he had already chosen to wear.

The cameras caught it and time stood still for a moment. Or at least for as long as it took every other watching would-be rocker (and his entire teenage audience too) to grab a pen and a shopping list and make a note for themselves.

Buy some glitter. It looks good.

John Springate, future mainstay of the Glitter Band, speaks for an entire generation of jobbing musicians when he recalls: 'At that time, I was basically doing the soul circuit; my brother and I had a three-piece group doing Cream, Hendrix and all that. And the stock look was flared jeans and the grandad shirt, long hair and a beard and a moustache, and everybody looked like that. And when Marc Bolan did what he did, that little bit of glitter on his face on *Top Of The Pops*, that's what started it. Everybody went on to look like that.'

Meanwhile, just three months after the band's initial hit, the print industry issued its first tribute to T Rex in the form of *Disco 45*'s *T Rex Special*. Right on top of that, the irresistibly budget-priced 'Flyback' was many newfound fans' first exposure to the music Marc Bolan was making before he hit fame. And what a shock it was.

Drifting through all four Tyrannosaurus Rex albums, plus a couple of unissued outtakes and single-only sides, 'Flyback's 13 songs look like pretty slim pickings today, while the packaging (matching others in the series: Procol Harum, the Move etc) was minimal, too. But it was good enough for the Music For Pleasure label to all-but duplicate it for the 1973 'Ride A White Swan' budget compilation, and when you play it today the magic comes flooding back.

March 1971: Hotlegs – Thinks: School Stinks (Phillips 6308 047)

Almost nine months had now elapsed since 'Neanderthal Man' and Hotlegs still refused to be rushed into anything. But with Philips demanding more of the same, the band were happy to comply. They had already proved their ambition with the single's B-side, 'You Didn't Like It Because You Didn't Think Of It', a beautiful mid-pace rocker that provided the blueprint for 10cc's debut-LP closer 'Fresh Air For My Mama.'

Godley: 'So we just kept going until we had an album, complete with our version of side two

of 'Abbey Road', 'Suite FA'. I think we also built the first Gizmo prototype during this period.'

A similar fate awaited the album. 'Thinks: School Stinks' arrived in a school desk sleeve that would prove very useful for Alice Cooper two years later, but he was probably the only person who paid it any attention. Which is a shame, because it's a terrific record.

Godley admits, 'It was great just to try to punch above our weight. It's not bad, but it's not us yet, is it? At the time, we didn't recognise "Neanderthal Man" for the inspired piece of nonsense it was. No tune. Stupid lyrics. "We can do better than this, chaps."

'We were young and subconsciously aping our heroes, like you do until the real you shows up, so "Neanderthal Man" was this bizarre anomaly that pointed one possible way forward but we failed to see it.' Decades later, in 2006, Godley sampled much of the Hotlegs album for the mid section of GG06 song 'Son Of Man', 'and I could hear something of what we eventually became, under all the other influences. In truth, we didn't fully discover our own musical identity until we stopped trying so hard and started feeling.'

On the road, Hotlegs toured the UK as support for the Moody Blues, again to little effect. 'Audiences were expecting "Neanderthal Man" and we were playing "Thinks: School Stinks". Consequently any momentum evaporated, the phone stopped ringing and it was time for a rethink.'

ON THE RADIO
29 March 1971 – Radio 1 Club: T Rex
ON THE BOX
11 March 1971 – Top Of The Pops: T Rex
18 March 1971 – Top Of The Pops: T Rex (promo film)
25 March 1971 – Top Of The Pops: T Rex

---

1 April 1971 – Top Of The Pops: The Sweet

Since its release at the end of January, 'Funny Funny' had enjoyed steady radio play. The band's gigs were respectable, but the record just wasn't moving and there was absolutely nothing anybody could do about that.

On 6 February, just a week after 'Funny Funny' hit the shops, a nationwide postal strike hit the UK, a six-week dispute that left the chart compilers scrabbling to collect returns from the record shops. The singles chart grew increasingly stagnant as the weeks went by. It wasn't that people weren't buying records. It's just that nobody was able to report the sales.

Even if they had, 'Funny Funny' itself wasn't exactly flying out of the door. Finally, management (Chinnichap and Wainman had formed a company, New Dawn, to handle the band) resorted to a practice all too common in those days, no matter how frowned upon it may have been. They purchased a list of the record shops whose sales figures were tallied to create the charts, then headed out to buy a few discs from each. Not too many, in case people became suspicious, but enough to edge the record into the lower reaches of the chart. By the time DJ Tony Blackburn picked 'Funny Funny' as his Record of the Week, nobody doubted that they had a hit on their hands.

'The postal strike nearly killed it, but I think it's levelled itself off now,' Brian Connolly mused at the end of February, and 'Funny Funny' finally entered the chart on 13 March, six weeks after release, to commence its slow rise up the listings. Number 28 on 3 April, Number 20, Number 15, Number 14 for two weeks as April turned to May, and then Number 13 for another fortnight. The Sweet had their first hit at last.

In the midst of this, on 1 April, the Sweet made their first ever appearance on *Top Of The Pops*, the show whose stage set they were to dominate for the next four years. T Rex were still Number 1 that week, but the show, as Connolly later remarked, was 'the making of the Sweet' – and that despite the band discovering, to their horror, that Georgie Fame and Alan Price, fellow guests on the show, were intending to appear wearing exactly the same red and black trousers as the Sweet had decked themselves in.

'*Top Of The Pops* was it,' Connolly continued. 'If you succeed there, you've done it. Fourteen million people watching every week, you knew what the next week's chart was going to be simply by watching it. If a band was on *Top Of The Pops*, they'd have to be seriously fucked not to be going up the chart the next week. Everything else we did, the gigs and the records and all the press, they all helped. But if we hadn't had *Top Of The*

Pops, none of that would have meant anything.'

Or, as Nicky Chinn pointed out, you could go to bed on a Wednesday night knowing nobody had ever heard of you. By eight o'clock the following evening, the whole country would know your name.

April 1971 – David Bowie: The Man Who Sold The World (Mercury 633804)

No less than the single that preceded it, Bowie's third album was destined for similar oblivion, and that's probably not too surprising. Anybody entering on the strength of 'Space Oddity' would have encountered a bludgeoning prog-metal blend that had far more in common with the one-off single that Ronson, Woodmansey, Visconti and Rats vocalist Benny Marshall cut for Vertigo Records than anything Bowie had recorded in the past...or would again.

A clutch of future Bowie favourites were included – the opening 'Width Of A Circle' remained a live staple into the mid Seventies as a showcase not only for Ronson but also his eventual replacement Earl Slick; 'Man Who Sold The World' itself would be a hit for Lulu (and, years later, Nirvana); and 'All The Madmen' would intrigue all the future biographers who wanted to prove that Bowie was obsessed by the notion of insanity.

There was also the album's original cover (replaced on the 1972 reissue), a gorgeous portrait of Bowie reclining in a dress. That would snag some press interest at the time and remain a constant image in Bowie's future.

But the album bombed and when *New Musical Express* later joked that it sold just 12 copies...maybe they weren't really joking.

April 1971 – Alice Cooper: I'm Eighteen/Is It My Body (Straight S 7209)

Alice Cooper himself was actually Vince Furnier, the son of a Michigan preacher man. Moving to Phoenix, he changed his name and, after experimenting with such titles as the Nazz, the Earwigs and the Spiders, he built a band around it. With schoolfriends Glen Buxton (guitar), Michael Bruce (guitar), Dennis Dunaway (bass) and Neal Smith (drums), Alice swiftly built a reputation as the worst band in Arizona. They moved to Los Angeles and became the worst band in California as well.

One night Alice threw a chicken into the audience. He thought it would fly away ('I mean, they have wings, don't they?'); instead the audience ripped it to pieces, and the next day the press swore blind Alice had bitten off the bird's head and sucked out its blood. 'After that we had to check in with the Humane Society every town we played.'

According to legend, Alice Cooper's big television break arrived when they were asked to appear in an advertisement for indigestion powder. They played your stomach before you took the cure.

But legend says a lot of things about Alice Cooper: how, at the Toronto Peace Festival, they beat each other up on stage. How, when they flew to London for the first time, the old lady in the seat beside Alice dropped dead. And how a 20-foot cardboard Alice, naked except for a strategically placed snake, brought London traffic to a halt when the lorry it was on broke

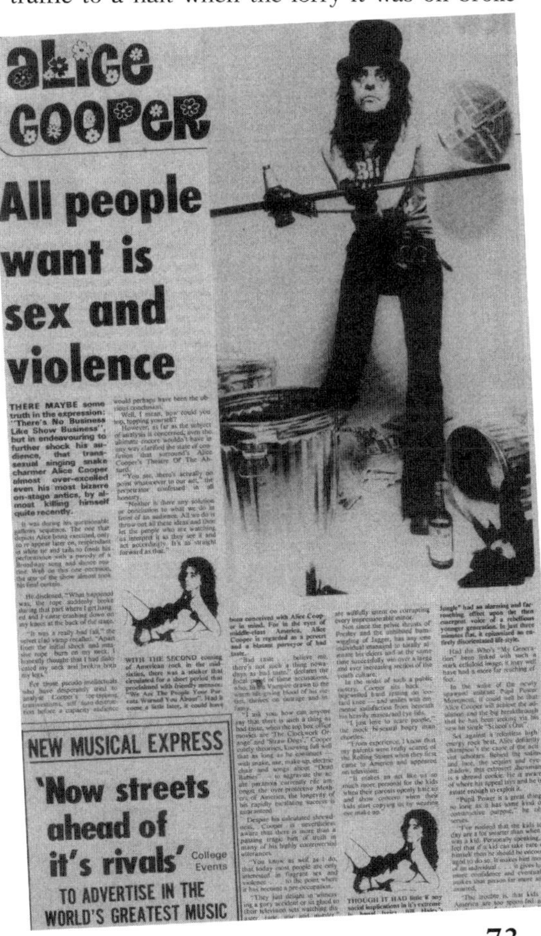

alice COOPER

All people want is sex and violence

THERE MAYBE some truth in the expression: "There's No Business Like Show Business", but in endeavouring to further shock his audience, that trans-sexual singing snake charmer Alice Cooper almost over-excelled even his most bizarre on-stage antics, by almost killing himself quite recently.

NEW MUSICAL EXPRESS

'Now streets ahead of it's rivals' College Events

TO ADVERTISE IN THE WORLD'S GREATEST MUSIC

down. 'We act as a mirror,' was the group's only explanation. 'People see themselves through us.'

They made two albums for Frank Zappa's Straight label, having woken him up in the early hours of the morning by auditioning on his lawn. But still they were on a hot rail to nowhere until they released 'I'm Eighteen' (they were all in their twenties at the time, but no matter), the ultimate teen anthem of the Seventies, and that's when everything fell into place.

'After our first two albums on Frank Zappa's Straight Record label failed to launch us into rock stardom, we desperately needed a hit single,' recalls drummer Neal Smith. 'The summer of 1970 all five members of Alice Cooper were writing brand new songs in a much more commercial vein. Michael Bruce came up with the original idea for a new song called "I'm Eighteen". A song celebrating the awkward teenage transformation from adolescence to adulthood.'

The band spent the summer of 1970 working up an eight-minute arrangement of the song for the stage, then entered RCA Studios in Chicago to record with Canadians Jack Richardson and Bob Ezrin. 'And finally, we got our first Alice Cooper hit single blistering the Top Forty radio airwaves.'

In America, anyway. The single didn't move in the UK. But Alice's time would come soon enough.

ON THE BOX
8 April 1971 – Top Of The Pops: The Sweet, T Rex
15 April 1971 – Top Of The Pops: T Rex
22 April 1971 – Top Of The Pops: T Rex

---

1 May 1971 – Glam Bang – Biba is Bombed

Biba wasn't the only boutique in town, but it was certainly one of the only places to be. Alkasura and Granny Takes A Trip, down on King's Road, were great as well. But Biba had a certain style, a certain look, that was all their own, and had done for almost a decade.

In business since 1964, when Barbara Hulanicki and her husband Stephen Fitz-Simon set up as a mail-order business, Biba geared itself towards whatever was the Moddest fashion around – Cathy McGowan, hostess of television's *Ready Steady Go!*, shopped there, and word quickly spread that whatever she wore on the TV on Friday night would be on sale at Biba the following morning.

Shifting with the times and swiftly developing its own ultra-glamorous style, Biba weathered the hippy boom of the late Sixties by concentrating on the more dandified elements that also crept out of that movement and, by the end of the decade, a succession of pop stars (and would-be pop stars too) had established it as the fulcrum around which the next five years of rock fashion would revolve.

Art Deco furnishings, dynamic designs, wild wigs and towering platforms were Biba specialties; so were lipsticks in colours that lips had never seen before, browns and greens and more vivid hues that would soon be matched by eyeshadow and powder.

The first store was outgrown within a year, the second within five. By 1973, Biba would be taking over the old Derry & Toms department store on Kensington High Street, redesigning the place in its own glorious image and becoming for a year or so *the* absolute heartbeat of rock'n'roll royalty.

Which means, when the left-wing militant Angry Brigade bombed Biba, the entire visual future of Glam Rock could have been altered overnight.

The Brigade's Communique 8, published in the 19 May edition of *International Times*, explained why.

'If you're not busy being born you're busy buying.

All the sales girls in the flash boutiques are made to dress the same and have the same make-up, representing the 1940's. In fashion as in everything else, capitalism can only go backwards — they've nowhere to go — they're dead.

The future is ours.

Life is so boring there is nothing to do except spend all our wages on the latest skirt or shirt.

Brothers and Sisters, what are your real desires?

Sit in the drugstore, look distant, empty, bored, drinking some tasteless coffee? Or perhaps BLOW IT UP OR BURN IT DOWN. The only thing you can do with modern slave-houses —

called boutiques — IS WRECK THEM. You can't reform profit capitalism and inhumanity. Just kick it till it breaks.

Revolution. '

Louis Price's documentary *Beyond Biba's*, was released in 2009.

May 1971 – T Rex tour

Home from a five-week American tour that peaked with four nights at the Fillmore East in New York (12-15 April), T Rex launched their first post-stardom UK tour in Bournemouth on 9 May, straight into scenes straight out of a Beatles movie. Sixty pence would buy you a ticket this time, and the riots that pursued the band around the country had the media already coining ever more extravagant titles to confer upon Bolan. Who just smiled in response. The biggest thing since the Beatles? Yeah, that'll do for the time being...

Prior to the long-delayed release of the *Born To Boogie* soundtrack album, T Rex were never treated to a truly stellar live recording, one which not only captured their incandescent energy but did so in a remotely listenable fashion. It is almost as if the only people with the foresight to record the band at its height were the ones with tickets for row Z, which they'd lost en route to the venue, so they taped the gig from the street outside.

Bolan's Eighties fanclub took a stab at breaking this particular duck, but it was the mid-Nineties release of 'Electric Boogie' (Burning Airlines PILOT 13) that finally ended the drought by serving up excerpts from four shows from this tour – that is, the period immediately after 'Hot Love' and prior to 'Get It On'.

Included are six medium-fidelity tracks from the Rotterdam show, plus two cuts apiece from Bournemouth, Wolverhampton (19 May) and Lewisham (9 July), with the first named unquestionably highlighted by a nine-minute rendition of 'Ride A White Swan'. If you're wondering how a simple three-minute pop song can be so elongated, remember Bolan's guitar-playing skills weren't limited to the brusque, choppy chords which highlighted his studio work. 'Elemental Child', from the Wolverhampton gig, makes the same point less surprisingly.

In fact, if there is any downside to 'Electric Boogie', it's the misleading packaging, conveying the impression that the recordings hail from another show that summer, the legendary Weeley Festival bash, outside Clacton over the long weekend of 27-29 August. Both the cover photo and Bill Legend's liner notes abet the deception although, in truth, such details probably matter only to the most committed collectors. For the rest of us, a rare chance to hear (and even enjoy) T Rex

at their live peak is simply too good to pass up.

And there was more to come. The Wolverhampton show, and a Stoke on Trent gig three months later (26 August) are also highlighted within the Easy Action label's 'Total T Rex 1971-1972' box set, with additional recordings (Bournemouth, 12 August; Rotherham 28 August) appearing on the confusingly titled companion 'The Electric Boogie, 1971'.

May 1971 – Slade: Get Down And Get With It/ Do You Want Me/Rasputin (Polydor 2058112)

Their hair grew out, their wardrobe was replaced and Slade had placed the skinhead shenanigans of the past far behind them, turning instead towards a brighter, more garish look that somehow put one in mind of a slightly deranged Max Wall.

Blue jeans were replaced by chequered suits. Doc Martens were supplanted by stack heels, shaven skulls by flowing manes. Vocalist Noddy Holder trained his sideburns down his face, guitarist Dave Hill sprayed glitter across his ample forehead. Noddy found a mirrored top hat, Dave came up with a bottomless range of indoor overcoats and an equally perverse collection of thigh boots. It was a slow process, one that would not truly flower for another few singles. But Slade were on the right track, and they received their first reward for their efforts with the success of 'Get Down And Get With It', a rousing revival of Little Richard's old-time chest-beater.

It was manager Chandler's idea that the band record it. It was a highlight of their live show and, in the studio, he told the band simply to 'play it like you do on stage. Blast it out like it's live, and pretend there's an audience in there with you.'

The result, cut in a single take, perfectly encapsulates the madness of a period Slade show and the band's only complaint was that, it wasn't half as heavy as it should have been. 'The equipment couldn't cope with it,' Noddy Holder reflected later.

No matter. The stamping and clapping accompaniment became a Slade trademark, while the record's overall aura of unrestrained power was simply too much for many radio DJs. Not until John Peel started airing it did 'Get

Down And Get With It' begin to move.

Success, however, came at an unexpected price. Like so many other fans, Slade assumed the song was written by Little Richard and credited it to him on the label. True composer Bobby Marchand sued and, while the record company soon sorted the problem out. 'We learnt to be more careful in future,' Holder recalled. So careful that, from now on, the band would write their singles themselves.

But it wasn't the simple process of having a hit that impacted the hardest on Slade. It was the realisation that, Marc Bolan's T Rex aside, there wasn't another band in the land to compete with them.

The first time Slade appeared on *Top Of The Pops*, bassist Jim Lea recalled, 'there were acts like the Pipkins, Edison Lighthouse [actually, they weren't] and Pan's People on.' The second time (29 July), they shared the stage with Cat Stevens, Shirley Bassey and the New Seekers. 'I remember thinking to myself that we could rule this situation. None of those acts had anything like the experience we had. I knew then that we were going to make it, and with Chas at the helm, it was impossible for us not to.'

Quite how much of Slade's reinvention had to do with Bolan we will probably never know. Slade themselves maintained that theirs was a gradual change – that while Bolan literally emerged overnight, they had already been experimenting with dress for some time, and that even their most garish costumes were simply a progression from the last.

Nevertheless, it was with the emergence of Slade that, at last, it became apparent that Bolan was not an isolated phenomenon.

His natural ebullience notwithstanding, Marc Bolan's appeal always verged on the more cerebral side of life, in that his whole approach to music possessed a fey other-worldliness. Slade, on the other hand, were almost brutally common,out-of-town yobbos having a night on the tiles and intent on raising hell everywhere they went. There was definitely room enough for them both.

'I think a lot of [our early success] was through the telly,' Holder mused. 'As soon as we'd got the colourful image sorted out, it just zoomed away for us. People just looked at us and thought "fucking hell, these guys are mad" and it just became an overnight thing.' And while Bolan concentrated on a narcissistic greatness, Slade went the opposite way entirely.

You could visualise Bolan camping up simply to mow the lawn, but Slade were pantomime dames, dressing up for the show and changing back into flat caps and clogs when they came offstage. Bolan lived his image; Slade kept theirs in the wardrobe with their parkas and wellington boots.

Yet their emergence a year after Bolan but a good six months before the rest of the pack was to set the scene for a sartorial struggle that could not help but translate itself into the music.

Just as it had taken the emergence of the Rolling Stones to challenge the supremacy of the Beatles before the Beat Boom could truly be born, so now the movement created by Bolan needed its own anti-Christ. Slade's leering thugs were the total antithesis of Bolan's lisping, bopping elf and, with a suddenly burgeoning New Wave of British Bubblegum caught on the fence somewhere in the middle, so the Glitter pack began to divide into two very separate camps.

May 1971 – The Dirtiest Show In Town, Duchess Theatre, London

Hair proved, in case there was any doubt at all, that there was a market on the London stage for nudity, sex and bad language, and the success two years later of Kenneth Tynan's *Oh! Calcutta!* proved that there was always room for more, at least in terms of headlines generated and controversy aroused.

Opening in July 1970, *Oh! Calcutta!* was an oft-times overly crude but nevertheless essential purging of earlier moralities through a celebration of the utterly immoral. Tynan referred to himself as the 'thinking man's voyeur' and revelled in pre-opening night rumours that the play would be the first to feature live copulation on the Broadway stage (*Oh! Calcutta!* had opened in the United States a year earlier).

In fact, *Oh! Calcutta!* didn't really live up to either of these promises, but audiences didn't care. To older theatre-goers, *Oh! Calcutta!* was the epitome of the new permissive society; to younger ones it was a taste of a reality that they'd maybe only read about; and to the artistic ones, it was a challenge that would soon be met.

London, sadly, never received David Newburge's *Stag Movie*, a five month off-Broadway wonder that starred the young Adrienne Barbeau and allegedly featured some of the finest sexual lyricism ever offered to the theatre world (no cast album was ever recorded). But May 1971 brought the next American sensation to London, and this one really steamed.

Tom Eyen and Henry Krieger's *The Dirtiest Show In Town* was produced (as were *Hair* and *Oh! Calcutta!*) by rock impresario Robert Stigwood and Michael White, and was controversial not only for its depictions of sex and flesh, but also for its own acknowledgement that gender should be no barrier to pleasure. 'My play has no sex preference,' Eyen said. 'It's homo, hetero and bisexual. I'm not sticking up for any of the three.'

Opening in May 1971 and destined to run for almost eight hundred performances, *The Dirtiest Show In Town* took the West End by storm. More so than either of its naked predecessors, *The Dirtiest Show In Town* worked in the realms of actual political comment as opposed to mere sound bite rhetoric; it had a plot (of sorts) and purpose.

In direct theatrical terms, it opened the door through which *The Rocky Horror Show* would sashay two years later; in cultural terms, it could be said to have furthered the democratisation of sexuality in a Britain that still thought in terms of seaside postcards and off-colour comedians; and in rock historical terms, it introduced the world to Michael Des Barres.

Public-school educated, titled (his father was a Marquis) and privileged, Des Barres was in his first year at drama school when he was plucked, alongside his fellow students, to appear in James Clavell's 1967 movie *To Sir With Love*. Three years, and a few TV roles later, he was being plucked again, nightly on stage at the Duchess, in the role of an androgynous rock star named Rose.

Des Barres was not the first Rose; he was cast after his predecessor dropped out shortly into the play's run. But he was probably the best, and that despite the fact that he'd never sung in public before, not unless one cares to consider 'a few drunken nights on Hampstead Heath where we used to get up to all sorts of trouble dressed in velvet.'

But Andrew Lloyd Webber, co-author of both *Joseph And The Amazing Technicolor Dreamcoat* and *Jesus Christ Superstar*, was impressed. 'He got hold of me and said, "What else you got?" I said, "Let me come back in a few days" and I wrote a song called "Will You Finance My Rock'n'Roll Band?"'

A few days later, Des Barres was invited to attend a dinner party Lloyd Webber was hosting. 'There's all this posh types, and I sat there and I played "Will You Finance My Rock'n'Roll Band?" and he said "all right".'

Lloyd Webber's first port of call in the summer of 1971 was to see John Coletta and Tony Edwards, Deep Purple's management. They were just launching the band's own Purple Records, and looking for new talent to sign.

'They bankrolled me to hold auditions and form a band,' Des Barres continues. 'So I put an ad in the *Melody Maker* and it said "wanted, erotic, relaxed musicians".

'But when it was published, it said "erotic relax*er* musicians", so I was sitting there waiting for the people to come in, and of course the most outrageous transsexual performance artists were filing in. I didn't get any musicians, but I got plenty of trisexual massage therapists.'

A second ad, better worded (or less prone to typographical misinterpretation) was more fortunate. 'A bunch of guys showed up, and we started to rehearse, and out of that there came this outrageous band in which everybody loved each other and respected each other. Every note they played, every article of clothing they wore, I loved. They were an incredible band.'

They were guitarists Rod Davies and Stevie Forest, bassist Nigel Harrison and drummer Pete Thompson. And they would become Silverhead.

May 1971 – Peter Noone: Oh You Pretty Things/Together Forever (RAK 114)
27 May 1971 – Top Of The Pops: Peter Noone with David Bowie on piano

In February 1971, manager Tony Defries played a tape of four new David Bowie compositions (including his latest *Tomorrow People*-inspired effort) to his old ally Mickie Most. Defries had worked for Most a few years earlier, helping him through some legal issues, and he thought the producer might like what he heard. Within weeks, Most had recorded one of them, 'Oh You Pretty Things', with former Herman's Hermits frontman Peter Noone, and taken it into the Top Twenty.

Noone recalls, 'David was writing these very thoughtful songs, a few of which he sent into Mackie's office because he thought they might work for me. And I really liked them. I played "Oh You Pretty Things", and it sounded a bit like something the Hermits could have done, a great British radio song. David came over to the studio when we were recording it to play piano on the track, and we got on fabulously. He was very shy, but we had a great time. I remember I erased the drum track by accident.'

The pair became firm friends. 'I'd go to his gigs, we'd go out for a pint, we'd hang out together. I think what interested him was I was nothing like he had expected, which was something I have always loved about the Herman character, the fact that when people met him there was a bit more substance to him than they ever expected.'

In early June 1971, Noone appeared on *Top Of The Pops* with a band that still boggles the mind – Bowie on piano, Tony Wilson of Hot Chocolate on bass and Luther 'Ariel Bender' Grosvenor on guitar. A week later, Noone's version of 'Oh You Pretty Things' was marching resolutely up the Top Thirty.

How cruel it was, then, that it subsequently became so fashionable to castigate Noone not only for recording such an unthreatening version of 'Pretty Things' but for changing the lyric as well. Where Bowie's version, taped later in 1971, is pregnant with foreboding, and knowingly snarls, 'the earth is a bitch', Noone's is simply a good-naturedly plod that merely opines 'the earth is a *beast*'.

How we mocked.

Ah, but Noone gets the last laugh. 'I just sang what was on the demo. That's what David wrote and, at that time, what would have been the point of him writing something which people might have considered offensive? He wanted a hit single; he wanted a hit single more than we did. He always used to say, "it's great, it's paying my rent!"'

'Oh You Pretty Things' peaked at Number 12 and, suitably emboldened, the team followed through by placing another Bowie composition, 'Right On Mother', on the B-side of Noone's follow-up, 'Walnut Whirl' (RAK 121), even recalling Bowie to reprise the deliciously hamfisted piano technique that distinguished 'Pretty Things'.

'Right On Mother' was a groovy little ditty dedicated to a parent who didn't object to her offspring living in sin with his girlfriend; so groovy, in fact, that the BBC took one listen to the lyric, then threw it in the bin. 'Nobody would play it,' Noone recalls. 'It was the most bizarre thing!' The only airplay the song received was from Vera Lynn, that bastion of pre-rock British entertainment. 'Vera Lynn loved it; I was on her TV show singing it. But we couldn't get a single other TV show. Everybody thought the song was "inappropriate".

'But that was something I loved about Bowie's songs at that time, they all had an element which wasn't Cliff Richard-esque, at the same time as sounding so fabulous.'

Noone would have a go at two other Bowie compositions. One was 'Bombers', a gorgeous song whose minor-key melody and querulous hook utterly belies its somewhat sobering subject-matter (nuclear devastation), and which remains unreleased to this day. (Bowie's own version, too, would stay in the vault before finally emerging 20 years later on the Rykodisc remaster of 'Hunky Dory').

The other was 'Life On Mars?', a song that remains one of the most strikingly beautiful that Bowie has ever written...and which Noone laughingly admits he'd completely forgotten recording.

May 1971 – Sweet: Co-Co/Done Me Wrong All Right (RCA 2087)
May 1971 – Sweet: All You'll Ever Get From Me/The Juicer (Parlophone R5902)
May 1971 – Sweet and the Pipkins: 'Gimme Dat Ding' (Music For Pleasure 5248)

Following hard on the heels of the breakthrough hit 'Funny Funny' (and rush-released after RCA got wind that former label Parlophone were planning a spoiler reissue), 'Co-Co' was an effervescent Chinnichapper blown straight in from the Caribbean, complete with steel drums, palm trees and sunny, unspoiled beaches.

The song, Brian Connolly explained at the time, 'is about a little Negro boy who loves to dance.' And that's about it. Although Connolly continued, 'it's probably a more commercial song than "Funny Funny" but it's not bubblegum,' it remained simplicity itself and the band were quick to confess that it had little to do with their own musical interests. Good job they didn't have to play on the record then. The usual team of sessionmen recorded the backing track (producer Phil Wainman played drums), and the Sweet were needed for nothing more than the vocals.

A monster hit worldwide, 'Co-Co' gave The Sweet their first ever US chart entry (Number 93) and topped the chart in 15 countries, from Chile to South Africa. At home, it reached Number 2.

The Parlophone poke, meanwhile, did nothing; Steve Priest had already predicted that 'Co-Co' would 'knock spots off the other disc. I don't know how people are going to receive the old disc, and we won't be promoting it on TV, although it's been included in our stage act for quite a long time. But, then again, if it was a hit, no-one would mind, although I don't really think it will be.'

However, Parlophone were not finished yet. The label also leased their full pre-Sweet catalogue to the budget Music For Pleasure label, alongside six songs by television-spawned novelty act the Pipkins, the oddly clothed duo of songwriter Roger Greenaway and session singer supreme Tony Burrows. The result, titled for the latter's solitary hit, was 'Gimme Dat Ding', with one side dedicated to the Sweet and the other a reminder of that moment, a year before, when the all-pervading chorus of the season was a duet between a piano and a metronome, an infuriatingly catchy ditty, riddled with novelty voices and a so-chirpy chorus.

May 1971 – Top Of The Pops Volume 16 (Hallmark SHM 735)

For an entire generation of teenage English boys, the *Top Of The Pops* albums represent their first ever brush with erotica.

Before that surreptitious first peek at *Penthouse*, before they wanked over *Whitehouse* or moaned at *Men Only*, those Top Of The Pops covers represented the pinnacle of adolescent fantasy. And, while it is not true that blue movie queen Mary Millington posed for one of them, early in her career (the blonde beauty bedecking Volume 29 is the usual mistaken identity), still there was a sensual beauty to some of those cover girls that could make the average men's magazine of the day hang its dangly bits in shame.

And then there was Volume 16.

It all seems impossibly tame today but, back in spring 1971, the appearance of a pair of female nipples on the sleeve of the latest Top Of The Pops album wasn't merely a bold step into territory that few pop records have ever taken in the past. It was enough for some observers to actually write letters of stern complaint to the record label, outraged that such smut, filth and degeneracy should be allowed to sully the minds of the young. And that's before any of them even played the actual record.

Ah, but maybe if they had, they'd have been a little more understanding. The UK charts of early 1971 were scarcely rampaging through their most vibrant era ever and, though the continued hysteria of T Rex suggested that the future would become brighter, little else in sight demanded more than passing glance. And Volume 16 echoes that blandness with chilling verisimilitude. Even 'Hot Love' feels lukewarm.

So, in an era when *The Dirtiest Show* was on the London stage, and *Percy* was poking the cinemas, *Top Of The Pops* kept abreast of the times in other ways.

ON THE RADIO
13 May 1971 – Stuart Henry Show: Slade
24 May 1971 – Terry Wogan Show: The Sweet

June 1971 – Arnold Corns: Moonage Daydream/Hang Onto Yourself (B&C CB 149)

David Bowie had some important news – and when *Rolling Stone* dropped by to visit him, shortly after the release of 'The Man Who Sold The World', he was bursting to let it out.

The album was already forgotten. There was some mileage, still, to be drawn from its cover art, a portrait of a simply gorgeous looking Bowie reclining on a *chaise longue* in a dress... 'A man's dress', he cautioned anyone who commented it. But Bowie was more interested in talking about the dress's designer than its inhabitant.

'I've got this friend who is just beautiful. When you meet him, you don't even question whether he's a boy or a girl. He's just a person called Freddi, who's very nice to look at. That's what's important, to be a person, to be an individual.'

And Freddi was so individual, Bowie continued, that he would be the first man ever to appear on the cover of *Vogue*.

He detailed his master plan. He'd written a song for Freddi, a far-out freak-out titled 'Moonage Daydream' and, accompanied by an extraordinary young guitarist named Mark Carr Pritchard, he'd built a band around the singer, the intriguingly named Arnold's Corn. He had even landed him a record deal with the small but successful B&C label. Bowie himself would produce and sing on the record. All Freddi had to do was stand there and look ravishing.

'The Rolling Stones are finished,' Bowie continued. 'Arnold's Corn will be the next Stones.' He had a high opinion of 'Moonage Daydream', too. 'This song is unique. There's certainly nothing to compare it with.' And because he believed that 'Freddi is right for now', the whole thing had been put together in just six days. 'There's no point in waiting.'

Freddi was less immodest. 'Actually, I can't just expect to bring Jagger back,' he admitted. 'Really, I'm just a dress designer.' And so he was. Like Carr Pritchard, Freddi Buretti was an art student from south London's Dulwich College who had wandered into the Bowie camp with his girlfriend Danielle and promptly become immersed in the flurry of sartorial reshaping Angela was in the process of executing.

'Every time David's band had an important gig,' Angela explained, 'Freddi would design new clothes for them.' She also worked hard to foster the belief 'that it was pointless going on stage in great clothes, if they were going to be wearing jeans offstage, so Freddi made them clothes to wear offstage as well, from mohair, cashmere, silk – anything that would make them look out of the ordinary when they were on the street.'

It was this look that Buretti would now be taking into the full public glare, as though Bowie wanted to check the reaction first before relaunching himself in equally audacious style. If Freddi was simply laughed out of sight, then Bowie would return to the drawing board. But if people accepted him in all of his finery, then the door would be open for anything else: an alligator, a space invader, a mama/papa coming for tea.

Arnold Corns, as the project would be slightly renamed, was announced to the world when Carr Pritchard was among the guests at Bowie's 3 June *Sunday Concert* broadcast on Radio 1, and led the ensemble through another of the songs earmarked for Arnold, 'Looking For A Friend'. Two weeks later, Buretti, Carr Pritchard and Bowie commenced a week of sessions at Trident Studios.

Tucked away in the darkened recesses of Queen Anne's Court, in London's Soho district, Trident was a small but implausibly intimate hangout that was just beginning to establish its name on the studio circuit, and which would become Bowie's favoured base of operations for the next year or more. There awaited the impossibly magnificently named drummer Timothy James Ralph St Laurent Thomas Moore Broadbent and bassist Polak De Somogyl – bandmates of Carr Pritchard in another group, Runk.

Arnold Corns were ready for action.

The group had four songs at their disposal: 'Moonage Daydream', 'Man In The Middle', 'Looking For A Friend' and 'Hang On To Yourself', a song Bowie had already taped once, incredibly, alongside Gene Vincent. Visiting the US for a brief promo trip at the beginning of the year, Bowie and the Be-Bop-A-Lu-lerr jammed together in a small Los Angeles studio, the only downside of the entire exercise being Vincent was inaudible on the finished recording. Much as Buretti would be inaudible on the Arnold Corns single.

Indeed, while Bowie was insistent that a full Arnold Corns album, 'Looking For Rudi', was in the works, it was difficult to shake the impression that the whole exercise was just another way of getting some music into the marketplace, without Mercury Records finding out.

Which, according to Bob Grace, over at Bowie's Chrysalis Music publishers, is exactly what it was. Bowie was spending so much time making demos, Grace explains, and getting 'really slick' in the process, that 'finally we decided to lease [four] of the demos to B&C, simply to try and get some money back. I think we got £300 for the masters. But because David was still contracted to Mercury, we couldn't use his name. So David came up with Arnold Corns. He never told anyone what it meant.'

No matter. While veteran publicist Bill Harry was engaged to tout pictures of Buretti, who really was as lovely as Bowie reckoned, around the Fleet Street papers, B&C's own PR machinery clanked into action, flooding the music press with copies of 'Moonage Daydream'.

Their travails went unrewarded. Fleet Street was apathetic, the music press was appalled. Even the best review was a stinker; commenting upon the single's B-side in the *New Musical Express*, journalist Charles Shaar Murray dismissed 'Hang On To Yourself' as 'a thinly disguised rewrite of the Velvet Underground's "Sweet Jane",' and the only consolation was that Bowie would not dispute that charge.

Having evaded even the bootleggers for 15 years, Arnold Corns' 'Moonage Daydream' was finally given an official re-release on the now fabulously scarce compilation LP 'The Great Glam Rock Explosion' (Biff BIFF 3) in 1986.

June 1971 – St Cecilia: Leap Up And Down (Wave Your Knickers In The Air)/How You Gonna Tell Me (Polydor 2058 104)

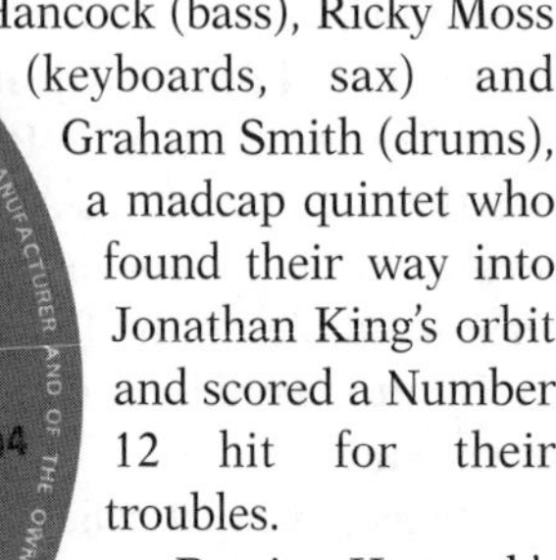

St Cecilia were Les Smith (vocals), John Proctor (guitar), Keith Hancock (bass), Ricky Moss (keyboards, sax) and Graham Smith (drums), a madcap quintet who found their way into Jonathan King's orbit and scored a Number 12 hit for their troubles.

Bassist Hancock's 'Leap Up And Down' remains one of the most joyously stupid records ever made (producer King penned the less than scintillating flip), an ode to doing precisely what it says on the label. And why not?

Because the BBC wouldn't like it.

'When the record was released it was very difficult for us to get radio plays because of stuffy old Auntie Beeb, and we were banned from doing *Top Of The Pops*,' Hancock recalled.

Not even a highly photogenic fan protest outside Broadcasting House, organised by the band and protesting the ban, could budge the Beeb. But 'Jimmy Young and Alan Freeman played it on their radio shows (bless 'em), and it was heavily featured on Radio Luxembourg.'

Video footage circulating today was shot in 1985 when the band guested on Noel Edmonds' *The Time Of Your Life* show – remarkably, the first time the song had ever been performed on television.

June 1971 – Alice Cooper: Love It To Death (Straight STS 1065)

'I'm Eighteen' gave the Alice Cooper band the American breakthrough they craved, but it was their third album, 'Love It To Death', that confirmed their arrival – a sprawling masterpiece that peaked with the twin psychoses of 'The Ballad of Dwight Frye' and 'Black Juju'.

Nine minutes of drum and basics, 'Black Juju' is a primal chant, a silent scream, a lullaby for the sleeping dead, a reminder that bodies need their rest – until it's time to wake up, and the voice that calls for resurrection is one of Cooper's most terrifying. It is the sound of a seething voodoo incantation that in turn becomes everything you've ever dreamed a dark mass could be without once suggesting that anything was out of the ordinary. Because the most frightening things are the ones you least suspect.

'It's not that we threw all the rule books out the window,' explains drummer Neal Smith, whose propulsive percussion is the heartbeat of the song. 'But we really had an open slate to work with. There were no preconceived notions. But we were honing our theatrics, and what we wanted was a way to kill Alice on stage every night, a song to perform while we did it. By the time we reached "Love It To Death", we realised that violence was around us all the time. We never focused on it, but we were thinking we should have an execution on stage.'

Bandmate Dennis Dunaway came up with 'Black Juju' in the first place. 'He didn't get the nickname Dr Dreary for nothing,' says Smith. 'He was one of the main creators of "Dead Babies", too.'

At first it was just an idea and a rhythm, pieced together while the Cooper band toured. 'It was worked on in hotel rooms,' Smith continues. 'We really didn't have a rehearsal studio, our rehearsal studio was the stage, so we sketched it out in hotel rooms on telephone books, and we all agreed it needed a heavy dark African percussion. I wanted to work on the percussion way beyond anything I'd done before. I wanted it to be a big feature drum song, and it was the perfect vehicle. There's a lot of music that uses that tribal primitive vibe, but for me it was like taking Gene Krupa and putting him on floor toms. Gene Krupa in Haiti.

'I was a percussionist. I learned all the rudiments early on and then went into orchestra, so my background was open to everything percussive, and one of my big influences was jungle drums, native American, African, raw percussion.'

So he did it.

Performed live for the first time on Midsummer's Day 1970 (a coincidence of timing that opens up its own can of neo-pagan worms) 'Black Juju' quickly found its feet. 'It was the end of the show, the finale, when we strapped Alice into the electric chair and fried him. And then Alice comes back to life...' while all around the undead rise in a choking sea of feathers and smoke and the band drives headlong into madness.

'We'd have the smoke bombs and Alice was ripping up the feather pillows, and Mike Bruce had some CO_2 canisters and would blast the feathers into the audience, and that was the finale of the show. It was,' Smith understates, 'very explosive.'

If 'Black Juju' chilled, 'The Ballad Of Dwight Frye' thrilled. Oozing out of the religiously tortured 'Second Coming', it faded in with a child's voice piping over the prettiest piano. 'Mommy? Where's daddy? Do you think he's ever coming home?'

'"The Ballad Of Dwight Frye" was the theatrical side of our group,' explains Smith. 'Most bands are influenced by others bands. But we were influenced by old Hollywood moves, horror movies in particular. The original 1931 *Dracula*, with Bela Lugosi, one of my favourites, featuring the insect-eating character Renfield, a lost soul and disciple of Dracula. Renfield is played by actor Dwight Frye. Hence the name and direction of our song.

'Michael and Alice crafted a song about a misunderstood mental patient who spends a lot of time institutionalised wearing a straitjacket. We brought our version of Dwight Frye to life when Alice appeared on stage wearing a straitjacket and made a Houdini-esque escapes from its restraints. The recording was [then] helped along the way with Bob Ezrin's classical musical influence and an atomic bomb explosion!'

'Love It To Death' did not chart in the UK upon its initial release. But it lurked in the background, waiting to strike when the moment was right.

June 1971 – Top Of The Pops Volume 17 (Hallmark SHM 740)

'Top Of The Pops Volume 17' is renowned among collectors as the first edition ever to include a David Bowie song, a full year before Bowie shot to fame. Peter Noone's version of the Thin White Zig's 'Oh You Pretty Things' is as foreboding as any look at the end of the world

could be – and it is to the Top Of The Pops team's credit that their version is no breezier than the erstwhile Herman's. Bowie purists will hate it, of course, but they're the only ones who will have a problem.

ON THE RADIO
3 June 1971 – In Concert: David Bowie and friends
ON THE BOX
10 June 1971 – Top Of The Pops: Peter Noone
17 June 1971 – Top Of The Pops: The Sweet

July 1971: New World – Tom Tom Turnaround/Lay Me Down (RAK 117)

Broad of collar and bright of shirt, New World exemplified the kind of bright-eyed, lightly sentimental folk-pop that threatened to devour the UK charts in the early Seventies.

Portrayed as an Antipodean import, the band was actually largely English; John Lee was born in Ashtead, Surrey, John Kane in Glasgow. Both had moved down under long before, though, and there they met Mel Noonan, a true-born offspring of Oz, and together they became one of Australia's most popular acts. Two hits, 'Try To Remember' (Parlophone A-8589) and 'Feed The Birds' (Parlophone A-8952), had already painted them as a younger and somewhat hairier version of the Bachelors, and they intended pursuing that line of thought when they relocated to the UK in 1969.

A Decca contract produced two further

singles, 'I'll Catch The Sun' (Decca F13031) and 'Something's Wrong' (Decca F13086), but New World remained undiscovered until they landed a spot on *Opportunity Knocks*.

In years to come, host Hughie Green's empire of clapometers and codswallop would be revealed (or at least depicted) as a hotbed of corruption and collusion. As the band's producer, Mike Hurst, explains, 'My manager signed [them] and did a dodgy deal with... *Opportunity Knocks*. They won the first show, and the next and the next. They went onto the final and...they won that too.'

So, when Inspector Knacker took an interest, he trained his truncheon towards New World.

They were acquitted of all charges. Only one dodgy vote could be proven in court, and that was placed by a college student who cast a vote for a friend who had gone to bed.

In fact, it appeared that people genuinely liked New World. Their winning song, and therefore their first single for new label RAK, was the country classic 'Rose Garden', and it swiftly became their first British hit. It made Number 15 in February 1971, and would doubtless have climbed higher had Lynn Anderson not been topping the chart with her own version at the same time.

Now, Mickie Most was sending New World into the studio with Chinnichap's 'Tom Tom Turnaround', a supremely mawkish ditty that Hurst confesses 'I hated. It was everything I disliked about pure pop, right down to the execrable talking bit.

'"Rose Garden" was fine,' he continues. 'It's a country song, I like country. But when we got to that schmaltzy stuff, no, that's not me. I couldn't get that together. But Mickie Most swore it was a hit, and even though I'd had plenty of hits myself, I had to say, if Mickie Most says in 1970-71 that a song is a hit, then it's a hit. I'm gonna believe it and I did.'

Most was right, as well. 'Tom Tom' reached Number 6 before he turned around, and Chinn and Chapman came back with another song in time for Christmas, an irresistible slice of rhyming nonsense called 'Kara Kara'. Hurst produced that as well, even though he swore that it 'was even worse than the track before.'

But New World had another hit, and while their British chart career fizzled out after that (they scored just one more major success, 'Sister Jane' (RAK 130) in May 1972, while their flops included a version of the future Smokie classic 'Living Next Door To Alice' – RAK 142), from here on in, RAK would become home to every significant act in the Chinnichap stable bar the Sweet.

July 1971 – T Rex: Get It On/Raw Ramp (Fly BUG 10)

Three hits in and already the universe had run out of superlatives.

'Get It On', described by Arrows' Alan Merrill as 'the ultimate Glam Rock anthem' was a smash before it even left the studio; its dizzying rise up the chart was simply a formality or even an afterthought.

Released on 2 July, it went from nowhere to Number 21, to Number 4 to Number 1, where it remained for the next three weeks. And all around, the summer seethed to the roar of the T Rex army.

21 July 1971 – David Bowie: The Country Club, Hampstead

At the beginning of June, a most peculiar bunch of aliens made it through passport control at Heathrow and took up residence in an Earls Court flat that was very swiftly renamed Pig Mansions. They were the cast of art dealer Ira Gale's presentation of *Andy Warhol's Pork*, hitting London for six weeks of rehearsal and auditions before their opening night at the Roundhouse in August.

Pork already had a reputation. Built upon what assistant director Leee Black Childers described as 'boxes and boxes and hours and hours of cassette tapes', telephone conversations between Andy Warhol and his friend Brigid Polk, *Pork* was 'nothing more than a lot of pointless conversation.'

A lot. When director Tony Ingrassia was first handed the tapes, he came up with a 29-act play that lasted a marathon 200 hours. Eventually he cut it to a more manageable two-act presentation that barely devoured an evening, and on 5 May 1971 *Pork* opened for a week at the La Mama Experimental Theater on New York. Now it was coming to London, and the nation was on tenterhooks.

Warhol's latest movie, *Flesh*, had already incurred the wrath of the anti-obscenity squad, who raided the cinemas where it was being shown, and made certain that the tabloids was apprised of every sleazy detail. Now here was Geri Miller, one of the movie's most unashamed stars, appearing in London in person.

Miller was, in fact, the only name Warhol associate in sight; the remainder were an ensemble that Warhol discovered during a night out at another off-Broadway play, *World: The Birth Of A Nation: The Castration Of Man* – an outrageous Atlanta-born showman named Wayne County; the laconic Tony Zanetta, the charming Leee Black Childers and the most beautiful woman in New York, Cherry Vanilla.

'Warhol came to see us, and he flipped out,' County recalled. 'At one point I saw him standing up, he was screaming so much because some of the scenes were so over-the-top and outrageous.'

Days later, Warhol was inviting director Ingrassia to oversee the production of *Pork*, suggesting that the core of the *World...* cast be retained for the new show. County, Childers and Zanetta were joined by Jaime di Carlo, Geri Miller and Patti Parlamann; while Vanilla's role would be taken by actress Cleve Roller for the New York run, Cherry returned for London.

They had an agenda. A few weeks earlier, all had thrilled at the pictures that accompanied that *Rolling Stone* feature on David Bowie, the singer who wore a dress. 'It piqued our interest,' Zanetta says simply, and they kept their eyes open for any mentions of him in the London press.

They found one in mid-July, an ad for an upcoming Bowie show at the Country Club in the northwest London suburb of Hampstead.

Childers recalls, 'when we got to London I was always looking out for David's name; "Hey, let's go see a man who wears a dress on stage." One day, we saw he was playing at the Country Club, so Cherry, Wayne and I went down there.'

The trio took their seats and tried their best to be impressed. But County spoke for all of them when he confessed he was outraged to discover that Bowie looked nothing like the Lauren Bacall he'd been led to expect, and was little more than "another fucking folkie with long stringy hair." A big felt hat with a feather, and yellow patent leather Mary Janes completed his ensemble. Bowie played acoustic guitar; Mick Ronson accompanied him on piano. Yuck.

But when Bowie introduced 'Andy Warhol', Cherry leaped up and flashed a breast. A fascinated friendship quickly developed backstage – one that, just days later, saw Bowie and wife Angela make their way to the Roundhouse to catch the stage show that would literally change his life.

ON THE RADIO
July 1971 – Radio 1 Live: The Sweet
ON THE BOX
1 July 1971 – Top Of The Pops: The Sweet
8 July 1971 – Top Of The Pops: T Rex
15 July 1971 – Top Of The Pops: Slade
22 July 1971 – Top Of The Pops: T Rex
29 July 1971 – Top Of The Pops: Slade, T Rex

---

2 August 1971 – Andy Warhol's Pork, London Roundhouse

Pork was an instant smash, and an absolute scandal.

Protestors, rallied by any one of the country's many watchdog fringes, descended nightly upon the Roundhouse, block-booking a row at the front of the auditorium and slow-clapping through any scene that dismayed them. Which, according to Cherry Vanilla, was most of them.

While Josie (Geri Miller) douched on stage, and Vulva (County) kept up a constant dialogue

Andy Warhol, the man who made a Campbell's Soup tin into an expensive piece of pop art, and filmed the Empire State building from one vantage point for 12 hours, has turned his attention to the theatre with a semi-autobiographical play called *Pork*. In these exclusive pictures, **Roger Finborough** discovers that this much-publicized debut is nothing more than a pig in a poke.

on the subject of shit, Pork (Vanilla) cavorted naked with the Pepsodent Twins, argued with her socialite mother (Suzanne Smith), masturbated with an egg whisk and 'shot something called vita-mega-vegimin' into her ass.

That maestro of the monotonous, Andy Warhol, is no longer satisfied with what most would regard as the substantial achievement of making a bore out of sex. In *Pork*, described by London's *Daily Telegraph* as "the nearest we have yet come to a theatrical emetic", he manages to debase it as well, with a treatment that puts it on the same level as a bowel movement. A stage play ostensibly depicting incidents in Warhol's personal life, *Pork* was originally written to last no fewer than 10½ hours. Mercifully director Anthony J. Ingrassia persuaded the czar of somnambulism to trim it by eight hours or so. The surviving scenes show wheelchaired Warhol (Anthony Zanetta) listening to and questioning a number of people whom Ingrassia describes as "like everyone else." They include Amanda Pork (Kathy Dorritie), a plump frustrated girl with a mother problem; Vulva (Wayne County), a hideous bushy-haired transvestite with a Southern American drawl; and Josie (Geri Miller), a topless dancer with a penchant for peeing in plastic basins. Real familiar, next-door, friendly neighborhood folk! In its dialogue *Pork* contrives to present sex, not as the joyful and

The mysterious B Marlowe (Zanetta) sat silent in his wheelchair, flicking through magazines or talking on the phone; and every moment they were on stage, this gang of freakishly coloured, occasionally costumed, weirdoes, deviants and degenerates were fucking and sucking and shooting up shit.

Across town in the West End, *The Dirtiest Show In Town* had just opened. It looked like a Persil commercial by comparison.

The following morning brought the first newspaper commentaries. 'We got reviews like you wouldn't believe,' County laughed. 'There'd be the really intelligent reviews about Andy's art and the socio-political side of it all, and we'd just say "What is he going on about?" Then there'd be *The Sun* saying, "Stop these perverts!"'

The Times described *Pork* as 'a witless, invertebrate, mind-numbing farrago', while the *News Of The World* complained that it made the London stage's last cultural nadir, *Oh! Calcutta!*, look like a vicar's tea party. 'Then there was someone who said '*Pork* is nothing but a pigsty. *Pork* is nothing but nymphomaniacs, whores and prostitutes running around naked on stage. The next night we were packed to the rafters!'

David Bowie loved it.

What Bowie saw in *Pork*, and what he took from it, was a mad sexuality that simply had no precedent in British society, and certainly not on the British stage. No matter that theatre was no longer bound by the Lord Chancellor's office, nor that *Hair, Oh! Calcutta!* and *The Dirtiest Show* had all shocked a nation.

Local attitudes towards sexuality and nudity remained locked in the grey straitjacket of post-Victorian formality and decorum, and the best that those other plays could be said to have done was loudly reject the status quo.

Pork cut to the chase. Conceived within an environment where none of society's favourite neuroses even existed, *Pork* approached sex (and drugs and, yes, rock'n'roll) not as a reaction against past behaviour, but as a lifestyle in and of itself. It was not 'liberated' because it did not believe it had anything to be liberated from. It simply existed.

There were no raincoated old men on the *Pork* stage (although there were plenty in the audience, particularly after the *News Of The World* got its teeth into the play), there were no repressed housewives or frustrated businessmen or any of the other tried and trusted staples of British alternative theatre. There were no hippies singing loudly about their right to fuck each other, or Alternative Christs saying 'It's okay to freak out'. *Pork* was pure sex, pure exhilaration, pure magic. And that was what Bowie pounced upon.

Wayne County details the transformation. 'We were all dressed up. You couldn't get Crazy Colour in those days so Leee had done his hair with Magic Marker. And David was just fascinated with us. We were freaks. We were doing things in 1971 that he was still doing four years later, like painting our fingernails different colours. We all had blue and multi-coloured hair, we were wearing big blonde wigs and huge platform boots and purple stockings. And he was wearing those floppy hats and the long, stringy hair, and he took one look at us and you could see that this was what he wanted to do.

'Leee and Cherry looked at him and said, "You can't keep on like you are. You've got to put on lots of make-up and freak yourself out a little." And then Angela and Tony Defries chimed in.'

That night, David Bowie went to sleep for the last time. When he awoke, he was Ziggy Stardust.

August 1971 – Tony Blackburn: Chop Chop/If You Were A Dream (RCA 2109)

Radio 1 morning DJ Tony Blackburn had already enjoyed a mildly successful singing career in the late Sixties. He returned to it in early 1971 and, after one flop 45 ('Is It Me Is It You'/'Happy' – RCA 2067), he turned to Chinnichap for a touch of their magic. They promptly handed him a song the Sweet had already recorded a demo of, 'Chop Chop', and with the Sweet backing him up on vinyl too, Blackburn at least scored a turntable hit.

It was not, says Steve Priest, an easy session. 'Blackburn had no timing. I'm trying to conduct it, trying to sing backing vocals on something that's not in time. We had to do each chorus separately over and over again, until we virtually got it in time with him.'

But Blackburn would become a staunch supporter of the Sweet, airing their music at every opportunity while they returned to the studio with him in mid-1972 to add further backing vocals to his next Chinnichap masterpiece, 'Cindy'/'Dusty' (RCA 2247).

10 August 1971 – Lift Off: The Sweet

The third series of *Lift Off* kicked in with Ayshea now joined as co-host by children's' TV personality Wally Whyton, the Fifties Skiffle titan (his Vipers were brilliant), who then swapped washboard and broom-handle for a career in children's television – earlier in the decade, Whyton was the host of the ever-popular *5 O'clock Club*, alongside *Lift Off* producer Muriel Young, and puppets Ollie Beak and Fred Barker.

It was this duo which welcomed the Sweet back to the studio; other guests on this edition include Miki Anthony with Sally Sunshine. The series would run through until 12 January 1972.

August 1971 – Top Of The Pops Volume 18 (Hallmark SHM 750)

Take a look, if you will, at the UK album chart for the week of 7 August 1971.

In at Number 48, 'Hot Hits Volume 5'.
Rushing towards Number 16, 'Top Of The Pops Volume 17'.
Sitting pretty at Number 1, 'Hot Hits Number 6'.

And embarking upon a three-month odyssey that would also peak at the pinnacle of the poppermost, 'Top Of The Pops Volume 18'. Five albums, 60 top hits, and you could buy the lot for two quid.

No wonder the rest of the UK music industry was upset. Decades before downloading, millennia before mp3s, aeons before Sony Walkmen and home taping and synthesisers and all the countless other things that the music industry has thrown back in our faces, complaining that they represent the End Of Civilisation As We Know It, Public Enemy Number 1 was the budget-priced hits compilation. And Top Of The Pops, Hot Hits and any other cut-price collection of top pop hits were in the direct line of fire.

The albums were a ripoff, claimed the major labels. In failing to openly state that the hit songs within were not the actual hit versions, the albums were guilty of misrepresentation on an almost criminal scale. For the sake of the innocent, gullible public, Top Of The Pops had to be stopped.

They cheated the performer. Sure, the publisher got paid, and the songwriter too. But what about the hapless band that recorded the song that was being so mercilessly aped? What did they get out of the deal?

And they cheated record shops, because the mark-up on a record that retailed for the price of two singles was an awful lot smaller than a full-price LP. You wouldn't want your favourite small record shop to go out of business, would you?

Meanwhile, it was business as usual across '*Top Of The Pops* Volume 18', as it predicts the

upcoming dominance of Chinnichap by serving up two of their earliest smashes, the calypso cataclysm of 'Co-Co' and the heartrending hubris of 'Tom Tom Turnaround'. From hereon in, there would not be a single significant Chinn and Chapman song that did not make it onto one volume or another. And Marc Bolan (whose 'Get It On' could easily be re-titled 'Turn It Off', so lukewarm does it sound here) wasn't far behind them.

But Chinn, Chapman and Bolan weren't the only people who had the world at their feet this month. 'Top Of The Pops Volume 18' became the series' first UK Number 1 album, shoving the Moody Blues out of the way in the process. Isn't life strange?

ON THE BOX
5 August 1971 – Top Of The Pops: Slade, T Rex
12 August 1971 – Top Of The Pops: T Rex
19 August 1971 – Top Of The Pops: Slade
31 August 1971 – Lift Off (Granada): Tony Blackburn

ON THE RADIO
23 August 1971 – Bob Harris (BBC): T Rex

---

7 September 1971 – Lift Off (Granada): Chicory Tip

With the Sweet debuting their forthcoming new single, 'Alexander Graham Bell' on tonight's show, all eyes tonight were on them. But Chicory Tip had something to say, too, in the shape of their third single, 'Excuse Me Baby'/'The Devil Rides Tonight' (CBS 7312) – a record that also landed them a berth on *Top Of The Pops* on 5 August 1971, while DJ Alan Freeman took a liking to the song and employed it as a jingle for *Pick Of The Pops*.

Which means everyone was surprised when it flopped.

But Chicory Tip were accustomed to failure. Two previous singles had already bottomed out – 'Monday After Sunday'/'Pride Comes Before A Fall' (CBS 5058) and 'My Girl Sunday'/'Doctor Man' (CBS 7118). And their follow-up, too, was destined for the junkshop: 'I Love Onions'/'Don't Hang Jack' (CBS 7595).

By the time *that* happened, however, the Maidstone, Kent-based quartet of Peter Hewson (vocals), Rick Foster (guitar), Barry Mayger (bass) and Brian Shearer (drums) already had a good idea of what their next single, and sound, would be. They'd recently got their hands on the first Mini Moog ever sold in the United Kingdom, and a new song written by German producer Giorgio Moroder. And when you put the two together...

September 1971 – T Rex: Electric Warrior (Fly HIFLY 6)

'Beneath the be-bop moon, I wanna croon... with you.'

They *really* don't write them like that any more, and they don't make albums like this any longer. Still so monumental that, when the end of the 20th century rolled around, even *Rolling Stone* included it in their Top 100 albums poll, 'Electric Warrior' not only epitomised Glam Rock, it transcended it as well. It truly is one of the greatest LPs ever made.

Divided neatly between the spacey ballads that were Bolan's forte ('Planet Queen', 'Girl', 'Life's A Gas'), and the seductive rockers that were his genius ('Mambo Sun', 'Motivator', 'Monolith'), 'Electric Warrior' was recorded just as T Rex hit superstar status and, with 'Get It On' showering its own glory over the grooves, it remains the consummate Bolan album.

But it's even more than that. Overwhelmingly exuberant, its flawless blending of Chuck Berry pop, Middle Earth imagery and

guiltless sexuality combines to forge a timeless musicality, for even as 'Lean Woman Blues' hurtles straight out of the Fifties the closing freak-out 'Rip Off' races equally pell-mell backwards from punk. 'Electric Warrior' was released at the dawn of the Seventies, and it still makes a difference today.

'Electric Warrior' was, is, and forever will be, perfection. It is one of those albums that neither needs, nor appreciates, augmentation – bonus tracks are superlative, outtakes and alternate mixes are tiresome.

Nevertheless, there have been several attempts to perform the same service for 'Electric Warrior' as has been gifted to Bolan's subsequent LPs, beginning with 'The Electric Warrior Sessions' (New Millennium, 1997).

It's hard to be subjective, because the sessions themselves were so economical. Much of '...Sessions' actually comprises live cuts ('Jeepster', 'Jewel' and 'Baby Strange') and older material that has no place in the same room– rough mixes of 'Summertime Blues' and 'Woodland Rock' date from around a year before the sessions commenced.

But, if one can overlook such discrepancies, 'The Electric Warrior Sessions' is a rewarding listen, all the more so since the parent album's own expanded edition, overseen by producer Tony Visconti in 2003, unearthed just *one* out-take, a demo-quality 'Planet Queen'. Here, two punchy stabs at 'Get It On', two more takes on 'Monolith', an echoey 'Cosmic Dancer' and a tremulous 'Life's A Gas' join a driving, and engagingly error-strewn warm-up through the old rocker 'Honey Don't' to at least lay the foundations for what would become one of rock's most treasured icons.

September 1971 – Bay City Rollers: Keep On Dancing/Alright (Bell 1164)

Ah, the Bay City Rollers.

For a few years in the mid Seventies, the Rollers were bigger than the Beatles, bigger than Bolan, bigger than anyone you could name, the tartan-clad centre of a firestorm that burned fiercer than fame. And even today, the devotion which the Bay City Rollers once inspired continues to nurture wild nostalgia in the hearts of those who were stricken.

But it wasn't always like this. In an age when bands conferred respectability upon one another by claiming to have 'paid their dues', the Rollers paid as many as anyone.

The Rollers first rolled in the mid-late Sixties, as Edinburgh-based schoolboys Derek and Alan Longmuir and their friend Nobby Clark occupied their free time in a makeshift band called the Saxons. Unabashed good-time pop merchants, the Saxons made their live debut at Cairns Church Hall in Edinburgh in mid-1967 and, over the next year or so, built a following on the local youth club circuit.

The group's line-up seemed to change with every gig. Dave Paton and Billy Lyall, later to find fleeting fame as members of Pilot, were members for a time, but through it all, Clark and the Longmuirs remained stubbornly constant. And when they left school in 1969, the threesome made the decision to turn professional.

They celebrated the move by changing their name. According to legend, having decided to utilise something that sounded American, they unfurled a large map of the United States and threw darts at it. One struck Bay City; Rollers would added because it sounded good, and that was it.

Newly christened, the band made their live debut with a Saturday night residency at Edinburgh's Top Storey Club. It was there they met Tam Paton, a bandleader at the nearby Edinburgh Palais. He would become their manager and, over the next year, Paton guided the Bay City Rollers ever higher up the Edinburgh live scene, which intriguingly also meant driving them further underground, to a venue called the Caves.

A regular hangout for those record-company talent scouts assigned to the Edinburgh beat, the Caves on this particular night were playing host to one who had come up from London to catch another band entirely. With time on his hands before his scheduled departure, the scout followed a local booking agent's advice and hung around for the Bay City Rollers, a band, he was told, with one of the most fanatical followings in the city. It is said that the scout signed the Bay City Rollers sight unseen. The crush at the door was too great for him to actually get in to see them.

Whether or not this story is true (and one sincerely hopes it is), he took the Bay City Rollers' reputation back with him to London and deposited it enthusiastically in the lap of one of Britain's top record producers, Jonathan King. A month later, 'Keep On Dancing' gave the Rollers their first hit record.

'The reason I recorded the Bay City Rollers,' King explains, 'is that I thought the time had come for a teenybopper idol to emerge, and the band had already got a following in Scotland of that ilk. So I thought, "Give them a hit and they'll start selling automatically." So I did that, but there was one terrible thing. As per usual with my art I was ahead of the times. In 1971, the kids were not ready to accept a teen idol. Then Cassidy and the Osmonds, everybody else who everybody knows, came along, and it was infuriating.'

A joyful rumble of a record, all rolling drums and coy chorus, 'Keep On Dancing' was a UK Number 9. But there was to be no hit follow-up. The Rollers returned to obscurity and it would take three years, and a change of vocalist, before they resurfaced. A re-recording would be cut following their hit breakthrough.

September 1971 – Hotlegs: Lady Sadie/The Loser (Philips 6006 140)

At long last, Hotlegs finally follow up 'Neanderthal Man' with a song that sounds nothing like it. 'Lady Sadie'/'The Loser' (Philips 6006 140) was, says Godley, 'a *faux* Rolling Stones song that explored Eric's love of dirty blues guitar. It was so obviously other people's territory. It had a nice feel but it didn't chart. Probably didn't deserve to.'

September 1971 – Top Of The Pops Volume 19 (Hallmark SHM 750)

It's official. Glam Rock has arrived, and where better to find it than lavished across the cover of the latest *Top Of The Pops* LP, in the form of a model whose star-studded hotpants and body-hugging necklace are as much a part of period imagery as any musical happening?

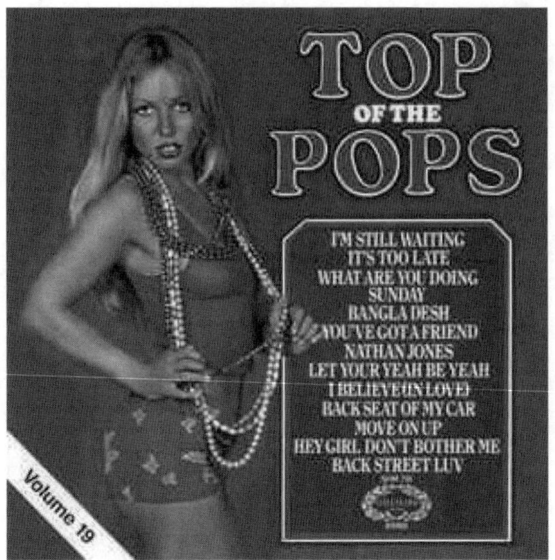

Which is just as well, as the album itself couldn't be less Glammy if it tried. T Rex and Slade were between hits, the rest of the pack were still awaiting their first. So, for one final season of non-genre-bound freedom, the UK charts danced to a myriad of different drums: Curved Air, the Pioneers, George Harrison, the Tams and Daniel Boone. As opposed to a pair of glitter-clad drummers.

ON THE RADIO
17 September 1971 – Terry Wogan: The Sweet
21 September 1971 – Sounds Of The Seventies: David Bowie

October 1971 – Sweet: Alexander Graham Bell/Spotlight (RCA 2121)

'Alexander Graham Bell', you'll be unsurprised to learn, was dedicated to the inventor of the telephone in much the same way (and with a similar lyrical bent) as the Mixtures' 'Henry Ford', a minor hit earlier in the year, was dedicated to the motoring pioneer.

It was an odd choice for a single; pulled from the stockpile of Chinnichap efforts that were being compiled for the Sweet's first album, and then thrust out into the stores with little heed paid to the fact that it sounded nothing like anything the band had done before.

There were all those lyrics, for a start. Washing over a suave musical arrangement by keyboard wiz Fiachra Trench, 'Alexander Graham Bell' was wordy wordy wordy, with Brian Connolly enthusing, 'Personally I like it. It's more involved and is more of a production than the others, which have been simple. I think we've said more on this one. It's a good change.'

But it was not a good choice. Reviews of the single were more or less positive but sales started slow and didn't pick up. A moodily atmospheric promotional film, placing the band in a tight circle in front of a vintage street scene backdrop, may have helped steer the record into the Top Fifty on its week of release, but that was just as likely predicated on the band's past reputation. It certainly had nothing to do with the subtle uncatchiness of the singing history lesson.

Because, whereas a berth on the very edge of the Top Thirty should have been the springboard for it to leap on to greater things, instead 'Alexander Graham Bell' reached Number 33 and hung up. The Sweet had flopped and, just to make matters even worse, the expense of hiring in a musical arranger had pushed the cost of the recording into the thousands of pounds.

October 1971 – Slade: Coz I Luv You/My Life Is Natural (Polydor 2058 155)

Slade's songs weren't music, they were aural graffiti, slabs of working-class consciousness spraypainted across the wall of the Establishment, each more crazily misspelt than the last. An wy not?

It was the magnificent 'Coz I Luv You', all manic stomp and spectral violin, that set the ball rolling. Written by Noddy Holder and Jim Lea, it developed out of a distinctive practice riff the band used to tune Lea's violin before shows. According to Holder, the song took just 20 minutes to write, layering a chord progression over the fiddle, then ad-libbing the first lyrics that came to mind. Then they played it to Chas Chandler the following morning, and he declared it their first Number 1. He booked a studio immediately.

Of course, there was still some revision to be done. Originally conceived as a straightforward ballad, the band toughened the song up by adding handclaps and more of the stamping sounds that gave 'Get Down And Get With It' such marvellous mayhem.

The title, too, needed work. The song was

originally called 'Because I Love You'. But, says Lea, 'that sounded wimpy, so we changed it to 'Cause I Love You', because that's what we sang. And then Chas suggested the changes in spelling [and] that was the way it came out.' The rest of the band's greatest hits simply followed in its wake – 'Look Wot You Dun', 'Take Me Bak 'Ome', 'Mama Weer All Crazee Now', 'Gudbuy T'Jane'. Slade were a lexicographer's nightmare as well as a dressmaking disaster.

But not yet. Out on TV to promote the new single, Noddy's flat cap and braces gave him the look of an avuncular sitcom uncle. Jim was the leather clad tearaway nephew; Don the silent psycho chewing gum outside the all-night café; and Dave? Well, Dave *did* have a look of his own, even when he dressed the same as the others, and he maintained that tradition now.

Things would soon change, that was for sure. Right now, though, it probably didn't matter. Within two weeks of release, 'Coz I Luv You' was topping charts across Europe, with the UK succumbing on 13 November. Pushing Rod Stewart's granny-shagging perennial 'Maggie May' out of the way in the process, 'Coz I Luv You' then held off both Tom Jones ('Till') and T Rex ('Jeepster') as it clung to the top. In fact, there was only one thing on earth that could displace Slade that season, and it was coming in so fast that you could hear the hoofbeats pound as they raced across the ground...the clatter of the wheels as they went round and round...

ON THE BOX
7 October 1971 – Top Of The Pops: The Sweet
21 October 1971 – Top Of The Pops: Slade
27 October 1971 – Lift Off (Granada): The Sweet
28 October 1971 – Top Of The Pops: The Bay City Rollers, Slade

---

November 1971 – T Rex: Jeepster/Life's A Gas (Fly BUG 16)
29 November 1971 – Jimmy Young Show (BBC): T Rex

Fly Records, the bughouse that Marc Bolan built, didn't want to lose T Rex.

But they couldn't afford to keep them either, particularly after Bolan approached former Move manager Tony Secunda to help him get away from the company. The pair were now negotiating a new deal with EMI, built around the creation of Marc's own T Rex Wax Co label, so Fly pulled one more cut off 'Electric Warrior' and sent it out as a single.

Bolan was furious, but he was even angrier when 'Jeepster' missed the top spot, held off first by Slade and then Benny Hill.

Slade, on the other hand, couldn't help but chuckle. 'Bolan said in a *Melody Maker* interview that Slade was no competition and I had it in for him from that day on,' Jim Lea told Slade biographer Chris Charlesworth. 'Bolan was huge, and I respected him because the records he made were tremendous. But I still had it in for him.'

He proved his point over the next two years. While Bolan's star waxed fast, then waned even faster, Slade remained inviolate through all the ensuing convolutions. 'Coz I Luv You' went to Number 1 in November 1971; 'Look Wot You Dun' dipped to Number 4, but from the moment 'Take Me Bak 'Ome' topped the chart in September 1972 the juggernaut was unstoppable.

November 1971 – Alan Merrill: Everyday All Night Stand/Ferris Wheel (Denon-Columbia/Mushroom CD-14M-2 – Japan)
November 1971 – Alan Merrill: Merrill 1 (Nippon Columbia, CD-7025-Z – Japan)

Alan Merrill was always going to be a Glam Rocker, ever since his ninth birthday. Or so he suggested to *Jackie* magazine when they asked him for childhood memories.

'I remember I had a big party with 25 of my friends, lots of food and a big cake in the middle. In the other room there was a huge object, all covered in brown paper, which I had strict instructions not to open until after tea. So when we'd finished eating, we all piled into the other room for the grand unveiling and inside was an eight-foot long spaceship. A commercial artist who lived downstairs [Ronald Fratell, designer of the Shadows of Knight's 'Gloria' LP sleeve] had made it for me out of boxes, luminous paper, silver foil, everything. It was really impressive.'

Beat that, Bowie.

'I eased into the glam scene organically,' Merrill explains. 'At 18, I was already recording for Atlantic Records' Japanese wing and I was the first male model to wear feminine make-up for a major Japanese TV commercial, in 1969, in a campaign for Nissan cars.'

Over the course of eight commercials in a two-year period, Merrill was the gleeful centre of a storm of controversy as Japanese society tried to figure out 'is it a boy or a girl?', a controversy Merrill quickly adapted to his pop career. 'I started to perform in make-up and frilly frocks. It got the girl fans excited, and that was good enough for me.'

The son of jazz singer Helen Merrill, Alan Merrill was still a teenager when he became an idol in Japan, the first foreigner ever to merit that status; the first, in fact, to even claim success in a ferociously parochial domestic market. American-born but based in Japan since 1968, Merrill essentially set the stage for every subsequent superstar import, and he still returns to the country on a regular basis to perform in front of delirious audiences.

Before heading off as a solo artist, Merrill was a member of the Lead, a Tokyo-based band who scored a hit with 'Blue Rose' and who cut a solitary album in 1968, 'Sounds Of Silence'. Two years later, in February 1971, Merrill scored a Top Thirty hit with 'Namida' (Atlantic L – 1014A), and that same month released a Japanese-language solo album, 'Alone In Tokyo' (Atlantic L5002A). (A second single, 'Taiyo To Ame', quickly followed.)

But it was 'Merrill 1' that truly established him, a solid blaze of distinctly Anglo-beat influenced pop songs that painted Merrill as an extraordinarily gifted songwriter, long before Arrows let the western world in on the secret.

Work began on what would become 'Merrill 1' in September 1971, with ten demos cut for music publisher Kuni Murai's Alfa Music. Two days later, recording kicked off in earnest with producer Miki Curtis, whose own solo album was being recorded (with Merrill on guitar) at the same time.

As if that wasn't enough, the boy was also pursuing a simultaneous modelling career and, in the midst of the sessions, on 22 September, he spent the afternoon on assignment with fellow model Mari Tachikawa (who, years later, married Don Powell of Slade), and was back at the studio by 6.30 to continue recording. 'Merrill 1' was completed by the end of September.

The album kicks off with the single, 'Everyday All Night Stand', tight and pretty pop-psych that set the mood for the rest of the record; one can only imagine the effect this album might have had if it could have been cut for Anglo-American consumption. In an age of Edison Lighthouse, Christie and so forth, Merrill's pop confections would have slipped right in.

And, in fact, one did. 1972 saw Tiny Tim become the first artist ever to record and release one of Merrill's songs in his homeland (Merrill included), when he cut 'Movies' as the B-side to 'Am I Just Another Pretty Face?' (Scepter 12351).

November 1971 – Arnold Corns: Hang On To Yourself/Man In The Middle (B&C CB 189)

Arnold Corns' debut single, 'Moonage Daydream' flopped ignominiously, as did its B-side, 'Hang On To Yourself', when released in its own right. Bowie still had high hopes for a projected third Arnold Corns single, 'Looking For A Friend', but B&C's interest in the affair was waning. The existing records were deleted, the follow-up was cancelled and Arnold Corns was left to founder in obscurity.

But from little A Corns big Ziggys grow and, sequestered in the studio as this latest prolusion stumbled, Bowie was busily watering those seeds. He had a new record company; one of Tony Defries' first concrete actions after taking over Bowie's management was to tear up his old Mercury contract and establish him instead at RCA. Defries was already talking of his charge as though he were the new Elvis, so what better home could there be for him than on Elvis' record label?

A trip to New York in September introduced Bowie to three of his idols – Andy Warhol, Iggy Pop and Lou Reed. Two of the three would soon be joining him in London to record albums of their own; the third, Warhol, at least liked Bowie's shoes. A new album, the chirpily titled 'Hunky Dory', was on the release schedule, and that was something to be pleased about. But Bowie was more excited about the album *after* that, the album he'd been writing in the months since he saw *Pork*.

Reprising two of the Arnold Corns song, 'Hang On To Yourself' and 'Moonage Daydream', it was going to be a concept record. But it was not the music that was the concept. It was the performer.

November 1971 – Sweet: Funny How Sweet Co-Co Can Be (RCA 8288)

Having made their LP debut with 'Gimme Dat Ding', half an album's worth of repackaged flops, the Sweet then followed through with an disc full of hits, drawing from both their own recent back catalogue and that of songwriters Nicky Chinn and Mike Chapman to create a record of almost unholy pop pleasure.

New versions of 'Tom Tom Turnaround' and 'Chop Chop' both joined the Sweet's hits catalogue on the platter, while B-sides 'Jeanie', 'Spotlight' and 'Done Me Wrong Alright' added some much-needed ballast to the light-headed line-up. True, their inclusion did mean the average fan might already have owned a full half of the record before even picking it up, but there was still the other half to listen to, right?

Wrong. The remainder of the record is pretty dreadful. A lacklustre rendering of 'Daydream' can be passed over immediately, while the soft rock stylings of 'Santa Monica Sunshine', Reflections', 'Honeysuckle Love' and 'Sunny Sleeps Late' are little more than bland filler. As drummer Mick Tucker grimly laughed, 'it must have been awful being a Sweet fan in the early days. Two albums to choose from and they're both shit.'

Brian Connolly, ever the optimist, effortlessly put an heroic face on the LP's contents. 'I think we are holding ourselves back musicianwise, because we don't want to get too complicated for the public. We want to keep people happy and dancing. It's all very well talking about progressive music, but I think in this day of musical progress, not many people can sit down and say they've written a string of hits like Mike and Nicky. And I don't think any guy in a band could turn around and say they didn't want that. It must be a one in a million chance to write five hits in a short time.'

Later, however, his opinion shifted dramatically, or maybe it didn't shift at all and he was just being diplomatic back then. 'It *was* a bad album.'

November 1971 – Top Of The Pops Volume 20 (Hallmark SHM 755)

'Now we're at Number 1,' declared the liner notes to 'Volume 19', 'we intend, with your help, to stay there.' And they did. On 27 November, 'Top Of The Pops Volume 20' not only displaced Rod Stewart's 'Every Picture Tells A Story' from the top of the chart, it also called up an impossibly laryngitic rendition of 'Maggie May' to help with the conquest. Then topped that with a 'Keep On Dancing' that features a Les McKeown soundalike a full two years before McKeown himself joined

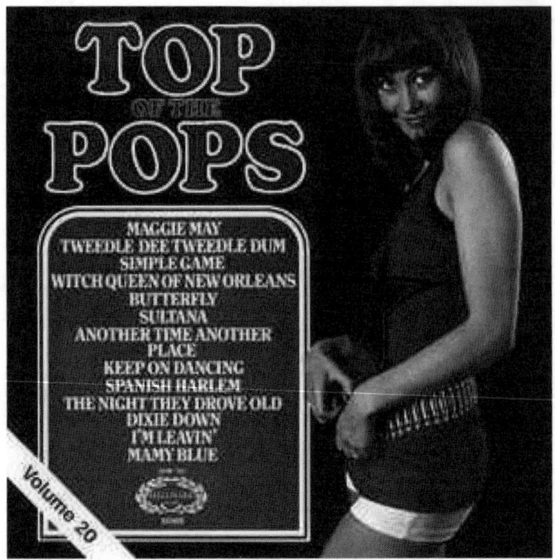

the Rollers! No wonder the album did so well.

But it was also the last hurrah. In early December, with Music For Pleasure/BWD Production's 'Hot Hits Volume Eight' at Number 2, the Powers That Be announced that, henceforth, budget-priced LPs would no longer be eligible for the chart.

It was, insisted *Record Retailer* (publisher of Britain's main album chart) purely a matter of pricing. If the perpetrators of these heinous discs brought their prices in line with regular LPs, they could come back in. But, of course, they were never going to do that. The charts aren't the only barometer of sales, after all, and these beasties were shifting 300,000 copies per release. They could afford to be smug.

ON THE BOX
4 November 1971 – Top Of The Pops: Slade
9 November 1971 – Old Grey Whistle Test (BBC): Alice Cooper
11 November 1971 – Top Of The Pops: Slade
18 November 1971 – Top Of The Pops: Slade
25 November 1971 – Top Of The Pops: Slade

December 1971 – Alice Cooper: Under My Wheels/Desperado (Warners K16127)
December 1971 – Alice Cooper: Killer (Warners K56005)

'Killer' was Alice Cooper's fourth album. If 'Love It To Death' was powerful, its successor was indeed the killer, a seething pit of violence and boa constrictors, with every track – all eight of them – presenting new vistas of horror for the impressionable pop kids: the swaggering 'Be My Lover', so laconically asking why the singer's name is Alice ('listen baby, you really wouldn't understand'); the spaghetti-western shootout of 'Desperado', the grinding 'Under My Wheels' – all building up to the album's three, count 'em, centrepieces.

First there's 'Halo Of Flies', created, says Neal Smith, from all the little bits of other tunes that the band had never completed. There's 'Killer' itself, a trial and death sentence set to music with the execution frying the felon as the needle spins out of the album; and there's 'Dead Babies', a song that had the concerned citizens brigade up in arms before they even read the words. By the time they'd *finished* reading them, it was all over.

'"Dead Babies" is another successful collaboration written by all five members of the band,' recalls Smith. 'The original idea for this song came from Mr Black Ju Ju himself, our dark side, Dennis. This maybe the first true shock-rock song, and it was written to be controversial. But listen to the lyrics closely. It's about killing babies, yes, but by parental neglect.'

'Dead Babies' would throw open the theatrical door that Alice had been banging on for so long, a swashbuckling Alice flaunting a sword to pierce a blond baby doll. Female mannequin body parts were scattered over the stage. The volume was nearing the pain threshold and your eyes were exploding from your head.

This ain't rock'n'roll, this is genius.

Right before launching upon a US tour with T Rex as support (poor T Rex; they didn't stand a chance), Alice played London to help promote 'Killer' as it rode towards Number 27 on the chart.

They shared the Rainbow stage with Mr Crazy World, Arthur Brown, who closed his act with a crucifixion. Nice one, Arthur. But Alice made it look tame.

December 1971 – David Bowie: Hunky Dory (RCA 8244)

Hindsight has painted this album in such glowing colours that it's difficult to remember just how little of an impression it made at the time.

True, the single 'Changes'/'Andy Warhol' (RCA 2160) became Tony Blackburn's Record of the Week following its mid-January release; and it gave Bowie a US hit later in the year. True, too, that 'Oh You Pretty Things' was dramatically reprised from Peter Noone's cover earlier in the year; and, of course, 'Life On Mars?', 'Quicksand', 'Queen Bitch' and 'The Bewlay Brothers' remain unimpeachable Bowie classics.

But it would be another six months before more than a comparative handful of listeners turned their attention to what might well be Bowie's most satisfying album by which time it was already ancient history, both stylistically and thematically.

Bowie seems to have known what he was doing, though, and it doesn't matter whether he designed 'Hunky Dory' in the knowledge of the themes he'd be returning to or if he deliberately returned to the themes because they'd already been mentioned before. But with the release of 'Ziggy Stardust' and the brouhaha that now erupted, all that was now 'known' (translation: believed/assumed/made-up-on-the-spot) could suddenly be backed up by the older record's contents.

Thus, 'Queen Bitch' confirmed the sexuality that would soon become part and parcel of the Bowie persona; thus 'The Bewlay Brothers' spoke of his brother Terry's mental health issues; thus 'Oh You Pretty Things', with its portents of Homo Superior paved the way for the end of the world. And so on, and so speculatively forth.

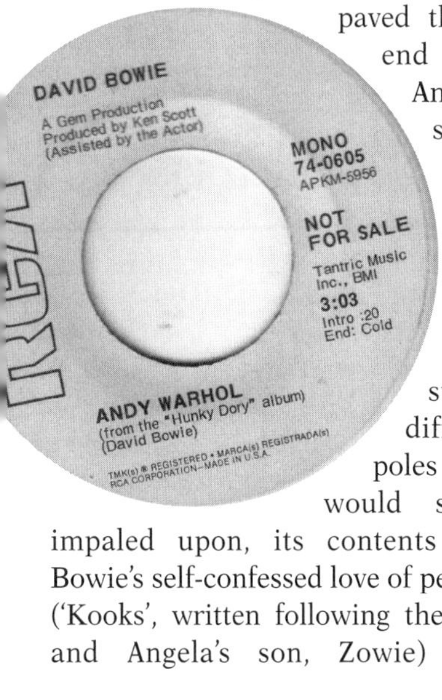

In its place and at the time, on the other hand, 'Hunky Dory' straddled very different musical poles to those that it would so swiftly be impaled upon, its contents ranging from Bowie's self-confessed love of period Neil Young ('Kooks', written following the birth of David and Angela's son, Zowie) to his equal admiration for both Bob Dylan and Andy Warhol; and on to a singer-songwritery bent that could have allied Bowie as readily alongside Cat Stevens or Paul Simon as it did Lou Reed and Iggy Pop.

'Hunky Dory' owed nothing to what was going on in the UK at that time and precious little to what Bowie himself was now working towards. The songs, some of which had been rattling around his live set for a year, were already old news to Bowie and his band; and by the time the rest of the world lent an ear to the disc, it might have been another artist entirely.

Which, if you really bought into the oncoming storm, is precisely what it was.

December 1971 – Top Of The Pops Volume 21 (Hallmark SHM 770)

It's a British chart tradition for the weeks around Christmas to be somewhat eccentric, as established superstars did battle with one-hit-wonders, and both were generally knocked for six by a clutch of wacky novelty songs. The end of 1971 was no exception.

T Rex maintained their domination with the boogie-rocking 'Jeepster' and Slade were still celebrating their first major hit. But Benny Hill was top of the pile with the spaghetti-western saga of 'Ernie (The Fastest Milkman In The West)', and Jonathan King had evidently overcome his disappointment with the Bay City Rollers by creating 'Johnny Reggae', credited to the Piglets. Wacky? It was downright weird.

All of the above are present, faithfully duplicated by the Top Of The Poppers – faithfully? John Kongos' 'Tokoloshe Man' is terrifyingly tribal and, as for 'Ernie', rarely have love, death and yoghurt been melded together with such delightful aplomb.

The violin cutting through the Slade song is even crazier than Jim Lea's original, while the vocals chirruping through 'Johnny Reggae' makes Jonathan King's original sound like the Royal Shakespeare Company. The rival Hot Hits series also tackled 'Johnny Reggae' within the intriguingly benippled cover of 'Volume 8' (MFP 5243), but it was never a match for this one – which can be said for most of that series' efforts, one reason why Hot Hits was dead by 1973 and Top Of The Pops kept going until 1984.

25/27 December 1971 – Top Of The Pops Christmas Special

A two-part round- up of all the year's Number 1 singles, and what a joy to behold. It was a positive treat to sit back as the last 12 months spooled past. 'Get It On' capturing Marc in pink trousers and Elton John on guest piano; Slade's 'Coz I Luv You' sounding as stompy as it ought to be; and the super-soulful Tams' 'Hey Girl, Don't Bother Me' offering up the mysterious disappearance of the frog-faced one in the band. One minute he's there, hamming uncertainly along with the rest of his bandmates; and the next – where's he gone? The five-piece is a four-piece and nobody even seems to notice.

'Ernie' gallops past via a filmed insert that still brings a smirk to your chops and Ashton, Gardner and Dyke turn up with the non chart-topping 'Resurrection Shuffle' for no discernible reason whatsoever. Which was one of the great things about *TOTP*; no matter how formulaic its critics claimed it to be, it could still surprise when it wanted to.

ON THE BOX

2 December 1971 – Top Of The Pops: Slade
9 December 1971 – Top Of The Pops: T Rex
15 December 1971 – Lift Off (Granada): Chicory Tip
16 December 1971 – Top Of The Pops: T Rex
22 December 1971 – Lift Off (Granada): The Sweet
25 December 1971 – Top Of The Pops: T Rex
27 December 1971 – Top Of The Pops: T Rex, Slade
30 December 1971 – Top Of The Pops: T Rex (Pan's People dance)

CHAPTER THREE

1972

The Sound of the Summer that lasted all year

'The sound of 1972,' announced the *Daily Express*, 'is your sound.' In late 1971, the newspaper published 'The Sound Of 72' album (with accompanying collectible 'beautiful colour cards'), a 14-page guide to the predicted giants of the forthcoming 12 months. And what they all had in common, it seemed, was their everyday mundanity.

'Never before have the people making music had so much in common with the people listening to it. The acts in this album are those that are likely to be playing throughout the coming year. They represent the Sound that will be coming out of your radios and stereo sets during 1972.'

Some, the majority in fact, must have felt like no-brainers. Who could have doubted that the likes of Melanie, Creedence Clearwater Revival, Judy Collins, the Who, Cliff Richard, Elvis Presley, the Bee Gees, Blood Sweat and Tears, Cilla Black, the Stones and George Harrison would all have successful years?

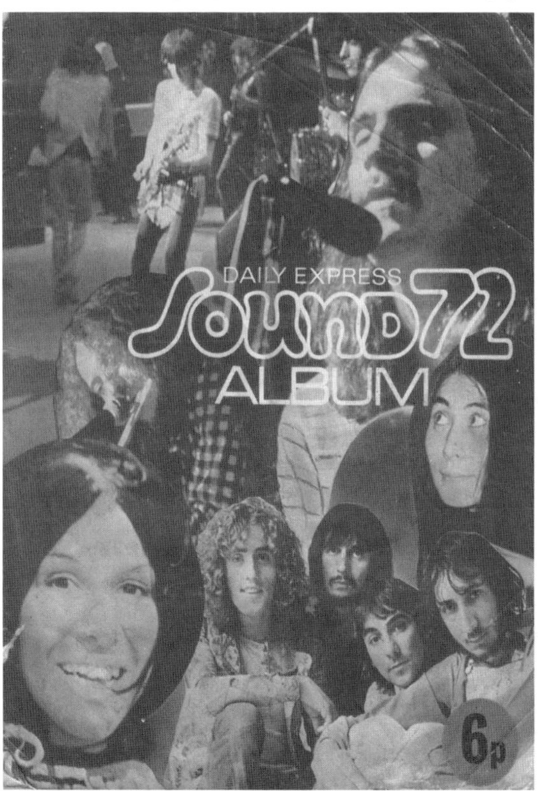

Less so Jimi Hendrix, whose death in 1970 seems to have passed the editors by, but more so for such recent hitmakers as Christie, Middle of the Road and Mungo Jerry. The jury was out on Magna Carta and the Strawbs, but it's true. At the dawn of 1972, these were the expected giants.

What happened?

Glam happened.

Just three of the booklet's 50-plus inclusions were destined to enjoy a memorable 1972 – Slade, Rod Stewart and the Faces and Gilbert O'Sullivan.

T Rex, David Bowie? Gary Glitter? Alice Cooper? Elton John? Nowhere in sight. There was no Paul McCartney, whose Wings became the biggest ex-Beatle band of the age; no Carpenters, Cassidy or Osmond.

In fact, if there was any single factor that unified the contents of 'The Sound Of '72', it was that 1972 wouldn't sound anything like it suggested.

Welcome to the Greatest Year In British Pop History.

January 1972 – T Rex: Telegram Sam/Cadillac/Baby Strange (T Rex 101)
15 January 1972 – T Rex: Live at Boston Gliderdome

Marc Bolan's first single of 1972 was also the first release on his own T Rex Wax Co label. A taut rocker, bristling with power and nailed by one of Bolan's most insistent riffs, 'Telegram Sam' was recorded in Copenhagen, Denmark, as the public's first glimpse into what would become T Rex's next album, 'The Slider'.

It was titled, appropriately, for the manager Tony Secunda. 'Telegram Sam' was Bolan's affectionate nickname for his 'main man' whose acumen landed him the label and an awful lot of money. In another verse, 'Jungle-face Jake' was Bolan's somewhat un-PC name for Sid Walker, Secunda's black personal assistant. Ever happy to muddy the waters, however, Bolan once added that the song was also 'written about someone I met in New York who used to do little services for me.'

Bolan was doubtless reconnecting with that mysterious bagman during T Rex's latest American tour, from which one show, in Boston, lives on as a savage highlight of the six-CD 'Total T Rex 1971-1972' box set (Easy Action).

In a blur of gutsy guitar, one disc captures the on-stage frenzy of T Rex at their height, building up towards the *Born To Boogie* movie,

and sounding ruthlessly liberated throughout. Other live recordings in that same package (Cardiff, 10 June 1972) complete the picture.

In their absence, meanwhile, 'Telegram Sam' entered the chart at Number 3 in the final week of January and topped the chart effortlessly. But it remained at Number 1 for just a week before dropping to Number 2 for two weeks.

January 1972 – Chicory Tip: Son Of My Father/Pride Comes Before A Fall (CBS 7737)

Subsequently commended by Saint Etienne's Sarah Cracknell for sporting two different haircuts at the same time, Chicory Tip singer Pete Hewson did indeed cut a genre-defining rug when the Tip turned up on television to plug their new single.

But the single itself deserved all the attention it received, a rollicking litany of singalong lyrics, a thunderous dancefloor rhythm, and *that* Mini Moog sound, squealing and wheeling across the airwaves almost a *decade* before the rest of pop caught up with what it was saying. Gary Numan? Visage? OMD? Chicory Tip rippers, every one of them.

In America, it was composer Giorgio Moroder's version that stormed the chart. At home, however, Tip had so much faith in this number that they all but abandoned their last single, November's 'I Love Onions', in their haste to get 'Son Of My Father' onto the shelves. To save even more time, the B-side was recycled from their 1970 debut.

'Son Of My Father' itself was recorded in two days and mixed on Christmas Eve.

But it was worth it. 'Son Of My Father' went to Number 1, and if you had seriously asked what the immediate future of Glam Rock looked like the answer would have been Chicory Tip.

So what went wrong?

January 1972 – Slade: Look Wot You Dun/Candidate (Polydor 2058195)
January 1972 – Slade: Coz I Luv You (Polydor 2383 100)

Slade were big, but they weren't yet the biggest. Or were they?

'Look Wot You Dun' was originally scheduled 'for release on the same day as T Rex's Telegram

Sam', a coincidence that so horrified Polydor that they pulled the Slade single forward a week, in the hope of getting a head start on Marc. So he pulled his single forward as well, and they marched out together after all.

In the end, 'Look Wot You Dun' could muster nothing higher than Number 4 behind Chicory Tip, 'American Pie' and 'Without You', but few people would describe 'Look Wot You Dun' as classic Slade; *Disco 45* called it 'typical', scarcely a compliment just three hits into their career.

Meanwhile, with 'Coz I Luv You' having topped charts across much of Europe, an LP of that title was rushed out to bridge the gap between Slade's last album, 'Play It Loud', and the forthcoming 'Slade Alive'.

There was little for the compilers to work, of course, and the album wound up simply adding the A and B-sides of the hits to half a dozen tracks culled from 'Play It Loud'. But it's still a marvellous snapshot, with the album cuts ('Pouk Hill', 'Shape of Things to Come' and the oddly affecting dying horse of 'Dapple Rose' among them) certainly consistent with the majesty of the hits. Indeed, of all the Slade compilations to have appeared over the decades since then, this – the earliest of them all – feels closer to a 'real' album than any of them.

January 1972 – Grunt Futtock: Rock'n'Roll Christian/Free Soul (Regal Zonophone RZ3042)

By late 1971, the Move were in a very strange place. The darlings of the late-Sixties psych-pop boom were still a going concern and were still ratcheting up the hits, albeit a little less memorably than they used to. 'Tonight' and 'Chinatown' were both Top Thirty in 1971; 'California Man' was poised to strike in early 1972.

But Roy Wood and Jeff Lynne were scheming a new project, the Electric Light Orchestra, and Wood was looking further ahead to a time when his innate gift for songwriting might again return to the pure pop pastures that he had once bestrode.

In the meantime, however, he had to do something for Andrew Loog Oldham.

Oldham was already a legend. In 1963, he discovered the Rolling Stones and produced them through their first four years of glory. In 1964, he followed through with Marianne Faithfull. In 1965, he launched Immediate Records, the first truly successful independent record label in the UK. And in 1971, he created Grunt Futtock, a Sixties rock supergroup camouflaged by some of the Glammiest photographs of the age.

'And when I tell you that the name was the most inspired part of the entire affair,' Oldham admits,' you'll have some understanding of precisely what I was trying to do.'

Teaming up with fellow manager Don Arden, and targeting Regal Zonophone label head Freddie Bienstock as their victim, Oldham first had photographer Gered Mankowitz 'take a group photo of some interesting-looking friends from the art and photography world. Then we had a guy...write up some anal fictitious bio, and then we gathered up a few old pals and clients.'

Roy Wood was joined by Peter Frampton, Steve Marriott, Andy Bown and engineer Alan O'Duffy 'and told that Don would break their legs unless they all made the record for nothing.'

According to Arden, the pitch was perfect. They contacted Bienstock and explained that they had just discovered the greatest band in the world. A meeting was set up with one of his A&R men, so they laid out the pictures and played the tape, and then came the moment of madness.

'Jesus, what do you call this group?' asked the record company man.

'Andrew just looked at him very calmly and, in a voice as quiet as a whisper, he said, injecting a little drama into his delivery, 'Grunt...Futtock'.'

The following day, a cheque for £10,000 arrived. Oldham and Arden went shopping – but they didn't buy Grunt Futtock. Nobody did.

The line-up's identity, stellar though it is, remained a secret at the time. 'We don't know much about Grunt Futtock,' bemoaned *Disco 45*'s review. 'But if they go on making records like this, they're going to be up there worrying the big 'uns before very long.'

'There were always projects like this going around,' Peter Frampton admitted 20 years later. 'I don't particularly remember it, though.'

21 January 1972 – Sounds Of The Seventies (BBC): Roxy Music

'There's a new sensation, a fabulous creation...'

With those words, Bryan Ferry introduced a new dance, the Strand, to open the second Roxy Music album, 'For Your Pleasure'. A year earlier, however, he could have been introducing Roxy Music themselves, for at a time when rock'n'roll was already launching itself full tilt into the new age Roxy Music erupted onto the scene, clad in space age stardust but wrapped in music that went beyond anything anyone else had conceived.

At a time when art as artifice was becoming common currency, Roxy Music reversed the roles completely. And not even David Bowie, whose own breakthrough would pre-date Roxy Music's by a matter of weeks, would pull that off. Quite simply, Roxy Music were the most explicit example ever of how the media could be put to one's own uses without degenerating into no-holds-barred hyperbole.

Essentially the vision of a northern-English schoolteacher, Bryan Ferry, Roxy Music had been around since the end of 1970 and, by late 1971, had evolved into a line-up comprising Ferry, saxophonist Andy Mackay, drummer Paul Thompson (replacing American Dexter Lloyd), bassist Graham Simpson and sound engineer Brian Eno, with a succession of guitarists coming and going as Ferry again and again made his bid for attention.

Nothing succeeded and what would now be a priceless treasure-trove of early demos circulated the music business to no avail. But then Ferry added former Nice guitarist Davy O'List to the line-up, and suddenly people began taking notice. Gigging around with his own Davy O'List Band at the time, the guitarist recalls, 'By the time I joined, Roxy Music had been rejected at least once by every record company in the land.'

And no wonder. One of the unsuccessful applicants for O'List's job, Quiet Sun guitarist Phil Manzanera, remembers, 'their tape was done with a very abstract, sort of classical drummer [Lloyd] and all that sort of thing. It was very different.'

Whether recruited as an astute exercise in self-promotion or, as he himself claims, a role model for Manzanera, who would become the band's eventual guitarist, O'List's arrival did alter Roxy Music's future.

The first notice came when the band's latest demo was reviewed in *Melody Maker* in December 1971. Writer Richard Williams described it as 'one of the most exciting tapes ever to come my way,' and that despite it having been recorded 'on a small tape recorder in what sounds like a Dutch barn.'

More succinctly, he later said: 'It was a mess. It sounded like people mucking around – and there was this bloke in the middle who wanted to be a pop singer.' Nevertheless his enthusiasm was contagious. Within days of the review appearing, Roxy Music were booked for a session on John Peel's *Sounds Of The Seventies* radio show. Five songs emerged: the fragmentary 'The Bob (Medley)', recreating the Battle of Britain over a series of musical vignettes, three shorter and marginally more conventional pieces and a lengthy, 11-minute version of 'If There Is Something' which remains among the most exciting and most evocative pieces in the entire Roxy Music canon.

Ferry's voice ranges in directions he would never dare walk again; the band shifts from overdrive to understatement without a moment's notice and the song's final coda, fading out on all the things we used to do 'when we were young', is pure poetry. It is a requiem for the past but also a hymn for the future – because there could, and would, come a time when we would all remember 'when you were young'; when the grass *was* greener, the trees *were* taller and the heels *were* higher. It was called 1972.

It would take another six months, and a little more tinkering, before Roxy Music were ready to reveal themselves to the world. But if they had never stirred again, their maiden Peel session – described by Richard Williams as 'the best set...since King Crimson's debut' – would be evidence enough of the days when giants walked this earth.

January 1972 – One Hit Wonders: Hey Hey Jump Now/Goodbye (CBS 7760)

A certain Mike Berry (not the Sixties hitmaker) was behind this grinding proto-Glam-in-the-garage epic, since unearthed by the compilation 'Glitterbest: 20 Pre-Punk'n'Glam Terrace Stompers' (RPM 265).

January 1972 – Worth: Don't Say You Don't/Polecat Alley (CBS 7728)

Liverpool's Worth had already cut two singles during 1970-1971, 'Shoot 'Em Up Baby'/'Take The World In Your Hands' (CBS 5309) and 'Let's Go Back To Yesterday'/'Let Me Be' (CBS 7460). They would release two more before breaking up during 1973 – Vanda-Young's 'Keep It In The Family'/'Hey Mister Lonely' (Epic S1009) and finally, June 1973's 'I Ain't Backing Down'/'I'm Not Fooling'. Band member Michael Baron, co-author of both sides of the final Worth single, would later co-write Tiger's June 1975 'I Am An Animal'.

22 January 1972 – Melody Maker: Oh You Pretty Thing

The crucial element was to create a persona.

From the very outset of his adventures with Tony Defries, and all the more so since *Pork* aligned his vision, it was obvious that if David Bowie was going to achieve his ambition of combining his passions for singing and mime into one devastating package, he'd better get a handle on theatre.

But because he was neither the world's best singer nor its greatest mime artist, he needed to create a persona who was. Somebody that would change plain old David Bowie into something intriguing, inaccessible and glamorous... 'James Dean as a girl', as Defries put it.

Defries himself had no more background in such a creation than Bowie. But he was a keen student. He looked back at how the great Hollywood studios of the past had worked, how they manipulated the media by walking in with a plan from the very beginning. He saw how Andy Warhol had convinced people to accept 'his delusion of things as art'. And everything fell into place. Bowie and Defries were not

Oh You Pretty Thing

DAVID BOWIE talks to Michael Watts

selling a pop star. They were selling the illusion of one, and an illusion can be anything you want it to be.

They started out small, supplying Bowie with a personal photographer (Mick Rock) when he was unknown. Hiring him a bodyguard when he was a nobody. It was theatre.

Why does an unknown singer need a photographer?

Because people must want photos of him.

Why does he have a bodyguard?

Obviously, because he must need one.

Bowie was the first rock star to have personal bodyguards around the clock, and just as Defries expected, 'people were so busy talking about that, that they forgot that he wasn't actually a rock star at the time.'

He wasn't a homosexual either. 'In fact,' avers Defries, 'he was one of the most resolutely heterosexual men I ever met.' But the media demanded a hook, something that it could get its teeth into, a slice of journalistic shorthand that summed the artist up in a word. And in early 1972, self-proclaimed homosexuality was one helluva hook.

Still, when David Bowie admitted, in the pages of *Melody Maker* (and, subsequently, elsewhere) that 'girls are super...almost as good as men...' it was headline news only for people who really cared to learn about the sexual predilections of pop's forgotten heroes. And he wasn't exactly convincing, either.

'I'm gay,' Bowie told journalist Michael Watts. 'And always have been, even when I was David Jones.'

'But,' cautioned the perceptive Watts, 'there's a sly jollity about the way he says it, a secret smile at the corners of his mouth. [Bowie] knows that in these times, it's permissible to act like a male tart...'

ON THE RADIO
3-7 January 1972 – Johnnie Walker: T Rex
10-14 January 1972 – Johnnie Walker: Slade
11 January 1972 – Sounds Of The Seventies (BBC): David Bowie
18 January 1972 – Sounds Of The Seventies (BBC): David Bowie
27 January 1972 – Pete Drummond Show (BBC): Slade

ON THE BOX
20 January 1972 – Top Of The Pops: T Rex
27 January 1972 – Top Of The Pops: Chicory Tip, T Rex
ON THE SHELVES
January 1972 – St Cecilia: Don't Want Women, Don't Want Wine/He's A Collector (Polydor 2058 193)
January 1972 – Alice Cooper: Be My Lover/You Drive Me Nervous (Warners K16154)
January 1972 – Gidian's League: Hey! Did You Know You've Got Your Face On Upside Down/You've Got A Mind Of Your Own (Parlophone R5933)

---

8 February 1972 – Old Grey Whistle Test (BBC): David Bowie

Bowie and his now renamed Spiders from Mars had been gigging since January, building a groundswell of support based partially on their music but more on their imagery, a dazzling array of increasingly (as finances improved) garish stage costumes that transformed three guys from Hull (Trevor Bolder had now joined Woodmansey and Ronson in the band) into creatures from another planet and Bowie himself into something even more bizarre.

They gigged wherever they could, starting in the smallest clubs and then working their way up the circuit, They executed a string of dazzling sessions for BBC radio and a brilliant *Old Grey Whistle Test* performance in February. They left audiences agape with the sheer theatricality of a stage show that incorporated mime, innuendo and tangible sexuality, as though Bowie were tapping into every movie, play and cultural reference that came to mind, then combining them into one seamless whole.

Which, of course, is *exactly* what he was doing.

Whistle Test brought three songs, the last album's 'Oh You Pretty Things' and 'Queen Bitch', all cool New York androgyny and lust; and the next record's 'Five Years', a solid premonition of the end of the world. Together, they established the twin bases within which Bowie's musical future would dwell, the sense of desperate decadence with which we all hope we will live out our last days. But, more than that, they were

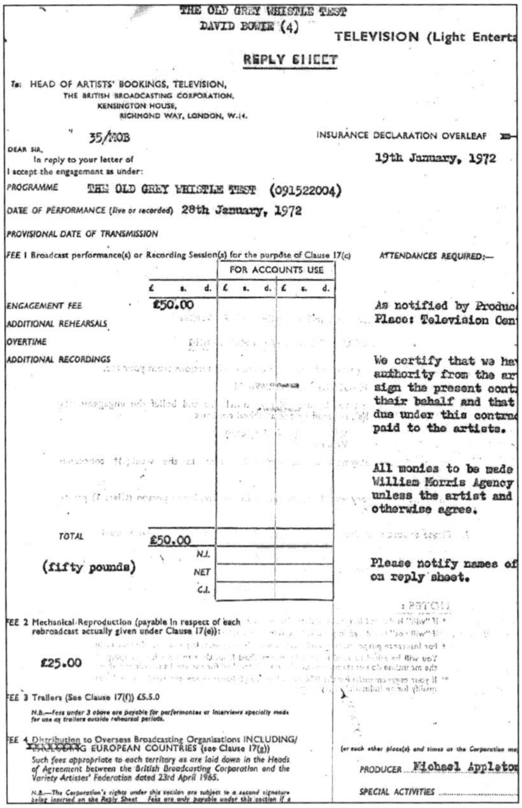
THE OLD GREY WHISTLE TEST
DAVID BOWIE (4)
TELEVISION (Light Enterta

REPLY SHEET

To: HEAD OF ARTISTS' BOOKINGS, TELEVISION,
THE BRITISH BROADCASTING CORPORATION,
KENSINGTON HOUSE,
RICHMOND WAY, LONDON, W.14.

35/MOB

INSURANCE DECLARATION OVERLEAF

DEAR SIR,
In reply to your letter of 19th January, 1972
I accept the engagement as under:

PROGRAMME THE OLD GREY WHISTLE TEST (091522004)

DATE OF PERFORMANCE (live or recorded) 28th January, 1972

PROVISIONAL DATE OF TRANSMISSION

FEE 1 Broadcast performance(s) or Recording Session(s) for the purpose of Clause 17(c)

	£ s. d.	FOR ACCOUNTS USE £ s. d.	£ s. d.
ENGAGEMENT FEE	£50.00		
ADDITIONAL REHEARSALS			
OVERTIME			
ADDITIONAL RECORDINGS			
TOTAL	£50.00		
(fifty pounds) N.I.			
NET			
C.I.			

ATTENDANCES REQUIRED:—
As notified by Produc
Place: Television Cen

We certify that we ha
authority from the ar
sign the present cont
their behalf and that
due under this contra
paid to the artists.

All monies to be made
William Morris Agency
unless the artist and
otherwise agree.

Please notify names of
on reply sheet.

FEE 2 Mechanical Reproduction (payable in respect of each rebroadcast actually given under Clause 17(e)):
£25.00

FEE 3 Trailers (See Clause 17(f)) £5.5.0
N.B.—Fees under 3 above are payable for performances or interviews specially made for use as trailers outside rehearsal periods.

FEE 4 Distribution to Overseas Broadcasting Organisations INCLUDING/ EXCLUDING EUROPEAN COUNTRIES (see Clause 17(g))
Such fees appropriate to each territory as are laid down in the Heads of Agreement between the British Broadcasting Corporation and the Variety Artistes' Federation dated 23rd April 1965.
N.B.—The Corporation's rights under this section are subject to a second signature being inserted on the Reply Sheet Fees are only payable under this section if a

(or such other place(s) and times as the Corporation ma

PRODUCER Michael Appleton

SPECIAL ACTIVITIES

great songs performed by a killer band, although it must be admitted that, back on the road, a lot of the audience was there out of pure, prurient curiosity. It was no accident, after all, that Bowie made his 'I'm gay' announcement on the eve of the band hitting the road, and none that he should be giving onlookers their vicarious money's-worth thereafter.

Later, Bowie admitted the only thing saying he was gay achieved was to sell lots of records. And, from his point of view, he was probably correct. He certainly distanced himself from both the quote, and the lifestyle, as his career wandered on.

But to the audience that would soon be flocking to his banner, his comment was considerably more important. Homosexuality was now legal. But it was also the butt of more jokes than a mother-in-law, and the source of more hostility too. In early-Seventies Britain, to admit you were gay was to confess to a moral, physical and emotional failing whose ramifications spread far beyond the boudoir and into every walk of life. The closet, from which today's gays emerge without even thinking about it wasn't simply closed, it was locked from both sides.

Bowie had the key, whether he liked it or not. But he would not be the first person to turn it.

February 1972 – Sweet: Poppa Joe/Jeanie (RCA 2164)
17 February 1972 – Top Of The Pops: The Sweet

In January 1972, David Bowie said he was gay. Six months later, everybody knew it. But, as he himself once remarked while excusing some of his more egregious musical borrowings, sometimes it doesn't matter who does something first. 'It's who does it second that counts.' And, while the Sweet's Steve Priest never actually said a word on the subject – not in earnest, anyway – by the time Bowie finally sashayed onto *Top Of The Pops* and let the world assume what it would about his love life Priest had already opened that door as wide as it would go.

And he did it with 'Poppa Joe'.

The Sweet's fourth Chinnichap single, 'Poppa Joe' is often mistaken for a close relative of the earlier 'Co-Co', not only through its repeated refrain of 'coconut' but also by virtue of the reappearing steel drums and arranger Fiachra Trench's tight calypso backing.

In fact, it is a far more accomplished composition, one of the first to illustrate writers Nicky Chinn and Mike Chapman's progression from pure pop constructions to more adventurous arrangements. Ignore the lyric, which is little more than mindless repetition and a maddening chorus, and 'Poppa Joe' is a fascinating creation, building in pitch and tempo as it progresses.

Less successful internationally than the best of its predecessors, 'Poppa Joe' nevertheless topped the chart in eight different countries and reached Number 11 in the UK, while *Top Of The Pops* pulled the band back into the studio on two separate occasions, on 17 and 24 February. And it was there that Steve Priest made Glam-Rock history.

History insists that it was Bowie who brought homosexuality out of the closet in the world of British pop. But Bowie had a bunch of other stylistic weapons in his arsenal, from the

distinctly science fiction cut of his music to the post-Warholian artistic tendencies that he espoused in every interview.

In terms of sheer sex and sexuality, he was actually something of a cold fish, and, while he expressed well-feigned amazement at just how quickly the 'news' of his sexuality spread and the impact it created (even Cliff Richard denounced Bowie for furthering the disintegration of society), he did so with a deliberately manipulative finger on the trigger.

Steve Priest, on the other hand, had no idea of what he was bringing to bear on the libidos of his audience. Noddy Holder had been introducing Dave Hill to Slade crowds as 'a queer' for years, and inviting the boys in the audience to come backstage to meet him, and Priest was only echoing that same vulgar humour and piss-taking.

Even before he started dressing up, he always seemed to be the target of homosexual advances and insults, associations that swiftly spread to his bandmates as well. So finally, he decided to go along with his look. 'Everyone thought we were queer, so I thought "Let's go to extremes!"

'At the time, I looked like a 12 year-old girl, and we used to go up north to mining country, and they'd hurl comments like "Do you like it up the arse?" so I thought instead of going "no", I'd say "Yeah, as it happens I do", and it was amazing how these guys would turn tail and run.'

The Sweet had already earned a reputation for their somewhat outlandish taste in television attire, and 'Poppa Joe's appearances on *Top Of The Pops* would be no exception. 'To start with,' Priest recalls, 'Michael Chapman said, "Let's go to Chelsea and start picking out some groovy clothes." But I hate buying clothes, so when "Poppa Joe" came out, all I had was a pair of green satin pants, and red and yellow platform soles.

'We were on *Top Of The Pops* the first time, and that's what I wore. Then the record got in the charts, and we had to do another *Top Of The Pops*, so I cut the legs off the green pants, used carpet tape and turned them into shorts. Then I got a pair of red tights... I can't remember what I was wearing on top, but I was the first man to wear hotpants on *Top Of The Pops*. And six months later, David Bowie wore hotpants on *Top Of The Pops* and it was "Bowie goes on *Top Of The Pops* with hotpants", and I'm going, "I did that six months ago, mate."'

February 1972 – UK Joe: Smoke Gets In Your Eyes/Deadwood Central (Bell 1212)

Bryan Ferry was not the only period personage to have fond memories of the old Jerome Kern ballad. Two years before the Roxy Music frontman wrapped his tonsils around this sweetest of melodies, the Esso paraffin company had the lyric rewritten for a TV commercial...

'They asked me how I knew/It was Esso Blue?/I of course replied/With lower grades one buys/Smoke gets in your eyes...'

There's a flexidisc preserving this particular version of the song; for commercial purposes, however, Joe returned to the original lyric.

February 1972 – Lieutenant Pigeon: Mouldy Old Dough/The Villain (Decca F13278)

Destined to become the hottest novelty of the year, 'Mouldy Old Dough' was everything you'd expect from three rockers and a piano-playing mother, and nothing like anything else on earth. The band's name, incidentally, was an anagram of 'Genuine Potential'.

Little more than Stavely Makepeace under an assumed name, with Rob Woodward's mother Hilda pounding the Joanna, Lieutenant Pigeon did not get off to the brightest start.

'When we'd finished the original recording of "Mouldy Old Dough",' Nigel Fletcher recalls, 'there was no elation. In fact, we went up the pub and were a little downcast because we thought it lacked mid-range drive. A few days later, we tried Stavely Makepeace guitarist Don Ker out on a rolling guitar track to try and fill the whole thing out. All it did was clutter the track so it went on the shelf, Don's guitar track wiped off it for good!'

It was two months before they returned to the track. 'We were doing some recording in Steve Wadey's SWM Studio in the Clerkenwell Road, London. When we had a lunch break, Steve stayed at his studio and nonchalantly picked up our seven-inch reel of master tapes which we took with us to add anything we did that day.

'He looked down the titles and "Mouldy Old Dough" caught his eye, so he wound the tape to find it. When we got back after lunch we heard the sound of "Mouldy" blasting out of the speakers. It was then that Steve came out with his famous prophetic line, "That's an international Number 1 hit".

'Of course, that gave us renewed enthusiasm to try and get a deal for Lieutenant Pigeon. Steve Wadey also tried to place it, but in the end we got our own deal with Frank Rodgers (Clodagh's brother) at Decca. And the rest, as they say, is geography.'

In fact, 'Mouldy Old Dough' still seemed to be stillborn until a newly launched current-affairs TV show in Belgium grasped it for its theme tune. The record rapidly rose to top that country's charts which, in turn, prompted Decca UK to look again at its potential. A relaunch was scheduled for August 1972 – and this time it went all the way.

February 1972 – Top Of The Pops Volume 22 (Hallmark SHM 780)

The controversy surrounding the exile of budget-priced LPs from the chart continued to swirl into the New Year, with the ban's supporters still grumbling about ripoffs and the like.

Top Of The Pops addressed them with 'Volume 22'. Traditionally a portion of the back cover of each album was given over to a paragraph or two of fluffy exhortations. From 1970, 'Hip hip, you hippies, and yippee, you yippies, go grab yourself this handful of rhythm and beat its brains out on your player.'

For 'Volume 22', the first release of 1972, the tone changed dramatically. 'We issued our first album some three and a half years ago and what has happened since then has been an uninterrupted run of success after success, a story based not on luck, but on hard work, imagination and more hard work. We wanted to give the world public a high-quality album of 12 current hit tunes recorded by the finest session musicians available to us; and at a price representing the best possible value. We believe we have succeeded.'

The public apparently agreed. Top Of The Pops' sales continued to rise and, while its competitors like Hot Hits slowly fell away, by late 1972 Top Of The Pops was firmly entrenched as the highest selling series of its kind in recording history.

And here's why. The first weeks of 1972 marked the emphatic dawn of the most exhilarating period in British chart history, and Top Of The Pops was there to chronicle it in all its spangly, starry, sparkling glory. And what better way to kick things off than with the record that rocked the New Year into place?

'Volume 22's furious remake of 'Telegram Sam', all scything guitars and honking horns, is one of the defining Top Of The Pops performances, and when you add the Faces' disreputably swaggering 'Stay With Me' and the Sweet's 'Poppa Joe' it's like you've died and gone back to pop heaven.

'Volume 22' also includes a performance

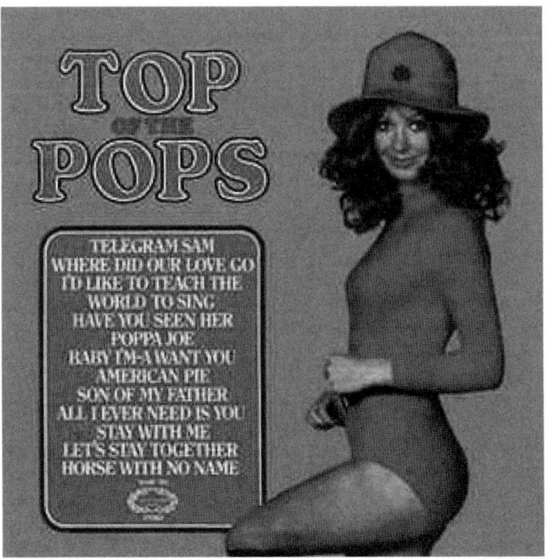

that, behind the scenes, would prove as integral to the Top Of The Pops series' growth and development as the music itself. Former Harmony Grass vocalist Tony Rivers makes his series debut covering 'Son Of My Father', and he would stay around even longer than Glam Rock.

ON THE BOX
3 February 1972 – Top Of The Pops: Chicory Tip, Slade, T Rex
17 February 1972 – Top Of The Pops: The Sweet, Chicory Tip, Slade
24 February 1972 – Top Of The Pops: The Sweet, Chicory Tip
26 February 1972 – Ask Aspel: Flick Colby

March 1972 – Slade: Hear Me Calling/Get Down And Get With It (Polydor 2814008 – DJ-only)
March 1972 – Slade: Slade Alive (Polydor 2383101)

No matter how brilliant they were in the studio, Slade were first and foremost a live experience. It made sense, then, to follow up their commercial breakthrough with an album that captured the full impact of a Slade concert; omitting both of their recent hits only added to the strength of the record.

Recorded over three nights, 19-21 October, at Command Studios in Piccadilly before a specially convened fanclub-only audience, seven extended tracks included only one familiar Slade hit, 1971's 'Get Down And Get With It'. Elsewhere, raucous covers of 'Born To Be Wild', 'Hear Me Calling' and 'Darling Be Home Soon' might not have advanced the cause of the Holder/Lee songwriting team, but did confirm the band's super-hard rocking credentials, at a time when their singles success might have dissuaded more 'mature' ears from giving them a chance. The result, Holder remarked later, was 'coarse, rare and gritty…just how we like 'em.'

'We knew from the start that it was important to appeal to everybody,' Chas Chandler explained. 'Marc Bolan had a very loyal following while he was doing the Tyrannosaurus Rex thing, which completely dropped away once he started having hits because the kind of people who liked the old stuff were suddenly embarrassed to like him now he was so successful.

'Obviously we didn't want to have the same thing happen to us, so we made a very conscious decision that the live and studio sides of the band would be very different, so even people who hated the records could hold their head up and say "But they're a great band live". And that's what happened.'

'Slade Alive' became Slade's first LP chart entry, peaking at Number 2.

March 1972 – Silverhead: Ace Supreme/Oh No No No (Purple 104)
March 1972 – Silverhead: Silverhead (Purple 7506)

Silverhead have been described, with some accuracy, as 'the greatest metal band ever to dress up like a bunch of weird-looking hookers.' Purveyors of 'strutting teenage trash of the first order', a distorted fun house in which 'guitars totter precariously on absurdly high heels, the rhythms are offering knee-tremblers in a back street alleyway some place, the lyrics drape lasciviously over anybody who'll hold them up, and the riffs will spend the night with anyone.'

Indeed.

'Silverhead grew out of the whole world of London velvet dandies,' singer Michael Des Barres explains. 'Rimbaud-affected Oscar Wilde mannerisms, while trying to grapple with slide guitar.'

It was a world in which he was already immersed, but his bandmates had no hesitation in joining him. 'Nobody told them what to wear,' explains Des Barres. 'But there's me sitting in an antique vintage dress over jeans with a brown hat with a feather in it. You're not going to show up in a boiler suit, are you?'

Silverhead's love was the circus.

Des Barres: 'Early on, when we were first starting out, we had white face, and we used circus motifs. I'd have that teardrop…it was very circusy. I've always found that imagery to be very scary with the clowns, but athletic as well with the trapeze. It's very Dada, a real world of painted faces.'

They hit the same live circuit as David Bowie and his Spiders from Mars were now playing, the smaller clubs and universities up and down the country, and often running into the same kind of audiences, dazzling all comers with the visuals while pummelling them with sound. And reactions, as Bowie was finding, were polar. 'The usual – the girls wanted to fuck us, the guys wanted to kill us. But the great thing is, we caught on very quickly in London, there was very quick acceptance by like-minded deviants, and there were a few break out places like St Albans as well.'

Unfortunately, before Silverhead could consolidate any of this, management rushed them off to Japan where labelmates Deep Purple were already superstars and Silverhead were certain to follow. It mattered not that their records were left to fend for themselves in Britain. Deep Purple had shown how much money there was to be earned elsewhere, and Silverhead were going to grab some of that.

Musically, 'Silverhead' occupies an odd position somewhere between Deep Purple and some of the late-Sixties Stones' sluttier-sounding moments – imagine 'Beggars Banquet' and 'Let It Bleed' fed through the kind of mushrooms that Turner would dine out on, and then raiding their sisters' wardrobe for stage wear. Music for a blood-soaked cabaret catwalk, then, and it doesn't really matter whether or not you like music. The package was perfect.

'It was the white-face thing,' reasons Des Barres. 'The Japanese, with kabuki and their sense of ritual and glamour, accepted it very easily. It's the tried and true joke "big in Japan", and we were. So we experienced that very quickly, and that drove us on to be even more eccentric. But the great wake-up came when we got to Cleveland and there were nine people in the club.'

An American tour followed the Japanese outing, Silverhead stuffed onto any bill that would carry them, and the group swiftly learned just how unprepared America was for five skinny Brits dressed up like Christmas trees.

Des Barres: 'Silverhead collectively weighed 160 lbs, and when we played down south I used to milk it. I'd come out in Mobile, Alabama, and I'd say "Oh I got such a red neck at the pool today", and people would go crazy, wanting to kill us. Which was great until you got into the parking lot at 3am.'

16 March 1972 – Portsmouth Mecca Ballroom. Miss World – yes. The Sweet – no.

The evening got off to a bad start, and it went downhill from there. Delayed on their way to the venue, the Sweet took the stage 20 minutes later than advertised with the anguished bellows of the ballroom's manager already ringing in their ears.

Now they were on stage and that same Mr Manager was storming onto the boards demanding that the Sweet exit the premises immediately, then calling down a complete Mecca Ballrooms-wide ban on the band. Never again, he swore, would these foul-mouthed yobboes sully the stages owned by the company that staged the Miss World beauty pageant.

'Their actions, words and everything were obscene. I made a report the following day to head office, and they were removed from the rest of the dates [Mecca controlled several other venues on the Sweet's latest tour]. We had complaints from the audience, and I was called from my office to see the performance. There were very few people left watching the group at the end of their act.'

Steve Priest recalled a slightly different version of events. All tour long, he explained, 'We had been getting some abuse from the male contingent [of the audience], usually questioning which way round we had sex. Our replies were generally in the area of "Go fuck yourself." This would send the young lads into a craze.

'Eventually, the managers of the clubs began to tire of our unruly conduct. At Portsmouth, the manager really got hostile. He pulled down the curtain on us and started ranting and raving. He called us degenerates and low-lifes, and questioned our parenthood. He then went on to complain bitterly about our foul language and got himself so worked up that he started using dirty words even *we* didn't recognise.'

'Sweet have been banned...following an alleged suggestive stage act,' reiterated the *NME*. 'Mecca claimed that the group swore on stage and simulated sexual actions, but Sweet insist there was nothing offensive in their act and that they received no complaints from the audience.'

Mecca head Eric Morley added his fury to the furore. 'Their gestures were not fit for the public. They swore and their actions could have provoked serious trouble.' Later, presumably feeling a little calmer, a Mecca spokesman admitted that the ban 'might be lifted in three months,' but Nicky Chinn fumed regardless. 'I think the whole thing has been vastly exaggerated and, in fact, I wish it was as bad as they said because Sweet would really be something!

'Also, I very much doubt that any of the kids complained. If they left, it's more likely they had to catch the last bus home.'

March 1972 – Captain Skidlid: Charlie Brown/She Knew Him Too Well RCA 2173)

Peter Shelley's time at the helm of Alvin Stardust's career was still over a year away when he donned the title of Captain Skidlid for an update of the old Coasters hit. With vocalist Alan Greed, Shelley's creation was, in his own words, 'funky and tough. I was really upset it didn't make it.' The B-side would subsequently distinguish the compilation 'Glitter From The Litter Bin: 20 Junk Shop Glam Rarities From The Seventies' (Castle CMQCD 675)

March 1972 – Gary Glitter: Rock'n'Roll (Parts 1 & 2) (Bell 1216)

'When I was a kid, my major influence was Elvis,' Gary Glitter declared. 'After that, I discovered people like Ray Charles; I liked his "What'd I Say" very much. Then I got into things like Gary US Bonds, Eddie Cochran, Gene Vincent's "Be Bop A Lula". Those were my real influences.' And those were the talismans he would carry through his greatest years.

When Gary Glitter first emerged in the spring of 1972, pounding on the ribs of 'Rock And Roll', the Glam Rock explosion was only one of the directions he was aiming in. The other was the rock'n'roll revival that was building slowly around the London underground, coalescing around increasingly regular visits by the likes of Jerry Lee Lewis, Chuck Berry and Little Richard.

It was the blending of the two into one seamless mass that made 'Rock And Roll' so eternally divine. Instantly nostalgic, but like nothing else on earth, 'Rock And Roll' cut through everything that was around that English summer, through the T Rex sparkle and David Bowie sashay, through Slade's patent stomp and Sweet's candied pop. And, though it didn't quite make Number 1, it hung around the chart for so long there's not another song on earth that recaptures the moment like it.

Even today, the pounding beat that opens the record, the chorusing guitars which carry the riff, and the opening calls of the Massed Vocals Of Hey convey a magic, a might, and most of all, an innocence which defies categorisation. It might not be the most important record ever made, but can anyone name a better one?

Gary did not always Glitter, of course. He was born Paul Gadd in Banbury, Oxfordshire, on 8 May – 1944 was the official year but estimates vary. He got his first guitar at the age of 13, but he never really took to it. He wanted to be a singer and recalled, 'I was the typical boy posing in front of the bedroom mirror with my collar turned up, trying to sneer like Elvis.'

The family moved to Croydon, just a short train ride from the big city, and Paul began heading up to Soho and the poky little coffee bars where all of Britain's rock aristocracy seemed to have been discovered.

'To me, aged 13, it was like entering a different world. As you went down the stairs into the club, you were hit by a wave of heat and sound and smells – it was like walking into a solid wall of excitement. There were always at least 200 people packed into a space that would have been crowded with 50 in it. Everybody was streaming with sweat, and the noise was deafening. But that was everything I imagined rock'n'roll should be.'

It was the era of Cliff Richard, still the local lad about to make good; of Vince Taylor and the Playboys; of Tommy Steele and 'Rock With The Caveman', and pretty soon it was the era of Paul Gadd as well. The Two Is, the best-known of all the capital's coffee bars, ran what was essentially an open mike. All you had to do to get in front of it was pester the club owner, Tom Littlewood, into giving you the green light. Still in his early teens, Gadd sang 'a few times down there', and his repertoire of Elvis and Buddy Holly was good enough for him to be booked into a few other clubs, the Laconda (owned by actress Diana Dors, but financed by the Kray twins) and the Latin Quarter.

The nightly fare at venues like this wasn't always to Gadd's taste. The Laconda, in particular, was nothing more than a hang-out for some of the city's most notorious gangsters with the Krays, of course, the most notorious. 'While I was on stage,' Gadd recalled, 'a crowd of frightening-looking characters would be sitting about getting legless. They'd make me sing soppy songs like "Teenager In Love", which I didn't really care for, but they paid me very well.'

It was to try and cut a more individual groove that Gadd formed his first band in 1958. Drawing from a pool of schoolfriends and with a drum kit made from cardboard boxes, Paul Russell and his Rebels (Russell was his stepfather's surname) continued thrashing through rock'n'roll standards, which was when a friend of the elder Mr Russell invited them to play at a club he'd recently opened.

The Safari Club, just off London's Trafalgar Square, was a demanding gig. Despite their tender years, the band was expected to play a full ninety minutes almost every night, and Paul often didn't get home till dawn, just in time to get up for school. After a year of this, and with the Rebels' own reputation beginning to spread out from the Safari, Gadd left home and moved into a one-room apartment in Clapham. He was 15, he'd just left school, and already he was a professional rock'n'roller. One wonders, though, if he'd have been as starry-eyed if he'd known how long he'd be waiting before his first hit.

Among the Safari Club regulars was a certain Robert Hartford-Davis, a small-time film producer with an eye for the easy money that rock'n'roll appeared to promise. He who organised Paul Gadd's first recording session, a two hour studio visit which produced the teenager's Decca debut, 'Alone In The Night'/'Too Proud' (Decca F11202). Gadd himself wasn't keen on the songs, but went along with it without complaint; 'I was desperate to get my name on a record.'

Even that was not to be. Neither Paul Gadd nor Paul Russell, it was felt, were sufficiently rock'n'roll for the modern pop market when up against the evocative likes of Billy Fury, Johnny Gentle, Vince Eager and Dickie Pride. 'Alone In The Night' was released in January 1960, under the name Paul Raven, a tag that would accompany Gadd for the next decade.

Despite an appearance on the *Cool For Cats* TV programme and a spot on Anthony Newley's latest tour, propping up a bill which also starred comedian Bernard Bresslaw, organist Cherry Wayner and 'Mr Blue' hitmaker Mike Preston, 'Alone In The Night' was not a hit. Neither were the Rebels. Midway through the tour, the promoter recommended that the band turn professional.

They refused. The tour was running at a loss, wages hadn't been paid. If this was professionalism, they'd rather get real jobs. Paul Raven completed the outing with backing from the rent-a-band musicians who accompanied the other artists.

His live set was just three songs long and, strangely for an artist who was promoting his latest single, didn't feature 'Alone In The Night'. Rather, Raven concentrated on music which was more to his tastes: 'Poor Little Fool', 'Baby I Don't Care' and 'Here Comes Summer'.Raven broke with Hartford Davis shortly after the tour came off the road; his last project with the man was a small role in low-budget movie *Stranger In The City*.

By April 1960, Raven was on the road again, part of a package tour headlined by Vince Taylor and the Playboys, and he continued touring through the year, utilizing a variety of backing musicians. 1961 then brought a new manager, Vic Billings, and a new record deal, with Parlophone.

With the company hailing him as 'our most exciting artist since Helen Shapiro' and *Disc* magazine describing him as 'Britain's first R&B singer', Paul Raven seemed on the edge of a major breakthrough. 'Walk On Boy', Wayne Walker's American blues hit, was his first single (c/w 'All Grown Up' – Parlophone R4812), and it was already selling well when Raven got a call from Parlophone head George Martin. He'd just heard a new Bacharach/David composition, 'Tower Of Strength', that he thought would be perfect for the young singer.

The problem was they'd have to get it out quickly before Frankie Vaughan released his version. It would mean abandoning 'Walk On Boy', but that was the price of fame.

Raven, of course, went along with the scheme and ended up with two flops for the price of one, as a national television strike removed all music-oriented viewing from the nation's screens. Almost all of it, anyway. Just one show survived the carnage, the weekly variety show *Sunday Night At The London Palladium.* And guess who appeared on that every week for a month, the duration of the strike, performing his latest single?

Frankie Vaughan. His 'Tower Of Strength' raced to Number 1, Paul Raven's (c/w 'Livin' The Blues' – Parlophone R4842) wound up in oblivion.

Parlophone dropped Raven after that, the corporate thinking being they'd given him two singles and neither had sold. Neither was another deal likely to be forthcoming, as the dawn of the Beatles/George Martin-led Beat Boom sent the age of the solo artist spinning into history.

Raven found work for a while as a studio warm-up man at *Ready Steady Go!*, racing around the studio trying to gee up the audience. He appeared in an advertisement for Cherry B wine; worked on sessions for Adam Faith, Tommy Steele and Engelbert Humperdinck; and even tried resurrecting his movie career, such as it was, by auditioning for the lead role in the rock musical, *Privilege* (he lost out to Paul Jones). Nothing seemed to work.

However, the mid-Sixties did provide him with one valuable link to what would become his future, when he was introduced to Mike Leander. One of the country's top arrangers and producers, Leander was following the prevalent fashion amongst the British music industry's backroom boys and forming his own 'Orchestra'; George Martin, Larry Page and Andrew Oldham had all tested the waters in recent months, but the Mike Leander Show Band was the most ambitious of them all.

A nine-piece outfit, it was to be fronted by Leander's regular songwriting partner Chas Mills and the proverbial AN Other. Leander wanted Paul Raven to become that Other.

He did not need asking twice and, by April 1965, the Show Band was on the road touring with Irish balladeers the Bachelors. It was a disaster. Audiences didn't understand the Show Band's music, promoters didn't understand the outfit's wages. The Show Band collapsed in disarray before the tour was even half over.

But Leander had not finished with Raven. Through his auspices, the singer won a handful of production jobs handling singles by Thane Russell ('Security') and the Poets ('Baby Don't You Do It', B-side to one of the Scottish rockers' Immediate 45s), and while Paul and Leander's paths were soon to separate they would keep in touch.

When the Show Band collapsed, Raven and baritone saxophonist John Rossall stuck together, forming Paul Raven and Boston International and heading off to Germany. Boston International (a name which was eventually truncated to the Bostons) would spend much of the next five years playing on the continent and, without Raven, would cut a number of singles for the German market: 'Time To Go'/'Wow Wow Wow', Apollo Flight'/'Count Down', The Swinging Creeper'/'Hitch Hike', Piccadilly Rock'/ 'Jenny Jenny', Hayride'/ 'Bang Bang Lulu', 'Hey Diddle Diddle'/'Come Over',' Open Up the Door'/ 'Everytime', My Crazy Family'/'Cornflakes' and 'Aquarius'/'Good Morning Starshine'.

In 1968, Mike Leander was placed in charge of the MCA label's UK operation. Raven became one of his first signings and June brought his first single for the label under the new guise of Paul Monday. 'Musical Man'/'Wait For Me' (MCA MU 1024) was the first of a host of Leander compositions the singer would make his own although, as before, few paid attention.

A similar fate met 'Soul Thing'/'We'll Go Where The World Can't Find Us' (MCA MU 1035), a reversion to the old Paul Raven name in August 1968; and with mind-numbing repetition he scored another resounding failure a year later, when 'We're All Living In One Place'/'Take Me Away' (MCA MK 5006) failed to give his latest pseudonym, Rubber Bucket, a hit.

That one really shook him up. 'We're All Living In One Place' remains one of the most bizarre but strangely captivating 45s of the era. According to Raven, a bunch of hippy squatters had recently moved into the vacant building next door to the MCA offices, spending their time chanting hymns of defiance at the efforts of the police to remove them.

Over time, the hippies became something of a *cause célèbre* in London, and one afternoon Leander hit upon the idea of recording one of their protests, adding some musical accompaniment and then putting it out as a single. He promptly wrote a hippy chant, sent Raven next door to get the ball rolling, and then hung some microphones out of his window. By the end of the day, he had a tape of a 3,000-strong choir of voices, with Raven's way up in the mix, shouting along to an arrangement of 'Amazing Grace'.

Intense media interest surrounded the recording, but it didn't help. '"We're All Living In One Place" was actually an awful record, and deserved what it got – absolutely no airplay or sales,' an older, wiser, Rubber Bucket would remark. 'But it marked another important stage in the development of my relationship with Mike. It was our first session with only the two of us. After this, Mike really got the bug to create a good record entirely single-handedly.'

Hiring the tiny Mayfair Studios in South Molton Street, Leander and Raven launched into a long period of experimentation. It was there, they later agreed, that the pounding roar of the Glittersound was born through the painstaking manipulation of tape loops and drum patterns.

'Famous Instigator', a track that would eventually appear on the first Gary Glitter album, was demoed around this time; so was a boiling rhythm that they called 'Shag Rag, That's My Bag' and which was tentatively scheduled as Paul Raven's next single. At the last minute, however, Leander changed his mind. The hook was right, the beat was correct but the song had something missing. It needed a bit more rock'n'roll.

In the meantime, Raven's vinyl career continued along its haphazard path. A cover of George Harrison's 'Here Comes the Sun' (c/w 'Musical Man – MCA MK 5006), powered by a remarkable falsetto, gave the Paul Monday pseudonym his second successive flop; Paul Raven then made it five misses on the trot when Sly Stone's 'Stand' (c/w 'Soul Thing' – MCA MKS 5053) went nowhere fast. The Sixties dribbled out of the egg timer around the same time.

A decade of failure hung behind him now, but Raven remained convinced that there was a niche for his favoured blend of soul, dance and rock'n'roll. He also knew 'Shag Rag, That's My Bag' was somehow the key to it all.

Good, strong and energetic dance music was coming back into fashion. Hits like T Rex's 'Bang A Gong' and Slade's Get Down And Get With It' proved that. If 'Shag Rag' could just be made a little more musically malleable, a touch more profound and a shade less obscene, it stood a good chance of following those classics up the chart.

Change! It was everywhere in the early years of the new decade. The Beatles had changed, from a superhuman unit to four fallible individuals. The Stones had changed, the Who had changed. Without placing himself into those same exalted circles, Paul Gadd knew he, too, must change. So must Paul Monday, so must Paul Raven, so must Rubber Bucket. The man of a thousand aliases needed to come up with the thousand-and-first, and even before he knew what he was going to record next he was desperately trying to create a new name.

Glam Rock was flowering everywhere; there was a clue in there someplace. Vicki Vomit, Terry Tinsel, Stanley Sparkle. Late at night, the calm of Upper Montagu Street, where he was now living, would be shattered by Raven leaping from his chair and announcing 'I want to be Horace Hydrogen!' Gary Glitter was simply the next alliteratively daft name he came up with. But this time it stuck.

'I wanted to project the whole glamorous

scene,' Glitter explained. 'Bowie was there, certainly...' – sharing the Gem management company, Glitter and Bowie 'used to bump into each other every day for some time' – 'and Dave Hill was wearing glitter in his hair. But you shouldn't go into a record store and ask for the title of a record. It should always be "Oh, I want to have the new one by so and so."'

And so-and-so had the new one everyone would want.

'Paul was very much into rock'n'roll,' Leander recalled, 'so I said to him "Let's go into the studio with a couple of friends, and you and I will write something as we go along...see what we come up with."'

Leander later described drawing upon influences as far removed as the Creole shuffle of Doctor John and the recent work of South African John Kongos, a Fly Records labelmate of Bolan, who hit during 1971 with 'Tokoloshe Man' and 'He's Gonna Step On You Again'. But it was a tape of 'Shag Rag, That's My Bag' that set the tone for the session.

'Friends dropped in during the evening, people came into the studio, played for a while and then drifted away, it was all very loose, and eventually this developed into an impromptu jam session as we started to get into a rock'n'roll rhythm, and then we built it up from there.

'And suddenly it all came together. We had produced something that was like all the records we had ever heard before, and yet was different to them all. We were writing and making the sort of record that we had both loved to listen to when we were 14 and 15 years old, yet it wasn't preconceived. We had not planned it that way. But when we played the tapes back the sound we heard was a revelation.'

What they came up with was a primeval mogadon stomp; 15 crunching minutes they titled 'Rock And Roll'. Edited down to a more manageable length, it became 'Rock And Roll (Parts 1 & 2)'.

'Rock And Roll (either part)' was to become one of the most unique records of its era, and they knew it. Leander continued, 'I took "Rock And Roll" to Dick Leahy at Bell Records, and they were all astonished when they heard it and more than a bit perplexed. There was nothing like it on the market at the time and yet they, like me, had this instinctive feeling that the record had something.'

Bell pressed 1,500 copies of the single and mailed them out to the usual BBC jocks. All turned it down flat. But in the clubs, the song was making an impact. Leander relates a conversation he had with Dick Leahy shortly after the single was released.

'He told me he'd been talking to the switchboard girl, and she'd mentioned that she was getting all these club DJs phoning up asking for copies, that kids were going up to them night after night and asking to hear "Rock And Roll". About a month after that, we started to get a change in the sales figures. Now record stores were starting to phone up and order copies because kids were coming in asking for that "Rock And Roll" record they'd heard at the disco.'

It took 'Rock And Roll' 11 weeks to get on the radio, 12 to get into the chart. And still they were left scrambling when the first call came to appear on *Top Of The Pops*. Gary Glitter, to them, was still just a name; they needed an image, and it wasn't to come cheaply. Clothes, stage and lighting equipment, staff for Leander's management offices; 'I wanted us to be a totally self-contained unit,' Leander explained simply. 'And I never had any doubts about our eventual success.'

18 March 1972 – T Rex: live at Wembley
March 1972 My People Were Fair And Had Sky In Their Hair...But Now They're Content to Wear Stars On Their Brows (originally released Regal Zonophone, 1968)/Prophets, Seers And Sages, The Angels Of The Ages (Regal Zonophone, 1969) (Fly TOOFA 3-4)
March 1972 – Tyrannosaurus Rex: Debora/One Inch Rock/Woodland Rock/Seal Of Seasons (Magnifly ECHO 2)

You want to know what Bolanmania was really all about? This is what the stage-door schoolgirl buttonholed by *Melody Maker* said. 'I used to like Keith Emerson. Now Marc Bolan is the only one for me. Keith is just a good-looking pop star whereas Marc has got everything. There's his fuzzy hair, for a start...'

If any single moment can be looked back on as the peak of Bolan and T Rex's supremacy – the moment when they creamed every other past incumbent of the rock'n'roll throne of time, the

TONY TYLER REVIEWS THAT INCREDIBLE WEMBLEY C

TWENTY THOUSAND SCREAMERS

THE DAY THAT POP CAME BACK

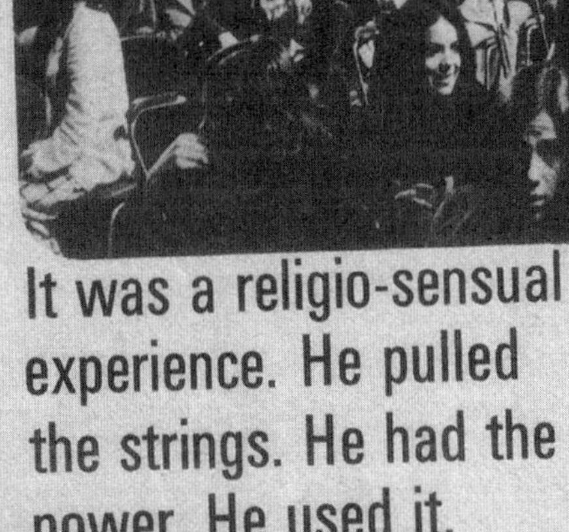

E WAS A POEM in silks, satins and nbroidered velvets. A soft cap, sewn ith astrological stars, clung to his ırly locks. Silken breeches encased his gs, where gleaming ose fell away to eveal silver-buckled hoes. Spangled dust, rtistically arranged eneath his lustrous yes, glittered, ref-ecting the powerful ighting in visionary lashes. He was an arch-priest of High Camp. He was beau-tiful.

And he, incredibly, was only a photo-grapher at Saturday's staggering T. Rex concerts at the Wem-bley Pool.

Indeed Wembley on Saturday night was many things to many people. For thousands of Rex-maniacs, secure in their fundamentalist faith, it burned with all the fervour of a religio-sensual ex-perience. A Diony-sian Rite of Spring in which they flocked to pay frenzied devotive offerings.

For Ringo Starr, whose film crew cap-tured the entire con-cert in living colour completely unnoticed by the crowd, it meant can after can of footage.

For the Job-sworths it brought a crush of climactic mania, unsurpassed since the Beatles.

And for Marc Bol-an, and T.Rex, it brought an unmiti-

tioned triumph. He is there. He has made it.

Boley's glory was not limited to the fact that nigh-on 20,000 people had packed themselves, precariously, into Wembley to hear the first T.Rex concert in England for six months.

Bolanolia

Nor was it merely because those same people paid him the sincerest compliment of all — flattery — by aping his hair, his clothes, his eye make-up and all the rest of the Bolanolia.

It was demonstrated by the almost-mesmeric control he had over them. By the ease with which he pulled the strings and they responded.

A raised eyebrow, noted more than 200 feet away, would be duly squealed over.

Voices would lift in joyful screams if he indulged himself with a bout of duckwalking. And he need only twitch a satined rear to bring forth a surge of thousands against the crash barriers, the metal warping visibly beneath the pressure.

He had the power, and he used it. Example: "Some of the people here are worried in case you're gonna get hurt up front there. They say they'll stop the concert." (instant worried silence).

"ARE any of you getting hurt?"

An enormous "NO" and Bolan, having pulled the rug, continues with the show.

Back to the concert.

It opened — d-j'd by Rosko with 1,500 watts and all the panache of a Baron Frankenstein of sex and sound atop his disco pulpit — with a fine set by Quiver, an interesting band with good lead-work, nice use of echo and a bassist who looked like Giglamps from the PC49 series in "Eagle".

I found them pleasant to listen to, although less pleasant to watch. They seemed nervous, or bored, or both. And it grew irritating.

Their speciality seems to

It was a religio-sensual experience. He pulled the strings. He had the power. He used it.

guitars, each with applied Binsons, topped by rumbustious vocals and a good, funky feel. They also rambled a little.

The audience, restive for T. Rex, occasionally thought so too. From where I was sitting the odd catcall ("Shout 'em orf" — "No, give 'em a chance") could be heard. But they finished their set unperturbed, and duly split, leaving the stage to an awesomely large crew of roadies who set up the T.Rex gear.

The excitement is intense. The guitars are brought onstage by a roadie. Vast screams of approval. Rosko takes the mike and asks "Are you READY?"

They are, indeed, READY.

His words are completely drowned at this point but we just make out ". . . T.

Noise, noise, NOISE.

Bill Legend straightens up from behind his kit, Mickey Finn vaults over the monitors, landing in front of his congas. And Steve Currie, in red pants, wanders on with his bass.

Then he's there. The Prophet of the New Age appears onstage with a built-in swagger that sends them potty.

Thrusts

It's incredible. They're actually baying their approval.

People hammer joyously on their seat-backs. On each other. On me.

The front row leaps impulsively to its feet, the second row follows suit; and so on.

The camera crews turn their spots on to the crowd. The Jobsworths move in

side, relieved of surveillance, instantly fill again.

Boley, all in smiles and green garb and a T-shirt with his own face, waves and plugs in. Now the crowd is a solid, waving mass as far as can be seen.

Peace signs, salutes, obeisances — the air is full of waving arms.

A girl next to me is screaming "MARC! MARC!"

Every now and again she stops, breathes deep to gain more cubic inches, then thrusts her chin out and lets fly once more.

The air is thick with screams. Flying sequins. Curses from the embattled Jobsworths.

And now, yes, T. Rex are actually playing. I can't hear properly. Is it "Cadillac"? People start falling all over me, and my lady.

It's time to leave the

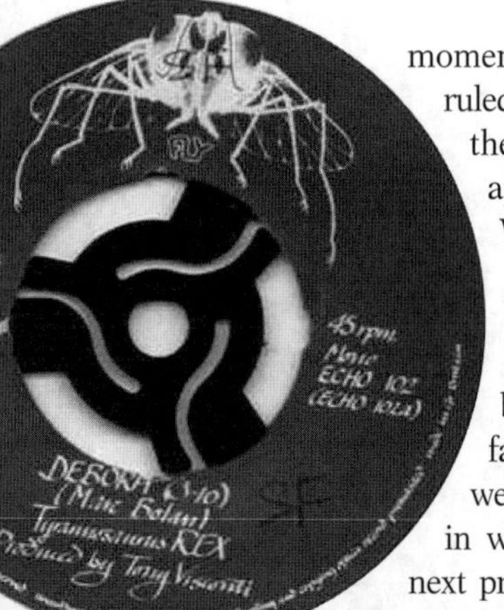

moment when fuzzy hair ruled the universe – it was their 18 March 1972 appearance at the Wembley Empire Pool.

Forget that they played two shows in one day, each attended by 10,000 screaming fans. Forget that both were filmed for inclusion in what would be Bolan's next project, the feature film *Born To Boogie*.

18 March was important because it was the day that the Sixties finally ended, and we could stop whinging on about how great the Beatles were. It was 'the day that pop came back', declared the headline over the *NME*'s review of the show. It was 'the end of an era', announced *Melody Maker* a few weeks later; 'fan-mania every bit as big as the Beatles.'

It was also the first miscalculation Bolan had made since his white swan first took wing.

Directed by Ringo Starr, and split between tempestuous live footage, backstage meanderings and some uproarious fantasy sequences, the movie of *Born To Boogie* was destined to become the Christmas hit of the year despite an uncertain response from the critics. A soundtrack album released alongside the movie would probably have outsold every other record in sight, and kept Bolan boogie-ing for at least another year.

He didn't release one.

Instead, it would be another 33 years (and several mis-labelled false alarms) before a full audio companion to the movie was released. You can't say that it was worth the wait, because we needed this record in 1972, when Bolan meant more than life itself and you couldn't just pop the movie into the player to relive the magic at home.

Losing the *Born To Boogie* soundtrack meant losing momentum – not musically, because of course Bolan was off in new directions by then. But commercially, it killed him and, though we can only say that for sure with hindsight, surely somebody, somewhere, must have given that a thought?

'There were a lot of people telling Marc to release the live album,' Tony Secunda recalled, 'but he refused because it would be cheating the kids. That's what his argument always was, it's why his B-sides were never on the LPs and so on, he didn't want the kids putting out money for songs they already had on the last record. What he didn't understand is that was what they wanted.'

Born To Boogie is not the greatest movie ever made. Its soundtrack is not the greatest live album. But the mood that explodes from the two together is one rock'n'roll has never recaptured, and it was obvious that Bolan would decline from here. Because there was no way he could ever go higher.

And he proved that on the record racks.

Until he joined John's Children in March 1967, Bolan claimed he had never even owned an electric guitar. And once he quit the band, it is said, he abandoned it as quickly as everything else that that band represented – freakbeat pop, adrenalined psych, electric soup.

In fact, Bolan never lost sight of his electric destiny, which means Tyrannosaurus Rex's debut album approaches the listener from a totally unique angle, the Incredible String Band with a hot wire to the brain. And it suddenly had a lot of listeners. A Number 15 hit in 1968, 'My People Were Fair' was now repackaged with Tyrannosaurus Rex's second album, and this time it went all the way. With the spin-off 'Debora' single climbing to Number 7 at the same time, if anybody ever asks you just *how* big T Rex were in spring 1972, you know what to tell them. *That*'s how big T Rex were at this time.

March 1972 – Bay City Rollers: We Can Make Music/Jenny (Bell 1220)

The long-awaited follow-up to 'Keep On Dancing' didn't even make it inside the disco.

March 1972 – Roxy Music: Remake/Remodel

Roxy Music's first *Sounds Of The Seventies* session was still reverberating as the band went on the road. Guitarist Davy O'List remembers shows at Reading University's Fine Arts Department and Battersea Art College, together with a handful of more mundane outings, opening for Quintessence in Bristol and Cambridge. The most incongruous of them all, though, was with the Pretty Things in Aylesbury.

'We were sitting in this freezing cold dressing room, while outside the place was filling up with greasers. We just wanted to get the gig over with, we were expecting it to be really bad. In fact, we went down great. Bryan had made a quick quiff with a pot of Brylcreem and there were all these greasers out there actually jiving to the music! It was an amazing sight!'

Listen to 'Would You Believe' from Roxy Music's debut album and it is very easy to relive that memory in your own head.

Interest in the unsigned Roxy Music was now approaching its peak, and in February 1972 Ferry decided to make overtures towards EG Management, a company to which he had been introduced by one of the band's few big-name admirers, Robert Fripp. Ferry actually auditioned for Fripp's King Crimson during 1971. He didn't get the job; according to legend Fripp advised him that with a voice and an approach like his, Ferry would be better off persevering with his own group.

EG was interested, but only in Ferry. They offered him a contract as a solo artist, but Ferry, to his ever-lasting credit, had not come through a year of intensive rehearsals simply to have his own masterplan discarded at the drop of a chequebook. Instead, he persuaded EG head David Enthoven to accompany him to a disused cinema in Wandsworth, where an apprehensive Roxy Music were preparing to go through their paces.

The scheme worked. Enthoven agreed to take the entire package and, within a week, had signed the band to Island Records, one of the companies that had rejected the group in the past.

Before Roxy Music could enter the studios, however, Ferry had one final adjustment to make, as he decided that Davy O'List's style of playing was no longer suitable. He sacked the guitarist, replacing him with Phil Manzanera, who had been killing time as the band's roadie.

That Ferry waited until Roxy Music was safely signed before he noticed anything amiss about their star guitarist does lend some credence to the suggestions, oft-repeated, that Manzanera was the man he had wanted all along and that O'List's recruitment had been for publicity purposes alone.

It has also been suggested that EG Management was behind the move in an attempt to keep O'List and another of their clients, Keith Emerson, safely apart. The years that had elapsed

Roxy Music

since O'List's Emerson-sponsored dismissal from the Nice had done nothing to heal the bad feeling that festered between the two virtuosos.

'No, none of that is true at all,' Manzanera insists. 'I went along for an audition after seeing the ad in *Melody Maker*, and I got on well with them, although they hated the tape I played to them. I auditioned, and I didn't get the gig but I used to bump into them in strange places, like a Steve Reich concert at the Queen Elizabeth Hall; they played the Friends of the Tate [Gallery] Christmas party, and my friend was doing the lights, and in they all traipsed.

'I continued to be a friend; I was at their audition for EG, sitting with the two managers from EG and Richard Williams from the *Melody Maker*. But Davy was their guitarist. And then, during the audition, Davy had a punch-up with [drummer] Paul Thompson, and that's when it was decided he had to go.'

As for his own hasty recruitment, Manzanera admits that he had been doing his homework. 'They asked me to audition again, and by that time I'd secretly learned all their material, sussed out what they wanted to do. I didn't tell them this, of course, didn't tell them for a long time, but I played and they thought, "Christ, he must be a genius!"'

March 1972 – Stavely Makepeace: Walking Through The Blue Grass/Swings And Roundabouts (Spark SRL 1066)

Stavely Makepeace released one further single for Concord, 'Give Me That Pistol'/'Sundance' (Concord 018) in 1971; then resurfaced on a new label in March 1972 (violinist Owen John replaced guitarist Tayton around the same time) and came close once again to chart glory with 'Walking Through The Blue Grass'.

Or, at least, it brought them a return to the *Lift Off* studios (26 April 1972), guesting alongside the briefly resurgent New World ('Sister Jane' – RAK 130 – would become their final Top Ten hit),and yodeller Dave Newman's impressive solo rendering of 'The Lion Sleeps Tonight'.

And while the single again failed to chart, it did attract some attention.

Two covers of 'Walking Through The Blue Grass' swiftly followed; one by Huntingdon-based band Slow Dog (c/w 'Ain't Never Going

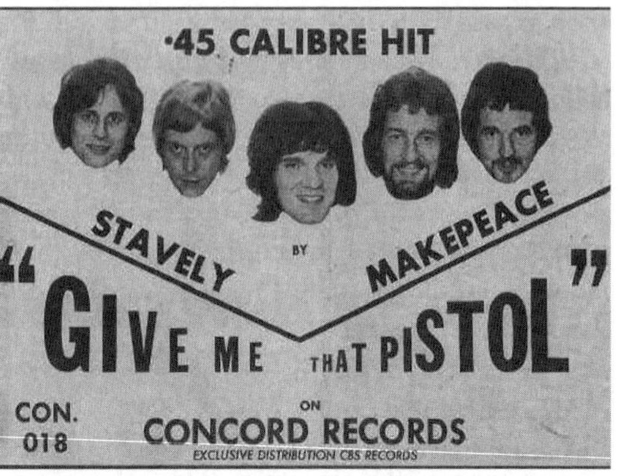

Home' – Parlophone R5942) the other (c/w 'Sardine' – Philips 6006 209) by Red Fox.

Rob Woodward was also able to hand a copy of the single to his idol Jerry Lee Lewis, at a reception in Kensington Palace Hotel. 'I doubt very much if he ever recorded it, though (I wish – I wish!).'

ON THE RADIO
13 March 1972 – Dave Lee Travis: The Sweet
13-17 March 1972 – Jimmy Young: Slade, T Rex
16 March 1972 – Pete Drummond: Slade
ON THE BOX
2 March 1972 – Top Of The Pops: Slade, Chicory Tip

April 1972 – David Bowie: Starman/Suffragette City (RCA 2199)

Drawn from Bowie's now imminent 'Ziggy Stardust' LP, 'we never thought of 'Starman' as a single,' admitted guitarist Mick Ronson. 'It just seemed to happen that way. It was never a song that worked well live, and there were far stronger songs on the album. I thought so, anyway.'

Bowie himself admitted that the song was based in part on 'Somewhere Over The Rainbow' from *The Wizard Of Oz*, and even delighted in singing a few lines from that song during concert performances of this gentle, acoustic rocker.

Yet it was 'Starman' which finally gave Bowie and his Spiders From Mars the British Top Ten hit six months of media attention insisted they land, and 'Starman' that unleashed the future legend of Ziggy.

But it wasn't this sweet little song about a spaceman that sent Bowie's career into overdrive.

It wasn't Bowie's spiky orange hair, or bassist Trevor Bolder's spray-painted silver sideburns. It was their appearance on *Top Of The Pops*, and that – like the record's chart entry, at the end of the June – was still a long way away. Until then, it looked as though you could chalk up another miss for the carrot-topped misfit.

April 1972 – Elton John: Rocket Man/Holiday Inn/Goodbye (DJM 501)

Salt? Meet wound. While David Bowie sat anxiously awaiting the hit that would justify the sheer amount of money and effort being poured into his career, Elton John looked back at Bowie's first hit, 'Space Oddity', and delivered a timely, and cruelly so, reminder of Ziggy Stardust's humble origins.

Later, Bowie could afford to tell the world how flattered he was that 'Elton John took so much out of ['Space Oddity'].' At the time, though, it wasn't so funny. 'Rocket Man' entered the UK chart on 22 April and, by the time 'Starman' stumbled onto the listings, Elton had already been to Number 2 with both single and the parent LP, May's 'Honky Chateau' (DJM 423).

And there was more. Portraying himself as the lonely spaceman of both songs' fame, Elton warned: 'I'm gonna be high as a kite by then.' It was to take Bowie another eight years before *he* discovered how Major Tom had been occupying his lonely orbit: 'Ashes to ashes, fun to funky/We know Major Tom's a junkie.'

April 1972 – Top Of The Pops Volume 23 (Hallmark SHM 785)

Capturing the best of spring 1972, 'Volume 23' rounds up two of the more unexpected hits of the day: 'Hold Your Head Up', a monster smash for the deeply prog Argent and 'Meet Me On The Corner', an even bigger hit for Lindisfarne, a folky crew from Geordieland who had hitherto seemed doomed to unremitting cultdom.

Of course, there was more to the mix than bearded weirdies and beetle-browed proggies. But it's not a barrel of laughs, either. Gilbert O'Sullivan's singing suicide note, 'Alone Again, Naturally' and George Harrison's deeply contemplative 'What is Life' both pondered deep existentialism, even if the latter is performed *à la* Olivia Newton-John's twangy guitar-led version.

But another former Fab saves the day with a song that captures every last soupçon of silliness for which 1972 is historically remembered, the stormingly nonsensical 'Back Off Boogaloo' – a song that also remedies the most glaring absentee of all. Marc Bolan was between singles at the time, so the fans made a smash of one of his favourite phrases instead. At least that's what Ringo said the song was about.

April 1972 – Hello: You Move Me/Ask Your Mama (Bell 1238)

North London's Hello were the band we all wished we could join – or, at least, believed we could emulate. So many other groups arrived on the scene fully-formed or were 'discovered' under dubious circumstances that already shrieked of hype and machination and then subjected to more by their songwriting puppeteers.

It's amazing to consider just how many Glam stars had already been around the block a few times – Gary Glitter and Alvin Stardust began recording before the Beatles; Bowie and Bolan in 1964-65, David Essex, Mud and Sweet before the end of the Sixties. Even the Bay City Rollers had a history. For the first time in the annals of British pop, a beast that traditionally thrived on young blood, genuinely 'new' talents were the exception not the rule.

Hello, on the other hand, really were four kids who'd put a band together for a laugh; who may have had a few lucky breaks along the way, but who remained in charge of their destiny throughout. Plus, they were young; still in their teens, just a couple of years older than their audience. Yeah, if you had to be in a Glam-Rock band, Hello was the one.

Vocalist Bob Bradbury, whose enormous blue eyes gazed out from the young band's frontline, was 11 years old when he started his first band in the summer of 1967. With friends Alan Osbourne, Robert Clark and Kevin Munn in tow, the Flashback Berries were 'a mime act, and the first song we did was "Fire Brigade" by the Move. We had girls running after us and asking for autographs, I was hooked.'

The following summer, he decided to learn to play guitar for real. The son of one of his mother's workmates was a bassist. 'She asked if he'd be interested in playing with me. He was older than me, so didn't want to do it but his younger brother wanted to play drums. This was when I met Jeff Allen.' (The bass playing brother didn't do so badly, though; he became Ultravox's Chris Cross.) Schooled on a borrowed drum kit, the first song the pair learned to play together was the Ohio Express' 'Yummy Yummy Yummy'.

Bradbury: 'Now to find another guitarist. I knew a kid at school who I thought would look good in a band; he joined, and I showed him what to do with a guitar.' This was Keith Marshall.

The Age, as the schoolboy trio named themselves, began gigging immediately, playing around the local youth-club scene. It was November 1969 before they realised that there was something missing.

'Oh yeah, a bass guitar! Jeff knew a kid who lived three doors away, Vic Faulkner, who we were convinced would be a good bassist. I showed him round the bass guitar and soon we were playing everything – Hendrix, Black Sabbath, Status Quo, Stones, Cream, right down to stuff like "Yellow River", Proud Mary", "I Believe", "Knock On Wood", and all the rock"n'roll greats; "Somethin' Else", "Bony Moronie", "Good Golly Miss Molly", "Carol", "Roll Over Beethoven", etc. 'There was even room for the first of the band's own compositions.

In April 1970, a female singer, Caroline Hall, joined the band; her name was appended to the Age's own and the group continued gigging, attracting some attention. In June, Caroline Hall and the Age appeared on the children's TV programme *Magpie*. 'We pre-recorded two songs in the morning [Creedence Clearwater Revival's 'Proud Mary' and 'Yellow River'],' Bradbury remembers, 'and then we performed the tracks on the *Magpie* boat. Jeff was playing the drums in a dinghy which was being towed behind the boat.'

That same month, they played before the 14th Army's annual Burma Reunion at the Royal Albert Hall, in front of the Queen and Prince Philip. But Hall departed in February 1971, and the core quartet continued on.

It was in June 1971, while playing at a local north London working men's club, that the Age were spotted by the brother of Argent frontman Russ Ballard. He mentioned them to Ballard and a week or so later, the band laid on a showcase rehearsal at Jeff Allen's house for Ballard and David Blaylock, a plugger at the Chappell Music publishing company.

By early July, the band was in the studio recording 'Can't Let You Go', a Ballard composition that would subsequently give Sixties' superstar Barry Ryan his first hit of the new decade. At the end of the month, they cut 'C'mon', another Ballard track that would become their own second single, and in September, the Age signed a management deal with Runidav Ltd, a company formed by Ballard, Blaylock and 'another partner called Nick, who was the studio owner and engineer. The following month the band changed its name to Hello, and by the time they signed to Bell Records on 16

January 1972, two further tracks were in the can, 'Ask Your Mama' and 'You Move Me' – both sides of their debut single.

'Our first recording experiences with Hello were a very exciting time for us,' Bradbury laughs, 'but we had no idea of the amount of work that was involved in recording and mixing a single. It had to be absolutely right, I remember it being very tiring and hard work although great fun. It was a real eye-opener for us and a great experience.'

12 April 1972 – Lift Off With Ayshea: The Move, Roy Wood

With hostess Ayshea Brough now penning a column in the weekly television magazine *Look In* and being hauled out as an expert on children's issues by other TV shows, Granada moved to imprint her even further on the national consciousness by appending her name to their flagship music show.

The premier edition of the fourth series was highlighted by appearances from both the Move (performing 'California Man') and a solo Roy Wood (his recently released solo single 'When Gran'ma Plays The Banjo' – Harvest HAR 5058), together with a band called Smile...not the pre-Queen Smile you're probably thinking of.

April 1972 – Dog Rose: Paradise Row/Sunday Morning (Satril SAT 2)

The first release by a band discovered by Dave Paramor, son of the somewhat better-known Norrie. The line-up of Dave Johnson (vocals, guitar), Rowley Henley-Jones (guitar), John Amis (bass) and Andy Hunter (drums) cut a second single, 'All For The Love of City Lights'/'All For The Love Of Each Other' (Satril 6) in 1973, alongside an album 'All For The Love Of Dog Rose'; 'City Lights' was the Dog's contribution to the compilation 'Glitterbest: 20 Pre-Punk'n'Glam Terrace Stompers' (RPM 265).

26 April 1972 – Lift Off With Ayshea: Stavely Makepeace, New World

Rob Woodward (Stavely Makepeace and Lieutenant Pigeon): 'With almost all the new single releases we had with both of our bands between 1970 and 1976, each successive one coincided with an appearance on *Lift Off*. The late Muriel Young, producer, was tremendous to our bands and gave us slots on the show whenever possible.

'I think one of the reasons why she warmed to us was the fact that we once cancelled a *Top Of The Pops* appearance in favour of a *Lift Off* one. Muriel was stuck for an artist on this particular occasion, and most bands prioritise the main TV slots above all others.'

April 1972 – Edwina Biglet and the Miglets: Thing/Vanessa's Luminous Dog Coat (RCA 2193)

The liner notes to 'Glitter From The Litter Bin: 20 Junk Shop Glam Rarities From The Seventies' (Castle CMQCD 675), which retrieved this jewel after three decades in obscurity, declare it's 'not really Glam at all'. But less puritan ears might beg to differ, as television host Jonathan Hodge rampages through three minutes of tomfoolery, and manages to encapsulate a lot of the burgeoning era for everyone who remembers sucking on an Old English Spangle to kill the smell of the Park Drive ciggies they just inhaled.

ON THE RADIO
29 April 1972 – Sounds For Saturday (BBC): Elton John
ON THE BOX
13 April 1972 – Top Of The Pops: Tyrannosaurs Rex
23 April 1972 – Music In The Round: T Rex
27 April 1972 – Top Of The Pops: Elton John
ON THE SHELVES
April 1972 – St Cecilia: C'mon Ma/How Come (Polydor 2058 222)

May 1972 – T Rex: Metal Guru/Thunderwing/Lady (T Rex Marc 101)
May 1972 – T Rex: Bolan Boogie (Fly HIFLY 8)

Arguably, T Rex's most eternal single, and certainly their most triumphantly flamboyant, 'Metal Guru' became their fourth chart-topper in a year by the simple expedient of bulldozing everything else to one side. It entered the chart at Number 9 and the following week, it was Number 1, displacing the military might of the Royal Scots Dragoon Guards Band in the process.

Everything is perfect, from the opening cry

of unadulterated joy, through a lyric whose buoyant nursery rhyme quality seriously belied its content, and on to the closing celebration. 'It's a festival of life song,' Bolan explained. 'I relate "Metal Guru" to all gods around...someone special, a godhead. I thought how God would be, he'd be all alone without a telephone.'

While Bolan lived only in the present, his fans were able to luxuriate in the past. Hot on the heels of the 'My People Were Fair/Prophets' double pack (whose chart-topping success it would effortlessly emulate), 'Bolan Boogie' served up another opportunity to experience the magic that was Marc, and a round-up of his first days of fame.

With the exception of one cut drawn from 'Unicorn', the entire album dated from the arrival of Mickey Finn, and the attendant headlong dive into electricity launched by 'A Beard Of Stars' and culminating with 'Electric Warrior'. 'Beltane Walk', 'The King Of The Mountain Cometh' and 'Fist Heart Mighty Dawn Dart' all proved that Bolan's early flair for myth-weaving had effortlessly survived the move to amplification, while 'Jewel' allied that assurance with some of the most gratuitously dirty guitar of the age.

'Raw Ramp', a five-minute rock opera buried on the back of 'Get It On', bristled with further dynamism. It opens gently, lavish strings and sad ballad sweet, pauses for a moment, then returns as a shuffling blues putdown ('You think you're champ, but girl, you ain't nothing but a raw ramp,' whatever that may be), then concludes with a heads-down electric boogie.

Perhaps the crowning glory, however, comes with another B-side, 'Summertime Blues', the ultimate anthem of youth disaffection utterly revised by the ultimate symbol of teenage rebellion.

May 1972 – Chicory Tip: What's Your Name/ Memory (CBS 8021)
May 1972 – Chicory Tip: Son Of My Father (CBS 64871)

'What's Your Name' was another Giorgio Moroder offering, and maybe just a little too

ON THE RADIO
16 May 1972 – Sounds Of The Seventies: David Bowie
22 May 1972 – Johnnie Walker Lunchtime Show: David Bowie
23 May 1972 – Sounds Of The Seventies: David Bowie
26 May 1972 – Sounds Of The Seventies: Slade
ON THE BOX
3 May 1972 – Lift Off With Ayshea: Bay City Rollers
6 May 1972 – The Sandie Shaw Special: Elton John
10 May 1972 – Lift Off With Ayshea: Chicory Tip
11 May 1972 – Top Of The Pops: Chicory Tip, T Rex
18 May 1972 – Top Of The Pops: T Rex
25 May 1972 – Top Of The Pops: Chicory Tip, Elton John, T Rex.

close to its predecessor to ape its success, as it faltered at Number 13. The album, meanwhile, doubled as a virtual story-so-far, looking back to 'Excuse Me Baby' for its contents but also giving that Mini Moog a good workout.

May 1972 – Slade: Take Me Bak 'Ome/ Wonderin' Y (Polydor 2058231)

Slade's second British chart-topper was what vocalist Noddy Holder later described as 'classic Slade – really rowdy and boisterous,' and the first to consciously drive into the heart of the band's live appeal.

Jim Lea later revealed that the song's genesis lay in an idea he'd been playing with for several years. 'I revamped it a bit and nicked a phrase or two from the Beatles' "Everybody's Got Something To Hide Except Me And My Monkey". Nobody ever noticed.'

Of course they didn't, they were too busy buying the record. 'Take Me Bak 'Ome' entered the chart at Number 25 on 3 June; climbed from 14 to 3 to 2, then opened July at the top. It remained there for just one week before Don McLean's 'Vincent' knocked it down again. But if he hadn't done it, the Osmonds would.

Don't look now, here comes Donny.

June 1972 – Donny Osmond: Puppy Love/Let My People Go (MGM 2006 104)

It all happened so suddenly.

The Osmond Brothers, a Mormon family hailing from Ogden, Utah, had been appearing as a quartet – the eldest of six performing brothers – on television for eight years now. Discovered playing an impromptu set on a disused lot in Disneyland in 1962, they graduated to *The Walt Disney Television Show*, from there to *The Andy Williams Show* and ultimately to *The Jerry Lewis Show*. They were a nice clean family, playing nice clean music.

With so much else going on, the Osmonds didn't even sign a serious record contract until 1970. Hitherto, they said, they had been too busy with their television career to worry about records, and the four singles released to no applause in 1967-69, 'I Can't Stop' (a worldwide hit upon reissue in 1974), 'Mary Elizabeth', 'Lovin' On My Mind' and 'Takin' A Chance On Love', were to play no musical part in what the family was now planning. For suddenly, something was suggesting the world was finally ready for their peculiar brand of all-round family entertainment.

That 'something' was the success of the Jackson Five and the Partridge Family. Augmenting their line-up with 13 year-old Donny; augmenting their sound with an adolescent falsetto lifted straight out of the Jacksons; the Osmonds' next single, 'One Bad Apple' chewed its way to the top of the US chart in January 1971. American politics had always revolved around the presence of a First Family. American pop now suddenly had three.

What made the Osmonds so appealing (or, from the other side of the fence, appalling) was that they were utterly faultless. They lived their lives free of drugs, free of alcohol, free of any artificial additives. As Mormons, their Church dictated their every action. They remained virgins until they were married, and when British journalist Charles Shaar Murray realised that the best musician in the band was also the only married one, his immediate reaction was to suggest the family's manager get them all hitched as soon as possible.

Everything about them was spotless. If David Cassidy was the Boy Next Door (albeit an incredibly well-fortified Next Door) and Michael Jackson was your favourite squeaky bath toy, to love an Osmond was to love Perfection itself.

And between the three of them, they reinvented the Teenage Idol.

There had been pretenders to that title in the past, of course. But they were mundane by comparison. Cassidy, Jackson and Osmond offered something far beyond any of them, an icon whose following was religious in its intensity, a shimmering, multi-faceted God-like being whose messages might have been received by every girl on the planet, but were really directed only at YOU.

There was nothing insincere about them, nothing unpredictable or dangerous. The Beatles would have been okay to date but you would never have wanted to settle down with one. Donny and David and Michael, on the other hand, were sensitive and loving, safe and predictable. There was nothing crazy about them, not like those Monkees who'd promise to be true to you in one song then trade you in for a dog in the next. And if anybody doubted that sincerity, all they had to do was listen to the music.

Yet it was a peculiarly asexual love affair. All that really mattered was that the idol existed, and did so on a plane where it didn't matter that you couldn't touch him, because neither could anybody else. Every girl dreamed of kissing Donny, of holding him and hugging him but beyond that, the mechanics of sex didn't really get a look-in. Ditty Michael, ditto (with some reservations), David.

Every detail of the star's family life was known, studied with an academic fervour that must have crippled any self-respecting schoolteacher with envy. But more importantly, and this was where the teen mags came into their own, every aspect of his personal life, his past, his preferences, his destiny, was also open to scrutiny.

A lot of it was pure speculation, of course, the impoverished hack cobbling together half-remembered press releases and out of context one liners, but it was all presented with such style, such panache, that it was impossible to believe the magazine did not have as direct line to The Adored One's heart.

'How to fall in love with Donny – and make

Donny fall in love with you' was a theme neither publisher nor public ever tired of. And if you didn't like Donny, next week they'd tell you how to fall in love with David, with Michael, with anyone you could possibly want to fall in love with. Even Little Jimmy, the youngest, fattest and most precocious child star of the age, was not spared.

Indeed, it was the teenybop press – in America, *16* and *Tiger Beat*; in Britain, *Popswop* and *Music Star* – that did the most to propagate the artists in the first place, keeping their names alive when the idols were out of sight and saturating the news stands with them when they weren't. Glossy colour photos and the stars' true confessions were only a part of it; a subscription to *Music Star* was like having a superstar penpal.

Osmondmania hit the UK for the first time in the summer of 1972. 'Down By The Lazy River', the brothers' third successive US Top Tenner, had made a fleeting appearance in the British listings back in March, but the group were still unknown as far as the country at large was concerned.

But with MGM's press office working flat out, it wasn't long before the teen magazines picked up on the fact that, taken altogether, the boys really weren't that bad looking. And that was all it took.

The American success in March 1972 of the solo Donny's 'Puppy Love' clinched it. It was his fourth US Top Ten hit, and immediately the British wing of MGM began planning a domestic release. The message of the song was perfect: 'We're young, we're in love, and our folks say we'll grow out of it. Boy are they wrong.'

It was a theme Donny had already aired a few times in the past; indeed it was one trotted out by every teenage balladeer who ever lived. But in June 1972, MGM bowed to what they described as 'public pressure' and released 'Puppy Love' in Britain.

And maybe there had been pressure, because it went straight to Number 1 and stayed there for five weeks. By the time the Osmonds announced they were coming to London in the autumn, the publicity machine had been running on autopilot for close on six months.

3 November 1972 saw war declared on three very separate fronts. For the rockers there was the Osmonds' 'Crazy Horses', an ecological stomper scarred by a truly demented synthi-whinny. For the romantics, there was Donny's 'Why', and for everybody else, Grandmothers to Grandchildren, there was little James Arthur Osmond.

In America, where Osmonditis was already beginning to die down, this unholy trinity barely caused a ripple, with 'Why' and 'Crazy Horses' peaking at 13 and 14 respectively, and the nine year-old Jimbo making a brief appearance way down the ladder at Number 38.

Britain, however, simply lapped it up, then came back begging for more. Donny made Number 3, the boys got to Number 2 and Jimmy reached Number 1 with 'Long Haired Lover From Liverpool'; could there have been a more pointed stab at the now superseded weight of Beatlemania?

T Rex didn't enter into it. For all the declarations that Bolanmania was the Beatles revisited, the Osmonds made him look like a seafront sideshow. Bolan's appeal was almost exclusively teenage. The Osmonds grasped every generation. But even more importantly, Bolan could release just one record at a time (maybe two if his old label was up to its tricks again). The Osmonds had a seemingly bottomless pit of performers to draw from, with sister Marie already poised to strike.

Not since the heyday of the Fabs had any one group been so dominant, but at least they had had the decency not to drag out the brothers and sisters to share the fun. (Mike McGear doesn't count for this particular analogy.) Suddenly the Osmonds stopped being the joke that most 'serious' pop fans had labelled them. Now they were a positive menace.

The group's arrival at London Heathrow was witnessed by nigh on 10,000 screaming fans. And, while rumour had it that many of them had been paid off by promo men anxious to curry favour with America's first family of pop, the hysteria which had even the hardest newsmen phoning through reports of Beatlemania (part two) was very genuine.

A chant taken up at one end of the airport communicated itself to the other within seconds. Periodically, everyone would scream for no reason whatsoever. Touts wandering through the crowd selling cheapo pins and Lurex scarves could hardly believe their luck. Normally, record companies frown upon that sort of thing. This time around, they didn't even seem to care.

Radio Luxembourg, which had done so much to publicise the band's arrangements over the previous week, later claimed that both Elton John and the Jackson Five flew into Heathrow immediately ahead of the Osmonds and were all but ignored by the waiting masses. 'The screams were quite astonishing, frightening,' wrote Mike Ledgerwood in *Disc & Music Echo* the following week.

And it wasn't only Heathrow that was under siege. The Finsbury Park Rainbow, where The Osmonds were to appear, became a campsite for three nights worth of teenage girls, all hoping to be amongst the lucky first ticket-buyers who would receive a free Osmonds LP for their troubles. And from there they rushed to the Churchill Hotel where, Radio Luxembourg DJ Tony Prince inadvertently let slip, the band would be staying.

When someone asked him why he blurted out the greatest state secret of the age, Prince replied 'Nobody told me not to.' It was a genuine mistake – or at least as genuine a mistake as could be made in a campaign that had been planned down to the last bathroom stop.

But Ledgerwood should have the final word, because it was he who invented the one that best summed up what was about to sweep the nation.

'The return of the new teeny idol is here. A new generation of fans has now arrived – the SCREAMAGERS.'

June 1972 – David Bowie: The Rise And Fall Of Ziggy Stardust And The Spiders From Mars (RCA 8287)

And talking of David Bowie...

With hindsight, it all seems so inevitable. 'Ziggy hit the nail on the head,' Bowie mused once it was all over. 'I wasn't at all surprised that [he] made my career. I packaged a totally credible plastic rock star. Much better than any sort of Monkees fabrication. My plastic rocker was much more plastic than anybody's.'

The trick was, he didn't *seem* plastic.

A lot of modern commentators concentrate on the bisexual aspect of the Ziggy phenomenon, but sex was only one part of Mr Stardust's message. Indeed, dig deep into the album that bore his name and it wasn't even an especially important one. True, 'Suffragette City' had a subtext, but it also had a meaty riff and one of the most triumphant kiss-offs in rock'n'roll history, a wham bam, thank you ma'am that leaped into the teenage vernacular harder than any ad-man's jingle.

Both 'Hang Onto Yourself' and 'Ziggy Stardust' itself were dramatic rockers, while 'Starman', as Bowie's publicist Cherry Vanilla (recruited, along with the rest of the *Pork* crew, to aid Bowie's American promotional campaign) once smiled, was simply 'a sweet little song about a spaceman.'

Elsewhere, 'Lady Stardust' (working title 'Song For Marc') might have raised prudish eyebrows with its off-hand reference to the make-up on *his* face. But the kids already knew who the Lady was even before Bowie started projecting the Bolanic beauty on a screen behind the stage and, suddenly, it mattered not that almost half of 'Ziggy Stardust' would never make the most generous Bowie Top Ten. Like Bolan before him and the *Rocky Horror Show* soon after, it was the totality that mattered, and individual songs were just flashes of the future that Ziggy was unfolding.

Even the sleeve, a guitar-toting Bowie resplendent in his quilted spacesuit staring up a dingy street packed its own message, of glamour amid the grimmest grime, while the now-long gone K West (quest – geddit?) furriers sign that hangs above Bowie's head remains one of the unlikeliest icons in rock'n'roll history. On the back, the same shimmering being poses in a telephone box. Again, the symbolism is hard to miss – magic and the mundane.

Because what happened next *was* magical. Released on 6 June 1972, at a time when Bowie and the Spiders had been building in-concert word-of-mouth for close to four months, Ziggy charted just three weeks later, and stormed to Number 5.

'The success was very overnight,' Mick Ronson recalled 15 years later. 'It [really] was like waking up one morning and finding that we were superstars, with no preparation at all.'

When they started work on the album, after all, Bowie and the Spiders were simply one of several Most Likely Tos on the music press agenda, and some way down that pecking order as well. Lindisfarne, Colin Blunstone, Silverhead, Blackfoot Sue, even Chicory Tip were rated just as highly, if not higher.

But still, Bowie applauded, '[Ziggy] just came at the ripest, rightest time.' It was already apparent, after all, that T Rex had peaked – how could anyone top 'Metal Guru'? – and in private conversation, Bolan was looking to pass on the glam-spangled baton.

Bowie grabbed it, gave it to Ziggy and, aware that he, too, would enjoy only the most finite lifespan before other flavours flocked to shunt him away, he wrote his own redundancy into the script. The albums closes with a 'Rock'n'Roll Suicide' that made it clear that Ziggy was not long for this world. And so inseparable were creator and creation that, when Bowie retired Ziggy in July 1973, a lot of people thought he'd be going as well.

But, of course, Bowie had long ago worked out precisely what he intended to do. For, not only did he pull the plug before his own star could slide like Bolan's before him, he then plugged the resultant void in another guise entirely. And so the world's first imaginary superstar became the world's first self-rejuvenating one.

13 June 1972 – Set Of Six: Slade

'Hands up all the girls with white knickers on!'

Cheer.

'Nice. Now, hands up all the girl with *no* knickers on!'

Roar. Slade slayed the stay-at-homes with their records, but it was in concert that the band truly touched perfection, a good time rock'n'roll band having a better time than anyone and punctuating every moment with one ribaldry or another.

From 'Slade Alive', there's that memorable moment in 'Darling Be Home Soon', that most tender of John Sebastian love songs, where Holder lets out a ginormous belch.

From memory, there's all the nights he asked if the audience were pissed yet?

And tonight, there's his suggestion that all the boys and girls in the audience get close to one another. *Really* close.

Set Of Six was exactly that, a blistering six song performance aired on ITV in the aftermath of 'Slade Alive' with the express intention of bringing the best of a Slade concert into your living room. Three hits and three album tracks are roared to perfection; the audience knows exactly what to expect and the band are dressed to damage your eyes.

We could complain (and we did) that we really only got five-and-a-half songs as the closing 'Born to Be Wild' was faded before its time, and the DVD release repeats those premature credits. But quality footage of Slade in concert from this period is scarce, and this is quality indeed. In fact, just three months after T Rex ruled the world, it's unlikely there was any live band capable of competing with Slade.

21 June 1972 – Lift Off With Ayshea: David Bowie, Hello

That two-year-old *Magpie* appearance notwithstanding, Hello made their television debut in Holland in mid June 1972, appearing alongside Sandy Beach and Mac and Katie Kissoon on the show *Eddy Steady Go*.

Bob Bradbury: 'Like our first recordings, these were an amazing experience for us, we didn't realise what went into making a TV show and how different the set looks on TV to when you are actually there!'

A week later they were back on home soil for *Lift Off With Ayshea*, this time sharing the bill with David Bowie. 'He came up to me on set and gave me some great advice on working with the cameras,' recalls Bradbury. 'That is advice I have never forgotten. Thanks Dave.'

Roxy Music: the sound of surprise

by Richard Williams

June 1972 – Roxy Music: Roxy Music (Island 9200)

20 June 1972 – Old Grey Whistle Test: Roxy Music

23 June 1972 – Sounds Of The Seventies: Roxy Music

Roxy Music had management and a record deal. The line-up was settled. Everything was going well. But Ferry's dreamboat was to run into troubled waters.

The handful of live performances they had played so far had gifted the band with a very Art-School crowd, cool, sophisticated and stylish, the Biba babes come out to play. It was exactly the audience Ferry had dreamed of courting, but to observers still desperately coming to terms with the pantomime androgyny of Bolan, the ice-cold fatales who followed Roxy formed an elite that immediately set outsiders on the defensive.

The band's music, too, permeated an otherworldly reserve. Roxy Music *looked* like Glam Rockers, Eno in feathers, furs and ladies' shoes, Ferry a mutant James Dean, Manzanera in human fly spectacles. But they sounded like computers locked into genetic overdrive.

Everything about the band, from the lyrics Ferry warbled with complete disregard for the conventions of melody through to the presence of musicians not as an integral part of the band but as 'featured soloists' seemed harsh and calculating. And when the band appeared on the BBC's weekly progressive rock show, the *Old Grey Whistle Test*, performing 'Ladytron' and 'Remake/Remodel', host Bob Harris admitted on camera that they were there entirely against his personal judgment; that, in his opinion, they were nothing more than a talentless hype.

Yet at the Lincoln Festival that summer Roxy Music were the stars of the show, despite competition from Slade (who first had to win over a decidedly hostile underground audience), the Faces and the headlining Beach Boys. And when the band released their eponymous debut album, the reviews might have been written by their record company staff members.

'The finest album I've heard this year and the best debut I can ever remember,' championed the *New Musical Express*. 'The answer to a maiden's prayer.'

Even Bob Harris seemed to have changed his tune. Introducing Roxy Music on the BBC radio *In Concert* programme, he told listeners, 'I don't usually say this, but I've been looking forward to this evening very much, particularly to see Roxy Music.'

Maybe he was simply being ironic. The next time Roxy Music graced the *Whistle Test* studios he was slagging them off as much as before.

If Bob Harris blew hot and cold, however, he was the only person who did.

A FISHY STORY FROM GARY

The image that most people have of pop stars is a pretty glamorous one. We see them looking absolutely stunning on stage or TV and sometimes it doesn't occur to us that there's another side to their lives when they unstrap their guitars or lay down their microphones.

In fact, very few of them carry over the glamour and the glitter of their pop lives into their private lives. Take their hobbies for instance — very few of them have a jetset existence all the time. Usually they occupy themselves in their spare time with things that are the total opposite of their working lives, so that they can quite literally get away from it all. Someone who does just that is Gary Glitter . . .

22 June 1972 – Top Of The Pops: Gary Glitter, the Sweet

Gary Glitter's earliest television appearances were to be restrained compared with what he would later accomplish. In a tight-fitting black jumpsuit that only accentuated the folds of blubber collecting around his midriff, and open to the waist to reveal his chest (or was it a chest-wig? The gossipmongers could never decide) in all its matted glory, he was no-one's idea of a teen idol.

Which was, no doubt, the idea behind it in the first place. While he was by no means ugly, Glitter could never hope to be teen-meat *per se*. So he exaggerated his faults, put on too much make-up, showed too much flesh and developed into the perfect caricature of a rock'n'roll superstar.

One of his best moves had him appear at the top of a staircase, a single gloved hand appear from behind a curtain. As the beat grew louder, an arm appeared, followed by a shoulder. And so on until Gary was finally revealed, his back to the audience, and voluminous cloak hanging to the ground.

Slowly he would shrug it off, and then turn, slowly again, to face the crowd. His eyes would be staring, his mouth open in a frozen 'O' as if he were astonished – or horrified – by what he saw.

Like an obscene vaudeville stripper, he used his body as a weapon to shock, to titillate the audience. 'Gary Glitter is the ultimate test of a liberated mind,' said the *New Musical Express*. 'If you can't live with the sight of Gary Glitter, the Michelin Man of Glam Rock, quivering like Fosdyke's tripe factory, you're just another bigoted straight. He looked,' the same organ reported, 'like a Yogi Bear li-lo disguised as David Bowie.'

It was as true then as it is today, a rock star growing fat is committing a revolutionary act. Under those terms, there really was no way he could fail!

June 1972 – The Sweet: Little Willy/Man From Mecca (RCA 2225)

'I hated that song,' snarled Brian Connolly. 'But that was the record where at last we had an image. Plus, coming on top of the whole thing with the Mecca Ballrooms, to go out singing about a little willy after everything we'd been accused of was really funny.'

And it's true. 'Little Willy' trails more playground innuendo than most people could fit into an entire album, let alone a three-minute pop song. It is utterly irresistible, a chanting, stomping ode to – well, that's best left to the imagination. But its wild, singalong chorus is as infectious as any of the band's earlier releases, layered over an arrangement that was moving closer and closer to the Sweet's own sound. The group, as usual, was not required to play on the record, but this would be the last time that happened, a pledge the distinctly Andy Scott-styled guitar line makes plain.

But back to the band hating it. Nicky Chinn recalled, 'Michael and I were definitely autocratic with our bands, and I became aware of that when we were told [by the Sweet] that "Little Willy" was a piece of rubbish and had no right to be released. It wasn't exactly a symphony, of course, but it was a hit, and we told them it was going to be released whatever they thought of it.'

And so it was. In the same week that T Rex's 'Metal Guru' left the Top Five and Slade's 'Take Me Bak 'Ome' went to Number 1 (Noddy was on the cover of *Melody Maker* too), Glitter's 'Rock And Roll' hit Number 2 and Bowie's 'Starman' made its Top Fifty debut, 'Little Willy' was sitting pretty at its own chart peak of Number 4.

Elsewhere in the Top Ten, Don McLean, Michael Jackson, Elvis Presley, Donny Osmond, Paul McCartney and the Drifters clung on with becoming but increasingly irrelevant tenacity. All were destined to maintain their own success throughout the years to come, but simply glancing at their faces on the *Top Of The Pops* chart countdown, it was clear that they had next to nothing to do with what was really happening, at the top of the charts or the top of the high street.

June 1972 – Blackfoot Sue: Standing In The Road/Celestial Plain (Jam 13)

Destined to become one more of the immortal sounds of that halcyon summer, 'Standing In The Road' was the debut single by a Birmingham band better known to its fans as Gift.

Active locally since the late Sixties, the band – the sibling rhythm section of Tom and David Farmer, guitarist Eddie Golga and vocalist Alan Jones – were still in their teens as they gigged behind local heroes the Move, Idle Race, Trapeze and Robert Plant's Band of Joy, and while their first attempt to relocate to London ended with them returning to the Midlands broke and hungry, they persevered.

Returning to London in 1971, Gift were invited to appear in a new BBC TV children's programme, *What Kind Of Life* – somewhat typecast, they were to play a starving pop group in the show. One song, 'Celestial Plain', was aired during the show, and the Gift gigged on.

United Artists showed sufficient interest in the band to place them in the studio with producer Roy Thomas Baker, then at the beginning of his career – among the songs cut during the spring 1972 session was Philip Goodhand-Tait's 'Jonathan Joe' together with a few band originals.

UA rejected the demo, but staff producer Noel Walker was more impressed. He became Gift's manager and landed a deal with Jam, a recently formed subsidiary of publisher Dick James' DJM empire.

'Standing In The Road', a song David Farmer built around something he'd dreamed, was the unanimous choice for their first single. Insistent and sibilant, but stomping and stirring too, it seems strange to think that it developed during an extended jam session by a bunch of longhairs whose in concert highlight was a revised version of Tomorrow's 'My White Bicycle' retitled 'My Right Testicle'. But the band knew that they had hatched a masterpiece; so much so that they didn't even perform it in concert too often, for fear that somebody else might rip it off.

Renaming the band after their shared household's pet cat Blackfoot, Jam released the single at the beginning of June, and then everybody sat back and waited. It would be 12 August before 'Standing In The Road' finally entered the chart at Number 44, but from there its progress was smooth. Three appearances on *Top Of The Pops* ultimately pushed it to Number 4 behind Slade, Rod Stewart and another band who most of their old fans would have denied had anything to do with Glam Rock, Herefordshire's Mott the Hoople.

But that was the funny thing about 1972. It didn't matter who you were or what you played. There was something in the air that year, and especially that summer. The whole world was going Glam.

June 1972 – Top Of The Pops Volume 24 (Hallmark SHM 790)

'It's almost four years to the day since we introduced the Top Of The Pops series to the world and, thanks to you all, we have gone from strength to strength.'

So celebrate the liner notes to 'Volume 24', and we're all invited to the party. 'As a birthday present from us to you, we have made an extra special effort to make this album the greatest yet.' And they very nearly pulled it off.

Even the best Top Of The Pops album was only ever as strong as the charts that it was based upon, but anybody denying that June 1972 was one of the hottest months in years had clearly had their ears cut off. 'Metal Guru', Rocket Man', 'What's Your Name', Little Willy' – Glam was glimmering all over the show and we hadn't even heard of Gary Glitter yet. 'Lady Eleanor', Isn't Life Strange'...it was going to be a simmering summer for sure.

Artist by artist, the performances wipe the floor with previous Top Of The Pops attempts to cover them. The Top Of The Poppers finally got Marc Bolan down all-but-pat; Brian Connolly no longer sounded like Widow Twanky's favourite plumber; and, if their Mick Jagger (a thunderous 'Tumbling Dice') comes across like a man whose lips are too large for his own mouth, then that just proves how well researched these albums were.

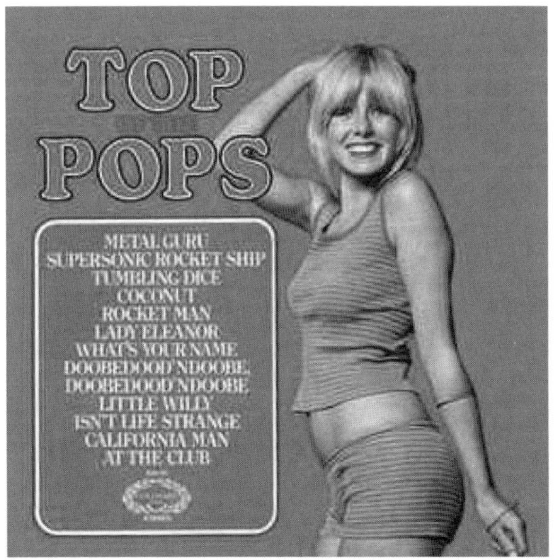

ON THE RADIO
1-2 June 1972 – Dave Lee Travis: The Sweet
1-2 June 1972 – Alan Freeman: Slade
5-9 June 1972 – Johnnie Walker: David Bowie
12-16 June 1972 – Dave Lee Travis: David Bowie
12-16 June 1972 – Alan Freeman: The Sweet
12-16 June 1972 – Jimmy Young: T Rex
19-23 June 1972 – Dave Lee Travis: The Sweet
19-23 June 1972 – Johnnie Walker: David Bowie, T Rex
19-23 June 1972 – Alan Freeman: Slade
ON THE BOX
1 June 1972 – Top Of The Pops: Slade, T Rex
7 June 1972 – Lift Off With Ayshea: The Sweet
8 June 1972 – Top Of The Pops: T Rex, the Sweet, Chicory Tip, Slade
15 June 1972 – Top Of The Pops: Gary Glitter, Slade, the Sweet
17 June 1972 – 2Gs and the Pop People (LWT): Slade
22 June 1972 – Top Of The Pops: Gary Glitter, the Sweet
28 June 1972 – Lift Off With Ayshea: Slade
29 June 1972 – Top Of The Pops: Gary Glitter, Slade

July 1972 – T Rex: The Slider (T Rex 5001)

'The Slider' was not Marc Bolan's best album; 'Electric Warrior' usually scoops that award. But it was, and is, his most perfect, a succession of taut rockers and introspective ballads that bristles not only with power and excitement (for those qualities were second nature to him now), but also with an otherworldly wordiness that rounds up some of Bolan's most eternal lyricism.

The ballads 'Ballrooms Of Mars' and 'Spaceball Ricochet', in particular, evoke candid memories of Bolan at his absolute peak. But every single second is perfect, the Bolan Boogie at its most majestic – which is why, 32 years later, it was fascinating to be permitted a glimpse into the workings behind the album, via 'Rabbit Fighter – The Alternate Slider'.

Igniting what would become one of the most fascinating series of archive releases the CD age had yet seen, 'Rabbit Fighter' set itself a formidable brief, to recreate the album in its incandescent entirety solely through outtakes, scraps and demos that Bolan left around the studio, yet still create a disc that deserved to share its (sub) title with one of the finest LPs ever made.

It succeeds. Of course, it cannot be compared to the full and final glory of 'The Slider' itself. But the largely acoustic take on 'Metal Guru' that opens the set is no less exuberant than its captivating cousin, while rough mixes of 'Rock On' and 'The Slider' pack an enervating scratchiness that quickly becomes compulsive. ('Telegram Sam', however, is a chaotic mess, with Finn's bongos sounding like a carpenter working in the next room.)

Not all of the original album could be located in an alternate form. 'Baby Boomerang' was replaced by an acoustic run through of the B-side 'Thunderwing', and it was fascinating to see how a jerking ballad was transformed into one of T Rex's most electrifying rockers.

A completely different song with exactly the same title replaces 'Buick MacKane', and two final tracks, 'Baby Strange' and 'Ballrooms Of Mars', were extracted from a live, eight-song radio session Bolan played in Los Angeles in February 1972. (This entire performance, together with a dozen other performances from sessions in Boston and New York, was also available on the 2CD 'Spaceball' and, alongside 'Rabbit Fighter' itself, delivers an intriguing snapshot of Bolan, the acoustic troubadour, at the electric peak of his career.)

Neither does the investigation end there. In 1995, as Edsel worked to restore Marc Bolan's entire 1972-77 catalogue to the shelves in both its original and 'alternate' form, the label launched a third series dedicated to documenting every surviving scrap of tape that Bolan left behind him that did not make it onto an official LP.

Across eight volumes, 'T Rex Unchained: Unreleased Recordings' would ultimately be responsible for swelling the Bolan catalogue by 184 new recordings, not one of which made it past Bolan's own sense of quality control. And the opening instalment confirmed, if confirmation were needed, that, for a moment there, Marc Bolan could do no wrong.

'Over The Flats', a slab of Bolanic autobiography that ranks among his finest compositions, 'Is It True', 'Children Of The World' and the shorter of two versions of 'Mr Motion' could all have graced 'The Slider' and would certainly have formed the foundation for a far greater follow-up than reality ever allowed.

Indeed, the evidence for 'Is It True' ranking among Bolan's most captivating compositions might be sparse, but it's certainly powerful. The song exists as just a brief sketch, its lyric nothing more than the repetition of the title and a haunting na-na-na refrain. But barely was this fragment in the stores than Saint Etienne conjured a luxurious interpretation, retaining the original's minimalism but extending melody and arrangement into precisely the territory one would have hoped to see the original journey. Few artists have ever topped Bolan's own vision when it comes to covering one of his songs. This is the exception to prove that rule.

For the most part, 'Unchained Volume 1' represents Bolan at his most unguarded. 'Sugar Baby' is musically identical to 'The Slider's 'Rabbit Fighter', while other tracks are present as mere fragments, the ghosts of abandoned classics-in-the-making. There's also a playfulness to Bolan's approach that would likewise fall by the wayside betwixt studio and pressing plant.

On vinyl, he was a furious self-mythologiser. Here, he lets slip an unguarded chuckle as he namechecks 'Jeepster' during 'Children Of The World' and, later, 'Alligator Man' clones that same song with a distinct lack of self-consciousness.

But, if the songs represent the exuberance of Bolan the pop star, a clutch of lengthy jams establish even greater credentials, reminding us that, before the screaming started, Bolan's core audience was embedded in the progressive rock underground. And, though they lost touch with him, he never lost sight of them.

6 July 1972 – Top Of The Pops: David Bowie, the Sweet

There are certain dates in rock history when you can say everything changed.

The Seattle morning that Kurt Cobain died; the London evening the Sex Pistols appeared on the *Today* show; the first time the Beatles set foot in America; the first time Elvis cut a record at Sun. And 6 July 1972, the first time David Bowie performed 'Starman' on *Top Of The Pops*.

It should not have been an overly auspicious occasion. 'Starman' had already been aired once before, when Bowie appeared on *Lift Off With Ayshea* and ran through the same song there.

But *Top Of The Pops* was different, not only because it received several million more viewers (by summer 1972, the show regularly attracted around 14 million pairs of eyes), but because those eyes tended to be a little bit older than the *Lift Off* crowd, a little more curious and a lot more comprehending of what unfolded on their screens as Bowie launched into the singalong chorus, the peroxided Mick Ronson stepped to the mike alongside him, and one colourfully quilted arm snaked out to drape across the guitarist's shoulders...

It sounds so *nothing* now. Evening soap operas don't even blink at same-sex kisses any more; Hollywood thinks nothing of full-on gay sex scenes. Homosexuality isn't simply 'acceptable' in the modern media, there are family-oriented TV shows that wouldn't exist without it.

But things were different in 1972. Back then, the lifestyle itself had only been legal for three years, and even the most prurient tabloids dropped little more than knowing winks when it came to detailing the dirty deeds.

Step into the schoolyards – *Top Of The Pops*' target audience, of course – and the mysteries were shrouded even deeper. And suddenly here was this David Bowie person (creature? space alien?), drawing back the veil and revealing so much. Two men embracing on the BBC?

Whatever next...full-on oral sex?

Well, yes, as it happens; a week or so earlier, *Melody Maker* published photographer Mick Rock's latest snapshot of the rising star going down on his guitarist in the middle of the show. And if there'd been any doubts about this Bowie-thing's sexuality before, now everything was out in the open, and that included the truths and promises that nothing in early-Seventies Britain, a world still of postwar prefabs and prewar superiorities, could ever have prepared us for.

As kids, we'd been warned to avoid people 'like that'. If a man should offer to show you a puppy, kick him hard and run like hell. Do not take sweets from strangers. And never, ever, go into a public lavatory without telling a policeman you were there.

Because some men weren't like other men.

Now here was one of those men-who-weren't-men on the telly and suddenly, life itself was nowhere near as frightening. Homosexuality wasn't as frightening. You might still not want to hang around certain parks after dark or bend over in the shower at the YMCA but, in the years since then, almost every musician of 'a certain age' (that is, somewhere in their early-mid fifties today) has spoken longingly, lovingly, of the night they saw 'Starman' on *Top Of The Pops*; and they whisper, almost fearfully, of the impact it had on their fragile, formative minds.

'I went into town the next day,' Bauhaus/Love and Rockets guitarist Daniel Ash remembers, 'and I was shaking when I went to buy that record. Because I knew it was going to change my life, and I didn't know if I really wanted to have my life changed.'

And after all that, what about those other stars of the evening's show? What about the Sweet? 'Little Willy' saw them sporting a comparatively restrained look – or maybe it was just the sight of Gary Glitter that left everything in the shade that summer.

Yes, they were bright and kind of beautiful, but all that had really happened since the last time they were on the show was Brian Connolly and Andy Scott had split a canary yellow suit between them (Connolly's tank-top remained regulation Woolworth's). And, if Steve Priest's sleeves were wider than they needed to be, the studio audience was scarcely more restrained in the fashion department.

They had no illusions about looking good, though, or appearing cool or even trendy. So far as the Sweet were concerned, they were simply playing dress-up, and the more absurd they looked the better. But something happened as they prepared to take the stage. Hanging out while the make-up girls made the final adjustments to the Sweet's appearance, David Bowie was growing ever more indignant as the Sweet's stagewear came to life. The clothes, the hair, the make-up...*especially* the make-up.

Sweet drummer Mick Tucker recalled, 'Bowie kept on saying "No, no, no – the eyes aren't right" and we all thought, "What a strange young man, taking it so seriously." As far as [we] were concerned it was all a piss-take. We just wanted to look like four old tarts...four dissipated old whores mincing about on *Top Of The Pops* and being as flash as arseholes.

'But everybody thought we were a bunch of poofs, that Brian and I were bumchums. Even the birds thought we were a bit sexually suspect...' And it was that assumption, the Sweet suddenly realised, which was going to raise them out of the pop swamp and into Glam Rock. The next time the Sweet were seen on the scene, they had undergone the most extreme makeover of all.

July 1972 – Suzi Quatro: Rolling Stone/Brain Confusion (RAK 134)

For all his magnificence as a producer, Mickie Most's influence did not end when the studio lights went out. Again drawing on his own experiences as a performer, he also understood the things that made an artist tick – and, perhaps more importantly, how to make sure they kept on ticking.

Most was producing the Jeff Beck Group in Detroit when he met Suzi Quatro, catching her on stage with her band Cradle. Elektra Records were also showing an interest in the band; Most won out, says Quatro, because Elektra saw her going solo 'and becoming the next Janis Joplin. But Mickie wanted me to be the first Suzi Quatro, so my instincts told me to go with him.'

Her instincts proved correct. 'Mickie was always there in every capacity,' she recalls. 'Manager, adviser, etc. He never let me put a foot wrong, he was very protective. He was my father, my brother, and the most important and longest relationship in my life.'

As a teenager leading her first band, the Pleasure Seekers, Quatro had already cut three singles in the US: 'Never Thought You'd Leave Me'/'What A Way To Die' (Hideout) in 1967; 'Light Of Love'/'Shame' (Mercury) and 'Good Kind Of Hurt'/'Light Of Love' (Mercury).

'We must have been mad to go out on gigs with a name like that, but we were so young we didn't understand the connections people might put to the group's name. Looking back, it was great fun. We used to support the big names like Mitch Ryder and the MC5.'

The Pleasure Seekers became Cradle in 1969; Quatro relocated to the UK in 1971.

'I put her in a hotel and kind of Anglicised her,' Most later explained, but their first single together, 'Rolling Stone', co-written with Errol Brown (Hot Chocolate) and Phil Dennys and backed by Peter Frampton and Micky Waller, went nowhere.

'None of the material we recorded was ever used,' Suzi slightly exaggerated later. 'For one thing, I can't write singles and for another I don't like being in a studio. I get high performing. I can't get a buzz in a studio because there ain't no audience.'

Which is when the producer decided to pair the Divine Miss Q with Chinnichap.

According to Chapman, Suzi was one of those rare artists Most knew ought to be a star, but didn't have a clue how to make her one. And why? Because he saw her as a singer-songwriter while Chinnichap knew she was more than that.

'I don't think I did anything consciously,' Quatro explains. 'All I know is that I knew I wasn't like other women, [and] that's what kept me going. I would see other girls and think "hmmmm, so where do I fit in?" That's usually what creates something new, the need to find a niche. In my case, since I didn't have any female role models, I had to create my niche – which many women filed through afterwards, and which made me happy. I was always a blue jean, T-shirt, leather jacket kind of girl – I guess kind of tomboy – and boy did it pay off.'

Well, it would. But not yet.

July 1972 – Alice Cooper: School's Out/Guttercat (Warners K16188)
July 1972 – Alice Cooper: School's Out (Warners K56007)

By June 1972, Alice's reputation in the US was hotter than hell. In Britain it took a little longer, but only a little, because all summer long, the entire country shook to 'School's Out', teenage perversity of the first degree, and an emphatic celebration of – what?

The end of term?

The end of the year?

The end of institutionalised education as we know it?

Nobody knew, but the sight of Cooper and his cronies whipping it up on *Top Of The Pops* was enough to outrage even the most liberal sensibilities.

'With the success of the singles "I'm Eighteen" and "Under My Wheels", we were climbing the charts all through the heartland of the US,' recalls drummer Neal Smith. 'Unfortunately, and unbelievably, we were still not able to crack the Big Apple on the east coast or LA on the west coast. We were being rejected by the two largest music markets in America. The powers that be thought, after two hit records, Alice Cooper was just a fluke.

'The music world also thought we had a theatrical rock show that overshadowed our questionable musical abilities. We desperately wanted to write a rock anthem that not only would not only get airplay in the US, but also in England and Europe as well. When it came down to crunch time our lead guitarist, the late Glen Buxton, came up with the intro rock'n'guitar riff for the ages and 'School's Out' was born.

'It was one of the most successful collaborations written by all five members of the band, and the rest as they say was rock'n'roll history. We got the national and international airplay we were looking for, only we never dreamt it would continue into the next millennium.'

The kids lapped it up, of course. Their elders, on the other hand, were less impressed. The British tabloid press took one look at Alice and began filing pictures of rock's latest sensation as seen on their most recent American tour.

It shuddered at the band's taste in lyrics, those songs about dead babies and killers, the way they re-enacted street fights and executions on stage. Their latest LP had been held up because they wanted it wrapped in a pair of frilly knickers, in flagrant violation of the fire code. They took snakes on stage with them, and inflatable sex dolls. If something was sacred they would spit on it, if it was holy they'd hack it to pieces.

'People put their own values on what we do,' responded Alice, 'and sometimes those values are warped. They react the way they do because they are insecure. They consider it shocking, vulgar; people who are really pure enjoy it. If Edgar Allan Poe were alive today, he'd do the same things as we do.' And to justify his on stage antics, 'Of course we're in bad taste. There isn't anything in America which isn't in bad taste. That's wonderful, isn't it?'

'School's Out' topped the singles chart, the album raced to Number 4, and the rest of the available catalogue started squirming as well; 'Killer's sales went up a notch and 'Love It To Death's went haywire, rocketing the record to Number 28.

July 1972 – Mott the Hoople: All The Young Dudes/One Of The Boys (CBS 8271)

It is, perhaps, the greatest three minutes 33 seconds worth of pop ever consigned to seven inches of vinyl. A rallying cry, a requiem, a love song, a death march, 'All The Young Dudes' has probably been covered more often, and more successfully, than any song outside of 'Louie Louie'. In fact, if Richard Berry's little chestbeater is the heartbeat of the American Sixties, then 'All The Young Dudes' is the soul of Britain ten years later, conceived at the height of the glam-rock explosion but so rapidly transcending that genre's limitations that, today, any one of a dozen different versions can be held up as somehow definitive.

There is the punk swagger of the Skids, gathering up the disparate tribes of late-Seventies rebellion and the rhinestone swagger of Angel, recasting suicide Billy and shoplifting Lucy in the malls of middle America.

There is the sultry harmonising of the Chanter Sisters, realising the song's inherent musicality and the rebellious folk vibe of World Party, redressing the injustices of a decade under Thatcher and Reagan. Bruce Dickinson injected the song with weary nostalgia; Mick Ronson, at his last recorded live performance, imbibed it with soaring sadness.

Gene Loves Jezebel have added a gritty gothic glamour; Jill Sobule a sad, sweet dreaminess. And, of course, there are the multitudinous renditions that the song's own composer has unveiled over the years, as he struggled to match the peerless perfection of Mott the Hoople's original, recorded back in 1972 and still as relevant today as it ever was.

'To be honest, I much prefer our version,' Mott the Hoople's Ian Hunter wrote of Bowie's first attempt at the song, later in 1972. '[His] seems too slow, and he's done it in a lower key.' And Bowie would appear to have agreed with him. Plans to include the song on 1973's 'Aladdin Sane' album were abandoned, and when Rykodisc remastered that same record for reissue in 1990, an hitherto adventurous flow of bonus tracks was staunched not only by the absence of any extra material on the record but also by label project manager Jeff Rougvie's indignant insistence that there wasn't any to include in the first place.

Responding to accusations that Rykodisc were 'holding back the good stuff' for some future Bowie rarities collection, Rougvie argued 'I'm not convinced there ever was a real studio recording of "All The Young Dudes". Every tape I ever got claiming to be the studio version was actually the radio session with the intro clipped off.'

Since that time, of course, Bowie's 1972 studio version of 'All The Young Dudes' has received a slew of official releases, and nobody has found the radio session Rougvie speaks of. But maybe, also since that time, Bowie himself has come to appreciate just how resilient 'All The Young Dudes' really is. Indeed, Bowie himself has bashed the song till it bled; rearranged it for soul and barbershop quartet; jangled it up and jungled it down – he has even given it away to his fans. 'This song was written 25 years ago,' he announced from the stage on his 1997 American tour. 'Do with it what you will.'

But then Reeves Gabrels would launch into the riff that once powered a generation's naive dreams, and a quarter of a century rolled back like candy wrappers until 25 years were 25 minutes. The kids still had hope and youth on their side, the old really were back at home with their Beatles and their Stones and T Rex and TV truly were all that mattered.

'All The Young Dudes' did more than zap the zeitgeist of early-Seventies pop. It created it.

Now the dudes are into their fifties or worse, and though the song remains affecting, it is heartbreaking as well. Play it, and remember how it felt to be young; play it, and relive the dreams that lie crushed by the years which have run over them. Play it and wonder – if it makes the people who bought it feel like that, what on earth must it do to the people who made it?

The story of Mott the Hoople began with a clutch of recordings by such Sixties R&B stalwarts as the Buddies, the Shakedown Sound, the Silence and Doc Thomas themselves; and before that, the ambitions of the Sandstorms, the Anchors, the Soulents and the Problems, hard-gigging bands who brought the semi-rural wilds of Herefordshire its first taste of native rock'n'roll but never progressed beyond the first rung or two up the ladder to fame.

Drummer Terence Dale Griffin and guitarist Peter Overend Watts were schoolfriends who'd been playing together since 1962. Lead guitarist Mick Ralphs was the brilliant young instrumentalist who forced Watts to pick up a bass instead; vocalist Stan Tippins was the wild frontman whose formative idol, Johnny Kidd, was never far from the musical surface; and organist Terence Verden Allen was a man who conjured wild Welsh nightmares from behind the organ in a then-unknown Jimmy Cliff's band – into which first Ralphs, and then Griffin, gently drifted. Together, they were bravely going nowhere and, despite regular name changes, slowly falling apart.

All five musicians were casting around for another opportunity. Griffin was offered the drum seat in Dave Edmunds' Love Sculpture, but turned it down to stay with his friends. Ralphs was arranging auditions with every band that needed a guitarist – Cartoone, managed by future Led Zeppelin heavyweight Peter Grant, was one. And Pete Watts spent a month in Italy, the Doc Thomas group's happiest hunting ground, planning a supergroup with the leader of local heroes I Giganti.

He came home when that fell apart, and headed straight down to London to try out with the recently shattered Free. And though he didn't get the job, he did find a soul mate.

Producer Guy Stevens is one of the unsung heroes of British rock. No matter that his legend today is as large as his ego was back then – 'There are only two Phil Spectors,' he famously remarked, 'and I'm one of them'; no matter that Stevens' pioneering role in the development of ska and R&B in Britain is a matter of public record; no matter that without him the magnificent eccentricity of the original Island Records would never have left the starting blocks. Stevens' greatest contribution to music was his absolute refusal to let 'the bastards' grind him down.

Interviewed in 1980, shortly after producing the Clash's landmark 'London Calling' album, that was Stevens' primary topic of conversation, the blinding brilliance of the musical path he mapped out for the bands he recorded, and the obstacles placed in his path by 'the bastards'. The fact the musicians themselves fell into this bag as often as anybody else did not seem to phase him in the slightest.

Free – 'I wanted them to conquer the world. All they wanted to do was kill each other.'

Mighty Baby – 'I saw them as Britain's answer to San Francisco. And if I could have got them out of the pub, they might have been.'

And Mott the Hoople – just for a moment, his eyes misted over at the thought of the ones that got away. And then he caught himself and let out a triumphant snarl. 'They were the worst ones of the lot. They wanted to kill each other, and *then* go down the pub.'

It was Stevens, however, who saw in Pete Watts the suggestion of a magic which needed to be teased out on its own terms. There was no point, Stevens knew, in grafting him onto Free, because the bassist had a dream and Free would simply be a job. Neither, once Stevens met Mick Ralphs, could he see any point in separating the two of them. As instinctively as everything else he did, Stevens perceived the chemistry between the musicians and when he heard that they had a band of their own he suggested they keep in touch. Then he suggested they find a new vocalist.

For Stevens, the defining moment in his relationship with this tenacious provincial outfit was not their music, but guitarist Ralphs' refusal to be messed about. The Silence, as the group was currently known, had recently recorded a demo tape, headed by the allegedly brilliant 'The Rebel'. But they'd mailed it out to a string of labels and were rejected by every one. Finally, Ralphs decided to deliver it to Island Records in person and drove down to London.

'I went to their office in Oxford Street and sat

there and waited, and in the end I got so frustrated I burst into Guy Stevens' office. "Listen! I've driven all the way down from Hereford and I'm pissed off that no-one takes any notice." And he says, "I like it. I like your attitude".'

The band continued to impress. At the audition, Verden Allen personally carried his Hammond organ up the stairs to the rehearsal room and Stevens was impressed. 'Anyone who carts that bloody big thing up the stairs deserves a record deal.' And once the band started to play, and the neighbours began to complain about the noise, that was it. Stevens, who thrived on confrontation and ruffled feathers, offered the Silence a deal on two conditions – one, they changed their name; and two, they changed their singer. Unhappy but unable to resist, the band agreed. Stan Tippins would become Mott the Hoople's road manager for the remainder of their career.

Like the band he was about to be grafted onto, Ian Hunter Patterson had spent much of the Sixties' going nowhere in a succession of guises. Born in Oswestry, Wales, raised in Hamilton, Scotland but latterly based in Northampton, England, his best-known band was the Apex R'n'B All Stars, a long-running local act with whom he played rhythm guitar, 'danced like an idiot' and possibly made his recording debut.

In 1964, the All Stars recorded a four-track EP for the local John Lever label (Lever was the band's drummer), but Hunter swears he cannot remember if he actually appeared on it or not. Music, after all, was never more than a hobby at this time; the All Stars paid few of his bills, particularly after he married and had two children. So he worked by day, gigged at night and tried to make ends meet in any way he could.

Leaving the All-Stars, Hunter's next band was Hurricane Henry and the Shriekers, best remembered today for featuring pianist Freddie 'Fingers' Lee – himself fresh from a glittering career fronting Screaming Lord Sutch's Savages. Lee joined the band in 1965, bringing with him his own record deal, but again Hunter is unsure whether or not he actually got to play on any of the pianist's singles.

In 1967, Hunter and his family moved to London and the singer soon became a familiar sight recording demos at Regent Sound Studios in Denmark Street. This led to a job as a staff songwriter at the publishing house Francis, Day and Hunter (no relation), while Hunter also reunited with Freddie Lee in a new band, At Last the 1958 Rock and Roll Show.

This time he did remember making a record; in fact, their first single, 'I Can't Drive'/'Working On The Railroad' (CBS 3349) was followed by a name change to Charlie Woolfe and a second release, 'Dance Dance Dance'/'Home' (NEMS 56-3675), quickly followed.

But neither release did anything, and soon Hunter and 1958 Show guitarist Miller Anderson were working the session circuit, backing faded rockers like Billy Fury and Mike Berry; auditioning unsuccessfully for the future

Gary Glitter's club band, and so on.

Hunter was also in line for a berth in the New Yardbirds, a group being planned by the original band's last manager, Mickie Most, to compete with a similarly named project being designed by guitarist Jimmy Page. Neither would really get underway (although Page's lot didn't do badly under another name) and Hunter returned to his job in publishing and his hobby at the demo studio.

It was while he was at the office one day, 5 June 1969, that Hunter received a phone call from Bill Farley of Regent Sound Studios. Guy Stevens was at the studio auditioning pianist/singers for a new band, the Silence, and getting absolutely nowhere. Farley thought Hunter would be ideal for the gig, and finally persuaded him to catch a bus to the studio and see what he thought. Hunter ran through a version of Dylan's 'Like A Rolling Stone' and, in the absence of worthwhile competition from any of the other auditioning aspirants, Stevens knew the band had no choice.

According to Watts, 'Guy was standing behind Ian pulling these horrific faces and giving the thumbs down and going, "crap, crap". Then Ian would sing a good bit, and he'd go "not bad, not bad". I could hardly keep a straight face. We didn't know which way to look. Ian wasn't a very good singer, but there was something there. After Ian had gone, Guy said "Look, that last bloke. Shall we get him in for a couple of weeks? Just so we can show we've got a group, and if somebody better turns up we'll get them in instead."'

Hunter was given the job in a phone call from Stevens a few days later. What he didn't get was his new bandmates' respect. 'I think the verdict was, we can't find anyone else, so let's try him for a few weeks,' Hunter agreed, going on to recall band meetings and rehearsals at Islington's Pied Bull pub where nobody even spoke to him. 'I think they were missing Stan Tippins. Yet Stan was the only one who would speak to me.'

Slowly, however, the mood lightened as Hunter showed what he was capable of, and Stevens' own manic enthusiasm cut through any remaining ice. The producer renamed the band – he toyed with Savage Rose and Fixable for a while, but finally settled upon Mott the Hoople from a novel by American author Willard Manus.

That task out of the way, he then renamed the band members. Michael Geoffrey Ralphs escaped unscathed, for reasons which probably aren't too hard to discern. But Ian Hunter Patterson was shorn of his surname, Allen and Watts were deprived of their first names; and poor Dale Griffin lost every name he owned, and was rechristened with a nickname he thought he'd shed years before. 'Buffin' dated back to a childhood cold, one which kept his nose running for what seemed like an eternity. For a time, his friends referred to him as a little sniffing bugger, then somebody spoonerised it and he became the Little Snigger Buffin. Now he was Buffin again.

Signing his new charges to Island Records, Stevens lost no time in ushering them into the recording studio in late June 1969. The way he saw it, there were two courses open to the band, the Dylanish angle that Hunter encapsulated and the semi-soft rock that was the band's stock in trade. Stevens being Stevens, however, he wanted to take both courses at once, simply to see what would happen.

According to Ralphs, 'Guy envisaged us as

being Bob Dylan's band and Ian being Dylan, that kind of electric folk thing. He encouraged us to work along those lines rather than the lengthy progressive stuff we'd been doing before.'

He was also skilled, Ralphs continues, 'at getting the most out of people in an unconventional way.' Discussing songwriting with Hunter, Stevens suggested playing a record backwards, to see what came of it – famously, Jimi Hendrix's 'Voodoo Chile' was created when the guitarist turned Cream's 'Sunshine Of Your Love' on its head. Hunter tried the same thing with Dion's 'Your Own Backyard', and ended up with 'Half Moon Bay'. ('Backyard' itself would resurface, the correct way round this time, on Mott the Hoople's fourth album, 'Brain Capers'.)

Ralphs goes on, 'We'd go into the studio, get drunk, have a huge meal sent in at great expense, all before we'd play a note. Then he'd say, "Right, let's wreck the studio." And we'd knock a few chairs over, and then we'd play.' Mott the Hoople's first album would reflect this attitude perfectly.

'Guy wasn't the slightest bit interested in production,' Hunter later said. 'He was called a producer, but people found out to their cost that he wasn't when they tried to emulate us later on. Guy would talk and talk and run around the studio. That was his game, because when you actually got to play, it'd come bursting out from his annoying you. He got you on the edge. [But] his talent was invisible, and it frustrated the shit out of him. He could also be destructive. I don't like Chris Blackwell of Island Records much, but you have to respect him because nobody else would have put up with Guy Stevens.'

The late-1969 release of 'Mott The Hoople' (Island ILPS 9108) was rewarded with a deserved, albeit lowly, chart placing – in May 1970, it breached the UK chart at Number 66, as Mott the Hoople set about establishing themselves amongst the hardest-gigging bands in the country. (An accompanying single, 'Rock'n'Roll Queen'/'Road To Birmingham' – Island WIP 6072 – did nothing.)

Mott the Hoople made their live debut in the Doc Thomas Group's old stamping ground of Italy, with a week-long residency at the Bat Caverna in Riccione in August. The following month, shows opening for Island labelmates King Crimson and Free were sandwiched in-between a show at the Chalk Farm Roundhouse in London and a couple of grammar-school gymnasium gigs.

They hit youth clubs, tiny clubs, anywhere that would book them, opening for anyone who asked, from Taste, Quintessence and the Liverpool Scene, to such forgotten names as Phineas Fogg, Castle Farm and My Cake. They simply didn't care who the competition was because once they'd taken the stage there wasn't anyone around who could touch them. And they blazed, through 20-minute renditions of 'You Really Got Me', 15-minute jams through 'Half Moon Bay'. 'We never used to move on stage,' Hunter once mused. 'Just in time to the music. There was never any flamboyance about it. And then "You Really Got Me" started to get more and more mad, and then we started leaping about. If [the audience] were losing control, why shouldn't we?'

It was a hectic schedule, but it paid off. On 29 May 1970, Mott the Hoople opened their first American tour in Detroit, less than nine months after they'd formed, proof of Island's conviction that Mott the Hoople's live success couldn't help but translate into record sales. And America could offer the highest record sales in the world. All a band had to do was go out there and find them.

It was to be a long tour, and a bizarre one. Mott the Hoople were not scheduled to return home until mid-July, and their itinerary boiled over with peculiar couplings. Quicksilver, Ten Years After, Mountain, Jethro Tull, Procol Harum, Traffic and BB King would all have the dubious pleasure of an opening set from these fiery unknowns, but it was the Kinks who made the biggest impression on the group.

Mott the Hoople shared the bill with Ray Davies and co on two occasions, two nights in Philadelphia, and two more in Port Chester, and 'You Really Got Me' was a highlight of both band's shows. The biggest difference was that Mott the Hoople got to play their one first, and of course Ray Davies was none too happy about that. 'We're going to end with a medley,' he told audiences, 'so Mott the Hoople can figure out which song to nick next.'

In fact, Mott the Hoople had no need for his

songs, or anybody else's. Their second album, 'Mad Shadows' (Island ILPS 9119) exploded out of a hard-rock sound which had barely been hinted at over the course of 'Mott The Hoople', beginning with what had already established itself as the band's live statement of intent, the appropriately thunderous 'Thunderbuck Ram' – a Mick Ralphs composition that remains quintessential Mott the Hoople. '["Thunderbuck Ram"] was a song with no title,' Overend Watts recalled. 'We found the name scrawled on as toilet wall in the Pied Bull, and it seemed perfect for the track. I think it was the name of a group. Guy Stevens heard it and he went pots over [it]. He thought it was great.'

Like its predecessor, 'Mad Shadows' would be a minor UK hit, coming to rest at Number 48 that autumn (1971). 'It's very introspective,' Hunter told *Disc And Music Echo*, 'not contrived, but that's how we all felt at the time. We were in this peculiar mood, and we went into the studio with the numbers, but no lyrics written. They just came as we recorded. It rather frightens us now.'

'Guy was giving us speed to keep us awake,' Overend Watts later revealed. 'Instead of recording, we'd have 12 hours sitting in the studio control room, talking.' And when they were recording, things did not always go as the band members would have preferred.

'Guy went purely by feel,' Watts continued. 'On "Walking With A Mountain", at one point Buffin breaks a stick and misses a beat. We said "We'll have to redo that, Guy, he's missed a beat." But Guy said, "No, no, it's fucking amazing as it is." And of course, every time you listen to it that mistake just gets bigger and in the end you can't bear to hear it any more.'

Unquestionably, Mott the Hoople were unhappy with the situation. They appreciated what Stevens had done for them, and they were well aware of how much they meant to him. But he was unstable, volatile; another musician who worked with him, years later, described him as 'the original mad, bad and dangerous to know.' Mott the Hoople were finding that out the hard way.

The end came in a heated exchange over the band's next move. Stevens wanted a live album, recorded in Croydon in September 1970, using the Who's mobile. Since released as 'Fairfield Hall Live 1970' (Angel Air), it captures the band in full flight, from the tumultuous opening 'Ohio', all ragged guitars and Verden Allen's foreboding organ, through a dynamite 'Rock'n'Roll Queen' and three slabs from the then-forthcoming 'Mad Shadows' and on to the closing oldies, 'Keep A-Knockin'' and 'You Really Got Me'. Alongside the Fillmore tapes recorded in the US earlier in the year, the true magic of the original Mott the Hoople was unleashed, a rock band that could have redefined 'rock' if only more breaks had gone their way.

Mott the Hoople, on the other hand, had set their hearts on an album that reflected the lighter side of the band, with songs like Ralphs' 'Wrong Side Of The River' already in place. They argued, they cajoled and, finally, Verden Allen snapped and broke a copy of 'Mad Shadows' in half in front of Stevens' astonished face.

The producer walked one way, the band walked another, and within two months of 'Mad Shadows' hitting the store, Mott the Hoople returned to the studio to record another album. And this time they would produce themselves.

It wasn't their smartest idea. 'We didn't understand the techniques of a studio,' Hunter later admitted. 'If something [went] wrong, we just had to cope.' But still, they created a remarkable record. 'I don't know what path our next album will take,' Hunter admitted as the sessions progressed. 'When we've been mucking about recently, we've been playing country music. So who knows?' What he was certain about was the fact that 'Wildlife' would emerge the polar opposite of its predecessor.

Where 'Mad Shadows' raged, 'Wildlife' (Island ILPS 9144) whispered; where 'Mad Shadows' stormed, 'Wildlife' sighed. And where 'Mad Shadows' eventually imploded with all the force of a rogue supernova, Wildlife looked abroad for its cacophonous finale, a raucous 10 minutes worth of 'Keep A-Knockin'' salvaged from Guy Stevens' projected live album.

'After the debacle of "Mad Shadows",' Hunter explained, 'I think it was Ralphs, the voice of reason, who suggested we do some nice songs.' Ralphs himself continued: 'Nice is a horrible word, but it is a nice album. We needed that to survive. And it was the first time that the band got a say in what went on. On the previous two, we were just told what to do.'

For all its understatement and softness, 'Wildlife' is the album where Mott the Hoople came of age, the one where Ian Hunter finally shed his lyrical self-consciousness. Ralphs' songs were the ones which grabbed your attention first, the lazy LA nightlife put-down of 'Whisky Women' (originally, if inexplicably, titled 'Brain Haulage'); the grown-up-wrong whine of 'Wrong Side Of The River'.

But Hunter's were the ones that hit home the hardest; the aching 'Waterlow', the haunted 'Angel Of Eighth Avenue', and the bitter 'Original Mixed Up Kid', 'probably one of the best songs I ever wrote,' Hunter later reflected. 'There were some very truthful songs on "Wildlife."'

'Wildlife' should have broken Mott the Hoople wide open. Island, however, barely gave its contents a second glance. Since the rush of wild enthusiasm which accompanied those early live successes, the company had now settled into the belief that that was all Mott the Hoople were – a live band. Their records were simply a sideshow to that attraction.

So while 'Wildlife' crept to a quiet Number 44 (total worldwide sales barely topped 14,000), the band returned to what they knew – the road, and what Buffin once eloquently described as 'an endless whirlwind of sweaty, jam-packed gigs the length and breadth of the British Isles, with increasingly large crowds of dancing dervishes, leaping, raging, wilding-out and passing-out. Through late 1969, 1970-71, we all but wore our own grooves in the British motorway system.'

Fitting the broadcasts in amongst the live shows, the band recorded its second BBC radio session on 8 March, this time for DJ Mike Harding. 'Keep A-Knockin'', 'Angel Of Eighth Avenue', 'Original Mixed Up Kid' and 'Whisky Women' all received airings, the latter pair being reprised the following month when Mott the Hoople recorded a session for TV's *Disco Two.*

There was a couple more days in the studio as well, recording a clutch of songs which would either make it out on subsequent singles ('The Debt', Neil Young's 'Downtown'), or else be forgotten until sundry future archive searches uncovered them (a cover of the Cliff Richard hit 'It'll Be Me', Ralphs' beautiful 'Until I'm Gone', Mountain's 'Long Red' and an early version of the future classic 'One Of The Boys'). And then it was back to America for a return engagement with the Kinks.

Mott the Hoople's second US tour was considerably shorter – and, without Stevens in tow, considerably more dignified – than their first. Still, the band was faced with some queer couplings; aside from the Kinks, they would also open for Emerson Lake and Palmer, Jethro Tull and Brownsville Station, although the highlight was the four nights they spent supporting Albert and Freddie King at the Fillmore West. Bill Graham's august venue had welcomed Mott the Hoople with open arms the previous year, and were delighted to see them return. Mott the Hoople responded with the kind of shows they always dreamed of delivering.

It was during this latest American sojourn that the band hatched one of their oddest ever ideas. Away from the naysayers at Island Records, they wanted to record a single, and that was fair enough. It was the fact that they wanted to record it with – Shadow Morton, a man whose studio mystique allegedly made Guy Stevens look like an open book – which raised eyebrows. That, and the fact that they didn't actually have a song for him to produce.

No matter! According to Hunter, the moment Morton had an opening in his schedule. 'We got on a plane and went straight to Long Island to record this thing I wrote on a bog in New York. We rammed through it, all out of tune, but we needed a single. It had a catchy "na na na" bit, so we thought it was commercial.' And once they'd changed its name, from 'The Hooker' to 'Midnight Lady (The Road To Rome)', it was.

Steve Marriott, in town with Humble Pie, was roped in for some backing vocals, and the moment Mott the Hoople returned to England they were anxious to show off their wares. 'Midnight Lady' was one of three songs recorded for a *Sounds Of The Seventies* session on 6 July, going out alongside 'Angel Of Eighth Avenue' and a cover of Dylan's 'Like A Rolling Stone'; it was encored when the band played a live show for Emperor Rosko's show 11 days later; and it remained a vital part of the set throughout a summer of touring. Island scheduled it for release in July 1971, and a live recording included on the 'All The Young Dudes' boxed set captures the mood of excitement that surrounded the record's first days on sale.

Despite influential BBC DJ Tony Blackburn claiming that he would shoot himself if 'Midnight Lady'/'The Debt' (Island WIP 6105) was a hit, Hunter told a devoted Birmingham audience 'It's doing well, it should go in [the chart] next week.' It was no surprise whatsoever, then, when the BBC invited Mott the Hoople to appear on *Top Of The Pops,* that most vital final step on the road to chart fame and glory.

The broadcast was 21 July 1971. 'And the day after the show aired,' Buffin sighed later, 'the single stopped selling.' And that was such a remarkable feat, he continued, that 'this should be in the *Guinness Book Of Records.*'

Meanwhile, Mott the Hoople were also celebrating their second anniversary, at the Royal Albert Hall on 8 July 1971. With the show sold out weeks in advance, the band spent some time deliberating over precisely what nature it should take. 'Wildlife', after all, had earned some phenomenal reviews, and in the weeks leading up to the gig, Mott the Hoople seriously considered recreating the entire record on stage, bringing in the London Symphony Orchestra to handle the lusher passages. 'We could have done it and got good reviews for it,' Hunter swore.

'But how can you kick three thousand kids in the head?'

So, rock'n'roll it was, and by the time the group took the stage the stately home of an eternity's worth of classical promenades was packed to the rafters and roaring like an express train, not from the polite applause of an appreciative audience but with the sound of the venue's hallowed seats being torn from the ground and cast into corners, a makeshift dancefloor for the wildest crowd the venue's security had ever seen.

Concrete floors cracked, a ceiling collapsed under the weight of partying fans, exclusive boxes were wrecked and two actually collapsed. Just to add insult to injury, when the show overran the venue started charging the band overtime.

Mott the Hoople were slapped with a lifetime ban from the Royal Albert Hall; rock'n'roll itself was outlawed for a long time. It was a national outrage, these long-haired rockers who descended like locusts onto the Holiest of Holies and stripped it like locusts. And Mott the Hoople were left to ponder the irony of being able to fill one of the greatest venues in England and not sell enough records to even pay for the damage.

The group consoled itself on the road. Through the rest of July, they toured alongside the Sutherland Brothers and Quiver; in August, they were a welcome addition to the Weeley Festival bill, terrifying the born-again teenyboppers pouring out to welcome T Rex and the Faces and the following month came close to blowing the Who offstage when the two bands played together at London's Oval cricket ground.

In the studio, however, matters continued lurching from bad to worse. Although much of the material was in place, work on the band's self-produced fourth album stalled in record time.

The very nature of the songs – dark, tumultuous numbers which were as different to 'Wildlife's West Coast pastorals as they were to 'Mad Shadows' biting rock – required more than Mott the Hoople themselves could give. Though one genuine masterpiece was completed, a sensational version of Hunter's epic 'The Journey', cuts like 'Mental Train' and 'How Long?' just didn't work. There was only one solution. They would have to bring back Guy Stevens.

But Stevens wasn't so easily brought back. Mott the Hoople had hurt him, and though he knew – and they knew – that the two were made for one other, he wanted to see them squirm. He would produce their new album, but he wanted £1,000 upfront for his troubles. Mott the Hoople paid up.

'Island weren't too flush with the money because we weren't doing well in terms of sales,' Ian Hunter later reflected, which is why just five days in September were deemed sufficient time in which to record the album; five days which began with Stevens and engineer Andy Johns turning up at the Basing Street studio on the first day dressed as highwaymen and armed with water pistols. Johns set the recording levels, Stevens told the band to start playing, then he and Johns pursued one another around the building with their weapons. The tape just kept on running.

'Guy went out into the lobby at Island and tore down all the framed album covers,' Watts recalled. 'He'd pick up something like King Crimson and smash it on the floor. "Fucking King Crimson," he'd be going. "They're shit. Mott the Hoople's the biggest band in the world".'

The studio looked like a bomb had hit it. Furniture was embedded in the walls, great blobs of tomato ketchup oozed from every surface. According to one legend, Stevens walked into the studio at one point and announced things just weren't sounding as good as they could. 'What we need,' he said, looking around the control room, and pausing while the band tried to second-guess his technical requirements, 'is to catch the place on fire.'

Then he piled up the chairs, desks and amplifiers, drenched them in even more ketchup and set them alight. The following day, when Island chief Chris Blackwell arrived, he took one look at the carnage and demanded to know what had happened. As sweetly as he could, Stevens explained, 'we were recording, and it got a bit out of hand.' Blackwell looked unconvinced. 'Did you get any tracks done?'

'Yeah, five.'

'Oh, well that's not so bad, is it?' And Blackwell left the room, while the band simply sat around, watching in stunned amazement.

'It was all done for a purpose,' Hunter explained later. 'We were getting complacent. I don't know if people understand, but if you are a band like us a lot of the adrenalin is set off by the audience. When you are in a studio, it's a very barren sort of atmosphere and it's hard to get the substitute – to get the same kind of adrenaline into your body.

'You have to get yourself into a kind of rage. Some people get stoned, some get drunk. We smashed a few things about.' And while he admitted that 'the thought of wrecking a studio seems rather stupid, I can assure you we were pretty dead when we went in there, and five days later we were really excited.'

The sessions blazed on through what Ian Hunter later called 'three days of madness, done very quickly'. Song titles were changed – 'Mental Train' became 'The Moon Upstairs', 'How Long' was reworked first, as 'A Duck Can Swim With Me', and then as 'Death May Be Your Santa Claus'; the album itself came perilously close to being titled 'AC/DC' before Stevens hit upon the far more suitable 'Brain Capers' (Island ILPS 9178).

Cover versions were experimented with, then either dropped or utterly rearranged – the Youngblood's 'Darkness Darkness' had been an integral part of Mott the Hoople's live set back in 1969 and Guy Stevens had always loved it. Verden Allen, on the other hand, hadn't, and protested its reappearance by refusing to play on the session. It didn't matter – even as a four-piece, Mott the Hoople steamrollered the song.

The intensity of the music, the intensity of the sessions – there simply was no way 'Brain Capers' could ever emerge as even a vaguely commercial entity, and Mott the Hoople knew it. So, of course, did Guy Stevens; indeed, there was a creeping suspicion that he had planned it that way from the start. Despite Chris Blackwell's long-time indulgence of his resident genius, there were clear signs the maverick producer's time with Island Records was growing short, and that is exactly how it turned out.

'Brain Capers', one final act of deranged genius, an album of such sonic dementia that it was unlikely it would ever be topped, would be his farewell to the company he had nursed through infancy. Stevens would leave Island Records for a staff position at Warners in Los Angeles around the same time as Mott the Hoople themselves quit the label. A decade later, on 29 August 1981, he overdosed on the prescription medicine he was taking to combat his alcohol dependency. Just 38 years old, Guy Stevens would never catch another studio on fire.

Despite advance orders of eight thousand, the best Mott the Hoople had ever achieved, 'Brain Capers' was a no-hoper from the start. So was the band's next single, an uninspired version of Neil Young's 'Downtown'/'Home Is Where I Want To Be' (Island WIP 6112). By the time labelmate Steve Winwood wrote a song called 'Low Spark Of High Heeled Boys', and the word went around that he was mocking Mott the Hoople, the band could sink no lower.

The group's latest tour ended in late November 1971, but of course they'd be back on the road again in the new year, around the UK through January and February, across to Switzerland in March, then back around Britain in April. All they had to do was grit their teeth and keep on keeping on.

But that, it seemed, was something they just weren't going to be able to do. Hunter explained the band's predicament. 'My mate Miller Anderson was in Keef Hartley's band at that time and they were slipping because they'd never had hit records, [although] they'd had a lot of people go to see them, and now we were in the same situation. Everywhere we went we sold out, but we knew it took hit records to sustain that attention; we knew it'd just fall off without a hit. So it was really worrying. We were trying to do it and we really didn't know how.

'The strange thing was, we were making money on the records, we weren't doing as badly as people thought. They didn't chart, but they kept selling. We were losing money on the live gigs because we had all these ideas of what we wanted to do and it cost so much, so we were losing money there. And because Island had us for publishing, agency, management, we couldn't get any money because the money we were losing live they were rolling over to the records. I got a cheque one morning for ten grand for the records, and it was cancelled about two hours later by the gig section of Island to go against that debt. So the records were doing well. It was the gigs – which were selling out – which were costing the money.'

The end of Mott the Hoople came in Switzerland, slogging around a hastily arranged circuit while back home Island Records despatched terse reminders of the group's failure. Cut back on the lighting, cut back on the PA; oh, and we've got you a gig tomorrow night in a converted gas holder in Zurich. It was there, on 26 March 1972, that Mott the Hoople broke up.

'Somebody played a wrong note,' Buffin recalled, 'there was a push and a shove, nothing very much, but a bit of snarling, followed by "There's better things to do in life than play fucking gigs in places like this." So it was decided, "That's it. We'll flounce off and not be a group any more."'

The following day, the five band members went to the pictures to see a John Wayne film. They were – a month's worth of outstanding commitments around the UK notwithstanding – finally free.

'We got home,' Overend Watts recalled, 'and I thought, "Well, it's all over now, what do I do?" So I rang David Bowie.'

This was not such a momentous event as it sounds. In the spring of 1972, Bowie was barely even as well known as Mott the Hoople, a one-hit wonder from three years before who'd had a few nice reviews for his last album, 'Hunky Dory'. Ziggy Stardom would be hitting hard and fast within the next few weeks, but when he picked up the phone to Watts he was no-one.

But he'd sent the band a demo a year or so before and, although Mott the Hoople just couldn't imagine themselves ever wanting to actually record 'Suffragette City', Watts wanted to thank him for the thought, tell him the news about the band's sad demise 'and ask him if he knew of any jobs going anywhere. We got talking for an hour, an hour and a half, and I was telling him about the group. He said, "Look, I've got a song I've half-written, let me ring you back in an hour or two, I have to speak to my manager."

'He rang back and asked if I'd like to go and listen to the song. I said I didn't know how the rest of the group would feel, but I'd come over. In fact, he came and picked me up in a battered old Jag. He was nervous to meet me, and I was nervous to meet him. We went round to [manager] Tony Defries' place in Chelsea, and David played part of "All The Young Dudes" on acoustic guitar. He'd got all the chorus words, he hadn't got some of the verse words, but you could tell it was a great song.'

From Defries' Gunter Grove house, the party moved on to an art exhibition and then to the Inn on the Park for a meal. Watts himself wasn't quite sure what was going on, Defries barely said a word all evening and the bassist got the distinct impression that he wasn't particularly interested in any of it. But once they sat down to dinner, Defries started talking. 'He was saying things like "What are we going to do with my new group?" and "We'll get you off Island Records for a start."

'I came home and phoned the rest of the lads and asked them if they wanted to hear the song. We still had some gigs to fulfil, so we hadn't actually broken up, and when they heard the song they thought it was amazing. David came to see us at Guildford Civic Hall [on 9 April], met everyone, and we fixed up a recording date. We came off Island and were suddenly on CBS. David was going to produce our album. Tony Defries had fixed it up, and said not to worry. It was a new lease of life.'

'All The Young Dudes', Mott the Hoople's first single for CBS, was released on 28 July 1972, and it was apparent from the moment Mick Ralphs' guitar chimed in the opening refrain that this was the perfect song for the summer. It crashed to Number 3 on the chart and Glam Rock had the only anthem it ever really needed.

July 1972 – Lynsey de Paul: Sugar Me/Storm In A Teacup (MAM 81)

Ultra-glamorous, blonde and beautiful, the erstwhile Lynsey Monckton Rubin 'studied textile design in college. And played classical piano – Bach, Chopin. But I had this job designing album covers for contemporary music. I had to listen to the records, and I thought when I played them, "I can write music as good as that".'

She could, too. In January 1972, the Fortunes took her 'Storm In A Teacup' to Number 7, and Rubin – now working under the name Lynsey de Paul – found herself offered a gig as a professional songwriter for a princely £20 a week. She accepted. 'I was living in a little flat and needed the money badly. It looked like a windfall to me then.'

A solo deal further sweetened the package, all the more so after the oddly-contagious and super-seductive 'Sugar Me' became her first hit that summer, climbing to Number 5. 'Getting A Drag/'Brandy' (MAM 88) followed in December, and de Paul continued scoring hits into the mid-decade.

Glam by nature, rather than design, de Paul never truly took advantage of her standing. Rather, she turned her attention to her sometimes co-writer Barry Green and the career that he would ignite as Barry Blue. She also penned further hits (or thereabouts) for Thunderthighs, Lena Zavaroni, Dana, Heatwave, Tony Blackburn and the Dooleys.

14/15 July 1972 – King's Cross: centre of the universe

Why did MainMan sign the Stooges? To keep David Bowie happy, of course. He'd been a fan for the band since his first visit to America in February 1971 – visiting a California radio station, the DJ asked if there was any record he'd like to hear. Bowie was just reaching for the Velvet Underground's final LP, 'Loaded', when the journalist who was accompanying him on the jaunt passed him the Stooges debut instead. 'Try this.'

Bowie was sold and, long before he actually met Iggy, in New York in September 1971, he was singing their praises to anyone and everyone, playing their two LPs ceaselessly and boning up on the legend of the Pop.

A man who poured molten wax on his bare flesh on stage.

A man who smeared his body in peanut butter.

A man whose loathing for humanity appeared to be topped only by his loathing for himself.

In September 1971, on the night that he met Lou Reed, Bowie also met Iggy Pop. But whereas Reed had a record deal, management and a career, all Iggy had was his reputation. Even his band had split.

MainMan to the rescue. They relocated the singer and guitarist James Williamson to London; paid for remaining Stooges Ron and Scott Asheton to join them, and now Bowie was promising to produce an album for them.

They turned him down.

The Stooges would play just two live shows

during their 18 months as MainMan artists; one in Detroit in early 1973, and one in London. Tonight.

MainMan were pulling out all the stops. On 14 June, Lou Reed was making his full London concert debut at the King's Cross Cinema in London. The following evening, Iggy and the Stooges would be making theirs. In-between times, David Bowie was playing Aylesbury Friars, with MainMan laying on coaches for journalists who wanted to hit all three.

Reed first. With only a totally unrepresentative solo album to show for the two years since the Velvets broke up, he was very much an unknown quality, and he revelled in that knowledge. Backed by the Tots, a new band formed especially for the touring he was about to commence, he took the stage a little after midnight and zeroed straight into 'White Light White Heat'.

The band was loose, the edges were rough, but Reed didn't care, deliberately messing with the timings to throw his under-rehearsed band further off their stride but maintaining perfect control. And if 'Rock And Roll' and 'New Age' received louder roars than 'Heroin', that just showed how much easier it was to find 'Loaded' in a British record store than any of the records that preceded it.

Either way, the Stooges would really need to be good to best Lou, and they were. This was the night that Mick Jones, later of the Clash, eulogised as 'the full-on quality of the Stooges was great, like flame

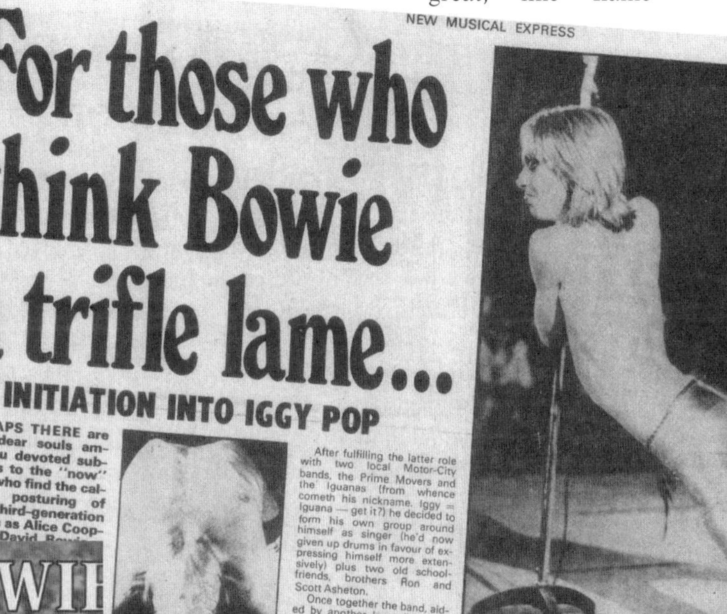

Page 28

NEW MUSICAL EXPRESS

For those who think Bowie a trifle lame...

AN INITIATION INTO IGGY POP

PERHAPS THERE are some dear souls among you devoted subscribers to the "now" scene who find the calculated posturing of such third-generation delights as Alice Cooper and David Bowie

studies in favour of finding the essence of "real black blues" in the gutters of Chicago.

Befriended by Sam Lay, the drummer responsible for making those great early Paul Butterfield sides even greater, he quickly built up a reputation for being a pretty nifty drummer himself.

After fulfilling the latter role with two local Motor-City bands, the Prime Movers and the Iguanas (from whence cometh his nickname, Iggy = Iguana — get it?) he decided to form his own group around himself as singer (he'd now given up drums in favour of expressing himself more extensively) plus two old school-friends, brothers Ron and Scott Asheton.

Once together the band, aided by another Iggy discovery, Dave Alexander, gained a definite measure of notoriety around the Ann Arbor district of Michigan.

The music wasn't just bad, it was downright offensive, while Iggy Stooge's movements struck fear and loathing into the hearts of all who failed to share our hero's concept of having a little fun.

Young girls could be seen running screaming from Stooges gigs, their eyes temporarily blinded by the sight of Iggy's deranged pout, their necks a mess of bites and scratches from attacks by the man unleashed.

Make no mistake, Iggy was a great performer — and an artist. While everyone from Mick Jagger down was stealing ideas on how to move from other performers, Iggy just worked out all his own gestures and took it from there.

Specialities in his act were back-bends, amazing acrobatic feats using the microphone stand, and some more involved and complex routines such as crawling like a lizard with infinite speed and precision around the stage and auditorium.

Then there were his direct assaults on the audience, such as reverso-rape which consisted of the incomparable Mr. Stooge provoking a member of the audience to attack him.

Iggy's whole act was based on the fact that he was bored to tears by everything going on around him. The Stooges were just four middle-class brats weened on the American way of life by their school-teacher parents.

Psychoanalysts would probably describe them as being a fine example of the new breed of spiritually-retarded youth, but to Iggy and the boys it was just a case of having to go to extremes in order to kicks.

Their first album, re Elecktra and produced Cale, is perhaps the f ample of pure punk-r to be recorded, captu actly what it's like to b hung-up horny and y this day and age.

The lyrics were of pu simplicity, the music v mal and stark to the p total banality: in other w great rock n' roll album.

As 1970 progresse band began to get really Iggy was now injuring regularly on stage, in broken ribs from his m spired moments, while s ing glass into chest or els ing candle-wax down his

His notoriety had s much further, having bee ed the world's sexiest m some girlie teen mag as w being No. 1 pin-up bo "Gay Power" and the ettes, the San Francisco drag theatre act.

The second Stooges al "Fun House", is the epi of joyful teenage debauc as wild as anything Reed could ever muster.

However, the band's ch life-style was not designe longevity. Problems not un nected with drug-addic were constantly appear Iggy became so sick he o vomited over the first row Ungano's in New York and band more or less broke up er their equipment van hi bridge scattering amplifi guitars and band members o the freeway.

For about six months, Ig spent his time at home with

throwers!' The night that Iggy thrashed out the rhythm of a song by shaking a fan by the head. The night he leaped into a girl's lap, then stared into her eyes while he sang into her face. The night the Stooges wore make-up for the first time.

And the night that photographer Mick Rock caught the defining image of Iggy, a waist-upwards portrait of him leaning on his mikestand, his face set and beautiful, staring into space. Pop later claimed he hated it.

But he hated everything about London by that point, including MainMan's continued insistence that the Stooges cut a record that might stand a chance of being a hit. Because that would mean letting Bowie produce it, and the Stooges wanted to do it themselves.

So they waited until he was out of the country, touring the US in September 1972, before entering the studio to lay down an album that has since been described as one of the most important bursts of noise ever recorded.

23 July 1972 – Eleven Plus: Marc Bolan

Russell Harty: 'Do you ever wake up in the middle of the night and think, "In another twenty or thirty years, I'm going to be 50 or 60. What shall I be doing?"'

Marc Bolan: 'I never think of that.'

RH: 'It doesn't haunt you?'

MB: 'I don't think I'll live that long.'

Bumping into *Eleven Plus* host Russell Harty in a restaurant the previous weekend, Bolan agreed to appear on the following week's show for a mildly confrontational discussion on the nature of stardom, privilege and the nature of being a rock'n'roll star – which Bolan promptly subverts by handing the question over to the audience.

It's not one of Marc's greatest interviews, or the oft-fascinating Harty's finest hour. But it's still great fun to see.

Russell Harty: 'Is your mum watching you tonight?'

Marc Bolan: 'No, she's watching *you.*'

July 1972 – Iron Cross: Little Bit O' Soul/ Sunshine (Spark SRL 1079)

Fronted by the gravel-voiced Dave Hill and Alan Saunders, Stoke on Trent's Iron Cross were Spark labelmates of Stavely Makepeace whose Nigel Fletcher and Rob Woodward produced three tracks with them at Southern Music Studios in London.

One of these, 'Sunshine', became the band's first B-side (the flip was handled by Barry Kingston) but was mysteriously credited to Fletcher alone. 'We can only put that down to the fact that my name was written first on the master-tape box. In fact both of us should have been credited.' Let the record be straightened here.

Fletcher continues: 'All of Dave and Alan's band had rich Stoke on Trent accents and they made us laugh with a book called *Half A Toe Crate In Staffordshire*. Which means "'How to talk right in Staffordshire"'

A second Iron Cross single, 'Everybody Rock On'/'All Of The Time' (Spark SRL 1112) followed in 1974.

July 1972 – Top Of The Pops Volume 25 (Hallmark SHM 795)

Some *Top Of The Pops* albums so perfectly encapsulate the moment they were recorded that it's like having your own private time machine. Others, though laden down with rubbish you wish you could forget, nevertheless remind you why you stopped buying records that month. It is rare, however, for any one to come along that leaves you scratching your head, asking 'Why don't I remember?' – especially when the year in question is 1972, and you've spent your entire life recalling that as the year when Glam Rock came of age.

Donny and David were inevitable, of course. Did a week go by in the Western world when one or both weren't somewhere near the top? And there's David Bowie's 'Starman' (a dreadful version, by the way, lacking all of the promise and magic of the man) to nail the chronology into place.

But when you recall a July 1972 Top Forty that included (deep breath) Slade, Gary Glitter, the Sweet, Alice Cooper, Hawkwind, T Rex, the Kinks, Free, Wings and B Bumble and the Stingers (eh?), it is an alternate universe indeed that would select Dr Hook, Johnny Nash, Scott English, Bruce Ruffin and *The Godfather* as a representative sampling of what the top pops really sounded like.

ON THE RADIO
3-7 July 1972: Alan Freeman: Slade, David Bowie
10-14 July 1972 – Johnnie Walker: David Bowie
17-21 July 1972 – Johnnie Walker: Slade
ON THE BOX
6 July 1972 – Top Of The Pops: The Sweet, Gary Glitter, David Bowie
13 July 1972 – Top Of The Pops: Alice Cooper
15 July 1972 – It's Lulu, Not To Mention Dudley Moore: Slade
20 July 1972 – Alice Cooper, David Bowie, Gary Glitter
27 July 1972 – Top Of The Pops: Alice Cooper
ON THE SHELVES
July 1972 – Wig Wam: Have A Cup Of Tea/Naughty Naughty (RCA 2243)

August 1972 – Slade: Mama Weer All Crazee Now/Man Who Speeks Evil (Polydor 2058274)

Noddy's in checks and a mirrored top hat, Dave's in a jacket made from what look like CDs and Jim and Don are as casual as you could look with bandmates like that. And that's before they even start playing.

Slade's third British chart-topper was the first tune Jim Lea ever wrote completely alone, and it could probably have gone anywhere from there. But Noddy already had the germ of a lyric. Standing on the stage after a London show and surveying the mounds of smashed seating left in the auditorium, 'I thought, "Christ, everyone must have been crazy tonight".'

'My My We're All Crazy Now' followed, before manager Chas Chandler changed the title a little and the band's traditions demanded the spelling be amended. Whatever. A full-on adrenaline monster, ear-splittingly loud with its lyrics a raw-throated bellow, the opening howl was recorded while Noddy warmed up his voice with some exercises; the closing 'Mama mama mama yeah' was made up on the spot and the rest was pure mania, spontaneous and controlled in equalled measure.

And the best was still to come. 'Mama Weer All Crazee Now' entered the chart at Number 2, behind Rod Stewart's 'You Wear It Well', then stayed at Number 1 for three weeks. Who did you say was crazee?

5 August 1972 – The London Rock and Roll Revival Show, Wembley

The first live concert ever to be staged at Wembley Stadium, the London Rock and Roll Revival Show was described, and is remembered, as a gathering of aged fossils. A decade had elapsed since most of the headliners meant very much; the Beat Boom of the Sixties may have still worshipped at the feet of Chuck Berry, Jerry Lee Lewis and Little Richard but to the average record buyer of 1972 they were old hat.

Bo Diddley? Bill Haley and the Comets? The movie that was made of the afternoon, Peter Clifton's *London Rock And Roll Show,* was almost relentlessly Jurassic in its adherence to the dinosaurs. Forget the movie's non-inclusion of the great Billy Fury. Where were the cameras when Gary Glitter was playing? Were the film crew on their tea break when Roy Wood's Wizzard came out to play?

In short months to come, and for several years thereafter, it became very clear indeed that the children of Glam Rock were as indebted to the Fifties as any of their older brothers might have been; that Glitter and Wood were indeed merely the first stirrings of a hybrid that rewired past rebellions into something new and exciting.

Forget Showaddywaddy, Mud and the Glam-Rock Presley-people. Shakin' Stevens stepped out of the early-Seventies ferment, as did Darts and

Chris Spedding. Malcolm McLaren built his empire around the revival, opening his Let It Rock store on the dog's-leg of King's Road, and clothing a succession of future retro-Teddy Boy types. The same Teds who celebrated the sight of their idols at Wembley by booing Little Richard and then beating the crap out of one another. Good times.

An interesting point, though. No matter how sad and ancient they might have looked on stage, it's worth remembering that Haley, Chuck and Diddley were still only in their mid forties, Lewis was only 37, and the one British talent to make it onto the movie, former Joe Meek protégé Heinz, was a baby-faced 29. The same age as Gary Glitter.

And it was Heinz, although he could not have known it, who also flagged a little piece of rock's future in his set. His backing band was a newly launched Canvey Island outfit called Dr Feelgood, the group destined to grant greatness to the still incipient Pub Rock movement. You probably wouldn't know it from the length of their hair, though.

August 1972: Smooth Loser sessions, Strawberry Studios

Smooth Loser was the latest project for Chris Gibbons and Jeff Pasternak, the son of American actor Joe and brother of popular Radio 1 disc jockey Mike (Emperor Rosko to his fans). Former members of the late-Sixties club band Krayon Angels, and the grandiose Bastardo Jones, they were fresh from cutting an ultimately unreleased album with the London Philharmonic Orchestra. Now they wanted a rock band. A hot rock band.

Recruiting American guitarist Danny Adler, newly arrived in the UK after a stint with New York's Elephant's Memory, Smooth Loser's first studio sessions in April 1971 caught them in full proto-glam mode, cutting 'Rainbow Horsemen' and 'You Said It Would Be' for a projected single (the sessioneer rhythm section of Brian Hodges and Barry DeSouza completed the line up).

The single never happened but, with a permanent line-up completed by Paul Huggette, Tony Lester and former Gentle Giant drummer Malcolm Mortimer, the Bristol-based Smooth Loser gigged constantly, opening for acts as diverse as Arthur Brown, Nektar and Roland Kirk.

Another studio visit in late 1971 saw the band lay down an embryonic version of Adler's later classic 'Cincinnati Fatback', at this point called 'Mr Fatback'. The group did find regular work accompanying Rosko on his roadshow tours, however, with the entire line-up resplendent in the latest Glam fashions... Adler cringingly recalls a trip to Kensington Market producing 'green platform boots, a bright red crushed velvet suit and a purple fishnet shirt that I wore with it. I had no colour sense at all.'

And Smooth Loser had no lucky breaks. Their final session, unreleased like its predecessors, took them to Stockport to record three songs with Graham Gouldman, including Adler's 'Water'. But in November 1972, Smooth Loser conceded defeat. Adler quit and, weeks later, was debuting a new band, Roogalator, at a Marquee Club talent night and preparing to join the Pub Rock boom.

August 1972 – Lieutenant Pigeon: Mouldy Old Dough/The Villain (Decca F13278)

Reactivating 'Mouldy Old Dough' following its chart-topping success in Belgium, Decca intended that this time everybody would pay attention, especially if they listened to Fab 208, Radio Luxembourg.

Three 'power plays' per night for six long summer weeks was not a cheap proposition. But it was money well spent. Entering the chart in September, a month after its re-release, 'Mouldy Old Dough' reigned undisputed for a month, repelling David Cassidy, 10cc and T Rex in the process.

In fairness, there was nothing Glam about Lieutenant Pigeon and, in any other era, the band would have been regarded as little more than a pop novelty act. But context is everything and, hearing 'Mouldy Old Dough' amid a run of other period pounders, it doesn't sound at all out of place.

Woodward: 'We felt at that time a fair contingent of the image was synonymous with gaudy make-up and somewhat '"camp"' posturing. Stavely Makepeace sat okay with Glam Rock, but retained the meaty and masculine persona more associated with the Fifties and Sixties. The image of Lieutenant Pigeon was also well in line with it, but the musical inspirations were etched from the likes of Jerry Lee Lewis and Little Richard's pounding style.

'Over the years, the general reactions to Pigeon music hit the extremes of either loving it or detesting it. We have lived with this reaction in terms of the fact that both Nigel and I prefer the music to be noticed even if slightly controversial! We are never afraid to push the boundaries. I believe it was an American record producer who exclaimed, "The worst thing you can say about a piece of music is that it's very nice!" I can never remember anybody making bland comments about either of our bands!'

Neither, although the group's subsequent chart history might convince you otherwise, was 'Mouldy Old Dough' the beginning and the end of the Pigeon's good ideas. And that despite their every song apparently revolving around yet another variation of the same drum/whistle/piano routine, punctuated by a gruff, growling hookline.

The throaty indolence of 'Desperate Dan' (Decca F13365) proved an adequate follow-up in December 1972 when it reached Number 17; later, the Jimmy Castor Bunch-meets-'Ain't That A Shame' surrealism of 'And The Fun Goes On' (Decca F13403), the locomotive breath of 'If Julia Sees Her' (from the 'Mouldy Old Music' album (Decca SKL 5154) and the Australian smash 'I'll Take You Home Again Kathleen' (F13486) all pack the same punch as the smash, a good-time packed-up party vibe that clashes mutant Gary Glitter with an album-long 'Neanderthal Man' and doesn't care how sick you get of stamping along.

August 1972 – Mott the Hoople: All The Young Dudes (CBS 65184)

'When I first saw [Mott],' David Bowie enthused, 'I couldn't believe a band so full of integrity and a really naive exuberance could command such an enormous following and not be talked about.'

He wrote them a single, then agreed to produce an LP, and admitted that he was fully expecting to have to nursemaid the band through the entire record, 'contribute a lot of material. Now they're in a wave of optimism, and they've written [almost] everything on the LP.'

Back in January, the band started demoing new material at Basing Street studios, and a couple of these songs were dusted off for a second look – 'Ride On The Sun' (now renamed 'Sea Diver', and gifted with a fabulous Mick Ronson string arrangement) and 'Black Scorpio' ('Momma's Little Jewel').

The year-old 'One Of The Boys' followed them in, and for a while, according to Hunter, Bowie thought it ought to be the band's first single. 'I said, "You've got to be fucking joking!",' Hunter recollected, but while the song ended up a mere B-side in Britain it became the follow-up to 'All The Young Dudes' in America.

New songs, too, were bursting through; the malignant 'Sucker', Verden Allen's grinding 'Soft Ground', Mick Ralphs' 'Ready For Love'/'After Lights' showcase, the impenetrably riff-heavy 'Jerkin' Crocus', the jokey 'Henry And The H-Bombs' and a cover of Lou Reed's 'Sweet Jane' that caused Hunter so many vocal problems that Reed himself dropped by the studio to lay a guide vocal down over Mott the Hoople's backing track.

'Before we teamed up with Bowie, we were all a bit thick,' Hunter confessed. 'We didn't understand the techniques of the studio. [But] this time, we were working with someone who had this basic knowledge, and could tell the engineers exactly what he wanted.'

The album's eventual peak of Number 21 was somewhat disappointing, but compared to what Mott the Hoople were used to it was a mega-smash. And, while there was little doubt that its success was in no small way attributable to Mott the Hoople's association with Bowie – who himself had broken through in a very big way that same summer – 'All The Young Dudes' really was not that far removed from the Mott the Hoople of old.

Of course it missed Guy Stevens' hand at the helm, but what it lacked in mad abandon it gained in cohesion and discipline; the pure timing of the band's emergence would do the rest.

It was with great reluctance, of course, that Mott the Hoople felt themselves being squeezed into the Glam bag. With the exception of Overend Watts, who had always boasted a sartorial flair to match his flamboyant name, the rest of the group were (as Buffin once delightfully put it) 'hoary old bastards' who really did not fit in with the air of studied androgyny and camp that was the new movement's favourite party trick. But they succumbed anyway, and while their old underground following burned its denim jackets in protest, furious that good ol' Mott the 'Oople had sold out to the painted Lucifer of Bowie and bubblegum, the band started plotting its follow-up single, another Bowie composition called 'Drive In Saturday'.

August 1972 – Roxy Music: Virginia Plain/The Numberer (Island WIP 6144)

'Seeing is believing where Roxy Music are concerned.' declared the boys' adventure magazine *Target* in January 1973. 'When "Virginia Plain" first bombarded the ears of the world's pop public, most of us probably thought "Well, okay! That's a masterpiece of electrical excellence, but can they make a noise like that outside a 16-track recording studio?"'

Yes, that's *exactly* what we thought.

But it didn't stop 'Virginia Plain' from shooting straight into the Top Five, its success so sudden that, by the time Roxy Music came to support first Alice Cooper at Wembley and then David Bowie at the Rainbow Theatre they might well have been even bigger than either of the headliners. 'Virginia Plain' remains one of the most memorable singles of an already overly memorable year, three minutes of wordplay and riffing that starts out with an orgasm and keeps getting better.

The song had its roots in Bryan Ferry's training as an art student; one of his paintings, of Warhol superstar Baby Jane Holzer modelling a pack of cigarettes, shared the same title. The lyric, meanwhile, was a pun-packed and utterly fascinating fantasy about life in New York City. Every line is eminently quotable ('just like flamingos look the same'), every chord is exquisitely placed. So, it came as something of a shock to discover that the whole thing was all but unpremeditated.

'The song came together quickly,' guitarist Phil Manzanera, recalls. 'We started with chords, no top-lines or anything. Bryan wrote the top-line without anybody having any idea what the song was about.' He also admits that he has never been able to duplicate the solo which explodes from the middle of the song; 'I just went "blam!"'

ON THE RADIO
1 August 1972 – Sounds Of The Seventies: Roxy Music
ON THE BOX
3 August 1972 – Top Of The Pops: Mott the Hoople
10 August 1972 – Top Of The Pops: Blackfoot Sue, Mott the Hoople, Alice Cooper
17 August 1972 – Top Of The Pops: Blackfoot Sue, Alice Cooper, Lynsey de Paul
24 August 1972 – Top Of The Pops: Roxy Music, Mott the Hoople, Slade, Alice Cooper
31 August 1972 – Top Of The Pops: Blackfoot Sue, Elton John, Roxy Music
ON THE SHELVES
August 1972 – Elton John: Honky Cat/Lady Samantha/It's Me That You Need (DJM 269)

September 1972 – T Rex: Children Of The Revolution/Jitterbug Love/Sunken Rags (T Rex MARC 2)

Recorded in August 1972, a none-too-convincing 'revolution in the streets' type lyric pinned to a none-too-original heavy metal melody, 'Children Of The Revolution' certainly packed a visceral punch with a lumbering two-chord intro that is worth its weight in gold. But it was considerably more style than substance, at a time when Bolan's manifold challengers were seeking the slightest sign that the world was tiring of the hot goblin.

They found it here. Kept off the top of the chart by David Cassidy and Lieutenant Pigeon, anybody researching the moment when Marc Bolan's hitherto iron-clad grip on the hearts and minds of his audience began to slip needs look no further. Not only did 'Children Of The Revolution' stall at Number 2, it also suggested that his once intuitive understanding of pop dynamics was beginning to falter.

Dig deep, however, and 'Children Of The Revolution' offers several valuable insights into Bolan's future intentions, not least of all the distinctly R&B-inflected backing vocals that float behind the song's hard-rocking immediacy. It would be interesting to discover where that led.

September 1972 – Pop printed pillowcases

The golden age of teenybop marketing kicks in, with the arrival (in the pages of *Disco 45*) of 'pop printed pillowcases. The pillowcases are really groovy and you can have either Marc Bolan, Donny Osmond or David Cassidy printed on them – or one of each! Did you ever think you would be that close to your dream?'

September 1972 – David Bowie: John I'm Only Dancing/Hang On To Yourself (RCA 2263)

Accompanied by a promo film shot (by photographer Mick Rock) during rehearsals for Bowie's August 1972 shows at the London Rainbow, with dancer Lindsay Kemp's troupe of fishnet-clad space mutants clambering around the elaborate stage, 'John I'm Only Dancing' was, according to Bowie, a simple message from one gay guy to another – 'I'm *dancing* with a girl, but that's all we're doing.'

A curiously understated song, it nevertheless followed 'Starman' into the chart, albeit peaking two places lower at Number 12, and consolidated Bowie's breakthrough better than almost anything else could. The fact that it wasn't culled from the album was a plus as well, the assumption being that already he was trailing his next LP. In fact, a punchier version cut during the sessions for that set, 'Aladdin Sane', with Ronson's guitar sublimating the original's sax, was ultimately omitted and only saw release when RCA, replenishing their stock of the original 45, utilised the later master instead.

September 1972 – Bay City Rollers: Manana/ Because I Love You (Bell 1262)

The Bay City Rollers' link with Jonathan King was sundered once it became apparent that there was no viable follow-up to 'Keep On Dancing' on hand. But Bell Records, with whom King had placed the group, showed more faith and, by summer 1972, the Bay City Rollers were working with another established hit-making team, Ken Howard and Alan Blaikley, the erstwhile brains behind Dave Dee, Dozy, Beaky, Mick and Tich.

'Manana', the first record under this new regime, did little in Britain, but sent the Rollers' stock soaring elsewhere. A hit throughout western Europe, it topped the chart in Israel and would eventually be voted Best Song in Radio Luxembourg's 1972 Grand Prix Song Contest.

September 1972 – Cabaret – London premiere

Its timing could not have been better.

Cabaret, Joe Masteroff's musical adaptation of English author Christopher Isherwood's memoir of pre-Nazi Germany, *Goodbye To Berlin*, opened on New York's Broadway in November 1966 with actress Jill Haworth as the transplanted American nightclub singer Sally Bowles, Joel Grey as the saucy, leering master of ceremonies and Brecht legend Lotte Lenya as Bowles' once-glamorous landlady Fraulein Schneider.

Within two years, it had transferred to the Broadway Theatre where it ran for another 12 months, by which time Judi Dench had made the Sally Bowles role her own at London's Palace Theatre. David Bowie caught at least one performance and later acknowledged borrowing the show's stark lighting effects for his own show.

But he – and many others – borrowed much more than that.

Director Bob Fosse's movie version of the musical premiered in New York in February 1972, with Liza Minnelli dazzling as Bowles, Michael York as Christopher and Grey returning as the emcee. An immediate hit in America, *Cabaret* was nevertheless received essentially as simply a souvenir of a smash hit musical, alive with toe-tapping songs and a shocking sexual subtext.

In the UK, however, its Technicolor rendering of the monochromatic decadence, struggle and irrational hopefulness that tints Isherwood's original novella fell upon soil that Bowie, as Ziggy, had already cultivated, and which the remainder of the Glam Rock pack was very quick to harvest.

For, within the realms that lay between music and movie, there lay an understanding, and a longing, that drove straight into the libido of a generation.

It was the mood of the film that mattered, the sense of living life on a knife-edge of vicarious thrill-seeking; of co-existing with mundanity even as you swept it from your sight. That was what caught the imagination; the glamour of the performers, the make-up, the glitter and the ever-pulsating undercurrent of sexuality that left its promises strewn throughout the film, and then exploded in a moment of delicious dénouement, somewhere ahead of the film's actual conclusion.

An exasperated Sally, sick of fighting against Christopher's attempts to domesticate her and convince her to shed her nightclub regalia of feathers, corset and boots, admits that she has fucked Max, a militaristic mutual friend.

'So have I,' replies Christopher softly.

The look on Sally's face when he says it is what Glam Rock was all about.

Surprisingly, in the light of just how much else was taken from *Cabaret*, only one of its songs.' Tomorrow Belongs To Me', ever made it into the Glam repertoire when the Sensational Alex Harvey Band adopted it as the title track to their first Top Ten LP in 1975.

'Cabaret' itself remains Liza Minnelli's personal theme song...but imagine what the 'Human Menagerie'-era Cockney Rebel might have made of it.

September 1972: Gary Glitter – I Didn't Know I Loved You (Till I Saw You Rock'n'Roll)'/Hard On Me (Bell 1259)

While Leander, Eddie Seago and solicitor Ray Brown busied themselves forming the management company that would oversee Gary Glitter's career, Rock Artistes Management (RAM), Glitter got on with the career itself.

'Rock And Roll' was barely out of the chart before the follow-up was unleashed and, aside from the fact that it had a longer title, 'I Didn't Know I Loved You (Till I Saw You Rock'n'Roll)' is all but the twin of its predecessor.

It's a little more lyrical, maybe, but it's no less primeval, its beat a Neanderthal thump and the guitars and sax an echo-laden leviathan, painstakingly riffing their way towards the inevitable (but always so gratifying) chants of 'hey' that punctuate verse and chorus alike.

None of which could stop it racing into the Top Five, of course, but it did give Glitter's critics something else to grumble about. In fact, 'I Didn't Know I Loved You' effortlessly confirmed the singer's ascendancy, and that in itself was a remarkable feat because Bell label head Dick Leahy had opposed its release.

Glitter had recently cut a cover of Dion's 'The Wanderer', and Leahy was convinced it had 'hit' written all over it. Glitter, however, would not budge. '"I Didn't Know I Loved You" was recorded at the same time as Mike was mixing "Rock And Roll",' Glitter explained. 'We had the flow going, it had the same vibe. We had found something unique – [a sound] that, even today, is second only to the Rolling Stones as rock's most easily identifiable sound. And we knew we could write more of it.'

The new single was debuted on *Top Of The Pops* on 21 September.

September 1972 – Geordie: Don't Do That/Francis Was A Rocker (Regal Zonophone 3067)

It's sad to think that Geordie have been relegated to little more than a bit part in the AC/DC story (vocalist Brian Johnson replaced the late Bon Scott in 1980); sad because, in their prime, they were at least as good as the Aussie rockers and a signal influence on them as well.

They were certainly a far cry from the handful of nowhere pub bands, and a schoolboy group which played Beatles covers that the histories now seem to treat them as, and they scored more Top Ten hits than the Australians. Not many people realise that.

Geordie developed out of USA, a Newcastle rock band formed by bassist Tom Hill with drummer Brian Gibson and guitarist Vic Malcolm from the Influence, a local act whose past membership also included Roxy Music's Paul Thompson.

They changed their name to Geordie shortly after Johnson joined in February 1972, around the same time as they signed with Red Bus Management. A deal with Regal Zonophone followed and, that autumn, Geordie tore down from the frozen north and demanded 'Don't Do That'.

They were a raucous bunch. No matter that the band members hailed from the same neck of the woods as Bryan Ferry and spoke with the same kind of accent. Flat caps, big boots and broadly belted blues, Geordie were the antithesis of all that was cool, calm and sophisticated in Glam. A few critics tried to compare them to Slade, and that sort of worked, but only in the same way as the early Pretty Things could be compared to the Stones.

Slade were loud, Geordie were louder.

Slade looked rough, Geordie looked rougher. And while Slade camouflaged their savagery beneath silks and silly hats, Geordie packed the same flared trousers you might have bought from Millets, the kind of stacked heels that you'd pick up on the high street, armless tunics, colourful vests, and could probably drink the whole band beneath the table.

Meaty fists pummelled the air. Drums drove tanks across shell-pocked muddy fields. Guitars scythed out of the sky like bombers, and a blitzkrieg bass completed the analogy. Then Johnson opened his mouth to sing with a range, a pitch and, most of all, a volume that exceeded simple pop stardom.

If Geordie had any rivals, it was Nazareth, the similarly blues-based Scots quartet who emerged on the chart scene just five months after 'Don't Do That'. But whereas Nazareth never ventured any deeper into Glammy pastures than Dan McCafferty's taste in tank tops, Geordie felt like the real thing. For a while, anyway.

16 September 1972 – Rock at the Oval

One of the largest outdoor events staged in London at that point, Rock at the Oval (London's Kennington cricket ground) served as a reminder to Britain's underground rock community that not everything was spangles and sequins.

Hawkwind, still riding their 'Silver Machine' round the chart, were the headliners. Jeff Beck was playing his first UK gig in more than two years, with his new buddies Carmine Appice and Tim Bogert; Frank Zappa was there with a 20-piece jazz orchestra. And squashed down at the bottom of the bill, with Quiver, Sam Apple Pie and the still little-known Man, a band called Biggles, of whom big things were expected.

Managed by impresario Rikki Farr, Biggles were – according to Ronnie Thomas, bassist with another band in the Farr stable, Heaven – a lot like Emerson Lake and Palmer; with Palmer's brother Steve as their drummer, did they have a choice? Their vocalist was Gary Holton, doyen of the drama-school degenerates who so brightly coloured the London underground at the very dawn of the decade. 'We'd smoke dope and watch Gary rehearse with them,' Thomas recalled. 'Caterwauling above all this synchronised jazz-rock. He was a complete looner.'

Holton's path into Biggles was unconventional, to say the least. 'I did opera for about two years, believe it or not, just small parts in Sadler's Wells productions. Then I decided I wanted to act, so I did a course at the National Theatre for three years. In the end I got thrown out of the course – for reasons I won't go into – and over a period of time I got chucked out of almost every other school possible. Then I saw this ad in one of the music papers, saying "Rock singer wanted..."' Biggles' backers were not skinflints. 'A fortune was spent on that band, it really was,' Holton recalled, including what all witnesses recall as a huge advance from an interested record label, none of which was spent on recording.

He got a terrific wardrobe out of it, though.

September 1972 – 10cc: Donna/Hot Sun Rock (UK 6)

By early 1972, Strawberry Studios was churning out so much material that its resident quartet – Lol Creme, Kevin Godley, Eric Stewart and Graham Gouldman – barely had time to consider their personal musical plans. They were too busy dealing with everybody else's.

The Scaffold, Mary Hopkin, Barclay James Harvest, Tony Christie, Shep's Banjo Band, Elias Hulk and the Fourmost (who cut a version of 'Maxwell's Silver Hammer' under the guise of Format) all passed through the doors in the first years of the new decade.

'Everything was pop, pop and more pop, with boozy northern showbiz thrown in for good measure,' laughs Godley. 'Anything vaguely artistic or experimental was disguised as 'novelty' and shoehorned invisibly into whatever came in the door. I think the key difference between most seminal production units and ourselves was this weird non-rock learning curve and a perverse policy to tackle any track, however dumb and outlandish. We recorded football teams, stand-ups, jingles, dancers, prancers, muggers, buggers queens, fairies, dopers, junkies, sick, venal. Someday a real rain will come...etc, etc.'

One particularly memorable session, he says, came with the call to cut a single with a local ventriloquist. 'I don't remember how many vocal takes it took before we realised the dummy didn't

ALICE COOPER COLOUR POSTER INSIDE

MUSIC IS THE MESSAGE

sounds

EXCLUSIVE

ZAPPA ROCKS BACK AT THE OVAL

CAT'S NEW ALBUM

ROXY— OSE OF ENO

RORY HAVING A BALL

CRAZEE SLADE! page ten

FRANK ZAPPA is to make an exclusive British appearance at next month's Oval rock concert, promoters Ron and Ray Foulk announced this week.

BANNED

CAPACITY

have to be there and it wouldn't actually matter if we saw the guy's lips move.

'It was an extraordinary time. It's just that Strawberry wasn't a place for "real" bands to record, at least not at first, and we found that frustrating. The vibe was more *Broadway Danny Rose* than rock'n'roll. Many weird and wonderful local acts passed through Strawberry's portals back then, plus the occasional genius (Peter Cowap) and the four of us using downtime to road test-our own ideas.'

The Strawberry team played on Solomon King's version of Lynsey de Paul's 'When You Gotta Go'. Dave Berry, Wayne Fontana and Mike Timoney, a virtuoso on the accordion, all recorded with them, Peter Cowap teamed up with Gouldman to cut a trio of singles for Pye, the Herman-less Hermits cut around 50 tracks over the course of a year, while the Hermit-less Herman, Peter Noone, also recorded a single with Gouldman, one of several sessions Mickie Most's RAK label sent Strawberry's way.

'At that period of time, Strawberry Studios was doing everything and anything,' says Gouldman, 'and it also was providing work for myself, Eric, and Kev and Lol as session musicians – we were the house band.'

Comedians, nightclub acts, you name it, Strawberry would record it, but the real money-spinner came from sport. In British chart terms, it was the age of the football (soccer) record – teams of sportsmen trooping into a studio to lend their often dubious vocal talents to their team's song.

Strawberry Studios would be responsible for many of these, including several big hits; Leeds United's imaginatively titled 'Leeds United' breached the British Top Ten, while both of Manchester's professional teams, United ('Willie Morgan On The Wing') and City ('The Boys in Blue') enjoyed Strawberry's services, with the former, an ode to one of the side's most gifted players, even earning a cover version by the Ted Taylor Orchestra.

'We did the football things,' Gouldman recalls. 'It was business for the studio. That was our attitude, and at the same time we were doing an album with Neil Sedaka, or an album with Ramases, and I think it showed we could turn our hands to anything – in other words, there were no depths to which we would not sink.'

Of all these projects, Ramases' 'Space Hymns' remains a genuine favourite. Ramases himself believed he was the reincarnation of the Egyptian pharaoh of the same name. 'It was great,' and Gouldman enthuses, 'a really fine album to make. We would sit down on the floor with acoustic guitars, that kind of vibe, very hippy and mystical.'

Released on Vertigo, in the days when its label design really could induce that feeling, 'Space Hymns' apparently did very well in Holland, but in terms of really putting Strawberry on the map, the most notable sessions were those with veteran rocker Neil Sedaka.

Sedaka had been drawn to Strawberry first after hearing Crazy Elephant's 'There Ain't No Umbopo', and then when Tony Christie recorded Sedaka's 'Is This The Way To Amarillo' at the studio and gave the songwriter his first hit in years. Sedaka would record two albums, 'Solitaire' and 'The Tra La Days Are Over', at Strawberry, a combination that gave his career a new lease of life with a return to both the UK and US charts.

Despite all this activity, however, the team were not neglecting their own musical ambitions, no matter how hard-pressed they were to find time for them. Early in 1972, Gouldman got together with producer Eric Woolfson (later a member of the Alan Parsons Project, and later still an aspiring solo artist whose 1990 album would feature contributions from Eric Stewart), to record a solo single, 'Growing Older'/'Nowhere To Go' (CBS 7739).

It was followed by a group decision that, while session work was all well and good, it was not making any of them feel particularly fulfilled. There and then, Gouldman remembers, they made a pact. They wanted to create 'something good and lasting.'

Godley: 'Ramases and Neil Sedaka were definite high points because they were album projects and gave us relief from the lunacy and solid opportunities to extend ourselves into more genuine experimental areas as in "Space Hymns" or hone our skills playing together as a band, as on both Neil Sedaka albums.'

'It was Neil Sedaka's success that did it, I think,' agrees Gouldman. 'We'd just been accepting any job we were offered and were getting really frustrated. We knew that we were worth more than that, but it needed something to prod us into facing that. We were a bit choked to think that we'd done the whole of Neil's first album with him just for flat session fees when we could have been recording our own material.'

But the previous years had been a valuable experience, as Godley explains. 'We suddenly understood why a studio control room looked like the flight deck of Concorde. The big window with all the flashing lights and buttons were there to take you places, so we set out to take ourselves to as many as possible. We didn't have the expertise or the focus we had later, but the sheer thrill of pushing ourselves and the technology was enough.

'I believe we pretty much learned the basics for everything during those years – CIA: Craft/Inspiration/Accident. Not necessarily in that order, and with a little hashish thrown in to help glue it all apart. It's also that certainty you feel at some point that what you're doing will stand up, and you actually might have something worth saying.

'I'd do it all again in a flash – particularly the ventriloquist.'

The first recording that the four made together, in the spring of 1972, was a Stewart/Gouldman composition, 'Waterfall'. Stewart took an acetate of it with him when he went to Apple studios to master that first Sedaka album, hoping that he could persuade Apple to release it. Months later, he received a rejection slip saying the song wasn't commercial enough to be put out as a single, by which time, Godley and Creme had come up with another song which was.

'Donna', a falsetto-voiced rock'n'roll spoof, was initially intended as a possible B-side to 'Waterfall'. 'But we knew it had something,' Stewart remembered, and with 'Waterfall' having been written off 'Donna' was immediately promoted to the top of the band's pile of potential singles. The trouble was, according to Eric, 'We only knew of one person who was mad enough to release it, and that was Jonathan King.'

The arch entrepreneur of British pop, King had known Eric Stewart since the early Sixties, when the Mindbenders were being followed around the country by a university student who claimed he could make them even bigger than the Beatles. The band laughed him off, 'and the next thing we knew he'd had a hit with "Everyone's Gone To The Moon". We never saw him again.'

Since then, King had gone from strength to bizarre strength. If an annoying novelty record came within even sniffing distance of the charts, King was usually behind it, whether protesting nuclear proliferation (and everything else) behind Hedgehoppers Anonymous, or conjuring up a version of 'Hooked On A Feeling' that was even sillier than Blue Swede's.

Most recently, he had launched his own label, UK, and promptly driven rock purists insane by unleashing Bubblerock, an album that took some of the best-loved songs in rock'n'roll history and did weird things to them. 'Would you believe "Rock Around The Clock Waltz"?' asked the album's liner notes. 'Twist And Shout' with a string quartet...and why had nobody else ever thought of recording 'Mr Tambourine Man' with an orchestra of 15 tambourines?

Stewart called King that same day, and by evening King was on his way to Strawberry. "He listened to "Donna",' Stewart remembered, 'and fell about laughing, saying, "it's fabulous, it's a hit". So we agreed to let him release it on his UK label, and he was right. It was a hit.'

It was King who also supplied the band's name, 10cc; apparently it came to him in a dream. However, a feature on BBC Radio 2 unearthed other accounts of how the name was conceived from Peter Tattershall and Graham Gouldman.

'It was either a very small motorbike,' Tattershall explained, 'or it was the overdose of a heroin addict.' Gouldman countered, 'Mythology has it that the name 10cc came from the average male ejaculation being nine cc, and, of course, being big, butch, Mancunian guys, we're gonna be, y'know, one cc more than that.'

It took Eric Stewart to end the speculation. 'No, the name actually did came from Jonathan King. He said he'd had a dream the night before he came up to Manchester to listen to "Donna". And, he saw a hoarding over Wembley Stadium or Hammersmith Odeon or something like that and said, "10cc: The Best Group in the World". So we said well, that sounds great to us, we'll call ourselves 10cc. And that's how it came about.'

Initial worries that the band would simply be dismissed as another of King's little jokes were dispelled when they appeared on *Top Of The Pops* on 28 September 1972. 'Jonathan said, "You can either go on as you are, or you can wear transparent hotpants",' Kevin Godley remembers. 'I think we probably made the right decision in hindsight, otherwise it would have been hindsight all the way.

'We all recognise now that pop music, rock music, has always had a strong visual component. But we could never have pulled it off. We were who we were. You can't be Glam Rock with a big beard – although it would have been interesting to try. No, we were serious artists, we were boffins, we were studio technicians. We weren't glitterball people. And to a certain extent I'm glad we weren't that way.'

As they walked into the studio, Tony Blackburn (whose choice of 'Donna' as a Pick of the Week had been instrumental in the record's success) greeted them with the words 'Good God, you're normal! What a great gimmick!'

'Donna', backed by the instrumental 'Hot Sun Rock' (based around a track Gouldman had had lying around for several years), reached Number 2 on the British chart; work immediately began on a follow-up.

September 1972 – The Sweet: Wig-Wam Bam/ New York Connection (RCA 2260)

On its way to Number 4, tribal drums, a tomahawk guitar line and a camp retelling of the poet Longfellow's *Hiawatha* epic...it has to be the Sweet. With Steve Priest dressed like an Indian chief.

The Sweet's sixth straight British hit was also the first the band recorded for themselves, and the group's own confidence and abilities shine through all the way. A meaty guitar riff, pounding drums and layered chorale vocals that might have been borrowed from the Turtles but certainly paved the way for Queen.

Another enduring Sweet tradition, a camp one-liner from bassist Steve Priest, also made its debut here – 'try a little touch, try a little too much...' The whole package was irresistible, although an article in *Music Star* asked just how much further they could go. Imagine, journalist Gordon Coxhill asked, how the Inland Revenue would feel 'when [they] come across Sweet's expenses chit, "Four pounds per month per man from the Biba make-up counter"?'

Scandalous!

September 1972 – Shakane: Love Machine/ Mr Jackson (Young Blood YB 1004)

Released in the same breath as the Young Blood label's biggest hit, Python Lee Jackson's 'In A Broken Dream', 'Love Machine' was the third single for a band that had been around since the late Sixties.

Brian Trusler, Adrian Castillo, John Strange and John Phillips were, in fact, already hitmakers in Sweden, after 1971's 'Big Step'/'Rhona' was a smash there; in addition, the band cut two albums for Young Blood, although little that they did can live up to this one. Thanks to 'Velvet Tinmine – 20 Junk Shop Glam Ravers' (RPM 251) for recovering it.

September 1972 – David Bowie US tour

While 'John I'm Only Dancing' battled with the likes of Faron Young, the Drifters and Judge Dread on the singles chart, its maker was on his way to the United States for his first ever full tour. And he was greeted on arrival by a handful of friends – *Pork* veterans Leee Black Childers, Cherry Vanilla and Tony Ingrassia, all recruited by manager Tony Defries to staff the American side of Bowie's management company, MainMan.

'There's an awful lot of assholes in the music business, and the idea of having to hire these people, to work with them, was nauseating,' says Angie Bowie. 'The most sensible thing to do was to hire actors to act the parts.

'Tony Zanetta became Tony's assistant, and within three years he was President of MainMan. That was great! He did it fantastically. He wears suits, he can nod, he's a brilliant actor, a brilliant set designer and a brilliant director. He would set the situation and he would direct the situation, and all the time he'd be acting out the role of President.

'Leee Black Childers had done a lot of press. For Leee to deal with the press, it was a fucking piece of cake. The same for Cherry, who was a writer. That is why MainMan was so successful, because those people did the things the way they had to be done, not the way they'd been done before, not because of 20 years in the music business.'

And the most amazing aspect of the entire scheme is – it worked. By the time Bowie released his next album, spring 1973's 'Aladdin Sane', MainMan and its distinctive logo were as familiar to fans as Ziggy himself.

September 1972 – Chicory Tip: The Future is Past/Big Wheels Rolling (CBS 8094)

With Chicory Tip overcoming the departure of guitarist Rick Foster for Edison Lighthouse, hopes were high for this one, as the band introduced new guitarist Rod Cloutt to their audience.

What audience? The single didn't even sniff the chart.

September 1972 – Top Of The Pops Volume 26 (Hallmark SHM 800)

Glam was a remarkably egalitarian beast, willing to spread its magic as far as its audience wanted it to go. Look back on the era through the plethora of compilations that litter the modern CD shelves, and some almost nightmarish visages leer out at you as virtually anyone who scored a hit between 1972-75 finds themselves tarred with a kohl and blusher-coloured brush.

Such decidedly unglammy creations as Mungo Jerry, the Wombles, Medicine Head and the Electric Light Orchestra (who at least had the decency to wear shiny clothes and tinsel hairpieces) have all come in for such revisionism, and so has Rod Stewart, a gravelly bluesman who made no more concessions to Glam than he could spray paint onto his legs. But listening to 'You Wear It Well' on 'Volume 26', all the old miscalculations come howling back into focus. The aura of the era is that intoxicating.

Elsewhere Lynsey de Paul's 'Sugar Me' may or may not be a riot of sexual innuendo, but vocalist Martha Smith provides a queenly reworking, the violin solo is straight out of Slade, and what is sugar if not Sweet? 'Wig-Wam Bam' might not get past the Political Correctness constables today but remains Britain's greatest-ever contributions to the theme of cowboy rock.

'Standing In The Road' chugs and hisses in all the right places. But if any two songs encapsulate the brilliance of this edition, 'Virginia Plain' (packed with even more Eno-isms than the original) and 'All The Young Dudes', are as anthemic as they ought to be. The dudes carried the news, and 'Top Of The Pops Volume 26' makes sure it stays as fresh as ever.

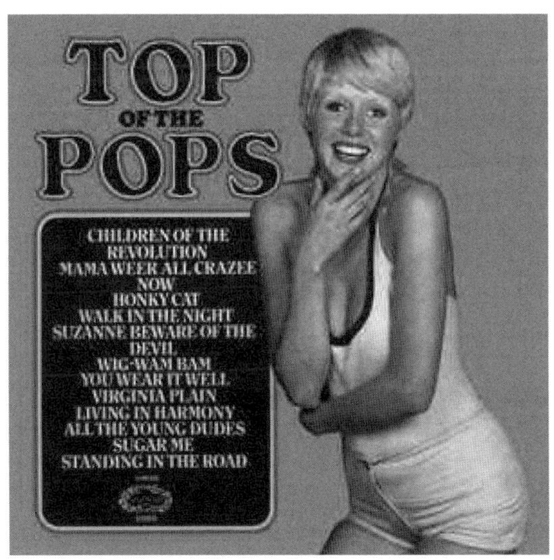

ON THE RADIO
16 September 1972 – In Concert: Roxy Music
18-20 September 1972 – Dave Lee Travis: The Sweet
18-22 September 1972 – Noel Edmonds: Roxy Music, Blackfoot Sue
18-22 September 1972 – Alan Freeman: Slade, Mott the Hoople
30 September 1972 – In Concert: Slade
ON THE BOX
7 September 1972 – Top Of The Pops: Lynsey de Paul, Roxy Music, Slade
14 September 1972 – Top Of The Pops: The Sweet, T Rex, Slade
21 September 1972 – Top Of The Pops: Gary Glitter, David Bowie, T Rex, Lieutenant Pigeon, the Sweet, Slade
28 September 1972 – Top Of The Pops: 10cc, Chicory Tip, David Bowie, Gary Glitter, T Rex

---

October 1972 – Alice Cooper: Elected/Luney Tune (Warners K16214)

And just in case you got to thinking that maybe it was all a con – that maybe Alice really was a beer-drinking, golf-playing vicar's son – wrap your ears around 'Elected'.

The US elections were just around the corner, Richard Nixon running for re-election to the most powerful gig in the world and there was Alice saying he wanted to run too. For the new party, the third party, the *wild* party.

He spoke of people's problems, because he

knew everybody had them, 'and personally, I don't care.'

In other words, the hidden subtext behind every party political bullshit broadcast ever delivered was placed on open display. And the worst thing was, Alice *still* seemed more trustworthy than the goons we wind up giving the job to.

October 1972 – Gary Glitter: Glitter (Bell 216)
Just two singles in, and already Gary Glitter's career was into hyperspace. He was everywhere and everything. Across the 12 months that followed 'Rock And Roll's chart entry, Glitter singles spent a staggering 51 weeks on the chart. His album added another 40 to that tally...which wasn't bad when you consider that it served up little more than a few hit singles ('Rock And Roll', 'I Didn't Know I Loved You'), a few potential hit singles ('Famous Instigator', 'Shakey Sue'), and a lot of old covers disguised as hit singles.

Present in both its vocal and near-instrumental incarnations, 'Rock And Roll' naturally dominates, the irresistible chorale of percussion, grunts and chanting still the sound of Glitter at its most purifying. But glitter-ised versions of 'Ain't That A Shame', 'Baby Please Don't Go' and 'School Day' build towards a crescendo that is delivered, finally, with a delightfully (and deliberately) ham-fisted rendition of 'The Clapping Song'.

There are a couple of sour notes. For all label head Dick Leahy's enthusiasm, 'The Wanderer', in particular, really does wander off the point. But the obvious pleasure with which 'Glitter' was created glistens through every moment.

October 1972 – Stavely Makepeace: 'Slippery Rock 70's'/'Don't Ride A Pillion, Paula' (Spark SRL 1081)
The mighty Makepeace's best-known release was what Rob Woodward recalls as one of their more 'self-indulgent efforts, as it leans towards our favourite feel of music – blues/jazz.

'[Hearing it again] brings back memories of a time when Nigel and myself were constantly experimenting with different sounds, and is synonymous with a period in time when we were extremely busy yielding a constant plethora of recorded output.'

'Slippery Rock 70's' was granted CD immortality following its inclusion on the 'Velvet Tinmine' collection, and Woodward glowed. 'Naturally, we are both extremely pleased that this track was chosen as a part contribution to this profoundly interesting album.' In 2007 it was revisited once more for the *Hot Fuzz* movie soundtrack.

October 1972 – Rodney's English Disco
'Rodney's was really geared to teenagers. They played all the British music that was coming out of England in the early Seventies that the American kids had never heard, because it was all disco in America in the mid Seventies. So I'd go to this club, and all the kids dressed outrageously with huge platform shoes and glitter. Everyone was very androgynous. The boys wore make-up. Everyone was very flamboyant. It was all really cool to me. That's where I was turned on to a lot of Bowie, T Rex, Sweet, Slade and Suzi Quatro. They were great records. They were three-minute songs with big choruses and handclaps and very prominent drums. Not to mention, I got to hear Suzi Quatro.' *Joan Jett*

A long-time fixture on the Los Angeles music scene without ever truly making a name for himself, Rodney Bingenheimer was the Mercury Records publicist assigned to look after David Bowie during the singer's February 1971 visit to the US. Six months later, the roles were reversed as Bowie hosted Bingenheimer in London, providing the visitor with a crash course in the Glam Rock currents that were beginning to sweep the radio waves.

Together the pair would visit the London club scene and marvel as an entire culture, or at least *couture*, sashayed out of the gay bars and into the mainstream, and long before Bingenheimer returned to LA he dreamed of being able to recreate a similar scene there.

He set the wheels in motion in October 1972, partnering with record producer Tom Ayres in the E (for English) Club, opened on the site of an old peepshow theatre on Sunset Boulevard. An audience quickly gathered, especially after word spread that visiting Brits Bowie and Roxy Music had both conferred their approval on the place; by year's end, the club had relocated to larger premises on the Strip and changed its name to the English Disco. A Hollywood legend was born.

The English Disco was *the* home for British Glam in the otherwise hostile United States. Radio never played it, most other clubs ignored it and, at that time, few of the bands were visiting. But Rodney's blasted it out all night, and with the musical liberation there came a host of other freedoms.

As Kim Fowley recalled, 'It was a great playpen for nymphets and older men. Everybody got fucked and sucked. There were great young bodies twisting and sweating in the half-light. People worked at it. It was like a red-light district in one club.'

The Disco oozed style. The long hand-carved wooden bar had, apparently, been imported to Los Angeles by a previous owner, and it dominated the room. Mirrors hung on every surface, even inside the DJ booth. Bright red carpeting gave it the feel of a down-market bordello. The audience did the rest, setting up a solid wall of glitter that kept Rodney's roaring for close to three years – years during which it made an indelible impact upon everyone who visited.

'That was our first taste of David Bowie bisexual glitter stuff,' reflected Joan Jett, one of the club's most loyal denizens. 'You'd get all these 11 to 13 year-olds in the club, dancing and being groupies, There were 11 year-old girls in silver lame miniskirts, dancing around, and all the rock stars – Barry Blue types – would come in and get all these 15 year-olds. It was insane!'

When *Newsweek* magazine descended on the place in January 1974, it noted incredulously: 'The dancefloor is a dizzy kaleidoscope of lamé hotpants, sequined halters, rhinestone-studded cheeks, thrift-store anythings and see-through everythings. During the breaks, 14 year-old girls on six-inch platforms teeter into the back bathrooms to grope with their partners of the moment. Most of the sex is as mixed as the drinks and the drugs the kids bring with them.'

Tony Zanetta, from Bowie's MainMan management company, added his own impressions. 'Nymphet groupies, stars in their tight little world. Some dressed like Shirley Temple; others wore dominatrix outfits or "Hollywood underwear", a knee-length shirt, nylon stockings and garter belts. These star girls streaked their hair chartreuse and like to lift their skirts to display their bare crotches. As they danced they mimed fellatio and cunnilingus in tribute to David's on-stage act of fellatio on Ronno's guitar.'

Some, apparently, didn't even bother miming it.

'It was a place where the kids could go and you could do anything and it was really fun,' Jett continued. 'You know, they never played that kind of music in America. It was the only place you could hear it. It was the only place you could hear all the Sweet, all the Mud, Alvin Stardust, Suzi Quatro, Gary Glitter, I mean, man, that was the only place you could hear that stuff. Even though everyone really liked it. Alvin Stardust, "My Coo Ca Choo". Wow!'

October 1972 – Jook: Alright With Me/Do What You Can (RCA 2279)

Stomping, stamping, crass and crazy, Jook was the brainchild of Marc Bolan's old John's Children bandmate, bassist John Hewlett. He was about to move into management, and it was he who introduced songwriter Ian Kimmet to guitarist Trevor White – the mastermind, two years previously, behind Inigo Jones' 'Noel Highway' Christmas single.

'We hit it off straight away,' remembers White. 'So we packed up our families and went to live in the wilds of Scotland.' They leased neighbouring cottages near Jedburgh, and spent the next nine months earnestly getting their heads together in the country, 'working every day and getting virtually nothing done. In the end, we decided to come back to London.'

Accompanied by a couple of Kimmet's friends from his Scottish homeland, bassist Ian Hampton and drummer Alan Pratt, the band launched into two months of intensive rehearsal, while Hewlett cast around for a deal and a name. He settled on RCA for one and Jook for the other, with the latter derived from what was then his favourite oldie, Gene Chandler's immortal 'Duke Of Earl'. Or so declared another John's Children refugee, Chris Townson, who replaced Pratt shortly after the band signed the record deal.

Jook launched amidst cries of 'There's nothing special about us at all, we just hope someone likes our music.' So did RCA, who apparently grabbed the band on the strength of one audition. For an unknown band, Jook had been signed for a huge fee – £5,000, plus instruments, amps, a PA and a van – and the company was anxious to exploit every possible selling point, including Townson's illustrious past.

Marc Bolan was at his peak, interest in his past was no less fervent and Townson at least shared a few months of that heritage. RCA promptly dubbed Jook 'the Seventies' John's Children', although Townson was swift to shrug it off. 'The only real comparisons were the anti-social attitude and the fact that I didn't like the records we made.'

What, none of them?

'No.'

It's a good job there was only four more to go.

October 1972 – Brian Wells: Paper Party/Just A Summer High (Spark 1082)

A glorious falsetto, a demonic violin – if Sparks had demoed 'Coz I Luv You', they might have reinvented it as this.

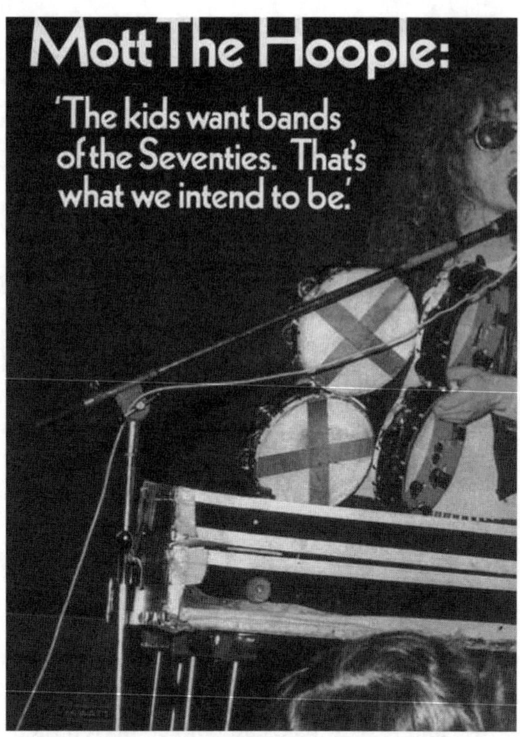

16 October 1972 – Bob Harris Show (BBC): Mott the Hoople

October 1972 – Mott the Hoople: Rock'n'Roll Queen (Island ILPS 9215)

Between February 1970, and October 1972, Mott the Hoople were regular guests at the BBC, recording a slew of sessions that have, for the most part, long since been erased. The bulk of the survivors finally appeared on the 1996 CD 'Original Mixed Up Kids', with the best of them dating from the 'Brain Capers' sessions, and the sound of a band tearing itself apart.

Of course, they didn't tear apart – or rather they did, but only for a couple of days, until David Bowie came along with his tube of 'Dudes'-shaped superglue, and kissed everyone better again. But anybody who believes that Bowie either reinvented or revamped Mott the Hoople needed only to tune in to their final BBC session for fiery versions of 'Ready For Love' (which the BBC's own records strangely retitled 'Ready For Me'), 'Jerkin' Crocus' (similarly mislabelled as 'Jerking Crows'), 'Sweet Jane' and 'One Of The Boys'.

Because any suggestion that Mott the Hoople had somehow been transformed went flying right out of the door. What Bowie did do was catalyse the individual elements which made up the group, exploring avenues opened up by the band's own ideas, but making sure that the band read the signposts as well. All they had to do was remember that they really were as great as he insisted they were.

'The first afternoon we met,' Watts concludes, 'Bowie said to me, "In the Seventies you are going to be enormous."' And it made me feel great, because I thought we were buggered.'

Instead Mott became superstars, Hunter became a demi-God and, if you really want a happy ending, ponder the fate of drummer Dale Griffin. It says something for the strength of Mott's Beeb sessions that, to paraphrase the shaver ad, he liked the company so much he took a job there. Griffin went onto become one of the BBC's top session producers.

Meanwhile, another reminder of earlier times appeared with the release of a quickie compilation designed to introduce Mott the Hoople's new fans to the music they made in the past. And it really didn't do a good job of it.

'Rock'n'Roll Queen's eight tracks included the claustrophobic hard rockers 'Walking With A Mountain' and 'Thunderbuck Ram', the singalong title song and the grinding 'Death May Be Your Santa Claus'. But the remainder can be summed up either as novelty fragments ('The Wheel Of The Quivering Meat Conception'), entertaining throwaways ('You Really Got Me' and the 'Midnight Lady' single) or live space fillers. Eight minutes of 'Keep A-Knockin'' were out of place enough on the otherwise sublime 'Wildlife' album. They have no business whatsoever on a putative best of.

Of course, it was that very inconsistency that made the original albums the minor ignored classics they were, and Mott the Hoople would never be this gloriously undisciplined again.

October 1972 – David Bowie: For The Collector, Early David Bowie (Pye 7N8002)
20 October 1972 – David Bowie, live Santa Monica Civic Auditorium

Just two hits old, and the oldies were already resurfacing, on an aptly titled EP that reprised four of the six songs that the young Mr B recorded during 1965-66. Understandably different to whatever you might have expected to hear, the quartet ('I Dig Everything', 'And I Say To Myself', 'Can't Help Thinking About Me' and 'I'm Not Losing Sleep') was nevertheless revealed as the sound of Bowie at his most endearing, mourning lost love and celebrating youthful promise, with his whole life ahead of him and fame still more than half a decade away.

They're classic mid-Sixties Britbeat and, though a world removed from all that he went onto, it's worth remembering that he would be looking at a few of them again, for the late-Nineties 'Toy' project.

There was no looking back on his American tour, of course, as Ziggy ground across the country and touched down in Santa Monica to record one of the most legendary shows of his career.

With RCA taping the evening for a possible live album (the Boston gig a few days later was also recorded), Bowie ran through his now-regular set with delicious aplomb, touching on songs dating back to 'Space Oddity' and looking ahead to 'Aladdin Sane' with the inclusion of the newly–written 'The Jean Genie'.

Swiftly to become one of the best-selling, and best-loved bootlegs of all time, 'Santa Monica 72' would finally be handed an official release in 1994 (Griffin/Golden Years GY 002).

October 1972 – Elton John: Crocodile Rock/Elderberry Wine (DJM 271)

What, exactly, are we supposed to make of Elton John – Glam Superstar?

On the one hand, and that which he turned to the most, he was an excellent singer-songwriter, cast in precisely the same mould as a string of fellow bards who wouldn't get a mention here no matter *what* they wore.

But on the other...well, he *did* have a sensational wardrobe, he wore glasses with more glitter than Gary's entire torso and when he rocked he Glammed like billy-o.

It's hard to disassociate his third hit in the year (a return to the Top Five after 'Honky Cat' faltered at Number 31) from Elton's later appearance on *The Muppet Show*, when this delightful Fifties-style rocker was voiced by crocodiles. And it was scarcely an accurate presage of his upcoming new album, 'Don't Shoot

Me, I'm Only The Piano Player', which naturally served up more of the syrupy stuff.

But if you remember when rock was young, and you and Susie had so much fun...

October 1972 – Harley Quinne: New Orleans/ In A Moment Of Madness (Bell 1255)

One of the most invigorating hits of the autumn was hatched by songwriters Roger Cook and Roger Greenaway (who penned the B-side) and enacted by a crop of sessionmen who may not have been too dissimilar to the current Blue Mink line-up.

Anonymity meant little, though, as Harley Quinne turned out on the telly in full glitter costumes, a-hey-ing and a-bellowing along to the old Gary US Bonds heartstopper, and well they deserved their Number 19 chart placing.

October 1972 – Hello: C'mon/The Wench (Bell 1265)

Recorded at Hello's second-ever recording session, back in July 1971, the A-side was another Russ Ballard original, but the B-side was a band original. 'We thought it would be a great follow up to "You Move Me",' says Bradbury. 'And it received the same huge amount of airplay. People like Alan Freeman were playing it all the time.' But, unfortunately, it was another miss.

October 1972 – Paul St John: The Flying Saucers Have Landed/Spaceship Lover (Pye 7N 45190)

St John was actually Welshman Laurie (Laurice) Marshall, a Leeds University graduate who moved to London and worked as a talent scout and in-house songwriter at Pye Records. 'I was a session singer, I did Abbey Road and all the studios in the late Sixties and early Seventies, I worked with various people...Alan Parsons a lot, when he was second engineer at Abbey Road,' he recalls. 'In England you had to be able to write everything and anything that was demanded of you. This wasn't a time for specialisation.'

His own musical tastes leaned towards the R&B side of things, but there was little outlet for such yearnings at that time. Later in the decade, Laurice would become the king of Canadian disco with 'We Will Make Love', 'The Disco Spaceship' and 'The Hit Line', but for now, he was writing and working with anyone and anything...

As 'The Flying Saucers Have Landed' reveals!

'The Flying Saucers Have Landed', together with another Marshall composition and production, Spiv's glorious 'Oh You Beautiful Child', was rediscovered aboard the compilation 'Glitter From The Litter Bin: 20 Junk Shop Glam Rarities From The Seventies' (Castle CMQCD675); 'Spaceship Lover', meanwhile utilises the same backing track as the A-side. 'I wrote a new song in two minutes.

'It was based on Erik Von Daniken's writing,' recalls Marshall and, after he relocated to Canada in 1975, he met the author at Toronto University and handed him a copy of the record. 'He was thrilled to bits!'

St John released several other records around this time. Hooking up with Roger Cook, he was responsible for 'All I Want To Do Is Sit And Cry' on London; 'Roger produced it, but I think he rushed it, and they didn't really push it. Then I produced "She Brings Me Love" for Odyssey, which was a Greek group, it's all bouzoukis and a heavy beat... There was "David Donny And Michael" by Weenybopper for Pye... (c/w 'Won't You Smile For Me' – Pye 7N 45203).

'That was amazing. It was so cute and that girl Weenybopper, I can't remember her name, was the most professional singer I've ever worked with. She was as cool as a cucumber, there were no dramas; for me as a producer that was a dream session.

'It was Cyril [Black, label owner] who pushed me to do it, he'd netted her, I had the song, Prudence financed it, but Pye released it.

ON THE RADIO
30 October – 3 November – Johnnie Walker: David Bowie
ON THE BOX
5 October 1972 – Top Of The Pops: Gary Glitter, Lieutenant Pigeon, Harley Quinne, the Sweet
6 October 1972 – Lift Off With Ayshea (new series begins)
12 October 1972 – Top Of The Pops: 10cc, Alice Cooper, David Bowie, Gary Glitter, Lieutenant Pigeon
18 October 1972 – Lift Off With Ayshea: 10cc
19 October 1972 – Top Of The Pops: Alice Cooper, Lieutenant Pigeon

25 October 1972 – Lift Off With Ayshea: Lieutenant Pigeon
26 October 1972 – Top Of The Pops: 10cc, Alice Cooper, Harley Quinne, Lieutenant Pigeon
6 November 1972 – Billy Dolls and a death from New York

The British music press was fiercely divided over the merits of the New York Dolls, an undisguised garage band from the city that named them, which then disguised itself as a bunch of dolls.

For every writer who proclaimed them the future of rock'n'roll (and there were several), there was another who thought they were the worst thing on ten legs and left the room every time their name was mentioned.

But the Rolling Stones came close to signing them to their own label until Mick Jagger decided they were ''orrible', and Rod Stewart was so infatuated that he flew them to England to support the Faces at the Wembley Festival of Music on 29 October.

And no surprise. The Dolls looked great, the misbegotten sons of Keith Richard's most unholy public image. Legend has it that, desperate to land a regular gig, they applied to the transvestite 84 Club in Manhattan, dressing up for the first time simply to add power to their argument.

The new look worked, and the costumes stuck. Shortly after, *Melody Maker*'s New York correspondent, Roy Hollingworth, caught them. His words would stick even tighter than the facepaint. 'The best young band I've ever seen,' Hollingworth enthused, 'subterranean sleazoid flash.'

In those days when people actually believed what they read in the press, people started paying attention. But tragedy loomed. Still in the UK after the Faces gig, Dolls drummer Billy Murcia died of an overdose in his hotel room on 6 November 1972.

8 November 1972 – ***Lift Off With Ayshea:*** **Bay City Rollers, Wizzard**
November 1972 – Wizzard: Ball Park Incident/The Carlsberg Special (Harvest 5062)

Making their television debut weeks ahead of the release of their debut single 'Ball Park Incident', Wizzard was the group Roy Wood formed following his short-lived dalliance with the almost-equally newborn Electric Light Orchestra. Having formed that band with Move cohort Jeff Lynne, Wood then fell out with his colleague over ELO's future direction during an Italian tour earlier in 1972.

He departed, taking with him keyboard-player Bill Hunt, cellist Hugh McDowell and sound engineer Trevor Smith, before picking up Mongrel members bassist Rick Price (also ex-Move) and twin drummers Charlie Grima and Keith Smart. The new band, dedicated to Wood's beloved Fifties' rock'n'roll, was completed with sax players Mike Burney and Nick Pentelow.

Wizzard made their live debut sharing the bill with Gary Glitter, Jerry Lee Lewis, Chuck Berry and more at the Rock and Roll Revival Show at Wembley on 5 August. 'For some members of Wizzard, the biggest gig they had [previously] done was the Queen's Head in Birmingham,' Wood later mused.

The following month Wizzard played the Reading Festival, before heading into the studio. Now they were out again, and an exclusive appearance on *Lift Off*, a show that Wood had favoured in the past, awaited.

So did a date with the make-up department. Plenty of other bands thought they dressed bizarrely and caked on the make-up. Roy Wood was out to make them all look like amateurs.

(Concurrent with Wizzard's output, Wood also maintained a solo career, beginning with the album 'Boulders' – recorded in 1969 but released in 1973.)

November 1972 – Lou Reed: Walk On The Wild Side/Perfect Day (RCA 2303)
November 1972 – Lou Reed: Transformer (RCA 4807)

'The thing about this album is, all the songs are hate songs. My first solo album was all love songs. This is all hate songs.' – Lou Reed, October 1972.

Everything about 'Transformer' squealed squalor…its very title suggested some kind of heavy deviation, and song titles like 'Vicious', 'Make Up' and 'New York Telephone Conversation' could only promise more of the same.

But the sailor with the salami down his pants on the back cover was only the first stop on the trip David and Lou had in store. So what if it was merely a caricature of what Reed was really capable of? 'Transformer' remained a lush and impeccably delivered catalogue of permutations and perversions. It has been described as one of the most decadent albums of its time; it was certainly one of the most camp, hustling its way through the soft white underbelly of New York and pulling back exactly the same curtains as the Velvet Underground used to, but looking in from a very different angle.

The sordid degradation, the hopeless wandering through a twilight world of sex-change kittens and midnight cowboys were the same as they always were. But for the first time, Lou wasn't taking things so seriously. Or at least his audience wasn't and, in the halls of legend, it all amounts to much the same thing.

'I can still empathise with all those songs I wrote before,' Reed said. '"I'm Waiting For The Man"? Yeah, sure. I went through all that and I can still relate to it. But old aficionados of mine are criticising my new work for all the wrong reasons. They want another "Sweet Jane" or "Sister Ray" and I can't give it to them.'

What he could give them was 'Goodnight Ladies', an oompah-powered Saturday night alone with the TV and a TV dinner; 'Perfect Day', the sweetest love song he would ever write; 'Satellite Of Love', 'Make Up', 'Wagon Wheel'...and 'Walk On The Wild Side', a duet for sly vocal and lascivious bass while the coloured girls go 'do-doo-doo'.

With a sense of bravado few record companies would ever dream of emulating, it was pulled off the album for release as a single in November 1972 and, at first, it did nothing. RCA put it to one side, issued a follow-up, 'Satellite Of Love'...and then, one week in early May 1973, it happened.

Lou Reed was having a hit single.

November 1972 – The birth of the Glitter Band

In summer 1972, with Gary Glitter's maiden concert tour looming, he and Mike Leander began piecing together a backing band, named – naturally – the Glittermen.

It was an ancient concept in shiny new trousers, a revival of the old Mike Leander Show Band with added glitter and pizzazz. The pair even retained that unit's unique two drum/two saxophone attack, and with Show Band baritone saxophonist John Rossall established as the leader, the line-up was completed around a nucleus of Gerry Shephard (guitar, vocals), Pete Gill (drums), Harvey Ellison (sax) and, finally, drummer Pete Phipps, from the jazz-rock band Heaven, the unlikely precursor to the Heavy Metal Kids. This line-up, augmented by a bassist and a second sax player, completed Glitter's first tour, but further refinements were required, including the recruitment of a new bassist, John Springate.

He recalls, '"I Didn't Know I Loved You" had just been successful and, up until that time they had a bass player who was like six foot, overweight and didn't look the part, so they were looking for somebody who was same height as Gerry, basically, and it just worked out I was that height. I got the job because I was five foot five.'

Prior to receiving the Glitter call, Springate had spent 18 months in Canada in a band with his brother; they returned to England and joined Clem Curtis and the Foundations before John quit, frustrated at the lack of opportunity to sing lead vocals. He turned, as did so many other out-of-work musicians, to the back pages of *Melody Maker* and soon has two bands vying for his attention – Glitter and a local group with a decidedly Beach Boys-oriented approach, a musical direction Springate was especially keen on.

He already knew Glitter's roadie, 'a guy named Steve who used to work for the Alan Bown Set, and the day before the audition he called and told me to watch Gary on *Top Of The Pops* that evening. So I watched it and I thought, "I don't know about this." But the funny thing was, Steve rang me back afterwards: "You're still coming tomorrow, aren't you?" "Yeah, okay."'

Although the majority of the band actually lived in London, band leader John Rossall was conducting the auditions in Sheffield; Springate arrived to find '20-odd bass players waiting, but nobody wanted to play because half the band was missing; they were all still in London. One of the drummers was there, Pete Gill, so Steve the road manager said to me "go on"; I just played along with him, John Rossall listened, said "great", and that was it.'

The second saxophonist left and wasn't replaced; drummer Peter Gill, too, departed, to be succeeded by Tony Leonard. 'It was a good line-up,' Springate enthuses. 'It looked good on stage, it balanced out – two brass, two drummers, Gerry and me in the middle.'

November 1972 – David Bowie: Space Oddity (RCA LSP 4813)
November 1972 – David Bowie: The Man Who Sold The World (RCA LSP 4816)

Among the terms of the deal that allowed David Bowie to break his contract with Mercury Records in 1971, prior to signing to RCA, was the pledge that his new home would buy up the masters to the music Bowie had been making (but nobody had been buying) between 1969-1971.

At the time, Mercury probably thought they got a good deal. A year later, 'Man Of Words, Man Of Music', sensibly retitled 'Space Oddity', was on its way to Number 17 and 'The Man Who Sold The World' was Number 26.

'Space Oddity' itself was rising to reissued glory in the United States, and Bowie's contemporaries were staring at him with undisguised awe. Every other artist lived in fear of their past indiscretions coming back to haunt them, or at least make waves on the release schedule; Marc Bolan was even forced to obtain a court injunction to prevent Track Records releasing an album's worth of his old demos.

Bowie, on the other hand, had complete control over almost every significant piece of music he had ever recorded. A debut LP for Deram in 1967, and a clutch of earlier 45s were all that lay beyond his grasp. And, as the Pye EP in October had proved, what possible harm could any of that do?

November 1972 – Kimono Bolan-o

Among the sundry quasi-legal attempts to fill the pre-'Born To Boogie' void in the live Marc Bolan catalogue, a pair of recordings from T Rex's November 1972 Japanese tour, 'TKY Blues' and 'Rockin' And Rollin'' found T Rex with the world at their feet. Certainly the gentlemen in the back rows of the Budokan, with their tape recorders apparently concealed within a large bag of rice, thought so. Whether they did the world any favours by switching them on, however, is another matter entirely.

You can make out there's a band on stage, and even discern who it is. The performance is sound, and while Bolan throws in all the usual rehearsed ad-libs, he is also in a playful mood. But the hyper-muffled sound is drowned by a howling crowd and Bolan himself is bedevilled by readily apparent monitor problems – 'No voice!' he complains during a protracted 'Jeepster' and the listener feels immediate sympathy. There's no guts to the recording, either, although a powerful (if feedback-ridden) 'Spaceball Ricochet' does cut through the murk with a certain soul-stirring majesty.

The gigs were great, the bootlegs are lousy. But Bolan didn't mind because, safely tucked in his luggage, he had a copy of the very first single by Japan's own greatest Glam band, Vodka Collins.

November 1972 – Vodka Collins: Sands of Time/Automatic Pilot (EMI-Express ETP 2857)

Our Glamerican in Tokyo, Alan Merrill, was still awaiting the release of his latest solo album 'Merrill 1' in late 1971 when work began on his proposed *next* one, 'Merrill 2'. And then stopped again.

He was not a happy camper. A dispute with his long-time management company Watanabe Productions left him forced to augment his income with session work instead of getting on with his own career.

But every cloud has a silver lining and, by the end of 1971, his decision to slip out of his earlier pop groove was confirmed when he and drummer Hiroshi Oguchi (of the Tempters) were recruited to ex-Spiders guitarist Hiroshi 'Monsieur' Kamayatsu's new backing band as he prepared to play his first solo concerts. (Masayoshi Takanaka, a founding member of the Sadistic Mika Band, was also in the group.)

At the same time, Merrill and Oguchi were block-booking Tokyo's Yotsuya Studios to demo a batch of Merrill's new songs. Kamayatsu joined them and, with bassist Take Yokouchi following, Vodka Collins was born.

Attracting attention as one of the first (if not *the* first) Japanese-based band ever to perform their original material in English, Vodka Collins took off immediately. They were making three or four public appearances a day as radio and TV piled into their concert schedule. Every record label in the country was hot on their trail, and the group even had their own fashion consultant. The young Koshino Junko designed Merrill's stagewear – in later years, she would become one of Japan's foremost fashion designers. Right now, she was still in high school.

'The early-Seventies glam scene in Japan was really amazing,' Merrill recalls. 'When Vodka Collins played Keio University's 1972 New Year's Eve party, it was mayhem. We played only four songs before the crowd went totally mad, and we had to stop. Police and riot squads were called in. It was quite an experience. Not your usual demure Japanese audience!'

The band signed with EMI/Toshiba in spring 1972 and set to work cutting their debut single, 'Sands Of Time'. 'We didn't get around to making an album until they saw how well the single was doing. After it sold, EMI went ahead with recording the album. That's how it went in Japan back then.'

For now, though, that didn't matter. 'Sands Of Time' was massive and, if Vodka Collins had one disappointment, it was that their fame had not, and never would, spread beyond Japan's borders. Bands from their neck of the woods seldom travelled out of country at that time; never braved Europe or America. If the western world was to hear them, it would have to come to them...and so it did.

Touring Japan that same month, Marc Bolan became an instant convert to the 'Sands Of Time' single, while David Bowie employed another of Vodka Collins' designers and friends, Kansai, to conjure up his own stagewear. Merrill himself continues, 'a young pre-David Bailey Marie Helvin was one of our Tokyo entourage, along with Tina Chow and her sister Bonnie (Adele), the Lutz sisters. Bonnie eventually married David Byrne.'

November 1972 – Dave Lee Travis Show: Hello

Hello were constantly gigging and touring, now, and regularly stopping off to record live radio sessions, too. This session featured three tracks, 'The Wench', 'C'mon' and 'You Move Me', and they were Radio 1 staples well into the new year.

November 1972 – Blackfoot Sue – Sing Don't Speak/2B Free (Jam 29)

The Brummies' less than monster follow-up to 'Standing In The Road' reached Number 36.

November 1972 – Sparks: A Woofer In Tweeter's Clothing (Bearsville K45510)

21 November 1972 – Old Grey Whistle Test: Sparks

A madcap California combo formed by the utterly dissimilar brothers Ron and Russell Mael in 1969, Sparks – or Halfnelson as they were originally called – had already cut an album with producer Todd Rundgren. This was titled both 'Halfnelson' and 'Sparks', depending which side of the name change you bought it on (Bearsville BV 2048).

Now, with their second LP in the can, they

were being shipped to England in the hope somebody might care more for them than the United States.

Guitarist Earle Mankey, his bassist brother Jim, drummer Harley Feinstein and road manager Larry Dupont accompanied the Maels for what promised to be a leisurely trip, comprising a couple of shows a week, with Bearsville's distributor, WEA, footing the bill for travel, meals, accommodation, the lot.

It was, the musicians agreed, like Rock Star Camp, at least until their first review rolled in, a merciless assault spread over far more space than it ought to have been. The band were devastated, but manager Roy Silver, paying a flying visit to London, was delighted. 'They were absolutely ripped to shreds by the journalist,' recalled Dupont, 'and they were terribly upset. And Roy said to them, "You don't understand! This is wonderful! Any publicity is better than none." He was correct, as well. The next time Sparks played out, it was to an audience at least partially comprised of people lured along by the vehemence of that review.

Sparks' London life kicked off with a residency at the Pheasantry on the King's Road; they also enacted guerrilla raids on the provinces and, occasionally, further afield. In Switzerland, they appeared on the *Hits A Go-Go* television show, performing 'Wonder Girl' (a minor US hit that summer) and 'Do Re Mi'; in Holland, they recorded Christmas greetings to the listeners of Radio North Sea International and played 'Wonder Girl' again on *Top Pop*. And then it was back to London for the *Old Grey Whistle Test* and another merciless roasting.

Just months after the show's genial host, Bob Harris, told the world he thought Roxy Music were an unimpressive hype, and almost exactly a year before he described the New York Dolls as 'mock rock', the bearded whisperer condemned Sparks as a cross between Frank Zappa and the Monkees, the worst thing he'd ever seen. It seemed that even England, the land that had inspired so many of their hopes and aspirations, wasn't ready for the Maels.

Fellow guest Neil Sedaka, then at the apex of his 10cc-fired renaissance, followed Harris' lead. Drummer Feinstein recalls, 'I remember hearing Sedaka say we represented a certain kind of band that was becoming more prevalent in music, a kind of band that he didn't like. The host didn't disagree. I wondered what kind of band he was talking about. *I* didn't know what kind of band we were.'

Harris and Sedaka's harsh words notwithstanding, the *Old Grey Whistle Test* turned Sparks' entire visit around. Their earlier sporadic gigging suddenly became a flood of dates, both in London and further out into the provinces. The crowning glory, however, came when WEA called up to inform them they would be playing the London Marquee every Thursday night throughout December, treading the same hallowed boards as so many of their own past heroes.

The opening night of the residency was 7 December 1972. The evening before, Sparks were at the immortally-named Growling Budgie in Ilford, playing to a small but genuinely enthusiastic audience that appeared to be comprised almost wholly of *Whistle Test* viewers.

The Marquee, on the other hand, was heaving and, when the show was over, the band simply stared at one another in amazement. 'It was the best gig the band ever did while I was with them,' Feinstein enthuses. 'The place was packed. The crowd was very receptive.' Everybody was looking forward to the following week's return.

Then Russell Mael fell ill. It was nothing serious, just one of those funky cold-or-flu bugs that always circulates in wintertime. But it robbed him of his voice and, while Dupont is adamant, 'If Russ could have made a squeak, he'd have been out there,' the band had no alternative. They cancelled their second Marquee show.

'It was a disaster,' Dupont laments. 'Afterwards, we heard there'd been lines around the block to get in. Everybody was so excited to see them, and they couldn't play.' A replacement band was hastily procured, and the line around the block was doomed to disappointment.

With Russell recovered, gigging continued to devour the band's time. Back from a short tour of the American East Coast, the Kinks embarked on a handful of dates around the UK; Sparks were added to the bill for one show, at Bournemouth Winter Gardens.

Another trip outside London took Sparks to the University of East Anglia, to open the show for the Electric Light Orchestra. 'We were on [that] one TV show [*Whistle Test*], then they booked some club dates and, as a result of that one TV show we were selling out these clubs,' Russell Mael marvelled. 'We thought, "God, this is so easy here. People actually respond to what you're doing."'

They began meeting local bands – manager Silver's UK office was headed up by one John Hewlett, the ex-John's Children bassist who now managed Jook. 'We went to see each other several times,' Jook bassist Ian Hampton recalls. 'Initially, I didn't know what to think. Chaplinesque Ron with his long curly locks, they didn't seem like siblings. The pretty one and the accountant one. But we hit it off socially, we went to all their gigs and they came to ours.'

Unfortunately, Sparks date sheet was about to come to a very abrupt halt. A meeting with the daughter of a Swiss club owner lured the band on an unscheduled return to Switzerland, where it turned out they were both unwanted and unable to get back to London.

The third Marquee date was cancelled and, when the band returned to London just before Christmas, it was to discover that the fourth show, too, was off; WEA, their financiers for the trip, had pulled the plug and were sending the band home that same day. Not even the promise of a small write-up in *Music Scene* magazine's February issue would change the label's mind. The album disappeared on both sides of the Atlantic and, months later, the Maels broke up the band.

November 1972 – Silverhead: Riding With My Baby/In Your Eyes (Purple PUR 110)

A second single that doesn't do any more than the first. Saleswise, anyway. Musically, both sides just hit you round the head.

29 November 1972 – Mott the Hoople and David Bowie, live in Philadelphia

A stunning show from Mott's autumn 1972 US tour, given further muscle by the appearance of David Bowie, both to introduce the band at the start of the show, and then join them on stage for 'All The Young Dudes'. A local radio broadcast preserved the show; the CD 'All The Way From Stockholm To Philadelphia' (Angel Air SJPCD 029) gave it a full release in 1998,

November 1972 – Top Of The Pops Volume 27 (Hallmark SHM 805)

Autumn 1972 fell upon the record-buying public like an eccentric aunt distributing candies to her cats, a six-week period during which all the big guns of the Glam pack were readying their Christmas broadsides so the charts were open to the weirdoes instead. The fact that a lot of them turned out to be more nuance than novelty was not known at that time. 'Mouldy Old Dough' was simply a ragtime revival and 'Donna' (shrieking here like dolphins on helium) cut into that Fifties scene again.

The Shangri-Las' 'Leader Of The Pack' was a surprise hit reissue, and the Top Of The Poppers crash their motorbike with deathly sweet precision. 'Elected' is disappointingly dull, and the majestic 'In A Broken Dream' is granted the sort of treatment it might have received had its guest vocalist been a slightly clumsy guitarist rather than a gravel-voiced shouter.

But Gilbert O'Sullivan's cloying 'Clair' is so exquisitely orchestrated it leaves the original in the dust. And then there's Jonathan King's 'Loop Di Love', originally released beneath the superbly childish name of Shag and here restructured as a remarkable collision between psychotic violin and Muppet innuendo.

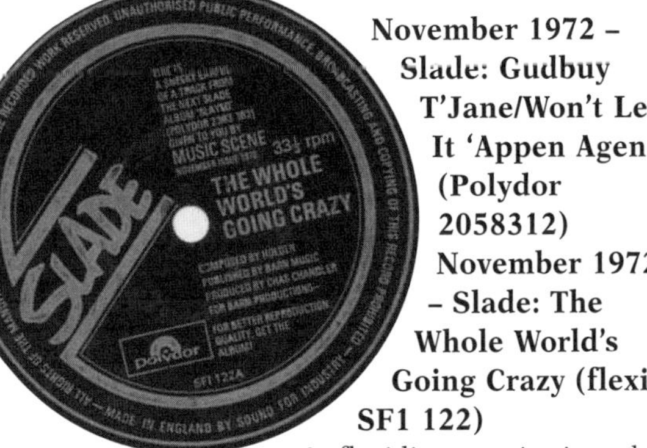

November 1972 – Slade: Gudbuy T'Jane/Won't Let It 'Appen Agen (Polydor 2058312)
November 1972 – Slade: The Whole World's Going Crazy (flexi SF1 122)

A flexidisc previewing the upcoming *Slayed* LP for readers of *Music Scene.*

Slade were touring constantly now. A late-1972 UK outing, with Suzi Quatro their unknown support act, and visits to both America and Australia filled the band's diary, and in the midst of all this, 'Gudbuy T'Jane' came within a ding-a-ling of giving the band their third successive chart-topper after coming straight into the chart at Number 8.

But Chuck Berry, fresh from the London Rock and Roll Show, was not budging from the top for anyone.

November 1972 – Ricky Wilde: I Am An Astronaut/The Hertfordshire Rock (UK 18)

The Jacksons, Osmonds and Partridges were not to have it all their own way. On both sides of the Atlantic, there was a growing need, primarily amongst middle-aged record company executives, to create further darlings in the hope of grabbing a slice of the teenybop pie, encouraged in the main by the simple mistake of confusing the natural growing pains that flooded into the Problems Postbag for fickleness.

'I don't think Donny loves me any more,' Heartbroken from Harwich would sobbingly write. 'And my best friend has already grabbed David. Are there any other singers who you think would love me forever?'

For some reason, most of the offenders appeared to be British.

The James Boys from East London, Darren Burns, the son of an EMI top dog, the Poole Family, the Handley Family – all emerged from the wasteland of Donny-mania, cut a few records, struck a few poses and ultimately succeeded in doing nothing more than turning even more people on to the originals.

But there was an unreal feel to them as well. David Cassidy was the boy next door, and he dropped by your house every Monday night to say hello. Donny was less visible, but by sharing, or at least acknowledging, his religious persuasions it was at least possible to get close to him. But what did Darren Burns have beyond a pretty face? Not very much.

Ricky Wilde was the best of the batch. The son of Fifties pop idol Marty Wilde (and brother, therefore, of Eighties songstress Kim), he was just 11 when he signed to Jonathan King's UK label and leaped straight aboard the glam-rock space race with 'I Am An Astronaut'. Further singles followed, together with blanket coverage of his activities in the teeny press of the day and, while he never made it as a nipper, he did give a great accounting for himself when he featured (with his dad) in the July 1973 *Man Alive* TV investigation into the creation of child stars, *Twinkle Twinkle Little Star.*

November 1972 – David Bowie versus the Sweet: blockbusting genies all the way

'Blockbuster!' Brian Connolly reflected, started life as 'a country and western number. In Australia they're very much into American country, so Chapman was writing that way.'

Nobody, Chapman included, ever expected the Sweet to record a country song, and a few rehearsals at the Hanwell Community Centre rehearsal space that they shared, among others, with Deep Purple and Uriah Heep, quickly saw the song take on a heavier demeanour.

'It was strange number because it had no chorus,' Connolly continued. 'We thought we were sticking our necks out, weren't that sure it was going to be a big hit. In fact we weren't sure it was going to be a hit.' But nobody doubted that it was the right record to release. 'It was everyone's decision to move to a heavier vein.

'There wasn't a decision to change the style of Sweet. Chinn and Chapman wanted a single that was more representative of the Sweet as we perform. They follow us, they don't guide us. Chapman is the musician of the duo and knows...we're a rock band. Anything before our hits, especially our most recent hits, wasn't representative of us, though I would say we're more commercial and more jolly than most groups.'

One thing that all agreed upon was, as Scott put it, 'It was one hell of a riff. I remember Mick Tucker and I discussing it, and saying there wasn't much song to "Blockbuster!" but there were a lot of elements.'

And so there were. The lyrics had a foreboding edge miles removed from the bonhomie of past releases, the rhythm section moved like a tank division. The hardest and sharpest production the Sweet had yet been treated to was layered around an American police siren which howled with such spinechilling precision even Nicky Chinn admitted that it made the hairs on the back of his neck stand up. (The siren would be removed from the US release of the single for fear of alarming or misleading motorists.)

And then there was the riff.

Steve Priest: 'I can remember when '"Wig-Wam Bam"' was out, we were doing it at *Top Of The Pops* [probably on 14 September 1972] and Mike Chapman went "I've got a great idea for a new song." He had an acoustic guitar and I went "That's 'I'm A Man'" and he went "Yeah, I know. Shut up." Then he went "You better take care, you better beware", and that was it.'

It was a behemoth of a record, a relentless roar in which so much was happening that, as they left Audio International Studios on 1 November with the mix still pounding in their ears, Tucker and Scott caught one another's eye and knew instinctively what the other was thinking. This was the biggest step the Sweet had yet taken, the heaviest record they had yet released.

For all their faith in the self-composed B-sides that had always been a feature of their records, the band had never pushed hard for one of them to be released as the A-side because they knew that the sonic shift would be too great for their audience. Now it was Chinn, Chapman and Wainman who seemed to be pushing the band out on a limb, and the musicians knew they were taking a chance.

But they also knew the only way they could ever advance the Sweet was to step outside of their audience's comfort zone, and if 'Blockbuster!' didn't work out then at least they'd have another chance; their name was too big and their momentum too pronounced for one flop single to derail them completely. All that mattered now was that they had created something completely unique.

How coincidental was it that, then, that on the other side of the Atlantic, midway through an American tour that opened in late September, David Bowie should have been toying with exactly the same old Yardbirds-out-of-Bo-Diddley riff for a song that he called 'The Jean Genie'?

Andy Scott: 'It's one of those anomalies! I can't believe David Bowie would think "That's a good old riff" [or song title, for that matter – the Sweet's 'Jeanie', after all, was just a few weeks old at the time] and immediately go off and write something, and I can't get my head around the thought that Mike Chapman would be skulking around RCA, he'd hear "The Jean Genie" and think "What a wag, what a great thing it would be to have two singles out there at the same time, with the same guitar riff." That would be a nightmare from his point of view.'

It was a nightmare that came true, all the same.

Steve Priest: 'I never knew what that was all about. I have a feeling... It was quite a while before "Blockbuster" was made that [Chapman] played it to us. But at RCA, people would walk around with the doors open, people playing songs and ideas, so who knows who heard what?'

Who knows, indeed? Bowie and his band departed for their American tour the week after that episode of *Top Of The Pops* was broadcast; 'The Jean Genie' was written in New York a few days later, using an old riff with which guitarist Mick Ronson had been amusing himself on the bus between the first two shows, in Cleveland (22 September) and Memphis (24 September).

'The Jean Genie' was recorded back in New York City on 6 October 1972, debuted in concert in Chicago 24 hours later and was already pencilled in for release – by RCA, the label Bowie shared with the Sweet – at the end of November. (c/w 'Ziggy Stardust' – RCA 2302).

'Blockbuster!' wasn't set to hit the schedules for another few weeks after that (c/w 'Need A Lot Of Lovin'' – RCA 2305). But still the coincidence was never going to be ignored, particularly as both singles seemed hell-bent on hitting the top of the chart.

In the event, Bowie's effort was halted at Number 2, trapped behind Chuck Berry's novelty hit 'My Ding-A-Ling' – a song that made 'Little Willy' sound positively wholesome by comparison. The veteran rock'n'roller not only spent four weeks at Number 1, but was also the recipient of a television ban after media watchdog Mary Whitehouse protested *not* at the song's lyric but the hand gestures with which Berry accompanied it.

'The Jean Genie' got tired of waiting for it to leave. But 'Blockbuster!' was destined to go all the way.

ON THE RADIO
9 November 1972 (9) – Sounds Of The Seventies: Roxy Music
13-17 November 1972 – Johnnie Walker: David Bowie
27 November – 1 December 1972 – Dave Lee Travis: Blackfoot Sue
ON THE BOX
2 November 1972 – Top Of The Pops: Lieutenant Pigeon
5 November 1972 – The Royal Variety Performance: Elton John
9 November 1972 – Top Of The Pops: Elton John, Geordie
16 November 1972 – Top Of The Pops: Slade
23 November 1972 – Top Of The Pops: Lynsey de Paul, Elton John, Slade
25 November 1972 – Full House: Roxy Music
ON THE SHELF
November 1972 – American Jam Band: American Jam/Nature's Child (Parlophone R5971)

---

2 December 1972 – In Concert: The Sensational Alex Harvey Band
December 1972 – Sensational Alex Harvey Band: Framed (Vertigo 6369 081)
December 1972 – Sensational Alex Harvey Band: There's No Lights On The Christmas Tree, Mother/Harp (Vertigo 6059 070)

'My name is Alex Harvey, and I would like to introduce you to my band. The Sensational Alex Harvey Band.'

It takes a lot of nerve to name your band something that unequivocal, a lot of nerve and a lot of self-belief. But Alex Harvey had both, and he was right as well. It just took the rest of the world a long time to cotton on to the fact.

For many rock musicians, if success is going to strike, it's going to strike early. Even those artists whose pre-fame history reads like an eternity of near-misses and unlucky breaks, seldom seem to be out of their mid-twenties when they do finally make it, and though there's always an exception to prove the rule, rock'n'roll is adamant about one thing. If you're still struggling when you're 30, nothing's going to change.

Alex Harvey was still struggling at 37, and he probably had resigned himself to a lifetime more of it. Questioned on the subject, he would even admit that was the only thing he knew how to do; 'I never wanted to be a star,' he once said. 'I just wanted to be happy.'

He was born in Glasgow's Gorbals district in February 1935, growing up on the streets and learning, very early on, to take the knocks that life sent your way – and pay them back with bountiful dividends. He left school aged 15 and, according to legend, spent the next few years simply drifting; according to one persistent legend, the young Alex Harvey had already tried 36 different jobs before he finally found one he could stick at, and around 1954 he made his professional debut as a musician, playing trumpet at a friend's wedding.

It was the age of jazz. Elvis Presley was still a truck driver only just introduced to the recording studio and rock'n'roll was simply Negro slang for sex. Certainly none of it meant anything to a young man from the Gorbals, and when Harvey joined his first band it was a Dixieland combo. He tootled through the latest standards while he glowered down his trumpet.

Harvey's own musical tastes were unusual for the time and place. Country and folk had both impacted on him, from the records that the seamen who thronged Glasgow's dock area brought home with them, and Harvey worked hard to introduce that music to his own bandmates...the Dixieland boys, and others thereafter. They usually sent him packing. It was the search for a kindred spirit that kept Harvey on the move, and finally he found one – a sax player named Bill Patrick, who shared

the same rehearsal space as one of Harvey's latest groups.

Entranced by the sight of a wild-haired hooligan bellowing his way through some song or other, battering out a rude rhythm on a protesting electric guitar, Patrick sought an introduction and suggested the two work together. Harvey agreed and soon they were playing live several times a week, either as the Clyde River Jazz Band, a traditional combo whose gigs paid the rent, or the Kansas City Skiffle Group, wild rock'n'rollers whose shows made the headlines.

By 1956, the two bands' roles had completely reversed. As rock'n'roll continued to explode upwards and outwards, and trad jazz fell into disuse, it was the Kansas City Skiffle Group who earned the most bookings. They were opportunistic as well. When skiffle, the British home-grown approximation to rock'n'roll, started to lose its flavour, they became the Kansas City Counts; and when Britain's own first rockers began to emerge they became the Alex Harvey Band.

Which in turn became the Alex Harvey Soul Band and, finally, the Alex Harvey Big Soul Band, which was soon a regular fixture on the Scottish live circuit. By the end of the decade they were making headway in England as well, and by the early Sixties they were regularly visiting Hamburg.

It was in Germany, that Harvey met the semi-legendary Kingsize Taylor, one of the catalysts of the pre-Beatles British beat scene; when Harvey signed to the German Polydor label in late 1963 it was Taylor's group, the Dominoes, who would back him on disc while the real Big Soul Band was left cooling its heels elsewhere.

Anybody coming across a copy of 'Alex Harvey And His Soul Band' (Polydor LPHM 46424) today will instantly recognise it for what it is. Recorded live at the Top Ten Club, it features two songs which, even today, are instantly associated with Harvey. Leiber and Stoller's 'Framed' and Willie Dixon's 'I Just Want To Make Love To You' were both included on the disc, the latter becoming Harvey's debut single (c/w 'Let The Good Times Roll' – Polydor NH 52264).

'Alex Harvey And His Soul Band' was released in March 1964, shortly after the Big Soul Band made its London debut at the 100 Club on 6 February. The group's appeal was instantaneous; rough and ready, genuinely snarling, they fit perfectly into the pigeonhole the Rolling Stones had created and which a slew of other, lesser, R&B bands was now hurrying to fill. Polydor even released a second single, 'Got My Mojo Working'/'I Ain't Worried Babe' (Polydor NH 52907) in June, and the Soul Band's profile had never been higher.

But when Polydor offered him the chance to record a second album, Harvey again left the group at home, this time flying to Hamburg with brother Leslie to record 'The Blues' (Polydor LPHM 46441) – a sparse collection ranging from 'Waltzing Matilda' to 'Strange Fruit'.

Harvey broke up the Big Soul Band in spring 1965, waving goodbye with what was also his final Polydor single, 'Ain't That Just Too Bad'/'My Kind Of Love' (Polydor BM 56017); in September, a solo Harvey released an audacious cover of Edwin Starr's 'Agent OO Soul' (c/w 'Go Away Baby' – Fontana TF 610). But a full year would elapse before next release 'The Work Song'/'I Can't Do Without Your Love' (Fontana TF 764), a period during which he all but quit the music business, disillusioned and directionless.

Harvey did make a stab at forming a new Big Soul Band, based around brother Leslie, his old bandmate Bill Patrick and singer Isobel Bond, but little came of it. As this latest union somersaulted through the Glaswegian underground, however, the rudiments of Leslie's next band, Stone the Crows, began to come together.

Alex, meanwhile, was toying with a new group of musicians, under the name of Giant

Moth. It was 1967 and, with psychedelia in full swing, Giant Moth knew precisely which way to fly. Unfortunately, they didn't get too far. Although Harvey landed a solo deal with Decca, and brought in his bandmates to back him, neither of his two singles that year did anything: 'Sunday Song'/'Horizons' (Decca F12640), followed by a cover of the Incredible String Band's 'Maybe Someday' (c/w 'Curtains For My Baby' – Decca F12660).

Giant Moth broke up shortly after, but Harvey remained a butterfly, abandoning psychedelia for the uncompromising sound of Progressive Rock and his first solo album. Recorded with brother Leslie and the largely improvisational jazz band Rock Workshop whose own self-titled album – CBS 64075 – was also partly recorded during these sessions, Harvey fashioned 'Roman Wall Blues' (Fontana STL 5534), one of the most uncompromising records of its age. Fontana, who released it, certainly thought so; the album went almost totally unpromoted, although a single, coupling 'Midnight Moses' with the title track (Fontana TF 1063), was released around the same time. It did nothing.

By 1970-71, Alex was again trying to put a band together, this time featuring former Clouds bassist Ian Ellis, Velvet Opera drummer Dave Dufort and, on occasion, ex-Kevin Ayers guitarist Mike Oldfield. Harvey and Oldfield did time together in the trenches of the London production of *Hair*, while Harvey continued working towards a new solo album. Demos recorded at Regent Sound Studios with his brother, plus drummer George Butler and bassist Jim Condron, included 'Penicillin Blues', 'He Ain't Heavy, He's My Brother' and Frank Zappa's 'Willie The Pimp' and would be released (in Europe in 1972) as 'The Joker Is Wild' (Metronome 15.429). Later, this same LP reappeared under the title 'This Is The Sensational Alex Harvey Band' (Metronome 200.173). But it wasn't.

Harvey was still drifting when he was introduced to Tear Gas, an equally directionless Scottish underground band. One rehearsal later (they played 'Midnight Moses'), a union was forged. And this time, the results would be sensational.

Originally named Mustard, Tear Gas was formed in 1969 by bassist Chris Glen, keyboard-player Hugh McKenna, drummer Richard Munro, vocalist David Batchelor and guitarist Zal Cleminson. The group cut two albums, the first, 'Piggy Go Getter' (for Tony Calder's Famous label, SFMA 5751) in November 1970, the eponymous second for Regal Zonophone (SLRZ1021) the following August.

Neither did anything outside of the band's immediate family circle and drummer Ted McKenna (who replaced Munro after *Piggy Go Getter*) later admitted, 'By June 1972, Tear Gas was in a deplorable financial position. There's no doubt the band would have broken up if we hadn't met Alex.'

With Tear Gas' erstwhile vocalist Batchelor taking over as the band's personal sound engineer, the combination proved potent. Keeping one eye on the increasingly theatrical Glam Rock scene that was exploding all around, and the other on his own comic-book mythology, Harvey began honing Tear Gas into a solid rock'n'roll band, complementing his own sense of on-stage dynamism with a showmanship that swiftly justified his choice for a band name.

They truly were the Sensational Alex Harvey Band.

The group was not in for an easy ride, at least not initially. Just two months after they got together, Leslie Harvey was killed, electrocuted on stage with Stone the Crows at Swansea Top Rank, a tragedy that almost prompted Alex to quit music altogether.

Neither was there much solace to be found in work. Early audiences hated SAHB, unable to comprehend why such a seemingly traditional rock group should so readily have embraced Glam-flavoured gimmickry. Cleminson even wore makeup, the thick white mask of a Pierrot.

Maybe it was that hatred which turned things around for them. People couldn't believe what they were seeing, so they brought their friends back to show them. Whatever it was, by the end of the summer SAHB was ranked amongst the biggest draws on the London club circuit, and in the early autumn the group signed to Vertigo Records, who despatched them straight into the studio.

Five days later, SAHB emerged with their

debut album, 'Framed', and a special Yuletide single, 'There's No Lights On The Christmas Tree, Mother, They're Burning Big Louie Tonight'.The album took its title from the Leiber-Stoller song already established as the centrepiece of SAHB's live show, one that would become increasingly more elaborate as time passed. With a silk stocking pulled over his head, Harvey acted out the part of a hard-done-by criminal as though his life depended on it; mid-song, the stocking would disappear into his mouth(!) as he busted his way through a polystyrene brick wall to plead his innocence before the audience. 'But no-one believes him,' *NME*'s Charles Shaar Murray wrote. 'Sure he did it, man, just look at him!'

Another epic was 'Isabel Goudie', a lengthy recounting of the legend of the Scottish witch, while some good old-fashioned boogie blues was provided by 'Hole In Her Stocking' and a lengthy reworking of Harvey's first ever single, 'I Just Want To Make Love To You'. Harvey also took the opportunity to rerecord the lost 1969 single 'Midnight Moses', then rang out the year with SAHB's first appearance on *In Concert*, a half-hour broadcast subsequently released on a Windsong CD.

December 1972 – Slade: Slayed? (Polydor 2383163)

Slade's fourth album was stuffed with so many mighty stompers the band could have taken the next year off and still not run out of steam. Even if one excises past hits 'Gudbuy T'Jane' and 'Mama Weer All Crazee Now' from the equation, it was a non-stop rock'n'roll riot, from the self-fulfilling prophecy of 'The Whole World's Going Crazee' to the downbeat but still eminently stompalongable 'Look At Last Night', the latter a reminder that, even at their loudest, Slade were still capable of some fetching balladry. Or should that be the other way around?

Further into the wax, did Blue Öyster Cult really borrow the tomahawk riffing of 'I Won't Let It 'Appen Agen' for their version of another Slade favourite, 'Born To Be Wild'? Maybe; they shared enough stages on tour in the States. But no-one could equal 'Gudbuy T'Jane', as a stirring Hill guitar break climbs aboard one of Noddy Holder's coolest vocals and rides it to oblivion.

A couple of covers break cover; a bass-heavy blues boogie through Janis Joplin's 'Move Over', and a closing medley of 'Let The Good Times Roll' and 'Feel So Fine' that sounds the closest you could come to the concert without buying a ticket. Of course, we don't have that option today. But stick on 'Slayed?', crank the volume really high, and the whole world will be going crazee again.

December 1972 – The Sweet: Biggest Hits (RCA 8316)

A straightforward dozen tracks culled from both the band's own chart-busting catalogue and Chinnichap's efforts for others. 'Tom Tom Turnaround' and 'Chop Chop' were originally reprised on 'Funny How Sweet Coco Can Be' and, if you'd already bought that set, you might not need this.

Several other songs sailed off that particular platter, but accusations of redundancy are quashed by the sheer flamboyance of 'Poppa Joe', 'Little Willy' and 'Wig-Wam Bam', the monster hits that saw the Sweet end 1972 as one of the biggest bands in Britain.

Plus, at a time when the band was starving

for respect, they also restate the Sweet's instinctive understanding of what made the Glam heart beat. They were fun.

December 1972 – T Rex: Solid Gold Easy Action/Born To Boogie (T Rex MARC 3)
December 1972 Unicorn (Regal Zonophone SLRZ1007, 1969)/A Beard Of Stars (Regal Zonophone SLRZ1013, 1970) (Cube)
14 December 1972 – Born To Boogie premiere at the Oscar One Cinema, Brewer Street, London

The follow-up to the comparatively under-achieving 'Children Of The Revolution' (by Bolan's standards, anything less than a chart topper was under-achievement), 'Solid Gold Easy Action' was written in France during sessions for T Rex's next album, 'Tanx'.

Generally regarded as having been very hastily conceived, and slammed out as a single only when it became apparent that 'Children Of The Revolution' was not destined for the Number 1 slot, it was based around a rhythm Bolan overheard drummer Bill Legend and bassist Steve Currie jamming in the studio one day.

Like its predecessor, it closed at Number 2 and now the knives were out. Overnight, it seemed, Bolan's bubble had burst. New stars had brought along new tricks, and he had only himself to blame.

Part of the problem was musical. T Rex's success was built on the T Rex sound, the result of everybody in the studio pulling together towards the same ends. The work ethic hadn't changed, but the personnel had. Mark Volman and Howard Kaylan, backing vocalists on every recording since 'Ride A White Swan', bowed out following the sessions for 'The Slider' as Bolan – now separated from wife June – invited his new girlfriend, R&B singer Gloria Jones, to take their place. But her attempts to recreate the same vibe from a more soulful base could not even begin to echo the classic sound, and no amount of fuzzy hair could disguise that.

Instead, Bolan might have been wiser to have flipped this latest single over because 'Born To Boogie' (title song to the just-released movie extravaganza) is one of his finest rock'n'rollers, a perennial live favourite and, more than any other song in his post-'Slider' arsenal, the one cut which could have effortlessly returned him to the top of the chart.

The single was a hit, and the movie packed the cinemas throughout the Christmas holidays. But the long-awaited successor to the two-for-one package that topped the UK chart earlier in the year, a pairing of the third and fourth Tyrannosaurus Rex albums, should have effortlessly followed it to Number 1 – or thereabouts, at least. Certainly that was the plan, and that was why it was held back until Christmas. Instead, it bombed; two weeks in the chart, no higher place than Number 44...then goodbye.

December 1972 – 10cc: Johnny Don't Do It/ 4% Of Something (UK 22)

In retrospect, 10cc admitted that their choice for a follow-up to 'Donna' was a mistake. 'Johnny Don't Do It' was another Fifties-style song, this time with the theme of a motorcycle accident. But the Shangri-Las' 'Leader Of The Pack' was reissued just beforehand and, while that epic tale of teenage dismemberment would reach Number 3, 'Johnny Don't Do It' sank without trace. You can have too much of a good thing.

December 1972 – Godzilla and Yellow Gypsy: Dai Go-Go-Party (Volume 1) (King Records SKM-1247/8 – Japan)

In the midst of Vodka Collins' hectic summer, Alan Merrill, pianist Haruo Chikada and drummer Jun Kanazawa plus guitarist Hiroshi Kato (aka the Yellow Gypsy and later of UK band Stretch) came together as Godzilla, a good-time rock'n'roll band who played a month long summer residency in the mountain resort of Karuizawa, toured Japan as support to the Bee Gees-soundtracked movie *Melody Fair* and cut a remarkable album full of red hot hit singles. Other people's red-hot hit singles.

'Metal Guru' and 'Rock And Roll', 'Highway Star' and 'Tumbling Dice', a year's worth of recent Anglo-American smashes were singled out for replay in a style that Merrill describes as 'kitschy fromage rock'. A shade unfairly, it should be said.

'Hiroshi Kato came from the old school, Ventures and Surfaris,' Merrill continues. 'He liked Santana as well. Not much vibrato from him without his using a whammy bar. I tried to show him [Paul] Kossoff's hand vibrato, but Kato wasn't interested. Still, he's a really great player, with lots of technique.'

The same session produced enough additional material for a second album to be released the following summer.

25 December 1972 – Top Of The Pops: David Bowie, Elton John, Slade, T Rex

28 December 1972 – Top Of The Pops: Gary Glitter, Lieutenant Pigeon, Slade, T Rex, Alice Cooper, Chicory Tip

From the annual round-up of the year's biggest hits, danced to by an audience of the year's most dazzling high street fashions, a reminder of just how pervasive all this spangly stuff was getting – the young man spotted bopping in the melee, his black T-shirt proclaiming his love of the Beach Boys…in glitter!

And then there were the performers; Bolan sparkled in metallic blue, Slade were resplendent in their happiest gladrags and Rolf Harris was called in to sketch sundry ding-a-ling-related mishaps over live footage of Chuck Berry.

But it was host Tony Blackburn who served up the biggest surprise of all, laughing in the company of a gentleman named Richard, a sound engineer on the show, who was dragged up better than all the bands put together.

Imagine that happening a year before!

December 1972 – Top Of The Pops Volume 28 (Hallmark SHM 810)

If any one act dominated the chart at the end of 1972, it was the Osmonds. For six months, the toothy siblings had been marching up the polls with a string of teen dream jingles.

And the Top Of The Pops team was ready for them.

They perfected the Donny sound by double-tracking vocalists John Perry and Martha Smith. They recaptured the thrust of the Osmonds by amping up the electronic organ and letting the nags go nutty. And when singer Tony Rivers introduced his son Anthony to the proceedings, they actually mustered a performance even chirpier than the original. In an age when pop stars were getting younger and more precocious by the day, little Anthony Rivers could have proved the biggest home-grown sensation since serial *Opportunity Knocks* winner Neil Reid.

But the Osmonds didn't have the chart to themselves. T Rex, Slade, and Rod Stewart and the Faces all get a look in; Michael Jackson is exquisitely aped in 'Ben', the sweet soundtrack theme to a movie about killer rats, while there's also a glorious stab at 'My Ding-A-Ling'.

ON THE RADIO

4-8 December 1972 – Dave Lee Travis: Wizzard

4-8 December 1972 – Johnnie Walker: Slade

18-22 December 1972 – Johnnie Walker: Slade

ON THE BOX

6 December 1972 – Lift Off With Ayshea: Stavely Makepeace

7 December 1972 – Top Of The Pops: Blackfoot Sue, Elton John, Lynsey de Paul, Slade, T Rex

14 December 1972 – Top Of The Pops: Slade, T Rex, David Bowie, Wizzard

20 December 1972 – Lift Off With Ayshea: Slade

21 December 1972 – Top Of The Pops: David Bowie, Elton John, Lynsey de Paul, T Rex, Wizzard

24 December 1972 – Lift Off With Ayshea: The Sweet

27 December 1972 – Lift Off With Ayshea: 10cc

CHAPTER FOUR

1973

Dancing With Your Lizard Leather Boots On

'I think all this posing stuff will be tolerated until – let's see – oh, the middle of 1974, and then it'll be dead.'
Mick Jagger, 1973

January 1973 – In the studio with Suzi Q
Suzi was still sweating from the Slade tour when Mickie Most took her back into the studio, to record a potential new single a cover of Clarence 'Frogman' Henry's 'Ain't Got No Home'.

She had a band now, likewise broken in by the tour – three mean-looking hombres named Len Tuckey (guitar), Alastair McKenzie (keyboards) and Keith Hodge (drums). 'I auditioned them,' she explained. 'We hadn't much time. I remember we had three of each type of musician to choose from. One was too clever, one was too flash and one was an oaf.

She picked the oafs.

But she didn't pick the Frogman song, and it wasn't working too well. It was finally scrapped around the same time as drummer Hodge decided to leave, to be replaced by Dave Neal, and Most made the decision to hand Quatro over to Chinnichap. They immediately handed her 'Can The Can'.

'They saw the aggression in Suzi,' Most said of the song, while Chapman added, 'It was a classic example of a record creating an artist, because "Can The Can" certainly created Suzi. It made her a superstar everywhere in the world except America.'

January 1973 – Gary Glitter: Do You Wanna Touch Me? (Oh Yeah)/I Would If I Could (Bell 1280)
Glitter's third successive UK hit was based on what would become one of his most enduring stage routines, leaning over the edge of the stage to shake hands with the audience while asking if they did, indeed, want to touch him.

'There?'

'Where?'

'There?'

'*Yeah!*'

It also represented a something of a departure from what was already hallmarked as the 'trademark' Glitter sound, faster and fuller, with the lyrics spat out like machine-gun fire, before returning to the basics of monosyllabic ejaculations – 'yeah, oh yeah, oh yeah.'

As it marched towards the Top Three, however, the artist formerly known as Paul Gadd, Paul Raven, Paul Monday and Rubber Bucket found himself facing an unexpected dilemma. What to do about his past?

Recent months had seen almost every one of his rivals, from Bowie to Bolan to the Sweet, being suddenly bedevilled by their Sixties past, reminders of the days when they were struggling unknowns, and the only spangles in their lives were the pocket-money priced sweets of the same name.

Decca, Parlophone and MCA all had their pre-Glitter skeletons in their closets – skeletons at least as embarrassing as the ghosts of his days as East London's Donovan, that led Marc Bolan to court to block a proposed album of demos; as ghastly as the Parlophone single that was resurrected the moment the Sweet hit it big; as shocking as the 'World Of David Bowie' collection Decca rushed out when Bowie hit it big, six years after he'd thought it was forgotten.

'As far as most of my fans were concerned, I hadn't existed before "Rock And Roll",' Glitter reasoned. 'There was no point to suddenly introducing them to Paul Raven and all the others.'

In a highly publicised move guaranteed to kill those spectres before they spotted him, Gary booked the floating museum, HMS *Belfast*, for the afternoon of 14 January, and staged a burial at sea as a coffin loaded with old cuttings and records was sombrely lowered into the depths.

Except it didn't stay there. 'Nobody had bothered to find out how these events are carried out, and we'd used an ordinary coffin which didn't sink. It just floated off down the river.'

Nevertheless, the ploy worked. Nobody reissued any of Glitter's old records, and they remain as rare and collectible today as they were in 1973. In hindsight, it's rather a pity.

January 1973 – Mud: Crazy/Do You Love Me (RAK 146)

Looking back on his initial encounter with Mud, and telescoping time just a little in his analogy, Mickie Most recalled, 'I thought they had something "tomorrow" about them. They had what every other band didn't have, they bridged the gap between Sweet and Slade.'

In early 1970, when he first encountered the quartet, neither of those bands meant a light. But you could see his point. Three years had passed since their first ill-fated encounter with Most, three years during which Mud had indeed left the Feldman's publishing company that so offended the great man and gone trotting back to Most. He shrugged them off – the moment had passed.

'So we went our merry way,' says Ray Stiles, 'working the clubs up north, working around. We were always popular, places were packed out, we were a good band. Word started getting around.'

Just like every other band on the circuit, Mud always asked club owners who else had played there recently. 'Places like the Cosmo in Carlisle, Rotherham Football Club...that was a great gig. The Imperial Ballroom in Nelson. We'd always go "What bands have you had here?" and there'd always be a band called Bitter Sweet, the Montanas and the Sweet, who'd just started having their first hits.

'The Sweet used to ask the same question because, apparently, they were on a recording session with Nicky Chinn and Mike Chapman and happened to mention that everywhere they went, this bloody band Mud had just been there, or were coming soon.

'So Nicky and Mike's ears pricked up and they tried to find out who this band was. They mentioned it to Mickie Most, and he said "I know them, I was going to sign them once", so they thought they'd better check us out.'

Mud were playing the Festival Hall in Trowell, near Nottingham, when Chinn and Chapman caught them for the first time. 'It was a Sunday night. They saw the first set and then they came into the dressing room; "We really like what you're doing." In fact, we didn't have a very good night as it happens, but they said "When are you back in London?" and we said, "Well, we'll be there tomorrow." So, tomorrow afternoon round to the office.'

Stiles missed the meeting; he was feeling unwell. 'But the others went, and they came round to my house afterwards to tell me what had been said; that we could have three hit records next year [1973], then three more the year after that, and more and more and more – and that's what happened.'

'They were incredibly prolific writers,' Mud vocalist Les Gray recalled. 'We had our ups and downs with them, but they were very talented and we had great respect for them.'

The feeling was mutual. Mud could not be described as ambitionless at this time, but they were very much directionless, content to grind around the same old circuit, making just enough money to keep things afloat but with little thought for life beyond the next gig. They were very professional and very polished. But they were also very small fry. Chinnichap intended changing that.

How did the Sweet feel about this? For two years, they had had Chinnichap to themselves. They had first choice of the songs they wrote, first call on their time. And now, recalled drummer Mick Tucker, '[Chinnichap] were walking around telling us that this was only the start, that they were going to build this empire of pop stars.'

At first, 'We thought [this] was great, because they also said that we were always going to be at the top of the queue when it came to new material. But you know, you're human. You can't help thinking "Well, they say that *now*..." and then you record something or do something you know is going out on a limb, and you look back at Mud going along with everything they're told to do and think "we're not as secure as we thought we were".'

Statistics would ultimately back those fears up. 'Sweet will be the group to provide us with the Number 1 hits,' Mike Chapman had said shortly after the release of Mud's RAK debut, 'Crazy'. 'Mud will have plenty of Top Ten successes, but they aren't really in quite the same league.' In the event, Sweet had but one Number 1, 'Blockbuster!' Mud hit the top three times and, like the Sweet, had *Top Of The Pops* to thank for a lot of that.

newscene

Bowie action '73

DAVID Bowie has begun 1973 in a burst of activity and a blaze of glory. As a performer, he had hardly returned from a much publicised visit to the States when he was off on a seven date tour of the home country, drawing capacity crowds to such famous venues as the Hardrock, Manchester and the Rainbow in London.

At the end of January he will be waving goodbye to England for yet another visit to America. He plans to mount a concert in the legendary Radio City Music Hall, home of the longest high kicking chorus line in the world.

Radio City, a monument of thirties architecture which has never previously permitted a rock musician to sully its hallowed stage, is equipped with all manner of strange and wonderful devices, including, a giant organ which rises with winking coloured lights, out of the orchestra pit. Bowie's show will be designed to take advantage of all these facilities. A spokesman for Bowie explained that Radio City were making this concession to rock because of the elements of theatre in Bowie's act. After this jaunt, a promotional trip to Japan is planned, though it is not yet clear whether this invoves a concert as well.

As far as records are concerned, an album of live material recorded at three of the gigs last time round in the U.S.A., is planned for release very soon. Also, while he was in New York, Bowie laid down four studio tracks and an album incorporating this material should follow hard on the heels of the live one.

Bowie's energy and influence also extends to the production of other people's records, notably Mott the Hoople and Lou Reed. One such record, which is due out anytime, is the latest offering of Iggy Pop.

David, as you can see, is hardly preparing to sink back into the obscurity which, in 1972, he dramatically escaped from

Byrds return

THERE is still some hope left in the rock world if things go on like this — the original Byrds have got together again and come up with an as yet untitled album that's due out here on the Asylum label in February (we hope).

Seems that Roger McGuinn, Dave Crosby, Chris Hillman, Gene Clark and Mike Clark were all brought together for a session that started off as a task and ended up as some sort of a gas, gas, gas.

Roger, Chris, Gene and Dave have two songs each on the album, plus there's Neil Young's "Cowgirl In The Sand" and Joni Mitchell's "For Free".

The album was recorded in Hollywood during November, thanks to Asylum boss David Geffen. Hassles over contracts there certainly were, but all that has happened is McGuinn would do that album just so long as Crosby did one for Columbia. Fair enough, it seems.

Looks like there may even be a tour to follow, though it's far too early at this stage to start talking about dates. Would be kinda nice if we could get the original Byrds over here for a while. The ball is in your collective court, promoters.

More Fairport

YET another line-up for Fairport Convention and a brand new tour to go with it. The fun begins at Mile End Sundown on January 18 and runs through to Portsmouth Guildhall where it winds up on March 23.

Guitarists Jerry Donahue and Trevor Lucas have joined Dave Swarbrick (mandolin and violin), Dave Pegg (bass) and Dave Mattacks (drums).

After Mile End, the tour's January dates are: Leeds University (19), Loughborough College (20), Grimsby College (22), Dublin University (25), Southampton University (27), York College (28) and Watford Town Hall (30).

In February, the tour visits Bolton Town Hall (1), Birmingham University (2), Hull University (3), Barnsley (4), Warwick University (8), Bradford University (9), Colchester University (10), University (16), L Imperial College Liverpool Manchester Har (22), Sunderland Glasgow (24), Jazz Club (25) Andrew's University

The March venue Luton Technical C (3), Nottingham University (9), Lan University (10), (16) and Essex Univ (17).

Blackfoot on the move

BLACKFOOT Sue the group that mainly to Red Go on, work it out off to Sweden, and Norway at the January for an promotional tour lucky people.

Latest British the group Lowestoft South (February 3), College (16), Maltings (17) and

Roxy waxing

HOTFOOT from the American tour ended at the January, Roxy have dashed recording their second should be March or nicely timed a British tour

The tour March 16 through to which also plays Italy, a the Golden Montreaux Paris Olympia

Dates being set concerts feature a Roxy type costumes

For Mud's first appearance on the show, clad in violently mismatched check suits, guitarist Rob Davis spent the entire performance locked in the lotus position while drummer Dave Mount played Groucho Marx from behind his kit. High-kicking guitarists, swinging machine heads, and the first steps towards a patent Mud dance were all in evidence, reminders of the band's days entertaining round the clubs. But Mud were only getting started.

Vivid greens and putrid pinks ensured that their stage outfits would clash violently with whatever fixtures bedecked the studios that week, and even Chinnichap were to express surprise at how adept the band became. Maybe those years on the northern cabaret circuit weren't a waste of time after all.

'We gradually developed things so that there was a different dance for every record and different clothes for every TV show,' Les Gray explained. 'There was no video in those days, so we had to do a live TV show every time. Of course it was meant to be tongue in cheek. The music was as good as we could get it, but everything else was rehearsed to look like chaos.'

In common with the Sweet, Mud would not play on their first or indeed their second RAK release. 'We were so booked up with all our work up north,' explains Stiles, 'so they said "we'll make the records, and then we'll just put your voices on when you get the chance. You can nip into the studio, do the voices and then be off again".'

Drummer Dave Mattacks (of Fairport Convention), guitarist Pip Williams, Fiachra Trench (keyboards) and bassist Chas Hodges (of Heads Hands and Feet and, later, Chas and Dave) duly performed the backing track. 'We came down and sang on them, and that was that.'

Released in January, 'Crazy' inched only slowly into contention. With the band on the road with crooner Jack Jones, it was March before it first sniffed the chart. But it ultimately rose to Number 12, and Mud were flowing.

January 1973 – Be Bop Deluxe: Teenage Archangel/Jets At Dawn (Smile LAFS 001)

A desperately serious young man fronting a desperately serious sounding band, Wakefield-born Bill Nelson had already grasped a smidgeon of attention when he self-released his 'Northern Dream' album (Smile AF 2182) in 1971, and won a few spins on John Peel's show.

The same homely set-up, the Holyground Studios in Wakefield, was also responsible for his next release, a union with local musicians Ian Parkin (guitar), Robert Bryan (bass), Richard Brown (keyboards) and Nicholas Chatterton-Dew (drums), beneath the oddly evocative Be Bop Deluxe banner...evocative because what do *you* think of when you hear those words? Not a bunch of po-faced pros furiously denying that they have anything to do with Glam Rock, that's for certain...

EMI had already shown an interest following 'Northern Dream', but were less convinced by the band. Echoing EG Management's disdain for the early Roxy Music, they instead offered Nelson a solo deal; echoing Ferry's dismissal of their advances, Nelson turned them down and suggested the label heads catch them in concert. Shortly after, Be Bop Deluxe had a deal.

January 1973 – Stavely Makepeace: Prima Donna/Swings and Roundabouts (Spark SRL 1085)

Previewed on *Lift Off With Ayshea* at the end of the year, once more into the breach for Stavely Makepeace and their final Spark single.

January 1973 – Elton John: Daniel/Skyline Pigeon (DJM 275)

January 1973 – Elton John: Don't Shoot Me, I'm Only The Piano Player (DJM 427)

And while we're on the subject of Stavely, was the majestic B-side to Elton's latest (somewhat wimpy) hit single *really* the Piano Player's tribute to the Lieutenant of the same species?

27 January 1973 – You can't block buster

The Sweet's 'Blockbuster!' made it to Number 1 on 27 January, finally toppling the long-haired lover from Utah in the process, and Nicky Chinn remembers being cornered at the London nightclub Tramp, shortly after. 'Bowie looked at me completely deadpan and said "Cunt!" And then he got up and gave me a hug and said "Congratulations!".'

Bowie's guitarist, Mick Ronson, was similarly impressed, both by the record and by the band itself. 'I kinda liked some of the Sweet's

singles around that time,' he said 12 years later. 'The Sweet were alright.'

The Sweet themselves were filming a *Crackerjack* performance (for broadcast on 2 February) when they heard they were Number 1. The moment filming was over they retired to celebrate in a nearby pub with fellow guests Lieutenant Pigeon.

January 1973 – Top Of The Pops Volume 29 (Hallmark SHM 815)

The British charts for 1973 opened as they closed in 1972, with the Yardbirds' 'I'm A Man' riff loitering around the top. The whole world was going Glam, and Top Of The Pops was there to capture it. From Owlish Reg from Pinner disguising his ordinariness beneath outlandish feathers and absurd specs; through the folky Strawbs rouging their cheekbones and singing songs in praise of industrial action ('Part Of The Union'); and on to Gary Glitter simply being Gary Glitter, ('Do You Wanna Touch Me? (Oh Yeah!)'), it was impossible to denigrate the difference a smattering of sequins and a quick dab of Max Factor could make to your career.

Even hoary old rockers Status Quo and Electric Light Orchestra were getting in on the act (remember ELO on the other *Top Of The Pops*, with Jeff Lynne's head encased in tinsel?), and 'Volume 29' sparkles with the best of them.

ON THE RADIO
1-5 January 1973 – Johnnie Walker: Slade
8-12 January 1973 – Alan Freeman: The Sweet
8-12 January 1973 – Johnnie Walker: Wizzard
8-12 January 1973 – Dave Lee Travis: Slade
22-26 January 1973 – Johnnie Walker: Wizzard
22-26 January 1973 – Alan Freeman: The Sweet
ON THE BOX
3 January 1973 – Lift Off With Ayshea: Lieutenant Pigeon
4 January 1973 – Top Of The Pops: David Bowie, Lieutenant Pigeon, T Rex, Wizzard
11 January 1973 – Top Of The Pops: Elton John, David Bowie, the Sweet, Wizzard
14 January 1973 – The Golden Shot: The Sweet
18 January 1973 – Top Of The Pops: Lieutenant Pigeon, the Sweet, Wizzard
21 January 1973 – They Sold A Million: Slade
25 January 1973 – Top Of The Pops: Wizzard, Elton John, the Sweet, Gary Glitter
27 January 1973 – Cilla: T Rex
27 January 1973 – Russell Harty Plus: Elton John

February 1973 – Lou Reed: Vicious/Satellite Of Love (RCA 2318)

One day, Andy Warhol asked Lou Reed to write a song called 'Vicious'.

'What sort of "vicious"?' asked Lou.

'Oh, "vicious, you hit me with a flower...",' Warhol replied. So Lou did it and the opening track to 'Transformer' ushered in the next half-hour as sweetly as any single song could, on board a riff as righteous as any he had conjured in the past.

It also had 'hit single' scrawled over it. So when 'Walk On The Wild Side' was stillborn in November RCA reached straight for the next best thing.

They backed it with another of the album's most translucent jewels as Reed delved back into the Velvet Underground's cupboard of unreleased songs and sketches for a gorgeous paean written in much the same frame of pioneering mind as David Bowie's 'Space Oddity' but shelved when the band broke up. 'If anybody asked me if we'd laid that down, I don't remember,' guitarist Sterling Morrison remarked, although he did recall the Velvets performing it in concert.

By the time of 'Transformer', the song had undergone a few lyrical and musical shifts but still its gentle arrangement and the cute backing vocals did their best to deceive the fact that the song is a bitter saga of jealousy, as Reed himself discovered on stage one memorable night.

'I was suddenly struck so hard by what it was really about. It stopped me in my tracks for an instant, just how intense that kind of jealousy was. I'm just glad that the melody was pretty.'

by Richard Williams

Favourite

Splendour

picture by Barrie Wentzell

Reed between the lines

February 1973 – Slade: Cum On Feel The Noize/I'm Mee, I'm Now An' That's Orl (Polydor 2058339)

Every fresh single turned the amplifiers louder and 'Cum On Feel The Noize' – released on the eve of a mega-gig at Wembley – was Slade's loudest yet.

The lyric had its roots in an especially chaotic night on the band's last British tour. Holder recalled, 'The audience was chanting along so loudly to every song that I couldn't hear myself sing.' Originally, the song was titled 'Cum On *Hear* The Noize' – Holder revised the title when he recalled 'how I had felt the sound of the crowd pounding in my chest.'

As usual, however, the studio allowed for some ad-libbing, and Slade's greatest moment sprang out of it. The opening seconds to 'Cum On Feel The Noize', full-throated and feral, fiery breath oxidising as it leaves Noddy Holder's lips, an opening bellow of 'Baby baby baby' that is so much more than the mere intro to a pop record.

It is a call to arms, the irresistible warcry of rampant youth at its most potent, primal and primitive. And you were never meant to hear it. Rather, it was Holder's customary cue for the rest of the band to come in at the start of a take. Producer Chas Chandler, however, left it in for the most distinctive intro of the age.

As for the burgeoning accusations that Slade records were all sounding very primitive, Chandler agreed wholeheartedly. But only because it led to its own set of challenges. 'Because the group have such a basic feel to their records,' he explained, 'producing them should be easy. But they are perfectionists and aren't satisfied easily. The special effects like the applause [on this one] was recorded in a corridor because they thought the echoes were better.'

Advance copies of the single went out to Radio 1 some three weeks ahead of release, in order to build up a nice head of airplay-shaped steam. They were rewarded when the record shoved 'Blockbuster!' rudely out of the way and entered the chart at Number 1, the first time any band had achieved that feat since the Beatles' 'Get Back' in 1969.

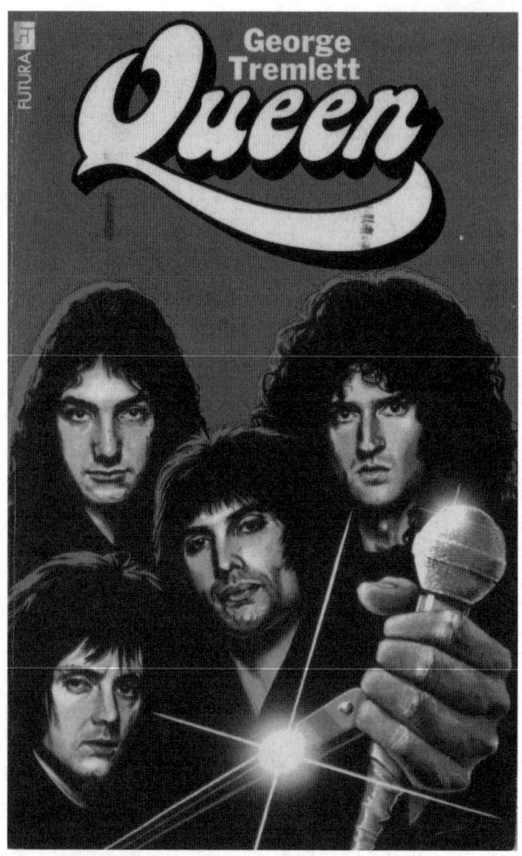

5 February 1973 – Sounds Of The Seventies: Queen

The union of singer Freddie Mercury with the rump of a prog band called Smile – Brian May (guitar) and Roger Taylor (drums) – was one of summer 1970's less reported events. True, Taylor and the immaculately flamboyant Mercury were running a clothing stall at Kensington Market at the time, and therefore had their fingers on the fashion of the day, but even after they were joined by bassist John Deacon in February 1971 the newly named Queen were more of a daydream than a drama.

Still, they made some demos at De Lane Lea Studios after a friend asked them to test out some newly purchased equipment and it was these tapes that eventually brought the band to the attention of Trident Audio Productions, owners of the Trident Studios and an aspiring management company.

In November 1971, Queen signed production, management and publishing contracts with the company and, by the new year, were reaping the first rewards via a booking at the Beeb. Queen's maiden session for DJ John Peel featured four tracks: 'My Fairy King', 'Doing All Right' and two instantaneous classics, 'Liar' and 'Keep Yourself Alive', that would be reprised five months later for a Bob Harris session.

They were raw, but they were powerful. 'It's a strange thing,' May reflects. 'You work for hours and hours in the studio for days and weeks to put down the structure of a song, but once you have it it's not too difficult to recreate it. It's doing it the first time which is the hard thing. So generally we recreated things quite quickly for a couple of tracks, because time was so short, then we'd sort of stretch out a bit on the others.'

Almost gleefully, he reiterates, 'You certainly couldn't spend all day in the Beeb because there just wasn't the time.' He will not be drawn on the relative merits of the performances. 'I think they were fun at the time and it's nice to look at them again. They have a roughness and a freshness which is enjoyable.'

February 1973 – Chicory Tip: Good Grief Christina/Move On (CBS 1258)

Good Grief. 'Christina' spent close to 12 weeks on the chart and didn't get any higher than Number 17.

February 1973 – Light Fantastic: Jeanie/You Don't Care (RCA 2331)

Light Fantastic – Sludge, Joe Dog, Twig, Spook and Buck – had been rattling around the Birmingham/Wolverhampton scene since the late Sixties. They toured with Carl Wayne, recorded demos with Roy Wood and even stormed the world of *Opportunity Knocks*. They finished second behind juvenile singer Neil Reid, but were nevertheless invited to return for the show's year-end special.

They had a fair amount of support, then, long before they were booked to open for the Sweet at the end of 1972. But friendship with the headliners followed and, although the band already had a deal with MAM (and had in fact released their debut single, 'Love Is Everywhere', in 1971), a new scheme was hatched to allow the Sweet to do for Light Fantastic what Chinnichap did for them.

'Jeanie' was a cover of a Roger Glover composition that Brian Connolly had co-opted for a Sweet B-side the previous year (and craftily tried to claim the writing credits for, as well). 'You Don't Care' was a spare Andy Scott effort. Amusingly, however, in the light of the Sweet's disapproval when the same stunt was pulled on them, Light Fantastic were not permitted to play on their own A-side. Rather, the Sweet's own backing track was employed, and Light Fantastic were required only to add the lead vocal.

'Yeah, we kind of stitched them up on that one,' Tucker grinned ruefully. 'But it turned out Phil Wainman was right. We only had a tiny bit of studio time, and it was just quicker and easier to use an old backing track, rather than try and coax the same performance from a band.'

February 1973 – Alice Cooper: Hello Hooray/ Generation Landslide (Warners K16248)
17 February 1973 – Alice Cooper: Excerpts From Billion Dollar Babies (Lyntone 2585)

Keeping up the pressure, 'Hello Hooray' reached Number 6, the latest taster for the next Cooper album. And, if that wasn't enough, you could also pick up the latest issue of the *New Musical Express* for a flexidisc that not only served up a fascinating medley of clips from the forthcoming LP but also offered one otherwise unavailable out-take, 'Slick Black Limousine', and one unused snippet from the album's 'Unfinished Sweet', a disembodied voice asking 'have you ever had gas before?'

This was the second of four *NME* freebie flexidiscs – others profiled new albums by the Faces, ELP and Monty Python.

February 1973 – Lieutenant Pigeon: Mouldy Old Music (SKL 5154)

The Pigeon were never happy with their debut album. Under pressure from Decca to follow up the hit as quickly as possible, says Rob Woodward, they turned to recordings that dated back as far as 1969, 'plus a few later ones we managed to complete. Most of these were from our home studio and, although caught with our pants down somewhat, it was released and the sales were very favourable.'

Two further Lieutenant Pigeon albums appeared over the next 18 months; 'Pigeon Pie' (Decca SKL 5174) in February 1974, and 'Pigeon Party' (Decca SKL 5196) that same November. A fourth album, a compilation within Decca's popular World Of series was scheduled for release in 1976 but withdrawn at the test pressing stage. Another compilation, 'Kathleen', was released in Australia, following the chart-topping success of 'I'll Take You Home, Kathleen' in 1974.

February 1973 – Barry Blue: Dancin' (On A Saturday Night)/New Day (Bell 1295)

Barry Ian Green was one of those teenage prodigies with which British pop once abounded – aged 13 in 1963, his schoolboy band the Dark Knights were seven-time winners of the Granada TV talent show *Stubby Kaye's Silver Star Show* and were rewarded with a recording contract at Columbia Records, signed by Norrie Paramor. His assistant, the then-unknown Tim Rice, produced the band's debut single, Green's 'She's All Around Me'.

Two years later, another Green composition, 'Rainmaker Girl', was covered by Gene Pitney and, in 1968, he penned the theme music to the newly launched Granada show *Lift Off.* He was also bassist and leader of the show's resident band.

A solo deal with Decca saw Green record three singles over the next three years, including 1971's bubblegummy 'Alexander the Greatest' and Swedish Top Twenty smash 'Papa Do' (c/w 'Boomerang', Decca DL 25508), his first co-write with Lynsey de Paul.

Green represented the UK at the 1972 Split Song Contest in Yugoslavia, finishing third, and signed to Bell later that same year, taking the decision to change his surname shortly before the release of his debut single. Originally penned for fellow Bell artists Mardi Gras, 'Dancin' (On A Saturday Night)' was another de Paul co-write and featured accompaniment from future Rubettes John Richardson and Alan Williams.

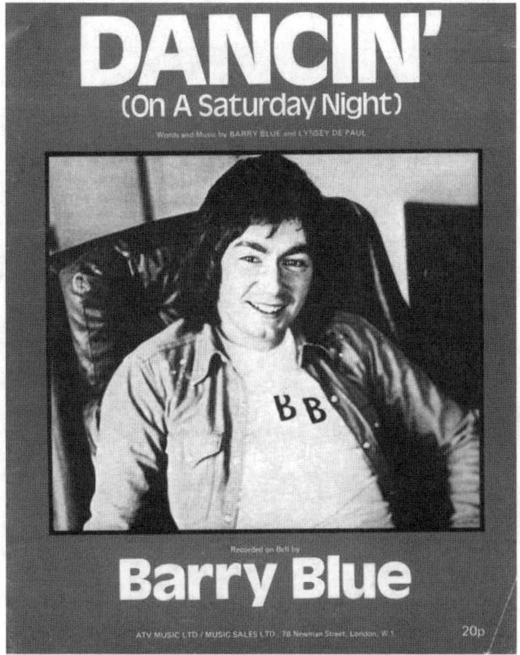

Initially, it looked like another non-starter. It would take the single no less than six months to finally sneak into the chart but, once it was there, only the perennial Donny Osmond could stop it. 'Dancin'' reached Number 2 in September, behind the toothsome 'Too Young'.

ON THE BOX
1 February 1973 – Top Of The Pops: The Sweet
2 February 1973 – Crackerjack: The Sweet, Lieutenant Pigeon
8 February 1973 – Top Of The Pops: Gary Glitter, the Sweet
15 February 1973 – Top Of The Pops: The Sweet
17 February 1973 – Russell Harty Plus: David Bowie
22 February 1973 – Top Of The Pops: Slade, The Sweet
ON THE SHELVES
February 1973 – Ricky Wilde: April Love/Round And Round (UK 28)
February 1973 – Scalliwag: Lazy Hazy Feeling/Stone (Bell 1290)

March 1973 – Alice Cooper: Billion Dollar Babies (Warners K56013)

Musically, creatively and in terms of sheer craziness, the Coopers reached their peak with 'Billion Dollar Babies'.

They talked of giving away real money with it, but backpedalled only when they realised how much it would cost if the album sold even a fraction of its predecessors. But the contents were alluring regardless – a dummy bill for a billion bucks, a pack of custom-made bubblegum cards and a collection of songs that paid homage to sick things, mad dogs and the dentist's drill. The last thing you heard was Alice screaming how much he loved the dead. *Loved* the dead.

Two hit singles, the ferocious Elected' and the admittedly-tame-but-it-did-the-job 'No More Mr Nice Guy' previewed the album... Over in California, Sparks – whose last album closed with the song of the almost-same-title – were counting the cost of refusing to allow Alice to

GLAM ROCK

Glamorous rock– brings with it glitt make-up and satir suits CAROLIN BOUCHER investigates the phenomenon and talks to the men who have put the show back into show business . . . and to those who still favour T-shirts and old jeans.

CASUAL DRESSER

borrow a lyric from the song 'Beaver O'Lindy' ('I'm the girl in your head, the boy in your bed') when he asked them nicely.

Because, they alleged to whoever would listen, he didn't even bother asking this time. 'Well, at least somebody discovered this song and made a buck or two out of it,' was Russell Mael's weary rejoinder.

The heart of 'Billion Dollar Babies', however, lay in the stage epics – the title track, all familial fiendishness and disembodied limbs; 'Raped And Freezing', with its vistas of degradation; a precious little jazzy piece titled 'Mary Ann' – and then the storm that succeeded that particular lull, 'I Love The Dead'. *Before* they're cold.

'Billion Dollar Babies' was reissued with a bonus disc of live recordings, outtakes and the *NME* flexidisc in 2001 (Rhino R2 79791).

March 1973 – Streak: Bang Bang Bullet/Blackjack Man (Deram DM 376)

Prior to his Japanese adventures, New Yorker Alan Merrill was a member of Watertower West, a band that grew out of various High School outfits before introducing him to guitarist Jake Hooker.

The band sundered when Merrill left for Tokyo in 1968 but the members remained in contact and, in early 1971, Merrill was in New York recording demos with Hooker and drummer John Siomos for a new band called Streak.

They completed four songs and took them to London, where they enlisted another American, David Wesley, on drums; 'Siomos had gotten a call from Stevie Wonder to tour,' Merrill laughs, 'and he wasn't going to turn that down!' Neither was Merrill going to stick around long; he returned to Japan but Streak continued with new bassist Ben Brierley.

What happened next is, perhaps, typical music-business shenanigans. Using the New York demo tapes, Streak landed a deal with A&M and took two Hooker/Merrill compositions, 'Be Your Rider'/'Gonna Have A Good Time' as their debut single, oddly substituting Merrill's name for Wesley's on the writing credits.

The single went nowhere, A&M dropped the band and Wesley quit. But Streak marched on, with drummer Paul Varley and guitarist Rick Steele, and in this form cut their second single, the now-immortal 'Bang Bang Bullit'.

'Instant punk rock!' declared the *NME*'s review three years before the term meant much (years, too, before Brierley joined the Vibrators), and in 2004, 'Bang Bang Bullit' would be rediscovered aboard the 'Glitterbest: UK Glam With Attitude 1971-1976' compilation (RPM 265).

In-between times, however, it rested in obscurity, its makers too. An album was commenced but never finished – four tracks, 'Snake Eyes', 'On The Ball', 'Dirty Dick' and 'Power Over You', were recorded with producer David Hitchcock (who also oversaw the single), but they never progressed further than monitor mixes before the band broke up.

March 1973 – Top Of The Pops Volume 30 (Hallmark SHM 820)

The Top of the Poppers let us down badly here. Unless, of course, you've always thought 'Cum On Feel The Noize' really needed to open with the sound of someone's dad calling the kids in for dinner. It doesn't make sense. The remainder of the performance is one of the finest Slade covers in the entire *Top Of The Pops* series. But that intro ruins the whole thing for everyone, which just about sums up this particular album.

Drawn from a chart simply clogged with clutter (and yes, sadly, that includes Chicory Tip's first hit in a year, 'Good Grief Christina'), it offers up little more than well-meaning nonentities, chirpy singer-songwriters, vaudevillian novelties, sundry singing siblings... You can tie on all the yellow ribbons you like, but they won't make this disc any brighter.

March 1973 – T Rex: 20th Century Boy/Free Angel (T Rex MARC 4)
March 1973 – T Rex: Tanx (T Rex 5002)

It was a harsh fact, but it was an inescapable one. Marc Bolan had created the Glam-Rock market, he had seen it flourish, explode. And now it had overtaken him. David Bowie, Gary Glitter, the Sweet, Lieutenant Pigeon, all were now out-charting the Bopping Elf.

Yet chart positions can lie. In 1996, Channel 4 TV's *Glam Top Ten* showcased the most successful artists of the era. Bolan romped home in second place – only Slade, the pantomime Stones to his sepulchral Beatles, outsold him, but not even they outperformed him. Bowie, incidentally, didn't even rank.

Even without their shared history, it was no coincidence that David Bowie's rise to glory should coincide almost exactly with Bolan's fall from grace. Bolan's success relied on his almost unaccompanied breakthrough; when he first hit the scene he was unique. The people who followed simply followed his example and with it, a facet of his personality. Gary Glitter grabbed the primeval stomp, Slade took the terrace-chant simplicity, the Sweet took the prepubescent awareness and David Bowie took the teenage hormones.

Bolan's own sexuality had never been dwelt upon. He could drag up and act the *prima donna* fag as much as he wanted, and rumours of his impending sex change and marriage to bongo-player Mickey Finn could circulate freely as they liked. But not once did Bolan step forward to end the speculation. That responsibility was left to Bowie, and with it the rewards.

After the fact, Bolan was furious that Bowie had beaten him to the bisexual punch, but it was already too late. With as much pride in his powers of invention as Bolan had, there was no way he was going to say – or do – something someone had already done. There was no point. 'Marc simply couldn't stand attention going in anyone else's direction,' Tony Visconti explains. 'David, on the other hand, always liked Marc. He liked to be with him. He would come home after a social session feeling quite hurt after Bolan had taken too many digs at him.'

In the end the strain, and the rivalry, simply became too much, and through much of the early-mid Seventies the two superstars were scarcely even on speaking terms, a sad turnabout from the days when they had been virtually inseparable.

There again, as Visconti continues, 'Marc was in rivalry with everybody. He was a total megalomaniac, God bless him, which is what a lot of stars are made of. You have to have a huge ego to be a huge success, Marc's was simply huger than most.

'He used to do things like buy 10 albums a day, James Burton guitar player records, then come round to my flat, play them, and ask me what I thought. So I'd say, "Pretty good, that's a good solo," and he's say "Yeah, but I'm better". Once I was listening to a John Williams album – I love classical music and I was off in a reverie somewhere, going "Oh, what marvellous technique", and Marc said, "I could play like that in two weeks". He was in rivalry with everyone. He couldn't stand competition. He'd meet it head-on, even if he had to make the most outrageous claims. He'd have the bravado to do it.'

Bravado, of course, is one thing, but once so-convincing boasts like 'I'm going to have four Number 1s this year, easy' now sounded shrill and empty. 'Glam Rock is dead,' he continued, but again, you only had to look around to see how hollow that was.

So, when 'Tanx' appeared in early 1973, the critical consensus was that Bolan had already shot his commercial bolt, and history would not break its back to prove otherwise. But divorced from the time and place in which it was conceived, there really is little wrong with the album. Its timing was faulty, that's all...that, and the vague sense that we'd already heard a few of the songs in the past. And so we had – 'Tenement Lady', 'Mad Donna', 'Country Rock' and the somewhat grating 'Life Is Strange' – were little more than below-par rewrites of the basic Bolan boogie.

But the phased acoustics of 'Rapids' were simply gorgeous if a little too short, while 'Shock Rock' wags a condemnatory finger at...well, Marc never said exactly who it was aimed at, but he clearly had someone in mind. 'If you know how to rock, you don't have to shock.'

The oddly Elton-esque 'Broken Hearted Blues' oozes affection, while the closing 'Left Hand Luke And The Beggar Boys' has the kind of street-fighting swagger that both Bruce Springsteen and Phil Lynott would subsequently claim as their own. And then there was 'Born To Boogie', *still* the biggest hit he never got round to releasing.

The memory of 'Tanx' takes further sustenance from 'Left Hand Luke – The Alternate Tanx' (Edsel), the 1994 recreation of the parent LP built around the outtakes that Bolan left behind.

As with the other albums in the 'alternate' series, 'Left Hand Luke' is an occasionally scrappy, scratchy listen. But it is also utterly reinvigorating, casting 'Tanx' itself in a brand new light and proving that, whatever else ailed Bolan at the time, he had not lost his passion. 'Mister Mister', hitherto a somewhat inconsequential little ditty, takes on unimagined power, while further enlightenment is drawn from a generous stack of demos – four played on acoustic guitar and bass, five more on the guitar alone, including a take on 'Mad Donna' with a slew of alternate lyrics.

In truth, little about 'Left Hand Luke' can be considered superior or even the equal of the original album, but that's as it should be. Rough mixes are scarcely the optimum source for variation, after all. But, as a window into the last stages of the album's completion, allowing us to see which bits were twiddled, which were twitched and which were omitted altogether, we also see what Bolan was trying to do with an album which, at the time, was dismissed as the abandonment of almost all his glam-rock principles.

And we know now that the impression wasn't wholly undesired.

Further evidence of Bolan's development is drawn from 'T Rex Unchained: Unreleased Recordings Volumes 3/4: 1973 Parts 1/2' (Edsel); indeed, any prevailing notion that Bolan's musical prowess was slipping as fast as his commercial invincibility is thrown out with the bathwater from the word go. Or, at least, from the moment 'Dance In The Midnight', 'Saturday Night' and 'Down Home Lady'

leap out to imprint themselves on your brain for all time, while his failure to take 'All My Love' to completion at least accounts for his failure to score any more Top Ten hits. Who could resist any song with the chorus 'My baby is a scooter and I love her'?

We also get a glimpse into the sheer wealth of projects that Bolan was then considering. At least one of the tracks, the sultry 'Metropolis Incarnate', was intended for 'Billy Super Duper', a concept album he continued toying with over the next two years; other stand-out tracks spread across these two discs (sold separately, but unquestionably destined to be considered as one) include 'Jet Tambourine' another of Bolan's cunning rewrites of both his own, and rock'n'roll, past, and the gentle 'High Wire'. 'Sad Girl' wouldn't have been out of

All Tanked u

Marc Bolan was very 'au fey' with the world when he turned into his office barely ten minutes late. He had just returned from Barbados and the shades were a dark shade of black. He flung himself into a chair, beamed broadly and asked for some coffee.

It turns out that the new LP, "Tanx" apart from being an excuse for Bolan to sit sexily across a large tank, with its barrel jutting into the text, is also another step towards musical aggrandisement in the shape of arrangements, instrumentation and cost.

He maintains however that the concept is the same. "When I met Tony Visconti I was doing acoustic things after trying electric things, and not feeling musically confident enough," he said leaning back.

"What I was doing then is no different from now, but I didn't have the economy to be able to cope with it. We used to borrow PA's; I used to borrow a guitar!

"If you listen through the albums each one gets thicker. The first one was basically pretty simple, the second one was the acoustic thing really tied up; the third one I used organ, drum kit, bass on it; the fourth one I used electric guitar and then we used the orchestras!"

They also used money. As a rough guide to Marc's LP expenditure; the very first album with Tyrannosaurus Rex, way back in July 1968, "My People were Fair and had Sky in their Hair" cost around £1,200. "Tanx" cost £12,000, and recording rates have only gone up from £28 to £35 an hour.

"When you're earning £50 a night or something there's not much point going out and spending £2,000 on an album, you know for a string session thing, if it's not going to work," Marc explained.

"Now I will try everything. I don't care you know. I'll

MARC BOLAN

Bolan aims at the future

words: Andrew Furnival

get ten Mellotrons and try them out, and if I don't like it I'll send them back. That's the nice thing that success can give you — it's freedom really."

Though Bolan has been a success himself, he doesn't recommend the rock business. "If I wanted to make money I wouldn't be in the rock 'n' roll business. I tell you that," he said tapping his finger on the table wisely. "I'd be in merchandising, cellophane stockings or plate glass earwigs or something. It wouldn't be rock 'n' roll."

On his last two English concerts, just before Christmas, he lost £12,000

which presum
£2,000 on the
that flashed a
the stab of a b
"I mean ob
got more mon
I ever had bef
probably thou
ever get. But y
don't know if
he remarked.
if I've ever me
was rich.
"I mean a r
a person who
to worry about
to worry about
— to run the c
£600 a week.
"I do have t
that if I stoppe
three months t
probably be br
continue for fiv
that won't be t
possible that w
royalties come
will be in a bett
but they take t
In common w
singers of the m
early sixties (re
Fabian, Bobby V
the 1973 Mr Bo
succumbed to p
films — as an a
has nothing to c
"Born to Boogie
Ringo.
"This is a nev
development fo
months ago (De
wouldn't have s
I would like to d
role where I wou
Marc Bolan. I co
lose myself.
"I wouldn't m
an 80 year-old m
"I'm pleased
development in
he went on. "I fi
refreshing not to
what you are for
I'm making a sile
Ringo, a 20-min
film.
"I haven't writ
It's serious. Have
Jekyll and Hyde,
original one with
Barrymore — inc
lots of, you know,
lighting.
"We've both g
and we'll just do
really nice illustr
and put a music
or something."
I asked Marc w
dependent on. "N
he replied withou
hesitation. "With
don't exist." You
makes sense.

place in the Rolling Stones' mid-Sixties' canon.

Other might-have-beens are conjured by 'Organ Thing', an infuriatingly brief glimpse into what could have been one of Bolan's most ambitious musical ventures and the otherwise untitled instrumental 'Jam', which harks back to the extended conclusion to 'Elemental Child', at the same time as looking forward to the funk basics which the forthcoming 'Zinc Alloy' album ultimately shied away from.

Almost 10 minutes of wah-wah soloing may not be to everyone's taste, but that's their problem. For anyone who doubts (or contrarily, doesn't doubt) Bolan's status as one of rock's greatest guitar visionaries, it remains essential listening.

March 1973 – The Sweet: The History Of Rock And Roll

Two years had elapsed since the Sweet's first album, two years during which they had run up the hits like they were going out of fashion, and talked a lot about what they wanted to do, once they got into the studio for more than a day.

Their new album, Andy Scott insisted, 'is already about half-written. It's going to be a concept album relating to rock'n'roll over a 20-year period, with the songs possibly joined together with monologue. We're not sure about that yet. Each of the songs will relate to a two-year period, although we won't date them, in case we might be a bit out! We're not aiming for authenticity of sound. It will be the Sweet sound, but we hope that people will be reminded of something from the era we're relating to, just by the flavour of the song.'

Brian Connolly continued: 'The album's going to start at 1956 – that's really when rock'n'roll began – with a song that'll be like a Presley. Then it'll change to a Little Richard sort of song, and so on, through the years. For 1965, it'll obviously be a song with a Beatles harmony. We'll also be doing a Stones type of number and to end we'll try and do a futuristic number for 1976. The problem now is just to get all the songs written.'

And it would be a problem. 'We got halfway through the album with the help of Mike Chapman and Nicky Chinn,' Priest reported, 'but when we listened to it in the cold light of day, we didn't find the songs very inspiring. So we shelved the whole thing.'

In fact, inspiration was one thing that the album possessed a lot of. One of the proposed inclusions, a Chinnichap newie called 'Touch Too Much', was later handed to Mickie Most for the Arrows. The Presley song surely was handed on to Mud. And the Sweet themselves would hang on to 'Peppermint Twist' and land an Australian Number 1 with it.

But everything else was simply scrapped and the band began work anew, pausing only to curse the schedule that kept the Sweet forever running back and forth to promote new singles, rather than knuckle down to the serious work of actually creating that album.

March 1973 – Geordie: All Because Of You/Ain't It Just Like A Woman (EMI 2008)
March 1973 – Geordie: Hope You Like It (EMI EMC 3001)

Destined to become one of the leading players over the next few years, the EMI label was the brainchild of A&R manager Joop Visser.

He arrived at the company's Manchester Square office in October 1972 and immediately set about trimming the fat off the label's books, beginning with a host of venerable old imprint. Parlophone, where the Beatles were born, Columbia, home to Cliff Richard, Regal Zonophone – all were given the chop. In their stead, just one label would flourish: EMI.

The roster, too, was drastically pruned. Eighty bands were on the various labels when Visser arrived. By the new year, there was just 40. Geordie were one of the lucky ones, and repaid EMI's faith immediately when the glam slam clatter of 'All Because Of You' became their biggest hit yet, a Number 6. But it was a less than trustworthy entrance into the world of their debut album. Because once they had you in there, they didn't really care whether you liked it or not. This was wailing blues-rock of the bluest degree.

It certainly makes few concessions to the band's new-found fame, a raw and raucous slam through 11 songs that only let the bombast slip when they tumble into the closing clown time of the traditional singalong 'Geordie's Lost His Liggie'. Elsewhere, Geordie go hell for rocking leather and – okay, maybe they did hope you like it. But would they like *you*? That was the real question.

March 1973 – Gary Glitter: Hello Hello I'm Back Again/IOU (Bell 1299)

No less than its predecessor, Glitter's latest single (and third Number 2 smash) was born from his stage act, this time his habit of returning from a costume change, of announcing 'Hello, I'm back!' And though its lyric was little more than a nursery rhyme, it nevertheless 'took hours to write. [It] was fantastically complicated to structure. It had to keep time with the beat and be easy enough to sing along with, but not so simple that the audience got bored.'

There was no danger of that. Over the years,

Glitter:

To date, Gary Glitter and colleague Mike Leander find commercial success with their records by sticking fairly rigidly to the same formula.

"Although, I don't like the word 'formula' that much, because I don't think that, in a creative industry, it *is* actually a formula," Glitter told me. "You find a sound and that's your identity. Then, you can work in and around it.

"If I thought it was just a formula, I could turn round to you and say 'Yes, the next record will *definitely* be a hit'. But, you're never really certain.

"Incidentally, I've thought that all my records have been totally different. But, I'm far more involved in them and know the different attitudes.

"Maybe, sometimes I don't know the subleties

on 'The Famous Instigator' (a track from the first album)?'. And I've said 'What thing?'. Then, they've demonstrated what, for them, really turns them on. *I* wasn't even aware of it.

"It was just something I did on the session because, towards the end of it, I felt that I had to be a bit humorous about what I was doing. That was my way of showing that it wasn't as heavy as I was making it out to be."

Glitter readily accepts that a sense of humour is essential to what he is doing.

"To me, 'Hello, Hello, I'm Back Again' wasn't the joke that some people considered it, but it wasn't heavy, either. It was quite humorous, in the same way as 'Touch Me' — which wasn't, as I was accused at the time, suggestive."

In the earlier days of the Glitter phenomenon,

'Hello Hello I'm Back Again' would become one of Glitter's personal signature tunes – not only on stage during concerts, but also as a herald of the various comebacks he made.

Those events were a long way away, of course. Simultaneous with the release of the single, March 1973 saw Gary play his first ever London concert. Although he had toured heavily in the wake of 'Rock And Roll', including a handful of shows which have ascended into legend for their inappropriate surroundings – village halls booked before the record took off, with Gary hugely incongruous in full costume on those little stages – he had purposely avoided playing the capital. Now, a full year after his breakthrough hit, there was no excuse. He would take the city by storm.

With true class, he booked into the London Palladium, a venerable old pile better known for hosting pantomimes and plays. It was one of the first rock shows ever staged there, and it would be one of the last for a long time. Afterwards, the theatre management swore they'd seen the balcony visibly swaying. That never happened during *Puss In Boots*.

roots of rock

are so many ways of doing a number — it's unbelieveable. And we try to explore every avenue. One likes to think that one's got it right, but you never know."

About the tracks on the current album, "Touch Me" (BELLS 222), Glitter observes:

"My personal favourites are 'Didn't I Do It Right' and 'Sidewalk Sinner'. We seem to have progressed a bit more with our writing on those particular numbers. And I enjoyed singing them as much as anything, too."

How does the singer react to critical qualifications, to the effect that the lyrics and the rest of the intrumentation on his discs are sactificed to the all-enveloping drum sound?

"Well, first of all, the drum thing is part of our sound, and I do like to make sure, that moment

But the other things are coming through a little bit more — we're letting them come through slowly. I suppose there probably will be a bit of a change, but I don't think it's good to change straight away.

"To suddenly say 'Right, OK, he's got a few hits, now we can change' would be a mistake. I think people still like our sound as it is.

"I kind of like the naive lyrics. And it's very hard to write such simple words, actually. But, think of the original rock 'n' roll: 'Long tall Sally saw Mary having it in the alley, oh baby', or something — you can't get any simpler than that! We try very hard to write like that."

Cont'd on page 46

March 1973 – Sensational Alex Harvey Band: Jungle Jenny/Buff's Bar Blues (Vertigo 6059 075)

SAHB toured Britain constantly through the first half of 1973 in support of both 'Framed' and a new single, the non-album 'Jungle Jenny' – a recording that had very, very little in common with the rest of the band's contemporary repertoire. The tale of a young girl who was raised in the jungle by monkeys, it is a novelty song with an intro parodying the Australian comedian Rolf Harris; its failure to chart is no more surprising than the band's decision *not* to include it on their next album. Instead, 'Jungle Jenny' would remain otherwise unavailable until Harvey dusted it off for 1975's 'Penthouse Tapes' collection of odds and sods.

March 1973 – Zakatek – I Gotcha Now/So Good to You (Bell 1289)

The Native American-styled Lenny Zakatek, says his Bell Records biog, was playing at Golliwogs, a London nightclub, when he was discovered by Lynsey de Paul. She immediately offered him 'I Gotcha Now', recorded at Strawberry Studios with in-house band 10cc behind him; de Paul produced, Eric Stewart engineered.

Zakatek learned his love of what was still called Red Indian lore from an aunt who lived on a reservation in Nevada.

March 1973 – Roxy Music: Pyjamarama/The Pride And The Pain (Island WIP 6159)
March 1973 – Roxy Music: For Your Pleasure (Island ILPS 9232)

Still regarded by many as Roxy Music' finest hour, 'For Your Pleasure' contained any number of future classics: 'Do The Strand', 'The Bogus Man' and the blow-up-dolly delirium of 'In Every Dream Home A Heartache' all peeled off the album, and are rightly considered among Bryan Ferry's greatest creations.

'Editions Of You' sparkles around one of Ferry's most contagiously breakneck lyrics, and Roxy made a further impact with second single 'Pyjamarama', a piece of knowing nocturnal nonsense that took a twisted take on every love-song cliché you've ever dreamed of ('how nice if only we could bill and coo').

Absent from the album, it made Number 10 on the chart. 'For Your Pleasure' peaked six spots higher.

But behind the band's most brilliant façade, all was sadly not well. Throughout the group's history, Roxy Music were to be troubled by vacancies in the bassist department. Graham Simpson, who recorded the first album, had already quit before its release; John Porter, a friend from Ferry's pre-Roxy band the Gas Board, stepped in briefly before producer Pete Sinfield

introduced Rik Kenton. He lasted eight months, before Porter returned.

The strength of the remainder of the band, of course, was such that these comings and goings meant little to the general public. During the summer of 1973, however, a far more tumultuous departure hit the headlines.

Eno quit.

March 1973 – Wizzard: See My Baby Jive/ Bend Over Beethoven (Harvest HAR5070)
March 1973 – Wizzard: Wizzard Brew (Harvest SHSP4025)

The sound of Roy Wood testing the Glam-Rock waters, 'Ball Park Incident' rose to Number 6 on charisma and chorus alone. 'See My Baby Jive', on the other hand, went all the way. Using every self-production technique in Phil Spector's book, then encouraging the band to dress up like their lives depended on it, Wood wrote and arranged the ultimate Fifties teen anthem, then spattered the whole thing in tinsel and glitter.

Add a taste for facepaint that could have stepped out of a Hammer film and Wizzard came across as the *very* last word in Glambitious madness. It took 'See My Baby Jive' just three weeks to get to the top of the chart, and three more for it to be dislodged from that perch, and while the single worked its magic 'Wizzard Brew' cast spells of its own.

Neither of the hits were included – a mere six tracks instead filled the vinyl with an even tauter approximation of Wood's beloved Fifties soundtracking, and it was that lack of familiarity that caused the LP to stall at a lowly Number 29. But it's a thrashing delight regardless, overflowing with mood and madness,

and if fans were maybe confused by its chronological proximity to Wood's decidedly dissimilar solo album ('Boulders' – Harvest SHVL 803 – was released in June) then that's the price you pay for admiring genius.

March 1973 – Lynsey de Paul – Surprise (MAM SS 504)
March 1973 – Lynsey de Paul: All Night/The Blind Leading The Blind (MAM 99)

Prefaced by a surprise flop single, de Paul's debut album rounded up many of the songs for which she was best known, but also included half-a-dozen co-written with Barry Blue/Green, including the hit 'Sugar Me', and a reprise of his own most recent single, 'Papa Do', retitled 'Mama Do'.

March 1973 – Jook: City And Suburban Blues/Shame (RCA 2344)

Where Slade had once trod doubtfully, Jook went full steam ahead. Undisguisedly skinhead in their looks and demeanour, they went out of the way to court that crowd, too, landing a residence at the Edmonton Sundown and pulling the entire skinhead population of north London in to fill it.

Their repertoire matched the masses. Although Jook weren't at all averse to their own material, it was the covers that went down best and their second single, taped in late 1972, hauled out two of them, the old Jimmy Reed chestbeater 'Shame Shame Shame', and a number composed by a songwriting duo whom John Hewlett had discovered a couple of years earlier, Gallagher and Lyle's 'City And Suburban Blues'. The gentle Scots apparently loathed what became of their song in Jook's meaty paws.

ON THE RADIO
5-9 March 1973 – Johnnie Walker: Slade
8 March 1973 – Sounds Of The Seventies: Roxy Music
12-16 March 1973 – Johnnie Walker: Roxy Music
26-30 March 1973 – Johnnie Walker: T Rex
ON THE BOX
1 March 1973 – Top Of The Pops: Alice Cooper, T Rex, Slade
2 March 1973 – Crackerjack: Slade
8 March 1973 – Top Of The Pops: T Rex, Slade
15 March 1973 – Top Of The Pops: Roxy Music, T Rex, Slade
22 March 1973 – Top Of The Pops: Slade
29 March 1973 – Top Of The Pops: Geordie, Mud

April 1973 – David Bowie: Aladdin Sane (RCA RS1001)
April 1973 – David Bowie: Drive In Saturday/Round And Round (RCA 2352)

'Drive In Saturday' had everything. With a Fifties revival always just around the corner, it luxuriated across a doowop backing. With a sci-fi future in everybody's eyes, it painted a portrait of an age next to come. It namechecked Mick Jagger and made a hero out of Twiggy, the sixties fashion icon whose frame was so delicate that she could have been a photo of herself. Later in the year, Twiggy would pose for the cover photo of Bowie's 'Pinups' album; later in the decade, she would relaunch herself as a TV host, with two shows – *Twiggs* and *Twiggy* – that became required viewing at the tail end of Glam.

Japan's David Sylvian took his surname from one line in the song; Bowie's own backing singer group, the Astronettes, took theirs from another.

And the single soared to Number 3, peaking the week before Bowie's latest tour got underway at Earl's Court on 12 May. The album, of course, was already Number 1.

'Aladdin Sane' was a piecemeal collection of songs and sessions from all times and places. Dipping back to 1970, it resurrected 'The Prettiest Star' with Ronno fearlessly duplicating Marc Bolan's old guitar lines; looking ahead, it predicted 'Pinups' with a grinding cover of the Stones' Let's Spend The Night Together'. 'Jean Genie' was the blockbuster that led to the album's finale; 'Watch That Man' and 'Panic In Detroit', the latter written after a night spent listening to Iggy Pop's autobiography, were the hard rocking treats that stepped into the realm of fresh Bowie anthems.

There was no room for either 'John I'm Only Dancing' or All The Young Dudes', but 'Cracked Actor' came out of Bowie's experiences in

Hollywood, and 'Time' mused, among other things, on the death of Billy Murcia, the New York Dolls' young drummer.

And then there was the title track, subtitled with the years that preceded the last two World Wars, and a question mark for the outbreak of a third. 'Five Years', opening 'Ziggy', had already hinted that things were not looking good. The ominous sequence of '1913, 1938, 197?' confirmed it.

12 April 1973 – That'll Be The Day premieres at the ABC2, Shaftesbury Avenue, London

It was the movie hit of the year, and further proof of the all-pervading influence of the old Fifties on the new Seventies.

That'll Be The Day, based upon a slice of rampant literary nostalgia by author Ray Connolly, starred the not-quite-risen star of David Essex as a typical English teen, doing typically English teenage things, in the typically English late Fifties.

Thrill as Jim MacLaine greases his hair! Swoon as he plays silly buggers at the funfair! Laugh as he trots out a script's worth of incomprehensible colloquial dialogue.

Culturally, then, it was a dead ringer for *American Graffiti* with one minor twist. Two, in fact. First, it was good – the best British pop music film since the Beatles, with sharp supporting roles from Keith Moon, Ringo Starr, Billy Fury and the stunningly lovely Rosalind Ayres; and second, it was believable.

Few of the fictional figureheads of *American Graffiti* seemed to exist outside of the period costumes into which they were thrust. Jim MacLaine, however, was a real-life would-be rock star long before his own attention began to stray in that direction; it was only natural, then, that the inevitable sequel should place him in precisely that position – even as the Bolanically good-looking Essex's own star rode roughshod over MacLaine's cinematic achievements.

Essex – David Albert Cook to his East-ender parents – had been around for a decade at this point, rising through the ranks of various under-achieving local bands before changing his name to David Essex around the same time as he signed his first record deal, with Fontana in late 1964.

'There was never any rock or theatre history in the Cook family,' he reflected. 'Only the docks, where my dad and all his brothers were. My mum wanted me to be an engineer.'

Nevertheless, what followed is a tale familiar to almost every major artist of the early Seventies, a succession of singles for a variety of labels, none of which went anywhere.

'And The Tears Come Tumbling'/'You Can't Stop Loving Me' (Fontana TF 559) and 'Can't Nobody Love You'/'Baby I Don't Mind' (Fontana TF 620) in 1965; 'This Little Girl Of Mine'/'Broken-hearted' (Fontana TF 680) and 'Thigh High'/'De Boom Lay Boom' (Fontana TF 733) in 1966; 'She's Leaving Home'/'He's A Better Man Than Me' (MCA – USA) in 1967; 'Love Story'/'Higher Than High' (UNI UN 502) and 'Just For Tonight'/'Goodbye' (Pye 7N 17621) in 1968; 'That Takes Me Back'/'Lost Without Linda' (Decca F12935) and 'The Day The Earth Stood Still'/'Is It So Strange?' (Decca F12967)...all floated by to zero reward.

So did his co-starring role in the duo David and Roza – 'Time Of Our Life'/'We Can Reach An Understanding' (Philips 6006 040) and 'The Spark That Lights The Flame'/'Two Can Share' (Philips 6006 094) passed by unseen in 1971.

But unlike so many of his contemporaries, Essex had another arrow to his bow. An accomplished actor, he made his debut in Rita Tushingham and Lynn Redgrave's 1967 swinging London comedy *Smashing Time* and, by the end of the year, he was in repertory, touring with *The Fantasticks*. The following year, he played the Sultan in a Yvonne Arnaud Theatre production of *The Magic Carpet*, and in December 1969, became Tommy Steele's understudy at the London Palladium's annual pantomime, *Dick Whittington*.

Twice he would be called upon to take the lead role (9 and 21 March 1970) before he moved onto the Mayfair Theatre to star alongside Michael Flanders and Sally Smith in *Ten Years Hard*. A few movie and TV roles kept him further occupied and, in October 1971, he was handed the role of Jesus Christ in the London stage production of *Godspell*.

It opened at the Roundhouse on 17 November and, days later, the *Sunday Times* elected him the best performer visible on the London stage of the day...this simple, wondering Christ.'

Godspell transferred to the Wyndham Theatre on 26 January 1972, days before Bell Records released the original cast album; Essex would also appear in a BBC documentary examining the sudden rush of religiously-themed plays, *The Box Office Christ*, on 18 June.

October 1972 saw filming commence on *That'll Be The Day*; Essex took seven weeks away from the play to make the movie and, six months later, there were kids out there who'd have said Essex was now even bigger than Jesus.

April 1973 – The Sweet: Hell Raiser/Burning (RCA 2357)

Topping 'Blockbuster' was a devil of a task, but Chinn and Chapman did it. 'Hell Raiser' was the Sweet's most dramatic single yet, a pyrotechnic rocker that opened with a hell-fire scream, rode a flame-thrower guitar through the opening verse, then exploded with volcanic riffs and rumbling drums, again and again and again.

The Hell Raiser in question was an especially *fatale* brand of *femme*, a 'starchaser, trailblazer, a natural-born raver'...although the actual content of the lyric is somewhat less important than Phil Wainman's near hard-rock production and the sheer energy of the performance.

In later years, the Sweet would make a concerted effort to 'go heavy' and lost a lot of their following as a consequence. In fact, 'Hell Raiser' was already a neo-metallic raver in its own right, and the fact that it stalled at Number 2 had more to do with bad timing than anything else. First, Dawn's yellow ribbons were standing in the way, then Wizzard's 'See My Baby Jive' made Number 1 its own. Three weeks at Number 2 is a cruel fate for any band, and Brian Connolly felt the pain more than most.

'People ask us if we're on the way down because we didn't hit Number 1 with "Hell Raiser", but that's exactly what we *don't* want people to ask,' he bemoaned. 'We want to be a household name like Cliff Richard. Every other release he has is a miss, but he's still Cliff Richard. Nobody says, "Do you think Cliff's finished because he's had a Number 15?" So why did they say it about the Sweet?'

April 1973 – Suzi Quatro: Can The Can/Ain't Ya Something (RAK 150)

They started out as songwriters, now they were empire builders. 'We're regarded by a lot of people as a sausage factory,' Nicky Chinn said. 'A hit a month'. But what does that matter if they're good sausages?

'There's nobody better in the world than we are,' Mike Chapman continued. 'Of course we're a hit factory. We can't help it.'

Mud's 'Crazy' was just departing the chart; the Sweet's 'Hell Raiser' was about to enter it and Chinnichap were turning their attention to their next teenage dream, five foot nothing of Detroit dynamite named Suzi Quatro.

And it's an indication of just how powerful they, and producer Mickie Most had become that the first time most of Britain saw Suzi she was already on *Top Of The Pops*, a bundle of leather-soaked lust, stomping through 'Can The Can'. David Bowie was launching his latest (final) British tour that same weekend, and the contradiction screamed out at everyone.

'The guys in my band don't wear glitter,' she snarled. 'They're *real* men.' It didn't take an Einstein to figure out what that made all the rest.

Or, 'Sure I'm a woman. But I like to keep my womanly charms for the bedroom.'

On 11 May, Quatro made that first appearance on *Top Of The Pops*. The following week, 'Can The Can' was at Number 34; the week after that it was Number 5. And on 16 June, she was Number 1, pushing Wizzard out of the way.

April 1973 – 10cc: Rubber Bullets/Waterfall (UK 36)

10cc's third single, 'Rubber Bullets' (backed with their proposed first single, 'Waterfall'), followed 'Johnny Don't Do It' into problematic waters, albeit of a very different kind.

The British army had recently started using rubber bullets in their bid to bring peace to embattled Northern Ireland, and with a title like that, the record *had* to have something to do with protest. Or so BBC radio thought, and banned the record accordingly.

In fact, the song dealt with a riot in an American prison, a fact BBC TV (who must have actually listened to the lyrics) were quick to recognise. Still, Kevin Godley remembers hearing that the record 'apparently became a big street anthem in Northern Ireland, even though the narrative was more akin to a James Cagney prison movie than political rhetoric.' And he 'loves those speeded up guitars. The only song appropriate to conclude our live shows.'

On 4 May, 10cc appeared on *Top Of The Pops* with barely a radio play to their credit. Six weeks later, 'Rubber Bullets' had knocked 'Can The Can' off top spot.

April 1973 – Ayshea: Farewell/Best Years Of My Life (Harvest HAR 5073)

27 April 1973 – Lift Off With Ayshea: Wizzard

Written, produced and played by Roy Wood, a solo Ayshea single had everything going for it...a great record, a beautiful singer, a lovely voice and a guaranteed spot on the first edition of the latest (sixth) series of *Lift Off*, with Wood and Wizzard also in attendance to make sure everything went well.

And still the single failed, living on solely as a curio in the Roy Wood discography prior to its rediscovery for the 'Glitter From The Litter Bin: 20 Junk Shop Glam Rarities From The Seventies' compilation (Castle CMQCD 675) in 2003.

But her performance on her show was not Ayshea's sole claim to fame that week. She also sang Gilbert O'Sullivan's 'Get Down' to her pet puppy Daisy-May...and surely planted the seed that would flower that Christmas into one of Pan's People's best-remembered dance routines. Same song, same set-up, only this time, there were five dogs. Big dogs. *Bored* dogs...

April 1973 – Whistle: The Party Must Be Over/Hideaway (York YR 201)

A highlight of 'Killed By Glam: 16 UK Junk Shop Glam Rarities From The Seventies' (Moonboot MB 01), the first of two co-produced (with Dave Hunter) singles for the northern-based Whistle; the second, later in the year, coupled 'When the Lights Go Out On Broadway'/'Lincoln Lullabye'.

April 1973 – Starbuck: Wouldn't You Like It/Manana (RCA 2350)

Starbuck was Brian Engel and Martin Briley, stalwarts of Mandrake Paddle Steamer and a clutch of other lost (but recently rediscovered) Seventies pop nuggets. It was no shock at all when they turned their attention towards Glam, but intriguing just how seriously they seemed to take it.

Teamed up with the same Howard/Blaikley team that had been working with the Bay City Rollers, the duo were perhaps surprised to be handed 'Manana', one of that band's old singles for their own release.

'Howard/Blaikley had run out of good ideas and soppy innuendo titles by this time, and were resorting to gimmick sound effects,' condemns Engel. 'I honestly remember a duck quack on this single…but I don't remember it being released.'

Briley is more forgiving. 'Now that was a good pop song with international appeal, a catchy song with a chorus that you could sing but didn't need to learn. "Na na na/Na na na na na." If you could remember those lyrics you'd got the song.' Outrageously camp on vinyl, Starbuck struck out even further on stage. 'We did do a few gigs. It actually was planned as a real entity. It was absolutely outrageously stupid, but I remember loving it because it was so unutterably silly. We were all ponced up with the most hermaphrodite look our girlfriends could devise, and it really appealed to my sense of the bizarre to be gyrating around, looking like Lynsey de Paul singing simple, pure Billy Fury songs like "Halfway To Paradise".'

Engel has a more chilling recollection, however. 'I seem to remember as a four piece we were booked to play a gig at some skinhead club in Chatham; the crowd looked so dangerous we had to decide whether to slip out the back or go the other direction and just totally camp it up. We chose the latter. I could never work out how we managed to get away with that; maybe they felt too sorry for us to get violent.'

April 1973 – Grudge: When Christine Comes Around/I'm Gonna Smash Your Face In (Black Label BL 002)

Punk-before-punk, Grudge was actually Welshman Paul St John, creator last year of 'The Flying Saucers Have Landed' and now purveying an even grander brand of madness.

The A-side's wild enough ('When Christine comes around, I'd like to smash her one'), but it's the flip that really gets the temperature soaring, a brattish stomp across a childish melody and the warning: 'I'll tie you to a great big chair, you'll live your life in fear/It's time for you to pay the price for saying I'm a queer.'

'What happened,' Marshall recalls, 'was my college chum Simon Potter, the co-writer, lived in a ground-floor flat in Wimbledon, I lived in London and used to go out and see him and stay the night, and every time I used to go this girl from upstairs – I think she had a crush on Simon because every time he had a visitor, there'd be a knock on the door and in she'd come. And her name was Christine. She was a very homely girl, and she it wasn't like she was a great conversationalist, she just sucked the oxygen out of the room. It was very difficult, and we didn't want to be rude to her, but she'd just sit there like a lump. It was terrible. After one of those nights, Simon said to me "Let's go out", he was in such a bad mood, and we're driving across London Bridge and I said "Why don't we write a song about this?" And it was done in about 20 minutes.'

A few weeks later, an industry contact introduced the pair to Cyril Black (younger brother of bandleader Stanley Black). 'Stanley Black was quite prestigious,' laughs Marshall. 'Cyril was his little brother.'

A Tin Pan Alley music publisher who was just about to launch his own label, Black, 'Cyril was really hungry for success,' continues Marshall. 'He had a little room in Denmark Street, he was very stereotypical, the little Jewish guy with glasses. But we sang him

"When Christine Comes Around" and he was knocked out. He loved it.'

Cyril in turn introduced them to a wealthy heiress named Prudence who apparently wanted to sponsor a band. 'She lived in a beautiful home in Richmond, and thought it was just wonderful – she loved "I'm Gonna Smash Your Face In" and we were in the studio [TPA in London] before you knew it.'

A studio band was gathered, one that rumour insists included Peter Frampton – unfortunately, Marshall can't remember. 'The only one I remember was the drummer, Dave, because he made a mistake and couldn't get over it.'

Recorded two weeks before Marshall oversaw Weenybopper's 'Donny, David And Michael' but released some six months later, 'When Christine Comes Around' became the first ever release on Black – and that despite being numbered 002. 'Cyril didn't want 001 because he didn't want everyone to think it was his first release.'

April 1973 – Stavely Makepeace: Cajun Band/ Memories Of Your Own (Deram DM 386)

With the band having signed to Decca's Deram subsidiary in early 1973, Stavely Makepeace's ninth single would be launched with yet another appearance on *Lift Off* (8 June 1973).

April 1973 – Blackfoot Sue – Nothing To Hide (Jam JAL 104)

November 1972's 'Sing Don't Speak' did a reasonable job of following up 'Standing In The Road', and at least rid the band of the stigma of being one-hit wonders. Now it was time for Blackfoot Sue to turn their attention towards the music press' insistence on labelling them a Glam band when it was clear that their antecedents lay in different areas entirely. They looked like the (Edgar) Broughtons, they jammed like the (Pink) Fairies, they were proggy hippies through and through.

Or were they? Period photos, shot once the first single made the chart, found the band kowtowing to whichever fashion demands were made of them, while their own *faux pas* included wearing matching dungarees on *Top Of The Pops*, posing for the teeny press and admitting that they painted moustaches on their faces, to make themselves look older.

Teen idols have been created from far less than that, and when you add the presence of identical twins Tom and Dave Farmer in the line-up; what more could a teenybop editor require? Plus, they *did* sound a bit like Slade.

And so to 'Glittery Obituary', a cut from the band's generally enjoyable and genuinely diverse debut album, and one of the most incisive assaults the Glam movement ever suffered. 'A future made from blue eyeshade/Max Factor's on a royalty,' they snarled. 'Saturated with infatuated girls/Last year they would have called you Nancy.'

Only Peter Hammill's 'Nadir's Big Chance', two years later and a little too late, did a better job of condemning Glam Rock than 'Glittery Obituary', but still Blackfoot Sue got the last word. 'One rainy day you'll rust away/But don't dismay/The scrapman he ain't fussy.'

Blackfoot Sue themselves would soon fade. Further singles distanced themselves from fame, while a second album, 'Strangers', recorded in 1974, didn't see release until 1977 – by which time two further albums had been recorded and likewise binned (excerpts appear on the 1996 compilation 'Best Of Blackfoot Sue' – Connoisseur Collection CSAP CD123), and the band itself had changed direction entirely as a Chicago-style harmony trio called Blackfoot.

ON THE RADIO
2-6 April 1973 – Dave Lee Travis: Roxy Music
27 April 1973 – Pete Drummond Sequence: Geordie
ON THE BOX
3 April 1973 – Old Grey Whistle Test: Roxy Music
5 April 1973 – Top Of The Pops: Geordie, Roxy Music, Gary Glitter
13 April 1973 – Crackerjack: Geordie
27 April 1973 – Top Of The Pops: Alice Cooper, Chicory Tip, Mud, the Sweet, Wizzard
ON THE SHELF
April 1973 – Hammerhead: Nice Girl/Little Girl (RCA 2326)
April 1973 – The Men: Oh What A Naughty Man/Rose Growing By The Sidewalk (Bell 1294)

12 May 1973 – Lou Reed has a hit

Lou Reed had been playing with 'Walk On The Wild Side' for over a year before he recorded it for 'Transformer', ever since he was tapped to score a stage show of the book of the same name. The play never happened, but Reed rewrote the lyric and came out with a song that he once insisted is the one composition for which he would most like to be remembered.

It takes the listener on a guided tour of the Warhol circus with Reed as the lascivious ringmaster introducing Candy Darling, who really lived up to her surname in the backroom, Holly Woodlawns, who 'shaved her legs and then he was a she', Joe Dallesandro, 'who never once gave it away', Jackie Curtis, 'who thought she was James Dean' and the Sugar Plum Fairy, 'looking for soul food and a place to eat.' Real people, real freaks...

'I thought they would all claw my eyes out when I got back to New York,' Lou later admitted. 'Instead, Candy Darling told me he'd memorised all the songs and wanted to make a 'Candy Darling Sings Lou Reed' album. It probably wouldn't sell more than a hundred copies!'

A single since November, six months had now elapsed since 'Transformer' became the most unexpected Christmas stocking filler of the decade. Already, then, the song's subject matter had been heartily discussed in every forum from the music press to the drag circuit.

'But she never lost her head, even when she was giving head,' sang Lou of Candy Darling, and knowing fans smirked quietly to themselves. They never dreamed that one day soon, 10 million daily listeners to Wonderful Radio 1 would become privy to that same piece of scuttlebutt, as the song suddenly burst out of radio and television alike.

DJ Tony Blackburn ('The poor deluded fool', one observer remarked) made the song his Record of the Week, and its ascent to Number 10 on the chart was achieved without any censorship whatsoever. In the US, RCA took the precaution of issuing radio stations with a cleaned up version of the song, only to find the DJs went with the unexpurgated version.

Reed, meanwhile, proved considerably less malleable than a lot of people might have hoped, at least in commercial terms. He followed 'Transformer' with the Shakespearean soap of 'Berlin' (a magnificent album, but Glam Rock it wasn't), before shaving Iron Crosses into his peroxided crew-cut and touring the world with a Heavy Metal vision of what the Velvet Underground might have become.

The two live albums that capture the ensuing carnage, 'Rock'n'Roll Animal' and 'Lou Reed Live', are devastatingly great, the finest in-concert recordings of Reed's entire career – at

When that Radio One D.J. said Lou Reed had once been associated with the Velvet Opera the surprise and pleasure of hearing "Walk On The Wild Side" was wiped away with irritating force.

That single was released months before our charts registered its presence and in fact the album from which it comes, "Transformer", made the first impact by coming into the NME Top Thirty on May 12, at No. 29.

"Transformer" was produced in England, yes dear old Britannia. Trident studios provided the location and producers were Mick Ronson and one David Bowie. Reed got the track "Walk On The Wild Side" from a book of short stories written by Nelson Algren.

The story of someone like Holly who shaved her legs and plucked her eye-brows and then 'he was a she' may sound pretty familiar in a time when sexual gender and role-play causes considerable discussion in all parts of society, yet within the context of pop single lyrics it diverges from the accepted enough to be risky.

Funnily enough when the single first came out in late '72 little was said as to whether it was desirable listening material for Radio One airwaves. Hit-parade entry was enough to create sudden interest in such discussion.

The theme is not an unfamiliar one to Lou Reed. Reed used to be associated with the Velvet Underground. To fans of the Underground he was the Underground. To them he is still the Underground, whatever the present format gets up to.

Velvet Underground were an historic New York scene group. The West Coast might have had its Grateful Dead and Jefferson Airplane, but the East had Andy Warhol and Nico plus Velvet Underground.

All belonged to what was called Warhol's "Exploding Plastic Inevitable" with among other things amplifiers turned up to ear-splitting distortion levels, chicks in black leather twirling whips and coloured lights flashing and changing shades all over the ballroom set off against underground films.

The scenes were heavily camp and some found them distasteful, as though some people were out to actually celebrate the depravity of man.

Reed through Velvet Underground and on his own has been continually expressive in lyric and to some extent in life-style of the unusual side of character and life — the wild side. Years back he achieved fame with the

song "Heroin" and other vintage ones include "White Light/White Heat" and "I'm Waiting For The Man".

His lyrics are pervaded with references to drugs and those on them, the sexually undecided and those unable to cope with the problems of living. Characters like the film star who has to face the anonymity of old age and gradual disintegration always remembering what it was to be liked and admired.

With the success of "Transformer" and the single from it, Lou Reed has become known in this country. Before that his following, though fanatical, was small. The influence of his music, however, reeking of the concrete New York jungle and the fantastical human permutations that people it, has been with us for some time. The style made an impact over here before the man managed it.

The Stones, Bowie, Roxy and Mott are just some of the big names who've responded to him in their own work. Bowie says that Reed occupies much the same place in his music that Chuck Berry did in the Stones'. At almost every performance he features his own versions of "White Light/White Heat" and "I'm Waiting For The Man".

Reed doesn't camp it up quite like Bowie, but there is the same self-conscious awareness of body and pose. It's just that Lou looks a lot more dangerous than David. He's coming over now on the strength of a scene that's just catching up with him, but not all the way. He's the fiercest, the most ambiguous, but it's on the style of his music not his image that he has to be immediately recognised throughout the city-music, glam-rock world as the original, unbelievable daddy of them all.

Lou influence of the Wild Side

least until his late-2000s reprise of 'Berlin'. But Reed had long since placed 'Transformer' behind him. Now he wanted the rest of us to do the same thing.

12 May 1973 – and Bowie has a chicken

Or, at least, his fans, the press, the promoters and MainMan did, after 18,000 people apparently rose as one to declare that they didn't want to attend concerts in vast auditoriums built for boat and Ideal Home shows.

Poor sound, lousy sight lines, uncomfortable seating, violent youths, sex and urine in the stalls...that's what the papers and the history books all say, anyway. But the view from Row K didn't seem that bad, and Bowie and the Spiders' latest – and, as it turned out, last – UK tour was underway.

DISC

Free poster: David Bowie

BOWIE OPENS 'ROCK ARENA' SEE PAGE 3

Rick Price—Move to Wizzard

SLADE

Part of the Glam Rock movement

Slade's Dave Hill (far right) on why we made it

Slade's new single reviewed by

FLOYD/FACES

NEW MUSICAL EXPRESS

BOWIE FIASCO

What went wrong?

Music scene NEWS

150,000 people expected at 31 date tour

DAVID BOWIE Is this Last Tour?

HE MAY NOT really beam in from Mars, but David Bowie is having a pretty hectic time dropping in on a whole host of British towns during one of the longest and most comprehensive tours we can remember. And all this follows a visit to America and Japan, a trip on the Trans Siberian railway, a few days in Moscow, then Paris and Calais!

David's aversion to flying is costing him and his entourage a lot of time as he insists on cars, boats and trains everywhere. Throughout his British tour which at present visits 31 venues between May 12 and June 24, he'll be travelling by road.

RCA, who are setting up the tour, hope that over 150,000 people will see David during his tour here, but with a possibility of still further dates, that figure could rise appreciably.

As he has announced his intention of going into films, this could be David's last tour for some time. It is on the cards for him to play Michael Valentine Smith, described as "a peace and love messenger from another planet" in "Stranger In A Strange Land" which sounds right up his street.

Meanwhile, his "Aladdin Sane" album and "Drive-In Saturday" single are out and about. With the exception of "Let's Spend The Night Together", all the tracks were written by the singer and the sleeve specially printed in Switzerland. Inside the cover is a near nude picture of our hero and the retail price £2.38.

The tour kicks off at the 17,500-seater Earls Court Exhibition building on May 12, then Ziggy and his Spiders visit: Aberdeen Music Hall (16), Dundee Caird Hall (17), Glasgow Green's Playhouse (18), Edinburgh Empire (19), Norwich Theatre Royal (21), Romford Odeon (22), Brighton Dome (23), Bournemouth Winter Gardens (25), Guildford Civic Hall (27), Wolverhampton Civic Hall ... Victoria ... Blackburn ... Hall (31).

June's ... begins at ... George's ...

Beatles reunion?

Sweet song

Fats Domino

EARLS COURT ARENA

(OPPOSITE WARWICK RD. EXIT EARLS COURT TUBE STATION)

MAIN MAN in association with MEL BUSH and R.C.A. Records present

DAVID BOWIE

Saturday, May 12th, 1973

at 8-30 p.m.

ARENA £2·00 Incl. VAT

FOR CONDITIONS OF SALE SEE OVER

BLOCK CC

ENTRANCE 40

ROW K SEAT 33

TO BE RETAINED

May 1973 – Mott the Hoople: Honaloochie Boogie/Rose (CBS 1530)

Had the fates been in a different mood, Mott the Hoople's follow-up to 'All The Young Dudes' would have been another Bowie composition, 'Drive In Saturday'.

And what a show that could have been. No matter how many classic records Bowie has made, he's written no more than a handful of truly great songs – 'All The Young Dudes' was one, 'Life On Mars?' is another, and 'Drive In Saturday' is an unimpeachable third. Of course he would have been mad to give it away, but if he had Mott the Hoople's next masterpiece would have been assured.

Sanity prevailed. 'I tried to get "Drive In Saturday" because I didn't think he was doing it as well as we could,' Hunter explained later. 'I had this real different kind of arrangement for it. Listening to the song now, God knows what was in my mind, because I can't see what we could have done with it. But anyway, he wouldn't give it to me.'

Instead, Bowie suggested Hunter cast around to see if he could come up with a suitable single of his own. Hunter obliged, and turned up a song called 'Honaloochie Boogie'; Bowie listened, suggested a tentative lyric change, then another and another; the single's eventual writing credit remained Hunter's alone, but he still admits (and the demo version featured on the Mott the Hoople box set proves) that Bowie's input went beyond a single line or two.

In fact, Bowie had a lot to say on the subject of Mott the Hoople. It was he, Hunter later revealed, who first addressed what he perceived to be the weak links in the group's makeup – revelations which led to the departures of both Verden Allen and Mick Ralphs. It was he, too, who pinpointed the void around which the band's power structure revolved, a void into which he suggested Hunter step.

'Bowie said to me one night that I had to take over Mott the Hoople because it was too diplomatic. They could never get a yes or no out of us, because you had to ask five people. They couldn't even get three to two, let alone five to none.'

Staff at Bowie's MainMan management office at this time agree. Tony Defries was accustomed to dealing with artists on a one to one basis. With Mott the Hoople, however, even the simplest decision required calls to all members of the group in turn, then a wait while they all called each other, to discuss the matter further. 'He even had to deal with the drummer,' one observer noted. 'And Tony hates drummers.'

He also hated waiting around. Maybe Hunter had already communicated Bowie's ideas to his bandmates, maybe he hadn't. But Defries had had enough. Mott the Hoople had never signed management contracts with him and so, shortly after the band returned home from their American tour, their relationship with MainMan came to a quiet and reasonably dignified close.

Defries turned the full weight of his attention back to Bowie, and his latest toy, Iggy Pop; Mott the Hoople found a new manager in Fred Heller and Hunter took centre stage.

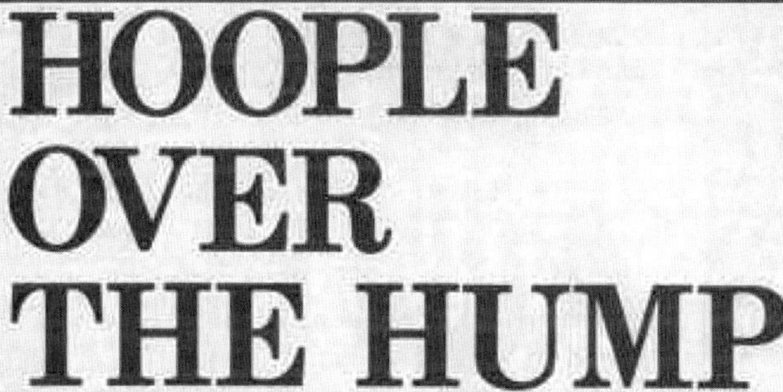

HOOPLE OVER THE HUMP

The single made the charts, the album from which it comes is just out and they've laid the ghost of David Bowie. Things are improving for Mott the Hoople, as MITCHELL PAUL found out.

Mott The Hoople (l-r): Ian Hunter, Buffin (at the back), Overend Watts (at the back) and Mick Ralphs.

Ian Hunter, frizzed hair and dark glasses, was hunched over a table

some credit is deserved to them.

The Bowie influence started with the great

accepted for what we want to play as opposed to finding ourselves doing certain kinds of music simply

mixer at the Rainbow, in London recently.

Funny really when you think of Mott The Hoople's

They keep popping up o radio and television. It wa John Peel who gave the

But Mott the Hoople didn't mind. With organist Mick Bolton (and, later, former Love Affair pianist Morgan Fisher) replacing Allen, work on their next album, 'Mott', was ready to begin. There were more shows around Britain, touring with the Sensational Alex Harvey Band; another American sojourn looming and another hit single. No matter that nine months had elapsed since 'All The Young Dudes', the dudes themselves were not forgotten. 'Honaloochie Boogie' climbed to Number 12.

May 1973 – Iggy and the Stooges: Raw Power (CBS 65586)
'Raw Power' wasn't merely a cardinal influence on Punk Rockers to come; for many of them, it was the first time they ever realised that rock music could even sound like this.

Ears were less forgiving, or knowledgeable, at the time. Bowie himself took one listen to the Stooges' original mix and hurried it back to the studio himself, to try and salvage something from the chaos; CBS, the band's label, took one listen to *his* efforts and decided he'd failed. And Tony Defries grew so sick of the Stooges' incessant complaints and misbehaviour that he dropped them from the MainMan roster in April 1973, before the album was even released.

May 1973 – The Sisters: Kick Your Boots Off/Driving Me Home (Bell 1307)
The female answer to Slade? Maybe so. Period reviewers certainly thought so, and the liner notes for 'Velvet Tinmine – 20 Junk Shop Glam Ravers' (RPM 251) recall the one that described this as 'Slade-tastic'.

May 1973 – Big Wheel: Shake A Tail Parts One And Two (Bell 1310)
Produced by Barry Green/Blue, who co-wrote it with Dave Jordan, this is a stomping little rocker about a girl who loves to ride. Bikes. Sound effects growl through it all, while a tougher alternate mix, complete with extra roaring motorbikes, also made it out on a Suzuki promotional flexidisc accompanied by an interview with racer Barry Sheene.

May 1973 – Hot Rod: I Want You/Love Is Alright (Hey) (President PT 397)
President was more adept at soul than Glam records, and this junkshop classic proves it.

ON THE RADIO
7-11 May 1973 – Noel Edmonds: Roxy Music
28 May – 1 June: Johnnie Walker: David Bowie
ON THE BOX
4 May 1973 – Lift Off With Ayshea: 10cc
4 May 1973 – Top Of The Pops: 10cc, Gary Glitter, the Sweet, Wizzard
11 May 1973 – Lift Off With Ayshea: Geordie
11 May 1973 – Top Of The Pops: Wizzard, Suzi Quatro, Alice Cooper
18 May 1973 – Top Of The Pops: Chicory Tip, David Bowie, the Sweet, Wizzard
25 May 1973 – Top Of The Pops: 10cc, Lou Reed, the Sweet, Wizzard
ON THE SHELF
May 1973 – Polly Perkins: Coochie Coo/Bad Girl (Chapter 1 SCHR 183)
May 1973 – Aquavitae: Softly As I Love You/ Saturday Morning Samson (Bell 1304)

June 1973 – T Rex: The Groover/Midnight (T Rex MARC 5)

He had made a rod for his own back. No longer spinning out the timeless classics, because where would be the challenge in that, Marc Bolan instead embarked on a voyage of musical discovery that cast him so far adrift from the commercial mainstream that when his critics said he'd blown it he didn't even bother replying.

How faulty was Bolan's timing, though? As it transpired, he was out by no more than a year, maybe less than six months. The era of disco was coming, and with it the wholesale transformation of a wealth of rocking talents, as they struggled to make headway against the looming hordes of soft soul and dance. Soon there would be weeks when watching *Top Of The Pops* was more akin to catching *Soul Train*, that leviathan of the Stateside airwaves, so many soulsters were on the chart.

Before Bowie began dreaming of 'Young Americans' fame, before Bryan Ferry even considered the pharmaceutical properties of *l'amour*, Bolan was up to his neck in American radio (and TV), working on music that exceeded his assumed capabilities no less than it shot straight over the heads of the kids who once bought all his hits.

'The Groover' marked the full-fledged birth of this new fascination, a simple but solid slab of funk-inflected rock that did, indeed, groove. And it really didn't do so badly chartwise, either. Straight in at Number 6 on 16 June, up to Number 4, then down to Number 5, only the seemingly perennial 'See My Baby Jive' and 'Can The Can' truly out-glammed it on a chart otherwise unhealthily preoccupied by Perry Como.

June 1973 – Mud: Hypnosis/Last Tango In London (RAK 152)

Like 'Crazy' before it, 'Hypnosis' had a dark, almost hard-rock feel to it, twisting around some memorably spectral backing vocals, a wizard guitar break and, once again, a snatch of lunatic laughter. Martial chanting beneath the final chorus completed the picture, and the overall impression was of drill practice at a military school for madmen. Which, of course, was not at all what Mud were all about.

The history books recall 'Hypnosis' as Mud's second UK hit. But in climbing no higher than Number 16, it also alerted both band and songwriters that the group was not yet firing on all creative cylinders – and would continue thus until Mud themselves were allowed to bring their own ideas to bear.

For Chinn and Chapman, the challenge now was to make sure they could deliver songs that matched the band's ambition.

Mud (l to r) Rob Davis, Dave Mount, Les Gray, Ray Stiles.

June 1973 – David Bowie: Life On Mars?/Man Who Sold The World (RCA 2316)
Hauled off the two-year-old 'Hunky Dory' album to accompany Bowie as he toured the UK, 'Life On Mars?' was based around a chord sequence that the future Ziggy borrowed from 'My Way', after he was one of several songwriters to attempt a translation of that song's original French lyric. (Paul Anka won.)

Bowie described 'Life On Mars?' as 'a sensitive young girl's reaction to the media', but it might also detail his own reaction to everything exploding around him at the time it was written – Bolan, *Pork*, the birth of Ziggy. Indeed, much of his own imminent eminence can be traced to 'the girl with the mousy hair' as she escapes the mundanity of fractious reality for a beckoning ferment where pop culture not only collides but also gleefully copulates with societal outrage. The freakiest show indeed.

None of which dawned on the likes of Marti Webb, the King Singers, Barbra Streisand and (in Swedish) Abba's Anni-Frid Lyngstad, all of whom have reduced the song to MOR slush. But Peter Noone's unreleased version is winsomely sweet, and one cannot help but wonder how history might have altered had he gone ahead and released it.

June 1973 – Slade: Skweeze Me, Pleeze Me/ Kill 'Em At The Hot Club Tonite (Polydor 2058377)
By summer 1973, as the old cliché (almost) says, Slade could have shouted out the phone book and they'd still have had a hit. They didn't go quite that far, but still 'Skweeze Me, Pleeze Me' was a formulaic racket, albeit more than vindicated by its superlative B-side, 'Kill 'Em At The Hot Club' – twisted violin, a pensive vocal and a murderous melody.

The A-side, Lea explained, was hatched in his local pub one night, listening to the regulars singing along with a piano player, and it sounds like that as well. But such details would be lost as 'Skweeze Me, Pleeze Me' became Slade's second successive single to enter the chart at Number 1, elbowing 'Rubber Bullets' aside and setting the stage nicely for the band's next UK tour.

June 1973 – Grumble: Da Doo Ron Ron/Pig Bin'n'Gone (RCA 2384)
10cc's Graham Gouldman and Strawberry Studios co-owner Peter Cowap unite on a fabulous piece of pop nonsense that really should have been a hit.

June 1973 – The Rocky Horror Show
In a year when sex – deviant sex, at that – was higher up on the cultural counter than ever before; with Lou Reed singing about blowjobs and David Bowie putting them into practise on stage; with the Sweet grinding harder every

time you saw them; and Gary Glitter turning the wheel full circle when the *NME* described him as resembling 'an epileptic getting a blowjob'; with all this going on, it was inevitable that, sooner or later, someone would wrap it all together.

And on 19 June 1973, in a tiny, 63-seat theatre in London, they did.

Rock and the theatre had never really seen eye to eye. A sickly hybrid throughout the Fifties and Sixties, when theatre's only concessions to the energies of rock revolved around slapping a handful of ballads into any passing stage show, the infant genre's finest hours so far had been of a distinctly religious bent – *Jesus Christ Superstar, Godspell, Joseph And The Amazing Technicolor Dreamcoat.*

There was the hippy luv-in *Hair*, of course, and *The Dirtiest Show In Town.* But anybody reflecting on the Who's 'rock opera' *Tommy* and comparing the messianic subtext of that creation with the bulk of the new arrivals would have been justified for believing that rock'n'roll had finally started to believe its own press. It *was* the new religion.

And then *The Rocky Horror Show* came along, with its cast of corset clad transvestite aliens, Frankenstein Ian muscle men, innocent college kids, a squealing groupie and a fabulous array of punch-above-their-weight rock'n'roll songs, and it altered the landscape forever.

Within days of the production opening, Jonathan King had signed *The Rocky Horror Show* for a full cast album; within a month, demand for seats every night had so outgrown the Royal Court's Theatre Upstairs that it was transferred to the Classic Cinema on the King's Road; and by the end of the year, it was selling out the 350-seat King's Road Theatre. It would remain there until 1979.

Not bad for a cult play that was the brainchild of an actor who was essentially forced out of the London production of *Jesus Christ Superstar* when he suggested that King Herod be played as Elvis Presley. The producers, on the other hand, wanted him to tap-dance. Neither party would budge and Richard O'Brien quit the play after just one performance.

He filled his suddenly spare time by writing a rock'n'roll musical that would allow Elvis full rein, penning songs around a plotline lifted straight from the Fifties B-movies he loved so much.

He was still hard at work when he landed a part in a Royal Court production of playwright Sam Shepard's *The Unseen Hand.* There he met Jim Sharman, famed director of the original Australian production of *Jesus Christ Superstar* and, together, they began building upon O'Brien's original vision. Sharman's involvement brought in a host of top line theatre personnel, including veteran stage producer Michael White and a cast that included Tim Curry, Patricia Quinn, Little Nell, Julie Covington and O'Brien himself. It was Sharman, too, who came up with a new title for the play. O'Brien originally called it *They Came From Denton High.*

Birthed at the critical and commercial peak of Glam Rock, *The Rocky Horror Show* was thoroughly a child of its times, the seamless blend of modern sexual sensibilities, a twisted sci-fi theme and (it suddenly seems inevitable) that mythical era which pop culture insists exists at the tail-end of the Fifties, when the younger generation was still divided between the nice kids and the bad ones (it was the bad ones who liked rock'n'roll).

American Graffiti meets *Plan 9 From Outer Space*; *That'll Be The Day* meets *They Saved Hitler's Brain. Cabaret* meets *Frankenstein. The Rocky Horror Show* became all of these things, as clean-cut Brad and Janet find themselves the unwilling visitors to the quintessentially spooky old mansion.

There, a bent and sinister butler informs them that they are to witness one of his master's 'events' – which turns out to be the creation of life in the form of Rocky, a Charles Atlas-style strongman who will meet every one of the master's needs.

Sex is everywhere; repressed in the shape of Brad (Christopher Malcolm) and Janet (Covington); outrageously in that of the master, Frank N Furter (Curry); unrequited in the form of the groupie Columbia (Nell); and possibly incestuous, in that of butler Riff Raff (O'Brien, and maid Magenta (Quinn).

But it was not alone. For *Rocky Horror* then threw in cannibalism, Government agents and a deep-seated love of old Hollywood to hit every cultural button it could find. And the fact that, just short of its fortieth birthday, the ensuing movie still pulls the kids in for a date with the midnight matinee proves that some things really haven't changed that much after all.

In the end, we still want to have sex with aliens.

June 1973 – Larry Lurex: I Can Hear Music/Goin' Back (EMI 2030)
On the eve of the release of Queen's first album, a Freddie Mercury solo single cunningly disguising its overwrought treatment of the Beach Boys classic (and a Goffin/King jewel on the flip) beneath a name tailor-made for Glammy consumption.

June 1973 – Gary Glitter: Touch Me (Bell 222)
More or less the twin of its predecessor, albeit with a few more originals on board, 'Touch Me' is nothing if not a reminder of just how timeless the old Glitter beat was.

The onboard hits – 'Do You Want To Touch Me?' and 'Hello Hello I'm Back Again' – set the scene, of course. But the almost-funky 'Sidewalk Sinner' gives a hint of how the sound might develop (it didn't), and 'Come On, Come In, Get On' is almost metallic in its delivery. There's a delicious cover of Paul Anka's 'Lonely Boy' to appeal to the romantic in us all, and Phil Spector's 'To Know You is To Love You' aches even harder. A solid gold gem and an instant Number 2.

June 1973 – Simon Turner: The Prettiest Star/ Live Around (UK 44)
Following on from Ricky Wilde, Simon Turner was Jonathan King's next stab at creating a British teenybop idol, and the campaign got off to a sterling start. 'The Prettiest Star' was always the prettiest song on Bowie's 'Aladdin Sane' album, and with Angie bestowing her husband's approval-by-proxy on the record, a hit probably seemed inevitable. It didn't materialise, but King and Turner would keep trying.

June 1973 – Top Of The Pops Volume 31 (Hallmark SHM 825)
A hot summer and a blazing showing for Top Of The Pops as the team got to grips with some of the most vital music of the year so far.

'Walk On The Wild Side' compensates in slippery bass lines for all that it lacks in Danny Street's distinctly non-New York-y sounding vocals (the series' producer later compared the rendition to 'a newsreader reciting a shopping list', although that's a trifle unfair); 'Hell Raiser' opens with what sounds like a yowl of agony, but rattles faithfully along thereafter; 'See My Baby Jive' emerges a garage-band approximation of the original's Spector-influenced purity, and series regular Martha Smith brings a proto-L7 shriek to Suzi Quatro's 'Can The Can', which is exactly how it should be performed. But the highlight has to be 'Rubber Bullets', because if you listen really closely, there's just the hint of an Irish accent in the backing vocals. Cheeky!

June 1973 – Geordie: Can You Do It?/Red Eyed Lady (EMI 2031)
A Number 13 hit, and Geordie's lowest Top Twenty entry (out of two) still finished only one place below AC/DC's highest (out of 30 or so).

June 1973 – Elton John: Saturday Night's Alright/Jack Rabbit/We'll Go Steady (DJM 502)
The first of two singles to be drawn, ahead of time, from Elton's 'Goodbye Yellow Brick Road' LP (DJM 9001) – the other was the yearning title track – 'Saturday Night's Alright For Fighting' lines up alongside another LP cut, 'Bennie And The Jets', as the moment when Elton got serious about his Glam-Rock credentials.

An incendiary rocker layers seething guitar over a vocal that almost cracks with aggression, and reached Number 7 on the chart – which, incredibly, made it his worst-performing single since 'Honky Cat'.

ON THE BOX
1 June 1973 – Top Of The Pops: 10cc, Suzi Quatro, T Rex, Wizzard
8 June 1973 – Lift Off With Ayshea: Stavely Makepeace
8 June 1973 – Top Of The Pops: 10cc, Mott the Hoople, Wizzard
15 June 1973 – Lift Off With Ayshea: Geordie
15 June 1973 – Top Of The Pops: Geordie, T Rex, Suzi Quatro
22 June 1973 – Lift Off With Ayshea: Slade
22 June 1973 – Top Of The Pops: Geordie, Mott the Hoople, Slade, 10cc
29 June 1973 – Top Of The Pops: Elton John, Geordie, Mott the Hoople, Slade
ON THE SHELVES
June 1973 – St Clement Wells: Lazy Lady/ Diven't Bar The Door (Bell 1317).
June 1973 – Johnny Farnham: Everything Is Out Of Season/It's Up To You (Columbia DB9002)

---

3 July 1973 – Slade crash and Bowie quits

Massively sold out weeks in advance, with the Sensational Alex Harvey Band a less than appreciated support, Slade's summer UK tour peaked at London's Earl's Court Arena, a venue that had earned all the wrong headlines after Bowie's opened his own latest outing there (12 May), and wound up with a disaster.

Bad sound, an unruly crowd and ugly security scarred the show, but Slade's appearance was a triumph, 18,000 fans screaming their approval as emcee Emperor Rosko introduced the band members onto the stage – Noddy! Dave!! Jim!!! Don!!!!

£4,000 worth of damage notwithstanding, it was the wildest party the capital had seen.

It would be the last for a while.

Back home in Wolverhampton three days after the biggest gig of his life, drummer Don Powell's white Bentley convertible flew off the road, through a hedge and into a brick wall. Powell's girlfriend, Angela Morris, died; Powell himself received a fractured skull, two broken legs and a broken arm.

That same night, 3 July 1973, David Bowie took the Hammersmith Odeon stage, and announced it was the final concert he would ever play. Waking up the following morning and scanning the newspaper headlines, it really did feel like an era had ended.

NEW MUSICAL EXPRESS
BOWIE QUITS
ZAPPA FOR WEMBLEY page 2
Ally festival album
CAROLE KING RUSH
'That's it.' page 3

But, of course, it hadn't. Bowie's retirement had more to do with the economics of his proposed next American tour than his need for a break... Envisioned by MainMan as a stadium-stuffing autumn outing, the tour was instead struggling to find a single promoter willing to present Bowie in anything larger than a theatre. But MainMan were in no mood for compromise. If Ziggy could play the omnidomes, then he wouldn't play anywhere.

Of course, Bowie would be back on stage in October, and back on the road in under a year; while Slade's recovery was even quicker. With Jim Lea's brother Frank sitting in, the band fulfilled their final engagement of the summer, at the Douglas Palace Lido, Isle of Man, on 6 July, and once Powell was off the critical list – after two days of anxious waiting – it was clear that Slade would continue. What else could they do?

July 1973 – Bay City Rollers: Saturday Night/Hey CB (Bell 1319)
For their next release, the anthemic 'Saturday Night', the Bay City Rollers were paired with Bill Martin and Phil Coulter, a songwriting and production team most associated with pop and bubblegum, but also capable of turning their hands to weightier material – Vertigo label prog mainstays Beggars Opera, for example.

Two years later, a rerecorded 'Saturday Night' would be the song that gave the Rollers their first American hit. Right now, though, nobody noticed it.

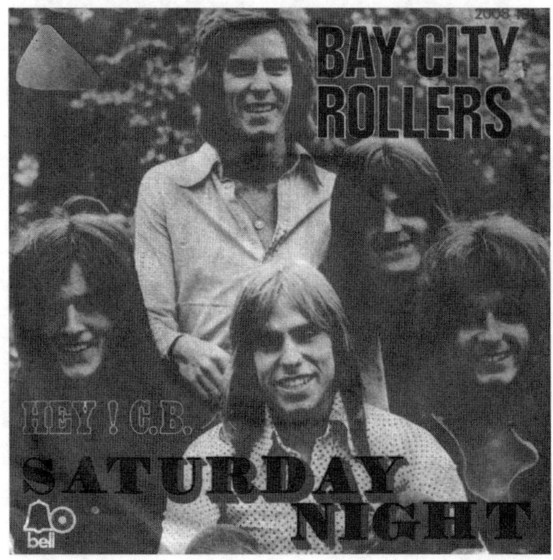

July 1973 – Glen: Lonely Here Tonight/Hey Little Girl (Columbia DB9010)
Popswop magazine was one of the market leaders of the era, a colourful weekly cluttered with photos of our fave-rave fab teenbeat heart-throbs. A move into music-making probably struck the publishers as a great idea, with a captive audience every week to peddle their wares towards. But the singularly-named Glen's balladic offering was a far cry from anything the average reader might have tapped her (the readership was primarily female) toes to, and the notion seems to have been abandoned.

July 1973 – Gary Glitter: I'm The Leader Of The Gang (I Am)/Just Fancy That (Bell 1321)
'Rock And Roll' is harder. 'Do You Wanna Touch Me' is raunchier. 'Hello Hello I'm Back Again' is wordier. But if any single record sums up everything Gary Glitter ever represented – to his fans, to history, to British culture in general, it is 'I'm The Leader Of The Gang'.

The opening roar of a souped-up Harley Davidson, the insistent chant of 'Come on come on', a lyric of pristine simplicity and a false ending that is almost heart-stopping in its abruptness, this is Glitter at his most glittering, an air-punching, foot-pounding, hip-swinging stomper that's frothier than Cresta, fizzier than Coke and so instantly recognisable that there probably wasn't a kid in class who didn't want to join the gang.

On 21 July, the smooching duo of Peters and Lee had knocked Slade off the top with the gruesome 'Welcome Home'. Glitter entered the chart one place behind them. The following week, the pair had swapped places and the Leader led the pack for the next three weeks.

July 1973 – Mott the Hoople: Mott (CBS 69038)
Ian Hunter: 'I wanted to lead the band because I was pissed off with the sloppy, slipshod way we were going. Pete and Buff were okay, they were all for it. But Mick [Ralphs] was dead against it – in fact, his actual words were "fuck you".'

Hunter wouldn't let the issue drop, though, and with a lack of forethought decided to broach the topic of the band's leadership during the recording of 'Violence', the fraught, fierce, fiery heart of Mott the Hoople's gestating new album.

The outcome was inevitable. 'We had a fight, and that was probably the crunch between Mick and I. But it would be the crunch between anyone. Try listening to that [song] for three days, it's murder.'

But it worked. 'Mick was doing the "Mott" album, but his heart wasn't in it, 'Hunter recalled. 'He was going out on weekends to see [Paul] Rodgers, and it was getting silly.'

With so much tension pouring into its creation, 'Mott' was never going to be a comfortable album, even without the seething 'Violence' cropping up amidships. Once again, Hunter turned in two stunningly gorgeous 'love' songs, the bitter-sweet 'Whizz Kid', and the almost painful 'I Wish I Was Your Mother'; once again, Ralphs' solo guitar number justified his annual ranking in the music papers' annual readers' polls.

But 'The Ballad Of Mott (March 26th 1972, Zurich)', ostensibly a celebration of the band's recovery from their now-forgotten Swiss crisis, simply reeked of embalming fluid, a requiem for the two crucial members stardom had chased – or was chasing – away. And 'Hymn For The Dudes', a wry poke at both Ziggy and stardom penned by Hunter and Verden Allen the previous autumn, lost a lot more than its mocking tone in the cold light of the band's ongoing dissolution. It also lost the air of hurt innocence that had hitherto characterised Hunter's most personal lyrics – maybe because it was he who was now doing the hurting.

'I don't think I was acting any different,' Hunter responds today. 'It was me that started writing the hits, it was me that started getting my picture in the papers. They were beginning to feel pushed out, but it was by circumstance. I wanted to keep the band as it was. When Ralphs left, it was a major blow.'

It just wasn't a fatal one.

July 1973 – Queen: Keep Yourself Alive/Liar (EMI 2036)
July 1973 – Queen: Queen (EMI 3006)

Queen were the first major signing to EMI following its reconstruction at the beginning of the year, Director of Repertoire Roy Featherstone picking them up on the strength of a half-complete LP.

Not everybody was convinced. On 9 April, with the album complete, Queen played the Marquee, and A&R head Joop Visser admitted, 'I was horrified'. There was no way, he believed, that this band would ever make it.

Queen, too, were unhappy. When they first came together, recalls guitarist Brian May, 'There was no such thing as Glam Rock. We were just a band who liked theatrics. We thought of ourselves as a kind of Led Zeppelin who enjoyed dressing up. By the time things started happening, though, people like Sweet and Slade, great pop groups who were also dressing up, were huge and what we originally thought of as a very original approach was suddenly the latest fashion.'

It was not a situation the band relished. 'Fashion, movements, really don't matter when you're a band. All you care about is what's inside you, and you really don't want to be fit into somebody's box. I'd much rather spend time finding out what the differences are between people than looking for the similarities.'

Not that Queen made any conscious efforts to shake off the unwanted baggage, 'Mainly because we were much too arrogant and pig-headed to care. We just did what we thought was worthwhile; there really was a terrible arrogance about us! But what that really means is, you're creating from the inside, rather than from an opinion poll. We never considered what people were saying as a guide to what we were doing.

'It doesn't mean we didn't care about our audience, because we cared deeply about them. But caring about your audience doesn't mean doing what they want you to do. It means treating yourself properly as an artist, so you are worthy of people's support. And if you're acting with integrity within yourself your audience will understand that.'

July 1973 – Wizzard: Angel Fingers/Got The Jump (Harvest 5076)
Another round of Fifties fantasy tarted up as much as you like and sent on its way with a slap on the bum that couldn't help but push it to Number 1. It only stayed there for a week, but it knocked Donny down a peg or two. It was a wonderful record as well.

WIZZARD WOOD CUTS

by BRIAN SOUTHALL

July 1973 – Suzi Quatro: 48 Crash/Little Bitch Blue (RAK 158)
Suzi Q's second Chinnichap single was ready for release before her first had even left the chart, crashing in at Number 6 in the first week of August and bouncing up to Number 3 before it faltered.

July 1973 – Godzilla and Yellow Gypsy: Dai Go-Go-Party (Volume Two) (King Records SKM-1258/9 – Japan)
More 'kitsch fromage rock' from Alan Merrill and co, this time rounding up 'Starman', 'The Jean Genie', Born To Boogie', 'Children Of The Revolution', 'Crocodile Rock' and Wings' 'Hi Hi Hi' among others.

July 1973 – Chicory Tip: Cigarettes Women And Wine/I See You (CBS 1668)
This loving ode to three favourite vices was, incredibly, banned by the BBC – and that should have given Chicory Tip's ninth single a genuine head start on the chart. Instead, it was as though the record didn't exist.

July 1973 – Top Of The Pops Volume 32 (Hallmark SHM 830)
When *Mojo* magazine ran a brief look back at Top Of The Pops in September 2000, one of performances that was singled out for special attention was 'Volume 32's assault on David Bowie's 'Life On Mars?'.

'Leaves the original standing,' affirmed author Kieron Tyler, but you'll have to take his word for that. While the orchestral arrangement is, indeed, superlative, the absence of any overt resemblance to the original (which was, of course, the whole point of the series), and a vocal that sounds like it's just coming off helium, almost transforms it into a completely different song.

Which wouldn't have been a bad fate for a few of the album's other inclusions. Was there anybody left in the land who wanted to hear 'Skweeze Me, Pleeze Me' again? Or 'Welcome Home', for that matter? But Mungo Jerry's 'Alright Alright Alright' resurfaces to remind us what stupendous 45s that band was capable of unleashing, and Elton's 'Saturday Night's Alright For Fighting' layers kick-ass guitar against a

suitably sassy vocal and should have been a single in its own right. And then there's 'I'm The Leader Of The Gang (I Am)'. Come on!

July 1973 – Jook: Oo-oo Rudi/Jook's On You (RCA 2368)

With former Dave Dee Dozy etc production mastermind Steve Rowland at the controls, this was Jook's most commercial single yet. It went nowhere.

ON THE BOX
6 July 1973 – Top Of The Pops: Slade
13 July 1973 – Top Of The Pops: David Bowie, Elton John, Gary Glitter, Mott the Hoople, Mud, Slade
20 July 1973 – Top Of The Pops: Suzi Quatro, Gary Glitter
27 July 1973 – Top Of The Pops: David Bowie, Mud, Suzi Quatro, Gary Glitter
July 1973 – Man Alive: Twinkle Twinkle Little Star: Ricky Wilde, Darren Burns
ON THE SHELVES
July 1973 – Hobokin: Collie Girl/Dirty Number 30 (Youngblood YV 1049)

August 1973 – David Essex: Rock On/On And On (CBS 1693)

The man who began the decade playing Jesus, and ended it as Che Guevara (in *Evita*) blended the twin roles of pop star and actor so perfectly it didn't even matter that a pair of flares was his only real concession to the demands of his

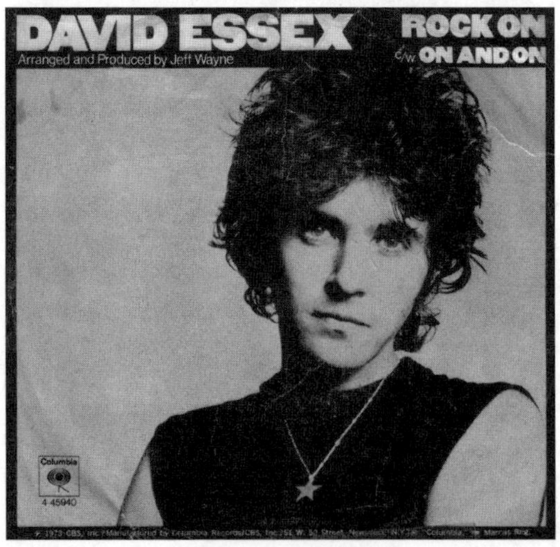

audience. If Glam Rock really was about creating an image, then sustaining it till it took on its own life, David Essex came as close to perfection as anyone.

With Jeff Wayne's production all echo and bass, united by a heartbeat as potent as the heart-throb he became, 'Rock On' arrived after almost a decade of trying, and of course it benefited from its placement on the chart-topping movie soundtrack. Essex had in fact already recorded a new Pete Townshend song, 'Keep On Rocking', for his debut, but shelved it when he wrote 'Rock On', on the set of *That'll Be The Day.*

Before the record was even released, Essex's *That'll Be The Day* fame had landed him appearances on the *John Denver Show* (BBC2, 28 April 1973) and a month-long stint hosting the Spike Milligan scripted *What Shall We Tell The Children* storybook show (BBC 1, 13 May-3 June).

He regaled fans of Radio 1's *My Top Twelve* with his dozen Desert Island Discs (24 May) and starred in a charity cricket match with Leslie Crowther and Henry Cooper. And the day 'Rock On' was released, he was fighting off over a thousand fans who had descended to see him make an appearance at Chappell's on Bond Street.

A month later, he left *Godspell*. 'Rock On' was Number 3.

August 1973 – Cockney Rebel: Sebastian/Rock'n'Roll Parade (EMI 2051)

A former journalist, Steve Harley (*né* Nice) was less a would-be pop star and more a rock'n'roll Cassius Clay, a man who insisted that he was the greatest, and did so with such intoxicating conviction that before long an awful lot of people were believing him.

'I was young, arrogant and fresh,' he reflected from 1976. 'I was really enjoying it and reckoned that any publicity is good publicity. It was great to be controversial and positive.' But it wasn't ego. 'In those days I didn't have [one]. It was juvenile over-excitement.'

At the same time, he did have a gift for putting people's backs up. 'Like Jesus said,' he once told the *NME*, 'just because I can turn water into wine, don't kick me and then nail me to a cross. I've got this gift. I'm not an arrogant, cocky little bastard in a long white robe. I'm not saying I'm better than you, just that I've got something that you haven't got, and I'm trying to share it with you. I'm doing you a favour.'

Er...are we still talking about Jesus here?

A challenge from the moment he gave his first interview, and essentially pissed on every other band in the land, Harley's group was Cockney Rebel, a name which conjured up visions of Pearly King jollity *à la* the Small Faces, Joe Brown, Tommy Steele and every other artist who made a virtue from dropping his aitches (and even David Bowie had tried that from time to time).

But the songs that Cockney Rebel carried painted a totally different picture. 'Come to a strange place,' he whispered here. 'We'll talk over old times, we never smile.' Even on the cabaret comeback circuit, 'Sebastian' remains chilling and, while Harley himself loathed the Glam tag, he never escaped it.

The satin and tat that draped the band's promo pics lasted 'for about five minutes', he swore. 'You never saw me, or anyone in my band wearing platform shoes. I've sung "Sebastian" in Belgium with an 80-piece orchestra, a 200-piece choir to 20,000 people. There's nothing Glam about that. "Psychomodo" [the band's second LP] was wild. There was nothing Glammy about that at all.'

He is, of course, utterly wrong.

August 1973 – Geordie: Electric Lady/ Geordie Stomp (EMI 2047)

Another clattering classic from the Newcastle lads, 'Electric Lady' rounded out a remarkable nine months for the band. Unfortunately, it also ended their chart career, faltering at Number 32. And when the hits stopped, so did the pretence. Geordie's second album, in 1974, was called 'Don't Be Fooled By The Name' (EMI EMA 764).

August 1973 – Rolling Stones: Angie/Silver Train (Rolling Stones Records RS 105)

It doesn't matter who, if anyone, the Stones were really singing about. In 1973 there was only one Angie that mattered, and she was married to David Bowie.

Cue rumour, lies and wild speculation...and the suggestion that Bowie's revenge was both swift and sweet as he persuaded Jagger's ex-lover, Marianne Faithfull, to break her own long silence by appearing alongside him during October's *1980 Floor Show* recording.

August 1973 – Mott the Hoople: All The Way From Memphis/Ballad Of Mott (CBS 1764)

Mick Ralphs confirmed his decision to quit shortly before Mott the Hoople's fourth American tour in July 1973 and played his final show with them in Washington DC on 19 August. Within weeks, he was in the rehearsal studio with his new band, Bad Company, even as Mott the Hoople's latest album, 'Mott', raced towards its UK chart peak of Number 7, and a new single, the rousing 'All The Way From Memphis', began its assault on the Top Ten.

Mott the Hoople were in Memphis when Hunter decided who should replace the departing guitarist, 'a flexible guitarist with brains in his head, who would understand.' Full stop. *Who would understand.*

Enter Luther Grosvenor or, as he would rapidly become more commonly known, Ariel Bender. And with him, enter what Hunter would christen – and history still recalls as – the Golden Age Of Rock'n'Roll.

Bender was a member of Spooky Tooth, a great guitarist in a pretty good band, when Hunter first heard him play. Although he was not Mott the Hoople's first choice – Americans Ronnie Montrose, Tommy Bolin and Joe Walsh were all tried out, then rejected – he was undoubtedly the best.

'He comes across as the yob,' Hunter remarked proudly, 'but he's probably the most complete professional in Mott the Hoople. It's a pleasure to walk into a rehearsal and see him. The first thing he's doing is tuning up. This is the crazy guy that everyone looks at and thinks is out of control.'

The Moils of Mott
—from 'Young Dudes' to Aerial Bender—

words: John Halsall/colour picture: Mike Putland

IF THERE WAS ever a suitable subject for a book entitled 'Rock 'n' Roll Saga' it would be Mott the Hoople. They've released six albums of original material plus another which was just a compilation of 'Hits' of the others. Each one, from about the third onwards, was heralded as the one that would finally break them into the big time, but to follow the chart progress of most of them, a Top 50 would be of more use than a Top 30, until the sixth, 'Mott', that is which planted them high in the charts with no messing.

It's strange that it should have taken so long, whenever they appeared live the crowds would always be there. But on record it didn't happen at all. The early part of 1972 saw the band thoroughly disillusioned and depressed with banging their heads against a proverbial re-inforced concrete wall and they split.

They were in Switzerland at the time and having made the decision, were enjoying the release from tension, getting drunk and having a good time. It was then that David Bowie got to hear of it. He got on the phone to a band he'd never met, told them how much he admired their work and pleaded with them to have one more try ... to get into the studios and he would try and help out. He presented them with one of his songs, 'All The Young Dudes' and it ultimately became one of the most successful records of 1972.

Ian Hunter recalls the group's first meeting with Bowie with a laugh. We were rather nervous about meeting him and, as it turned out, he was even more nervous about meeting us. We weren't quite as he expected us to be. I'm sure that, from seeing us on stage, he thought we would be very camp and theatrical ... and then, there we were, a crowd of very straight roughs. His wife was obviously a bit put out as well, because she talked far too much and kept on saying, 'It really is nice to meet you all at last'.

Bowie not only wrote and produced the single for Mott, but also handled production of their album of the same name, and got them a management deal with Tony de Fries who was masterminding his own career.

The working partnership between the fey sophisticate Bowie and the ultra-masculine, aggressive Hunter, who often tends to call a spade a bloody shovel, was certainly a strange one, but it worked. Perhaps it was that each recognised the other's natural intelligence and sense of purpose, or perhaps it was, as Ian reckons, "because we are so totally different from each other in every possible way".

The band are still on friendly terms with David even though both parties have gone their separate ways. Not so, though, with de Fries. At first their faith in him was unshakable. After all, he'd worked wonders with Bowie, could he not do the same for them.

He tried to build up a mystique for them by refusing to allow the media anywhere near them and they co-operated, then, just around the time that they needed him for advice about a follow-up single, he had to leave for America to supervise Bowie's tour there. Mott remained in England cooling their heels and wondering what was going to happen next.

"David was going to write another single and produce it for us," says Ian, "and said he would have time to do so. De Fries told him he would not have the time and he was right, so we had to think about doing something on our own."

Eventually the inevitable split with De Fries came. "He pretty well told us in so many words that he didn't think we were star material," explained Hunter candidly. "But we all think it was for the best because that's one of the reasons why the new album worked out so well. We all thought, 'we'll show him'."

'Showing him' proved to be quite a job. Before recording even started the band's keyboard player Verden Allen quit. They decided no to replace him and this left them with a quartet.

"Then, during the recording, everything didn't seem to be going as well as it might. We were working on one track for a whole day and we just couldn't seem to get it right. Tempers started to fray and, at one point, Mick and I started arguing and very nearly came to blows. Then I walked out swearing that I'd never work with him again. But the following morning I listened to the track again and it sounded great ... so I apologised to Mick and we were O.K."

As a single 'All The Young Dudes' hadn't altered Mott's situation as recording artists. Most people were of the unfair opinion that it was 10% Mott 90% Bowie. After all, it didn't sound very much like the stuff they'd been churning out before. 'Honaloochie Boogie', the follow-up, was the big test!

It was the first single that the band had written, recorded and produced without any help from third parties at all ... and it was a hit. They could all afford to relax a little, feel more secure. But, even after it smashed its way into the charts, a cautious Hunter confessed: "As a band we are still searching for mass acceptance."

So, with two hits under their belts, the enigmatic Mott started to shudder at the foundations yet again. It was rumoured, for a time, that both Mick Ralphs and Buffin the drummer were leaving. A new single, 'All the Way from Memphis' was released and quickly raced into the charts. A long, hard, American tour was completed to critical reviews which would have pleased the most doubtful of bands. It was decided that capitalisation on the initial American success was necessary and a second tour of the States was hastily set up which gave the group a mere two weeks breathing space between returning and setting off again. In that two weeks Mick Ralphs finally made up his mind and quit.

Rumours flew around the British press for a time giving vent to the thought that this time it might well all be over but, once again, Mott have come up still breathing with a chap who calls himself Aerial Bender and who is, in fact, a much respected Rock musician, Luther Grosvenor late of Spooky Tooth.

Aerial, as we shall call him, had just about ten days to get it on with Mott before the second tour loomed up and, basically, this was just about enough for them to get on 'Top of the Pops', play 'All The Way From Memphis', pack a bag and disappear in the direction of Heathrow. It was, in fact, at Heathrow, that I caught up with him and asked him why he'd chosen such a peculiar name ... what was wrong with Luther Grosvenor

Mott the Hoople on 'Top Of The Pops' on the eve of their second visit to America this year. They are currently doing a month long U.K. tour.

Bender joined the band in September 1973, on the eve of their next American tour. 'When I joined,' Bender reflects, 'I believe that I gave them a shot in the arm. They were very down when I joined Mott the Hoople, so it was great for them, but it was also great for me, and the fact is, we spent the most commercial time together.

'Before I joined Mott, I knew them all very well through my relationship with Island Records, so when they offered me the job, it was quite natural. The only problem I had when I joined was, I didn't have enough rehearsal time with them. I went into a tour, I had to pull all that together in five days, and you never get a full day, something always happens. But it was wonderful.'

Hunter agreed. 'We gave him the job, and within eight days this maniac had the whole act off, and we did two TV shows' – promoting 'All The Way From Memphis' on *Top Of The Pops* in England, and *Midnight Special* in the US. 'He was crapping himself, but he did it.'

August 1973 – 10cc: 10cc (UK UKAL 1005)
August 1973 – 10cc: The Dean And I/Bee In My Bonnet (UK 48)

The success of 'Rubber Bullets' more than paved the way for 10cc's eponymous debut album. It ensured it would walk into a hailstorm of applause as well.

All three of the band's A-sides to date (although both 'Donna' and 'Johnny Don't Do It' were remixed, while 'Rubber Bullets' appeared in an extended form) were on board, with a fourth, 'The Dean And I', quickly joining it.

But six other tracks further compounded the belief that 10cc were fast developing into a force to be reckoned with, as the band turned in one of the most compelling albums of the year. Which is all the remarkable because the songs we got were the songs they recorded. There would be no outtakes or overflow; there will be no bonus-stacked CD remaster.

'Because we were a complete self-produced entity, there was very little self-editing,' drummer Kevin Godley mourns. 'We wrote until we had ten or 12 tracks, and then stopped. It wasn't like we recorded 20 songs and then looked to see which would make an album.

'We would write and record it, and when we had 12 songs we'd stop. An album lasts 40 minutes, we've done 40 minutes, so let's stop and mix it.' There were no tracks left in the vault that didn't end up on albums. You don't make five legs for a table, you make four and then you stop. Except when Lol [Creme] and I were doing "Consequences" (their first post-10cc project), when we built a table with 300 legs.'

As for 'The Dean And I', Godley continues, 'if Daniel Day Lewis was Doris Day's son in a retro psychedelic art movie about making a fucked-up high-school musical, the theme song might sound like this.'

Guitarist Eric Stewart apparently disliked the song intensely – 'Too much cheese, perhaps, and a serous challenge for any guitar hero,' Godley speculates. 'God knows why it was a hit. It was structurally bizarre and had no chorus to speak of it. One of my favourites.'

'The Dean And I' reached Number 8, and the Top Forty success of the album prompted the band to make their first foray onto the live circuit. On 26 August 1973, with Paul Burgess as second drummer (to allow Godley to take his own vocal parts), 10cc debuted at Douglas Palace Lido on the Isle of Man.

This particular show was a success, but 10cc swiftly found themselves catching the wrong end of the critical stick when it came to live performance. Maybe the music was too complicated; maybe the live environment was too primitive. Either way, what their studio output suggested was one of the best bands in the world could not make a similar claim in concert.

Godley: 'We had a lighting guy, and we just got on with the music. Maybe our brains weren't big enough to think of doing both. The visuals took a back seat, or maybe we had terrible taste. Or maybe both. I remember we played somewhere in England and Queen were supporting us, and they had a full lighting rig and we had a plug which was on or off, more or less.

'We did have various presentation ideas but they were all pretty shabby, pretty crap. There was no cohesion which was very strange because there were a lot of bands who were contemporaries who took care of the whole package, the full service...something we never did.

'The only two people in the original band who were capable of doing something like that were myself and Lol, who were visual. For some reason we couldn't be bothered to think of stage sets and wardrobe ideas, how we should dress. It was almost like we prided ourselves on being anonymous which in retrospect was pretty stupid – although it also made us stand out.'

August 1973 – David Bowie: The Laughing Gnome/The Gospel According To Tony Day (Deram DM 123)

In 1973, at the height of David Bowie's post-'Aladdin Sane' fame, a tiny smirking skeleton came creeping out of his closet, paused to adjust its pointy hat, then rocketed to Number 8. It was, of course, 'The Laughing Gnome', a reminder of David's days drifting through the Sixties, and a cause for ribald amusement wherever it played.

Today, of course, Bowie is no stranger to embarrassment, nor to 'The Laughing Gnome'. What, after all, was his role in the *Labyrinth* movie but a twisted reprise of the Gnome's

naughtier excesses, while his 'Earthling' album even offered its own return to the varispeed vocals that made the Gnome laugh.

At the time, however, how he must have cringed as the gnome punned and pattered its way to immortality. Or, as the *NME* sniggered in its review of the single, 'Oh by jingo, how embarrassing.'

August 1973 – New York Dolls: Jet Boy/ Vietnamese Baby (Mercury 6052402)
August 1973 – New York Dolls: New York Dolls (Mercury 6338270)

Stunned by the death of Billy Murcia, the Dolls returned to New York and rebuilt. Jerry Nolan (whose bright pink drum kit Murcia had been borrowing) was drafted in to replace him; weeks later, Rod Stewart's label, Mercury, stepped in to sign the band. The Dolls promptly started auditioning producers, and having turned away 20 they went with Todd Rundgren.

At this point the band's set consisted largely of covers: the Kinks' 'All Day And All Of The Night', Bo Diddley's 'Pills', Archie Bell's 'Showdown' and Sonny Boy Williamson's 'Don't Start Me Talking'. Rundgren insisted they replace them with a self-composed repertoire of their own, a thrashing, tatty, adrenalined barrage that may, as some critics continued to complain, have been little more than a few old garage licks lashed together with lipstick and lace, but would also become the yardstick by which all future glitter-trash merchants would measure themselves.

New British bands the Hollywood Brats and the Winkies would both be early disciples of the Dolls daunting discipline; later in the decade, a host more would sing their praises.

August 1973 – Big Secret: Samson And Delilah/OK Alright (Youngblood YB 1037)

A cover of the Middle of the Road hit makes a deceptive opening to a career that deserved more than the occasional Internet footnote it now receives. Big Secret – aka July and Enry – released a couple more singles, including the punchy 'Ride Captain Ride' and a rocking 'King Kong'.

August 1973 – Leo Sayer: Why Is Everybody Going Home/Quicksand (Chrysalis CHS 2014)

Like Elton John and, to a lesser extent, Gilbert O'Sullivan, Leo Sayer was one of those singer-songwriter types whose true Glam credentials lie in their proximity to the action, as opposed to their active involvement, and to whoever was designing their clothing at the time.

O'Sullivan had got over his dressing-up days before the ball really started rolling; Elton would not stop for decades to come. And Leo – Shoreham-born Gerard Hugh Sayer – kept it up for just one single, the follow-up to this, his Chrysalis debut.

But it's interesting to look back on what he started with.

Sayer had already come to attention after no less than eight of his songs, co-written with producer Dave Courtney, were featured on Who vocalist Roger Daltrey's debut album. The remaining pair were penned by Courtney and Adam Faith, the Sixties icon-turned-actor who was also Sayer and Courtney's manager.

The resultant album (particularly the Courtney-Sayer team's 'One Man Band' and 'Giving It All Away') lifted 'Daltrey' into completely unexpected territory, a record that was almost cinematic in scope, exultant in its promise. Even more importantly, *it* provided the blueprint for four further LPs over the next 18 months, all of which developed that theatricality even further: Sayer's 'Silverbird' and 'Just A Boy' (a line from 'Giving It All Away'), Faith's 'I Survive' and, finally, Courtney's 'First Day'.

'The theatrical style in my writing was not thought out,' explains Courtney. 'It just evolved naturally.'

His earliest influences, from childhood, came from 'listening to the likes of Danny Kaye, the classic children's record Sparky and his Magic Piano, and great melodic pieces like Chaplin's 'Terry's Theme' from *Limelight*, *The Greatest Show On Earth* and an early television programme titled *Circus Boy*, starring the young Mickey Dolenz. And he loved circuses. Now he was marrying those fascinations to more recent favourites, from *Cabaret* to Cat Stevens, Brecht to Bowie, Tchaikovsky…and the rewards came quickly.

Sayer and Courtney road-tested their vision in 1972 with the first and only single by Sayer's then-current band, Patches: 'Living In America'/'Quicksand' (WB K16201) is one of those great rocking 45s so beloved of the Junk Shop Glammers and definitely deserved more than the handful of pleasant reviews it received. It did nothing else, however, and with the newly solo Sayer packing no image beyond an Afro and a nice line in stripy tank-tops, neither did 'Why is Everybody Going Home'.

But Courtney wasn't concerned. It wasn't only the sound of the circus he was in love with. He liked the look of the circus, too.

August 1973 – American Jam Band: Jam Jam/ Back On The Road (Young Blood YB 1056)

The follow-up to 1972's 'American Jam' was a pulsating monster that put Blackfoot Sue through a phaser, mixed in a little John Kongos and came out sounding like the best of everything. It would just take thirty years for more than a handful of people to hear it – 'Jam Jam' is one of the so-called proto-punk jewels uncovered by the compilation 'Glitterbest: 20 Pre-Punk And Glam Terrace Stompers' (RPM 265).

13 August 1973 – Bob Harris: Queen

Reprised from their Peel/*Sounds Of The Seventies* session earlier in the year, 'Liar' and 'Son And Daughter' were joined by the then-unreleased slow blues 'See What A Fool I've Been' on this initial broadcast. 'Keep Yourself Alive' was held over until later.

August 1973 – Big Carrot: Blackjack/Squint Eyed Mangle (EMI 2047)

Still road testing his new R&B direction, Marc Bolan and T Rex convened for a one-off instrumental 45 that remained anonymous even in its choice of label – his regular releases appeared on his own T Rex Wax Co imprint. It mattered not. The single passed unnoticed by all, and Bolan's own career would continue having to bear the brunt of his ambition.

August 1973 – Daddy Maxfield: Rave'n'Rock/ Smiling Again (Pye 7N 45266)

An American band, forerunners of the Graham Daddy and Louis Maxfield-powered Charm School, Daddy Maxfield were exhumed on the compilation 'Glitter From The Litter Bin: 20 Junk-Shop Glam Rarities From The Seventies' (Castle CMQCD 675)

August 1973 – Stumpy: Make Me A Superman/Keep It Coming (Dawn DNS 1080)

A vehicle for ex-Neat Change vocalist Jimmy Edwards, and former Love Affair keyboard-player Lynton Guest. 'Keep It Coming' was rediscovered following its inclusion on the 'Blitzing The Ballroom: 20 UK Power Glam Incendiaries' compilation (Psychic Circle PCCD 7021).

August 1973 – Slade: Slade Talk To Melanie readers (Lyntone 2645)

A fun flexidisc!

August 1973 – Top Of The Pops Volume 33 (Hallmark SHM 835)

'Volume 33' is another of those albums that doesn't put a foot wrong, even if it doesn't always get everything right. A turbulent version of 'Rock On' concentrates not on the original performance's musical attributes, but on the effects-laden vocal that still echoes through your ears. Contrarily, Barry Blue's long-slumbering 'Dancin' (On A Saturday Night)' is reiterated with such gusto that the original record's own multitudinous gimmicks are subverted by a new musicality.

In traditional Top Of The Pops style, two of the most immaculately produced records of the season, 'The Dean And I' and 'Angel Fingers', are reiterated with glittering panache, and 'Angie' aches as slyly heartbreakingly as the original ever did.

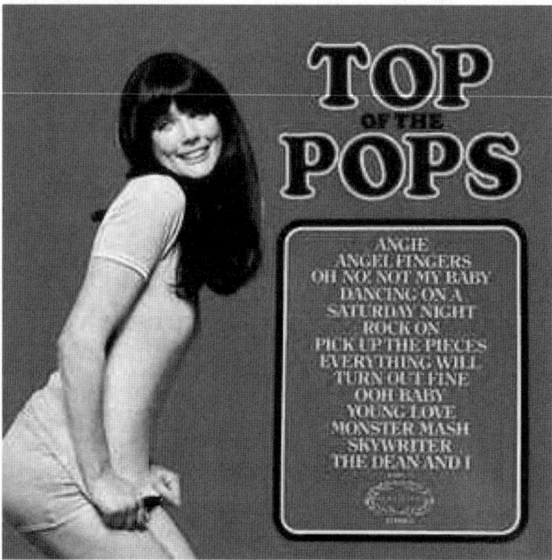

ON THE BOX

3 August 1973 – Top Of The Pops: Barry Blue, Suzi Quatro, Gary Glitter

5 August 1973 – Russell Harty Plus: Wizzard

10 August 1973 – Top Of The Pops: 10cc, Barry Blue, Mud, Suzi Quatro, Gary Glitter

17 August 1973 – Top Of The Pops: Geordie, Gary Glitter

24 August 1973 – Top Of The Pops: Barry Blue

31 August 1973 – Top Of The Pops: 10cc, Barry Blue, David Essex, Wizzard

ON THE SHELVES

August 1973 – Van: Keep Stomping/Love Is A Lady (EMI 2045)

September 1973 – The Sweet: The Ballroom Blitz/Rock And Roll Disgrace (RCA 2403)

Other Sweet singles were bigger and several were more memorable. But 'The Ballroom Blitz' is the archetype, a turbulent tornado of preternatural yelping, blistering guitars and a lyric that says nothing, but sounds like it means a lot regardless. Producer Phil Wainman later confessed that the breakneck drumming was borrowed directly from old Sandy Nelson records and it shows. But it works as well. The percussion drives the record like a racing car.

Steve Priest's quavering camp peaks here, his one-liners stretching to virtual paragraphs, while the instrumental break – nothing less than a drum solo mud-wrestling with a classic rock guitar – packs a vivid madness all of its own. And that's before we even consider the ear-catching rehearsal-studio intro ('Are you ready, Steve?') or the manic outro; 'It's – it's – the ballroom blitz.'

'We were trying to write songs that had no meaning,' Michael Chapman later recalled, 'and "The Ballroom Blitz" was one of them. I suggested the title and we sat down and wrote a song about a guy having a horrifyingly bad dream that his latest record hadn't made it. He was in this ballroom, in a discotheque, and maybe he was on drugs because he started hallucinating.'

Straight into the chart at Number 2 on 22 September, riding advance orders of 80,000, 'The Ballroom Blitz' might even have gone all the way had Wizzard (who'd halted the ascent of 'Hell

Raiser' as well) not had 'Angel Fingers' at the top that same week.

Hopes that 'The Ballroom Blitz' would maintain its push to the top the following week, however, were to be dashed. Wizzard slipped from the top to be supplanted by 'Eye Level', the instrumental theme to the TV detective drama *Van Der Valk* that was destined to rule the chart for the next month. 'Ballroom Blitz' clung to Number 2 for three long weeks, before it finally ran out of patience. It then commenced its gradual slide down the chart. Foiled again.

'It crucified me that Simon Park's Orchestra beat us to Number 1,' Nicky Chinn reflected twenty years later – and all the more so considering that it was simply a reissue of a record that barely made Number 42 a year before.

'I remember ringing Radio 1 to find out if ['The Ballroom Blitz'] was Number 1. I knew them all very well down there, and one of the girls held the 'phone away from her mouth and whispered "Who's gonna tell him it's not Number 1?" I heard Robin Nash say, "I'd better do it." And he said "Dear boy, I'm very, very sorry," and I said, "You're not half as sorry as I am."

'We'd made this fantastic record, it was a Number 2 smash and all we had was depression in our camp. We were all slaughtered, because this was the record, above all those that Mike and I and the Sweet had made, that deserved to be Number 1...it was Number 1 everywhere else.'

September 1973 – Hello: Another School Day/C'Mon Get Together (Bell 1333)

Having been working in the studio with producer Mike Leander since January, Hello signed with his Rock Artistes Management (RAM) empire on 14 May and, days later, were back in the studio with him, recording a new song offered by Nicky Chinn and Mike Chapman, 'Dyna-Mite'.

They never got to meet the writers, recalls Bob Bradbury, but 'It was a great track; we were pleased with it, and thought it had a very high chance of charting.' At the same time, however, something held the band back from releasing it – a fear, perhaps, that they would instantly be labelled another Chinnichap puppet act and castigated accordingly.

Plus, their own material was now coming on strong and a new composition, 'Another School Day', was sounding just as good as the Chinnichap effort.

The record company agreed. A rebel cry for everyone who ever thought education was simply an adult plot to keep them from more interesting pursuits ('I'm just a bopper with the schoolboy blues'), 'Another School Day' was recorded in early September (the B-side was held over from the 'Dyna-Mite' session), just weeks before its release, elbowing 'Dyna-Mite' aside.

Chinn and Chapman took the song back, handed it to Mud and promptly scored a massive hit. 'Another School Day', on the other hand, went nowhere. 'We all make mistakes!' Bob Bradbury admits.

September 1973 – Kid Dynamite: Call Me Sunshine Superman/Breaking The Ice (Pye 7N 45274)

Slade were already moving in a similar direction to this, a cross between a terrace anthem and a rowdy pub singalong. They were also more successful at it. The neatly named Kid would remain obscure until exhumed by the compilation 'Glitter From The Litter Bin: 20 Junk Shop Glam Rarities From The Seventies' (Castle CMQCD 675)

September 1973 – The Hollywood Brats make a splash

Always more of a fashion statement than a functioning outfit, the now-legendary Hollywood Brats formed around Canadian-born singer Andrew Matheson, guitarist ES Brady, bassist Wayne Manor, pianist Casino Steel and drummer Louis Sparks.

Firmly cast in the shadow of the New York Dolls, with whom their fashion sense, at least, was routinely compared, the Brats spent most of their time hanging out and as little time as possible actually playing.

'The Brats were always being booed offstage,' Mathieson later explained, 'sometimes even beaten up by all these people who only ever wanted to hear Barry White or Billy Paul. They never wanted fast rock'n'roll music. We went round every record company, even the small ones, and all they kept saying was that rock'n'roll was dead and that that kind of raunchy music would never come back.'

He is, of course, exaggerating. More than one Dolls-loving witness to the Brats' dishevelled sense of self insists they were booed offstage became they were terrible, 'more interested in posing and insulting the audience than playing.' And it is as a precursor to the Punk movement that the Brats are best-known today.

That, and the fact that Keith Moon once declared them the greatest band he'd ever seen. It was Moon's endorsement that led to the band entering Olympic Studios to record an album during 1973; largely comprising originals, it remained unreleased until 1975 (when it appeared in Norway), by which time the Brats had long since faded.

Steel, however, reappeared in the punk-pop Boys and resurrected the Brats' 'Sick On You' as that band's first single in 1977.

September 1973 – Winston: Mona/Rockerdile (Bradley's BRAD 306)

Barry Blue produced this stunning single for the north London quartet Winston. 'Mona' was another Blue/Lynsey de Paul co-write, rediscovered following its inclusion on the 'Blitzing The Ballroom: 20 UK Power Glam Incendiaries' compilation (Psychic Circle PCCD 7021).

September 1973 – David Bowie: Sorrow/ Amsterdam (RCA 2424)

Within weeks of his on-stage retirement, Bowie, Ronson and bassist Trevor Bolder travelled to France, to begin work on their next album – drummer Woody Woodmansey, after three years in the Spiders from Mars, was gone, replaced by the legendary Aynsley Dunbar. Bowie's notebook of new compositions was left behind as well as he reacted to a recent dispute with his publishers by declaring he wouldn't record another new song until it was settled.

'Pinups', as the new album would be called, was his way of proving that point, and any number of tales exists about the nature of the record he initially intended recording.

A visiting journalist only had to see the sheet music for a song lying about the studio for a whole wave of conjecture to arise. Roxy Music's 'Ladytron', the Velvets' 'White Light White Heat', The Stooges' 'No Fun', the Lovin'

Spoonful's 'Summer In The City', the Beach Boys' 'God Only Knows' and the then little-known Bruce Springsteen's 'Growin' Up' and 'It's Hard To Be A Saint In The City' have all been grafted onto the project, while other whispers insisted Todd Rundgren would be producing.

According to Mick Ronson, however, the album's ultimate theme of London in the mid Sixties was never far from anybody's mind, and the only real question was what songs they should seize upon.

'I forget how many we tried. We didn't record that many extra songs, mainly we just played things to see how they would sound, picked certain ones out and that was it. It wasn't like we recorded all this stuff.

'The concept was just an album of covers, Sixties covers, which was all right with me because I'm a big fan of that music. When we did the Pretty Things' songs ('Rosalyn' and 'Don't Bring Me Down') it was great because I'd been such a Pretty Things fan. When their records came out originally, each one was the greatest thing I'd ever heard. To actually play on them was such a thrill.'

Which brings us to 'Sorrow', a mawkish ditty even in its original incarnation (a hit for the Merseys in 1966). It was certainly the least single-like track on an album full of proven smashes, especially in the current climate. But Bowie selected it himself and, up against 'The Laughing Gnome', it did him proud. 'Sorrow' went to Number 3 in November, one spot higher than the Merseys' original managed and five better than the chortling troll. You didn't need to study at the London School of Eco-gnome-ics to know what *that* meant.

It meant his publishers would soon be capitulating.

September 1973 – Bryan Ferry: A Hard Rain's A-Gonna Fall/2HB (Island WIP 6170)

Bob Dylan songs can be a bugger to cover. Not because they're difficult – has the bard ever written a number that someone or other hasn't made their own hash of? They're a bugger because, no matter how primitive Dylan's own version might be, nothing else sounds so perfect.

That's why David Bowie wrote a song *for* him ('Hunky Dory's 'Song For Bob Dylan') rather than attempting to cover one himself...and anyone who heard his Nineties assault on 'Like A Rolling Stone' will be grateful. And that's why the entire Glam movement gave Dylan a miss when most other composers were fair game for some fun.

The entire Glam movement, that is, aside from Bryan Ferry. And guess what? He got it right, taking the protest-era Zimmerman's most apocalyptic epic and grafting on a dark, claustrophobia that made the original sound anaemic.

Over five minutes long, with little embellishment beyond the occasional interjection of wired electricity from guitarist Phil Manzanera and a suitably frazzled backing chorus, 'A Hard Rain's A-Gonna Fall' was a fascinating choice for Ferry's first ever solo single.

But, so compulsive was the performance (and so threatening the accompanying promo, a black-clad Ferry glaring over a piano) that the record had no difficulty in climbing into the UK Top Ten.

The only question was, we already knew that David Bowie was making an album filled with cover versions. Could Bryan Ferry be doing one as well?

September 1973 – Slade: My Friend Stan/My Town (Polydor 2058407)
September 1973 – Slade: Sladest (Polydor 2442119)

It couldn't be said too loudly, and nobody would have believed it if it was, but Slade singles were *really* going downhill now. Noddy had a friend named Stan. To rhyme with 'funny old man'. Oh yeah.

Compared to everything else they'd released (even the tiresome 'Skweeze Me, Pleeze Me'), 'My Friend Stan' didn't even deserve to be a Number 1 and, mercifully, it wasn't. In at Number 4, outsold by 'Monster Mash' and the Simon Park Orchestra, 'My Friend Stan' would push Sweet out of the way to get to Number 2, but that was the end of it. The following week, he was on his way out and attention turned to the other attraction, Slade's first (or second, if you count 'Coz I Luv You') hits collection.

A cynical Christmas offering, to be sure, but the events of the last few months had scarcely given the band much time in which to write. Don Powell had recovered sufficiently to rejoin the band, only to discover that he needed to relearn all his parts as well – he was suffering from amnesia, as well as walking with a cane and learning to live without the senses of taste and smell.

But no sooner was he back than the band was off to America for their next tour, postponed and rescheduled after the accident, but essential therapy for the drummer. They would have just

NODDY CONQUERS THE YANKS

one studio break to record another new single; the hits album filled in the gap. And some gaps in the collection, as well – its contents went all the way back to 1970 and the only biggie missing was...'My Friend Stan'.

Smart move.

September 1973 – Mighty 'Em: Dr Jekyll And Mr Hyde/What A Way To Go (Decca FR13446)
The mysterious Mighty 'Em's solitary single, since saved from oblivion by 'Killed By Glam: 16 UK Junk Shop Glam Rarities From The Seventies' (Moonboot MB 01).

September 1973 – Suzi Quatro: Daytona Demon/Roman Fingers (RAK 161)
Quatro's third successive hit was, again, less than the convincing monster its makers expected, drifting in and out of the lower Top Twenty (it peaked at Number 14) in a matter of weeks in November.

27 September 1973 – Top Of The Pops
It's Number 1, it's *Top Of The Pops*. On 27 September 1973, the venerable institution was approaching both its tenth birthday and its 500th showing. But first, it had to get pass the 499th and, with the chart dominated by 'Eye Level', the Simon Park Orchestra's instrumental rendering of TV's *Van Der Valk* theme music, we were guaranteed as mixed a bag as the show ever served up.

Ike and Tina Turner played us in, Status Quo turned up the volume with 'Caroline', which might well be the archetypal Quo rocker. Rod Stewart weighed in with the seldom seen promo film for 'Oh No Not My Baby', a vision in green tartan and spandex – yes he *did* look like a plank, but it was 1973 for heaven's sake. Everyone looked like planks back then.

The Hollies and Perry Como (yes, *that* Perry Como) reminded us that *Top Of The Pops* wasn't just for the kids, and Manfred Mann's Earthband brought some gravity to the situation with a grin-laden 'Joybringer' and an astonishingly serious-looking drummer. Not *everybody* looked good in a kung fu sweatband and beard, just as not every member of the Pan's People dance troupe was ravishing when painted green. But Babs goes for it, regardless, and 'Monster Mash' will never look the same again.

29 September 1973 – Showaddywaddy win New Faces
Just what we needed, another talent show, as if *Opportunity Knocks* wasn't bad enough. But *New Faces* promised to be different. For a start, it wasn't the viewers who would be determining the winners, with all the pitfalls (in terms of honesty and taste) that entailed. It was a panel of judges, selected from all walks of entertainment life and instructed to judge the contestants on just three criteria: presentation, content and star quality.

No more 11 year-old sopranos appealing to Granny with their innocence. No more six year-old redheads. No more MOR songbirds and U-certificate comedians. This was the big league, and a panel of judges that included Mickie Most, Tony Hatch, Ted Ray and disc jockeys Ed Stewart and Noel Edmonds was going to make sure it stayed that way.

So cue the theme music, Carl Wayne's 'You're A Star' and some words of introduction from host Derek Hobson: our very first finalists are...Showaddywaddy!

Showaddywaddy were a Leicester-based rock'n'roll revival band, formed after two local groups, the Choice and the Hammers, both regulars at the Fosse Way pub, decided to pool their considerable resources after realising how great they sounded when they got together to jam.

At a time when Gary Glitter was making a virtue of having two drummers, this new aggregation could also boast two bassists (Al James and Rod Deas), two guitarists (Russ Field and Trevor Oakes) and two singers (Dave Bartram and Buddy Gask). Drummers Malcolm Allured and former Black Widow percussionist Romeo Challenger completed the line-up, a full Fifties-style wardrobe completed the experience.

Veterans already of intensive gigging up and down the country, Showaddywaddy concentrated on the entertainment-starved north. They took on management, a Newcastle-based team that wasn't about to take any nonsense, and when the telephone began ringing the morning after *New Faces* they were ready. Producer Mike Hurst was the quickest off the mark.

Earlier in the decade, the ex-Springfield-turned-producer had worked with rock'n'roll revivalists Fumble, one of those bands who are often declared Glam Rock by default by virtue of having toured with Bowie in 1972. They weren't, of course, but even if they had been the world might not have yet been ready for the ensuing cultural hybrid. It was all very well paying stylistic lip service to the past. But full-on drape coats and duck's arse hair-dos? Crepe souls and bootlace ties? Cupping cigarettes between thumb and forefinger and mouthing 'be bop' at the passers by? That looked good on the King's Road, hanging over the railings outside Let It Rock. But would it have worked on *Top Of The Pops*?

Hurst thought it would. 'I was sitting watching television one night, *New Faces*, and on came this group in drape jackets and everything, all the different colours of the rainbow. They won the evening's contest and I thought to myself, because Mud were already up and happening, "Not bad. It's all a bit freaky, they look like 1957 but, on the other hand, why not?"'

The following morning, Hurst rang the television station, got a number for the band's management company and called. 'I said, "I'd like to produce this band's records," so they said, "Let's have a meeting." Three days later, I went up to Newcastle to meet with the band and their management, and they said '"What can you bring to the table?" And I said, "I can bring you the best singles label in this country," which was Bell. Now I hadn't mentioned this to Bell, but I knew Dick Leahy who ran the company and I knew I could get in to see him.

'I went to see him the next day and I said, "Dick, I have this group that I want to bring to your attention – they're called Showaddywaddy" and he said, "That band that was on *New Faces* at the end of last week? God, my secretary's been talking about them." I said, "There you go, do you want them?" And he said, "Yes please".'

An open and shut case, then? Not quite. Back in Newcastle, Hurst learned that another label had entered the pursuit, Polydor A&R man Wayne Bickerton. Not only was he offering to sign the band, he had also written a sure-fire hit for them called 'Sugar Baby Love'.

Hurst shrugged. 'Forget Polydor. We have a deal with Bell. As for "Sugar Baby Love", I told them not to worry about it. I wanted Showaddywaddy to write and record their own songs.'

Showaddywaddy went with Hurst.

September 1973 – Kristine Sparkle: Gonna Get Along Without You Now/I'll Be Your Baby Tonight (Decca F13445)

With a name like that, she has to be Glam. Well, not really. A former member of the band Family Dogg, Sparkle was poppier than some, softer than most, as evidenced by her choice in covers: 'I'll Be Your Baby Tonight' was a Dylan song, her next-but-one single, 'Eight Days A Week' (c/w 'The Drum' – Decca F13515) was a Beatles numbe and, on either side of that, 'The Hokey Cokey'/'Baby I Love You' (Decca F13485) and 'It's In His Kiss'/'The Highway Song' (Decca F13544)... well, you get the picture.

So don't be fooled by the name!

September 1973 – Top Of The Pops Volume 34 (Hallmark SHM 840)

'Volume 34' arrived as the heroes of the hitherto inviolate Glam Rock pack were beginning to alter their focus. Slade's 'My Friend Stan' and David Bowie's 'Sorrow' both served first notice that their makers had more on their minds than their next pot of facepaint, but how curious that they should do so simultaneously. Was there something in the water? Or was it just bad timing?

Having ridden Glam more successfully than any other genre that would come into its orbit, the Top Of The Pops squad greeted – and treated – such meanderings with obvious trepidation. Any collector curious enough to assemble, say, every one of the series' Bowie covers into one long listening session will instantly recognise 'Sorrow' as one of the weakest, and the Slade slam is pretty lacklustre too.

But Joni Mitchell's 'This Flight Tonight', as gnarled up by Nazareth, is a solid roar, while '5.15' overcomes some hiccups in the vocal department to emerge a barrage of bombast that leaves the Who sounding almost saccharin. But the (perhaps unexpected) highlight has to be 'Eye Level', not because it's a spot-on orchestral recreation of the first TV theme ever to top the British chart but because it annoyed everyone else so much.

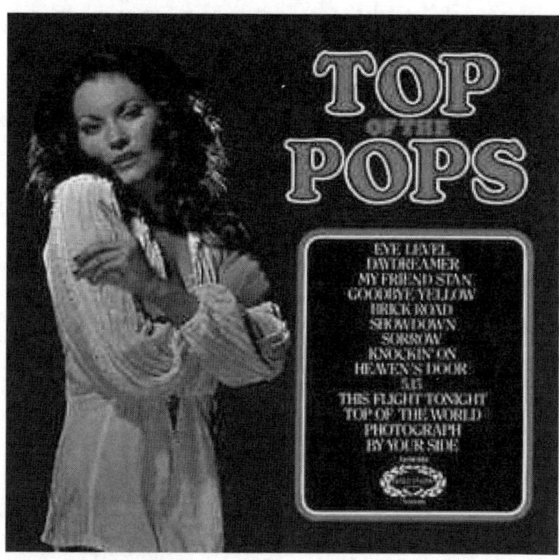

ON THE BOX
2 September 1973 – Russell Harty Plus – David Essex
7 September 1973 – Stanley Baxter Picture Show: Blackfoot Sue
13 September 1973 – In Concert (BBC): Queen
13 September 1973 – Top Of The Pops: 10cc, David Essex, the Sweet, Wizzard
20 September 1973 – Top Of The Pops: Mott the Hoople, the Sweet, Wizzard

ON THE SHELVES
September 1973 – Electric Dolls: Doctor Love/Love A Little Longer (Jam 52)
September 1973 – Fantasy: Politely Insane/I Was Once Aware (Polydor 2058 405)
September 1973 – Chunky: Albatross Baby/Road Runner Girl (Orange OAS 214)
September 1973 – The Thieves – Ali Baba/ Can I See You Today (RAK 160)
September 1973 – Blackfoot Sue: Get It All To Me/My Oh My (Jam 53)
September 1973 – Hot Rocks: Chopper/Roly Poly (Bell 1326)
September 1973 – Kidrock: Ice Cream Man/ Dream Dream Dream (Youngblood 1058)
September 1973 – X Certificate: Don't Stick Stickers On My Paper Knickers/Come Home Baby (Spark 1096)
September 1973 – Peter Henn – Flip Flap/Song Of The Rising Country Wind (Bradley's BRAD307)

---

4 October 1973 – *Top Of The Pops 500th Edition*
This was the big one. Five hundred episodes is a milestone for any show, not least of all one about pop music, and *Top Of The Pops* was not going to let it pass unheralded.

Filmed inserts by some of the biggest acts of the day – Slade, the Jackson Five, Gary Glitter, Slade and the Osmonds – were secured, all of them paying tribute to the greatest pop show on earth; an hour of Thursday evening viewing time was surrendered to a double-length programme, and the evening's billing was astonishing.

Gary Glitter, Lynsey de Paul, Bryan Ferry, Cliff Richard, Dawn, the Tremoloes, the Who and the Simon Park Orchestra all turned out to perform; David Bowie was celebrated with a film for 'The Laughing Gnome', Lieutenant Pigeon were on hand to say a few words, and it was all capped off by a will-he won't-he make it in time adventure with David Cassidy.

The show opened with footage of Cassidy's plane in mid-air, somewhere over the Atlantic we were told. Forty minutes later, we saw him land at Heathrow and say a few words to a waiting Tony Blackburn. And then, right there on the tarmac, on live television, he mimed to his latest hit, 'Daydreamer'. The fact that he'd already been in the country for a few days; the plane had simply been taxied in from a private airport, and the whole sequence was shot the previous day should not diminish the memory. It was good TV, either way.

But that was also the night, sadly *off*-camera, that the Who's Pete Townshend got into a loud and almost violent argument with a member, or members, of the Simon Park Orchestra – about what we do not know. The correct way to treat a guitar, perhaps?

October 1973 – Alvin Stardust: My Coo Ca Choo/Pull Together (Magnet 1)
5 October 1973 – Lift Off With Ayshea – Alvin Stardust

On paper, it all looked so fresh. On vinyl, too, it was a revelation.

But then you actually caught a glimpse of Alvin Stardust first appeared, all tight black leather and a-glowering into the camera, and wasn't there something ever so familiar about him? A face in an old magazine, for example; or a dimly remembered clip from a Sixties television show?

Oh my God, it's Shane Fenton.

Bernard Jewry was merely the roadie for a band called Shane Fenton and the Fentones when 17-year-old vocalist Johnny Theakston died, victim of the rheumatic fever he had suffered as a child.

It was a crippling blow, all the more so since the band had sent a tape into the BBC's *Saturday Club* a few weeks' earlier, putting themselves forward for an audition. The response came back a few days after Theakston's death; they had been accepted.

At first they ignored it. The band was finished. But Theakston's mother asked them to continue as a tribute to her son, and to retain the band name, too. Roadie Jewry became Shane Fenton that same afternoon.

Early in 1961, the newly reconstituted Shane Fenton and the Fentones not only sailed through the audition, they had also acquired a manager, Tommy Sanderson and, by the end of that same week, a deal with Parlophone. September 1961 saw the band release their debut single, 'I'm A Moody Guy'/'Five Foot Two, Eyes of Blue' (Parlophone R4827); their television debut, on *Thank Your Lucky Stars* followed, and the record peaked at Number 19.

In early 1962, Shane Fenton and the Fentones joined one of the era's great package tours, sharing the bill with Billy Fury and the Tornadoes, Karl Denver and Peter Jay, under the aegis of entrepreneur Larry Parnes.

Their live show went over well, but three successive singles passed by unnoticed: 'Walk Away'/'Fallen Leaves On The Ground' (Parlophone R4866) and 'Why Little Girl'/It's All Over Now' (Parlophone R4883) by the full group, the instrumental 'Lover's Guitar'/'The Mexican' (Parlophone R4899) by the Fentones alone.

June brought a respite when 'Cindy's Birthday'/'It's Gonna Take Magic' (Parlophone R44921) returned the band to the upper echelons of the chart. But then it was back to square one as 'Too Young For Sad Memories'/'You're Telling Me' (Parlophone R4951) and 'I Ain't Got Nobody'/'Hey Miss Ruby' (Parlophone R4982) sunk into oblivion, to be joined by another of the Fentones' instrumental efforts, 'The Breeze And I'/'Just For Jerry' (Parlophone R4937).

A second Parnes tour in early 1963 found the band bottom of the bill and, that April, Shane Fenton and the Fentones broke up. Fenton went solo, but further 45s 'A Fool's Paradise'/'You Need Love' (Parlophone R5020) and 'Don't Do That'/'I'll Know' (Parlophone R5047) sank.

The tides were changing; the Beatles had arrived and the Beat Boom was in full swing. For a time, Fenton moved into management, linking with Tommy Sanderson to oversee the early days of the Hollies. It didn't last long, however, and Fenton was soon performing again, touring the northern cabaret circuit with his wife Iris Caldwell (the sister of Rory Storm) as Shane Fenton and Iris. Fenton released a final single, 'Hey Lulu'/'I Do, Do You' (Parlophone R5131) in 1964, and that was it for the next near-decade.

It was a reunion with Hal Carter, Billy Fury's road manager on that first Larry Parnes tour, that brought Fenton back 'up-to-date'. He was touring now with his Shane Fenton Rock'n'Roll Trio and, he explains, 'In the late Sixties, Hal became an agent and a part-manager; he ran an agency with Marty Wilde and Billy Fury, and getting gigs for people like Joe Brown, and he

Alvin
STARDUST
George Tremlett

asked if he could represent me, as the Shane Fenton Rock'n'Roll Trio. So I said, "Okay, try and get me some work", and he did. I started working with him about 1970.'

By 1972, Carter was operating his own Fury record label, named of course for Billy, but Shane Fenton became his second signing. But the two singles he would release for Fury were not to appear under what was now considered 'his' name.

'We thought...to be honest, it was Hal who suggested that Radio 1 probably wouldn't play a new Shane Fenton single because it was such a Sixties name, and he wanted something more down to earth.' Jo Jo Ellis was born, 'and I just went along with it.' 'The Fly'/'Persona Mia' (Fury FY 302) and 'Eastern Seaboard'/'Blind Fool' (Fury FY 305) followed, but the name change ultimately made no difference. The singles still didn't get played.

Meanwhile, Marty Wilde was working with Peter Shelley, a songwriter and producer who had just become a cornerstone of a brand new label, Magnet Records, owned by music-biz accountant Michael Levy and otherwise staffed only by plugger Ann Bishop and a school-leaver named Joanne.

The first release was scheduled to be a new song Shelley had written, a dark, coiling guitar anthem titled 'My Coo Ca Choo'. He recorded with a band that included guitar legend Big Jim Sullivan, Terry Britten and Brian Bennett; the only problem was he couldn't find anyone to sing it. Finally Hal Carter cornered Shane Fenton.

'Peter had made the track and he didn't want to sing, he wanted to be a producer, so he asked Marty [Wilde] if he'd sing it and Marty didn't want to. I think he asked two or three other people and everyone said no. So Hal came to me and said "Look, there's a track going here, it's going to be on a brand new label, it's not going to cost you anything, why don't you do it?"

'And the next thing I know, they said "We're going to need a new name, something that's going to be current with the Glam Rock feel." Originally, I was told it might be Alvin Star, and somewhere down the line it changed to Stardust.'

What they needed now was a look. Shelley's chief thought for the performer was that it needed to be someone 'who could sing rock'n'roll, but who looked pretty mean.'

But *how* mean? There was some uncertainty on that score when Alvin Stardust made his television debut on *Lift Off With Ayshea* (5 October), a vision in pink and blue – but Shane Fenton takes no responsibility for that. It was Peter Shelley.

The record started out very slowly. 'I recorded the track, and then went back to Manchester or wherever. We were playing the working men's clubs and I thought that's the last we'll hear of that. I really didn't think we had a cat in hell's chance of doing anything with a name like Alvin Stardust and a song titled "My Coo Ca Choo". It was too crazy to work.'

Then one night on Radio Luxembourg, DJ Tony Prince span the record and declared at the end that he recognised the voice. 'Magnet tried to say this was some unknown person, but Tony Prince said "I know this voice. I think I know who it is, and I think he had a couple of records in the charts in the early Sixties."'

He started playing the record regularly, challenging Fab 208's listenership to call in and guess who it was. The more he played it, the more it sold, 'and suddenly the record company got the chance to do *Lift Off.* I was working and couldn't do it, but they said "We can't turn it down, we'll have to do it," and someone told Peter you'll have to go.

The media had recently been besieged by a series of photographs depicting what Chrysalis Records believed would be the Next Big Thing, a singer-songwriter named Leo Sayer, all togged up in a clown outfit. His new record was still some weeks from release, though, so the look was, technically, still up for grabs.

'So someone at Magnet told Peter, "We'll do that. You can paint half your face in pink and half your face in blue and wear a blue and pink clown's outfit." So Peter went on and sang it like that.'

October 1973 – David Bowie: Pinups (RCA 1003)

October 1973 – Bryan Ferry: These Foolish Things (Island ILPS 9249)

Bryan Ferry's solo ambitions, dormant throughout Roxy Music's rise to ascendancy, were finally uncaged during the hiatus initiated by Eno's departure. 'These Foolish Things' was a collection of standards, old and new, each given the distinctive Ferry touch, and even the album's detractors had to admit it fulfilled that brief.

With its contents ranging idiosyncratically from 'Sympathy For The Devil' and 'A Hard Rain's A-Gonna Fall' through to 'The Tracks Of My Tears' and 'It's My Party', Ferry created an album that remains one of the weirdest records ever cast towards a rock audience, even one as enlightened as the British Glam scene.

As versatile in his arrangements as he ever was as a songwriter, Ferry imbued the most innocuous lyric with a sense of genuine malice, even when he was aiming for heartache. His version of 'It's My Party' is sheer genius, although he saved his finest performance for the title track.Journalist Robert Cushman, author of the book *The Lives Of The Great Songs* (Pavilion 1994), surveyed almost 60 years' worth of recordings of the song, including performances by the likes of Billie Holiday (1936), Bing Crosby (1955) and Frank Sinatra (1961). Ferry's version was deemed superior in virtually every department. High praise indeed.

But how did that make David Bowie feel? He, too, had spent the summer musing an album of covers; he, too, had formulated a concept that would unite them all, and although it all seems very trivial today, at the time there was a very real possibility that one or other of the artists was going to start whistling up the lawyers and waving round injunctions.

Common sense ultimately prevailed; 'Pinups' gave Bowie his expected Number 1; 'These Foolish Things' rewarded Ferry with a seasonal Number 5 and it has to be said that the two records were so dissimilar that neither had much to complain about.

The only really aggrieved party was the Sweet. They'd been talking about making an album like this a full year before either Carrot-Top or Smoothie Chops even thought of it.

October 1973 – Spiv: Oh You Beautiful Child/ Little Girl (Pye 7N 45293)

A great Laurie Marshall composition and production, and a highlight of the 'Glitter From The Litter Bin: 20 Junk Shop Glam Rarities From The Seventies' (Castle CMQCD 675) collection, Spiv were a London-based pub band fronted by a singer named Glen.

'People seem to love "Oh You Beautiful Child",' Marshall recalls, 'although if they heard the demo they'd love it even more. The demo was incredible. I asked the guy at Pye, Robin Blanchflower why we didn't just release the demo, but he was a new operations manager and he knew nothing. He didn't have a clue, he didn't know who I was, so he was "No no, we have to do it all again", and it came out well enough… But I knew the demo had it. If that demo had been released, and had a little promotion, it would have rocketed up the chart, it was incandescent. It was that good.'

Unfortunately the single was doomed, running up against the BBC's growing predilection for play-listing American talent over British. 'For British artists on independent labels at that time, it was a terrible situation. Unless you were with RAK or [Elton John's] Rocket, you didn't get played.

'They were literally dumping records outside the Beeb, and when I heard they were doing this with Spiv I got a sandwich board, "BBC unfair to British artists", and walked up and down outside the building for a day, protesting the BBC's policy.

'How do you tell a band that they're not getting played because the promo guy from Pye left your record on the BBC doorstep? I was so angry I didn't know what else to do. Avenues for independent stuff, you just had Radio Luxembourg and Radio Caroline out near the Dutch coast...they were all into American records, which I loved, but come on.'

October 1973 – Hello Sailor!

The Norwegian-born son of a Russian prince, Pavel Tchegodieff, and French-Finnish sculptress Johanna Kajanus (granddaughter of composer Robert Kajanus), the young Georg Kajanus grew up in Paris and Canada, where he fell into the local (Montreal) folk scene.

Relocating to London in 1967, Kajanus formed a new folk-rock band with Canadian Michael Rosen, Australians Trevor Lucas and Kerrilee Male and Englishman Gerry Conway – an eclectic blend friend Joni Mitchell promptly christened Eclection. The band cut one album for Elektra and performed at the Isle of Wight festival before Kajanus left following disagreements with his bandmates' proposed jazz direction.

'Eclection was my first attempt at breaking into the professional pop music scene, and I became a lot more serious about creating compositions that would fulfil me. It was important that I secured a publishing deal. I had to compose 10 songs and submit them to Chappell Morris Music in order to sign a contract with them.'

It was one of these, 'Flying Machine', that introduced Kajanus to the world. 'It was selected by Cliff Richard's management team as a single. I was even asked to perform on the recording. Bruce Welch of the Shadows was trying to replicate the 12-string guitar part from my demo, but ultimately didn't think he had the right feel for it. So they called me. They were looking for my demo-style of simple, yet powerful straight strumming with fingerpicks, which I could do very easily.

'I also played the penny whistle part from the demo, but that proved to be much more of a challenge. Not being a professional penny-whistle player, I needed a lot of takes to get it right. We recorded "Flying Machine" at Abbey Road Studios. Sadly, it was one of Cliff's lesser hits, [Number 37 in July 1971] but it still raised my profile as a songwriter since it did get into the Top Forty.'

It was at Chappell Morris that Kajanus met fellow songwriter Phil Pickett. The pair joined forces as an eponymous duo and cut a demo comprising three of Kajanus' songs and two of Pickett's. 'Phil took the tape to GTO Records, who signed us virtually on the spot. We were very impressed with such a rapid result.' The duo cut an album for GTO's Signpost subsidiary, 'Hi Ho Silver', and prepared to go out on the road. However, after just one gig, at the Troubadour folk club in Earl's Court, London, they abandoned the idea.

'I played guitar, as well as a tambourine mounted on to a bass drum pedal, creating the offbeat. Phil had a similar set-up, but he was playing a real bass drum, doing the on-beat, as well as other string instruments such as mandolin and electric guitar. I guess we just weren't destined for live work with our set-up.'

At the same time as Kajanus-Pickett was underway, Kajanus was also working on a musical titled *The Red Light Revue*. He had just one song completed, 'Sailor's Night On The Town', about the Madame of a brothel preparing her girls to receive the next influx of sailors on shore leave. The remainder of the set would continue in a similar vein, both lyrically and musically – darkly continental, alive with accordions and acoustics, *chanson*-esque tempos and rhythms, and closer to Brecht or Brel than Bowie, with short songs and vignettes being handled by a variety of different singers.

'The material, image and direction for this project was all coming from a powerful fantasy of mine. This concept was a romanticised account of some of my personal experiences in Paris as a young man and was influenced by music that was alien to Phil.' It was also massively ambitious, and very slow going, so when Pickett suggested putting together a new band around the Kajanus-Pickett project, Kajanus agreed.

Both brought along a couple of new songs, Kajanus' 'Brag Brag Brag' and 'Traffic Jam', and Pickett's 'Lost My Mode' and 'Medallions'. Joined by keyboard-player Henry Marsh (ex-Gringo) and drummer Grant Serpell (ex-Affinity, alongside Fancy's Mo Foster), they began rehearsing the old Kajanus-Pickett back catalogue, as well as the four new songs.

'However, one morning during the latter half of 1973, we met at my place, as usual, to discuss the band's musical direction. Grant was curious about the *Red Light Revue*.' Kajanus played some of his demos and was immediately rewarded when 'Henry and Grant felt that this was what we should do as a band, rather than the more folk-rock, West Coast style of Kajanus-Pickett.'

Kajanus agreed; Pickett, suddenly squeezed out of the group's vision, quit, and it was a three-piece band, now renamed Sailor, who auditioned for Epic Records performing 'Sailor's Night On The Town'.

Label head Dick Asher, delighted to find a band that wasn't the usual guitar-led rock combo, signed them and, with Pickett returning to the fold, work began on Sailor's first album – a record that both musically and stylistically, would delve into realms that Glam Rock had always acknowledged, but never truly visited, the twilight world of the red-light district, matelots, *roués* and the romance of sleaze and disgrace.

October 1973 – Mud: Dyna-Mite/Do It All Over Again (RAK 159)

Who was 'Dyna-mite' really written for?

Hello, of course. But once they'd rejected it…according to Brian Connolly, it was offered to the Sweet, only for them to turn it down as well. So it was passed onto Mud, and they grasped it with all eight hands. Steve Priest says no. 'We were never offered it. That's another urban legend. I actually went to Nicky Chinn and said did you offer us "Dyna-Mite"? And he said no, that was always written for Mud.'

Or Hello. Either way, Mud made it their own.

Ray Stiles: 'Mike and Nicky bought it up to a gig in Birmingham and played it to us, and we thought "Yeah, that's great, we'll do it".'

'Dyna-Mite' would be the first of their records Mud played on. Gray continued: 'The first time we heard the demo, which was just Mike on acoustic guitar, we could see what a great song it was. So Mike was playing the song on acoustic guitar, Rob [Davis] picked up his guitar and began playing around him, and Mike realised that we really did know what we were doing.'

But, as Stiles explains, everything bar the playing was being done for them at that time. RAK picked out their wardrobe, Chinnichap selected their singles, Mickie Most decided who played on them, the lot. 'Then, after the first two hits weren't as big a hit as Mickie would have liked, we were summoned into RAK and they said "Well, lads, you've had a couple of hits but they weren't big enough, so get your act together or you're out."'

'And we thought, "Hang on, you told us what to wear, you chose the clothes, you told us what to do, you gave us the songs, you recorded them, and now you're blaming us because they weren't big enough?"

'Anyway, Mickie made it clear that if "Dyna-Mite" wasn't a big hit we'd be out. Then he said, "This is what you'll be wearing"' and pulled out

these silver shirts and flared trousers. We said, "We're not wearing that. If we're going to be out on our ears, let's wear what we want to. It's a rock record, and we're not going to go up there in gargantuan shirts and flares!"'

Stiles selected a Teddy Boy outfit, 'because my Uncle Len was a Ted.' Gray agreed and ordered the same. Mount decided to stick with trousers and a shirt because nobody could see him behind his drum kit, and that left Davis alone to make his decision.

'When "Dyna-Mite" started getting into the charts and we had to do *Top Of The Pops*, he had this catsuit kind of arrangement,' Stiles laughs. 'So we said to him "Go down to wardrobe and see if you can yourself one of those little gold clip-on earrings." So Rob goes down there and comes back with a pair of long diamanté ones. They never had any little gold clips, but they had these, and we were "Great, put them on". We worked out that sılly dance, the rock'n'roll Teddy Boy thing, and it just went wild for us.'

Mud had found their niche. There as certainly no further mention of dropping them.

Stiles: 'Once "Dyna-Mite" took off, the next time we were on television our jackets got bigger and our trousers got shorter. I'd have one red sock and one green, Les would have one green and one red, and Rob's earrings just got bigger and bigger.

'My wife used to make earrings, and there'd be Christmas trees that lit up, and earrings down to his waist, and his clothes became more like dresses. Rob's mum phoned me up one day: "Oh dear, I just saw Rob on the television wearing earrings. Does he have to wear all that?" So I said to Rob, "Your mum's been on the blower and asked if you could tone it down a little?" He turns round and says, "Tell her to fuck off".'

They could tell Mickie Most to fuck off, as well. 'Dyna-Mite' halted at Number 4, as big a hit as anyone could have dreamed of. Nobody ever mentioned throwing Mud out again.

October 1973 – Suzi Quatro: Suzi Quatro (RAK 505)

Suzi discusses fan art with *Jackie* magazine: 'I got a lovely one from a little boy who'd drawn me in my leather gear – only he'd given me a bust of about 66 inches.'

No matter how much you'd loved Suzi Quatro so far, by the time 'Daytona Demon' rolled around it was difficult to deny the formula was wearing thin. Which means even fans viewed the arrival of her debut album from the querulous side of uncertainty, and it was only when they delved inside that they – or anyone else, for that matter – discovered just how much more there was to the girl.

Her fame and, of course, her hits were unquestionably built upon Chinnichap's ability to crank out the classics. But away from the glare of TV and radio-play, with Quatro and partner Len Tuckey granted full musical rein, 'Suzi Quatro' emerged a shattering demonstration of the sheer power of the Quatro personality.

The heart of 'Suzi Quatro' lies in the band's choice of covers. Omitting both 'Can The Can' and 'Daytona Demon', it instead harked back to

Quatro's years in Detroit clubland. There's a Slade-meets-Stones-ey grind through 'I Wanna Be Your Man', a raucous blast through Elvis's 'All Shook Up' recalling her teenage love of the Jeff Beck Group (the song was a standout on their second album). And, restating the song's status among the best rock'n'roll any Briton ever wrote, Johnny Kidd's 'Shakin' All Over', with garageland sexuality oozing out from every pore.

Chinnichap's 'Primitive Love', the finest song the duo ever allowed to remain an album track alone, boasts a similar intent, seething percussion and unearthly crowd sounds building around a jungle chant that reduces Quatro's cries to a breathy growl that is pure animal seduction

Of Quatro/Tuckey's own contributions, 'Glycerine Queen' (already familiar from a B-side) and 'Shine My Machine' are the most in-character, straightforward rockers bolstered by the band's already-trademark roiling rhythm. 'Skin Tight Skin', on the other hand, is the most adventurous, bucking the formula in favour of a slow swing and a vocal straight out of *West Side Story*. But all combine to confirm 'Suzi Quatro' as one of the most nakedly sexual albums of the glam-rock era.

October 1973 – Zappo: Rock'n'Roll Crazy/ Right On (Magnet MAG 2)

Not content with relaunching one pseudonymous pre-Beatles rocker onto the Glam scene, producer Peter Shelley had another one up his sleeve, Marty Wilde, fresh from turning down the opportunity to perform 'My Coo Ca Choo'.

Showing considerably more artistic credibility than one might have expected (or maybe just narked that he'd been rumbled), Wilde told *Record Mirror* he adopted the name Zappo to ensure that people bought the record because they liked it, 'rather than because of having a following.'

It seemed cruel to point out that following had not bought one of his records since 1962 and would pass this one by as well. Twelve months later, 'Right On' would be revisited by another Peter Shelley/Magnet Records discovery, Yellow Bird; Zappo would be reprised on the compilation 'Killed By Glam: 16 UK Junk Shop Glam Rarities From The Seventies' (Moonboot MB 01).

October 1973 – Chicory Tip: IOU/Join Our Gang (CBS 1866)

Returning to songwriter Giorgio Moroder, Chicory Tip unleashed one of their most compulsive singles yet. Unfortunately, it wasn't compulsive enough. Another miss.

October 1973 – Zakatek: Get Your Gun/Gotta Runaway (Bell 1335)

Lenny Zakatek once again, a great song, and a terrific Lynsey de Paul co-write and production to match.

October 1973 – Cozy Powell: Dance With The Devil/And Then There Was Skin (RAK 164)

By 1973, Cozy Powell was highly renowned among Britain's most respected drummers; he had recorded with Jeff Beck and his own band Bedlam, and was probably the hardest-hitting player around. So when Mickie Most decided that the Next Big Thing was going to be a drum solo, he called up Cozy. And Powell replied 'why not?'

He was doing a session for Alexis Korner's CCS when Most first broached the notion. 'It was a great idea,' Powell recalled. 'A mad idea, but a great one, and that's what Mickie was good at. I'd loved all those Sandy Nelson singles, "Let There Be Drums" and so on when I was a kid, and so had Mickie, and that's what we wanted to recreate, a record that we built from the drumbeat up which would shake things up a bit.

'It took us 20 minutes, and then I forgot all about it. About six weeks later, Mickie told me he'd finished the track, put some backing vocals on and played it to me. Great. I didn't think any more about it until someone told me that it was going up the charts.'

With a guitar riff unapologetically borrowed from Jimi Hendrix's 'Third Stone From The Sun', and a backing chorus straight out of Mud, 'Dance With The Devil' was nevertheless wall-to-wall drums, and when Powell appeared on *Top Of The Pops* – the first solo drummer to chart since Nelson, trailed the dailies – the country sat still to watch.

'Dance With The Devil' would not chart until early December, and didn't peak until the New Year; it reached Number 3 in February. But Mickie Most was already certain of one thing. He had a new hit machine on his hands. The only thing he needed to do was convince Cozy to cut a follow-up.

October 1973 – Spiv: Oh You Beautiful Child/ Little Girl (Pye 7N 45293)
A highlight of the 'Glitter From The Litter Bin: 20 Junk Shop Glam Rarities From The Seventies' (Castle CMQCD 675) collection, Spiv were a London pub rock band who boarded the Glam bang-wagon for one stunning single. Their lead vocalist, according to one review, was named Glen.

October 1973 – Starbuck: Do You Like Boys/ You Never Wanna (Bradleys BRAD 312)
The Brian Engel/Martin Briley partnership resurfaced under their Starbuck guise, still working with Ken Howard and Alan Blaikley. Another one for the 'Glitter From The Litter Bin: 20 Junk Shop Glam Rarities From The Seventies' (Castle CMQCD 675) collection.

October 1973 – The Jets: Yeah/Rusty Corinthian Pillar (Cube BUG 35)
What the A-side lacks in title, the B-side more than compensates for. Find 'Yeah' on 'Killed By Glam: 16 UK Junk Shop Glam Rarities From The Seventies' (Moonboot MB 01).

October 1973 – Spunky Spider: You Won't Come/Perchance (Phoenix NIX 143)
On the off-chance that the same people who bought Judge Dread singles might fancy a little rock as well, clashed with post-'Popcorn'/Chicory Tip-like electronics, Spunky Spider bemoan the death of love in the form of a lover who positively refuses to orgasm. Another proto-punk jewel unearthed by the compilation 'Glitterbest: 20 Pre-Punk'n'Glam Terrace Stompers' (RPM 265).

October 1973 – Wild Angels: Clap Your Hands And Stamp Your Feet/Wild Angels Rock'n'Roll (Decca F13456)
The final 45 by future Flight 56-er Mal Gray's long-running rock'n'roll revival band, and you can't help but wonder what might have happened if they'd just held on for a little longer, donned some brightly coloured drapes and changed their name to Showaddywaddy...

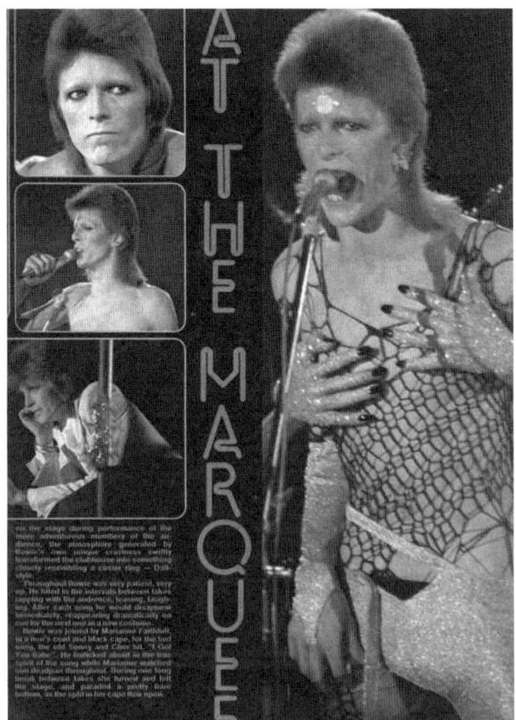

20 October 1973 – David Bowie: Midnight Special: The 1980 Floor Show (NBC TV)
Staged over three days at the Marquee Club in London's Wardour Street, *The 1980 Floor Show* was alternately the theatrical climax of everything Bowie had been working towards over the past two years, an early taste for his next project, a musical version of George Orwell's *1984* and the final death knell of Ziggy Stardust and Aladdin Sane.

Whichever you choose, it was a riotous occasion. Before a live audience culled from friends and his fanclub, Bowie was back on stage for the first time since retiring to dance once more in the arms of the painted, costumed creations who had cosseted him for his first 15 months of pop superstardom.

Statuesque beauty Amanda Lear was peeled off the latest Roxy Music LP cover and invited to compere the event; a handful of guests including the Troggs and Marianne Faithfull were on hand to help entertain the masses and retain the Sixties vibe of the 'Pinups' album. And Bowie even found too to foist some new talent onto the world, an Anglo-American flamenco rock band called Carmen currently being produced by Tony Visconti. They were complete unknowns as far as the public was concerned, but a sprinkle of Bowie stardust would surely alter that.

'Tony arranged for Bowie, Angela and friends to meet us at his house for dinner one night a couple of weeks into our first album,' Carmen frontman David Allen recalls.

'We offered to cook and Roberto [Amaral, the band's vocalist] made Mexican food – he's a great cook – and the night went well. The following week, Bowie asked Tony if he could bring the head of *Midnight Special* down to the studio to hear some of our music, as he was interested in including us. Tony said sure, and played them a rough mix of "Bulerias" when they arrived. They let us know right then and there that we were on. We were very cool and said thanks. Then – once they'd left – we went down to the pub and got drunk!'

The Marquee was teeming. MainMan were out in force, Wayne County a centre of attention for everyone, Cherry Vanilla and Angie radiant in the throng. The Spiders were there, only looking a little

LEFT: The Nun's Tale. ABOVE: Reg Presley BELOW: Wayne County

Zigs and Troggs and backless nuns

CHARLES SHAAR MURRAY reports on that BOWIE Marquee gig

bryonic superstar soloist, is wearing white.

tle, and his vocals are thin and languid.

in one of his Ziggy spaceman

lop-sided since Woody Woodmansey's replacement by Aynsley Dunbar. There was even room for the Astronettes, the backing singers whom Bowie first unveiled at the Rainbow, and whose debut album, he was planning to produce in November.

And there was a live show that drew equally from 'Pinups' and its immediate past and future... two new songs, '1984' and 'Dodo' were medleyed as a taster for his next solo project, a musical version of George Orwell's *1984*. 'Space Oddity', 'The Jean Genie' and 'Time'; a fabulous performance, a wealth of weird costumes; and Marianne Faithfull returning to the stage in backless nun's habit to croak 'I Got You Babe' alongside a Ziggy who could scarcely believe his luck.

Bowie talked of running *1984* as a stage show in the new year, and if this was intended as a dry run for that ambition then there was no doubt that he could pull it off. But Orwell's widow Sonia nixed the notion of the musical; the Astronettes project was completed but stillborn and Bowie was bored with everything else. His next album would bid farewell to Glam Rock... although he'd be giving it a great send-off.

The *1980 Floor Show* would be screened in the United States only, in the *Midnight Special* concert series, on 16 November 1973. It has never been granted an official release.

ON THE RADIO
13 October 1973 – Rock On: Sensational Alex Harvey Band
20 October 1973 – In Concert: Queen
21 October 1973 – Sounds On Sunday: Geordie
ON THE BOX
11 October 1973 – Top Of The Pops – Slade
18 October 1973 – Top Of The Pops: Bryan Ferry, Mud
25 October 1973 – Top Of The Pops: David Bowie
ON THE SHELF
October 1973 – Cool Bananas: Been And Gone/ Cool Bananas (Penny Farthing PEN 817)

November 1973 – Gary Glitter: I Love You Love Me Love/Hands Up! It's A Stick Up (Bell 1337)
While Bolan, Slade and Bowie were ensconced in their search for new directions, Gary Glitter had no such dilemmas. 'I Love You Love Me Love' completely shattered the classic Glittersound bubble by slowing everything down to half the speed, and it still hit Number 1 without even breaking sweat.

It remains one of the Glitter/Leander team's all-time greatest singles, but it was one of the all-time greatest surprises as well. Glitter had tried his hand at the slow stuff before, after all, although never as much more than filler on his albums. But 'I Love You Love Me Love' came out of the traps as the successor to 'Leader Of The Gang', one of the biggest hits of the decade so far – and wound up even bigger. It entered the chart at Number 1 on 17 November, and sold over a million copies in Britain alone.

The song itself came about almost by accident. Glitter was still bathing in the success of 'Leader' when the record company called to ask if he had a follow-up ready to go.

Without thinking, Glitter said he did, and reeled off the first phrase that came into his head. 'I'd always been fascinated by the title of the Elvis record 'I'm Left, You're Right, She's Gone', and had been playing around with phrases like that for a while. So I shouted back "How about 'I Love You Love Me Love"?' And then he panicked because, 'with a title like that, it had to be a ballad.'

He needn't have worried. Even in full-on love song mode, 'I Love You Love Me Love' packed all the necessary ingredients of a great Glitter hit, while its so simplistic lyric would become one more permanent concert staple, all the more so during his triumphant comeback of the early Eighties. We were still together after all that we'd been through, and the Leader's gang was still intact.

Glitter toured as the single did its business, four shows in Paris, Manchester, Newcastle and Glasgow and one extravaganza in London, taking over the Rainbow for two shows on 17 November to film a planned documentary on the Glitter phenomenon.

But the end result was so stunning that the shows eventually became the backdrop and climax to a full-fledged feature film, one in which an ever-so-ludicrous plot allowed our hero to indulge in his wildest rock star fantasies. The Kung Fu sequence alone is worth the price of admission. *Remember Me This Way*, it was called, and we will.

November 1973 – T Rex: Truck On (Tyke)/ Sitting Here (T Rex MARC 6)

Scarcely a song, let alone a single, 'Truck On (Tyke)' remains a nadir from which Bolan's career was lucky to recover. His slowest-selling and lowest-charting new single since the hits began, it took a fortnight to make the Top Twenty and another month to decide it wasn't going any higher. 'Truck On' trucked off at Number 12.

November 1973 – David Essex: Lamplight/We All Insane (CBS 1902)
November 1973 – David Essex: Rock On (CBS 65823)

Record Mirror fans had already voted Essex the year's best newcomer (ahead of Suzi Quatro, Barry Blue and Marie Osmond) when 'Rock On' arrived, but it wouldn't have changed their minds. With its title track instantaneously established among the defining songs of the Seventies, the album had a lot to live up to. So it says much for the quality of Essex's collaboration with producer/arranger Jeff Wayne that, from the moment 'Lamplight' kicks the needle into play, 'Rock On' asserted itself in the most convincing manner possible – by spinning that track off as a second worldwide hit.

More pseudo dub echo and yearning, sly vocals, the semi-soundalike made the Top Ten easily, and Essex's debut album consolidated its success with its Christmas berth at Number 7.

Neatly divided between the darkly percolating, percussive rumbles that characterised his breakthrough ('Streetfight', 'We All Insane', the singles), and the broader ballads that would ultimately ensure Essex's longevity as a performer, *it* was a supremely confident debut.

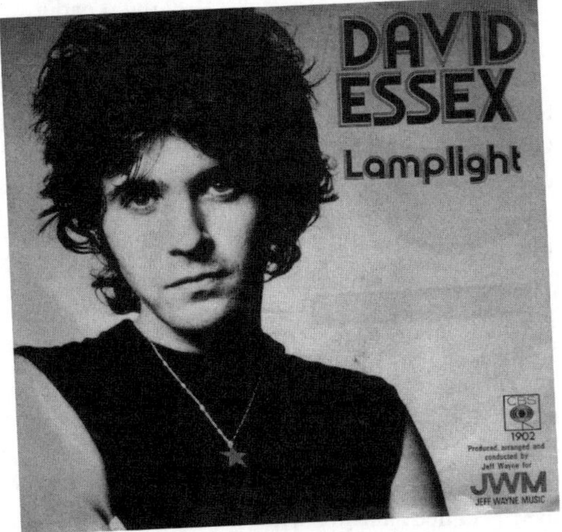

Of course his roots showed in sweet covers of Paul Simon's 'For Emily, Wherever I May Find Her' and Doc Pomus/Mort Shuman's 'Turn Me Loose', while there was also a reverb-drenched stab at proving further versatility with the mock-Caribbean swagger of 'Ocean Girl' (to rhyme with 'I love the way you twirl'). And another cover, 'Tell Him No', became even more persuasive, its lyric drawing such emotion out of Essex's voice that it overcame all the effects and proved that the boy could really sing.

November 1973 – Leo Sayer: The Show Must Go On/Tomorrow (Chrysalis 2023)

He still had the Afro, and stripy tank tops too. But when Leo Sayer appeared on *Top Of The Pops* for the first time on 20 December, he had something else as well.

He had a clown costume, and Sayer could say all he wanted about how the character was simply intended to illustrate the protagonist of the song. For the three minutes or so that he was on screen, Leo Sayer played the most convincing role of his life.

David Courtney: 'Leo, Gerry as he was then, was always very animated, and reminded me of Al Jolson so I went out one day and bought him a pair of white gloves which he was bemused by. One day photographer Graham Hughes, Roger Daltrey's cousin and the guy who did all the early Who album covers, came down to see me at my Brighton apartment to discuss the concept for Leo's "Silverbird" album sleeve.

'He listened to some of the tracks we had recorded and asked me how I envisaged Leo's image. I told him about the white gloves and that sparked it off. Graham came up with the Marcel Marceau image and later brought a real clown in to create the makeup. I remember Adam [Faith] and I taking a two-track recorder to record "The Entry Of The Gladiators" on an actual fairground organ that we used as the intro for "The Show Must Go On". I guess it must have been those early circus influences behind it!'

The clown sold the record. Yes, it was a great single and deserved all the success both it and parent LP 'Silverbird' received.

But like Bowie's draping arm, and Stardust's twisted grip, when you bought Leo Sayer you bought into an image that was as English as fish and chips and as dark as Punch and Judy. And it was only when you got it home, and played the B-side (if you were smart) or the whole album (if you were given record tokens for Christmas) that you realised that Sayer had been right all along. It was just one character, it was just one song.

'We were aware we were producing something unique and original,' says Courtney. 'The clown image added to the mystique, but it would have only ever have been a gimmick if it had not been backed up with substance, with Leo's voice and the songs.'

The next time Sayer was on the charts, he was bemoaning the life of a one-man band. The time after that, he had long tall glasses. They were still great records, but the clown was in the closet again and that's where he would stay.

Which is probably just as well. Imagine how boring it would have become if he'd dragged it out for every new single.

November 1973 – Silverhead: 16 And Savaged
9 November 1973 – Silverhead at the Rainbow

Album title of the year, and album cover of the year as well. Chelita Secunda, wife of Tony, put it together, meeting a fan at the Speakeasy one night, lining her up in the ladies room and taking her picture.

The album itself was (nearly) as memorable, a second helping of the same dissolute dance that made the debut so fabulous, with new guitarist Robbie Blunt (replacing Steve Forest) adding further metallic punch to the punishment. Yet '16 And Savaged' was as ignored as its predecessor, as Michael Des Barres recalls.

'Nobody took to Silverhead on a mass level. We were very unappreciated by the majority, and the reasons for that are up for grabs. Ahead of our time perhaps; not promoted perhaps – in America the label crashed within two weeks of us being on tour. There were a thousand reasons why we didn't become the next Rolling Stones and none of them interest me whatsoever.'

The band continued to work hard. Touring to promote '16 And Savaged', Silverhead rolled up at the London Rainbow for a show, recorded for a Japan-only live album, that captured the essence of a band that was too metallic for Glam but too flash to be much else.

Adored in the east, abhorred in the west, Silverhead would break up the following spring. But not before playing out a few final dramas, such as, touring the United States with the so-called bogus Fleetwood Mac, a line-up put together without any of the group's actual members by a disgruntled manager the real Mac were trying to rid themselves of. Legal action ultimately ended the dispute, but Silverhead made their own contribution to the situation once they realised what was going on by playing Fleetwood Mac songs in their own live set.

The band also commenced work on a third album to be titled 'Brutiful', 'and it was fucking amazing,' recalls Des Barres. 'There's a few songs floating around that we cut that got out, we were obsessed with Americana – James Dean and Marilyn Monroe, I wrote songs for both of them. It was Kerouac with three chords, it was amazing, but I was too fucked-up to continue and, as the guy in the middle and the front, that did not help. Drugs became more important, the tangents that one took were governed and determined by narcotics and the music and the enjoyment of that became second to that.'

November 1973 – Cockney Rebel: The Human Menagerie (EMI EMA 759)

At a time when Glam Rock was either growing brighter or getting softer, Cockney Rebel restated everything it had once represented by returning their vision to Glam Year Zero and rebuilding everything from scratch.

There was no glitter or Glitter, no Sweet, Mud or Slade. Even Bolan was excised from the equation as Harley looked instead to the movement's cinematic roots – the sexuality of *Cabaret*, the darkness of *Performance* and beyond them to the nightmare conclusion of Roeg's *Don't Look Now*, to a world of grand guignol where every shadow shivers, and you can't wake up from the nightmare because it's reality that's a dream.

The labyrinthine 'Sebastian' was already familiar to anyone who picked up the single; the loquacious 'Death Trip' would soon be oozing too, the shellshocked collision of a band poised on the edge of shambles and a producer (Roy

Thomas Baker) with ideas enough for everyone. Absurdly orchestral, leviathan ambition, 'The Human Menagerie' in general, and 'Death Trip' in particular, was rock at its most bombastic, the stuff of madness meets the music of the spheres and if, a few years later, Meatloaf had confessed that his 'Bat Out Of Hell' flew straight out of this record, no-one would have batted an eyelid.

There are no rules. The accompanying lyric book abandoned the songs, and told peculiar stories about the band members instead...Milton Reame-James wandering onto a darkened stage and only realising after 10 minutes that he was performing with the wrong band. The lyrics themselves went wherever they liked; it took a brave man indeed to rhyme 'bravado' with 'guard-o' and still sound like a genius. And though we may never discover the significance of somebody calling the singer 'Sebastian', we can't help but wish they'd do it to us.

What really marked Cockney Rebel out, though, was the fact that they felt so believable. Other artists sung about absinthe and sweet Ipomoea and scratched their heads as they did so. Harley knew what he was on about. And while he wasn't the first cultural genius of his age, he was the first who wasn't content to merely zap the zeitgeist. He wanted to suck out its soul.

November 1973 – Mott the Hoople/Queen: UK tour
November 1973 – Mott the Hoople: Roll Away The Stone/Where Do You All Come From (CBS 1895)

Mott the Hoople rang out 1973 with a tight and delightful piece of Fifties-flavoured fluff called 'Roll Away The Stone'. Originally recorded with Lynsey de Paul on backing vocals while Ralphs was still in the band, it was reworked to a wilder pitch with Ariel Bender and Thunderthighs, the backing trio first spotted on Lou Reed's ''Transformer'. Buoyed by a positively triumphant (if appallingly mimed) *Top Of The Pops* performance, 'Stone' rolled all the way to Number 8, Mott the Hoople's highest chart position since 'All The Young Dudes'.

Their latest UK tour, their first with Bender, meanwhile, kicked off less than fortnight after the band returned home from America, and there would be no easing their foot off the accelerator. The opening act was Queen, and the critics were already calling them one of the most exciting live acts seen in years.

Every night was a battle, Queen pulling out all the musical stops (they couldn't afford many visual ones at that time) to upstage the headliners; Mott the Hoople fighting back with a show that was so tight, so sharp and so immaculately crafted that it was impossible to believe this was the same band who...long-time fans, insert your favourite pre-'All The Young Dudes' moment here. And of course, it wasn't. It was actually a better one.

'Bender goes into the middle,' Hunter explained, 'and I shove him out. He comes up and he tries to upstage me, and the majority of the audience hate me for it. If I was in the audience I'd be with him. I wouldn't like that flash bastard in the middle, I'd dig the guy that was coming on cheeky. But it's great. After laid-back Ralpher, I love to see this punk come and challenge me for my turf.'

Bob Ellis / Barry Stacey

IAN HUNTER is a worried man. He doesn't show it too much, and besides there's the shades between him and the rest of the world but . . . he's most definitely deeply concerned — and things don't look like getting better.

Starstruck is the word that could describe his malady, yet not in the usual sense of the word. It's more to do with being actually aware of the position he's in. Mott The Hoople is now one of Britain's top ten bands, and that's official. On the outside it looks like Hunter and the rest have got it made. Why, they could even do the traditional house in the country and rest on their laurels for a while.

Not this man. A rock 'n' roll star, he most definitely is; a slouch, no way.

Inside his publicist's flat he burns energy just looking out the window. He shifts about from one foot to t'other, lights another fag, then flicks it nervously.

Action man.

Champagne corks are popping, everybody got to have a good time. Ian leans forward to make his point: "I've always been below the belt energy y'see," eyes flicker behind the shades. Carries on: "I like the American New York way of life y'know? Same as Lennon. He was drawn by it. I'm being drawn by it too — 'cause it's below the belt energy."

He's got an American wife too, so it all adds up: Ian Hunter must become at least a part-time New Yorker. The band will remain British, that's not the problem. The problem is . . . inspiration.

"Y'need inspiration because as you go further up the lyrics become harder because you've less life to draw on. Mott's very first album was very good but it had like 20 odd years to draw on. Now, if you forget about tours and all that, I get about two months to write an album."

And it's a problem?

"Look," he says reaching for another Benson: "When you sit in the front row looking at a guy who's making a lot of money and doesn't go to work Mondays, Tuesdays, Wednesdays etc. y'think to y'self, 'Christ if I was doing that I'd be on top of the world.' But people don't change.

"I'm just the same miserable sod as I was when I had nothing. I figured this would be the answer to my problems.

"If someone had told me four years ago that Mott The Hoople would do what it's done, first I'd have said 'you're joking' and second I'd have been on top of the world. But I'm just the same person I always was.

"People don't change. If you're an unhappy sort of person, you won't get any kind of material rewards. Material things won't change you that much.

"I'm just the same. I can still see the shit in everything and with the awareness of travel and seeing

So did audiences. When the band played London's Hammersmith Odeon at the end of the tour, the gig ended in a veritable riot, the venue staff lowering the safety curtain to keep celebrating fans off the stage. The fans just carved their way through it.

November 1973 – Sensational Alex Harvey Band: Giddy Up A Ding Dong/Buff's Bar Blues (Vertigo 6059 091)
November 1973 – Sensational Alex Harvey Band: Next (Vertigo 6360 103)

B-sides first. 'Buff's Bar Blues' had already been culled from 'Framed' for the flip of 'Jungle Jenny', so why did it turn up again? Because nobody bought it then and they wouldn't buy it now. The A-side more than made up for that, a frenetic reworking of the 1956 Freddie Bell hit which previewed in turn SAHB's imminent second album, and served advance warning that Harvey was now out for blood.

Throughout SAHB's career, the most constant criticism was that their vinyl never reflected their live performance. 'Next', dynamically produced by Sweet mainman Phil Wainman, would change that forever.

Once again, the title song was a cover; a dramatic version of Jacques Brel's 'Au Suivant', transformed into the apocalyptic tango. Viewers of the band's *Old Grey Whistle Test* performance cannot help but have it seared into their skulls forever and, at a time when Brel was simply a name dropped by David Bowie, Harvey's recitation of this homo-erotic tale of army whorehouses, gonorrhoea and having his ass slapped by 'the queer lieutenant' while a masked string section sawed away behind him was absolutely captivating.

Certainly it was leagues away from Bowie's effete renditions of the same writer's 'Amsterdam' and 'My Death', and it would take the emergence of Marc Almond almost 10 years later for Brel to have such a sympathetic English supporter. But even *he* couldn't touch Harvey's 'Next'.

Equally important within Harvey's own iconography was the pulsating 'Faith Healer'. Soon to become the band's traditional set-opener (replacing a manic version of the Osmonds' 'Crazy Horses'), 'Faith Healer' has since ascended to the status of a rock anthem, aided again by a *Whistle Test* memory.

But there is so much more to 'Next' than those songs. The distasteful drama of 'Gang Bang', the sexual edginess of 'Swampsnake' and that most autobiographical of all Harvey's compositions 'The Last Of The Teenage Idols', a song recounting his long-ago triumph in the Scottish Tommy Steele competition.

November 1973 – Roxy Music: Street Life/ Hula Kula (Island WIP 6173)
November 1973 – Roxy Music: Stranded (Island 9252)

With Eddie Jobson, Curved Air's young violinist and another of Ferry's pre-Roxy friends, recruited to replace the errant Eno, bassist Johnny Gustafson was drafted to plug the now-habitually vacant bass stool and work began on 'Stranded', the band's third album.

The album was heralded by the 'Street Life' single, and first impressions were very much of business as usual. Sliding in on an industrial approximation of the partyscape that opened their debut album, 'Street Life' is a fabulous incantation of modern life in all its kaleidoscopic brilliance, a cunning construction that allowed us to listen in as Roxy shed the brittle skin of their earlier persona and acknowledged that they were a great pop group as well.

Across its length, 'Stranded' felt considerably closer to the rock'n'roll mainstream than its predecessors, a factor which some people put down to the lack of Eno, while others pointed to Ferry's experiences with 'These Foolish Things'. Having spent time working on other people's 'classics', he was now writing his own to similar conventions, and certainly Ferry/Mackay's dolorous 'Song For Europe' meets many of those criteria.

But they were also inching towards a maturity none of their contemporaries were yet ready to embrace, but which seemed to suit Roxy like one of Ferry's own dinner jackets. 'Amazona', 'Mother Of Pearl' and 'Serenade' are brittle beauties; 'Sunset' and 'Just Like You' are plain jewels. And, while the single climbed to Number 9, one place higher than 'Pyjamarama', 'Stranded' gave Roxy Music their first chart-topper.

November 1973 – Carmen: Fandangos In Space (Regal Zonophone SRZA 8518)

Unexpected heroes of Bowie's *1980 Floor Show*, Carmen were an Anglo-American rock band that seemed poised, for one gloriously giddying moment, to usher in a musical hybrid that was unlike any we had heard before. Flamenco Rock!

What a combination it was. Across two songs on the TV broadcast, and an hour's worth of alternate takes that were shot during the three-day filming, Carmen were simply electrifying, a swirl of colour and musical dynamics laden with imagery and swimming in ideas. And the two songs they performed, 'Bulerias' and 'Bullfight', still stand out as highlights of a show that was bristling with the things.

The difference was that, while Bowie, the Troggs and Faithfull all raised their game for the occasion, Carmen simply played through their regular routine. They were always this good.

'The stage show was fairly hard work to achieve,' recalls founder David Allen. 'It required a lot of rehearsal. Roberto [Amaral] is a choreographer as well as a dancer, so we were able to bring professional skills to the dance sections. We used the heelwork as percussion by attaching Barcus Berry Hot Dots [a percussive device used by tap dancers and the like] to a custom-built dance stage.

'We were then able to amplify that sound, and mix it with Paul [Fenton]'s drums at very high volumes.'

Allen and sister Angela had been in the UK for less than a year by the time they filmed *Midnight Special*, but already they had caused a major stir. In a land fixated with the Glam Rock Bowie, T Rex, Gary Glitter and so many more had already made their own, Carmen's blur of costume and stomp slipped effortlessly in alongside the genre's more cerebral contenders, at the same time as wowing the prog crowd as well.

'We always thought of ourselves as a cross between Led Zeppelin and Genesis via Spain, with a healthy dollop of glam thrown in,' admits Allen. 'We didn't really know where our audience was for sure, so we just kept playing to every audience that was available.'

It was that uncertainty that held the band back throughout its earliest years. The Allens formed Carmen in Los Angeles in July 1970 – the Spanish influence was drawn from the flamenco restaurant, El Cid, their parents ran on Sunset Boulevard, the rock from the arrival of the Beatles that set the youngsters' minds reeling. The quest to combine the flamenco music they grew up with and the electric rock they loved became a passion.

The band's primary gig was at the restaurant. 'When I put the first version of Carmen together there were seven of us,' says Allen,' including a second guitarist and a lead singer. Angela and a male flamenco dancer – not Roberto yet – came on stage only when they danced.

'We survived because my parents turned the restaurant into a music club, three days a week, for us. Fortunately, our live act was popular enough that they were able to afford to do that for three years.' Attempts to break out of the restaurant, however, were doomed. Although several record companies expressed an interest, none could see how Carmen's live show could ever translate onto vinyl.

Allen was not discouraged. A keen student of UK music tastes, he had watched as Glam solved that very equation and, in January 1973, he and Angela, Amaral and bassist John Glascock flew to London to start again. (Drummer Brian Glascock chose to remain in the US, Englishman Paul Fenton recruited in his stead.) They found a manager, Brian Longley, and just weeks later, they found a producer. 'The band saw Tony Visconti interviewed on the *Old Grey Whistle Test* soon after we'd emigrated to London. We all decided on the spot that he was our producer. Brian Longley happened to know Tony's business manager and arranged an audition for us. A few weeks later we were recording our first album.'

Visconti 'adored them from the second they walked into our offices wearing facial make-up and their hybrid rock/flamenco outfits. When they opened their mouths to sing I felt I was gloriously transported to an alternate universe.'

'Fandangos In Space', Carmen's debut album, should have been enormous. Instead, it stiffed, as did two singles, 'Flamenco Fever'/'Lonely House' (Regal Zonophone RZ3086) and 'Bulerias'/' Stepping Stone' (Regal Zonophone RZ3090). Unperturbed, work quickly began on a second set, 'Dancing On A Cold Wind'.

November 1973 – Vodka Collins: Tokyo-New York (EMI-Express ETP8274)- Japan)

With the 'Sands Of Time' hit single still selling, it took months, it seemed, for EMI to finally approve a Vodka Collins album; months that the band members could scarcely afford. 'I was wondering if we'd actually ever do an album,' Alan Merrill admits. 'It was dragging on so long with us touring for months, doing radio and TV promoting the single all up and down Japan...'

But once the album sessions did begin they were spectacular. 'The Sadistic Mika Band and Vodka Collins both had the same producer at EMI, a Mr Hashiba,' Merrill continues. 'He let me do whatever I wanted, a nice luxury in the studio.' (The Mika Band's Kazuhiko Kato was among the backing vocalists on the sessions.)

Had the band ever got around to finishing the record, it could have been amazing. But having spent months keeping the band out of the studio, EMI were now demanding the record be delivered as soon as it was long enough, regardless of mixing, production, and finishing touches. And what the label wanted they received.

Still the resultant 'Tokyo-New York' album is a milestone in the annals of Japanese rock, effortlessly establishing itself among the new year's biggest hits. Three hit singles swung off the album, 'Sands Of Time', 'Automatic Pilot' and the paranoid gender-bent 'Billy Mars' (the first record in Japanese recording history to employ a backwards guitar!), while another cut, 'Scratchin'', became the theme to a hit TV series, featuring singing actor Kenichi (Shoken) Hagiwara.

There appeared to be no limit to Vodka Collins' ascent. Behind the scenes, however, the group's alchemy was being strangled by the manipulations of management. No matter that Vodka Collins were one of the most successful groups Japan had ever seen. They weren't actually seeing any of their earnings.

'The Japan glam-rock scene was very healthy, but the country had yet to "boom" fiscally speaking, so the pay was still very low,' Merrill explains. Factor in a few sharks feeding off the Yen that were available, and life was becoming extremely difficult. Merrill had had enough.

'We were headlining over famed Japanese Glam acts like the Sadistic Mika Band. We were very popular and, this one occasion, we were supposed to do a Budokan show, headlining the 10,000-seat arena. It was completely sold out…and the day before the show, I left the band. The manager was cheating me out of money, so I wanted to teach him a lesson. The story is legendary in Japan. A one of a kind situation. No-one had ever done anything like that before.'

In fact, he didn't simply leave the band. He left the country as well.

Throughout 1973, Merrill grew accustomed to receiving calls from his old friend Jake Hooker, asking him to abandon the Land of the Rising Sun and return to London. Hooker was still in the Streak, but Deram were on the point of dropping them 'and he was getting desperate. He was assuring me that Dick Rowe at Decca thought I was amazing and wanted to sign the band, based on some demos he'd heard, on condition that I be the lead vocalist.'

Finally, in early autumn, Merrill agreed. 'If what Jake had been telling me on the phone was true, England might be a good place to move to and start over to teach a lesson to the thieves who managed Vodka Collins.'

A plane ticket arrived. 'Jake had told me it was paid for by Decca. Not true. Jake had sold a Marshall amp. And when I got to London Dick Rowe was far less enthusiastic than Jake had made him out to be. "Sorry boys, I really can't see you having a hit situation."

'Being turned down by you is hardly a kiss of death,' Merrill shot back.

The Man Who Turned Down the Beatles did not respond.

Meanwhile, back in Japan, Vodka Collins' album had finally seen the light of day.

'The album has an official press release date of 3 November 1973,' Merrill laughs. 'But when I left Japan, the album wasn't finished, so EMI released an incomplete album because they had already paid the management a large advance and wanted to recoup, even though the front man (yours truly) had flown the coop.

'In fact, we had three or four more songs, including "TNTeenager" [which he subsequently re-recorded on his 'Cupid Deranged' solo album] on tape, but I simply couldn't carry on. Management were stealing every penny. I was a star in Japan, and I wasn't even being paid enough to cover the most basic expenses, rent, food, etc.

Merrill finally received a copy of 'Tokyo-New York' in spring 1974, when Vodka Collins' old roadie Taiji Hashimoto brought one over on a trip to London. 'It was the first time I knew it had been released.'

15 November 1973 – Top Of The Pops

The pink and blue debacle that was Alvin Stardust's *Lift Off With Ayshea* appearance had been forgotten. The record continued to sell as Radio Luxembourg continued to spin it, and as it moved onto the Radio 1 playlist it became clear that a more permanent image – and performer – was called for.

And then the call came in from *Top Of The Pops*.

'Everyone was in deep confab as to what I should wear,' Stardust recalled. "We think maybe a white suit and a silver wig," they said, and I thought, "No thank you very much." The day before the show…I thought I'd have a go at my hair and make it more distinctive.'

It was, he says, 'a chance for me to do anything I wanted. I'd always been a massive Elvis Presley fan, and he'd just had a big comeback where he wore a black leather suit and I thought that looks amazing, I'm going to go with that, because no-one in the Glam Rock thing was wearing black leather.' (No guys, anyway; Suzi Quatro would argue the point otherwise.)

'They were all wearing sequinned suits and whatever, wacky colours and everything, so I thought I'll wear black.'

Off he trotted to Woolworth's, bought some black dye… 'and to my total horror, I discovered my hands were bluey-black from the dye and there were dark streaks on the side of my face.'

He was due back at the Magnet offices the following day to firm up his ideas for his costuming. Thinking quickly, 'I went to see some people who designed wigs and got some sideboards to cover the streaks up.' He borrowed a pair of gloves from a ladyfriend to cover his blackened hands, then realised he missed wearing all his rings. So he put them on over the gloves.

'I used to be a big Gene Vincent fan and Gene used to wear leather gloves, so I thought I'm gonna do the lot, I'll dye my hair black, I'll do the leathers and the gloves. Now, Gene used to hold the mike stand at an angle and crouch down. I thought I can't do that because it'll be too obvious, but if I imagine I've got the mike on the stand and take the stand away; it'll mean the mike is kind of sideways, so I'll do that. It was just having a bit of fun.'

A dash of pancake make-up hid any remaining telltale stains. The following morning, Stardust walked into the meeting in full leather and dye. 'They all took one look at me and said "That's it!"'

Stardust's *Top Of The Pops* debut was like nothing on earth (apart from 'Spirit In The Sky', of course), and the very best BBC special effects were in place. CGI imposed Alvin against the bearded mystery of his backing band, sideburns crept down his face like the plague and his hair was so black that there was no way of telling where his coiffeur ended and the leather began.

Frankly, he was terrifying, looking old enough to be your dad (in an age, of course, when 31 years of age was considered positively ancient), his perma-scowl etched in stern disapproval, poised to pounce like a leonine Gene Vincent.

Elsewhere on the chart and, thus, on the show, the Osmonds were enormous, Wings were shooting wacky videos ('Helen Wheels' really was a jewel), and the Wombles were turning up everywhere.

But the now classic clip of Mott the Hoople caterwauling atrociously through 'Roll Away The Stone' made its first appearance here, with Thunderthighs having a riot on backing vocals and Ariel Bender looking every inch the Guitar God he was. David Essex pouted through a super-sultry 'Lamplight', and Kiki Dee lost her virginity in the kind of jacket that Adam Ant would have given his mandibles for.

And Pan's People were the right colour again. So, all in all, another fabulous feast from the BBC archive and another reminder that Glam Rock isn't just for Christmas, it's for life.

By it was Alvin Stardust everyone was talking about afterwards and, by the time the media at large, and Tony Prince in particular, realised who he really was, an entire generation of pop fans were so entranced that it really didn't matter.

The media was already showering him with mystery and malice: 'The Man In Black', 'The Untouchable', 'The Star Who Is Forbidden To Smile', 'The Son of Gary Glitter'.

He didn't object. 'Most of the other acts went out a lot,' he admits, 'Slade and Sweet and Mud and Gary. But I've always been a bit...not a recluse, but I've never been a socialite. I think it was from being an Elvis fan. I always noticed he had a humility about him which made him interesting, and I respected that. I thought "Yeah, not a bad yardstick", so I wasn't that flash all the time, I just used to be a bit outrageous in the stage shows.'

Outrageous? Children's television even spoke of outlawing him altogether in case he scared the kiddies, but 'My Coo Ca Choo' had its momentum now. The single rose to Number 2, to be held off the top spot by fellow veteran Gary Glitter.

November 1973 – Light Fantastic: Alley Oop/ Peace And Love To The World (MAM 112)

Light Fantastic's final MAM single was backed up with a memorable appearance on *Lift Off With Ayshea*, pounding out the old Hollywood Argyles hit in gorilla suits and leopardskin togas.

The single failed to move, however, and despite a successful tour with Mud in the New Year the band's next deal was with the tiny Blue Jean label. Three further singles followed during 1974-1976: 'Take Me Shake Me'/'Don't Let Go' (Blue Jean BJS 701), 'We Are The Song'/'Raining' (Blue Jean BJS 704) and 'You Have Got Such A Lovely Mind'/'Blue Rain' (Penny Farthing PEN 980). Showaddywaddy's management, for a time, was also handling the band.

But Sludge, Joe Dog, Twig, Spook and Buck would never again sparkle like they used to...

November 1973 – Geordie: Black Cat Woman/ Geordie's Lost His Liggy (EMI 2100)

Early reports detailing Geordie's next single claimed a song called 'Rock'n'Roller' would be the A-side. Instead, another non-LP cut, 'Black Cat Woman', came yowling out, although she didn't get very far.

November 1973 – Barry Blue: Do You Wanna Dance/Don't Put Your Money On My Horse (Bell 1336)

November 1973 – Barry Blue: Barry Blue (Bell BELLS 238)

Excerpted from Blue's debut album, 'Do You Wanna Dance' was a weaker follow-up than Blue deserved, but a Number 7 hit regardless. In fairness, of course, the album itself was less than stellar, with Blue too frequently defaulting to a lighter (and less glammier) vein than that immortal first hit. But he was never that keen on this pop star stuff; was always much happier behind the scenes. And as soon as he got through his contract he'd return to that.

November 1973 – Jook: King Kapp/Rumble (RCA 2431)

Still convinced that Jook were a hit machine that simply needed to be guided, rather than allowing the band to follow its own musical instincts, RCA now placed them in the hands of producer John Porter of Roxy Music fame. 'King Kapp' was composer Kimmet's tribute to Reg Smythe's cartoon hero Andy Capp and featured guest piano from Pete Wingfield. It didn't help.

November 1973 – Hector: Wired Up/Ain't Got Time (DJM DJS 289)

Fronted by Pete Brown, who also designed the band's cartoon logo, Hector were a Portsmouth quartet (Phil Brown, Nigel Shannon and Alan Gordon completed the line-up) with an ear for Slade and an eye for matching stripy shirts and dungarees, Jook-ish turn-ups and booties. And they were launched by DJM hysterically proclaiming them 'the ultimate in Bovver Rock.'

Unfortunately, nobody seemed certain what Bovver Rock was, and while the publicity machine would insist that 'Wired Up' was 'the biggest thing to hit pop music since "Coz I Luv You",' ultimately it wasn't even as big as 'King Kapp'.

Which, remarked Chris Townson upon being shown a picture of Hector a decade later, was one hell of an achievement.

27 November 1973 – Old Grey Whistle Test: New York Dolls

When Biba opened its own venue, the fifth floor Rainbow Rooms restaurant in November 1973, there was only one band worthy of inaugurating the stage. The New York Dolls.

Declared by its attendants as one of the pivotal moments in Seventies rock history, for no reason other than the opportunity to catch New York's garage finest in surroundings that actually made them feel at home, Biba's was in fact just one of several engagements the Dolls had.

They took the opportunity, too, to trek down the King's Road to Let It Rock, to browse the Teddy Boy finery that shopkeeper Malcolm McLaren had on display (he was out at the time), and they were also booked onto rock's most serious show, the *Old Grey Whistle Test*.

There, the Dolls postured and purred through a triumphant 'Jet Boy' and a sassy

PREVIEW

Dolled up and rarin' to go

Lisa Robinson from New York

'Looking For A Kiss', but the hosting Bob Harris simply winced. 'Mock Rock', he murmured once the performance came to a close, and a nation of would-be Punk Rockers apparently rose up as one and screamed abuse at their television.

If any one event, they all bellowed later, fermented the angst and agonies that would become the punk movement, it was Horrible Harris dismissing the Dolls.

And three years later, they reacted.

Three years. They must have been *very* cross indeed.

November 1973 – Beggars Opera: The tale of Diana Demon

The opening act at the Dolls' Biba showing was the long-running prog band Beggars Opera, newly reshaped by Mellotron player Virginia Scott's shift to lead vocals. The band was now scheming a rock opera featuring what Scott described as 'a Glam-Rock figurine called Diana Demon', although none of that was in evidence tonight.

'Biba's was very influential,' recalls Scott. 'There were many interesting people in the audience...I remember Brian Eno was there.'

So was Angie Bowie and, in conversation with Scott and guitarist Ricky Gardiner, she was fascinated by the duo's plans for Diana Demon. 'We were setting up the imaginary landscape of a tour of Germany,' Scott continues.

With costumes by Jean Bramble of Made to Measure (Alkasura), outfitter to so many Glam artists, and photographs by Tactics, Diana Demon had already taken on a dazzling appearance. Haughty and proud, Diana (modelled by Scott)

appears clad in sequined drainpipes, wildly dragon-winged boots, high collars, a diamante-studded cape – imagine a space-aged Siouxsie Sioux clashed with cartoonist Tony Benyon's wings and codpiece-clad Rocky Thighs and you'll be on the right track.

Scott: 'Then I met Angie Bowie at Biba's one night, I think it was when we played with the New York Dolls. We hit it off and she offered some beautiful costumes for a photoshoot with Terry O'Neil, which developed Diana Demon even further.'

Demon, Scott explains, 'was a space traveller. The songs were postcards from the universe, abstract visions curated from news, sci-fi feminist commentary, songs, technology, experiments on my Fender Rhodes, overtures, interludes, extra-terrestrial surrealism and astrology.'

'Fresh visions from the pitch and sensibility of the female voice; a cliché-less, more dynamic visual element, and presentation more akin to the burlesque credo of the original *Beggars Opera* by John Gay, which had spontaneously inspired our original band in overtures, bawdy songs, arrangements, orchestrations and solos from which we seemed temporarily to have strayed. I think the "Diana Demon" idea came to mind as a way of generating some new Beggars Opera material from a new perspective.'

ON THE RADIO
10 November 1973 – In Concert: Sensational Alex Harvey Band
ON THE BOX
1 November 1973 – Top Of The Pops: Elton John, Mud, Suzi Quatro
8 November 1973 – Top Of The Pops: Barry Blue, Gary Glitter, Mud, Suzi Quatro
15 November 1973 – Top Of The Pops: Alvin Stardust, Mott the Hoople, David Essex, Gary Glitter, Barry Blue
22 November 1973 – Top Of The Pops: Mott the Hoople, Mud, Barry Blue, Alvin Stardust, Roxy Music, Gary Glitter
23 November 1973 – Russell Harty Plus: Gary Glitter
29 November 1973 – Top Of The Pops: David Essex, Leo Sayer, Mott the Hoople, T Rex, Gary Glitter

ON THE SHELVES
November 1973 – Harley Quinne: Such A Night/We Go Down (Bell 1328)
November 1973 – Claggers: Primo/Ania (Jam 57)
November 1973 – Simon Turner: California Revisited/Simon Talk (UK-52)
November 1973 – Dazzling All Night Rock Show: 20 Fantastic Records parts one and two (Magnet MAG 4)

December 1973 – Wizzard: I Wish It Could Be Christmas Everyday/Rob Roy (Harvest 5079)
December 1973 – Slade: Merry Xmas Everybody/Don't Blame Me (Polydor 2058422)
December 1973 – Elton John: Step Into Christmas/Ho Ho Ho, Who'd be A Turkey At Christmas (DJM DJS 290)

It's strange, but rock'n'roll history books often refer to the British pop tradition of releasing Christmas singles, as though it's something that has taken place every year since the beginning of time.

Yet if you actually dig into Santa's sack (and excuse those middle-of-the-road-shaped songsters who would sing a song about Saint Werburgh's Day if they thought some grannies would go for it), Christmas-themed hits had *never* been a part of the British holiday season until 1972, when both John Lennon ('Happy Xmas (War Is Over)') and the Royal Scots Dragoon Guards ('Amazing Grace') came tumbling down the chimney.

There were records that might only have become big hits because it was Christmas... 'Ernie', Two Little Boys'. But novelty records can strike any time of any year.

No, Christmas did not become synonymous with song until 1973. And these were the records that made it so.

Wizzard first, and it must be said that their festive offering is probably best remembered for the *Top Of The Pops* footage of a grotesquely made-up Roy Wood clutching in his arms an apparently bemused little girl plucked from the gaggle of littl'uns recruited to pipe the song's so-festive refrain; 'When the snowman brings the snow...' And she looks terrified.

'For *Top Of The Pops*, I really wanted to use

the schoolkids [who appear on the record],' Wood mourned later. 'But we had to use Equity children, so we got them from the Italia Conti acting school. I was really brassed off because the kids they sent were much too big and they didn't even know the song, so half of them just stood there. They didn't even sing the words.'

A glorious taste of December whenever you happen to hear it, 'I Wish It Could Be Christmas Everyday' deserved to rise higher than its ultimate placing of Number 4 – especially when Elton John's proved such a non-event. But Slade were in Santa-mode this year as well, and that made all the difference.

Having already enjoyed two seasonal Number 1s without even dreaming of Christmas, this one was probably a no-brainer. Composed, as usual, by Jim'n'Nod and recorded at the Record Plant in New York during Slade's last American tour, 'Merry Xmas Everybody' was based around the chorus of a long-forgotten and never-recorded song the band had been playing back in 1967 while they were the N'Betweens.

The melody was Holder's first ever solo composition but, with admirable selflessness, he acknowledged the chorus alone was worth salvaging; Lea added elements of another song he was then writing, to which Holder appended a lyric detailing every single thing he could think of that people associate with the holidays. It took him an entire night to write, but his first draft was the final one.

The original recording session lasted five days – more than twice as long as the band usually spent on singles and, when it was finished, they hated it. A re-recording was more satisfactory, although the studio was soon considered far too small for Slade's purposes. The background vocals ended up being recorded in a suitably echoey stairwell.

Predictably, 'Merry Xmas Everybody' entered the UK chart at Number 1 on 8 December and it remained at the top throughout December. Indeed, it upset all sensible predictions by clinging on doggedly until well into January. To this day, Noddy Holder wonders what reason anyone could have had for buying it two full weeks after Christmas! The record's continued success in the years since then, meanwhile, has established it among Britain's best-loved festive traditions.

December 1973 – Jobriath: Take Me I'm Yours/ Earthling (Elektra K12129)

Jobriath was America's first attempt at creating a Glam Rock idol of its own, and he might as well have been its last. Others would follow, and some even preceded him. But none glittered as brightly, or as outrageously, and none so perfectly summed up what the image meant to everyone without actually giving out anything that his audience might have wanted.

He was described by manager Brandt as being as different from Bowie as 'a Lamborghini is from a Model A Ford (they're both cars, it's just a question of taste, style, elegance and beauty)', but in the motor showroom of life, it was Bowie who had the wheels. Jobriath was the guy at the side of the road with his thumb hopefully out for a lift.

Bruce 'Jobriath Boone' Campbell was born in 1946 in Pennsylvania, smack in the heart of Amish country. He appeared in the original LA run of *Hair*, recorded one album with a long-forgotten group called Pidgeon ('Pidgeon' – Decca DL 75103); and spent some time under the aegis of former Hendrix manager Mike Jeffery. And then Columbia Records president Clive Davis spoke the words that alerted the world to the fact that Jobriath was somehow different: that Jobriath was 'mad and unstructured, and destructive to melody.'

Jerry Brandt, Carly Simon's manager, signed the singer on the spot.

Brandt's enthusiasm was contagious, as Elektra Records chief Jac Holzman later confessed. 'I made two errors of judgment in my days at Elektra, and Jobriath was one of them.' Some $80,000 was poured into Jobriath's eponymous debut album, with close to half of that going on promotion; full-page ads in *Vogue, Penthouse* and *New York Times*, a giant billboard in Times Square, the works.

An air of exclusivity was cultivated; even after the singer's eponymous debut album was released in America in October 1973 (UK release followed 11 months later), there would be no interviews, no live shows beyond an airing on American TV's *Midnight Special*, nothing for the media to gets its teeth into beyond the fact (for which they should all be jolly grateful) that Jobriath existed.

If it had worked, it would have been one of the greatest publicity campaigns in rock history. But it didn't.

A great unveiling was announced, at the Paris Opera House. The world and its mother would be flown to France to watch Jobriath perform for the first time.

It wasn't. The concert never happened and, although 'Jobriath' certainly landed some good reviews, Elektra seemed already to be regretting their profligacy – all the more so since a second Jobriath LP was already underway. The problem, Jac Holzman said, was that 'the music seemed secondary to everything else. It was lacking in any sense of reality. It's an embarrassment.'

But Brandt has no regrets. 'It was a lot of fun. It was very hard work because it was all mirrors and acrobatics. But it was fun. He only played one show in his life, and that was at the Bottom Line, but everybody thinks he worked the Paris Opera House and he worked the Albert Hall and etcetera etcetera. What I would do, I'd hit three countries in a day and show the *Midnight Special* tape; then we checked into a hotel in Paris and stayed two months because they saw our show at the Opera House! So that was the life of a manager.'

He had no idea, of course, how any of this would play out. 'I made it up as I went along, and that was a bad thing, meaning I made critical mistakes such as promoting a show before having a hit record, building the set before having a show, creating the costume and not having a record. It was all ass-backwards. But public relations-wise, it worked. To this day, Jobriath lives because I am Jobriath, and that's the truth.'

So how much of your own ambition and dreams were bound up in that package?

'I'd say 100%'

And how much of young Jobriath's?

'100%.'

Snap.

December 1973 – The Donettes: My Donny/ Your Love Is Warm (Jam 55)

No surprises who this is about...or why the Donettes' true identity remains shrouded in mystery.

December 1973 – David Bowie and the Astronettes

Ava Cherry, Jason Guess and Warren Peace first appeared alongside David Bowie as backing vocalists at the Rainbow in August 1972. Name-checked as the Astronettes in 'Drive In Saturday' then reborn at the *1980 Floor Show*, they were now to record an album of their own. Bowie, of course, would produce.

It was, he declared, the first time the group ever worked together in a studio, a statement backed up by several witnesses. David proudly announced, 'Eva [Ava Cherry] used to be a cocktail waitress [they met backstage at a Stevie Wonder gig – Tony Defries was Wonder's representative while the singer was battling Motown in 1970], Jason Guess made leather clothes. The only one with any musical experience is Geoffrey MacCormack [Peace].'

To which Tony Defries adds: 'Eva might have been a great waitress and she looked good – the first blonde black girl I ever saw – but she couldn't sing. Jason couldn't dance – of all the coloured guys in the world David had to get involved with the only one who had no sense of rhythm. He couldn't sing either. And then there was Geoff, who used to drive a minicab.'

David and the Astronettes recorded several songs, four of his own compositions including the scorching 'I Am A Laser' and another that was destined to re-emerge (in 1980) as 'Scream Like A Baby'; songs by Frank Zappa, Roy Harper and

Bruce Springsteen, a Beach Boys cover and more. Puerto Rican arranger Luis Ramircz was flown in to handle the string and brass arrangements and the album was scheduled for release in February 1974.

But Bowie tired of making it long before then, and announced he wanted to make a solo Ava Cherry album instead. That, too, went by the board after just a handful of sessions, and the Astronettes ascended to the annals of Bowie legend for the next 30 years, until a mid-Nineties release for the project, as 'People From Bad Homes', revealed he'd been right to can it in the first place.

Generously, one can squirm through its weak R&B-isms and trace the evolution of the blueprint that would one day become Bowie's 'Young Americans' album, but which now sounded more like left-over T Rex outtakes.

Honestly, one never needs to listen to the record again.

21 December 1973 – The Sweet: live at the Rainbow

Originally released (in part) on the Sweet's 'Strung Up' odds and sods collection, and since cherrypicked for a wealth of subsequent comps and cash-ins, the Sweet's Christmas 1973 London headliner is the cat's whiskers as far as peak-period concerts go.

The band played the same venue earlier in the year and it was a disaster, as every conceivable gremlin came out to destroy the event. This time around, nothing was left to chance.

A dozen-strong backstage crew oversaw every detail, even down to spraying a festive greeting across Mick Tucker's drum riser. A BBC camera crew was on hand to record the event for the *All That Glitters* documentary, and the entire evening would be rounded off with the ceremonial demolition of the on-stage Christmas trees. Later, in the age of VHS (and, after that, DVD) compilations, footage from this show would later be immortalised as the 'official' video for the 'Hell Raiser' single. The whole performance was as good as that clip.

'Ballroom Blitz' sensibly opens the show, 'Little Willy' and 'Hell Raiser' pop up soon after; and there's a stunning medley of B-sides 'Burning' and 'Somebody Else Will'. But with the band still under the Chinnichap thumb, the stage was the Sweet's solo outlet for their hard-rock alter ego, and they made sure everyone knew that.

Andy Scott later described the Rainbow show as one of the best the Sweet ever played, while Mick Tucker laughed, 'We were so hopped-up that night that we were running a sprint at the end. Somebody timed us and said that we finished the show 12 minutes earlier than we should have, we were playing so fast!'

22 December 1973 – Elton John: live at Hammersmith Odeon

Boy, but he could be good when he wanted to. Recorded at Elton's creative, if not artistic, peak, smack in the middle of the 'Yellow Brick Road', John hit the BBC with a festive party that still wipes the floor with every subsequent live recording he's unleashed himself.

The opening 'Funeral For A Friend'/'Love Lies Bleeding' (has anyone had a better intro than that?) sets the stage, the first swirling, stirring and utterly uplifting, the second a fleet-footed rocker *par excellence*. Elton himself is in strong voice, and even stronger fingers; never prone to the kind of consummate showoffery that scarred the performance of so many other early Seventies pianists, he still hammered the keys into submission, coaxing genuine emotion where others would go for mock majesty and having a bloody good time while he was at it.

He's chasing Davey Johnstone's guitar lines with his tonsils during 'Bleeding', slowing 'Bennie And The Jets' to a vaudevillian grind, getting playful for 'Honky Cat', baleful for 'Alice', and positively encouraging the audience to bossa nova through 'Daniel'.

And all that despite suffering from an audibly crippling cold.

A throwaway 'Rudolph The Red-Nosed Reindeer' conjures up memories of the music-hall piano turns from which Elton's own showmanship was most obviously descended, while storming versions of 'Crocodile Rock' and 'Saturday Night's Alright For Fighting' bookend positively the most heartfelt 'Your Song' you're ever going to hear.

But the most important thing to bear in mind is, for all the sins he's committed in the years since this show, Elton was once a jobbing, slogging musician in a real rock'n'roll band, hitting the highways in a sweaty van and eating greasy food with the roadies. And this was recorded while he still remembered what that felt like. It might be the best album he never made.

25 December 1973 – Top Of The Pops: Slade, Suzi Quatro, the Sweet, 10cc, Wizzard

1973 saw television become a sartorial battleground among a certain class of band.

'It was just a crazy time, but why not?' asks Mud's Ray Stiles. 'The Glam-Rock era was great for television, because Gary Glitter would be doing something one week, then the Sweet, and then we'd go on and say "How can we go one better than them?" Then someone else would come on, and they'd do the same thing. And the net result was we used to get slagged off by the press, but the public loved it because it was such a lot of fun.'

The hour-long Christmas *Top Of The Pops* was to be the final conflict. '[That was] the epitome of it all,' recalls the Sweet's Andy Scott. 'Steve dressed up as a homosexual Hitler. I had three legs, Jake the Peg, and Mick was in a suit cut right down to the meat and veg. Earrings, makeup...'

'*Top Of The Pops* was a big contest to see how stupid you could look,' Steve Priest explains. 'I don't even know what my parents thought about it. They never really said. They never actually came out and said, "Your appearance on *Top Of The Pops* was amazing." They didn't know what to say, I don't think.'

And, if his own parents were speechless, one can imagine what the rest of the country was thinking.

Priest: 'We took it to the stupid extreme, but even then we weren't the stupidest. Wizzard joined the Sweet on the Christmas show, and the guitarist or the bassist, I can't remember, he's on roller skates with angel wings. He took it to the extreme, but again it was a competition to outdo each other with stupidity. We didn't do too badly.'

Priest's televised turn as a stormtrooper remains one of the most memorable images British music television has ever broadcast. The Sweet were performing 'Blockbuster!' and, Priest recalled, 'the stormtrooper was totally...it wasn't quite right, actually, because I wanted to be full-blown SS. The helmet was wrong, it was from the First World War, but what could I do?

'I just wanted to be a gay Hitler, and I offended so many people...how many years ago was it, and it's still being brought up! "Don't mention the war. I mentioned it once and I think

I got away with it." John Cleese just about got away with it at that time, and then all of a sudden, "Oh no you can't say or do that, you'll upset the Germans."

'We had free rein in the costume department, but I have no idea what was in my head at the time. I just thought, "I want to go on as a stormtrooper", and everyone was "what?" "I want to do a gay SS stormtrooper, what's the matter with that?"'

What indeed?

December 1973 – Top Of The Pops Volume 35 (Hallmark SHM 845)

The final Top Of The Pops album of the year was probably the most adventurous, too. Between 'Lamplight', 'Street Life' and 'My Coo Ca Choo', it appeared the British singles-buying public wanted nothing more than another heavily phased, weirdly accented, electrifyingly jerky three minutes of noise. And that's exactly what they got.

'My Coo Ca Choo' is the revelation here, as dark as Stardust's black leather outfit, as sinister as the snarl with which he performed the song, and further dignified by a guitar that sounds like it's being garrotted, fuzzed and filthy from the moment it plugs in.

Against that, of course, can be weighed the album's makeweights – lacklustre versions of such lacklustre songs as 'Paper Roses', 'Solitaire' and 'You Won't Find Another Fool Like Me' win no friends among even pappy pop enthusiasts. But the demon guitar noise returns on 'Truck On (Tyke)', which barrels out of the speakers like a truck of its own, and 'I Love You Love Me Love' swings like the wildest party in town – wilder even than that ignited by a raucous take on 'Roll Away The Stone'. Which couldn't have been easy.

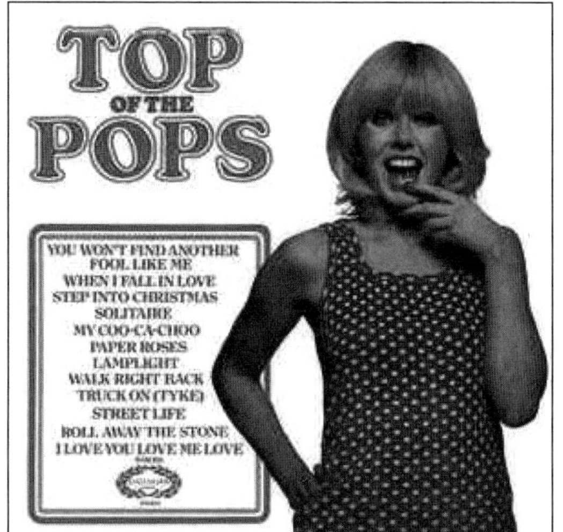

ON THE RADIO
6 December 1973 – Sounds Of The Seventies: Queen
25 December 1973 – Sounds Of The Seventies: Elton John
ON THE BOX
6 December 1973 – Top Of The Pops: David Essex, Roxy Music, Slade, T Rex, Wizzard, Gary Glitter
13 December 1973 – Top Of The Pops: Slade, Alvin Stardust, Cozy Powell, Mott the Hoople
18 December 1973 – Old Grey Whistle Test: Sensational Alex Harvey Band
20 December 1973 – Top Of The Pops: Cozy Powell, Leo Sayer, Roy Wood, Slade, Wizzard
25 December 1973 – Top Of The Pops: Slade, Suzi Quatro, the Sweet, Gary Glitter, 10cc, Wizzard
27 December 1973 – Top Of The Pops: 10 Years of Pop Music: David Bowie, Wizzard
ON THE SHELVES
December 1973 – Smiley: Saturday Woman/ Zoo Baby (Mooncrest MOON 21)

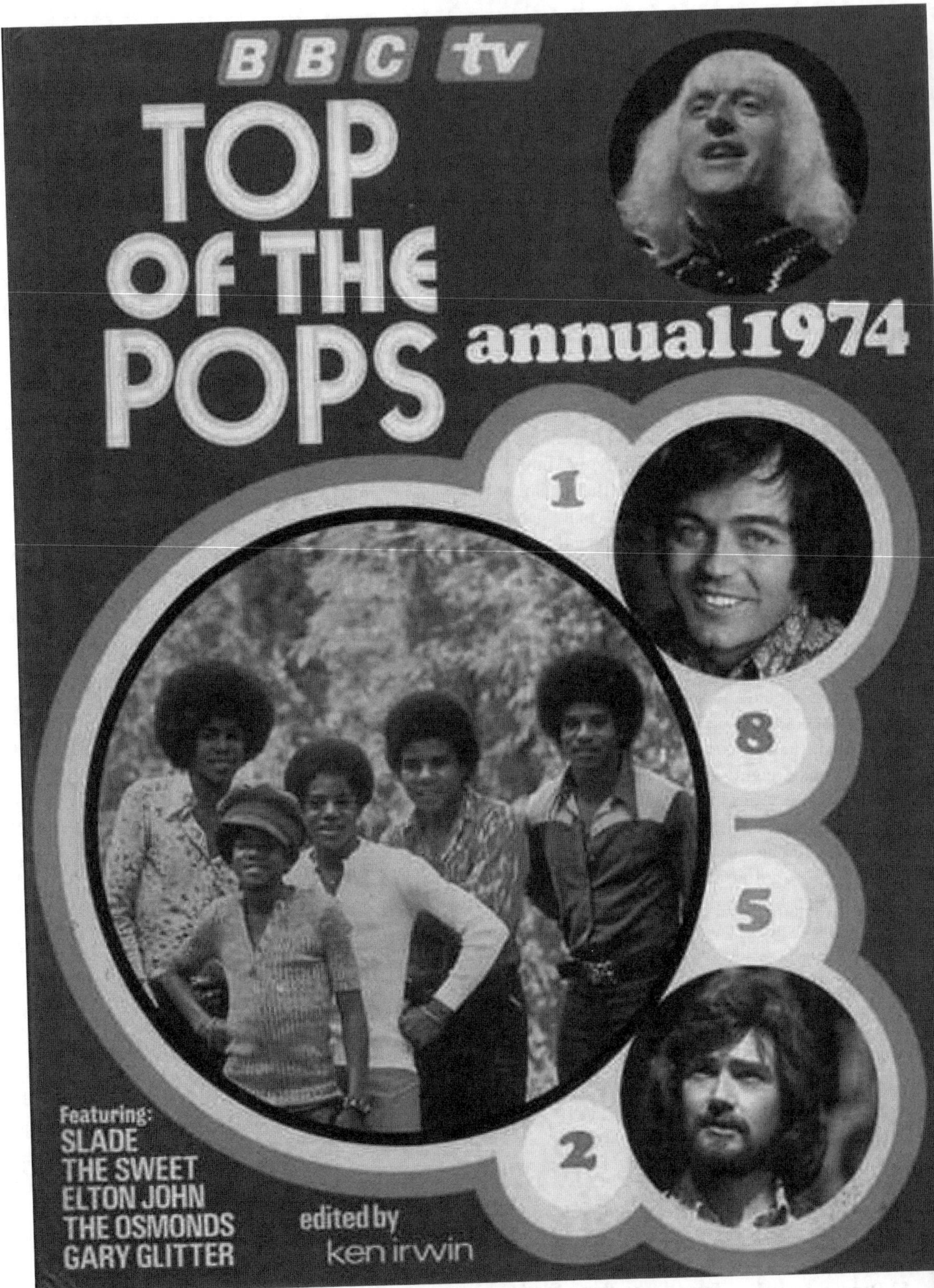
BBC tv
TOP OF THE POPS
annual 1974
1
8
5
2
Featuring:
SLADE
THE SWEET
ELTON JOHN
THE OSMONDS
GARY GLITTER
edited by
ken irwin

CHAPTER FIVE

1974

Tumbling Down

LOOKING BACK AT 1974 – OR WHY GLAM ROCK NEVER MADE IT IN AMERICA

'All this Glamour scene will run its course. The only one who'll come out full intact is Bowie, and maybe he's gone too far. But the rest are all in his wake.'

Lou Reed, 1974

1974 was the year in which the revolutionary fervour of the Sixties gave its final defiant roar, as the Symbionese Liberation Army burst onto the American stage with a high-profile kidnapping and a five-month reign of rhetoric.

It was the year in which the American dream sat stalled on gas-station forecourts, as the OPEC oil embargo sank its teeth into the western world.

The year in which an American President admitted he had lied to the nation and resigned his office.

And the year in which the biggest selling single of the summer was a reflection on life through the eyes of a dying man. 'Goodbye to you, my trusted friend…'

'Seasons In The Sun' was written by Belgian Jacques Brel, then translated into English by poet Rod McKuen – Brel's most loyal interpreter. It was not one of Brel's best-known numbers; neither Scott Walker, who recorded so many of his songs in the Sixties, nor the cast of the hit musical *Jacques Brel Is Alive And Well And Living In Paris* had shown it any regard. But Canadian Terry Jacks would change all of that and, in so doing, he gave the season – indeed, the entire year – an icon that remains instantly identifiable.

It was a strange year in pop-chart terms. Jacks was Number 1 for what felt like an eternity, although if we had it bad in Britain think of poor America. There, only Barbra Streisand ('The Way We Were'), Paul Anka ('You're Having My Baby') and Ray Stevens (the headline-hustling 'The Streak') could match his longevity. Elsewhere, no fewer than 35 different records sat at the American summit that year, the highest number ever to have made it that far.

They all seemed to shift with the nation's mood. While Richard Nixon waffled through the last weeks of his Presidency, Steve Miller sang of 'The Joker' and Al Wilson demanded 'Show And Tell', while the week after Nixon was pardoned by the incoming Gerald Ford Eric Clapton topped the chart with 'I Shot The Sheriff'. When 148 tornadoes ravaged 13 states and killed 300 people, John Denver hoped for 'Sunshine On My Shoulder'. While the Hues Corporation pleaded 'Don't Rock The Boat', a military coup shook the island of Cyprus, paving the way for the Turkish invasion. And, just days before a certain George W Bush was discharged from the US Air Force Reserve, Bachman-Turner Overdrive warned 'You Ain't Seen Nothing Yet'.

Nor had we. *Dungeons And Dragons*, UPC bar-codes and *People* magazine all made their debut in 1974 and, all these years on, they're still going strong. Abba won the Eurovision Song Contest, an event that meant (and still means) nothing to America, but they established themselves as the Swedish Beatles all the same.

The Towering Inferno singed the pants off the

NEW MUSICAL EXPRESS

1974 Hot Rock Guide

Rock, Soul, Jazz, Folk

— not to mention oldies, goldies, hotsies, groovies, and a touch of vicious controversy in NME's annual music survey.

planet, igniting a trend in disaster movies that would soon become a genre in itself; Kung Fu moved from the martial-arts underground to a national obsession (and spawned its own end-of-year chart-topper); and, when Seattle hosted a Champions World soccer match in July 2004, did the semi-unclothed character who raced past the cameras realise she was helping celebrate the thirtieth anniversary of streaking? Ray Stevens' hit record was actually the least amusing facet of the entire fad, but it does remind us of just how much we envied those free-spirited nudists when a record about taking your clothes off could go gold.

But not all was new and shiny. Stevie Wonder and Paul McCartney grasped their umpteenth Grammys and *All In The Family* was America's most-watched TV show. Again. For the second year in succession, meanwhile, three former Beatles had Number 1s (George was the odd bug out), while the American Civil War was remembered by Bo Donaldson and the Heywoods piping 'Billy, Don't Be A Hero' through the last days of America's involvement in Vietnam and proving that, the more unpopular a modern war becomes, the more fascinating older ones seem to the entertainment industry.

To paraphrase Barbra Streisand ('The Way We Warred', heh heh), could it really be that things were so much simpler then? Or has time rewritten every line?

It has certainly rewritten great swathes of 1974. Mention the year in mixed company today and people of a certain age can get quite misty-eyed about the whole thing. That was the year they saw Peter Frampton live or bought their first triple concept album. It was the year Jefferson Airplane metamorphosed into Starship. And it was the year Harry Chapin's 'Cat's In The Cradle' was the US Christmas Number 1, as though the usual familial squabbling and guilt wasn't already sufficient to scar the festivities.

But the memories are fragmented and scattered. The music industry moves in cycles, with every half-decade or so kicking a new trend into play, whether we want it to or not. 1974, however, was one of those years that fell firmly between two stools – and boy, did it fall.

Caught between the hard rock of the early decade and the disco craze of the later, such years usually have no choice but to founder. Because, no matter what one's feelings are about either (or both) of those movements, *at least something was happening.*

Rock, on the other hand, was almost static despite its dramas. Eric Clapton made his comeback, Paul McCartney made a great album ('Band On The Run'), Dylan was working on 'Blood On The Tracks'. Good Things. But they were isolated moments. Even en masse (and you can add Bowie's 'Diamond Dogs', Stevie Wonder's 'Fullfillingess' First Finale' and half of the Stones' 'It's Only Rock'n'Roll' to the roll call), they did not add up to some great renaissance of the things that made rock tick.

Nor, though latter-day historians grow quite giddy at the memory, did the first flourishes of Pub Rock (in Britain) and CBGB (in New York) mean a light to anyone bar the handful of adherents who wandered in off the streets to find out what the noise was?

It would be two or three years before two very disparate scenes conjoined as Punk Rock, and rewrote their origins as something significant; until then, even the Grammy's gang were simply grasping at straws when it came to pinpointing new talent.

Poster-boy David Essex, the funky Graham Central Station and soul man Johnny Bristol were all among the nominees for the Best New Artist of 1974 and, in terms of hitting the nail on the head, we can only hope that the committee never tried to erect a bookshelf.

All three contenders scored a memorable hit during 1974, but would they so much as peep at the American Top Forty ever again? With the exception of GCS frontman Larry Graham they wouldn't; and neither, though it seems strange to relate, would Terry Jacks. But there again, maybe he didn't need to. Every year takes on a flavour in the national consciousness; each one resonates to the sound of a certain song or symbol, and 'Seasons In The Sun' embedded itself so deeply that, even today, you cannot hear the song without being catapulted 30 years back in time. For we did have joy, we did have fun, no-one could deny that. Unfortunately, just like the song's ailing protagonist had discovered, it was all buried deep in the past.

Is it 1975 yet?

January 1974 – Bay City Rollers: Remember/ Bye Bye Barbara (Bell 1338)

At last, the Bay City Rollers were assuming the form in which they would conquer the world. Lead guitarist Eric Faulkner had already been recruited from another local band, the Kip, and in January 1974, rhythm guitarist John Devine was succeeded by Faulkner's replacement in that same group, Stuart Wood.

Without realising it, of course, and probably with no more sense of permanency that any past incarnation had enjoyed, the Rollers were finally approaching what would become their 'classic' line-up: Alan and Derek, Eric, Woody – and Nobby.

Nobby?

16 January 1974 – On Tour With The Osmonds (BBC TV)

In dark days such as these, when our senses are constantly being pounded by one manufactured idol after another, it's difficult to remember a time when such talents were actually forged organically, arising fully formed from a distinct environment, to take the world by storm *without* the assembled hordes of multi-media hell to first hold our noses till we finally open our mouths.

The Osmonds were such a phenomenon and, though this marvellous BBC TV documentary does not really get into the machinations that thrust the toothsome siblings into view in the first place (nor the manipulations that kept them there), this snapshot of a week in their lives is a fascinating reminder of the sheer pandemonium that those magical names – Donny, Alan, Merrill, Wayne, Ringo and Bert – were capable of arousing.

Opening with the Osmonds' traumatic arrival at London airport at the outset of their 1973 visit where a balcony packed with screaming fans collapsed and ending with them slipping back out of the country after a handful of gigs and a few thousand broken hearts, *On Tour With The Osmonds* is a portrait of a world we will never see again as the most fabulously adored young men of their generation are smuggled from one grimy provincial backstage to another by minders and associates who could have stepped out of the crowd scenes for *Only Fools And Horses.*

Shabby facades and uniformed commissionaires, spotty teenagers in full Donny drag and the whole family along for the ride as well, mom and pop Osmond, shy sister Marie, and the dreaded Little Jimmy...a little less chubby than we remember him, but just as irritating. He wants to be your long-haired lover from Liverpool, but the tour goes no closer than Manchester and you could strip paint with his speaking voice.

The full glory of the Osbros stage show is here, from the karate routine to the rock'n'roll oldies and onwards to the brutal 'Crazy Horses' – a song so heavy even 'grown-up' music fans agreed that they kinda liked it. We see Donny hurt his hand on stage, and the whole clan head for a Mormon church to murmur dutifully in all the right places.

And, just to confirm how bizarre the whole thing is, there's no drinks, no drugs, no swearing...and only the tiniest hint of sex, as we see married Merrill wriggling on a bed with his wife of one month, Mary. But they're fully clothed and the rest of the family are watching...and you have to admit, they all look so happy that you really feel for the teenies who have taken their place in the modern firmament. Will they ever experience such joy as the Osmonds?

17 January 1974 – Wayne at the Trucks

Of all the characters that permeated the fantasies of MainMan, David Bowie's management company, none exercised the imagination more than Wayne County. First sighted on British shores in *Pork*, but an established member of New York's arts underground for a couple of years before that, County was never given an official position at MainMan. He was retained as a kind of house freak, always on hand to jolly up journalists on the big occasions, while making sure that reports of his live shows, back in New York with his band Queen Elizabeth, were never far from the headlines.

Bowie was often described as being overtly sexual. County was obscenely so, his songs and costuming alike ramming every organ into every orifice – even his shoes were shaped like cocks. He was also writing a regular advice column for the American *Rock Scene* magazine (you can imagine!) and with a nationwide readership impaling itself on his every word it was time to launch the lad into an even brighter spotlight.

MainMan vice president Tony Zanetta hatched the idea of County staging the ultimate theatrical rock show; Cherry Vanilla declared that it ought to be filmed and set out on the midnight movie circuit. County selected the location, 'an area of New York, very depraved, very S&M', and on 17 January the full might of MainMan descended on the Westbeth Theatre, on the fringe of New York's docklands for a night of condoms, vomit, cock shoes and rock.

The night was a success, the movie looked spectacular. And it all went to waste. 'It got out of hand,' Zanetta lamented. 'Defries was not very keen on Wayne and basically got involved with him because of Leee [Childers] and me. I think he thought that he was doing it as a favour to us and as long as we did all the work and it did not cost him too much he didn't mind. But he was never committed to it, so when conflicts arose and a real budget was done in order to edit the footage into a film he abandoned the project.'

The tapes were shelved, the film was canned and when fire destroyed the warehouse where the recordings had been buried, that was the end of the tale.

Or was it? Thirty years on, an old Wayne County acetate was discovered in a box left for the dustbin outside a now-closed studio. Salvaged and sold through eBay, it made its way back to County, who revealed it to be the audio portion of *Wayne At The Trucks* and sounding as fabulous as legend always insisted. More than three decades after the fact, that same soundtrack was released on CD ('Wayne County At The Trucks' – Munster 267).

January 1974 – Lulu: The Man Who Sold The World/Watch That Man (Polydor 2001490)
With the basic tracks recorded at the Chateau d'Herouville during Bowie's 'Pinups' sessions, and completed in London a few weeks later, this coupling of two heavily rearranged Bowie classics became Lulu's first Top Fifty hit in five years, a success that possibly compensated her for the non-recording of the LP she was also

promised by the dynamic Mr B. (She wound up voicing just two more songs with him, and both remain unreleased: 'Dodo', in January 1974 and 'Can You Hear Me' in New York in April.)

He didn't join her on any of her TV appearances, either. But he posed for a terrific series of photographs, Lulu resplendent in Mafiosa chic, Bowie looking somewhat shabby alongside her.

But they were not, insists Lulu, such an odd couple as they might have seemed at the time; had, in fact, 'been friends for a long time. We both sought fame together in the early Sixties, when Marc Bolan, David Essex and a lot more of us were struggling pals. 'And now? 'He wanted to make a hit single with me, and he did.'

January 1974 – Mick Ronson: Love Me Tender/Only After Dark (RCA 0212)

Six months earlier with Bowie's retirement still fresh in the headlines Mick Ronson informed journalist Michael Benton: 'I can tell you Mick Ronson will continue. He may even go out on the road as Mick Ronson one day, and a solo album is pretty likely.'

Pretty likely? Bowie's 'Pinups' sessions had just wrapped up when Ronson, and the rest of the band – bassist Trevor Bolder, drummer Aynsley Dunbar and pianist Mike Garson – moved on to Trident Studios to record that solo set.

'Love Me Tender' was the herald that proclaimed it, a mournful take on the Elvis Presley oldie aimed more at proving Ronson could sing than reminding us he could play guitar. And because it was mournful and distinctly un-Ronsonic, it missed the chart by a mile.

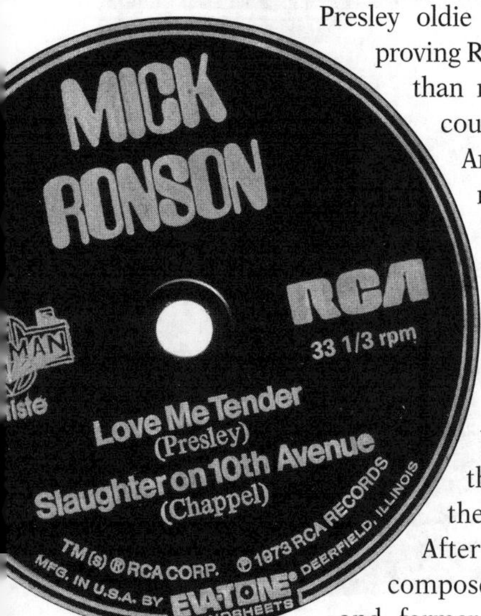

A far better bet would have been the song that warmed up the B-side. 'Only After Dark' was composed by Ronson and former SRC frontman Scott Richardson during the latter's 1973-74 London sojourn, a solid riff riding above a distinctive backing chorus and Ronson again in fine voice.

Oh well, too late now.

January 1974 – 10cc: The Worst Band In The World/18 Carat Man Of Means (UK 57)
20 January 1974 – BBC Sounds On Sunday: 10cc

The first trailer for 10cc's upcoming second LP, 'The Worst Band In The World', was not the band's first choice for a single. But Jonathan King had a track record for being phenomenally right when he made up his mind, and the only occasions when he failed was when he was phenomenally wrong instead.

This was one of those occasions.

10cc were well-accustomed to airplay starting small and relying on *Top Of The Pops* to kickstart their singles. Well, it worked for 'Rubber Bullets'. This time, however, the TV was dubious too, wary of the phrase 'up yours' in the chorus, and also a couplet in the first verse which rhymed 'admit' with 'we don't give a...'

An amended version was hurriedly produced and rushed over to the broadcasters but it was too late. 'The Worst Band In The World' flopped, and that despite a B-side, '18 Carat Man Of Means', that might well have been an A-side in its own right.

Still, the offending song did make it onto the BBC at least once, when 10cc recorded a session for *Sounds On Sunday*. They performed six songs, 'Worst Band', 'Somewhere In Hollywood' and 'Oh Effendi' from the new album, plus 'Sand In My Face', 'Rubber Bullets' and 'Headline Hustler' from their debut, their last act before embarking on their first American tour in February. And that was an adventure in itself.

'We used to have some interesting combinations the promoters used to put us together with,' recalls Graham Gouldman. 'Slade. Slade and 10cc. That is pretty bizarre, but you know what? It didn't work. It was strange. Slade were topping the bill and most people came to see them. We just went on, played, then went off again. Interesting.'

Rory Gallagher was another regular star of 10cc's American shows, but the band were spared further, even more incomprehensible couplings when Kevin Godley fell victim to illness. The band took the change in plans as an excuse for a holiday.

January 1974 – Alice Cooper: Teenage Lament '74/Hard Hearted Alice (Warners K16345)
January 1974 – Alice Cooper: Muscle Of Love (Warners K56018)

If it seemed an age since the last new Alice record, that's because it was. Eight months separated 'No More Mr Nice Guy' from 'Teenage Lament', as band member Neal Smith explains.

'After the overwhelming success of the 'Billion Dollar Babies' album and tour, we returned to our Connecticut mansion to recuperate and begin thinking about writing songs for our next album. I, like Michael and Dennis, was always writing songs. After that tour, I was in a very melancholy mood and started composing some new songs; one of those songs was the original version of "Teenage Lament". None of us ever knew for sure if our songs would make it to the next album, much less be our next single.

'The band rehearsed the song and Alice did a rewrite of the lyrics, which was his job. The song got better and better and we ended up recording it for our "Muscle Of Love" album. It was recorded in Los Angeles and produced by both Jack Richardson and Jack Douglas.

'While the vocals were being recorded it was decided to add some female background vocals to the song. Not just any female singers, but an all-star line up that included the Pointer Sisters, Ronnie Spector and Liza Minnelli. Now I loved our theatrics, I loved our outrageous stage shows, I loved my monster drum sets and I loved my wild clothes, but I am a purist and didn't like outsiders singing on our records. Personally I was surprised that "Teenage Lament" was chosen to be the first single off the album. "Muscle Of Love" was my first choice for single. I still dig the hell out of that song and love to play it live!'

Despite Smith's reservations, and those of a lot of other people too, 'Teenage Lament '74'

would reach Number 12. The parent album, on the other hand, crashed at Number 34, and it's not hard to work out why. Relaxed and casual, it dispensed with all of the fascinations that had hitherto marked out an Alice Cooper album, and delved instead into what Alice described as 'love, American style.

'It's mostly do to with sex and violence, and not a very subtle sex and violence. [But] "Muscle Of Love" was just more of a laid-back album. We weren't doing any sort of horror on it. We just thought we'd sit back and make the album we wanted to, a fun album that didn't have any kind of concept. Usually we pressure ourselves into an image... the diabolical, notorious Alice Cooper. This time we thought we'd just sit back and have fun.'

Bad move.

POSTSCRIPT: The Alice Cooper Band broke up shortly after coming off the road. An attempt to keep the band going without either Alice or guitarist Glen Buxton, the Billion Dollar Babies, cut one LP ('Battleaxe') but faded fast; a 'Complete Battleaxe' collection, featuring additional demos and live material, was released in 2001 (New Millennium PILOT 77).

Glen Buxton passed away on 19 October 1997.

26 January 1974 – In Concert: Cockney Rebel

The media acclaim, Steve Harley later mused, 'was inexorable' and Cockney Rebel were in suitably uncompromising form tonight. Their breakthrough hit was still some months away, but did they care?

Nothing on display suggests that anything remotely resembling the Top Twenty could ever cloud the band's horizon. Nor do they appear to want it to. Not when they conclude their first ever national radio show with an unabridged tramp through 'Death Trip', 'The Human Menagerie's epic closer and possibly the first rock song ever to demand of its listeners, 'have you ever thought of dying slowly?'

Even without the orchestration that takes the album version to such Wagnerian heights, it is a powerful, affecting and utterly terrifying performance. And when, as the climax comes closer and the band is building louder and faster, Harley suggests 'let's go out with a bang', he sounds like he means it. The world could have ended, but that song would just keep playing.

January 1974 – The Smoke: Shagalagalu/ Gimme Good Loving (Decca FR 13484)

Yes, it's *that* Smoke, the Sixties psychedelic heroes whose good friend Jack ate sugar lumps. But seven years have passed since then, and that remains their finest hour. So they did what a lot of bands seemed to be doing, cadging a ride on the Glam Rock omnibus for a single that really had nothing to do with the glories of old and was soundly ignored accordingly.

Other Smoke-y Glam moments, largely unreleased at the time, surfaced on the band's 2002 'High In A Room' anthology.

January 1974 – Eno: Here Come The Warm Jets (Island ILPS 9268)

26 January 1974 – Melody Maker: Tight and Hard and Eno Wants Them.

Eno's role within Roxy Music was one that few people could ever have described. A self-confessed non-musician, he originally joined as their sound engineer, advancing from behind the mixing desk when it became apparent that he did not so much mix the band's sound as mix it up.

But though he looked great out on the stage, and certainly seemed to be having fun, Eno never intended becoming a pop star, and had even less intention of making pop music. And if he was ill-defined musically, he was even more obscure in person. Towering squatness, beautifully hideous, flamboyant, fey, freakish – there were more rumours in the air than there were hairs on his head.

Was he was heir to a vast pharmaceutical fortune (Eno's was a well-known indigestion remedy)? Was he gay, was he Glam, was he an alien, was he the Lord Himself? Eno is an anagram of One.

In fact, he was plain old Brian Peter George St Baptiste de la Salle Eno, an East Anglian whose only real claim to fame was that he was bore the longest name in rock history. As a youth, he dreamed of painting, first with oils on canvas, but then with sounds on ears. So he studied electronics, and published a book, *Music For Non-Musicians.* Then he met saxophonist Andy Mackay in a London tube station, and was enrolled into Roxy as their 'technical adviser'.

Eno's departure for a solo career left outside observers aghast, and totally oblivious to the irony of that emotion. A mere year before, Eno's presence had been regarded as just another gimmick in Roxy Music's bag of tricks. It is certainly a testament to the sheer power of the band that, just 12 months later, people didn't even remember their original hostility towards the man.

At the time, however, there was very much a sense that if Eno had not quit, Bryan Ferry would have been forced to. Two such powerful personalities simply could not exist side-by-side in one band, particularly as Eno himself was not averse to donning the increasingly outlandish costumes that, in other bands, would have suited the frontman alone.

'It was a very interesting combination of people that got together,' Manzanera says of the early Roxy Music. 'We all had our own agendas, and when any one of those agendas got out of sync with the other peoples', like Eno's did with Bryan, then they sort-of jumped ship.'

He reveals that he and Andy Mackay almost followed Eno out of the band at this same time. 'I was very good friends with Brian, and it did affect me a lot when he left. I almost left, I came very, very close, but in the end, at that point, I still wanted to be in a pop band that was being successful. It would have been perverse to quit, and that's when I realised there was an avenue to do both, to be in Roxy Music and to work with Eno.'

In fact, Eno did set himself up, at least briefly, as a genuine competitor for Roxy Music's core audience. Having broken his post-split silence by combining with King Crimson's Robert Fripp to create the impenetrable electronic soup of 'No Pussyfooting' (an album, he was astounded to learn, David Bowie could hum), Eno then body-swerved back to something approaching conventional song and cut an album that could actually have *been* Roxy Music if Ferry had felt he had to go.

He even used the same band – Mackay, Manzanera and Paul Thompson all performed on the record and, while Manzanera doesn't remember if it bothered Ferry to see his bandmates' loyalties so clearly split, he admits, 'I suppose it must have done. Either I was oblivious to it, or he was busy enough not to notice.'

No sooner was the album complete than plans were being laid for Eno to tour. Nobody had any doubt that, with the right musicians behind him, he could easily set himself up alongside Roxy Music – one reason for Bryan Ferry to be grateful that his own bandmates were back on board Roxy now, touring the 'Stranded' album. So Eno looked elsewhere.

The Winkies were Glam superstars that never quite made it. Feted by the UK press as London's answer to the New York Dolls, but considerably more accomplished than that, the band formed in summer 1973 when Canadian native guitarist Phil Rambow, newly arrived in London, was spotted jamming at the Lord Nelson pub on Holloway Road by manager Paul Kennerley.

Kennerley was in the throes of putting together a band around ex-Holy Rollers guitarist Guy Humphrys, and the rhythm section of Brian Turrington and Mike Desmarais. Songwriter and guitarist Rambow was the ideal fit and, within weeks of meeting, the Winkies were up and running.

It was a remarkable band from the start. 'Nothing was an accident,' says Rambow. The idea of having my Canadian twang, the folky thing, we wanted to go down our own road, and everything we did planning-wise, like Guy playing a Les Paul and me playing a Telecaster, was all deliberate.'

The Winkies debuted back at the Lord Nelson on 24 October 1973, slipping effortlessly into the capital's now-vibrant Pub Rock scene, even as their musical and sartorial ambitions soared far from those sordid surroundings. Laughingly Rambow recalls 'the clothes and the make-up and me with the black eyeliner and doing up my nails in pub loos...which was a lot of fun; blue nail polish, kohl, mascara and shit.' And it took just a week for the band to catch their first glimpse of Pub Rock's harsh underbelly, when an audience member was stabbed at their show at the Cock, in Kilburn. (The incident was the inspiration behind Rambow's 1976 solo single 'Dem Eyes'.)

They were at the Brecknock in Camden

Town, 10 and 12 November, and it was at one of these that all eyes turned to the door as Brian Eno walked in, with American singer and beauty Judy Nylon on his arm. 'Everybody went 'Who's he?' That's Eno. And who's *she*? But between sets he came up and we had a chat...'

With his debut album already complete and his first tour imminent, rumour had it that Eno was now looking for a band to back him and had turned to the pub circuit in search of it. Indeed, he had apparently already approached and been turned down by Dr Feelgood. 'That was the rumour, that they turned him down because the Feelgoods were too masculine and he was too effeminate and wacky, not what they were doing.'

The Winkies themselves were divided on the idea, with Humphrys especially negative. But Rambow 'put my foot down and said "Listen, this pub-rock circuit is driving me mad and here's an opportunity to go on the road..." And I loved Eno, I thought he was great. Whatever he wanted to do would be fun, so we negotiated – we'd do our set, and then come on and do his. We'd record together, he'd produce us and it became a marriage made in heaven creatively. Plus he really liked our playing.'

Rehearsals began immediately and, true to Eno's already burgeoning avant-garde reputation, they were like no rehearsals the Winkies had ever experienced.

'As an example of how he worked, one day he said to me and Guy, "Listen, when we play together, there's just one thing I want to do." We said "What's that?" and he replied, "Actually, it's one thing I *don't* want you to do. You can play anything you want on any of my songs, just don't ever play the blues. Whenever you even come close to even trying to sound like a blues note, just don't do it." So everything we did with him, there was this little jewel of instruction, and that what makes him so great as a producer and someone to work with.'

The team went into the studio soon after meeting, recording two Eno numbers, his own 'Seven Deadly Finns' and a distinctly loopy cover of 'The Lion Sleeps Tonight', plus the proposed first Winkies single, a Rambow original called 'Last Chance'.

Opening on raw guitar with a vocal that deliberately hangs around the same kind of pitch that Eno himself was comfortable with, 'Last Chance' is a solid punch in the gut, Stonesy-vibrant but glam-electrifying too, with a teasing two-word chorus that hovers above the ghost guitar solos for what seems like minutes longer than the track's less than three-minute lifespan. It was phenomenal – and Chrysalis, with whom the Winkies had just signed, turned it down. The single was abandoned, and further recording placed on hold until the tour was over.

That would come a lot sooner than anybody expected.

January 1974 – The Sweet: Teenage Rampage/ Own Up, Take A Look At Yourself (RCA LPB0 5004)

Rooting around for the next Sweet single, Chinnichap came up with 'Moonlight In Baskerville', a rocking little number that appeared, on first hearing, to offer up plentiful possibilities for clothing and imagery.

But rehearsing the number saw its musical charms fade quickly, and the visual angle lost its appeal as well, once it became apparent that the entire idea was predicated on the success, that same season, of a reissue of the old Sixties' novelty shocker 'Monster Mash'.

'Mike wanted us to go from glam rock to horror rock,' Tucker recalled. 'And my attitude was, "Well I don't know. I think we should move on but..." I didn't wanna stand still because, you know, never be afraid of anything new, so to say, but I wasn't sure whether that was the way to go. Thinking about it now...we [could] had made something of that. It would have been a hit record. But when I heard the chorus, I said to Mike Chapman, "It sounds like a Mud song".'

'Moonlight In Baskerville' was abandoned, 'and two days later,' Connolly laughed, 'Mike walked in with "Teenage Rampage" and said "Here you go, it's the Nuremberg Rally".'

'Right, we'll have it,' Scott replied.

A raucous call to arms, with liver-than-live applause pouring through it, 'Teenage Rampage' was utterly primal, purposeless, violent, a demand for rebellion for rebellion's sake. Which is what rock'n'roll is all about.

But why was it released in the same week as a new Mud 45?

January 1974 – Mud: Tiger Feet/Mr Bagatelle (RAK 166)

Mud's best-loved hit was a riot of excitement. Their best-remembered record was a broiling ball of energy. The finest three minutes was the peak of idiot dancing.

'Tiger Feet' was all of these things, and that still doesn't begin to sum up its magnificence. But it set the whole country frantically bopping round their living rooms to the most explosive chorus of the age, and four years later, Gordon the Moron would still be doing the dance to Jilted John's eponymous lament.

On *Top Of The Pops*, it was Mud's road crew and friends who clenched flying fists at the ends of outstretched arms, and they probably incited more dancefloor casualties than any other routine on earth. 'This song is like my pension!' singer Les Gray recalled years later, but then he confessed that the first time he heard it he wasn't even sure that it would be a hit. And even after he was convinced, 'we never realised it would be quite so huge.'

'It is the defining sound of Mud,' Ray Stiles agrees. 'People who weren't even born at that time love that record, and when it gets played people still get up and do that Mud dance. And I listen to it today, and think it's a bloody good record.

'But we weren't too keen on it at the time. Mike gave us that, and we played it to a few people and they were "Ooh, they could give you something better than *that* to record".'

Their reticence communicated itself to the recording session. 'Mike got the vibe that we weren't that knocked out with it. It seemed a bit

silly to us, and it wasn't happening. We got a track down but it just wasn't sitting right.

'When Mike gave you a demo, he always wanted the recording to sound just like the demo. But this time, he got the hump with us, and said "Oh bloody hell, just do it your own way." So Dave suggested we use a fuzz bass, and it started to become a bit more lively; then we started adding more and more, growing into it in the studio.'

Mike Chapman agreed the band's input was vital to the song's success. 'One of the most interesting parts of it is a lick that was played on the bass which Ray Stiles came up with.' And, by the time the session was finished, 'it was one of those records that you knew was going to be a Number 1 as soon as you listened to it.'

And if you still weren't convinced, wait until they got it onto *Top Of The Pops*.

'My favourite memory of that whole period,' Stiles says, was 'when we were in rehearsals over at Ealing for a tour, and left home about 9 o'clock in the morning; our tour manager picked us up in the car, and the charts were up that morning. But we got caught in traffic, and by the time we got to this huge cinema in Ealing they'd already been published. So we walked in, and before we could even ask how we'd done our managers were screaming that we were Number 1.'

'Tiger Feet' became the third Number 1 single of the new year, and January wasn't even over yet. Slade had clung on for two more weeks; the New Seekers squeaked them out of the way for seven days, and then 'Tiger Feet', which entered the chart at Number 10, bounded up to devour them all.

The Sweet's 'Teenage Rampage', on the other hand, may have entered higher, but it stopped shorter...for two weeks at the end of January/beginning of February, Chinnichap occupied the top two spots on the chart and when somebody asked Brian Connolly what he thought about it, his response would have been funny if it hadn't been intended so seriously. Or maybe it was funny regardless.

'The day that Mud sell four million of anything, then we'll be impressed. In this business, he who has the last laugh, laughs longest. Mud have been dead lucky so far. But one hit single isn't the point. We're second with "Teenage Rampage", but we're not only second, we're *second*! You mark my words. Mud will be well pleased if their next single makes second place.' In fact, it would.

Connolly raged on. 'Mud are quite nice-looking lads, all of 'em, but you'd never remember them, would you? I know I'm not the most beautiful man on earth, but when the kids see me on the box they recognise me straight away. The same goes for Steve, Andy and Mick. One thing that makes us more visually striking than other groups is the colour of our hair. They don't even have to know my name. They can just talk about the blonde one. Then there's Steve's red mop and Mick's ebony tresses. But Mud, they all look the same. I can't tell 'em apart.'

Steve Priest looked back and admitted, 'The only rivalry we had with Mud was the fact that Chinn and Chapman were being greedy; they wanted one Number 1 after the other and we, being their first band, thought we should be higher on the food chain. But all of a sudden, we ended up with Number 2s and everyone else ended up with Number 1s, and that's all down to timing. I'm not saying they didn't deserve it, it's just that you get remembered in history for having a Number 1, not a Number 2.'

That's right, that's right, that's right, that's right...

January 1974 – The Rubettes: Sugar Baby Love/You Could Have Told Me (Polydor 2058442)

Wayne Bickerton, the head of A&R at Polydor, and Tony Waddington had written a song nobody wanted. It was originally penned for a rock'n'roll musical that they were working on, alongside a number that singer Pearly Gates had already cut, 'Johnny And The Jukebox' (Polydor 2058 443), and the duo knew 'Sugar Baby Love' had hit potential.

But having offered it around to all the usual suspects, they found they were the only people who did.

'Sugar Baby Love' was rejected by the team responsible for selecting Britain's Eurovision Song Contest entrants. It was turned away by Showaddywaddy, the Leicester rock'n'roll band that had just won TV's *New Faces* talent contest. It was even handed back to them by Carl Wayne, the man who sang the *New Faces* theme tune. So they decided to record it themselves.

They returned to two of the musicians who played on the original demo, vocalist Alan Williams and drummer John Richardson, and asked them to recruit a band. Referring back to sessions they'd recently completed with Barry Blue, the pair recruited Pete Arnesen and 'Do You Wanna Dance' backing singer Bill Hurd (keyboards), plus vocalist Paul Da Vinci, guitarist Tony Thorpe and one-time Tremeloes bassist Mick Clarke.

'We were all experienced musicians,' recalls Hurd, 'and some of us were good friends who had worked together on sessions for various other artists together and individually. Some of us had also been in previous bands together at some time in our lives.'

Recorded in October 1973, the song continued to lie around for another couple of months, while Bickerton arranged its release on Polydor. He already had a name for the band, the Rubettes, and by December, the bulk of the musicians – Da Vinci alone ducked out – had decided to stick together, at least until the single had done its business.

The Rubettes' first photo session, in December, crystallised the band's image. Hurd: 'Wayne and Tony had chosen the name, basing it on the song's rock'n'roll/doowop influence, a play on Diamonds/Rubys/Ronettes etc. It made sense to follow the theme through, and the first publicity photographs taken as the Rubettes leaned heavily towards Sha Na Na rocker-style dress.'

That scheme was stymied as the first photographs of Showaddywaddy began to appear in the media, and with Bell's publicity machine already gearing up around that band's debut single a quick rethink was required.

'We decided to go completely different, with tailored suits etc,' Hurd continues. 'Also at this time, Wayne said he had seen Gene Vincent with his band the Blue Caps, and that idea prompted us to wear the caps.'

An image was in place, the record was in the shops and media response was good. Unfortunately, no-one was buying the record, while the bulk of the band (Hurd, Williams, Richardson and Clarke) were in any case preoccupied, preparing to tour the UK as Barry Blue's backing band.

After all that work, it still seemed as though Bickerton and Waddington were the only people who believed they'd written a hit.

ON THE RADIO
26 January 1974 – In Concert: Cockney Rebel
ON THE BOX
3 January 1974 – Top Of The Pops: Roxy Music, Cozy Powell, Leo Sayer, Mud, Slade
10 January 1974 – Top Of The Pops: The Sweet, Alvin Stardust, Cozy Powell, Lulu, Slade
17 January 1974 – Top Of The Pops: Alvin Stardust, Cozy Powell, Mud, Sweet
19 January 1974 – Russell Harty Plus Pop: David Essex, David Bowie, Gary Glitter, Wizzard, Elton John
24 January 1974 – Top Of The Pops: The Sweet, Suzi Quatro, Mud, Lulu
31 January 1974 – Top Of The Pops: Mud
ON THE SHELVES
January 1974 – Granny: Lady/Weirdie Deirdre's Dilemma (DJM DJS 291)

---

2 February 1974 – In Concert: The Winkies
13 February 1974 – Eno and the Winkies on the road

'Here Come The Warm Jets', Eno's first solo album, had already proved him to be a force to be reckoned with in the studio. But then he linked with the Winkies, and the live arena opened wide to him too. Especially if you were listening as the Winkies geared up for action with a tremendous solo *In Concert* broadcast, recorded on 25 January and broadcast the following week.

Twenty dates were booked for Eno's maiden outing, opening at the Derby Kings Hall on 13 February. Rehearsals turned up a devastating set that opened with 'Blank Frank' and moved on through a little more than half of the album, interspersed with a few favourite covers – the Velvets' 'What Goes On' (which Bryan Ferry would pointedly cover himself four years later), Peggy Lee's 'Fever' and a positively petulant, proto-punkoid assault on the Who's 'I'm A Boy', plus a couple of new songs – 'Dignified By The Loop' and 'Love Slips Away'. The encore was Neil Sedaka's 'I Go Ape'.

It was a devastating show, and absolute torture for Eno.

Rambow recalls, 'rehearsals were fine, everybody was really looking forward to getting on the road, including Brian. And then, the very first night, reality hit. He hated being in the centre of the stage, in the spotlight with a synth and having to sing the same things we'd rehearsed. That great look he had with Roxy Music, the Mad Professor on the side with the feathers, that was gone. In its place was the naked man in the spotlight. You could see he didn't like it. It was just too limiting a lifestyle and required too much of a discipline he didn't have.'

Worse was to come. 'It was at the second or third show. At the end of the set, Eno would introduce the band – "ladies and gentlemen, I'd like to introduce the Winkies to you," and he went through us – Guy, Phil, Brian – and he comes to the last of us. From the back of the crowd this huge great voice comes booming out, "And who the fuck are you?" That was the beginning of the end.'

The tour ground on. Sheffield, Swansea, Bristol, Dunstable and then, disaster as Eno was suddenly rushed into hospital with a collapsed right lung.

'It was the only project I've been involved in during the last few years that I would say was abortive,' Eno reflected from his hospital bed. 'But I decided that I didn't want to be a star, the kind of figure Bryan [Ferry] became. I knew that becoming that would only inhibit what I really wanted to do, because my ideas are so diverse and frequently apparently unrelated that I need a low-profile position from which to produce them.

'The momentum of my career had been toward becoming a sub-David Bowie,' he continued. 'But what I like is sitting in little rooms fiddling with things until they suddenly hit a chord.'

With the UK tour already cancelled, he wrote off a projected European tour as well. 'Jumping around the stage is the most self-conscious activity for me. I knew it was the wrong decision from the first night of the tour. I was happy when my lung collapsed.'

14 February 1974 – Bearded Lady at the Marquee

Stepping out on the Marquee stage, if singer Johnny Warman had known that, in 29 years' time, his band would be hailed as one of the greatest unsung acts of Glam Rock he would probably have said something rude. Bearded Lady were on the way up right now, and nothing was going to stop them.

Bearded Lady had already been around four years by the time they played their first Marquee show. Warman recalls, 'In 1970, I was approached by Fred Sherriff and Chris Peel, who came to my house and brought their gear with them. They were after a singer and, after playing one of their songs, I thought that I would give it a try.'

'The band was originally called Elmo's Fire' recalls Sherriff, 'but we chucked the singer [D Wilcox] out because he was a prick. Chris and I tried to do the vocals ourselves, but we had little notion of changing keys and the like so we sounded like donkeys. I was going out with Yvonne Castro at the time and she said, "I used to go out with a geezer and he's mad about playing guitar, that's all he thinks about."

'So she took us round in our old Transit unannounced to Johnny's home and he turned out to be an old schoolfriend. He was indeed keen on his guitar and kept it slung around his neck the whole time we were there. When Chris asked, "You don't sing at all do you?" he replied, "No mate, I just stick to one thing", patting his Gibson SG like a puppy. But he *could* sing and our first number together was "Hear Me Calling" by Slade. It worked and we were off!'

With drummer Paul Martin completing the line-up, Bearded Lady gigged constantly.

Warman: 'I remember an open-air gig we did with Strider and Kokomo; gigs at the Speakeasy with Gary Holton in residence and Ollie Halsall from Patto. Chuck Berry came to check us out, and I remember a night at the Speakeasy talking to David Bowie about the band.'

'When we first started,' Sherriff continues, 'the music was rough and rocky, maybe some Faces stuff, Stones. But we had a few original songs, "Rat In A Trap", "I'm A Rocker", and Johnny added his own song 'Ultrasonic Bombardment' (I still use it to check my tuning!). After that song. Johnny became more and more prolific and his stuff became more sophisticated.'

'I don't think we were directly influenced by anyone in particular,' says Peel. 'We mostly liked the same sort of music, so just played what we liked to hear. At the same time, we always were of the mind that the audience needed to be entertained and our music shouldn't be too self-indulgent.'

It seemed to work. Sherriff used to jam every Sunday the King's Head on Upper Street, Islington, close by the Hope and Anchor. 'The pot man from the Hope and Anchor, Dave Robinson, approached me to see if I had a band to play there. We played there a lot and Johnny proved himself as a great rhythm guitarist, singer and frontman and we all learned our stagecraft. Bearded Lady became a tight and powerful rock band.'

A couple of gigs stand out in the memory. One night at the Hope, Sherriff dressed as Father Christmas, 'and we let a David Bowie impersonator get up and sing. But little did he know that we had custard pies (plates of shaving foam) at the ready. At the right time, we let him have it. Another time at the Marquee, we swung a dummy out over the audience in a mock hanging. It was a particularly strongly-made dummy but the audience grabbed it and tore it to shreds, a weird sight from the stage.'

Looking back at such travails, Warman is adamant. 'I think that four years from being just adequate (yet so confident, bordering on arrogant) to headlining at the Marquee is pretty good. Remember, we did everything ourselves and we had jobs and children to feed. The music was what drove us; we would play anywhere, any distance because we truly believed in all we did with total conviction.

'We were special, we were cheeky, I had learned my stagecraft well and everyone was gifted in their own departments. And I will never forget the Marquee audiences, when some of our songs were 15 minutes long and we would come off completely soaked.'

He would not forget the clothes, either. 'I don't think we considered ourselves to be glam at the time,' Sherriff shrugs, 'although we evidently were. Chris and I got our stage clothes from Malcolm Hall. Johnny would wear his wife's trousers with a zip up the rear—how *outré*! But I don't remember us wearing makeup.'

'We certainly didn't go out to copy any glam acts,' Peel confirms. 'I don't think my Pearly King outfit or John's sparkly bowler hat were copied from anyone else.'

But one thing, concludes Warman, was certain. 'We loved to dress up and look outrageous. I used to colour my hair and then spray my boots the same colour. I used to go on as the guy from *Clockwork Orange*, and we used to come on to that music as it had a profound effect on me. It was pure theatre and looking great, as we were young handsome men who loved women and the air of androgyny was useful too.'

February 1974 – Slade: Old New Borrowed And Blue (Polydor 2483261)

The two years that elapsed between 'Slayed?' and its follow-up were tumultuous years in which the band's success outstripped even T Rex's role as the decade's great phenomenon and the band's musical sensibilities adapted accordingly. They'd sewn up the rockers and the rebellious teens market; now they were looking to expand their horizons even further and start nabbing the parents and grandparents too – the generations who had quite enjoyed the early Sixties but had only bought one single in the Seventies so far, and that was 'Merry Xmas Everybody'.

Certainly the group's songwriting was moving in that direction. The placid 'Everyday', the homesick 'Far Far Away', and the so-pretty 'Miles Out To Sea' were not the sound of the bellowers of old; indeed, as the album sped along, it was the more raucous rockers that sounded out of place and the mellow new sounds your ears kept returning to. And with good reason. It was boring listening to admiring critics compare Slade's success to that of the Beatles. It was time to compare their songwriting, too.

February 1974 – T Rex: Teenage Dream/Satisfaction Pony (T Rex MARC 7)

Like Slade, Marc Bolan had had a precipitous couple of years. Unlike Slade, he was rolling in the wrong direction. But if he ever paused to consider his career, and wonder where it had all gone strange, 'Teenage Dream' – as in 'Whatever happened to the teenage dream?' – was the song he'd have written. The fact that it was one of the least Bolan-like songs he had released in years only pounded the irony home.

Five minutes of virtual mini-opera, 'Teenage Dream' was blessed with both a captivating lyric and a sharp self-production – Tony Visconti's services had been dispensed with, as Marc continued stripping the past away, but the master was a keen pupil. Skyscraping strings, lamenting guitars, soaring chorales and palpable drama were the 'Teenage Dream's defining hallmarks, while the plaintive chorus served up a slice of autobiographical pathos quite unlike the self-aggrandisement of old.

IS THIS THE END OF GLAM ROCK?

Colour picture: Richard Fitzgerald.

Marc Bolan, who three years ago led the Glam-Rock cult, has now cut out the glitter ... as this latest picture of him so starkly reveals. Explains the new-look Bolan: he was the first to start the trend, but now so many others have copied him he doesn't see the point of continuing with it any longer.

It won't affect his music, but, could this be the beginning of the end for Glam-Rock look?

There are changes too for Micky Finn (below), with a nice new line in hats.

The black and white picture is also of Bolan, of course, taken when he first came into the music business.

For an answer to that question you needed look no further than its ultimate chart placing, a dismal Number 13; and the fact that it remained his last hit until 1976.

February 1974 – Suzi Quatro: Devil Gate Drive/ In The Morning (RAK 167)

'Devil Gate Drive' was Suzi Quatro's second Number 1, but it was a far greater occasion than that for its composers. For Suzi knocked Mud off the top of the chart and, although she remained there for only a couple of weeks before being displaced by the similarly leather-clad Alvin Stardust, how many songwriting teams since the Beatles had had that kind of success?

21 February 1974 – Alvin Stardust versus the Daleks: Last behind the sofa's a cissy

On 23 February 1974, BBC 1 broadcast the latest adventure in the *Doctor Who* series, *Death To The Daleks*, and an ocean of newsprint warned Britain's children to book their place behind the sofa now.

They were already there. Two nights earlier (and a week before that, too) Alvin Stardust was back on *Top Of The Pops* and familiarity had not dulled the danger. If anything, he looked even more sinister, still wringing that microphone cord like a neck, still crouched like a cobra

preparing to strike. And whereas 'My Coo Ca Choo' had merely been pregnant with danger, 'Jealous Mind' (c/w 'Guitar Star' – Magnet 5) was dripping it from every chord.

The whole point of 'Jealous Mind', explained composer Peter Shelley, was to 'accentuate that evil look Alvin had in his first TV appearances. There was a combination of that, and the thing about jealousy which is an emotion that kids of today feel a great deal.'

But it was also designed for the top, and it got there. If a job's worth doing, it's worth doing twice, and so 'Jealous Mind' rocked out along much the same lines as its glorious predecessor, sold half a million copies in the process and, as if to compensate Stardust for being locked into second place the last time around, 'Jealous Mind' bumped 'Devil Gate Drive' off the Number 1 slot on 9 March.

And was that the ghost of a smile on Stardust's face when he sang? Yes, it really looked like it was.

February 1974 – David Bowie: Rebel Rebel/ Queen Bitch (RCA 5009)

Today people would say he had Attention Deficit Disorder. In late 1973 and early 1974, they simply assumed his butterfly intellect was working overtime.

How many different projects did Bowie say he was juggling? There was a movie of *Octobriana*, a Czech comic-book hero, that would star Amanda Lear. He talked of playing sax for Adam Faith as the old idol not only relaunched his career with Dave Courtney and Leo Sayer, but also prepared for a lead role in the follow-up to *That'll Be The Day*, *Stardust*. And he did get into the studio with Steeleye Span to wheeze laryngitic saxophone across their cover of 'To Know Him Is To Love Him'.

He flirted with the Astronettes and co-wrote some songs with Mick Ronson. He spoke of producing Wayne County and was rattling off the planned stage shows as if Broadway was going out of fashion. *1984* and its *1980 Floor Show* doppelganger were already taking shape; but there was also a *Ziggy Stardust* musical, and when he was finally forced to choose between them – and wound up mashing all three together – 'Rebel Rebel' was salvaged from the latter.

It might have been the best song he wrote all year. 'Rebel Rebel' is magnificent, a sassy, slashing teenage anthem, built around a circular riff and a lyric that celebrates trash at its brightest. His finest new single since 'The Jean Genie', his most meaningful stomp since 'Hang On To Yourself', 'Rebel Rebel' entered the chart at Number 6 and, though it rose just one spot before fading away, its sheer ubiquity makes it feel like his biggest hit single yet.

Which is probably why he couldn't leave well alone. Perhaps conscious that the original version was way too Glammy for American ears, Bowie concocted a less stomping and heavily-phased revised version for American consumption. DJs turned out to prefer the original, but while the alternate take was withdrawn from the schedule it was never abandoned. Bowie stuck with that same rearrangement for his upcoming live show.

February 1974 – Queen: Seven Seas Of Rhye/ See What A Fool I've Been (EMI 2121)

The A-side, drawn from the upcoming 'Queen II' LP, is one of the best-loved songs in the Queen catalogue, while the B-side is one of the least-known of all.

'It was a little bit out of the scope of our main thrust,' Brian May admits. 'But it really represented us on stage in the early days, doing bluesy things which was a lot of fun. From the beginning we knew fairly clearly what our direction was, although it was argued about all the time. We always went for the maximum colour and experiment and scope and breadth, and things like "See What A Fool" didn't really belong in that.

'In fact, it was an adaptation of an existing blues standard – you're going to ask me which one, and I don't know! I heard it on a TV broadcast, it was one of those things where I remember hearing how the Beatles heard "Apache" on the radio and wanted to do a version of it, but they weren't able to remember it properly so they put together an instrumental which became "Cry For A Shadow". It was the same sort of thing.

'I heard this song once on a TV programme and remembered about a third of it and put together something which, in my mind, is the same thing. And I don't know how much accurately I did it because I still haven't found the original! It's funny, we were actually looking…to see if we could discover what the song was, and who the original author was. I'd love to find out, because I'd like to pay the guy!'

February 1974 – Alan Lee Shaw: She Moans/ Bollweevil (Alaska ALA 15)

Junk Shop Glam of the first degree, 'She Moans' was the work of Cambridge students Alan Lee Shaw and Rod 'Bell' Latter. Veterans of various college musical projects and bands, including one in harness with former Pink Fairy Twink, Shaw was scouring the classifieds in *Melody Maker* one day in late 1972 when he spotted an ad placed by one Kenneth Pitt seeking new talent.

Shaw made contact and 'after a few phone calls, I went to meet him at his office/flat in Manchester Square. We got on okay, and he said he wanted to manage me. I found out that he was the first to manage David Bowie and had got him the "Space Oddity" record deal.'

That was the cream on the cake. Shaw was a solid Bowie fan, and was happy to be 'regaled with many stories about…how Ken had got him a job at a graphic design studio to make ends meet and how he had brought all these records from the Verve record label in the States; how he was non-stop playing the Velvet Underground "just over there in the corner" and how Marc Bolan used to pop round and sit on the couch where I was sitting. I mentioned that I had seen Bowie sitting cross-legged on a tiny stage at 4am in a marquee at a Cambridge May Ball singing "Memory Of A Free Festival". Ken immediately went to his files and pulled out contract. "Ah, yes, we got £115 for that show."'

Pitt immediately set to work landing Shaw and Bell a showcase at the Marquee supporting Daddy Long Legs (19 January 1973). 'The act was myself and Rod on timbales and the image was definitely Glam, as with everything else that was groundbreaking at that time. Lots of satin, I seem to remember. I think the music would be Glam

Punk if anything. But the image was definitely Glam. I still have some of the costumes, very Japanese Bowie style, made for me by a fantastically talented fellow art student.

'It was cool to have the odd painted fingernail and swan about with red hair and a cloak. You got the same response from Joe Public that you did for being Punk a few years later. Strangely, the chicks loved the whole gender-bender thing like mad. I think it may have been a forbidden fruit thing. Definite sexual intrigue on their part...'

The duo continued gigging through 1973, until one night Pitt brought down an old contact of his, A&R man John Schroeder – a gent whose credentials stretched back to Cliff Richard and Helen Shapiro but were more recently hung around Man and Status Quo.

Schroeder was just getting his own label, Alaska Records, off the ground. 'We signed to him for the grand sum of £500, which went on buying a tape machine and Ken Pitt's commission. John booked us into Pye Studios in Marble Arch, and I think we did the recording in one or two days. This was early summer 1973, and the single came out in February 1974. I remember it being a long wait. I was very impatient and headstrong in those days.'

'She Moans' received what Shaw recalls as 'the very basic airplay and promotion, and it pretty much disappeared.' It did receive a review in the *NME*, beneath an all-encompassing 'Pünke Rock' headline, 'and odd other bits here and there. But I felt Ken and John were out of touch even then and we just went our separate ways.'

Shaw and Latter subsequently morphed into the Maniacs, moving onto a darker Lou Reed-type musical journey and then embracing the full-on Punk explosion two years down the line.

February 1974 – Buster: Superstar/Rainbows And Colours (Bradleys BRAD 7401)

'Let the girls all tear my clothes,' demanded Liverpudlians Rob Fennah (vocals, guitar), Pete Leay (guitar), Kevin Roberts (bass) and Leslie Brians (drums) on this fabulous slice of teeny glam, produced by Adrian 'Sherry' Baker and Roy Morgan.

The girls did not respond.

A second Buster single, 'Sunday' (RCA 2678) was a minor (Number 49) hit in 1976; a third, 'Beautiful Child'/'Daybreak' (RCA 2732), wasn't. 'Superstar' was resurrected by the compilation 'Glitter From The Litter Bin: 20 Junk Shop Glam Rarities From The Seventies' (Castle CMQCD 675).

February 1974 – The Rats: Don't Let Go/Dragon Child (MAM 113)

No relation to the Hull-based band from which Mick Ronson emerged, but nevertheless good enough to have their name dropped by a host of industry mavens in the weeks before they were signed, former World Of Oz frontman Dave Kubinec's new band have become something of a hero in the Glitter-Bin annals, although nobody cared at the time. ('Kubie' was also signed briefly to Motown and in 1978 cut solo album 'Some Things Never Change' with producer John Cale.)

February 1974 – Iron Virgin: Jet/Midnight Hitcher (Deram DM 408)

Marshall Bain, Gordon Nicol, John Lovatt, Stuart Harper and Laurie Riva were a Glasgow hard-rock band who may be best remembered for donning American Football outfits for their first promotional pictures almost two years before a Glasgow pop-rock band, Slik, donned American baseball outfits for some of theirs.

Fortunately, Iron Virgin also cut some great records, beginning with a Nick Tauber-produced cover of a track from the last Paul McCartney/Wings LP, 'Band On The Run'.

It was definitely a good idea, as Paul McCartney acknowledged when, the moment he got wind of it, he rushed the same song out as his own latest single.

February 1974 – Kiss: Kiss (Casablanca 4003)
Alice Cooper's comic rock horror show aside, Glam Rock meant little in the United States. Primal sleazeballs the New York Dolls scarcely escaped from New York, while Flash Cadillac and the Continentals were more concerned with reviving mom and dad's memories of their own Senior Proms, going so far as to excise any reference to glittered jackets from their cover of Barry Blue's 'Dancin' (On A Saturday Night)' and replace it with faded denim.

Brownsville Station made a gallant, but fairly ponderous, stab at Gary Glitter's 'Leader Of The Gang', and lifted some neat wardrobe tips from the Sweet for a short time; and while Grand Funk's Quaalude plod through Little Eva's 'Locomotion' itself owed more to Gary than it did to being an American band, the majority of the action was confined to the handful of Anglophiliac strongholds scattered up and down the east and west coasts.

Joan Jett talks nostalgically of Rodney Bingenheimer's Glam Rock discos in LA where she grew up on a diet of Glitter, Bolan, Bowie and Slade; Joey Ramone was almost beaten up when he tried to buy the first Gary Glitter album from a tough neighbourhood record store; and Iggy Pop had a great pair of shiny silver trousers. And there was Jobriath.

But aside from all that, the reason for the music's Stateside failure was simple. Americans hate having fun. At least, that's what the visiting Brit bands would say when they came home from another desultory tour, although maybe it wasn't as simple as that.

Glam Rock was a singles-oriented phenomenon revolving around one classy song, one classy line, one classy lick. Just as the American Bubblegum scene was born out of the songwriter's struggle to sound sharper and snappier than the competition (and with the Beatles out of the way, the competition was never that awesome), so in Britain Radio 1 and the imported Radio Luxembourg became a battleground in which the first 30 seconds of a song were all that mattered and a handful of hooklines were worth a lot more than the most profound of philosophies.

Of course the bands made albums, but still they revolved around a handful of singles. They'd never have cut it on American FM, and with AM having followed up the universal appeal of the Osmonds and Cassidy by venturing even further into the realms of adult-oriented soft rock, there was no room at that inn either.

But people *did* still like dressing up, *did* still want their idols to put on a show for them. And while the British side of things was just too weird-looking (and faggy) for middle-American tastes, the only workable solution was to go back to the comic books and see what developed there. Which is where Kiss entered the equation.

Perhaps the story that best sums up Kiss was told by producer Bob Ezrin. He'd already worked with Alice, he knew what it was all about. And when he first saw Kiss he knew what they were all about as well. But one day, his curiosity was aroused during a conversation with a high-school kid.

'Kiss? Oh man, they're great. The kids at school love them. The only problem is, their records are so shitty. But we buy them anyway, simply 'cos they look good.'

That was Kiss' secret. Musically they were little more than another stultifying Heavy Metal band singing about sex, sex and partying all night. Nothing special there. But visually they were the tops. They were Over The Tops.

No-one knew what they really looked like because they never appeared in public in anything less than full performance drag – disfiguring facepaint, teetering heels, bulked body padding, the lot. The guitarist fired rockets from his guitar, the bassist breathed fire, the drummer levitated. Flash bombs would detonate across the stage, and the dry ice would choke the first 15 rows. Manager Bill Aucoin claimed it cost $10,000 a week simply to keep the band on the road. But they sold a million with every record, so clearly they were doing something right.

The Kiss operation was marketed on three fronts. While Aucoin hyped the media and Kiss hyped the kids, backstage sat Neil Bogart, the crown prince of Bubblegum and president of Kiss' record company, Casablanca. As his track record suggests, he'd never been that keen on Heavy Metal.

But Kiss, he said, were different. 'I am dedicated to them,' he declared. 'They are everything I've ever looked for in a rock band. 'He paid $15,000 for Kiss' signatures, and by the end of the first year he and Aucoin had sunk over a quarter of a million bucks into them.

'We put in everything we had. We undertook what was to become one of the most exciting promotions of my career. We believed in Kiss, so we crossed our fingers and hoped that the money would hold out. At the time, Kiss *were* Casablanca. We were trying to establish the label at the same time as trying to establish the group.'

'The whole concept of Kiss is unlikely,' singer Gene Simmons said later. 'The fact that we started in 1972 when the Glam-glitter rock scene was dead [sic] was crazy. So was the fact that we wanted to grow our hair at a time when everybody else wanted to look like Patti Smith. Everybody became "Hey, we're just like you." We didn't want to be just like you.'

February 1974 – Mick Ronson: UK tour

MainMan put Ronson on the road to accompany his debut album's release, a 13-date British tour that opened at the London Rainbow and, from Ronno's point of view, went downhill all the way. While he never experienced quite the same road-to-Damascus style conversion that beset Eno earlier in the month, he was clearly a lot less happy commanding his own stage than he was when snatching the spotlight on somebody else's, and looked even less amused when the evening's biggest cheer was reserved for his version of 'Moonage Daydream'.

Bowie was in the audience that night and, according to his personal assistant Suzi Fussey (the future Mrs. Mick Ronson), only the fiercest exhortations prevented Bowie from joining Ronson on stage. If Ronson was to cut it as a solo artist, he would have to do it unaided.

In the end, it probably wouldn't have mattered. As Charles Shaar Murray wrote in the next week's *NME*, Ronson was 'an exceptionally gifted man. His album proves [that] he has a coherent and convincing musical identity of his own, and his live work with Bowie demonstrated that he is an exciting and original guitarist as well. But he cannot hope for superstardom by divine right, which is what all MainMan's hype and flummery were trying to set him up for.'

In the event, a projected live album and movie from the Rainbow gig were canned. One cut from the show, 'Leave My Heart Alone', was later employed as a B-side; three others appeared on the 1997 reissue of 'Slaughter On 10th Avenue'.

February 1974 – Top Of The Pops Volume 36 (Hallmark SHM 855)

First, Volume 36 reminds us of one of those peculiar little coincidences with which pop history occasionally abounds, as Marc Bolan, the Sweet and Alice Cooper all chose the precise same moment to unleash new singles which had the word 'teenage' in the title. Of course they're all here, together with everything else that made early 1974 seem so promising.

'Tiger Feet' opens the show, an instant chart-topper performed with vivacious zeal. 'Dance With The Devil' is executed with such panache that the guitar and chanting are almost irrelevant as the drums play the whole track themselves. Future hit songstress Tina Charles, the latest recruit to the Top Of The Pops team, turns in a spot-on Lulu impression, while another of Ziggy's progeny, Mick Ronson, is represented via his solo warbling of 'Love Me Tender' – a timely reminder that the Top Of The Pops albums didn't simply reflect the chart of the day. They also had a go at predicting them, and it's a sign of the skill with which the series was compiled that there are very few occasions they got it wrong.

This time they did it twice. 'Love Me Tender' was joined on the junk heap by 10cc's 'The Worst Band In The World'.

February 1974 – Dana Gillespie: Weren't Born A Man/All Gone (RCA APBO 0211)

Although Dana Gillespie was probably best known for her early-Seventies' spell among David Bowie's most visible cohorts, a presence at every major concert and event, and was in fact his schooldays girlfriend, her own recording career dates back almost as far as Bowie's.

A former British water-skiing champion, the former Richenda Antoinette de Winterstein Gillespie was, like Bowie, signed to Pye Records in the early Sixties, under the aegis of Donovan. She cut three singles for the label: 'Donna Donna'/'It's No Use Saying If' (Pye 7N 15872), 'Thank You Boy'/'You're A Heartbreak Man' (Pye 7N 15962 – both 1965) and 'Pay You Back With Interest'/'Adam Can You Beat That' (Pye 7N 17280 – 1967); like Bowie, she then moved to Decca, and producer Mike Vernon.

Her debut album, 'Foolish Seasons', was released in the US only in 1967; her second, in the UK in 1968, was 'Box Of Surprises'. Both evidenced an adventurous ear for folky pop, but Gillespie would lapse into vinyl silence now, as she turned to theatrical work and embarked uon a run as Mary Magdalene in *Jesus Christ Superstar*.

She returned to the studio in 1971 to record the rudiments of a new album with Bowie and Mick Ronson – two songs from this partnership, 'Mother Don't Be Frightened' and Bowie's own 'Andy Warhol', were then included on a split promotional LP pressed up by Tony Defries (500 white-label copies – BOWPROMO 1); also included were 'Never Knew', 'All Cut Up On You' and a Ronson production, 'Lavender Hill'.

Whereas RCA moved quickly for Bowie, Gillespie remained unsigned until 1973 and it would be almost three years before she finally cut her sophomore album without either Bowie or Ronson to help. The title track became her first single.

February 1974 – Nobby Quits Rollers

With its ingredients cherry-picking the best of contemporary British pop – a sax straight out of Wizzard, a plinking old-time piano (shades of Lieutenant Pigeon) and a lyric you memorised the first time you heard it, 'Remember' was, in a nutshell, perfection. And it was starting to sell at last. What the Bay City Rollers needed now was a classic image to match.

It would be another few months and two further singles before the Rollers adopted the tartan colouring that would become synonymous with their rise. But manager Tam Paton had some ideas anyway, modelled around the skinhead image of the early Seventies, and most recently spotted adorning the four members of Jook.

They, too, were poised on the brink of a step forward; a tour opening for the Sweet was imminent, and Mickie Most liked their look so much that he signed the band to a publishing deal without even having heard them perform.

One evening, however, Jook played a ballroom in Edinburgh and it was there that their death warrant was signed. The show was over when an admirer appeared backstage. He represented what the Jook drummer Chris Townson remembers as 'a very scruffy local band, and had dropped by to rave about yon bonny image.' A few weeks later, Jook sat back in disbelief as that very same admirer and his cronies cavorted around *Top Of The Pops* in Jook's own skinhead outfit, hiked up trouser-cuffs and all. The Bay City Rollers had arrived ('and that was the end of Jook').

But the Rollers had undergone one final trial before that moment, as vocalist Nobby Clark announced he was leaving the group to launch a solo career. He was replaced by Leslie McKeown, one of the band's regular backing vocalists, whose first task was to re-record the lead vocal on 'Remember', and then placate

Nobby's loyal local following. No more than 5,000 copies of the Clark vocal are believed to exist. The McKeown one, on the other hand, would soon go into overdrive.

ON THE RADIO
24 February 1974 – Sounds On Sunday: Slade
ON THE BOX
2 February 1974 – Cilla: The Sweet
5 February 1974 – In Concert: Leo Sayer
7 February 1974 – Top Of The Pops: T Rex, Lulu, Mud, the Sweet, Suzi Quatro, Bay City Rollers, Alice Cooper
9 February 1974 – Russell Harty Plus: Lulu
10 February 1974 – Old Grey Whistle Test: Cockney Rebel
14 February 1974 – Top Of The Pops: Alvin Stardust, Mud, Suzi Quatro
15 February 1974 – Crackerjack: Slade
21 February 1974 – Top Of The Pops: Suzi Quatro, Alvin Stardust, Bay City Rollers, Queen
23 February 1974 – Cilla: Bryan Ferry
28 February 1974 – Top Of The Pops: David Bowie, Suzi Quatro
ON THE SHELVES
February 1974 – Blackfoot Sue: Bye Bye Birmingham/Messiah (DJM DJS 296)
February 1974 – Ricky Wilde: Mrs. Malinski/ Cassette Blues (UK 59)
February 1974 – The Farm: Fat Judy/Gypsy Mountain Woman (Spark 1105) (GLIT

---

5 March 1974 – Top Gear: Eno and the Winkies
March 1974 – Eno: Seven Deadly Finns/Later On (Island WIP 6178)

Eno's tour was cancelled and, while Island went ahead with the release of his first single, they clearly did not have their heart in it. Minimal radio play and promotion awaited this devastating union of Eno and the Winkies, although the BBC session did go out on schedule.

Two songs from 'Here Come The Warm Jets', 'Paw Paw Negro Blowtorch' and 'Baby's On Fire' (medley with the otherwise unheard 'Totalled') led up to a bafflingly brilliant rendition of the live favourite 'Fever' (assuming a few roars at the end of a mere handful of performances permit any song to be considered a favourite), and the energies of the stage show shone through every second. Rambo's guitar is screaming the odds, but Eno won't allow it to riff in peace, layering treatments and tricks onto every solo and creating an entire new instrument for 'Fever'.

'Seven Deadly Finns', meanwhile, creates a whole new style of music as it mangles and baffles itself towards sonic glory. A convoluted saga of the good, the bad and the ugly, the French girls making daisy chains as the lovelorn mate lots descend upon their town – and, just when you think that a good time will be had by all, Eno starts to yodel.

Let's repeat that. Eno. Starts. To. Yodel.

March 1974 – Gary Glitter: Remember Me This Way/It's Not A Lot (Bell 1349)

'I Love You Love Me Love' proved that Gary Glitter was more than a hard-rock maven, even as it retained all the characteristics that made him look like one. Now it was time to pull things even further back, and reveal Glitter as something that even he probably never imagined becoming – the most accomplished pop balladeer of the Glam Rock generation.

'Is the teenybopper's favourite dirty old man trying to do an Elvis and win the hearts and *directoire* knickers of the blue-rise brigade?' asked jazzman George Molly, guest reviewer in the *NME* that week.

Maybe so. A Number 3 hit, 'Remember Me This Way' is almost painfully melancholy, the heartbroken strains of a broken-down brass band the sole distraction from a shattered Glitter lyric, half-breathed, half-sobbed and so moribund even the funeral march sounds upbeat by comparison.

Had Glitter chosen to retire as the record faded out, rock theatre would never have reached such heights again. If anybody ever complains that Gary Glitter's records all sound the same, play them this. And hide the bread knives.

March 1974 – Glitter Band: Angel Face/You Wouldn't Leave Me, Would You? (Bell 1348)

A solid presence behind the Leader on stage, the Glittermen quickly gathered a following that was almost as devoted as his; or, at least, that was the thinking behind Leander's next plan, launching the Band on their own, parallel career – and that despite the fact they never performed on Glitter's discs.

'Mike Leander played all the instruments on the records,' Gary revealed two decades later. 'Sometimes I'd help out a bit, and between us, we did it all. They were like garage records. Occasionally, they would overdub a few things, but generally it was easier for Mike and I to get on with it because we were writing it as we were doing it.'

Bassist John Springate agrees. 'We were out touring with Gary, and Mike used to do all the backing tracks, except for Harvey and John, who would do the brass parts. When it came to doing *Top Of The Pops*, we did all the backing tracks for that and Mike always said it sounded better.'

It was with that in mind that Leander began thinking about pushing the band to the fore in its own right. But Springate admits 'There were egos arising, including mine, and Gerry's as well. We both wanted to get success as singers.

'When I joined the band, I turned around and said, "I'll give it three singles and an album", which is usually the sort of length of that sort of act. "It ain't gonna last long." Everybody laughed at me and said "It's going to last a lot longer than that", and it did last longer, but I was beginning to get a bit frustrated because all I was doing was backing vocals and I wanted to be the singer.

'So it was suggested to Mike, "How about the band doing some recording?" so he gave us a day in Mayfair Studios, and John and Gerry had come up with the idea of "Angel Face", which got partially recorded, along with about six other songs. "Angel Face" eventually was picked out to be the single and that was the start of it.'

Gorgeously outfitted by Jean Bramble of Alkasura, a boutique on the King's Road, Chelsea, the newly-renamed Glitter Band made their solo live debut at the Aquarius Club in Lincoln on 15 December 1973, a venue most of the band members had visited at some point in their musical past, but 'with all these other bands that hadn't had hits, or who had had hits but not in a long time,' laughs Springate. 'And suddenly I'm in a group that's going out there as a hit act.'

'Angel Face' was sliced directly out of the Glitter mould, a blur of pounding drums, cries of 'Hey' and guitar lines that swooped from the heavens. And, following exquisitely in their bandmate's footsteps, 'Angel Face' took just three weeks to make the Top Five before halting at Number 4.

9 March 1974 – Russell Harty Plus: Alvin Stardust

March 1974 – Alvin Stardust: The Untouchable (Magnet 5001)

The agony commenced as Alvin Stardust stepped out onto the studio floor and studiously ignored the host's outstretched palm. Harty demanded to know why. Stardust hemmed and hawed.

RH: 'You obviously felt some kind of marginally hostile reaction to me. Didn't you?'

AS: 'Er, no. But I wasn't sure what to expect, because you're interviewing me and you've got a bit of a reputation.'

RH: 'I have? So have you. *So have you.* What kind of reputation do I have that you know about?'

AS: 'I don't know. I was told I was doing the *Russell Harty* show and I thought it was like a kind of talk-in version of the *Basil Brush Show.* That was the first impression it gave me. I thought you were a little dog or something, which surprised me because I'm not supposed to do children's television.'

Game and set and match to the man in black.

With hindsight, it's difficult to understand what all the controversy was really about. Yes, Stardust wore black leather and chains. Yes, he glared and glowered, and didn't like to smile. And yes, he called his first album 'The Untouchable' and he liked his girls to 'lie down and groove on the mat.'

There was even (or there would be) a German television play, Stardust later found out, 'about this murderer who gets young ladies back to his flat, then he locks the door and he plays "My Coo Ca Choo" while he murders them. I couldn't believe it. He sits her down, "Let me get you a drink", then he goes over and puts this record on...'

Are you sure that was only a play, Mr Stardust? My schoolfriends and I would have thought it was just another day in your life. But even so, that was no reason to label him a deviant pariah, was it? Apparently so. The city of Hull even banned him from performing there, stating 'he is not the sort of act we want in Hull.' Mick Ronson, a man who had spent 18 months getting on-stage blowjobs from his lead singer, was a Hull boy, but nobody moaned about him. So why pick on Alvin?

Because the Untouchable left them without any options. We didn't know then that Stardust would soon be abandoning the armour and the knuckledusters –and even if we had, he was wearing them now, and even singing a song about them, the battered Bolan blues of 'Dressed In Black'.

Elsewhere, too, violence seethed across the grooves, and it didn't even attempt to hide itself away. Who but a latter-day Mr Punch would invite his lady to 'Be My Judy'? Who but a madman would celebrate his 'Jealous Mind'? Even when boy met girl in brooding ballad land, 'You're My Everything' left you wondering just what the sentiment meant. 'Don't ever leave me,' his sibilance warned, and was it simple paranoia? Or did he really leave unspoken what will happen if you do? 'Sha la la la la.'

The Untouchable was secret sex and sordid secrecy.

It was bound-and-gagged subversion and bruising intent.

It was Elvis and Gene Vincent on a highway to hell and maybe Stardust didn't, as the playground whispered, really have a torture chamber in his basement, where he lashed his groupies with a microphone cable. But it didn't matter either way. Right here, right now, though, The Untouchable was touching us all.

March 1974 – Barry Blue: School Love/Hi-Cool Woman (Bell 1345)

Slipping into balladic mode, Barry Blue's third hit single reached Number 11.

March 1974 – Mott the Hoople: The Golden Age Of Rock'n'Roll/Rest In Peace (CBS 2177)
March 1974 – Mott the Hoople: The Hoople (CBS 69062)

Mott originally intended calling their next LP 'The Bash Street Kids', in honour of the long-running stars of the *Beano* comic book. Publishers DC Thomson, however, weren't so enthusiastic, and swiftly let it be known that the Kids were not available for a parallel career in rock'n'roll.

The album became 'The Hoople' (which made sense after 'Mott'); its former title track became 'Crash Street Kidds' and, although there was no way that anyone could have known it at the time, Mott the Hoople got on with what would become their long-playing swansong; one that possesses a personality, and a sense of inner purpose no Mott the Hoople album since 'Brain Capers' had captured, a grotty grandeur and a weary wisdom which takes its cue from the opening line of its finest cut, 'Pearl'n'Roy (England)', and never lets up from there.

'It's "clean the chimneys, kids", and it's 1974.'

The Hoople was the sound of Mott the Hoople taking reality by storm. Hunter's confidence was at an all-time high, and his songwriting reflected that. "Marionette" is the best track that Mott's ever done,' he announced at the time. 'I wanted to do a five-minute opera as opposed to an opera that went on for 40 minutes, which I feel might be a bit trying.'

Another epic, 'Crash Street Kidds', meanwhile, foretold the downfall of British government with a foresight which all but anticipated punk. '[It's] the story of a street gang that is getting pretty pissed off with the way things are run in this country. They decide they're going to take over Britain.'

It didn't matter that not every other song was a classic. From the moment the opening 'Golden Age Of Rock'n'Roll' kicks in, to the last dying seconds of 'Roll Away The Stone', the rollercoaster doesn't let up for a moment. And if 'The Hoople' sounded great on wax, it was a revelation live.

Which is why the end of the band; the real end, this time, not another of those are-they/aren't-they pastiches of the past, came as such a total surprise.

March 1974 – T Rex: Zinc Alloy And The Hidden Riders Of Tomorrow (T Rex BNLA 5002)

'I was allowing the madness to move away,' Bolan explained when asked about his fall from commercial grace. 'I'll accept that I'm blatantly commercial because I enjoy it, but I would like to do something beyond the simple Bolan rock'n'roll. And if only a quarter of the kids come with it, it wouldn't matter.'

'I've got good taste,' he continued. 'I only wore glitter five times and a bit of makeup. When people like the Sweet started wearing makeup, it was embarrassing, so I moved away from it. You have to stay ahead. I enjoyed the madness and being born to boogie, but I can see more clearly now.'

But when former manager Tony Secunda caught up with him in early 1974, for the first time since they severed their partnership two years earlier, he was amazed he could see anything at all. 'Marc had started getting heavily into coke on the American tour,' Secunda recalled, but now cognac had joined it as Bolan's only other principal form of nourishment.

Fat, bloated and directionless, it is said that Bolan himself addressed his decline only after he – and a fortuitously passing journalist, the *NME*'s Roy Carr – caught sight of his corpulent mass in a hotel mirror. 'Oh God, just look at the state of me,' Bolan groaned. Over the next six months, he would work hard to exorcise that particular demon forever.

The spectre of his decline in popularity, of course, could not be so easily dismissed, but Bolan kept trying. The last album to feature drummer Bill Legend, 'Zinc Alloy And The Hidden Riders Of Tomorrow'

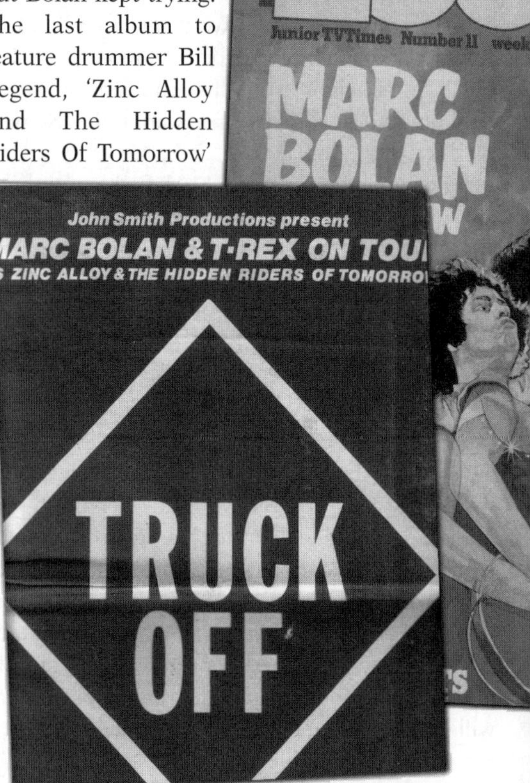

is not classic Bolan, even if one overlooks the transparency of its title. After all, hadn't Bowie already done the Fictional Someone and the Somethings routine? Actually, he had, as his fans kept reminding us at the time. But Bolan did it first and, although Spiders have two more legs than Earwigs, Dib Cochran had two years on Ziggy Stardust.

Besides, hindsight proves that, far from losing his muse, Bolan's only real sin was the loss of his once-impeccable sense of occasion. He talked of recording albums of poetry and electronic music, and made a start on both. 'Billy Super Duper' rolled on, and so did a notion he'd been talking about for four years, a full-length reinvention of 1970's 'The Children Of Rarn'. None came to fruition, and it was only with the release of the 'Unchained' series that we discovered how close (or far) they came. The material was already in place. Intransigence was his enemy.

The reflective 'Teenage Dream' notwithstanding, the heart of 'Zinc Alloy' was cast firmly in the R&B shadow of 'The Groover' and 'Truck On (Tyke)', the James Brown drive of 'The Avengers (Superbad)', 'Interstellar Soul' and 'Liquid Gang', and the implausibly slight, but impressively groove-ridden 'You've Got To Jive to Stay Alive'. Period B-sides 'Satisfaction Pony' and 'Sitting Here' continued the explorations to prove that Bolan wasn't simply taking a new direction. He was erecting the signposts that would soon take so many other British rock talents down some the same unfamiliar alleyways.

'Zinc Alloy' was released in March 1974. Bowie began rehearsing his own soulful Philly Dogs tour in July. Yet, even with such credentials to uphold it, this isn't quite Bolan's soul album. Neither can it be neatly pigeonholed in the same way as Bowie's 1975 'Young Americans'. Bolan scoured the spectrum for his influences, but he never once went to Philadelphia. Rather, he investigated the same rocking R&B landscape that intrigued the early Funkadelic and Sly Stone, neither grasping a direction nor abandoning one.

This uncertainty is most apparent across the outtakes that make up 'Change – The Alternate Zinc Alloy' (Edsel). Looser and far less self-conscious than the 'real' thing, it ranges from the gritty proto-punkisms of 'Venus Loon' to a brief, gentle demo of the horribly underrated 'Spanish Midnight' and on to a 'Teenage Dream' that marries the nightclub smoke of Bowie's 'Aladdin Sane' to a positively bad-tempered guitar-shaped grumble.

'The Groover', shorn of its grating backing chorus, and an acoustic take on 'Truck On (Tyke)' are both superior to their familiar versions, while a blood-soaked slur through the B-side, 'Midnight', proves that Bolan's vision was still intact, and it was only the delivery that was at fault. Bolan called his new music 'space-age funk'. Now we know what he meant.

It's ironic, then, that the best indication of Bolan's state of mind during 1974 is gauged not by 'Zinc Alloy' but another aborted project, an album he was producing for backing vocalist Sister Pat Hall. Easily dismissed as simply his attempt to do an Astronettes, the album (finally released by Edsel as 'Marc Bolan Presents…') is actually one of the era's strongest slices of pure British soul, its necessary acknowledgement of the black American influence balanced perfectly by white London sensibilities.

It's not a Glam album, and its relevance to the Bolan story itself probably depends upon the listener's own devotion. But if you've stuck with the story this far then you owe it to yourself to hear it.

March 1974 – Cockney Rebel: Judy Teen/ Spaced Out (EMI 2128)

'Judy Teen' would work hard for her glory, languishing for almost three months before quietly gnawing her way into view.

The single that made rebels of us all, impossibly short though it was, was already a hit in Holland as Cockney Rebel prepared to go out on the road to push it. And with EMI forking out an unprecedented £10,000 to make sure the tour went with a bang, that's exactly what they did. Gigs ranged from the traditional theatres, to Biba and beyond – Rebel even played a short set at the Biggin Hill air show. Rebel were on the move, and the memory of Harley on *Top Of The Pops*, barely moving but conveying the lyric with his body, swaying on his cane, the queen of the scene, makes you curse the BBC for wiping the tapes.

There was a strike on at the Beeb the week the band appeared. The 'humpers' union', as Harley called them, there to hump the gear around, were out, and union rules prevented anyone else from filling in for them.

So there the band were, 'First time on *Top Of The Pops*, ambition fulfilled, our big day and no equipment.' But no worries. They gathered up all the guitars they could, one for every member of the band, and Cockney Rebel had their day in the sun. Harley would later call the memory 'a little embarrassing', but it was great television regardless. 'Judy Teen' peaked at Number 5 in late June, and we all went 'Psychomodo'.

Oh, and flip the single over for the so-cool 'Spaced Out' – a song that could have been just as big a hit without even having to try.

March 1974 – Queen: Queen II (EMI EMA 767)
March 1974 – Queen, first headlining UK tour.

Queen, too, were breaking through. 'Seven Seas Of Rhye' had given them their first major hit; the half-heavy, half-conceptual 'Queen II' was entrancing an entire generation of Glam-hungry prog fans; and a new song being heard on stage for the first time, 'Now I'm Here', was still a reliable diary of the band's recent tours with Mott the Hoople, and not just another oldie to be dragged out in the greatest hits bit of the set.

And it shows. Compared with many later Queen live shows, the band's enthusiasm was utterly contagious. Material from 'Queen II' – itself adventurous far beyond anything their debut had presaged – was executed with a flair that often exceeded its studio counterpart, while the older 'Keep Yourself Alive' and 'Liar' completely overstepped their metal margins to reveal themselves as veritable Glam-opera epics – a feat Queen wouldn't officially achieve until the advent of 'Bohemian Rhapsody'. By the time the show hit 'March Of The Black Queen', Queen could have come out in T-shirts and jeans and still out-glittered the world.

March 1974 – Slade: Everyday/Good Time Gals (Polydor 2058 453)

Drawn from the already chart-topping 'Old New Borrowed And Blue', 'Everyday' was anything but an everyday Slade record. No misspelling, no stamping or clapping, no maniacal bellows at beginning or end. Noddy didn't even shout. Not too much, anyway.

Instead, a crowd-swaying singalong of such scarf-waving majesty became Slade's most memorable new single in a while and, as the cue for further airborne anthems, it became one of the most crucial songs in their entire repertoire.

It was certainly the most sensitive.

Which might explain why it peaked at Number 3, a poor performance by the band's usual standards (all but one of their last nine 45s had reached either Number 1 or Number 2), and a lot of people wondered why they'd even bothered releasing such an un-Slade-like single.

Why do you think? 'We'd done all we could in that department,' Holder reasoned. 'We didn't want to keep just churning out the same sort of song.'

From here on in, they wouldn't.

March 1974 – Dana Gillespie: Andy Warhol/ Dizzy Heights (RCA 2466)
March 1974 – Dana Gillespie: Weren't Born A Man (RCA 0354)

Work on Dana Gillespie's third album had started almost three years before, and several of the songs included on the 1971 promo LP were still in contention. Two Bowie productions 'Mother Don't Be Frightened' and an alternate mix of 'Andy Warhol', plus a longer version of 'All Cut Up On You' were all featured on the finished disc ('Never Knew' would be held for her second RCA album; 'Lavender Hill' remained unreleased until the 'Andy Warhol' compilation).

And if Bowie's involvement was restricted to just those two songs, the fact that Gillespie's 'Andy Warhol' wiped the floor with his version was surely compensation enough. Ronson's guitar weeps through the mix, Gillespie sounds

both sultry and savvy and, besides, the rest of the album was red hot, too.

As was the artwork.

Resplendent in a boudoir corsage, black silk stockings and a bright red feather boa, Gillespie chose the image herself. 'It was my own decision, they were my own clothes. I actually enjoy wearing suspender belts and I like the way stockings feel, it's as simple as that. The cover was a laugh as much as anything else.'

Unfortunately, RCA didn't see it that way, at one point even threatening to wrap the LP in a plain brown bag for fear of over-exciting passing shoppers. They relented in the end and it is only with hindsight that Gillespie admitted it might not have been a bad idea.

Plough through the music papers of the day and it swiftly becomes apparent that Gillespie was, absurdly, better known for her bust size and past liaisons with both Bowie and Bob Dylan, than she was for her music. The 'Weren't Born A Man' cover might have done much to cement the glamorous image, but it also ensured that when Dana's next album, 'Ain't Gonna Play No Second Fiddle', appeared, it was discarded by most people before it even reached the turntable. You couldn't see her underwear.

March 1974 – Mick Ronson: Slaughter On 10th Avenue (RCA 0353)

First things first. 'Slaughter On 10th Avenue', Ronson's first solo set, is brilliant, a solidly excellent set that never deserved its ho-hum reviews and should have sold bucketloads more than it eventually moved.

It had everything going for it. Forget the hype with which MainMan layered its release and which may, to be honest, have put a lot of people off. Forget, too, the fears that Ronno was just a surrogate Bowie, sent out to keep the punters happy while the fat man's Cadillac was at the garage.

True, Bowie contributed two songs to the set, the freakish Glam reverie of 'Growing Up And I'm Fine' and the mixed-up madness of 'Hey Ma Get Papa'. But both were shaped so far beyond Bowie's current musical leanings that the worst thing you could say about them was that 'Growing Up' was not that different to the *Ziggy*-era 'Velvet Goldmine' and 'Sweet Head', neither of which had been publicly aired at that time.

'Hey Ma', on the other hand, was simply savage, a litany of weird, wired convolutions while a bizarre, sinister carnival is in full swing in the background. Cockney Rebel would have killed for a song like that.

Italian murder ballad 'Music Is Lethal' and a cover of jazz pianist Annette Peacock's 'I'm The One' take an altogether different tack, allowing Ronson to explore his own musical tastes, but it's the title track that truly nails 'Slaughter On 10th Avenue' into place and confirms Ronson's position as the most important guitarist of the era.

His instrument sings, it weeps and it dances. It does everything, in fact, apart from the one thing it needed to – which was persuade the public to part with its money and buy it.

March 1974 – Wizzard: Rock'n'Roll Winter/ The Dream Of Unwin (Warner Brothers K16357)

A decidedly *un*seasonal Number 6. 'Rock'n'Roll Winter' was, according to Wood, originally scheduled for release in January. The continued sales of the Christmas hit stymied that plan and there was some thought given to holding it back for another year.

'But for all I knew, Wizzard might be into something completely different by then,' Wood explained, 'so I decided to put it out anyway. A lot of people slagged me off for releasing it when the sun was out.'

The band made the most it anyway, turning out on *Top Of The Pops* with a Pythonesque Gumby, a costumed gorilla and a sax-playing wizard, while Wood played the strings of an upright vacuum cleaner.

So, silliness as usual and a great song as

wouldn't call myself a musician'

DISC MUSIC POLL AWARDS 74

Roy 'They must be mad' Wood talks to Rosemary Horide

well, but Wood was correct. Wizzard were getting into 'something completely different', best evidenced by their second album, 'Introducing Eddie And The Falcons', later in the year – a pastiche of Fifties rock and pop that hit so close to its putative home that it wasn't even much fun to listen to. It was fine for Glam to *update* the period sound – in fact, that's one of the things that the genre did best. But recreating it perfectly? You might as well have bought the original records.

March 1974 – Sweet tour cancelled

Brian Connolly was enjoying a night out in Staines, close by his home, when a bunch of local thugs jumped him. He was left nursing such a badly bruised throat that even a Harley Street specialist could not coax his voice back to action. He was in a very bad way.

The original plan was to hush it all up. The Sweet's latest tour, due to start in mere days, had to be cancelled, of course. But it was because Connolly had a cold, they said. That was all. Only as the extent of the damage became apparent did it become obvious that some kind of official statement needed to be made, if only to quell the whispers that were now circulating around the music industry and beyond. Because they made it sound even worse than it was.

Connolly detailed the events of the evening. 'I was just getting into my car, when these two guys hit me with a bottle. They knocked me to the ground and began kicking me. I didn't even get a chance to see them. They ran off and left me lying unconscious on the pavement beside my car. Fortunately, a young couple found me, picked me up and took me to hospital.'

Further details leaked slowly. There remained an element of Connolly having been in the wrong place at the wrong time, but one of the most recognisable faces in the country really should have known better than to be acting the superstar in public – which, a decade later, he admitted he was. 'I was a bit of a flash Harry when I'd had a few, and that night I had.'

He also acknowledged that, when his behaviour began attracting attention from a bunch of heavies in the corner, he should maybe have toned it down, 'and not gone wading into them, offering to take them outside.' He'd been talking with some local girls and Connolly suspected that jealousy may also have played a part in what happened. 'If I was at my local and some flash cunt came in and started chatting up my bird, I'd probably have had a go at him as well.'

What nobody could have expected was the damage that handful of indiscretions caused. 'I'd had two of my teeth kicked out. I had to have stitches in my head, mouth and ten more in my lip. And I was covered all over in bruises. The doctors told me that I wouldn't have any injury, but I've been left with this weakness in my throat...it's an internal bruising of the muscles which control the vocal chords and this can take months to heal properly.'

Neither were the Sweet and the ticket-buyers the sole casualties. The support band, Jook, were out of luck as well; and after the disappointments of the last two years, as single after single slipped into the dumper and the Rollers ran off with their wardrobe, the Sweet tour was the best thing that had ever happened to them.

A new single, 'Bish Bash Bosh', was in the can and on the schedule for release once the tour got going. If anything was going to break the band big, it would be their first ever major tour. And now it had all been snatched away.

Could anything else possibly go wrong for them?

March 1974 – Chris Hodge: Beautiful Love/ Sweet Lady From The Sky (RCA LPBO 5007)
Hodge had been around since the end of the Sixties, most notably recording for the Beatles' Apple label. His career continued on, generally in a poppy singer-songwriter vein, and then this jewel appeared, a rocker built almost plink for plonk around the discordant piano that haunted the Stooges' 'I Wanna Be Your Dog'. Brilliant, and awaiting rediscovery aboard 'Killed By Glam: 16 UK Junk Shop Glam Rarities From The Seventies' (Moonboot MB 01).

ON THE BOX
7 March 1974 – Top Of The Pops: David Bowie, Barry Blue, Bay City Rollers, Alvin Stardust
14 March 1974 – Top Of The Pops: Queen
21 March 1974 – Top Of The Pops: Barry Blue, Gary Glitter, Mott the Hoople
28 March 1974 – Top Of The Pops: Glitter Band, Queen, Slade
30 March 1974 – Russell Harty Plus: Elton John
ON THE SHELF
March 1974 – Ant: Banana Pie/No Road Goes Your Way (Pye 7N 45332)
March 1974 – Kiss: Nothin' To Lose/Love Theme From Kiss (Casablanca 503)
March 1974 – Simon Turner: She Was Just A Young Girl/I'll Take Your Hand (UK 60)
March 1974 – Ricky Wilde: Teen Wave/Round And Round (UK 63)
March 1974 – Willy Flascher and the Raincoats: Everybody Wants To See A Streaker/Run Rabbit Decca (F13506)

April 1974 – Bay City Rollers: Shang-A-Lang/ Are You Ready For That Rock'n'Roll? (Bell 1355)
'Shang-A-Lang' is the Bay City Rollers' masterpiece.

They may have made more successful records, they certainly made better ones. But in terms of laying out the terms and conditions of what would soon become known as Rollermania, 'Shang-A-Lang' single-handedly confirmed the one thing that Cassidy and the Osmonds didn't have. A sense of fun.

Even at their hungriest, the teenybop titans seldom boogied. They might rock on occasion and you could tap your toes to the beat. But did either of them once leap to his feet, throw his fist in the air and shout 'shang-a-lang'? Would Cassidy ever have 'ran with the gang'? Could Osmond even pronounce 'doo-wop shee-doobee-doo-ay'?

Yeah, boys, ballads are lovely. But sometimes, the kids wanna *rock*.

It was with 'Shang-A-Lang', which reached Number 2 and should have gone higher, that the phenomenon that became Rollermania was first sighted on the streets of Great Britain, platoons of hard-faced Rollergirls stalking the streets, daring anybody to denigrate their heroes. The tartan uniforms had yet to arrive; the Rollers would not unleash them until later in the year. But soon those platoons would become an army, and the army would conquer the world.

You bet we all ran with the gang and sang shang-a-lang. It was the only way anyone could get a look-in with the girls...

April 1974 – Alvin Stardust: Red Dress/Little Darling (Magnet 8)

To be truthful, the record itself was fairly shallow, sonically reducing the Stardust formula even closer towards its lightweight destiny. The ghost of old guitars still clung around the rhythm, though and there was one line of lyric that lives on in the mind, long after the rest of the song's been forgotten.

'I'm not your brother, you're not my sister/Lord above, you're a girl and I'm a mister.'

Sheer poetry.

A Number 7 hit, Pete Shelley wrote 'Red Dress' after noticing Stardust's penchant for singling out a particular girl in the audience and dedicating his attention to her for a song. Days later on the road, the first female fans turned up in scarlet – and by the end of the year Alvin, too, would be wearing red.

11 April 1974: 45 – Alvin Stardust

Launched in late 1973, *45* was the Granada TV network's latest stab at a national pop show to try and rival *Top Of The Pops*, broadcast on whatever schedule the individual independent companies felt best suited... Saturday mornings in London and the south, other days in other regions.

Hosted by Radio Luxembourg DJ Kid Jensen and entertainingly open-minded in its choice of guests, it never would beat the BBC show, but it did give early exposure to a wealth of new bands (including Dr Feelgood the following July), while the old hands flooded to the studios, too.

11 April 1974 – Top Of The Pops

It's interesting to compare this edition with one from a year or so before. Slade were still with us, only now they were singing 'Everyday' and Noddy was giving it some serious Tony Bennett. Mud were describing how 'The Cat Crept In' and the Gary-less Glitter Band extolled the virtues of 'Angel Face'. But the chart rundown at the beginning was still full of Little Jimmy, because the sounds may change but the names remain the same.

Or do they? Abba celebrated victory in the Eurovision Song Contest by suggesting that they're not going to take the same sudden exit as past foreign victors of that grisly competition...and dig that crazy hole-in-the-ice-shaped guitar! And Limmie and the Family Cooking's 'Walking Miracle' is shrill enough to frighten dolphins.

But you're not meant to enjoy every act on the show or to buy every record you hear. *Top Of The Pops* is a bit like having your temperature taken; the only question is where the doctor will stick the thermometer this week.

12 April 1974 – Mott the Hoople: Santa Monica Civic Auditorium, USA

Mott the Hoople's antipathy towards bootlegs was legendary. The underground vinyl industry was at its peak now, Trade Mark of Quality and the Amazing Kornyphone Label pumping out the discs the 'real' labels didn't think you needed... *In Concert* radio broadcasts, Peel sessions, the view from Row Z, studio leavings; if it was hot and unreleased, the bootleggers would blag it.

But Mott had always seemed boot-resistant; were, in fact, renowned on the live circuit for the treatment they'd mete out to anybody spotted with a tape recorder in the audience. And then they played a show for the American *King Biscuit Flour Hour*, a sponsored, syndicated concert broadcast, and just weeks later one of the finest boots of all time materialised, mockingly titled 'Behind Enemy Lines' and serving up four sides of primo, Bender-led Hoopling.

Since released as 'Two Miles From Live Heaven\ (Angel Air SJPCD 099), a 2CD set packaged with earlier live cuts and demos, this is the sound of Mott at their mightiest, certainly inching out the original 1973-74 'Live' album released later this same year and maybe even eclipsing anything else in the discography. No matter how great Mott were when they reformed in October 2009 for a week of sold-out shows in Hammersmith, they weren't *this* great.

The crowd would still be making their way back to the seats when the show began, to the strains of Gustav Holst's 'Jupiter' – the section that became the hymn 'I Vow To Thee, My Country'. Above the stage, a giant video screen hung blankly, flickering into life only as the overture began to fade and for a second several thousand pairs of eyes struggled to make sense of the blur up above them.

It resolved itself slowly, a face, a leer, a mouth, a song. Cracked, uncertain, backed only by a raw piano, the first lines of Don McLean's 'American Pie' floated across the room, each syllable strained, every nuance stretched, while below, an accusing spotlight sought out the singer, locked on him and froze.

But the voice croaked on regardless, sounding less sincere with every passing phrase and turning the final couple of lines into an absolute mockery. 'But something touched me deep inside...the day...the music...died.' Then a pause and the savage, final denouement. 'Or did it?'

The stage would explode, in lights, sound and action and 'The Golden Age Of Rock'n'Roll' would flatten the first 15 rows like a herd of bewildered wildebeest.

The group's live set spanned the years, the hits as well. It was a non-stop celebration, and while Overend Watts' contribution to 'The Hoople', the *American Graffiti*-esque 'Born Late '58', and a track from Bender's 'Under Open Skies' solo album, 'Here Comes The Queen', gave Hunter a few minutes of mid-set respite, such moments were probably unnecessary.

In taking control of the band, Hunter had taken control of its history, too. A couple of co-writing credits for the dear departed was the only indication in the live set that there had ever been a Mott the Hoople before this one, and so much water had passed under the bridge that the bulk of the audience didn't know (or care) either way.

We can argue all day whether or not Mott the Hoople were the greatest live band that ever walked the earth. On this evidence, however, you'd be hard pressed to find one better.

April 1974 – Mud: The Cat Crept In/Morning (RAK 170)

It must have felt a thankless task attempting to follow-up 'Tiger Feet', established as one of the biggest records of 1974 before the year had even got under way. But the crazy cat grabbed all the momentum and, in reaching Number 2 (trapped behind 'Seasons In The Sun'), it proved 'Tiger Feet' was no fluke.

Les Gray's Elvis-shaped vocals are the dominant feature, with the rest of the band pursuing a similarly retro vibe, only to shatter it with the guitar break. For there, Rob Davis lets rip with a performance which was immediately cast as one of the defining solos of the Glam age – at least until he came up with an even better one during 'Rocket'). That's a damned good scream he lets out, as well.

'Once we had got the dancing thing together and "Tiger Feet" was so successful, we tried to take it further,' Les Gray remembered. 'Everything seemed to fall into place with the driving guitar riffs and it seemed like we had found the right formula. Although the songs were all different, the whole team knew what it was doing.'

'We were always a visual band, even back in the days before we had any success,' continues Ray Stiles. 'And it started because, we were at the Fiesta in Stockton one night, which is a cabaret club, I remember somebody saying "You're a really good band, but you could look away, go to the bar, come back and you wouldn't have missed anything." So from that point on, we always concentrated on having something always happening on stage.

'It wasn't a case of going up there and playing the song. We'd mess around, we'd change words in songs and that's why we used to get booked back, because our approach was kind of showbizzy. We'd give people something to watch as well as listen to.

'So when *Top Of The Pops* came around and there was a bit more money floating around, it was natural for us to do that and then just go berserk with it. We would get TV shows even when we didn't have a new record out, *Cilla* and *Lulu*, things like that. We always used to go on *Jim'll Fix It*. People loved us because we were great live television.'

April 1974 – Beggars Opera: Diana Demon spreads her wings

The first demos for Beggars Opera's 'nano-opera' *Diana Demon* (now titled *The Immortal Show*) were recorded at TW Studios in London, by Virginia Scott and drummer Mike Travis, with Alan Winstanley overseeing the session. April then saw Scott and guitarist Ricky Gardiner go into the Workhouse Studios to record a possible single, 'Jet Set Lover' and 'Don't Turn Me On'.

They were also talking with producer Tony Visconti, introduced to them by Angie Bowie, but it was not yet time to move further on the project.

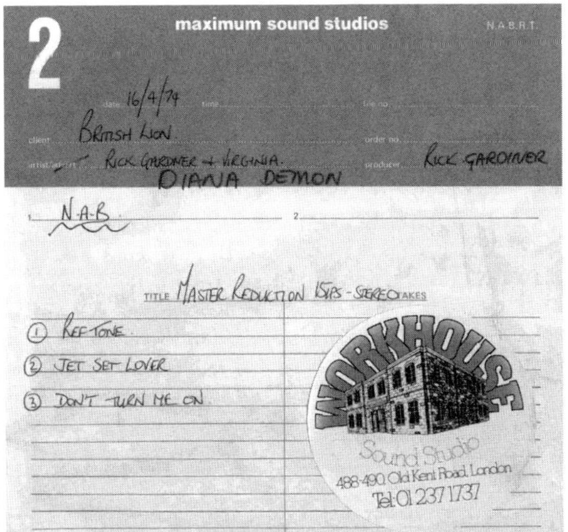

Scott: '*The Immortal Show* was gestating for some time in the background as we were catching up with two Beggars Opera albums promised to Jupiter Records in Germany, with experimental line ups.'

April 1974 – The Sweet: Sweet Fanny Adams (RCA 5039)

After all their nagging and raving and moaning about how much they wanted to make a new album, what happened? They pulled it off.

It was not an easy process. For all their expertise on laying down singles, the Sweet had little idea of how to behave over a longer studio stint. Songs were brought in and recorded long before the lyrics – and sometimes, even the melodies – had been completed, while the band's drive to produce a record that would be taken seriously by the media (the over-riding concern in everything they did) saw the most mediocre decisions drawn out interminably, while producer Phil Wainman looked helplessly on.

But when the process worked, it worked well.

Chinnichap were effectively sidelined; even dispensed with as Connolly positively refused to sing 'The Kid's Gone Mad', a song about a young man having his penis torn off. The dynamic duo wound up with just two songs on the album, 'No You Don't', which Steve Priest sang after Connolly's mishap put the singer out of action, and 'AC DC', a potential single before the band put their foot down. The gay angle they had always championed was good for a laugh. But the lesbian triangle painted by 'AC DC' hammered the point home harder than anybody was comfortable with. Thirty-two years later, Joan Jett *would* release a cover as a single and landed one of her most successful singles in years. But she had Carmen Electra in the video. The Sweet would probably have just dressed up Steve Priest.

Elsewhere, a relic from the abandoned history album, that frenzied (and yes, distinctly Mud-like) rendering of 'Peppermint Twist', was resurrected, while the band's contributions included the maniacal 'Rebel Rouser', such a solid stab at writing their own Chinnichap song that it could have been an alternate version of 'Hell Raiser'. And RCA were so impressed by 'Heartbreak Today' that there was talk of releasing it as a single, only for the band to turn them down. They, too, knew it was a great song. But was it a major hit? Probably not.

For all their demands for critical respect, the Sweet still wanted the hits as well.

April 1974 – David Bowie: Diamond Dogs (RCA 0576)

April 1974 – David Bowie: Rock'n'Roll Suicide/Quicksand (RCA 5021)

Tony Defries had a dream, that one day David Bowie would become an artist who was instantly recognizable by a single name alone. Elvis was Elvis, with no further word needed. Dylan was Dylan. Lennon was Lennon. And Bowie would be Bowie.

The plan was put into action now. The new single would be credited to Bowie alone, with no David to distinguish him from any others of that name…the knife, the cowboy, the jazzman. And it might have worked. Had they chosen a more appropriate single.

'Rock'n'Roll Suicide' could be, and was, passed over without much comment – hauled out from the two year-old 'Ziggy' once it became apparent that 'Diamond Dogs' had already surrendered its best stab at a success ('Rebel Rebel'), it stopped selling more or less before it started and became Bowie's worst-performing 'new' single yet; an indignity that was only hammered home harder when the label changed its mind and issued 'Diamond Dogs' itself on 45. The closing track from one of the most important albums of the decade died at Number

22. Six-odd minutes of self-conscious sci-fi rambling went to Number 21.

'Diamond Dogs' was Bowie at his most uncompromising, the tattered remains of his *1984* stage show grafted onto a clutch of other songs and given the semblance of a conceptual form by luck as much as judgement. Certainly the closing triptych of '1984', Big Brother' and the wordless 'Chant Of The Ever Circling Skeletal family' are magnificent; so, on side one, is the medley that combines the two-part 'Sweet Thing' with the foreboding 'Candidate'. 'Rebel Rebel' is peerless and 'We Are The Dead', another Orwellian hangover, possesses one of Bowie's most alluring lyrics.

Yet 'Diamond Dogs' still feels strangely unfinished, as though the opening 'Future Legend' poem had a lot more to say than he ultimately allowed it, and the frankly drab 'Rock'n'Roll With Me' would never have made it into view if he'd just had more time to work.

Less than six months had elapsed since 'Pinups', which itself arrived six months after 'Aladdin Sane'. Bowie was tired, but more than that he was bored. Maybe the massive American tour he set up to accompany the album's release would give him something new to think about?

PAN'S PEOPLE

THE GIRLS WHO BRING GLAMOUR TO THE SHOW!

Pan's People – a handful of very dishy, very dolly dancing birds – are now a household name. Thanks entirely to Top of the Pops.

For it's the TV show which has been responsible for shooting the girls to the top in their particular dancing field.

It's Pan's People who add the sex appeal to the show, with their intricate and exhausting, yet exciting dance routines.

They've been dancing on the show for six years. They followed in the pretty footsteps of the Go Jos, the first dance group to flit in and out of the TV show. The Go Jos, who were run by Miss Jo Cook, danced regularly on the programme for a couple of years.

Pan's People first came together as six talented girl dancers, all determined to set a new trend as an entirely "different" group. They had done a little TV before, but mostly on the Continent.

Five were English, one American. The odd girl out was Felicity (she likes to be called Flick) Colby, born in New York and originally trained as a ballet dancer.

It was Flick who did … of the choreography. The gr… was always a pretty close-… unit, and they decided am… themselves on the sort of w… they would tackle.

The group was made up … Flick, Ruth Pearson, Dee … Wilde, Louise Clarke, Bar… (Babs) Lord, and Andrea (An… Rutherford.

When Andy Rutherford … to have a baby, last year, a … girl, Cherry Gillespie, came i… join the group.

Flick Colby quit the ac… dance line-up a couple of ye… ago in order to work solely … the group's choreographer. … now spends most of her t… dreaming up new dance routi… for the girls, and puts th… through their paces every we…

"We were always much m…

PAN'S PEOPLE . . . in action in front of the cameras, 1973.

April 1974 – Streakers: Turn Me Down/Wake Up Sunshine (Dawn DNS 1066)
April 1974 – D'Jurann Jurrann: Streakin'/Oh! Janine (Dawn DNS1068).

Streaking, the art of publicly disrobing and then running across a public place, had been around for decades, even centuries, before the Seventies transformed it into an art form. But isolated incidents in America during early 1973 became a rash before the end of the year and by 1974 they were a veritable epidemic.

And just like every other public craze, somebody wrote a song about it.

American comedian Ray Stevens had the hit; his strangely unfunny 'The Streak' topped the UK chart in June, weeks after the pastime received its most notable exposure at the England v France rugby match at Twickenham on 20 April. Australian Michael O'Brien was captured by a policeman, who then found his own way into streaking folklore when he shielded O'Brien's genitals with his hat. A helmet for a helmet, it was said.

Even before that, however, streaking had taken off in the UK and the wryly-named Willy Flascher and the Raincoats were the first off the ball in March. Producer Tony Hiller's prosaically named Streakers followed them up, then came the phonetically prophetic D'Jurann Jurrann, a one-off guise for former Mungo Jerry man Paul King.

None of the records sold, or even received much airplay, and once Stevens got in on the act there was little need to say anything else on the subject. But the Streakers were resurrected by the compilation 'Glitter From The Litter Bin: 20 Junk Shop Glam Rarities From The Seventies' (Castle CMQCD 675) and the rest are out there somewhere.

April 1974 – Jook: Bish Bash Bosh/Crazy Kids (RCA 5024)

Jook's most pop-tastic single yet was produced by the sure-fire fingers of AIR Studios co-owner

a dance team. More of a
," says Flick. "Except that
irls don't sing. They do
they're best at – which is
ng.
were kinda like session
ians. We just got together
ise we all liked dancing.
ist wanted to go out and
eaping around. So we did.
we've stuck together ever
"
describes their style of
ng as "kinda funky."
a long time, dancers
treated as moving wall-
. Now all that has changed.
ing has become an involved
of any TV show.
a dance group, Pan's
le have always had 'some-
to say'. And this, I hope,
s in our dancing."
girls were all picked, says
because they were good
ers, not necessarily good
rs. Although good-looking
obviously help any act
.
she admits: "The more
dance, the more sexy they
– to watch. But Pan's
le have never been 'teasers'.
e never tried the alluring
ique."
re is, nevertheless, a great
of sex which comes into
ct when the Pan's are on
. It's there, in their dancing.
this is what makes them so
nating.
k came to Britain in 1966.
the last few years, she
also been involved as a
ographer, away from Pan's
le. She was the choreo-
her on the musical "Catch
Soul" in London, and then
in Paris. She has also
ed on the Les Dawson
s, "Sez Les", for Yorkshire

ce she changed to become
choreographer, she says,
relationship has changed
endously with the girls."
he has no trouble from the
when it comes to them
ing a new dance routine.
ll a matter of practise, hard

But just look how dancing styles have changed. This is The Gojos, resident dancers on the show, back in 1965.

PAN'S PEOPLE, relaxing out of the studio, 1971. Left to right: Louise Clarke, Andy Rutherford, Flick Colby, Ruth Pearson, Dee Dee Wilde and Barbara Lord.

work, and more practise.

"I often receive letters from young girls who think it is very attractive to be a dancer on TV. But I have to tell them, quite honestly, that it's really one hell of a hard slog," says Flick. "It's groovy. But hard work."

The girls rehearse three days each week for the TV show. They do a new routine in each programme, and work starts on Monday morning with Flick "scripting" the dance routine. Then they have a costume fitting. And rehearsals go on, right up to the dress run-through a few hours before the final show.

"Chicks change tremendously from, say, the age of 18 to when they become 24 or 26. All this has got to be taken into consideration when you are working with a group of girls," says Flick. "All their varying personality changes are reflected in their dancing. They often have a completely new attitude to the job in the space of those half-dozen years or so."

Why Pan's People? the name is simple. "Pan is the name of the Patron of dance," explains Flick.

As well as appearing on Top of the Pops, Pan's People have also appeared on many other TV shows, including the Cilla Black series, the Bobbie Gentry shows, the Frankie Howerd shows, and the Georgie Fame/Alan Price show "The Price of Fame". They dance a lot in night clubs and discos, too.

It's not so surprising, either, that they have a great many admirers. Their unofficial "Fan Club" extends around the world. For Pan's People have been claimed as official Pin Ups to many Armed Forces units, including several ships. And also to prisoners serving jail sentences.

This, they find extremely flattering.

John Burgess and, had the Sweet tour gone ahead, it might well have done something.

RCA certainly thought so, probably spending more money on this single than on all its predecessors put together – and that may or may not have included the cost of hiring someone to walk the London streets at night, spraying JOOK RULE OK on every available surface.

But all to no avail. The band scratched together a few last minute club dates to replace the cancelled nationwide scouring, but that was all they could do. 'Bish Bash Bosh' came and went unnoticed and they knew the end was near.

April 1974 – The Damned: Morning Bird/ Theta (Young Blood YB 1067)

Not, obviously, to be confused with the punks of the same name, the Damned were a Miki Dallon production who, said their press release, 'are deeply involved in ancient Druid knowledge.'

It only followed, then, that 'Morning Bird' should be 'an invocation chant calling up an unknown force or maybe an alien spacecraft.' Neither arrived and 'Morning Bird' would next be sighted on 'Velvet Tinmine – 20 Junk Shop Glam Ravers' (RPM 251) in 2003. That same album, incidentally, also brings us another Miki Dallon production, Crunch's crunchy 'Let's Do It Again'.

17 April 1974 – In Concert: Pan's People

By early 1974, Pan's People's popularity had reached such proportions that it made sense to establish them as a performing troupe in their own right, as opposed to a pleasant interlude during *Top Of The Pops*. *In Concert* was the first step (an Epic Records deal would follow), although the team initially viewed the performance with mixed emotions.

Already nervous at facing an audience that had come exclusively to see *them* perform, Louise recalled, 'Dee and I were given the most expensive costumes the BBC had ever bought and it was the smallest thing I'd ever seen in my life' – tiny pads for the nipples and flesh-coloured fabric for the lower zones. The pair then crouched over cushions and gyrated very slowly...

'It was also the first time we ever sang,' she lamented. 'There were only a couple of us who could sing, and I'm not one of them.' A tap routine provoked similar reservations.

But when the performance was good, it was excellent – and today, the team rightly regard *In Concert* as the pinnacle of their time together. The records, on the other hand...

April 1974 – Arrows: Touch Too Much/We Can Make It Together (RAK 171)

Turned down by Decca, the newly reunited Alan Merrill and Jake Hooker started again from scratch. They briefly shared management with Barclay James Harvest, but a demo taped at Trident Studios with drummer Clive Williams was a poorly recorded disaster. But then Peter Meaden, the Who's original mentor, took over their affairs and things started moving.

Meaden already knew Hooker; had, in fact, penned the Streak's Deram press release. Now he insisted that instead of going to all the bother of recording a demo tape, Hooker and Merrill should simply visit the record companies and play their songs in person.

Some listened, some threw them out. And Mickie Most at RAK flipped – on one condition. 'He wanted us to record a song called 'Touch Too Much', written by Mike Chapman and Nicky Chinn for David Cassidy. Cassidy rejected it, so Most wanted to teach him a lesson and prove the song would be a hit. He played them a demo, voiced by Brian Connolly. 'If you record "Touch Too Much", you've got a deal.'

Two conditions. Dump the drummer and bring in Hooker's old Streak bandmate, Paul Varley. 'If you get Paul and record "Touch Too Much", you've got a deal.' Three conditions. Lose Pete Meaden. Most didn't want the competition.

Merrill and Hooker accepted all three. 'We called Paul Varley who was between gigs. He was in. RAK put us on retainer and I got off Jake's floor and got my own flat, and then we went into Morgan Studio and cut "Touch Too Much" with Mickie Most producing.'

A prolific songwriter himself, Merrill did feel a little uneasy recording a cover for his first UK single. But he also understood the necessity. 'I liked Mike and Nicky personally. They were always cordial in the office at RAK. They were also the hottest writing team in the UK pop charts in the early Seventies.'

Buoyed by the newly-christened Arrows' dreamy good looks and with RAK rallying the teenybop press to their side, 'Touch Too Much' entered the chart in the last week of May. It rose to Number 8.

April 1974 – Giggles: Glad To Be Alive/High School Girls (EMI 2288)

A semi-regular support band for the Sweet, Giggles were rediscovered following their B-side's inclusion on the 'Blitzing The Ballroom: 20 UK Power Glam Incendiaries' compilation (Psychic Circle PCCD 7021).

April 1974 – Abacus: Indian Dancer/Be That Way (York YR 207)

April 1974 – Paul Ryder and Time Machine: Are You Ready/If You Ever Get To Heaven (Penny Farthing PEN 834)

Further obscurities rediscovered following their inclusion on the 'Blitzing The Ballroom: 20 UK Power Glam Incendiaries' compilation (Psychic Circle PCCD 7021).

April 1974 – Sparks: This Town Ain't Big Enough For Both Of Us/Barbecutie (Island WIP 6193)

'Without drawing overworked comparisons,' announced Island Records' first Sparks press release, 'we believe that Sparks, with their music and unique visual identity, will capture the imagination and affection of roughly the same audience sector which has made Roxy Music such an overwhelming success.'

With manager John Hewlett adding that the band were trying 'to recapture the excitement of the Small Faces and the Who,' two very different sets of expectations were carefully being nurtured. Both were shattered when the band's first single, 'This Town Ain't Big Enough For Both Of Us', was released and ended up sounding like nothing on earth.

Marvellously produced by Muff Winwood and backed by an equally phenomenal non-album cut, 'Barbecutie', 'This Town Ain't Big Enough' was a riot of guitar, gunshot and Russell Mael's falsetto, primed across two earlier Sparks albums but now honed to glass-shattering perfection.

Truthfully, it was a record you either really loved or utterly loathed, the most idiosyncratic release of the year and one of those songs that was either going to be an enormous hit or a resounding flop. Elton John was among those who predicted the latter and went so far as to wager £5 on the fact. Muff Winwood, with whom he made the deal, had no problem collecting his winnings.

The original Sparks broke up within months of returning from their first London visit in December 1972. They'd hung on in LA for as long as they could, but when the only venue that still regularly booked them, the Whisky A-Go-Go, stopped returning their calls it was the beginning of the end. The cancellation of a projected tour with Bearsville labelmate Todd Rundgren was the final straw.

Contacting John Hewlett, the English manager (of Jook) whom they'd met in London, the Maels announced they wanted to relocate. Hewlett contacted Winwood, who was interested enough to guarantee that Island would at least listen to anything the brothers had to show them and coughed up £500 to prove it.

Over the next few months, the Maels worked to piece together a band: bassist Martin Gordon, drummer Norman 'Dinky' Diamond and guitarist Adrian Fisher, formerly with Gary Moore's Skid Row and ex-Free bassist Andy Fraser's Toby.

It was hardly the 'unknown band' the Maels maintained they discovered at a party thrown by their biggest fans, the Kennedy family, but the brothers, with their astute knowledge of the power of the media, were more than aware that a good story could sell as many records as a good song. It was also a lot more glamorous than the truth and in England, as 1973 slipped into 1974, glamour still held a lot of appeal for the kids.

Rehearsals saw a solid set of songs developing, with Ron explaining, 'Our music is a weird combination of a gutsy backing and Russell's falsetto,' and Russell adding, 'The singing is dictated by the way the songs are written. When Ron writes, he happens to use the right hand a lot on keyboards and comes up with songs without any regard as to whether they can be sung like that.' Indeed, 'This Town Ain't Big Enough' was written with so little regard for Russell's abilities that there were doubts it could even be sung.

Ron himself claimed the song developed out of an evening spent playing Bach *études* on his piano at home, but Russell continued, 'He'll go from high notes to low notes without singing it himself, so he doesn't even know if a person can possibly sing like that. But it's quite interesting, occasionally, to force yourself to sing like that and not transpose it to a key that's easier. The result is, I sing whatever's there. Actually, my voice hasn't changed since I was 12. It hasn't broken yet and I'm keeping my fingers crossed that it doesn't otherwise we're going to be in for a lot of trouble.'

An album, 'Kimono My House', was recorded and 'This Town' readied for release. A promo film, directed by Rosie Samwell-Smith (wife of ex-Yardbird Paul) was shot at Beaulieu Palace House and the first review copies went out. And by the end of April, 'This Town Ain't Big Enough' was poised on the edge of the chart. A month later, it would be Number 2, pipped to the post by the Rubettes.

And therein hangs a tale.

25 April 1974 – Top Of The Pops: Sparks vs the Rubettes

By the end of April, the Rubettes' 'Sugar Baby Love' had been in the stores for three months and the best thing you could say for it was that it was 'bubbling under'.

Meanwhile, Sparks' 'This Town Ain't Big Enough For Both Of Us' had been available for less than three weeks and was already on everybody's lips. When *Top Of The Pops* producer Robin Nash drew up the next *Top Of The Pops*, it was obvious who he would have to include.

Unfortunately, it was apparently not so obvious to Sparks and their management precisely what kind of official hoops they needed to jump through before they could take Nash up on his offer.

Russell Mael: 'We went to re-record the song [as per Musicians' Union requirements] and Robin Nash, came down to meet us. A very British gentleman, he says with a perfect BBC accent, "Hullo, Robin Nash, *Top Of The Pops*" and I went, "Hi, I'm Russell from Sparks" with my best American twang. And he said, '"Oh, excuse me, I must make a telephone call." And they pulled us off of the show because they'd assumed we were British and we weren't part of the Musicians' Union here.'

Sparks were replaced by the Rubettes. 'Robin Nash, bless him, said "Quick, get another band",' recalled Rubette Alan Williams. 'There were two or three bands bubbling under and [we] got the call.'

The Rubettes took their bow alongside the Bay City Rollers and Alvin Stardust on the show. Bill Hurd is still flabbergasted when he recalls 'just how big an impact we made and that first unforgettable TV appearance.'

The suits were Persil-perfect, the choreography – Williams at the front, bandmates Clarke and Thorpe on his flanks and moving in exquisite harmony, Richardson stepping out from behind the kit for his spoken-word cameo – breathtaking. All the trademarks for which the Rubettes would become renowned were in place and they blew the rest of the show away.

The following week, the Rubettes were Number 27 and Sparks were Number 48. The week after that, Sparks were 27 and the Rubettes were Number 2. A month after that, Sparks were at Number 2 and the Rubettes had been at the top for three weeks.

April 1974 – Barry Blue and Starbuck On Tour

While 'Sugar Baby Love' still slumbered, Barry Blue scooped up four Rubettes to accompany him on his first ever tour. It was a nerve-wracking outing all round, as keyboard-player Bill Hurd recalls.

'It was a unique experience because Barry is a good songwriter and producer but not a great singer. And it was his first ever tour, so he was very nervous and inexperienced.'

Even worse, the tour was still ongoing when the Rubettes' single finally started to move. '"Sugar Baby Love" charted and, once we had been seen on *Top Of The Pops,* we were being recognised by the concert audiences. On occasion the audience were even calling for us to sing "Sugar Baby Love" and saying "send him off", etc! A bit embarrassing, but I have to say Barry took it all very well and was always complimentary about the band and our success.'

Another outing sent Blue to Germany for a short but highly successful tour that also provided the highlight of Starbuck's live career. Martin Briley recalls, 'We were halfway through the tour and wondering why Germans seemed so keen on giving blokes flowers when it dawned on us that we had been booked into a series of gay bars.'

April 1974 – Top Of The Pops Volume 37 (Hallmark SHM 860)

One of the most unappealing albums in the entire Top Of The Pops series, 'Volume 37' is as drab as the spring-so-far had shaped up to be. Secure at Number 1 was *Opportunity Knocks*' latest gift to mankind, Paper Lace's 'Billy Don't Be A Hero'. When it finally fell from grace, we had 'Seasons In The Sun', which slithered in to take its place. And fighting it out beneath them, 'Long Live Love' simpered on about wet days, dry days and great to be alive days; the tiniest Osmond threatened to knock on your door and, squeaky-cleaner than all of them, the New Seekers were getting sentimental over you. But only a little.

'Angel Face' raised the temperature a little,

but 'Remember Me This Way' was a dismal drone. Hot Chocolate's 'Emma' found herself with another reason to kill herself and 'Seven Seas Of Rhye' went awry. You could probably skip this one.

ON THE RADIO
7 April 1974 – Sounds On Sunday: Wizzard
15 April 1974: Bob Harris: The Winkies, Queen
ON THE BOX
4 April 1974 – Top Of The Pops: Gary Glitter, Glitter Band, Mott the Hoople, Mud
11 April – 45: Slade
11 April – Top Of The Pops: Mud, Slade, Glitter Band
18 April 1974 – Top Of The Pops: Mott the Hoople, Bay City Rollers, Glitter Band, Wizzard
25 April 1974 – 45: Geordie
25 April 1974 – Top Of The Pops: The Rubettes

May 1974 – Bilbo Baggins: Saturday Night/ Monday Morning Blues (Polydor 2058 479)

Edinburgh-based Bilbo Baggins were the 'other' band in Rollers manager Tam Paton's stable, but despite the connection and the manifold advantages that brought them they never threatened to approach their stalemates' fame.

Formed in 1972 and lining up as Colin Chisholm (vocals), Brian Spence (guitar), Gordon 'Tosh' McIntosh (guitar), James 'Dev' Devlin (bass) and Gordon 'Fid' Liddle, the band was named by manager Paton from the *Lord Of The Rings* character. They had already built up some local support when Paton took them into the studio in January 1973 to record a demo; Polydor took the bait.

Entrusted to Rubettes masterminds Wayne Bickerton and Tony Waddington, Bilbo Baggins' debut single 'Saturday Night' was *not* the Rollers number; rather, it was the producer's own composition, a punchy ditty whose promotion included several photos of the band clad in just a hint of the tartan that the Rollers would soon (but not just yet) make their own.

'Saturday Night' was included on the compilation 'Killed By Glam: 16 UK Junk Shop Glam Rarities From The Seventies' (Moonboot MB 01).

May 1974 – Renegade: A Little Rock'n'Roll/ My Revolution (Dawn DNS 1067)

A solid Slade soundalike, resurrected by the compilation 'Glitter From The Litter Bin: 20 Junk Shop Glam Rarities From The Seventies' (Castle CMQCD 675).

May 1974 – Thunderthighs: Central Park Arrest/Sally Wants A Red Dress (Philips 6006 386)

When they appeared as backing vocalists on Lou Reed's 'Transformer' in 1972, the rumour spread that Thunderthighs were actually David Bowie and Mick Ronson – a supposition that Reed first denied and then, laughing, insisted was the case after all.

In fact they were the trio of Karen Friedman, American Dari Lalou and ex-Gringo vocalist Casey Synge; a fourth member, Jacki Hardin, left before the group made any recordings.

Thunderthighs' profile soared after they appeared on *Top Of The Pops* recreating their cameo on Mott the Hoople's 'Roll Away The Stone'. Lynsey de Paul (who sang the same sequence on the LP version of the single) their debut single, and it made it to Number 30. de Paul's version of the song appeared as the B-side to 'No Honestly' in November.

May 1974 – Cozy Powell: The Man In Black/ After Dark (RAK 160)

Not a paean to Alvin Stardust, but the long-awaited follow-up to 'Dance With The Devil'.

'I wasn't keen at first, but Mickie could be very persuasive,' Powell admitted years later and Alan Merrill, bassist on the session, recalls the line-up that accompanied Powell into the studio – Jake Hooker on lead guitar, Merrill on electric bass (Most's own Fender Precision) and Clive Chaman on upright double bass. Phil Dennys played keyboards, said Merrill, 'but Don Airey may have also contributed and the primitive ooh, aah and sung chorus chants were Suzi Quatro, Len Tuckey, Jake Hooker, Paul Varley and me, triple-tracked. A RAK team effort.

'The B-side was just Cozy, Phil Dennys, Jake Hooker and me. To Mickie, B-sides were an annoyance that had to be dealt with quickly – we did the flip side fast but it sounds pretty good!'

Less successful than its predecessor ('The Man In Black' stalled at Number 18), it nevertheless prompted Most to demand a third single for late summer.

May 1974 – Bryan Ferry: The 'In' Crowd/ Chance Meeting (Island WIP 6196)

Interviewed in *Melody Maker* during the sessions for his second solo album in 1974, Bryan Ferry happened to mention Davy O'List's brief time as a member of Roxy Music, remarked how much he'd enjoyed working with him and expressed the hope that he would do so again. O'List, for whom the past two years had swept by in a flurry of inactivity, was on the phone immediately.

'I just called and said, "Come on then, here I am." Bryan turned around and said he had just the track for me to play on, a version of 'The "In" Crowd' – that's what happened.' (The pair also recorded a new version of 'Sea Breezes', one of the songs O'List had been playing during his tenure with Roxy Music.) The electrifying result, a riff that opens, closes and altogether dominates the song, remains one of O'List's career-best creations. But the single, unjustly, climbed no higher than Number 13.

May 1974 – Mick Ronson: Slaughter On 10th Avenue/Leave My Heart Alone (RCA 5022)

Destined to become Ronson's private anthem, Broadway playwright Richard Rodgers' 'Slaughter On 10th Avenue' has an immense pedigree, but this is surely the definitive take. Not an especially wise choice for a single, though.

May 1974 – Sparks: Kimono My House (Island ILPS 9272)

May 1974 – Jook: final sessions

Sparks' third album, 'Kimono My House', was released to almost unprecedented acclaim and unprecedented confusion, two weeks after 'This Town Ain't Big Enough'. The title was debated endlessly – what did it mean? Schoolyards echoed with increasingly surreal (and often obscene) explanations, some so convincing that it was actually disappointing to learn, a decade later, that it was all quite innocuous. 'It was just a pun,' Russell explained. 'Kimono my house, come on over to my house.'

Ian MacDonald, in the *New Musical Express*, proclaimed the album an 'instant classic' and few listeners disagreed. From the opening fade-in of 'This Town Ain't Big Enough' to the closing sax and squawk-driven 'Equator', a song that *still* boasts one of the greatest endings in recorded history, it was an astonishing record.

By the end of May, 'Kimono' had joined 'This Town Ain't Big Enough' in the UK Top Ten. Yet, within days of that, everything had changed. Bassist Martin Gordon was fired after one grumble too many and manager John Hewlett was on the lookout for replacements.

He didn't have far to look.

Jook were fading fast. Still suffering the fall-out from the cancelled Sweet tour and sensing that the end was near, the group opted to have one final hurrah in the studio, booking into RG Jones Studios in Morden and simply blasting

away through every song they fancied.

Some of them were new – 'Moving In The Right Direction', 'Hey Doll' and 'Cooch'; others reprised the group's favourite covers – Bobby Parker's 'Watch Your Step' and Charlie Rich's 'Mohair Sam'. All, however, sounded more relaxed and natural than anything the band had recorded before and all were doomed to obscurity. RCA passed on the entire tape and the group was in disarray even before manager John Hewlett called up to ask if Trevor White and Ian Hampton wanted to become stars?

Sparks needed a bassist, and they wanted a second guitarist as well.

POSTSCRIPT: Jook's entire recorded canon is compiled on 'Jook: Different Class' (RPM 295); 'Moving In The Right Direction' was also released as the B-side to Trevor White's 1976 solo single 'Crazy Kids' (Island WIP 6291).

16 May 1974 – Top Of The Pops: Alvin Stardust, Arrows, Bay City Rollers, Wizzard, the Rubettes

Alan Merrill: 'One day we got a call from Mickie Most; we had been asked to appear on *Top Of The Pops*. We were all over the moon, happy as larks dancing around the room. We all knew clearly we now had a real shot at the Top Ten. Our record was hovering just outside the UK Top Thirty at that point in time. It just needed a nudge.

'We dressed in the black and white leather jackets that Mickie Most had custom made for us. His own design, it was sort of glam cowboy. Very short, tight and form-fitted. He'd then sent us down to London's Carnaby Street, to a place where we also had black tight gabardine trousers made up. The same place he sent Suzi Quatro for her leather jumpsuits. An Italian man with an accent worked furiously measuring and making stage pants as quickly as he could for all the bands.

'Last but not least, I wore some white seven-inch platform shows for the show that I had bought in Tokyo. They made me about six and a half feet tall.

'I wasn't nervous. I just wanted to get up there and get "Touch Too Much" moving further up into the charts. Suddenly I felt someone touch my arm. I turned around and it was Cliff Richard. "I know you may be nervous, but don't worry. I like your record, it's very good, and you look great, so go on and knock them out. You'll have a hit." This was becoming lots of fun. I had a star the stature of Elvis in England wishing me luck. The same guy whose records I had listened to in school when I was a young lad. It was one of those surreal life moments. I loved it.

'We launched into "Touch Too Much". I sang and played the song for all it was worth. The camera was mine. I'd had plenty of TV experience in Japan already, and I wasn't going to let this opportunity slip away. The performance went without a hitch, and was greeted with plenty of enthusiasm by the studio audience. Some girls, teenyboppers, were screaming and I smiled to myself. It had worked. We had made it over this major hurdle. There was a sudden buzz about the band in the music industry. It was everywhere. The record started to sell. Lots. Week by week, we were going up the charts.'

May 1974 – David Essex: America/Dance Little Girl (CBS 2176)

Inexplicably (or maybe not; it wasn't that good) halted at Number 32.

May 1974 – Angel: Good Time Fanny/Who D'Ya Think You're Fooling (Cube 2016072)

Angel were originally known as Pebble, in which form they played several dates opening for the Sweet. They broke up soon after, but when Andy Scott and Mick Stewart called up looking for a new outlet for their production and songwriting ambitions, the band was persuaded to reform as Angel.

Ultimately the project came to naught at home, but Angel would go on to considerable continental success, with and without their Sweet mentors.

26 May 1974 – David Cassidy/Showaddywaddy at White City

May 1974 – Showaddywaddy: Hey Rock And Roll/You Will Lose Your Love Tomorrow (Bell 1357)

Showaddywaddy were initially reluctant to releases one of their own compositions as their debut single. They'd have been an awful lot happier digging out a favourite cover.

But producer Mike Hurst wouldn't hear of it, especially after he heard what they had. 'They played me this thing that they didn't think had a chance called 'Hey Rock And Roll', and I was – "Hold on a minute! You *have* to do that. Not only is it a wall-shaker, you're also going to have every kid in the venue punching their fists in the air." And sure enough, they played White City Stadium with David Cassidy, they played "Hey Rock And Roll" and the whole place was on their feet, punching their fists in the air.'

There would be little time in which to congratulate the band. That same night, a crush at the front of the stage saw some 750 fans injured as a large part of the 35,000-strong audience surged forward to greet the headliner. Thirty were hospitalised and one, 14 year-old Bernadette Whelan, had stopped breathing. Emergency workers were able to restart her heart but the girl never regained consciousness.

She died on 30 May.

A tape made of the night's concert, played at the coroner's inquest, reveals the chaos as the expected barrage of impassioned screaming was transformed into cries of terror; the show was just 20 minutes old when Cassidy realised something had gone horribly wrong.

'Get back, get back. They're going to stop the show, they're going to pull the plug on me. Cool it!' But like Mick Jagger at Altamont five years earlier, his words had no effect. He left the stage and the PA kicked into whatever lightweight pop was to hand in an attempt to calm the crowd.

The tape kept recording, only it wasn't picking up the keening cries of 'David, I love you'

any longer. Against a backdrop of 'The Wombling Song', crushed and battered fans were screaming for help.

Later, the promoter would argued that the majority of supposedly injured fans were faking it; that they assumed the stretcher-bearers would take them backstage where they might catch a glimpse of their hero and recovered the moment they realised they were going the opposite way. Even more cruelly, it was claimed that Bernadette was suffering from a congenital heart defect and could have died anywhere. The fact that it decided to give out when she was lying on the floor, crushed beneath several hundred other girls, was pure coincidence.

The coroner swiftly put paid to that, citing her cause of death as 'traumatic asphyxiation'. His report condemned the 'trendy, high platform shoes' that many of the victims were wearing and suggested that many of the girls who fell were literally toppled off their heels. And taking a well-aimed pot shot at the entire teenybop phenomenon, he described Bernadette as a 'victim of contrived hysteria'. The British Safety Council called it a suicide concert.

They were terms the shattered Cassidy recognised instantly. For two years he had been complaining at the absolute lack of control he had over the star-making machine that surrounded him; condemned the fact that he could not even buy a box of breakfast cereal without having his face stare back at him from the packaging.

Musically, he was already pushing as fast as he could away from the teenybop milieu; had already taken the decision to step out of the concert limelight. 'I feel burnt up inside,' he told the *Daily Mail*. 'I'm 24, a big star, in a position that millions dream of, but the truth is I just can't enjoy it.'

White City and a Manchester show two days later were billed as his farewell performances and within hours of the stampede (incredibly, the concert was resumed once the injured had been cleared away), he was considering cancelling the Manchester show altogether.

In the event it went ahead, but a muted affair was further diminished when it became clear how many of the 20,000 ticket-holders were staying away. The venue was less than half full as anxious parents, horrified by the previous morning's newspaper headlines, returned their children's tickets. Devastated by the tragedy, it would be 10 years before Cassidy regained his appetite for live work, but his days as a teenybop idol were over.

Showaddywaddy's on the other hand, were just beginning. One of – if not *the* – finest rock'n'roll revival bands of the Seventies, Showaddywaddy also proved one of the most successful and enduring, the suddenly-elected spearhead of that vein of Glam that – having watched *That'll Be The Day* and liked what it saw – already included Mud and Wizzard and would soon be embracing the Rubettes as well.

Showaddywaddy brushed them all to one side. 'Hey Rock And Roll' had already entered the lower reaches of the chart the week before the Cassidy concerts, the same time as a reissue of Bill Haley's 'Rock Around The Clock' dropped out. The week after, it crashed into the Top Twenty at Number 6, its eyes already fixed on the Rubettes' roost at the tip. Ultimately, its progress was halted at Number 2 behind the unfunny humour of 'The Streak'. But five weeks in the Top Five suggested that Showaddywaddy would soon be back for more.

ON THE BOX
2 May 1974 – Top Of The Pops: Bay City Rollers, Alvin Stardust, Wizzard, the Rubettes
9 May 1974 – Top Of The Pops: Bay City Rollers, Sparks, the Rubettes
16 May 1974 – Top Of The Pops: Alvin Stardust, Bay City Rollers, Wizzard, the Rubettes, Arrows
23 May 1974 – Top Of The Pops: Cockney Rebel, Sparks, Bryan Ferry, Cockney Rebel, Showaddywaddy, Sparks, the Rubettes
25 May 1974 – 45: Bay City Rollers, Showaddywaddy
25 May 1974 – Saturday Scene: Geordie
30 May 1974 – Top Of The Pops – 10cc, Cockney Rebel, Arrows, Showaddywaddy, the Rubettes
ON THE SHELF
May 1974 – Rocky Horror Show: Sweet Transvestite/Time Warp (UK 67)
May 1974 – Be Bop Deluxe: Jet Silver (And The Dolls From Venus)/Third Floor Heaven (Harvest HAR 508)
May 1974 – Jobriath: Street Corner Love/Rock Of Ages (Elektra K12146)

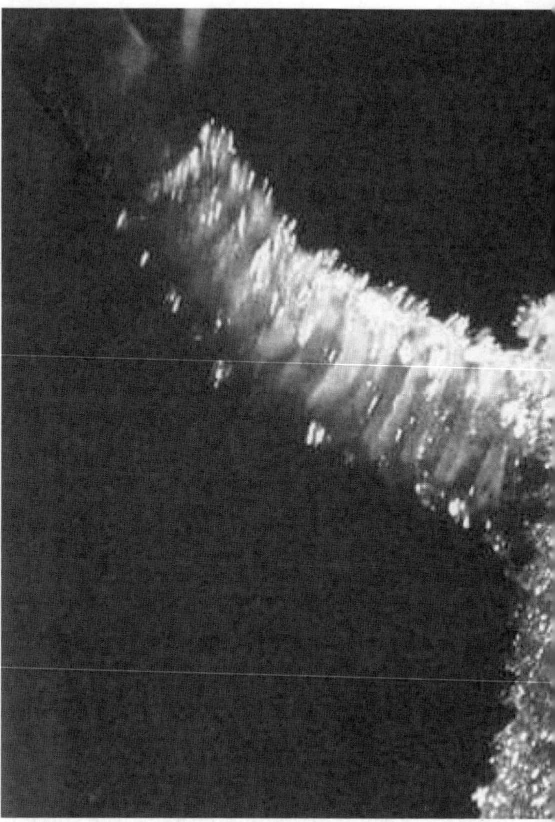

---

1 June 1974 – Eno at the Rainbow
Putting his loathing for the live arena aside, Eno agreed to appear briefly at the Island Records showcase at London's Rainbow Theatre alongside Kevin Ayers and former Velvet Undergrounders John Cale and Nico.

All had new (or new-ish, in Eno's case) albums out, with the headlining Ayers widely tipped to have his first hit. In the event, he didn't, but a live album of the proceedings, the sensibly titled 'June 1 1974', preserved highlights of all four sets for posterity, including Eno's 'Baby's On Fire' and 'Driving Me Backwards', performed with a band featuring Cale, Robert Wyatt, Ollie Halsall, John Bundrick and Eddie Sparrow.

June 1974 – Gary Glitter: Always Yours/I'm Right, You're Wrong, I Win (Bell 1423)
June 1974 – Gary Glitter: Remember Me This Way (Bell BELLS 237)
A return to the high-energy thump of old but shot through with the emotional gravitas that paid off so well the last few times, 'Always Yours' gave Gary his eighth successive hit. Straight in at Number 5, it then became his third Number 1 before Charles Aznavour came crooning along and normal life paused for a moment.

Glitter's new album had no such problems. The soundtrack to the movie of the same name, 'Remember Me This Way' was recorded live at the Rainbow the previous November, a show bassist John Springate recalls as one of the best the team ever played.

'That was a good night. Afterwards, when we listened to the multi-track in the studio, there was very little needed to be done with it. There were a few little things we had to sort out, but everybody was playing so well that night it wasn't doctored at all. I was very pleased with that one.'

So were the fans. Eight of the album's 11 tracks were Top Five smashes; three more could have been; and the entire package remains the perfect document of Gary Glitter's peak period. The music is only part of the experience, however. Glitter seemingly lived for the live performance, involving the audience in every gesture, every nuance, every bellowed 'hey'.

The sense of excitement that builds around the opening 'Leader Of The Gang', before Glitter himself takes the stage, is palpable even today, while the massed singalongs that erupt every time he opens his mouth testify to the sheer majesty of the event. Only the absence of Glitter's greatest ballads marred the track selection – in later years, watching Glitter emote his way through 'I Love You Love Me Love', for one, was akin to seeing Judy Garland sing 'Over The Rainbow'. You knew she'd done it a million times, but the tears still looked real.

'The Glam thing was always great fun,' Gary reflected years later. 'We – Marc Bolan, David Bowie, myself, Slade, Sweet – were working in pre-video times, but we'd be thinking visually. When we did *Top Of The Pops,* which was our major outlet, we devised some outrageous props. I used to come out on motorbikes, or moons to stand on.'

Surviving clips of Glitter's TV performances back him to the hilt. Papier-maché dragons, vast crescent moons, if a prop looked proper he would utilise it. And his visual extravagance was only half the story. Tales of Gary's spending were manifold and tended to be true; importing sequins from Switzerland, he thought nothing of dropping between £2-3,000 on one suit.

Clothes had always been important to him – 'Even when I was earning one hundred pounds a week in the clubs, most of it went on clothes,' he revealed. But now they were important to his fans, as well, and he wasn't going to let anybody down.

At one point he owned 30 glitter suits, maybe 50 pairs of monstrous silver platforms; questioned later about his expenditure, he happily admitted: 'I needed that many because there were always people around. It's what they wanted from me, just like anybody today would be disappointed if they dropped in on Prince and found him slopping about in an old cardigan.'

June 1974 – Slade: The Bangin' Man/She Did It To Me (Polydor 2058 492)

Home from their first Japanese tour, their second Australian, and their *fifth* American, Slade's attention now was focused on a feature film, hatched by filmmakers Andrew Birkin and Richard Loncraine. They accompanied the band to the US, but not to capture the shows; rather, they were working on their screenplay, the tale of a fictitious band that rises from obscurity in a grim midlands city to become the biggest group of the age. Yes, completely fictitious.

THE BANGIN' MAN

NOT DISTRIBUTION

SLADE

So 'The Bangin' Man' was knocked out while their minds were understandably elsewhere, and though it climbed to Number 3, it was *only* Number three. Charles Aznavour and, strengthening the MOR logjam even further, the Drifters, stood between Slade and the top. Once, the boys would have annihilated them both.

June 1974 – Marty Wilde: All Night Girl/She's A Mover (Magnet MAG 110

Zappo had already proved that Marty Wilde was not the only Fifties veteran to be suddenly invigorated by the sight of Alvin Stardust on TV, but he was probably the most convincing. Sadly, this reversion to his own name fared no more successfully than its predecessor but Wilde probably wasn't too disappointed. He was about to join Adam Faith and David Essex on the set of the most eagerly awaited new movie of the year – *Stardust*, the sequel to *That'll Be The Day*.

13 June 1974 – Top Of The Pops: Meet the new boss, prettier than the old boss

Not everybody welcomed the crop of new bands that were creeping into the chart (or leaping onto the Glamwagon) as 1974 marched on. Even among the kids who had welcomed Bolan and Bowie aboard, and who had themselves had to face down the disgust of their elders, there was a sense that pop had taken a turn for the worst and talent had finally been sacrificed to Max Factor.

The old guard took it hardest, though. They were the people who had fought for rock to become established; who had battled in the trenches of the early-Sixties beat boom to face down the enraged military veterans ('I fought in two world wars to guarantee your freedom, so get your hair cut because you look like a girl') and outraged London cab drivers ('string 'em up, the lot of them') who viewed pop as a serious affront to their morality.

Now they were complaining that this new noise wasn't music, that the boys all looked like girls these days, and 'You'd never have lasted five minutes at the Star Club if you'd gone out dressed like that.'

Arrows were back at *Top Of The Pops* when they encountered their first taste of vintage pop distaste, sitting in the make-up room alongside Alan Price. Promoting his latest single, the vaudevillian throwback 'Jarrow Song', Price was having just enough powder applied to his face to ensure that it didn't go all shiny when the studio lights hit him. Seated next to him, meanwhile, Jake Hooker was going the whole hog.

Alan Merrill: 'Jake went through a whole menu of what he wanted for his make-up. Eyeliner, blush, lipstick, the lot. Sitting close by and in earshot and not to be outdone, I said to my makeup girl "Please make mine the same". Alan Price made a thoroughly disgusted face and stormed off out of the makeup room. Glam rock was obviously something he loathed.'

The evening's host, incidentally, was Paul Burnett, making his first ever appearance on the show following his arrival at Radio 1 (to host the Sunday morning show) earlier in the year. His first jingles for the show were recorded by a dream combination of Arrows plus John Miles. 'Paul Burnett's really gettin' it on/All there is to hear.'

June 1974 – Bullfrog: Glancy/In The City (Cube BUG 44)

Originally known as Mandrake, this Consett, County Durham hard-rock band took third place in a talent contest sponsored by EMI – and wound up on Cube. Their one and only 45 was titled for the band's former vocalist, Mick Glancy; Pete MacDonald was now fronting the group.

June 1974 – Fancy: Wild Thing/Fancy (Atlantic K10383)

It had hit single written all over it. A lascivious bass line that throbbed hot and nasty. A guitar that drooled across one of rock's most memorable riffs; a synthesiser line which felt like K-Y dripping from vertiginous heights and, over it all, a young lady in a seemingly serious state of sexual arousal moaning, 'Wild thing, I think you…move me?'

Donna Summer had nothing on Helen Caunt, and Helen Caunt had nothing on. October 1971's *Penthouse* Pet and well-versed, therefore, in the vicarious manipulation of juvenile male hormones, Ms Caunt turned in what remains one of the most pointedly sexual vocal performances ever to transfix an American radio audience. No wonder her band was called Fancy.

'One night back in summer 1973,' producer

Mike Hurst explains, 'I thought the time was right to do a new, rocked-up version of the Troggs' classic "Wild Thing". I knew a great many good musicians, but my favourite guitarist by far was [the Spencer Davis Group's] Ray Fenwick.'

Fenwick introduced former Affinity bassist Mo Foster to the proceedings, enticing him away from a sessions career that included work with the likes of Jimmy Helms and Olivia Newton-John. Then, with Henry Spinetti adding drums and Alan Hawkshaw supplying keyboards, they got to work on 'Wild Thing'.

Hurst continues, 'Ray immediately went for the idea of using a female vocal for "Wild Thing". It made it sound more raunchy, especially when we found Helen to sing, or perhaps I should say breathe, the words.' The result was a dirty, low-down track, with all the heavy breathing and suggestive orgasmic guitar and bass work.

Hopes to have their creation storm the UK charts were dismissed when Hurst could not find a single label in the land willing to unleash this smorgasbord of squelch upon a naïve and innocent public. The American Big Tree label, however, was nowhere near as squeamish and in June 1974 'Wild Thing' commenced its rise up the Hot 100. It finally peaked at Number 14, earning Fancy a gold disc in the process. Then, having reduced American radio to a sweaty, breathless heap, 'Wild Thing' crossed the Pacific to seduce the Australian Top Twenty. It charmed most of Europe and became one of the biggest hits of the year in Holland and Belgium.

It even, in the end, impacted in Britain in an odd sort of way, when the Goodies released their own take on 'Wild Thing' (c/w 'Nappy Love' – Bradleys BRAD 7524) and took Fancy's original sexiness to its ultimate conclusion.

'Come on, hold me tight,' breathes vocalist Bill Oddie. And then, 'Uuurrgggh, not THAT tight.'

June 1974 – Cockney Rebel: Mr Soft/Such A Dream (EMI 2191)
June 1974 – Cockney Rebel: The Psychomodo (EMI EMC 3033)
June 1974 – Top Gear: Cockney Rebel

The most intoxicating album of the year and the most unexpected as well. 'The Human Menagerie' could easily have painted Cockney Rebel into a psychotic cul-de-sac, where serial-killer strings and orgiastic orchestras were the only shadows they could dance beneath. Instead, they stripped back to basics, all weirdo fiddle and exotic

intonation and let the drama breed with its own sense of bravado.

Add on one of the most elegantly menacing cover photos of all time (the work of Mick Rock, who also pictured Queen) and 'The Psychomodo' was madness on the rocks, the death trip at the end of the rainbow that 'Judy Teen' sent the country pirouetting across.

Upending the intentions of its long-playing predecessor, 'The Psychomodo's key cuts moved away from the epics – the swirling 'Ritz' and the ponderous 'Cavaliers' were little more than litanies of one-liners that haunted via their very length.

Instead, it was the vignettes, the paranoid streak of stardom that stutters through 'Sweet Dreams', the oddly romantic 'Bed In The Corner' and the skulking intimacy of 'Mr Soft' – their latest hit single (it reached Number 9) – that marked 'The Psychomodo's territory. And even they were only the lead-up to the final decay of 'Sling It' – every disaster movie ever made, crammed into the length of a heartbeat – and 'Tumbling Down', a lament for the death of innocence and youth, capped by a chorus that the fans still mourn today. 'Oh dear!' declares Harley. 'Look what they've done to the blues.'

No, Steve, look what *you* did to them.

June 1974 – 10cc: The Wall Street Shuffle/ Gismo My Way (UK 69)
June 1974 – 10cc: Sheet Music (UK UKAL 1007)

At the beginning of November 1973, 10cc returned to Strawberry to begin work on their next album, sharing the studio with Mike McGear, who was recording his 'McGear' album under the auspices of his brother Paul McCartney.

Working nights while the Maccas worked days, 10cc nevertheless made their presence felt on 'McGear', with Godley-Creme in particular lending a hand; ever since the Hotlegs days, they had been developing the Gizmo (note different spelling), a device which enabled a guitarist to achieve maximum sustain while duplicating a variety of orchestral sounds.

The McCartneys returned the favour. 'We often overlapped,' Graham Gouldman remembers. 'The studio was completely crammed with equipment and there was this tremendous buzz – y'know, Paul would come in and we'd play him our stuff and vice versa. And I think that kind of inspired us as well. There was just a tremendous atmosphere.'

Destined to become one of the most successful albums of 1974, 'Sheet Music' remained on the British charts for over six months and qualified for a gold disc. It was also the album that cemented 10cc's reputation among the most inventive and exciting British bands of the decade.

'It grips the heart of rock'n'roll like nothing I've heard before,' raved *Melody Maker*, before describing 10cc as 'the Beach Boys of "Good Vibrations", the Beatles of "Penny Lane", they're the mischievous kid next door, they're the Marx Brothers, they're Jack and Jill, they're comic cuts characters and they're sheer brilliance.' Eric Stewart agreed; he told that same paper, 10cc's music is 'better than 90 per cent of the sheer unadulterated crap that's in the charts.'

Kevin Godley singles out the haunting 'Somewhere In Hollywood' as one of the key tracks: 'A long and complex song detailing Godley and Creme's abiding love for all things "movie". We didn't have the tools or the talent to make a proper film so we made our sonic ode to film instead. The electric piano harp effect that starts the track still gives me goosebumps, too.'

Gouldman agrees. 'Sheet Music' is probably the definitive 10cc album. What it was, our second album wasn't our difficult second album, it was our best second album. It was the best second album we ever did.'

June 1974 – Be Bop Deluxe: Axe Victim (Harvest SHVL 11689)

They may have signed a major label recording contract and they might have seen a new single hit the stores. But did Be Bop Deluxe have anything to smile about? They probably did, but they didn't let it show. Because Be Bop made it plain from the outset that they wanted nothing at all to do with this Glam business.

A tour with Cockney Rebel was their first reward for getting this far, facing a 'somewhat more 'poppy' crowd' than Be Bop had encountered in their past – their only previous experience of touring was with the decidedly un-poppy Peter Hammill. Even when Bill Nelson acknowledged that Be Bop had 'sprung to life from the same glittering root' as Steve Harley's boys, 'the more interesting fringe of Glam Rock', he sounded dismissive. His ambition was to 'develop a more hybrid flower.'

In concert, Be Bop were spectacularly garish. In the shops, they were a painted nightmare, peeping out from behind a guitar on their album sleeve. But on vinyl, they hit you with what they really thought: 'You came to watch the band,' they sang, 'To see us play our part/We hoped you'd lend an ear/You hoped we'd dress like tarts.'

June 1974 – Michael Des Barres: Teenybopper Death (He Loves You, Bernadette)

With Silverhead having broken up in everything but name (the end would be announced in July), Michael Des Barres announced his next project would unite him with Brinsley Schwarz songwriter Nick Lowe for a solo single mourning the death, in May, of Bernadette Whelan at David Cassidy's White City show. Or, rather, it was announced for him.

'I was at the Speakeasy with Nick Lowe and [journalist] Nick Kent and we were talking about the David Cassidy thing that had happened the day before. I found this unbelievably relevant and incredibly important to pop culture, so I said let's write a song called 'Teenybopper Death (He Loves You, Bernadette)' and thought this was genius.

'Well, Nick Kent wrote about it. We hadn't even written the song, it was never written, never recorded. But he put it in the *NME* and the shit hit the fan. The father went bonkers, the national press had pictures of me with skulls and pound signs all around my picture. I was a pariah.'

Des Barres tried to explain. 'Bernadette's death upset me a great deal. I expect somebody to be killed at Altamont, at a Stones gig or a Silverhead gig, but I don't expect them to be killed at a light entertainment concert.'

But an opening lyric like 'Crushed at the front, it was no publicity stunt' (the only line, in fact, that was ever composed) was scarcely likely to endear Des Barres to a tabloid press that – then as now – looked for the worst intentions in everyone bar itself. Particularly at a time when so many people were still scrutinising the media's own role in inciting the kind of hysteria that led to Bernadette's death.

'I figured it was sociologically interesting and I am very media-conscious,' he told the press. 'I am not an offensive person.' His explanations fell on deaf ears. 'Even the degenerates who I was getting coke from; even the coke dealers turned their backs on me,' he recalls, 'because I was this awful exploiter of this poor girl's memory while being completely innocent and wanting to point out the absolute awfulness of this pop star having to deal with this poor young girl...it was a very interesting story,

'It didn't make sense and I wanted to make sense of it. But it was seen in another light. I understand the grief of the father, but what it did was, it propelled me to make some changes.'

June 1974 – Mott the Hoople: Foxy Foxy/ Trudi's Song (CBS 2439)

Mott the Hoople's latest single was a magnificent slice of faux Spector and should have been at least as big as the similar statements that Wizzard were making. Instead it scratched to a lowly Number 33 and the band were still contemplating their follow-up when Ariel Bender quit.

'They were going through another change, another downer,' Bender recalls. 'Even while I was in the band, they were talking about changing Mott the Hoople, going for another sort of style and my leaving really was six of one [he jumped], half a dozen of the other [they pushed], if you know what I mean. But it was biggest mistake they ever made and the biggest mistake I ever made.

'What you had there, and what had probably been there for years before I came into the band was, I believe, that when Ian came into the band he stole the show because he became what they were, Mott the Hoople.

'So you had all this backstabbing, jealous stuff going on and it was still going on while I was there, you could never get rid of it. Ian had come in and he was Mott the Hoople, the others were the others. And when I came in, when this creature called Ariel Bender came in, he joined Ian at the front, whereas before Mick Ralphs had always been at the back with Overend Watts and Buffin.'

If that was the case; if Bender's departure really was at least partially engineered by Watts and Buffin in an attempt to restore some false sense of balance to the band. Hunter's solution to the departure of Mott the Hoople's second guitarist in under a year was nothing short of patricidal. He asked Mick Ronson to join.

June 1974 – Sparks: Girl From Germany/ Beaver O'Lindy (Bearsville K15816)

How does a band know that they've made it? When the oldies start getting reissued.

June 1974 – Marc Bolan: The Beginning Of Doves (Track 2410 201)
June 1974 – Marc Bolan: Jasper C Debussy/ Hippy Gumbo/The Perfumed Garden Of Gulliver Smith

And how does a band know that they're past it? When they no longer care that the oldies are getting reissued. In 1972, Marc Bolan took out an injunction to prevent this gathering of pre-Tyrannosaurus Rex demos and outtakes from being released. Two years later, it came out with a murmur.

June 1974 – The Rats: Turtle Dove/Oxford Donna (Good Ear EAR 101)
June 1974 – The Rats: First Long Play Record (Good Ear)

The first signings to former Joe Cocker manager Nigel Thomas' Good Ear label, Rats accompanied their second single with their debut album, an almost-self titled set cut with future Babys mastermind Adrian Millar.

As a dry-run for Millar's future project, it's a great glam-pop confection that has deservedly been reissued (RPM 322) since the band's rediscovery via the 'Boobs' compilation.

June 1974 – Suzi Quatro: Too Big/I Wanna Be Free (RAK 175)

A lesser hit than Quatro's reputation demanded but a lesser record than her fans deserved, the oddly pedestrian 'Too Big' peaked at Number 14.

June 1974 – Hector: Bye Bye Bad Days/Lady (DJM DJS 303)

The second and last single by 'the ultimate in Bovver Rock', as they dropped the bovver and donned black velvet catsuits and then broke up after a particularly atrocious gig at that Sweet-endorsed of permissive tolerance, Portsmouth's Mecca Ballroom. 'Bye Bye Bad Bad Days' would be reborn aboard 'Killed By Glam: 16 UK Junk Shop Glam Rarities From The Seventies' (Moonboot MB 01)

20 June 1974 – Everybody out

The mid-Seventies were rife with strikes, but none hit the music industry as hard as the technician's dispute that closed down *Top Of The Pops* for a heart-stopping seven weeks in the summer of 1974.

The 13 June edition was the last to be broadcast before the techs downed tools; it would be 8 August before matters were resolved. In the interim, the mighty suffered, the minnows perished and the general public was forced to make up its own mind as to which records it wanted to send to the top.

It was a bitter time, but Mickie Most – of course – saw its commercial possibilities. He asked Alan Merrill to write a song called 'Strike' as

a possible new Arrows single. Recorded at Morgan Studios it was shelved when it became apparent that the strike would be over before the single was ready (Merrill later rewrote it as 'Wake Up').

June 1974 – David Bowie: Diamond Dogs/ Holy Holy (RCA 0293)
'Diamond Dogs' was released as Bowie commenced his first post-retirement tour in the United States, a massive outing that would scour the country with a vast and immobile Hunger City stage set designed to replicate the mood of 'Diamond Dogs' but which he swiftly tired of as the tour went on.

By the time the outing took a summer break, he had turned his back both on the tour's theatrical concept and rock'n'roll itself, delving into the same funk and R&B roots that Marc Bolan had already been playing with for a year and preparing to re-emerge as the Philadelphia Soul Boy of 1975's 'Young Americans'.

Breaking from manager Tony Defries and the MainMan organization in March 1975, on the eve of that album's release, furthered his removal from his past, so we will say goodbye to him now with a single that struggled to Number 21 and was best bought for its B-side, a seething Spiders remake of his first single of 1971, 'Holy Holy'.

Cut during the 'Aladdin Sane' sessions and unreleased until now, it returned Bowie, in spirit at least, to the state in which he opened this book; as Gary Glitter would say, we should remember him this way.

June 1974 – Iron Virgin: Rebels Rule/Ain't No Clown (Deram DM 416)
Stunned by the perfidious Macca's decision to upstage their startling cover of 'Jet', Iron Virgin selected a riotous original for their follow-up. Sadly, it did no better than its predecessor.

'Rebels Rule' was rediscovered following its appearance on 'Velvet Tinmine: 20 Junk Shop Glam Ravers' (RPM 251).

June 1974 – Top Of The Pops Volume 38 (Hallmark SHM 865)
Dolphins quake, dogs block their ears…yes, it's 'Volume 38' and here are both 'Sugar Baby Love' and 'This Town Ain't Big Enough For Both Of Us' to punish you for turning the bass up on your music centre. Former Sparks bassist Martin Gordon reflects on the latter, which he purchased at the time and remembers feeling 'vaguely flattered that someone would go to the trouble of transcribing the bass parts' and took it as a compliment. The end result didn't sound too bad, as I recall. But then you add the similarly shriek-laden 'Sugar Baby Love' to the show and the human ear should not be subjected to such sounds.

Which is unfortunate, because 'Volume 38' tries hard to please all comers. 'Shang-A-Lang' rocks with knowingly daft enthusiasm and 'Red Dress' seethes harder than Alvin's original. Other period hits have their own set of charms, too. But still one's ears return to the Rubettes and Sparks and, though the *Top Of The Pops* studios might not have been big enough for both of them, this album is.

ON THE BOX
6 June 1974 – Top Of The Pops – Sparks, Gary Glitter, Cozy Powell, the Rubettes, Bryan Ferry
13 June 1974 – Top Of The Pops: Arrows, Cozy Powell, Elton John, Gary Glitter, Showaddywaddy
22 June 1974 – Saturday Scene: Mott the Hoople
29 June 1974 – Saturday Scene: The Sweet

ON THE SHELF
June 1974 – Zippers: Streak Up And Down/ Funk 74 (Youngblood 1070)
June 1974 – Fuzz: I'm So Glad/All About Love (Pye DDS 104)

---

1 July 1974 – Lift Off With Ayshea: Slade
The eighth and final series begins with guest appearances from Slade ('The Bangin' Man'), Angel and the Flirtations. The series ran until 17 December.

July 1974 – Chicory Tip: Take Your Time Caroline/Me And Stan Foley (CBS 2507)
Two years after 'Son Of My Father', but not long after this became their third flop on a row, CBS dropped the band.

July 1974 – The Sweet: The Six Teens/Burn On The Flame (RCA LPBO 5037)
Having taken the top two slots last time, and with the new Suzi Quatro single, 'Too Big' still rising up the chart, Chinnichap were aiming for the Top Three this time.

They didn't get it. 'Too Big' was way too small and perished at Number 14. Mud peaked at Number 6. But they had higher hopes for the Sweet.

Brian Connolly was still fighting to recover his voice when the Sweet cut 'The Six Teens' at the end of May 1974 and thanking Chapman for at least turning in a song that 'isn't such a screamer as "Teenage Rampage".'

Indeed, slower and more studied than its predecessors, tinged with a hint of bitter-sweet nostalgia, 'The Six Teens' was scarcely even related to the Sweet singles of old. An acoustic base washed the rhythm and Connolly's vocal, a little deeper and darker since the attack, sounded almost haunted – and that despite a lyric that itched with cynical nostalgia.

'The Six Teens' traces the fates of Bobby and Billy, kids growing up immersed in the revolutionary rhetoric of the late Sixties ('Where were you in '68?'), as they come to terms with the fact that the revolution they fought for was simply another mass-marketed gimmick.

Heady stuff for a simple pop song, although by this time – mid-1974 – the Sweet had developed so quickly that the only real shock was that Chinn and Chapman wrote this. It could have been a Deep Purple B-side. Or a new Queen anthem. That band borrowed an awful lot from the Sweet in the vocal department, and it is one of rock history's saddest ironies that, when the Sweet themselves tried to reclaim their harmonies during 'The Six Teens', the UK media promptly condemned them for copying Freddie Mercury and co.

It was only later, Tucker growled, 'that I discovered that it had actually been written for Suzi Quatro and they were expecting us to turn it down, the same as we had all her other hits.'

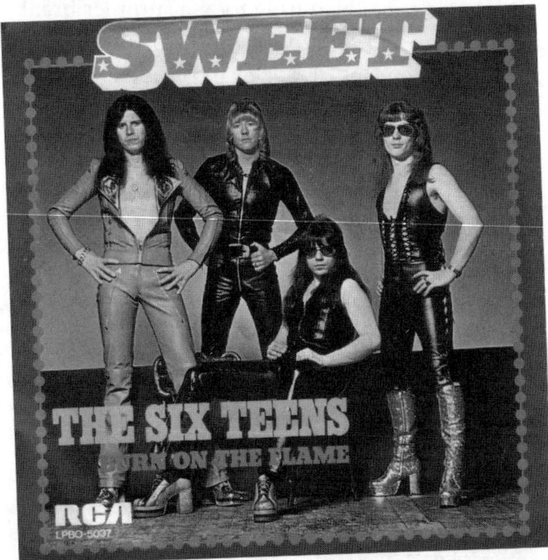

The BBC technicians' strike hit just as 'the Six Teens' commenced its rise and, deprived of their most traditional ally, *Top Of The Pops*, the Sweet seemed to flounder. An appearance on *Lift Off With Ayshea* on 8 July 1974 did as much as it could to push the record up the chart, but the week after 'The Six Teens' breached the Top Ten, the first in August, it was back down to Number 11. It had one more week in the Top Twenty and that was it

'There was the blackout and the BBC strike,' shrugs Scott, 'but you can't make these excuses, because a lot of other records still managed to sell a hell of a lot, other records still made it to Number 1.'

The week that 'The Six Teens' hit Number 9, the Three Degrees, Stephanie De Sykes, George McCrae, Charles Aznavour, the Drifters, Wings,

Slade and a reissue of the sixties anthem 'Young Girl' all stood between the Sweet and the Number 1 spot, 'and it was at that moment,' Scott continues, 'that we realised there was a difference in where we were going, what we should be doing and that we should not be trying to convince people who didn't want to be convinced.'

July 1974 – Mud: Rocket/Ladies (RAK 178)

The super-stellar 'Rocket' made it six hits out of six for Mud, rising to Number 6 and standing among the band's most ambitious releases ever. 'If you listen to this one, you can hear how hard we worked,' Gray recalled, although the session was probably a lot more difficult than it should have been.

The singer continued: 'I sat down for 24 hours doing the vocals on this one day and night with Mike Chapman. We had it all down on tape and the next morning we came into the studio and found the junior tape operator had made a mistake and wiped everything that we'd done.' With time running out, Chapman hustled Gray to the microphone and told him to simply do his best. In just two takes, Gray turned in a performance for the ages.

The band, too, rose to the occasion, with Rob Davis confirming his status as the great unsung guitar hero by turning in a solo that still sounds amazing. Triumphant and tricky, soaring and silly, it ends with a flourish that was ideal for kicking your leg in the air to. Which is just as well, because when the sickly green-clad Mud unveiled their latest dance, that's precisely what it involved.

Oh, and thanks, Les Gray, for *the* deathless catchphrase of the day. Long pause... 'Second verse.'

July 1974 – Glitter Band: Just For You/I'm Celebrating (Bell 1368)

The follow-up to 'Angel Face' was, once again, a chip off the old block, an echo of Gary's own latest efforts in its shifts from pounding Glam towards a more romantic approach. It did grow a little tiresome with repeated listens, but that didn't stop it climbing to Number 1, and making the Glitter Band an all but ubiquitous presence on television, and everywhere else.

John Springate: 'I don't think we ever thought about the Glitter band being a separate entity as such; it was just a thing that we did. What made it more difficult was we were doing his tours and our tours, we were constantly on the road, all the time, non- stop, and television all the time.'

By the time 'Just For You' completed its chart run in August, the Glitter Band had made no less than ten appearances on *Top Of The Pops* since Christmas, and Springate laughs, 'I remember I was out cleaning my car one day and my mum came out and said "Haven't you got *Top Of The Pops* tomorrow?" We were doing it so often it just got to that point. Which is a really bad attitude, but you can't help it.'

July 1974 – T Rex: Light Of Love/Explosive Mouth (T Rex MARC 8)

And speaking of foundering, 'Light Of Love' became Marc Bolan's first new single to miss out on the Top Twenty since 'King Of The Rumbling Spires' in 1969.

July 1974 – Eli Cuthbertson: I Need Your Love Tonight/Boogie Queen (EMI 2207)

With a Fifties rock'n'roll sound breaking out everywhere, Les Gray was surely not the only person wondering what might happen if the real Hound Dog singer turned his tonsils towards Glam Rock?

Elvis wasn't interested. But an Elvis impersonator, American Cuthbertson, was not so reticent, and with former Pretty Thing Wally Allen producing, he turned in this gigantic clash of the cultures.

July 1974 – New York Dolls: Stranded In The Jungle/Mystery Girls (Mercury 6052615)
July 1974 – New York Dolls: Too Much Too Soon (Mercury 6338498)

The Dolls' first album reached Number 116 in America, with an opening spot on the latest Mott the Hoople tour exposing the band to audiences their New York City stardom had never prepared them for. People genuinely did not enjoy the Dolls, not even Mott the Hoople fans, while their European profile wasn't much better.

The French, apparently, loved them, but British audiences preferred to measure them up against local talent and then write them off as lacking in almost every department.

By the spring of 1974, then, the Dolls were virtually back where they started, playing small clubs around the east coast and saving up songs for a second album, the prophetically titled 'Too Much, Too Soon'.

It was produced by Shadow Morton and *was* an improvement on its predecessor. But it fared even more poorly and, while the Dolls would struggle on for a while longer, even coming under the pre-Pistols managerial aegis of a pre-Pistols Malcolm McLaren (who dressed them up in red leather and sent them out to pretend to be Communists), their demise was a lot more important than their legacy.

Within a year of the Dolls splitting, the first punks were singing their praises. But even before that, their influence was being felt as Kiss guitarist Ace Frehley admitted that the Dolls had a lot to do with Kiss' own decision to make-up.

'The Dolls were the hottest thing around and we always wished we could be the Dolls because we were nobody at the time. But we weren't physically like the Dolls, who were small, skinny guys, so we decided to come on in black and silver instead.'

POSTSCRIPT: The New York Dolls hung on with Malcolm McLaren as their manager until late 1975. Frontman David Johansson subsequently launched a solo career, under his own name and as Buster Poindexter; guitarist Johnny Thunders and drummer Jerry Nolan formed the Heartbreakers.

Thunders passed away on 23 April 1991 and Nolan on 14 January 1992. The three surviving Dolls reformed in 2004, shortly before the death of Arthur Kane (13 July 2004). The remaining pair subsequently toured and released a new album.

July 1974 – Paul Da Vinci: Your Baby Ain't Your Baby Anymore/She'll Only Hurt You (Penny Farthing PEN 843)
July 1974 – The Rubettes: Tonight/Silent Movie Queen (Polydor 2058499)

The success of 'Sugar Baby Love' not only provoked a rapid-fire follow-up from the Rubettes. Paul Da Vinci, the hit's original, absentee vocalist, surfaced as well to enjoy a minor (Number 20) hit in silk bowtie, pressed white suit and an opening falsetto that, even on TV, you could see him working hard to muster.

With Alan Williams taking over at the front and white jackets switched for red, 'Tonight' was a magnificent record, heroically stepping beyond the parameters of its predecessor to emerge an almost pristine ballad (Nick Lowe later penned an exquisite rewrite, also titled 'Tonight') into which the Rubettes' own musical quirks brewed like a good cup of coffee.

'There was a conscious effort to retain the falsetto vocals within the Rubettes sound,' Bill Hurd explains, 'and also to keep and build on that big vocal harmony sound that had introduced us with "Sugar Baby Love". Over the years we've always kept that in mind and strong vocals have become a trademark of the Rubettes sound throughout.'

So has a good sense of humour. Listen closely and you could almost believe that the backing vocals are poking fun at those newly arrived upstart claimants to the Rubettes crown, Showaddywaddy, then getting a poke in at Sha Na Na as well. Unfortunately, Bill Hurd denies the charge. 'We always had a lot of input into vocal arrangements and the chant was not pointed in any way at Showaddywaddy.'

Still it raised a knowing smirk among fans and, with all that going for it, it was incredible to see 'Tonight' falter at Number 12, another apparent victim of the BBC technicians' strike that blotted out *Top Of The Pops*.

July 1974 – Bryan Ferry: Another Time Another Place (Island ILPS 9284)

No sooner was 'These Foolish Things' complete, than Ferry was contemplating its follow-up. 'It seems a pity not to do another solo,' he smiled. 'There are thousands of other songs I'd like to have a crack at destroying.'

His final solo release for the time being (he now returned his attention exclusively to Roxy Music) 'Another Time Another Place' duplicated its predecessor's format with dramatic class and triumphed both in performance and content. 'You Are My Sunshine' is dark clouds and rainstorms, and that is one of the bright spots.

Another pleasure, albeit one for which he cannot take the credit, was following the *New Musical Express*' campaign to rechristen him with any name but his own. Over the next year or so, readers would thrill to the musical adventures of El Ferranti, Brain Fury and even Brown Furry. Journalist Nick Kent later dismissed this campaign as childish, but it was highly amusing at the time.

July 1974 – Mr Big: Ee I'm Alright/I Ain't Been A Man (Epic EPC 2464)

It was one of rock history's funny little tricks that decreed Mr Big should not become big until after the era that spawned them was over. That the musical currents that brought them to life should already have mutated into something else; and that they themselves should have mutated too, so that 'Romeo', their biggest hit, was so different to the Punk Rock of the day that it's sometimes difficult to remember they even co-existed.

It was not always like that. Once, Mr Big were so firmly in tune with the scene around them that their breakthrough seemed imminent for months. And, before that, they were knocking so loudly on the door that even the deaf had heard of them.

Like so many of his contemporaries, frontman Jeff 'Dicken' Pain had already been around the houses a few musical times. 'After leaving school, I tried a few wretched jobs that I hated,' he recalls, while blotting out that necessary misery by playing with his band.

The brilliantly named Chaulkie's Painful Legg formed around 1967-68 and played 'village halls covering songs like "Lazy Sunday". I'd also written a couple of songs by then, so we recorded a demo that was produced by the late Colin Saunders at his mother's house in Oxford. [Saunders later became the founder of SSL Solid State Logic].'

A short time later, in mid 1969, the band descended upon London, demo in hand. 'The Beatles were recording their 'Abbey Road' album at the time, so my brother Dave and his friend (would you believe it) gatecrashed the studio and, amazingly, they were allowed in to watch and chat for a while. The rest of us just waited outside in our van with all the other Beatles fans. Then my brother came out and told us what they had been doing; I remember being so excited.

'Not long after that Mary Hopkin arrived at the studio, so we got her autograph and then Dave handed her our demo tape, which she said she would give to George Martin for us, and that was that.'

Though they never did hear from Martin, the band returned to London, marched into the Apple offices and demanded to know what was happening. They learned that Bill Collins, the manager of the band Badfinger, had heard the tape and loved Dicken's voice.

'We were given an audition at the Abbey Road Studios. I can't remember who was listening up in that control room, maybe Mr Collins, but we were completely useless. I sang, but the others – bassist Paul Harris and drummer Vince Chaulk – just couldn't play a note.' Turning them down on the spot, Collins did suggest Dicken leave the band, move to London and start again from scratch, but the boy said no. 'It all seemed so frightening and lonely for me. I didn't want to leave all my friends, so that was the end of that.'

A new band formed. Burnt Oak lined up as Dicken, Chaulkie and bassist Peter Crowther and by early 1971 were regulars on the London nightclub scene before graduating to the Top Rank ballrooms. Which they promptly fell out of, following a gig where they opened for Slade. Dicken swore at the audience, the newspapers got hold of the story and the band was banned from the Top Rank circuit amid a howl of tabloid condemnation.

Weeks later, Burnt Oak had a regular gig at the Marquee Club – they played there for the first time on 10 July 1971, ran a month-long residency through October-November and, by the time they played there for the final time, in 1977, had trod those boards almost 20 times.

Chaulkie left and new drummer John Burnip stepped in. A publishing deal with Red Bus followed...an unfortunate deal that saw Dicken sign his entire output away, including numbers that had not even been written yet.

'I naively thought that I was just registering my songs/titles for the PRS when actually I was signing my copyrights over to them. They also asked me to put down all my ideas/titles as well. "Aleyloo", "Bernadette", "Buffalo Bill" etc. I didn't bother to finish these titles, but the melodies do exist somewhere in my mind. The song titles that I did go on to finish Red Bus claimed, even "Goodbye World" which was just a title – no lyric. And if that wasn't enough, they rarely accounted to me.

A record deal did materialise with one of EMI's imprints and a Burnt Oak single, 'All Together', was apparently released – Dicken recalls the release, but neither he nor any known collector actually possesses a copy. Clearly it failed to sell and, 'after a bit of PR and a few promises, we moved on to do more gigs around the country.'

Burnt Oak became Mr Big one night at the Marquee. 'We were looking at the headline in a tabloid newspaper, all about a porn king and we toyed with the idea of changing our name to Mr Big. Contrary to what has been written about us using the song title from the rock band Free. Marquee club manager Jack Barrie got wind of it inside the club and, without much fuss, he put the name up on the front door and refused to change it. And that was that.'

The name-change prompted an image change, as Dicken recalls: 'Someone came up with the idea that we should dress as Pearly Kings and pretend to be Cockneys.'

It was not a unique image; Bearded Lady were touting a similar look at the same time. Undeterred, 'We got some pearly buttons and each of us then went about making our own waistcoats and trousers. It was amazing; we certainly sparkled!'

CBS swooped, A&R chief Dan Loggins picking them up late in 1973. A label showcase in the East End furthered the group's new image and their next single was scheduled for June. But a last-minute change of heart with the A-side saw 'Genevieve' shelved and replaced by 'Ee, I'm Alright', 'me doing my Steve Marriott thing.' It brought the band an appearance on *Lift Off* on 19 August and, the following month, a role in an episode of the police drama *Softly Softly*, singing actor Paul Nicholas appearing as their vocalist.

July 1974 – Sparks: Amateur Hour/Lost And Found (Island WIP 6203)

With Jook guitarist Trevor White and bassist Ian Hampton replacing the sacked Martin Gordon, the new Sparks line-up debuted on *Top Of The Pops* on 23 May with the performance that pushed 'This Town Ain't Big Enough' to its peak

of Number 2. And, while the single slipped from the Top Twenty with unprecedented haste, from Number 9 to nowhere in the space of a week, Island lost no time in following it up.

Just a fortnight after its predecessor left the chart, 'Amateur Hour' entered the chart at Number 42. The following week, this beginners' guide to adolescent sex was Number 17; it ultimately crested at Number 7 without *Top Of The Pops*. That damned strike again.

Still, it was all very confusing for the new boys. White and Hampton still recall the absolute disorientation into which they were suddenly flung and the sense of frustration that went with it. To be appearing on countless television shows, performing the hits they had no part in creating was, admitted White, even worse than hearing one or other of the album tracks on the radio and thinking, 'That's the biggest band in the country, I'm a member of it and nobody even knows.' But that was all to change as Sparks went out to meet their adoring public for the first time.

July 1974 –Heavy Metal Kids: Hangin' On/ Rock'n'Roll Man (Atlantic K10465)

The Heavy Metal Kids' genesis lies in a jazzy-blues band called Heaven who plied the UK club circuit as England's answer to Chicago. By early 1972, however, their original four-piece brass section had been reduced to a lone sax/trumpeter and an ever-revolving line-up had just one original member left.

The end drew even closer in May 1972 when,

in short succession, drummer Pete Phipps left to join Gary Glitter's band and manager Rikki Farr called time on his involvement and took back their van, amps and equipment – only to loan it back when newly arrived guitarist Mickey Waller suggested a farewell show with bassist Ronnie Thomas, singer Terry Scott, keyboard-player Brian Johnston and two members of Long John Baldry's touring band, drummer Keith Boyce and guitarist Bob Weston.

'Rikki Farr thinks we're doing one gig in England,' Boyce laughs, 'but in fact we absconded with the van and gear to France where Mickey had set up some gigs. We ended up staying there for five months and went from rags to riches, there and back again.'

Only at the end of the summer did the band return to England, minus frontman Scott who decided to remain in Paris. 'So we decided that we'd try this singer, Gary Holton, Mickey and Ronnie knew from another of Rikki Farr's bands, Biggles. Gary came down and sang with us and we thought he was great, so that was the beginning of the Kids.'

With Weston having departed to join Fleetwood Mac and Johnston, too, leaving (he later reappeared in Whitesnake), the newly named Heavy Metal Kids recruited Argentinean keyboard player Danny Peyronel and played a handful of shows as a four-piece before Boyce and Holton spotted guitarist Cosmo in another band. 'We thought he was amazing, so we asked him to join us.'

From the outset, the Heavy Metal Kids were playing with image, wrapping their raucous blend of streetwise rock, reggae and balladry into a Dickensian image of street-urchin chic – an homage of sorts to one of Holton's old acting gigs, playing the Artful Dodger in a production of *Oliver*, crossed with a trip through Biba's dustbins.

Boyce: 'I used to share a house with Gary and his French model girlfriend and a couple of our roadies in Kennington in South London and we used to like going down the East End on a Sunday morning to Brick Lane, where we used to buy lots of stuff for the house. You could pick up some great gear in them days for next to nothing there.

'We furnished the house with all sorts of Thirties, Forties and Fifties gear. Lots of kitsch stuff that we were really into. We thought our

place looked like something out of the film *Performance*, which we all loved, but it probably looked more like *Steptoe And Son*'s house! We used to buy tons of old clothes down the Lane and that's how our early look came about. All old second-hand clobber, but we liked the look of it and it was dirt cheap.'

They were also unrepentant Glam fans. 'We loved it, as we thought music had got too serious and everyone was looking terrible dressing down in tatty jeans and T-shirts. It was great to see some flamboyant styles and colour come back and hear some good, short, sharp, poppy songs.'

But audiences did not necessarily agree. At the Gibus Club in Paris, the bottles rained down so hard Holton had to hide behind the amps and there were several UK shows where the crowd left the room, long before the band stopped playing.

There were some magnificent performances, as well, though. 'The Kings Road Theatre in Chelsea for one. We did a few nights there, all the darlings were out and they loved us. We also did a few nights at Biba's Rainbow Room in Kensington and that was great as well. Very Glam and such a cool room, with all those pretty, skinny girls dressed up in their Biba dresses and makeup and the guys in their snakeskin and leathers. That was *real* style.'

'It's the performance that counts,' Holton explained. 'That's what you're up there for. What you do offstage is boring, no-one really cares. So what you have to do is, make what you do offstage as exciting as what you do when you're on, or at least make people think that's what you're doing.'

The Kids were treating the Speakeasy to a typically irreverent set when Dave Dee, of Dozy, Beaky, Mick and Tich fame 'discovered' them. 'One of our managers, the late Laurie O'Leary, managed the club,' Boyce recalls, 'so we played there every few weeks at the start of the band. It was a great club to go to but it was a really tough audience to play to, mainly full of older serious musos, some of them big names and music-business types.

'Most bands died a death there and we had a hard time at first. But Gary became more lippy and funny with the crowd as the weeks went on and pretty soon we were going down a storm there. So I think that sold Dave Dee on us, because if you could go down well there you could go down well anywhere.'

By the end of the year, the band was signed to Atlantic and recording at Olympic Studios. Now it was time for the real work to begin.

July 1974 – Bay City Rollers: Summerlove Sensation/Bringing Back The Good Times (Bell 1369)

Fan loyalties had never been so divided. Supporters of the previous kings of the teenybop pile, the Osmonds and David Cassidy, had at least regarded one another with a mutual respect, tempers flaring only when the subject of looks came about.

Hardfaced and not at all frightened to use their fists, Rollergirls had no time for diplomacy. They would fight to the death if necessary for the honour of the adored objects and the soundtrack to the ensuing carnage was 'Summerlove Sensation'. No matter where you went, the Rollers' finest hour by far was to be heard drifting out of beach transistors and fairground sound systems all season long. With a title like that, how could it not have been?

Fifties production, Beach Boys harmonies, strings and lyrics that utterly predict the opening scenes from *Grease*, 'Summerlove Sensation' is up there with First Class' 'Beach Baby' among the quintessential summertime singles of all time, though it ultimately faltered at Number 3 on the chart.

July 1974 – True Adventure: Where The Roxy Used To Be/Outlaw Love (Decca 1974)

Another side project for Mandrake Paddle Steamer mainstays Brian Engel and Martin Briley, last seen masquerading as Starbuck. They're still glamming it up furiously, though, with pianist/drummer Sandy Davis' flatmate, DJ Mike Reid, on board to help with the singalong chorus. And next time a pub quiz demands to know which member of Soft Machine once played on a Glam record...it was bassist Roy Babbington. Another track exhumed by the 'Blitzing The Ballroom: 20 UK Power Glam Incendiaries' compilation (Psychic Circle PCCD 7021).

July 1974 – Would you like milk and cookies with that?

American Glam was a sickly creature, as Jobriath had both discovered and proved. But maybe he was too po-faced about everything. What American kids really wanted was fun and Milk'n'Cookies were out to give them some.

A flash-looking four-piece with a predilection for white bow-ties and pink dungarees and an endearing line in what future generations would describe as Power Pop, Milk'n'Cookies had formed the previous year. But nobody really paid them any attention until the secretary of the Sparks fanclub, a fellow New Yorker named Joseph Fleury, called up yet another ex-pat American, Sal Maida, and suggested he give them a listen.

A brilliant bassist, Maida was one of the aspirants who called Sparks for an audition as they were putting together their first British band. He disqualified himself when he admitted he was American – the brothers wanted a British band. But Roxy Music were more cosmopolitan; weeks after the Sparks disappointment, Maida auditioned for the revolving bassist role in the band, as they prepared to go out on the road with 'Stranded'. It was only a temporary gig but he knew he would land on his feet.

Maida: 'The Roxy Music tour was over, so Joseph said "Hey, what you gonna do now?" I hadn't really thought about it, so they asked if I wanted to join this new band they were working with – "They sent us their demo, they're fantastic and the first thing we want to do is put you in the band".'

Fleury elaborated: 'Ian North, the singer, had written to us saying that the band were great Sparks fans and asked if we would come and see them next time we were in New York. At the time, things were getting really difficult with Adrian Fisher (Sparks' lead guitarist). He hated the band, he hated the music, he was simply in it for the money.

So Ron and Russell were looking for someone to replace him and for a while it looked as though Ian might be suitable. In the end he proved otherwise...'

Maida: 'They played me the stuff, I said okay and they said "They're like 17 years old and really good, really raw. They need some work, but you would be a great addition, give them some musical credibility." Whatever! So I listened to the tape and said "Yeah, these guys are great." I still didn't know if it was right for me but they talked me round, gave me this whole sales pitch. So I went down to play with them and the chemistry was through the roof.'

Things moved quickly. Fleury had already interested Sparks manager John Hewlett in the band; now Hewlett, just as he had with Sparks, piqued the interest of Muff Winwood at Island. Only this time, it was Winwood who flew to America to see the band, travelling to their Long Island base to witness the quartet running through its paces, as Maida recalls.

'He immediately said "Let's do it, I'll sign it, I'll produce it..." We went over to London, Island put us up in a big house, Muff produced, Rhett Davies was the assistant, it was pretty amazing.'

July 1974 – Washington Flyers: Another Saturday Morning/The Comets Are Coming (Dawn DNS 1076)

Another vehicle for Jimmy Edwards (ex-Stumpy), lost and then found by both 'Velvet Tinmine – 20 Junk Shop Glam Ravers' (RPM 251) and 'Glitter From The Litter Bin: 20 Junk Shop Glam Rarities From The Seventies' (Castle CMQCD 675).

July 1974 – Shelby: (Dance With The) Guitar Man/Jump Into The Fire (Santa Ponsa PNS 21)

Terry Clark fronted the Sixties band Jason Crest before finding himself lured into UA promo man Roger Easterby's Santa Ponsa set-up. He made several pseudonymous recordings for the label, including this neat rendering of the old Lee Hazlewood/Duane Eddy number, presciently released almost a year before Eddy himself made a comeback with the Tony Macaulay-penned 'Play Me Like You Play Your Guitar'.

July 1974 – Top Of The Pops Volume 39 (Hallmark SHM 870)

Check out the British charts for early summer 1974 and the middle of the road couldn't get any wider. From Charles Aznavour to Philly soul's Stylistics; from *Crossroads* crooner Stephanie De Sykes to the fuzzy rodent romp of the Wombles; it was the kind of season that should have prompted riots and rebellion. Instead, it all kicked off here instead.

'Top Of The Pops Volume 39' is spellbinding. A handful of the bigger baddies do creep aboard, but even Aznavour 'as no voice in the face of 'The Six Teens', Bolan's 'Light Of Love', Quatro's 'Too Big', Slade's 'The Bangin' Man' and Mud's magical 'Rocket', crazed guitar solo and all. Glam rock may have been on its way out as an all-consuming commercial force, but you wouldn't know it from the recreations here – now it's the originals that sound like less-than-perfect covers, and Top Of The Pops that spangles and sparks.

ON THE RADIO
16 July 1974 – Sounds of the Seventies: Andy Mackay
23 July 1974 – Top Gear: The Heavy Metal Kids
ON THE BOX
8 July 1974 – Lift Off With Ayshea: Hector
15 July 1974 – Lift Off With Ayshea: The Sweet
22 July 1974 – Lift Off With Ayshea: Barry Blue, Paul Da Vinci
29 July 1974 – Lift Off With Ayshea: Bay City Rollers, Bilbo Baggins
ON THE SHELVES
July 1974 – Shane: Hold On Billy/Shape Of Things To Come (RAK 176)
July 1974 – Starbuck: Heart Throb/Ricochet (Bradleys BRAD 7411)
July 1974 – Carmen: Bulerias/Stepping Stone (Regal Zonophone RZ3090)
July 1974 – Jack and the Giantkillers: Somebody's Been Sleeping In My Bed/People Don't Like Me (UK 71)
July 1974 – Ricky Wilde: I Wanna Go To A Disco/Bad Boy (UK 70)

August 1974 – Heavy Metal Kids: The Heavy Metal Kids (Atlantic K50047)

Having signed to Atlantic on the strength of their live performance, the band's eponymous debut album emerged in mid-1974. Produced by Dave Dee, the 'Heavy Metal Kids' took an already streamlined live show and honed it to needle sharpness, although Holton insisted, if you listened carefully enough, you could hear 'all the same mistakes we used to make on stage.' No matter. 'The Heavy Metal Kids' was one of the most exciting albums of 1974, no question, and their record label knew it.

Keith Boyce: 'Atlantic were right behind the band and they did splash out a lot of money on promotion, which led to some people were saying we were a hype. I guess because we had these full-page ads in all the music papers and we were on the TV and stuff like that. But we had been building up to it since late 1972, so it wasn't an overnight thing, although it might have looked like we just burst onto the scene to some people.'

In fact, the Heavy Metal Kids never became stars, never won any readers polls, never had a hit record. But, if you could roll back time to that moment in 1974 when the very first needle hit the very first pressing of their eponymous debut album, that would be impossible to prophecy.

'We had so much fun,' Boyce recalls of the sessions. 'Gary was an extremely funny guy. Ronnie Thomas is hilarious as well, so with the pair of them carrying on we used to laugh ourselves silly.'

The music was pretty entertaining, as well. Part unrepentant boogie band, part pub-rock leviathan and part good-time distillation of the best of Slade and the Faces, fronted by Holton's irresistible cackle, the Kids' flash slash-and-sashay assault had a cosmic energy that could transform even their ballads ('It's The Same', 'Nature Of My Game') into air-thumping anthems. 'We Gotta Go' is unadulterated bliss and the laconic reggae of 'Run Around Eyes' became a dry run for the Stones' later romp through 'Cherry Oh Baby', although they were not the only souls impressed by that particular track.

'We were in Olympic Studios recording "'Run Around Eyes",' Boyce continues, 'and I sensed someone was behind me. I looked round and there's this guy all dressed up from head to toe in green, with a cloak on and a hat with a feather in it, looking just like Robin Hood and he had a black girl on each arm.

'I was pretty taken back by this sight. Ronnie turns round and we all stop playing. Suddenly I realised who this guy is. Ronnie says to him, "What the fuck do you want? We're trying to record here mate," and I'm whispering to Ronnie "Shut up, don't you know who it is?"'

It was David Bowie, apologising for disturbing the band but explaining that he'd so enjoyed what he'd heard from outside the room that 'he couldn't resist coming in to have a look at these white boys playing reggae.

'He then invited us into the studio next door where he was recording and he played us this new song he'd just finished. It was "Rebel Rebel". It sounded incredible! Anyway we spent a good while there talking to him. Really great interesting guy and easy to get on with.'

'Ain't It Hard', 'Always Plenty Of Women', 'Hangin' On'... 'Heavy Metal Kids' walloped so many highs that the end of the album arrives much too quickly. But the closing 'Rock'n'Roll Man', heralded by one of the most resounding screams in history, is followed not by the sound of needle scraping label but a violent reprise for what remains the Kids' finest hour, the stomping, storming 'We Gotta Go'. But they would be back.

August 1974 – Be Bop DeRebel

The Night of the Long Knives. In August 1974, with the world at his feet, Steve Harley suddenly announced that he'd sacked his entire band and had already replaced them. Indeed, by the time he returned to *Top Of The Pops* on 22 August, riding 'Mr Soft' for a last few weeks, the familiar faces had already gone and with it the mad instrumentation that defined Cockney Rebel for the ages.

Only drummer Stuart Elliot survived the cull. Now, Harley was surrounded by 'real' musicians: former Family guitarist Jim Cregan, keyboard-player Duncan Mackay and bassist George Ford. It is true that future Cockney Rebel recordings would be better played. But would they sound as exciting?

Meanwhile, Be Bop Deluxe were undergoing some changes of their own, as Harvest Records buttonholed Bill Nelson one night and suggested the band really wasn't capable of matching its obvious potential. Nelson, too, disbanded his group and rebuilt it around Milton Reame-James (keyboards) and Paul Jeffreys (bass), both ex-Cockney Rebel, plus drummer Simon Fox.

'The four of us went out to do some quietish concerts to see how the line-up bedded in,' Nelson recalled. 'We played around 14 concerts, I think, but for me it didn't really gel.' Fox alone was retained; otherwise, 'It was back to the drawing board.'

POSTSCRIPT: Paul Jeffreys and Milton Reame-James remained together, forming their own band, Chartreuse, in 1976 and releasing a fabulous version of 'You Really Got Me' (c/w 'Rock And Roll Blues' – Klik KL 64). Jeffreys died on 21 December 1988, a victim of the Lockerbie air disaster.

August 1974 – Andy Mackay: In Search Of Eddie Riff (Island ILPS 9278)

Roxy Music's identity crisis took on another facet as saxophonist Andy Mackay released his solo debut, 'In Search Of Eddie Riff'. As was becoming the custom with Roxy Music spin-off records, the rest of the gang, plus Eno (but minus Ferry) convened for the sessions, but while the results had little in common with the main affair, still there is a honking grandeur to the proceedings.

From 'What Becomes Of The Broken Hearted' and 'The Long And Winding Road', through to Schubert's 'An Die Musik', 'In Search Of Eddie Riff' takes the aural imagery its title suggests and spraypaints the walls with the outcome.

The highlight (and, sensibly, the single) was 'Walking The Whippet'. One of only four Mackay originals on the album, it rides an R&B beat of breathtaking purity, reeking of the same streets that Bowie's 'Pinups' knew so well, while Mackay and guitarist Manzanera duel to decide who will buy the first drink.

8 August 1974 – Top Of The Pops

And the bells did toll! The BBC strike was finally over. Seven long weeks had elapsed since the technicians downed tools and the big guns rolled out to celebrate: Mud, Paul Da Vinci, the Glitter Band, the Rubettes, the Bay City Rollers – and George McCrae, whose soft soul 'Rock Your Baby' had taken advantage of the confusion to top the chart for the last two weeks.

August 1974 – Arrows: Toughen Up/Diesel Locomotive Dancer (RAK 182)

Among the more surprising inclusions on the 'Velvet Tinmine' collection of Junk Shop Glam were Arrows, turning up with 'Toughen Up' – their second single, a Chinnichap gem and the follow-up to the Top Ten smash 'Touch Too Much'.

Surprising because this should have been an even bigger hit than its predecessor.

As with its predecessor, the song was handed over as a Brian Connolly-voiced demo and Alan Merrill was instructed 'to copy Brian's vocal as closely as possible, I guess since it was a method that worked very well for them. I tried my best to do that, but inevitably anything I sing sounds like me.'

No matter. It was a great-sounding record and success seemed inevitable, particularly now that *Top Of The Pops* was back on the screens. Unfortunately, Arrows weren't the only band whose label was thinking that way. RAK itself had acts on each of the returning show's first three episodes, Mud and Cozy Powell (twice); and there a new Suzi Quatro single was coming up fast.

'We were made to believe that at some point, if we waited, that we would get a *Top Of The Pops* with 'Toughen Up', even six months after it was released,' Merrill recalls.

'Dave Most, Mickie's brother, had us convinced that the single could get a second life and he assured us that we would get a *Top Of The Pops*. 'It happens all the time,' he said. 'Singles get re-released and are hits.' And we bought it. So our record hovered around the Top Fifty from the radio play and then it dropped. It was then that I knew we had a problem with the label, but the deal was signed and we were trapped in our contract.'

Merrill and Most would, later in life, become friends. Throughout the band's years in his stable, however, 'Mickie really hated The Arrows' – and he kept on hating them for some years more. As late as 1982, the year from which the producer's contributions to the 'Velvet Tinmine' liner notes were drawn, he still recalled them only as a vehicle for his sense of sartorial humour. 'We used to record them because we liked to see them dress up. They were the greatest poseurs in the world.'

'The fact is,' Merrill laughs, 'he bought us each one leather jacket, two pairs of black gabardine trousers and one cowboy-style shirt with our names on it. Not a vast wardrobe.'

'Toughen Up' was not, in fact, the first choice for single; 'Dreamin'', recorded with the regular line-up supplemented by guitarist Chris Spedding and drummer Cozy Powell, was cut first only for Mickie Most to scrap it and have Merrill/Hooker write a new song over the same backing track. The result was 'Bam Bam Battering Ram', but Most wasn't impressed by that, either, and finally went back to 'Toughen Up'. And after all that...

21 August 1974 – In Concert: 10cc

A performance that makes a mockery of period criticisms of the 10cc live show, the band unchain five songs from the recently released 'Sheet Music' album (plus two from their debut) and uncork an energy that actually amplifies the perfection of their studio work.

The opening 'Silly Love', 'Wall Street Shuffle' and the closing 'Rubber Bullets' are easy, of course...in the words of the age-old maxim, fuck art, let's boogie. But, in between times, 'Fresh Air For My Mama', 'Old Wild Men' and the strangely topical 'Oh Effendi' all offer up an unfamiliarly ferocious face, while the voodoo stew of 'Baron Samedi' serves up the best of both worlds.

August 1974 – The Osmonds and David Bowie by George Tremlett (Futura Books)

The first volumes in what became, over the next two years, the most essential library available to the teenage pop fan. GLC councillor and former music writer Tremlett's biographies seem fairly slim today, averaging around 150 pages and drawing liberally from the press releases and cuttings retained in the author's legendary files.

But he had also interviewed many of his targets during his years as 'London correspondent for TV and pop music magazines in Japan,

Holland, Sweden, the United States, Belgium, Germany, Australia, New Zealand and Finland,' and while modern critics do mock his books, they remain invaluable period source material for researchers. It was Tremlett, after all, who revealed the existence of Bowie's first ever single, 'Liza Jane', recorded with the King Bees in 1964 and, just days after the book was published, staff at the Vintage Record Centre in Caledonian Road (at that time the capital's premier oldies store) were tired of turning away requests for it. 'You read that bloody book, didn't you?'

Over the next two years, Tremlett published further, similar, biographies of Gary Glitter, David Essex (both November 1974), Marc Bolan (1975), Queen, Alvin Stardust, Slik and 10cc (all 1976), alongside a number of less spangled titles (Rolling Stones, Rod Stewart, the Who, Paul McCartney, John Lennon, Cliff Richard). You can usually pick them up for under a pound today.

August 1974 – Floating Opera: Keep On Streaking/Home Run (DJM DJS321).
Probably more interesting to Kinks fans than Glammers, a Ray Davies production dedicated to the spring and summer's favourite hobby just as it began to fall from vogue. You've seen one naked sprinter, you've seen them all.

August 1974 – The Sisters: There's A Raver Coming Home/Help The Music (Warners K16445)
A very belated follow-up to the Sisters' earlier 'Kick Your Boots Off'.

August 1974 – Cozy Powell: Na Na Na/Mistral (RAK 180)
More successful than its predecessor (it rose to Number 10) the third percussive Powell hit single broke the mould by incorporating full vocals by former Bedlam bandmate Frank Aiello, now a part of new group Cozy Powell's Hammer. But it would be the last single. 'I was well and truly sick of the whole thing,' Cozy confided.

August 1974 – Alvin Stardust: You You You/ Come On (Magnet 13)
Released in near tandem with mentor Peter Shelley's decidedly un-Glammy 'Gee Baby', 'You You You' appeared as Stardust – shockingly to those fans who still thought of him as something out of the ordinary – established himself on the cabaret circuit.

A conventional theatre tour earlier in the year, supported by fellow Magnet stars Fable, proved Stardust was a brilliant live performer, a decade-plus of experience being poured into every show. 'But then the record was taking off all over the place and the record company wanted me to promote it. I went to Germany and did a couple of dates with a promoter named Rainer Haas, who is still a big promoter [and Suzi Quatro's second husband], then came back and did the cabaret. I hated it.'

He made his debut with a week-long gig at the Stockton Fiesta in June; he was now about to commence a similar engagement at the Sheffield Fiesta. And while he insisted that his fans be catered for by having free Sunday matinee performances written into his contract, where would you really want to see the Star Who

Doesn't Smile? On stage in a theatre with two thousand other fans? Or in with the chicken-in-basket crew? 'Although we were doing a week in one place and it was called a cabaret club, we were still doing a rock show.'

'You You You' climbed to Number 6 in the face of all such reservations, but it would be his last Top Ten hit. In this guise, anyway.

August 1974 – Showaddywaddy: Rock'n'Roll Lady/I'm A Traveller (Bell 1374)
August 1974 – Showaddywaddy: Showaddywaddy (Bell 248)

'Showaddywaddy' celebrated the success of 'Hey Rock And Roll' (and, fast-tracked to join it, the imminent Number 15 'Rock'n'Roll Lady') by corralling 12 solid stompers, sharply divided between spot-on band originals and remarkable classic covers.

Showaddywaddy's version of 'Johnny Remember Me' is one of the finest around, with producer Mike Hurst layering chill upon thrill, while a wild 'Bony Moronie' simply screams out for more. 'Temptation' is terrific as well and drummer Malcolm 'Duke' Allured later revealed where the band got all their favourite oldies from. The Duke would sing all contenders to his pet parrot. If it ignored him, the song was scrapped. But if Polly went potty...

August 1974 – Martin Gordon is Alive and Well...

The classified ad in the back of *Melody Maker* said it all. 'Martin Gordon is alive and well, his bass playing is as stunning as ever, so any suitable offers please...'

Just weeks after being bounced out of Sparks after one moan at the Maels too many, the hero of *Kimono* was ready to return, although the first call he received came as quite a surprise.

'When Trevor [White] and Ian [Hampton] went to Sparks, I was furious,' admitted Jook drummer Chris Townson. 'I knew I was being unreasonable; if it had been Ian Kimmet and I who were asked to join Sparks we'd have done exactly the same thing. But when [manager] John Hewlett phoned to tell me the news, I was livid. I slammed the phone down on him and rang Martin. John told me that he was feeling pretty despondent, so I thought we might be able to get something together.'

Townson's first inclination was to try and keep Jook together with Gordon and a new guitarist joining Kimmet and himself. But Kimmet was already hatching plans of his own and Hewlett wasn't exactly enthusiastic either. The pair set off on a new course of their own.

Gordon: 'The thought process which began this whole affair was "How can I pay my rent at the end of this month?" I had to do something and as the other avenue seemed to be joining Peter Banks and his band Flash, I figured that I would stay with what I was comfortable with rather than embark on headache-inducing widdly-widdly and compound time signatures.'

Renting a rehearsal space in Stoke Newington and overcoming the immediate theft of Townson's drum-kit, the pair spent their time going over the vast backlog of songs Gordon had accumulated during his time with Sparks while building a band around themselves.

Townson suggested vocalist Andy Ellison, alongside whom he'd played in John's Children; Gordon added Peter Oxendale, a keyboard player hired briefly by Sparks to flesh out their stage sound. And guitarist Davy O'List was recruited after they heard his guitar lines on Bryan Ferry's 'The "In" Crowd' and knew he would be perfect.

Or so they hoped. 'Davy would fall over in the middle of a solo and *just carry on*! Random! This was the majesty of rock, the mystery of roll, the effectiveness of elephant tranquillisers. He showed me a royalty cheque he had received from the Nice one day at Chris' house in Friern Barnet. I was impressed, no question.'

Jet was born that summer. 'We rehearsed a bit, recorded some demos and distributed them liberally. One ended up at the desk of Jamie Turner of Firefly Records, who took it along to Mike Leander and his company Rock Artistes Management. They signed us on the spot.' And it was only later, Gordon sneers, that 'we discovered there was also a Rock Artistes Music Publishing operation and a Rock Artistes Agency, as well as a Rock Artistes Anything Else That We Have Forgotten And Can Get Some Money For.' And Jet were signed to all of them.

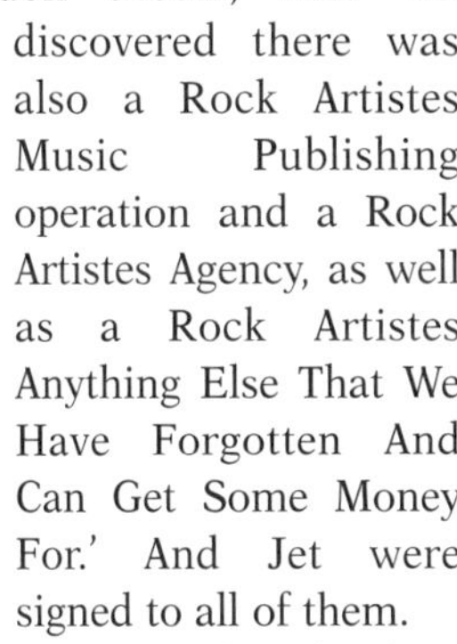

Jet played their debut show at the American submarine base in Dunoon, where Andy Ellison broke up a fight in the audience by grabbing a rope that hung from the ceiling, swinging out over the dancefloor and kicking out at the combatants as he flew.

RAM and CBS had no doubts of the band's potential – the first Glam Supergroup of course, a mix'n'match combo of Sparks, Bolan, Roxy and Queen. Producer Roy Thomas Baker was drafted in to oversee the band's debut album, clothes were crafted by Elton John's tailor and they shared their management with Gary Glitter. In dream-team terms they were unbeatable. And the fact that Gordon was a songwriter of intense originality, gifting Jet a repertoire that was equal parts humorous, quirky and memorable, was the little silver balls on the icing on the cake.

In fact, the outfitting was a source of considerable discontent. Gordon: 'I remember Leander and his sidekick Ray Brown came to an early Jet gig. Mike insisted upon applying make-up personally to every band member, declaiming about showbiz values or some such. I submitted with as much grace as I could muster, which wasn't much. We all looked like raging queens except for Davy, who looked like a homosexual stegosaurus.'

The band had already submitted to what they thought of as a perfectly reasonably photo-shoot with Gered Mankowitz – moody, side-lit, no costumes. But it wasn't deemed Glam enough. Instead, Leander suggested they get together with designer Jean Seel.

'She it was who came up with the various designs for each member of the band in a scene worthy of *Spinal Tap*. "I see Martin on horseback," she said, "and I have Davey as a rampaging primeval being." Well, that was it, I was doomed for the foreseeable future to appear wearing jodhpurs, riding boots and a monogrammed silk scarf. Davey got a black satin costume that had spines all over it and Peter Oxendale flaunted a white tail suit. Chris got off relatively lightly, togged up as a kind of glamorous boxer with poodle hair, while Andy went down the saintly flowing white route. It was all most odd.'

Another show. A college in Scotland. 'It was a fresher's ball,' recalls Gordon, 'and all the action was going on somewhere else. The curtains drew back to reveal us on stage and two people at the back of the hall. One was comatose, the other left shortly after we began our deafening racket. Andy, dressed in flowing white robes like some kind of wizard, read out interesting titbits from the current issue of *The Sun*. We played grimly on.'

August 1974 – Sailor: Traffic Jam/Harbour (Epic 2562)

'Traffic Jam' was one of the songs Sailor frontman Georg Kajanus brought to the band's first rehearsals, which meant it had no part whatsoever to play in the *Red Light Revue* that was to shape their debut album. Epic Records, however, liked it, insisting that it became their first single.

Kajanus, too, remained a fan. 'Although it wasn't part of the Sailor project, I liked it as a song. It was based on my experiences in big cities

SAILOR Ahoi-Hit in Sicht!

Das ist die neueste Hitgruppe aus England: Sailor (= Seemann). Die vier «Seeleute» – mit nicht zu langem Haar und gar nicht kurzem Verstand – bringen einen völlig neuen, stimmungsvollen Sound. (Gruppen-)Käpt'n Johan Tijedopiev-Sakonski Kajanus, Sohn eines russischen Prinzen, ist der Erfinder des elektronischen Nickelodeons – einer synthetischen Ausgabe jener alten elektrischen Kneipenklaviere, die erst nach Einwurf eines 5-Cent-Stückes (Nickel) losklimperten.

Mit dem metallischen Tastenhämmern dieses ungewöhnlichen Instrumentes und mit harmonischem Gruppen- und Ziehharmonika-Spiel zaubern «George» Kajanus (Gesang, Gitarre), Henry Marsh (Nickelodeon, Piano, Akkordeon, Gesang), Philip Pickett (Nickelodeon, Piano, Bass, Gesang) und Grant Serpell (Schlagzeug, Gesang) einen mitreissenden, neuen Klangstil zwischen verträumter Seemanns-Romantik und stimmungsvoller Kneipenmusik. Sehnsucht und Einsamkeit auf See, Mädchen und kurze, (feucht-)fröhliche Stunden an Land – so ist das Leben der Seeleute. Und das ist die bunt schillernde Musik von Sailor. Zwischen Melancholie und ausgelassener Tingel-Tangel-Stimmung.

Henry Marsh · Philip Pickett · Grant Serpell · George Kajanus

Gruppenboss George Kajanus erfand das Nickelodeon, eine Nachbildung des alten Kneipenklaviers

«Die Hafenviertel – Seeleute und Huren –, das alles fasziniert mich . . .»
George Kajanus

Die Story von Sailor beginnt vor 6 Jahren in Paris:

«George» studierte an der Sorbonne, und Henry, Grant und Philip kamen auf den verschiedensten Umwegen in die Stadt an der Seine. Abenteuerlich wie ihr Weg nach Paris, war auch ihr Leben dort. Wo wohnt man in Paris? Natürlich im Studentenviertel Quartier Latin. Auch die vier Engländer hatten ihre «Buden» in den typisch kleinen Gassen der Pariser Altstadt. Dort, wo tags Caféhäuser, rauchige Pinten und kleine Lädchen das Bild bestimmen und nachts Kaskaden von Neonlicht und Leuchtreklamen die Strassen überfluten. Dort trafen sich «George», Henry, Philip und Grant. Und es war schon eine ziemlich verrückte Tat, als die vier Engländer ausgerechnet mitten in Paris eine Gruppe ins Leben riefen. Ihre ersten gemeinsamen Auftritte waren in einem gewissen Café namens «le matelot» – und «le matelot» heisst nichts anderes als «Sailor» . . .

Pariser Caféhaus-Atmosphäre, russisches Prinzenblut, musikalische Bohème und die Rastlosigkeit der Seezigeuner, das alles prägte schon damals die Musik von Sailor.

Doch 1971 schien das jähe Ende für Sailor gekommen. Das Café brannte bis auf die Grundmauern ab. Für die vier «Matrosen» aus England bedeutete das musikalischen Schiffbruch. Sie verloren ihr Dauerengagement und mussten sich auflösen. C'est la vie.

George, Henry, Grant und Philip gingen wieder ihre eigenen Wege – bis Philip im Sommer 1974 mit Steve Morris, dem Sohn eines schwerreichen Musikverlegers, zusammentraf. Die beiden beschlossen, Sailor wieder zusammenzubringen. George Kajanus, Initiator von Sailor, Hauptsongschreiber und Nickelodeon-Erfinder, war von diesem Vorhaben besonders angetan: «. . . denn das gibt mir die Möglichkeit, meine ganzen musikalischen Einflüsse voll auszuwerfen.»

George ist seit seiner Pariser Studentenzeit weit herumgekommen. «Die Hafenviertel – Seeleute und Huren –, das alles fasziniert mich», lächelt George.

Philip und George waren also fest entschlossen, die alte Mannschaft erneut anzuheuern. Das war gar nicht so einfach, es dauerte viele Monate und kostete Hunderte von Telefongesprächen, bis die beiden überhaupt herausgefunden hatten, wo sich die anderen aufhielten. Doch als Henry und Grant dann gefunden waren, brauchte es nicht viel Überredungskunst, um sie wieder für die Sailor-Idee an Land zu ziehen.

Wenige Wochen später feierte Sailor den zweiten Stapellauf. Beim diesjährigen Weltkongress ihrer Schallplattenfirma CBS hatten sie einen riesigen Erfolg. In der bekannten TV-Reihe «in concert» von BBC London begeisterten sie Englands Jugend, und jetzt kann man sie auch bei uns hören.

Nach dem melodischen Single-Hit «Traffic Jam» erschien jetzt das erste Album unter der Flagge von Sailor. «The Girls Of Amsterdam», «The Street» und «Sailor's Night On The Town» – das ist herrlich gesungenes Seemanns-Latein mit melancholischem Ziehharmonikaklang und dem typisch metallisch klimpernden Nickelodeon-Sound.

Da kann man nur sagen: Sailor ahoi, Hit in Sicht.

SAILOR

„Warum wir unsere Frauen verstecken"

Oben: Immer nur allein lassen sich die vier von Sailor in der Öffentlichkeit sehen. Ihre Familien sollen ein „normales" Leben führen.

Georg Kajanus schaut verträumt eine Fotografie seiner hübschen Frau Chris an: „Je länger ich sie kenne, desto besser gefällt sie mir. Schade nur, daß wir uns so selten sehen können!" seufzt Georg. Das ist der Nachteil, den die Sailor schweren Herzens in Kauf nehmen, seit sie ständig auf der Erfolgsleiter nach oben klettern. Für ihre Frauen und Kinder haben sie nur wenig Zeit. Die Familienväter sind auf Tournee.

Es gäbe eine ganz einfache Möglichkeit, dieser Misere abzuhelfen – die Frauen mitzunehmen. Doch Georg winkt schon ab. „Wir wollen nicht, daß unsere Frauen Tag für Tag in dieser Hektik leben müssen. Und unsere Kinder sollen fern von diesem ganzen Starrummel aufwachsen können." Leicht fällt es vor allen Dingen Georg nicht, wochenlang ohne seine Chris auszukommen. Die schöne Japanerin, die in Kanada aufwuchs, lebt mit dem adlig angehauchten Georg seit über zehn Jahren zusammen. „Ich möchte es ihr aber auf jeden Fall ersparen, immer hinter mir herrennen zu müssen, wenn wir von Termin zu Termin hetzen."

Aber auch Henry Mash, der seit 1971 mit Susan glücklich verheiratet ist, weiß inzwischen die Vorzüge dieser Abmachung zu schätzen. „Wenn ich zu Hause mit meiner Frau und meinem Sohn Thomas durch die Straßen bummle, kann ich tun und lassen, was ich will!" meint Henry, der zur Entspannung gern in die Anonymität verschwindet.

Grant Serpell ist der einzige, der sich in Gesellschaft am wohlsten fühlt. Daß er trotzdem gern nach Hause fährt, liegt an der hübschen Französin Michelle. „Ich finde es toll, daß Michelle immer wie selbstverständlich zu Hause auf mich wartet und immer für mich da ist. Und das genieße ich eben mit ihr dann am liebsten allein", meint Grant schmunzelnd.

Auch Phil fällt es sehr schwer, ohne seine Familie auszukommen. Sein kleiner Sohn ist gerade ein halbes Jahr alt. Und zudem befindet er sich mit seiner Frau Ann fast noch in den Flitterwochen. Erst im vergangenen Jahr hatten sie geheiratet. Phil: „Ich hätte die beiden zwar gern immer bei mir, aber so ist es besser." ●

like Montreal, London, Paris, New York and especially Mexico City, with all their problems of endless jams and pollution, but also some of the romance associated with the automobile throughout human history.'

'Traffic Jam' attracted some kind reviews but little else in the UK. It reached Number 4 in Holland, however, at a time when the Dutch market was widely considered the most influential in mainland Europe. With that success behind them, it would not be long before what the press regarded as a cunning blend of Sparks, Roxy Music and a dry continental mystique would pay dividends.

August 1974 – Barry Blue: Miss Hit And Run/ Heads I Win, Tails You Lose (Bell 1364)

Its Blue/de Paul parentage notwithstanding, another in a growing sequence of weak Blue 45s struggled to Number 26.

August 1974 – Geordie: She's A Teaser/We're Alright Now (EMI 2197)
August 1974 – Geordie: Don't Be Fooled By The Name (EMI EMA 764)

Another characteristic powerhouse, although it was becoming increasingly clear that Geordie and the UK chart were no longer on speaking terms. And the title of the band's second album made it very clear they didn't care, although they can't have been thrilled being beaten to the Chicago mobster look by Lulu a few months earlier.

Inside, of course, the music remained much the same, that patent Geordie crash and bang, an exhilarating cacophony that took savage originals and established classics alike ('House Of The Rising Sun' and 'St James Infirmary' were both primal Geordie fodder) and made magical mincemeat of any preconceptions anyone ever had of them.

August 1974 – Slack Alice: Motorcycle Dream/Ridin' The Wind (Fontana 6007 038)
August 1974 – Slack Alice: Slack Alice (Philips 6308 214) 1974

Fronted by the superbly-named Alice Springs, Slack Alice were a hard rocking quintet also comprising John Cook (keyboards), songwriter Pete Finberg (guitar), Mick Howard (bass) and Eddie Leach (drums). Usually caught somewhere between a bluesier Cado Belle and SAHB, if both were brought up on Pub Rock, they are said to have peaked with 'Motorcycle Dream', a genuinely cool, hard-hitting Quatro-meets-'My Coo Ca Choo'-style rocker with Springs packing a defiantly tough vocal. Even better, though, is the album's lispy, squeaky 'Slack Alice' which oozes the same kind of silent-movie nostalgia sleaze the *Rocky Horror Show* monopolised. Springs later reappeared in the band Darling.

August 1974 – Pandora (approximate date): Talk about obscure!

Pandora are so unknown that even their record company didn't know they existed until 20 years after they broke up. Nobody seems to know who they were; where they came from, where they are now, their very names and credits are lost in the mists of time.

But the seven track Eva-Tone flexidisc they recorded in a Cleveland warehouse under the supervision of Granicus drummer Joe Battaglia in 1974 which went unheard for almost two decades, then resurfaced in a desk drawer in the mid-Nineties, stands today as one of *the* pre-eminent slices of American Glam Rock – the kind of record which, if it had only been heard at the time, could have wiped the smirk off a lot of foreign faces. The Brits still believe they had the Glam market sewn up, and they probably did. But then Pandora come screaming out of the speakers and all bets are off.

The easiest point of reference for Pandora was the New York Dolls, at least in terms of the trash aesthetic. But they were deeper than that, and darker. If the Spiders From Mars had been invaded by Badger, then forced to play extemporised Silverhead jams; if the Alice Cooper Band found a singer who sounded like Roger Wootton of Comus; if Jobriath had joined Led Zeppelin instead of Robert Plant and 'Whole Lotta Love' had been written by Marc Bolan.

Pandora played Glam Rock, but it was Glam with a decidedly demented bend in the middle, a harbinger of all that would be perpetrated in that name during the mid-late Eighties but so utterly a child of its own time that the comparison falls flat. Which in turn simply lends oodles of mystique to what became Pandora's deeply posthumous debut album. Passions inflamed by the rediscovery of the flexidisc, the producer then unearthed the full Pandora session, a 10-track collection finally released in 1997.

Comprising all seven of the tracks on that original flexidisc, plus three more ('Crack Your Skull', 'Don't Put Me' and 'Daze Of Madness'), 'Space Amazon' (Arf Arf AA 064*)* was freaky, frenzied and frantically fey and it withstood the test of obscurity better than pretty much any other album of its ilk. Whether or not anyone ever finds out who Pandora were, sometimes the image just speaks for itself. Which is what Kiss were relying on all along.

August 1974 – Bryan Ferry: Smoke Gets In Your Eyes/Another Time Another Place (Island WIP 6205)

Spinning out of Ferry's second solo album, a Number 17 hit.

August 1974 – Sensational Alex Harvey Band: Sergeant Fury/Gang Bang (Vertigo 6059 106)

In July 1974, SAHB appeared at the first Knebworth Festival, down the bill from the Allman Brothers, John McLaughlin, Van Morrison and the Doobie Brothers – a soporific line-up that didn't stand a chance. Harvey pulled out all the stops, building both his show and the stage set around the forthcoming new album and then unleashing the power of Vambo – 'a cross between Father Christmas and Captain Marvel', as Harvey himself explained.

The following month, SAHB headlined the first night of the Reading Festival above 10cc and Camel while a new single, 'Sergeant Fury', paid tribute to Harvey's favourite Marvel comic book, the tale of a grizzled old warrior leading his merry band of misfits into action. Sound familiar?

ON THE RADIO
10 August 1974 – In Concert: Elton John
17 August 1974 – In Concert: The Winkies
ON THE BOX
5 August 1974 – Lift Off With Ayshea: Mud
8 August 1974 – Top Of The Pops: Mud, Paul Da Vinci, Glitter Band, the Rubettes, Bay City Rollers
12 August 1974 – Lift Off With Ayshea: Glitter Band
15 August 1974 – Top Of The Pops: Bay City Rollers, Cockney Rebel, Cozy Powell, Glitter Band
19 August 1974 – Lift Off With Ayshea: Alvin Stardust, Mr Big
22 August 1974 – Top Of The Pops: Alvin Stardust, Bay City Rollers, Cockney Rebel, Cozy Powell, Showaddywaddy
26 August 1974 – Lift Off With Ayshea: Geordie
29 August 1974 – Top Of The Pops: Bryan Ferry, Showaddywaddy
ON THE SHELVES
August 1974 – Simon Turner: Sex Appeal/Little Lady (UK 74)
August 1974 – Jobriath: Ooh La la/Gone Tomorrow (Elektra K12156)

September 1974 – 10cc: Silly Love/The Sacro-Iliac (UK 77)

With 10cc touring the country and playing the Reading Festival, it was time for a new 45. But 'Silly Love' wasn't merely the *third* single to be lifted from 'Sheet Music', it was also the first to have an album track on its B-side. 'A cheat and a chiz,' cried the band's loyal fans, who repaid them by staying away in droves. Appearances on

Top Of The Pops and *Lift Off With Ayshea* didn't help. 'Silly Love' grabbed a mere fortnight in the lower reaches of the Top Thirty, then vanished.

4 September 1974 – In Concert: Sailor
September 1974 – Sailor: Sailor (Epic 80337)

Were Sailor a Glam band? Captured by *In Concert*, all togged up and as visual as you like, they could scarcely be anything else. But Georg Kajanus is less certain. 'In many ways, our image was very anti-Seventies. I insisted that we dress in sailor suits and cut our hair short to best reflect the content of my songs, which were about sailors on shore leave. We basically re-invented ourselves, to the extent of even creating a fictional biography for the group.

'But because our image was so powerful and so specific, it was easy for the English media and audience to misunderstand the concept and categorise us as part of the Glam trend, failing to see that our image was a product of the theatricality inherent in the musical material that I'd written.

'Personally, I wasn't that fond of the whole Glam Rock scene: image or music, but it was a lot of fun. And also, quite glamorous!'

Still, listening to Sailor's debut LP felt like being initiated into the greatest secret you'd never been told. Comparable in its underground impact to the first, similarly overlooked, albums by Cockney Rebel and Sparks, Sailor inhabited a darker world than either of them, simply by virtue of its reality – we'd all heard about the Reeperbahn, we'd all heard Bowie's version of Jacques Brel's 'Amsterdam' and Alex Harvey's take on the same writer's 'Next', but it was left to Sailor to truly indoctrinate us into the world where all three merged into one deliciously voyeuristic whole.

Or almost. 'Epic insisted on including "Traffic Jam" [the band's first single], which I thought grossly challenged the conceptual beauty of the rest of the album. As much as I could understand the commercial value of the song, it had nothing whatsoever to do with the *Red Light Revue* or the romantic and sensual motifs running through it.'

Nowhere are those motifs better revealed than across 'Sailor's Night On The Town' and 'Blue Desert', the songs that Kajanus still pinpoints as the linchpins around which the concept revolved, 'setting down both a thematic and musical direction for the two worlds of the *Red Light Revue*; the sailors and the sea on the one hand, the harbour town with the girls on the other.'

Sonically, too, 'Sailor' is a delight, conjuring up the imagery that we all dreamed about after listening to *Cabaret* and Brecht, while foghorns pumped mournfully through the self-defining title track and 'Josephine Baker' oozed melancholy over the rainswept boulevards. And we puzzled over the Nickelodeon, the mighty Heath Robinson-style contraption that created the landscape over which all were laid.

Kajanus: 'In the process of reproducing the

Ihr Markenzeichen ist der Sound des Nickelodeon, eines zweiseitig bespielbaren, klavierähnlichen Instrumentes mit dem scheppernden Ton eines Honky-Tonk-Pianos, mehrstimmiger Gesang und ausgefallene Kleidung: Die vier von Sailor lassen sich – dem Namen gemäss – zumeist in Seemannstuch und Schiffermützen ablichten. Von den Freuden und Leiden der Matrosen an Bord und Land, von Freudenmädchen, Bordellen und lärmigen Seemannskneipen handeln auch ihre Lieder, die allesamt von Sailor-Gitarrist Georg Kajanus geschrieben werden. Denn er hat eine ganz besondere Beziehung zu Seeleuten und Nutten:

SAILOR: Es begann im Freudenhaus...

Der scheppernde Sound des Nickelodeon, eines zweiseitig bespielbaren Tasteninstrumentes, ist das musikalische und optische Markenzeichen von Sailor

sound of my demos many unusual instruments were used in the recording of the album, so we would've needed several backing musicians if the instrumentation and the arrangements of the songs were going to be reproduced live. 'After a lot of thought, I came up with the plans for what was to become the Nickelodeon. It became a two-sided contraption capable of accommodating all the instruments required, with the exception of my acoustic 12-string guitar and Grant Serpell's drums.

'The idea involved two small upright pianos back to back – rigged up mechanically with an electric doorbell-triggered glockenspiel, a bass keyboard, chasing lights and an array of synthesisers. The whole concept was very expensive, but it was funded by Sailor's first manager and publisher, Steve Morris.

'We bought two Kemble upright pianos and I built the Nickelodeon at the Nightingale Public House in Wood Green – an Irish pub which had become the rehearsal home to the band. The Nickelodeon was played by Henry Marsh on the treble side and Phil Pickett on the bass side, who faced each other. They were effectively able to play seven musical sounds between the two of them.

'The concept was like an early form of MIDI (in other words, a mechanical MIDI) and, if I may say so myself, it turned out to be quite a magnificent device. Not only did it provide the sound that we needed in order to remain a unit of four people but it could also serve as a musical trademark for Sailor. So, we ended up with this surreal, mad, Victorian-looking music machine that was to become Sailor's ultimate logo.'

September 1974 – Glitter Band: Hey! (Bell 241)
September 1974 – Mud: Mud Rock (RAK 508)

Recorded in eight days, Mud's debut album was an all-out party, orchestrated by the grooviest jukebox in the land. Their own hits alternate with vintage covers, while the studio became a crowded dance club, with the sound of the revellers (friends, roadies, studio staff) a constant backdrop to the music itself. The result was as contagious as it was pulsating, one of the wildest parties of the year.

One of them. The other was 'Hey!', a Glitter Band debut that could have been conceived in the same breath as 'Mud Rock' and adheres to much the same musical agenda. The hits are here, of course, and a clutch of covers that range from an effective 'Sea Cruise' and a furious 'Twistin' The Night Away' to 'Tell Him', an old Exciters number rearranged so successfully that it would soon be a hit in its own right.

Only not by the Glitter Band. Hello were taking notes.

September 1974 – Jobriath: Jobriath (Elektra 75070)

Daftly delayed for a year after its US counterpart was released, Jobriath's debut finally touched down in England and was everything the promo photos led us to hope for.

Grand, grandiose, obsessive, precocious, pretentious, a smorgasbord of overbearing rock hooks ('World Without End' and 'Earthling' are even funky), fronted by a singer who dreams of operatics and over-run with aliens, pierrots and forgotten movie stars. A few years later, Meatloaf would take a similar grasp on the vastness of excess and make a million. Jobriath made a millstone, but the parallels are apparent all the same. Heartfelt ballad as medieval battering ram.

September 1974 – Sensational Alex Harvey Band: The Impossible Dream (Vertigo 6360 112)

SAHB were one of the biggest live attractions in the land now and, as they celebrated their first Top Twenty LP, they turned out to play that most hallowed of venues, the London Palladium.

Just watching the audience file in, one knew immediately just what an impact Alex Harvey had made. It was as though every kid in the crowd was wearing the same striped T-shirt Harvey had sported for years.

The sessions for the album were scarcely so harmonious. A full LP recorded with producer Shel Talmy earlier in the year was abandoned after band and management lost faith in the sound and delivery. The tapes were shelved and presumed lost forever – when they were rediscovered in 2009 (for release as the 'Hot City' album), even the surviving band members had forgotten about one of the songs, 'Ace In The Hole', while all professed amazement at just how radically rearranged favourites 'Vambo' and 'Man In The Jar' were. No sooner was it scrapped than the album was reborn as 'The Impossible Dream' and emerged as their most successful yet.

In fact, 'The Impossible Dream' is infuriatingly patchy. Several tracks – notably 'River Of Love', 'Long Hair Music' and 'Weights Made Of Lead' – are little more than throwaways. But when 'The Impossible Dream' was good, it was startling.

'Tomahawk Kid', retelling Robert Louis Stevenson's *Treasure Island*, was already a dramatic live staple, inciting entire theatres to join in with the compulsive 'yo ho ho' chorus. 'The Impossible Dream', heartfelt and hurting (and segue-ing out of a violent 'Money Honey') was another. And it all wrapped up with the so aptly titled 'Anthem', the song with which SAHB now closed their live show and which allowed Harvey to live out all his Scottish fantasies with bagpipes, fife and drum.

September 1974 – The Hammersmith Gorillas: You Really Got Me/Leaving 'Ome (Penny Farthing PEN 849)

Beloved of Glitterbin connoisseurs everywhere, the Hammersmith Gorillas were one of several bands fronted by the maniacally sideburned Jesse Hector throughout the Glam era, albeit bands that purposefully had little in common with the energies surrounding them.

The others were Crushed Butler, who opened the decade cutting demos for any label that would allow them but never getting past that phase; and Helter Skelter, who recorded one single ('I Need You'/'Goodbye Baby' – Sticky 102) for the predominantly soul-oriented Sticky label, only to see it canned until 1978.

This menacing demolition of the Kinks' debut hit was better starred, if only by virtue of being released while the band was still in existence. But the BBC stopped playing it, allegedly, after one of their DJs actually removed needle from vinyl live on air and railed instead about how badly played the record was.

The Gorillas relocated to France until the UK climate became a little more understanding; two years later, as the Gorillas, they were one of the first bands to appear on the Chiswick label as it bridged the gap between Pub Rock and Punk.

September 1974 – Alice Cooper: Alice Cooper's Greatest Hits (Warners K56043)

The tombstone on the grave of the now sundered band, a sensible round-up of hits and key LP tracks to keep us occupied while we awaited the now solo Alice Cooper's next move. Because, of course, the old devil kept churning it out, sometimes good, sometimes bad and sometimes so damned ugly you couldn't help but admire his nerve.

He would start well, though. Ferociously theatrical, with dancers, deaths and giant spiders, 1975's 'Welcome To My Nightmare' album and tour spawned some of the best reviews of his life and even gave Alice a shot at MOR credibility when actress Julie Covington covered his 'Only Women Bleed'.

Another track, 'Department Of Youth', two or three years earlier, might even have given him the biggest hit of his life, it was that good. Especially the bit where Alice asks the kiddie chorus who gave them their freedom.

He expects them to say he did.

They tell him it was Donny.

Alice's roar of surprise gives the record player palpitations.

But his greatest triumph came a couple of years later, when he delivered 1977's 'Whiskey And Lace'. In the US, it was regarded among the most forgettable things he'd ever done. In Britain, though, an extra song, erased from the American release for reasons of taste and decency, proved there was still schlock left in the old rocker after all.

'The King Of The Silver Screen' was the tale of a construction-site worker who wanted to be a Hollywood starlet. 'I could have been Greta Garbo if I'd been born in another time,' he mourns, before the band strikes up 'The Battle Hymn Of The Republic' and the singer fades out telling the world how much he loves wearing dresses, make-up, long hair. 'I don't care any more! Just don't hit me!'

Again, a few years earlier...

September 1974 – Carmen: Dancing On A Cold Wind (Regal Zonophone SLRZ1040)

Carmen's second album was, deliberately, a denser set than its predecessor, 'I seem to recall the record company being unsure as to the commerciality of the second album,' says David

Allen. 'It was more introspective and self-indulgent. But it remains my favourite in parts. I thought the harmonies were great and loved the sound Tony got with the bass. We were really getting good together; we went in and more or less made it up on the spot.'

Again, however, there were no rewards for the vinyl. *The Midnight Special*, however, had raised the band's American profile high enough for them to spend much of 1974 on the road, touring with the likes of Santana, Rush, Blue Oyster Cult and ELO. Hopes for a slot on Bowie's US tour that year fell through, but Carmen entered 1975 with almost four months on the road with Jethro Tull.

The band's tenure alongside Tony Visconti, too, came to an end; he later described Carmen's failure as one of the greatest regrets of his career. Instead, the band recorded a third album under their own auspices, laying down 'The Gypsies' 'within two weeks of coming off a year's touring.

'We didn't go in thinking we were going to make a commercial album,' Allen admits. 'It was a true reflection of where we were at the time. Playing live in constantly changing circumstances, with different bands of all types, taught us to pull out all the stops quickly and head for a higher gear.'

'The Gypsies' (Mercury SRMI 1047) went unreleased in the UK and Carmen's American label barely seemed aware they'd released it. Plans to open for the Rolling Stones on their next tour fell through; Paul Fenton was seriously injured in an accident with a horse and could no longer drum, while John Glascock turned out to have so impressed Jethro Tull when the two bands toured together that he was invited to join them. By summer 1975, Carmen had folded.

Allen: 'The last months were a mixture of sadness and relief, mainly sadness. We all loved what we were doing with Carmen, it was a passionate and intense experience.' But their energy and enthusiasm had finally reached its end.

September 1974 – David Essex: Gonna Make You A Star/Window (CBS 2492)
September 1974 – David Essex: David Essex (CBS 69088)

Essex had spent the last few months working on his second feature film, *Stardust*, alongside Adam Faith, Marty Wilde, Keith Moon, Paul Nicholas and Dave Edmunds. He returned to action in time for the movie's release and to have some fun at the expense of his own critical stature.

Shrugging off the disappointment of his last single, the deeply under-performing 'America', 'Gonna Make You A Star' ran through a shopping list of his own perceived failings – 'Is he more than just a pretty face?' – then answered them for the naysayers with a mocking sneer. 'I don't think so.'

With the Stardust premiere set for 24 October and Essex's first nationwide concert tour kicking off one week later, he was rewarded with his first Number 1, sweeping reggae icon Ken Boothe out of the way to get there, then followed through with a sophomore album that proved just how powerful his forward momentum was. Less than 12 months had passed since 'Rock On' and already he had left it behind.

September 1974 – Brett Smiley: Va Va Va Voom/Space Ace (Anchor ANC 1004)
20 September 1974: Russell Harty: Brett Smiley

Russell Harty: 'Are you aware…'

Brett: 'Aware? Sure.'

Russell Harty: 'Are you aware of the weight…'

Brett: 'I'm not that heavy.'

Russell Harty: 'Are you aware of the weight Andrew Oldham places on your young shoulders?

Brett: 'I don't think he's ever been on my shoulders.'

He was beautiful – the most beautiful boy in the world, according to a *Disc* headline in October 1974. Pouting, blonde and so pretty in pink, everything about the boy screamed 'pay attention!' – including the fact that Brett Smiley really is his own name.

Radio Luxembourg took a shine to the effervescent 'Va Va Va Voom', Smiley's breathtaking first single, and played it half to death. *Disc* splashed Smiley across its 12 October 1974, front cover in vivid, living colour (headline: 'BEAUTIFUL BRETT'). And he made his UK television debut on *Russell Harty*, a pink gabardine-suited vision who didn't even flinch when the tape operator played the wrong backing track and he found himself miming to his latest B-side.

What really caught the eye, though, was the

expression of absolutely exquisite detachment with which Smiley regarded the entire proceedings. When Harty asked Smiley to sit quietly for a moment, while he talked to manager Andrew Oldham, Smiley asked if he could put his sunglasses on. When Harty questioned that, Brett offered them to him.

Rival teen idols shuddered at his audacity. 'I thought he was a bit pathetic,' complained Simon Turner. 'He kept putting his glasses on and off.' And later, Brett confessed that he was out of his head on the show thanks to a thoughtless cocktail of sleeping pills and tranquillisers.

But it was studied languor, not stupefied lethargy, that shone through his performance: that and a Noel Cowardesque air of decadence that, for even the most casual viewer, made the act of watching television almost painfully raw and personal. Russell Harty thought he was interviewing just another would-be pop star. In fact, he was greeting a Greek God.

Smiley had only been in London for week when the call came through to appear on *Russell Harty* and it didn't phase him in the slightest. Why should it? He was 17 and sexy, he was an American in England, he had an enormous deal with Anchor Records, the UK wing of ABC, and he had been discovered by Andrew Loog Oldham, the greatest starmaker/image creator in British pop history.

Harty was hostile from the start. He opened by complaining how his show was constantly being deluged by requests to give young talent a step up the ladder and admitted that tonight was an experiment, to discover whether it was actually worth doing. There were enough other shows dedicated to preening pop wannabes, he seemed to be saying; did his programme really need to descend into the same mire?

So he started rough and got rougher.

Unfortunately, Smiley and, seated beside him, Oldham were in no mood to be manhandled.

Harty mentioned the fact that $100,000 had already been spent on Smiley's career.

Oldham agreed. 'Mainly in airfares.'

It was Detroit promoter Russ Gibbs who introduced the pair. Oldham recalls: 'one glimpse of Smiley set my mind train rolling in the same directions that Marianne Faithfull had. The boy was beautiful, and beauty doesn't simply sell, it flies off the shelves. So everyone's into Glam Rock are they? Brett was Glam with a capital hard-on.'

The Indiana born Smiley's credentials were already impressive: a four-year stint in the Broadway production of *Oliver* which saw him rise from the chorus to the lead role (and only just lose out to Mark Lester in the race for the movie) and a clutch of television ads had long since groomed him for stardom.

But a handful of recordings with future Knack supremo Doug Fieger's band Sky proved insufficient to land him a deal and Smiley returned to the US, first to the family home in Seattle, doors away from what would later become famous as the Kurt Cobain residence, then to Hollywood, where he leaped headlong into the Glitter scene revolving around Rodney Bingenheimer's English Disco.

'There was a whole crowd of us that sat around in velvet and boots and makeup. We weren't really from wealthy families, but you could always get by; if you were cute you could get by real easy.'

A previous manager had already tried launching the teenager in England in 1972 at the height of the country's fascination with the teenybop dreams of Cassidy and the Osmonds. That failed, but Oldham wasn't deterred.

A single was called for, a statement of intent and Smiley delivered. 'Va Va Va Voom', an amalgam of vintage Bolan and manic Mud brought to a breathless three-minute climax by Steve Marriott's guitar and a characteristically dramatic Oldham production. 'Andrew's favourite record was "River Deep Mountain High" by Ike and Tina Turner,' Smiley reasons, but even that doesn't explain it all. Oldham may have learned his craft at the altar of Spector, but he was never content to remain a mere pupil. 'Va Va Va Voom' was more than a pop single. It was a way of life.

Smiley recalls: 'I wrote "Va Va Va Voom" here in New York and I thought it was just a throwaway. But I was playing some songs for Andrew and he loved it. At the time, I couldn't for the life of me understand why, but later I did. He loved it because it's simple and it doesn't say that much.'

'Va Va Va Voom' was only the beginning. Armed with Anchor Records' $100,000 recording advance (plus another $100,000 for publishing), they headed down to Nashville to record the basic tracks for a Smiley album.

'Then we took them to New York and added more, then Andrew would take the tapes to Olympic Studios in London and come back with something totally different.'

And then it all went belly-up. 'Va Va Va Voom' barely registered a flicker on the sales-o-meter; Brett himself was just one more pretty face on a scene which, quite frankly, already had more pretty faces than it knew what to do with. A projected US release on Sire fell through, despite the support of New York DJ Scott Muni's *English Hour*, and to crown it all, says Oldham, Anchor got cold feet and pulled the plug on everything before the album had even been paid for.

Smiley returned to the States where he now lives in New York, still writing, still playing and still recording. And, 30-plus years later, that LP, 'Breathlessly Brett', finally found a release. Judy Garland meets Jobriath, a teenage T Rex with a Bryan Ferry bent, the Shangri-Las with stun guns bristling.

The songs were exquisite, the arrangements were heavenly and Oldham's production was astonishing, a liquid wall of sound that melts around the teenage Smiley's every affected inflection. Hearing it for the first time in three decades, Oldham declared. 'It remains a beautifully recorded, exquisitely paced and deliciously organised record.'

September 1974 – In the studio with the Winkies

The brevity of their liaison with Eno notwithstanding, the Winkies were firmly in the spotlight now. And while Chrysalis staggered everybody with their rejection of the band's own choice for single, the Eno-produced 'Last Chance', the label had a back-up plan already in place.

Phil Rambow: 'Ten Years After had just broken up and Chrysalis were going to do something with Alvin Lee, but the other guys – Leo Lyons and Chick Churchill – had made them a lot of money so they wanted to do something for them. Leo wanted to try production and Chrysalis thought we would be perfect for him Chrysalis said, "If you do this for us, it will be a favour and we'll do something for you, a lot of money on marketing, etc." So we said yes.'

But the plot thickens. 'All this came about with the background that Guy Stevens was the hugest Winkies fan you could imagine. When we played Dingwalls one night, Guy came backstage, completely mad, telling us, "You were fucking great, it's gonna be brilliant, I'm gonna produce you, you're better than Spooky Tooth."

'But our manager got together with Chrysalis and said, "We can't put our valuable band in these crazy hands," so they ignored him. Then the Lyons thing came up, and there was all this money and promotion, so we went into the studio with Leo.'

What followed is one of those tragedies for which Seventies rock became so renowned. 'There was a huge amount of money, and so much nonsensical bullshit like Chick Churchill writing orchestral parts, and mountains of cocaine. £26,000 for a month in Morgan Studios, and we came out with something that was almost unlistenable, let alone unreleasable.'

A couple of what Rambow concedes were 'interesting tracks' made it out of the morass, including a soaring cover of the Jackson Five's 'The Love You Save'. 'But the rest was so devoid of soul and bottom end, and warmth and good sound, it was just devoid of everything. And we had to start over.'

Lyons' own inexperience notwithstanding, the producer was not wholly to blame for the debacle. The Winkies, too, 'completely got lost in our ideals.' But the disaster, Rambow concludes, 'ruined the band. We were never the same afterwards.'

Desperately, Chrysalis sought a solution, finally returning to Guy Stevens – who, thankfully, was quick to forgive. 'Guy didn't have any ego, so he goes "Well, you've wasted all this time and all this money, so let's rehearse as a live band, do it all live so it'll be really quick.'

Chrysalis coughed up another £10,000 and band, producer and engineer Keith Harwood moved into Olympic Studios. Ten days later they moved out again. 'We recorded the backing tracks live. No overdubs, nothing. We bashed it all down in three days, mixed it in a week and finished under budget.' By mid-September, the album was complete. All they needed now was for Chrysalis to release the thing.

September 1974 – Pan's People: You Can Really Rock'n'Roll Me/Singer Not The Song (Epic EPC 2606)
Disco strings, Chris Spedding guitar and a truly magnificent Mike Batt production conspire with a faintly Halloweeny lyric to produce a genuinely great 45. Cherry Gillespie's vocals are sultry enough to conjure up images of the group themselves and the whole package deserved a lot more than the oblivion that awaited.

September 1974 – Barry Blue: Hot Shot/ Hobo Man (Bell 1379)
September 1974 – Barry Blue: Hot Shots (BELLS 249)
Rounding up Blue's last three singles behind a very camp cowboy cover, Blue's second (and final) solo album was accompanied by his last UK hit – 'Hot Shot' reached Number 23.

September 1974 – Top Of The Pops Volume 40 (Hallmark SHM 875)
When 'You You You' is a Glammy as it gets, you know that this is one Top Of The Pops set you probably won't be listening to very often. Thrill, if you will, to a buoyant rendition of 'Y Viva Espana' and allow 'Kung Fu Fighting' to recall a time when the whole world went chopstick crazy. But summertime has always been sleepy time in chart terms, and this year's was positively comatose.

ON THE RADIO
9 September 1974 – Bob Harris: The Heavy Metal Kids
ON THE BOX
5 September 1974 – Top Of The Pops: 10cc, Alvin Stardust
10 September 1974 – Lift Off With Ayshea: Showaddywaddy
12 September 1974 – 45: Alvin Stardust
13 September 1974 – Top Of The Pops: Bryan Ferry
17 September 1974 – Lift Off With Ayshea: Wizzard
19 September 1974 – 45: 10cc, Glitter Band
20 September 1974 – Top Of The Pops: Cozy Powell
26 September 1974 – 45: Showaddywaddy
27 September 1974 – Top Of The Pops – 10cc, Alvin Stardust

ON THE SHELVES
September 1974 – Blackfoot Sue: You Need Love/Tobago Rise (DJM DJS 326)
September 1974 – Giggles: Maria (Enchilada Song)/Your Mother Wouldn't Like It (EMI 2212)
September 1974 – Brendon: Make Me A Dollar, Make Me A Dime/Find Me (UK 79)
September 1974 – Thunderthighs: Dracula's Daughter/Lady In Question (Phillips 6006 413)

October 1974 – Slade: Far Far Away/OK Yesterday Was Yesterday (Polydor 2058522)
The first hit from the now-looming *Slade In Flame* movie was this spectacular ballad, a travelogue of the worldwide travels the band had undertaken, shot through with a healthy dose of homesickness.

Chas Chandler later admitted that he had reservations about its release, but it was a beautiful record and when it entered the chart at Number 3 a return to the top seemed inevitable. Instead, it got tangled up behind Ken Boothe ('who the hell was Ken Boothe?' asked Jim Lea) and Number 2 was its limit.

October 1974 – The Rubettes: Wear It's At (Polydor 2383 306)
Looking back on that first year of Rubettemania, Bill Hurd laughs: 'The Rubettes were around at the time of Glam Rock, but really that refers to Sweet, Gary Glitter, T Rex etc with the sparkly/glittery clothes. We were somewhat slicker-looking and, apart from being there at the same time, we were not a Glam-Rock band as far as we were concerned. That said, we are often referred to as such and it's not something which we feel insulted by or take offence to at all. We just never saw ourselves that way!

Grasping a copy of 'Wear It's At', the band's denial is easy to accept. Slick and suave they were, with the album all but recreating that Fifties-themed musical that their songwriters had abandoned. The opening 'Way Back In The Fifties' sets the scene, of course, and 'Rock Is Dead' is a pointed reminder that, for many folk, it was.

'Sugar Baby Love' arrives surprisingly late in the cycle, bookended by the sparkling 'For Ever' and 'Teenage Dream', and just to make certain that everyone got into the spirit of things early copies of the album arrived complete with a free cardboard beret. So you could wear your own 'at while you listened.

October 1974 – Hello: Tell Him/Lightning (Bell 1377)

Hello's breakthrough had always been threatening. Caught on the phone during Glitter's *Remember Me This Way* movie, producer Mike Leander is heard proudly announcing that Hello were 'taking off' a full six months before they finally did. That they then promptly came back to land is one of those guilty mysteries that British pop will always have to live with.

The band spent most of 1974 on the road, both at home and across western Europe and Scandinavia and they looked as great as they sounded. Developing their stage image in the years before they were signed and predating any common notions of Glam Rock by six months, Hello's original garb of crushed velvet or satin trousers, Grandad vests and Bob Bradbury's omnipresent top hat had now given way to cut off denim jackets, jeans, patches and badges. They still glittered, but it was understated, a slightly spangled Status Quo look that added to their appeal. Not only could you imagine being in a band like this, it was easy, too, to dress like them.

By the end of the year, Hello had built up sufficient acclaim to take seventh place in the *New Musical Express*' Best New Band readers' poll, but there was one final act to play out before that happened – at last, a hit single.

It was producer Mike Leander's idea that Hello re-record one of the better cuts on the Glitter Band's first album, the old Exciters hit 'Tell Him'.

Bradbury: We recorded it in May 1974 along with the B-side 'Lightning'. This period was just crazy – we were so busy, gigging, radio shows, TV, press, interviews, photo sessions, anything they could put us in, we did it.'

'Tell Him' reached Number 6 during a three-month chart run and also became the band's first hit in Germany.

October 1974 – Roxy Music: All I Want Is You/ Your Application's Failed (Island WIP 6208)

Casual as you like on *Top Of The Pops*, with Ferry even affecting what looked like a stained grey T-shirt, 'All I Want Is You' is what a sentimental love song would sound like if the Four Horsemen of the Apocalypse formed a band.

Essentially a shopping list of all the things Ferry doesn't want to hear about, because they all pale in comparison with his true love, it's a little like Sam Cooke's 'Wonderful World', except instead of not knowing about history, biology and science, Bryan simply doesn't care.

No matter that the lyric is miles away from the word-weaving of former glories. 'All I Want Is You' heralded the 'Country Life' album with irrepressible excitement.

16 October 1974 – Cherry Vanilla: Pop Tart Compositions

David Bowie's publicist and the uncrowned queen of the MainMan office, Cherry Vanilla left MainMan when Tony Defries closed down the abortive film division and cast around for new diversions.

She settled on the prose and poetry she had always written. 'I had once given out about 30 Xeroxed copies of a collection of excerpts from my diaries. I called it *Pop Tart* and it was a hit with my friends. So, I decided a book – a professionally produced, signed, numbered,

limited-edition book of my poetry, with pictures – was the vehicle I needed for my next step. And since the cover was going to be a photographic reproduction of one of the classic compositions books I always carried around with me, I simply worked that into the title, calling it *Pop Tart Compositions*.'

The book was launched with Vanilla's first ever public poetry reading, upstairs at an Italian restaurant, Ratazzi's, on New York's West 48th St.

A ferociously limited edition of 250 hard covers at $25 each and 500 soft covers at $6, *Pop Tart Compositions* sold out almost immediately.

October 1974 – Glitter Band: Let's Get Together Again/Jukebox Queen (Bell 1383)
The Glitter Band's third successive hit reached Number 8.

October 1974 – Yellow Bird: Attack Attack/Right On (Magnet MAG 16)
Tony Sando (vocals), Rob Fowler (guitar) and brother Steve (guitar), Jeff Gibs (bass, keyboards) and Barry Everleigh (drums) were Magnet's latest tip for the Glam-Rock top, and how could they fail with both Peter Shelley *and* Marty Wilde producing them?

Well, they could have looked for a different B-side. 'Right On' marked the first anniversary of its appearance on the Zappo flip by returning here.

October 1974 – Zig Zag: Bump/Sleeping Blue Nights (Magnet MAG 17)
Zig Zag were the featured dance troupe on Granada TV's pop show *45* and comprised Marianne Brown, Julie Dean, Guy Lutman, Ken Martyne, Victoria Shellard, Lamona Snow and Robert Finch. Their debut single was duly promoted on the show, with added audience participation, but it didn't help...

24 October 1974 – London premiere of Stardust
On record it's a beating heart, but on film the blood has already stopped pumping and it's the final slamming of the hospital door that ushers in the funereal beat which runs through the national anthem of rock – 'Stardust', the most sobering reflection yet on that most clichéd of glorious rock'n'roll ambitions, 'live fast, die young and leave a beautiful corpse.'

Jim MacLaine, the hero both of *Stardust* and its predecessor, *That'll Be The Day*, did all three and, in so doing, he dragged British cinema out of a rut it had been riding for half a decade.

No longer tethered to the twin bankable gods of Hammer horror and sitcom spinoffs, the mid-Seventies saw British pop music movies explode into a focus unseen since they heyday of Merseybeat. Glam Rock was a visual extravaganza even before the cameras started rolling, but its screen test took a lot of folk by storm.

Unfortunately, that's about as far as it got. Bolan's *Born To Boogie* seems quaint today; *Slade In Flame* merely dated, Glitter's *Remember Me This Way* was always absurd and Bowie's much delayed *Ziggy Stardust – The Motion Picture* had all the guts and guitars mixed out of it to try and make its tenth anniversary release sound more 'Eighties'.

Then there was *Stardust*, and celluloid really doesn't get much better than this. *That'll Be The Day* ends with Jim MacLaine buying an electric guitar; *Stardust* picks up with him already on the road, co-leader of the Stray Cats and happily grinding round the clubs until MacLaine talks an old fairground acquaintance – Mike, Leo Sayer's real-life manager Adam Faith – into managing them.

There's another managerial spot for Marty Wilde, the singer who wouldn't become Alvin Stardust, and dazzling cameos for Keith Moon, Paul Nicholas and Dave Edmunds. And the movie moves quickly, the industry standard hybrid of hard graft and crafty hardness ('fancy a drink?') propelling the Stray Cats to the top, even as Mike's behind-the-scenes machinations push MacLaine to the fore. When *That'll Be The Day* was released on DVD in the US in the late Nineties, the promotional material suggested that it was based on the life of the young John Lennon; it wasn't. *Stardust* embarks upon a journey even more tragic than his.

With Larry Hagman stepping into an Allen Klein role years before the Rutles conceived Ron Decline, and Faith perfect as the archetypal Mr Fix-It, *Stardust* slips effortlessly from a simple tale of rock'n'roll excess into something approaching a Shakespearean tragedy as an increasingly messianic MacLaine first breaks down, then burns out and finally blows away, a brilliantly-depicted OD in the midst of his first live television appearance in two years.

The final scene shows Faith shouting angrily into the cameras. 'It's a good story, isn't it?' Then the door slams shut.

Ever dream of being David Essex's girl? Well . . .

If Only That Had Been The Day

I'D BEEN standing in a long queue for hours but it didn't seem to matter at all. Even though the wind bit into my cheek, I wasn't miserable. I knew that soon, soon I would be meeting David who'd warm me with his smile. And as he smiled he'd look deep into my eyes . . . which was all I dreamed of. So I didn't let anything else enter my mind. When you're in love with someone you just shut out everyone but that person. And we'd been so close for so long, him and I.

Did we really meet in school and eventually start dating in the fourth year—although I'd had a crush on him for years? He was certainly the best looking boy in the form and of course one of the cleverest. I envied him when he came top in most of the exams but I felt proud at the same time. It was like an extra boost for me when he did well but success never used to affect him at all. Every break he'd sit listening to the radio and all the other girls would crowd around pretending to be interested in an Elvis song but really wanting to be nearer to David. Hardly surprising!

The first time he took me out I wore my hair in a ponytail and I must've blushed when he said I looked cute. Then, as I looked into his blue eyes, I realised two things with absolute certainty. I knew he was dreaming of many different things and I knew too that I would follow him anywhere. We dated for a couple of months but I knew that if we were going to last, it couldn't be a plodding, steady relationship. And I knew he understood when I said that I had to set him free because I dreamed of being the girl he needed, needed so much to be waiting after everything else had gone wrong. Even if he dated other girls I wouldn't mind too much, because I'd understand.

Was the first thing I knew about his running away from home his mum coming round to see if he was at my house? I told her I'd heard nothing but I wished I could have settled her mind. Wherever he'd gone, I knew he was safe. A few weeks later I got a postcard telling me he was working as a deck-chair attendant on the coast. But his later letters told me that he'd moved on to a fairground and was going around with a new friend called Mike. In one letter he asked me to go and see him because he was feeling really down. So of course I had to travel down to see him the following Saturday. Even though he looked pale, I couldn't ask him to go back with me. I knew he wouldn't listen so I didn't try.

The worst blow came when he did eventually return. I saw him a few times but I knew he was seeing a blonde, the sister of one of his friends. I didn't mind that—but when I heard they intended to get married I couldn't pretend not to care. All I could do was hide my feelings and I even smiled for the wedding photographs. When their baby was born I made a shawl for the christening and felt happy because David looked happy.

I was the only one who knew his plans when he packed his bags and left again. He wanted to get in a band, be someone like the rock 'n' roll stars he heard at dance halls. His voice was good and I believed he had talent. If anything I'd encouraged him to take chances, and I knew he was a wanderer. There was something special in him that attracted me but I didn't realise then that he'd become a superstar.

Slowly th[illegible] started following him, writing his name on walls, crowding around his dressing room. It was a strange feeling, all those girls feeling exactly the same way as me. Wanting to be near him, waiting, hoping. I watched him on television waving to the crowds as he stepped off a plane. Singing to the camera he was singing to thousands of girls but I always knew it was for me.

Yes, I'm the one who could tell his story better than the closest friend who thought they knew him. Now that he's coming back to me from TV, the cinema screen and magazines I can watch him again. Each movement that I know so well, the habit he has of smiling that crooked smile when he's not sure of himself, I've noticed every little thing about him, I could almost tell you the number of eyelashes on each eye. Each decision he's ever made I've decided along with him and I've always backed him up—even when the going has been hard.

Eventually I got as far as the ticket office and went in to see 'Stardust' for the second time. Next week I'm going to my fourth performance of 'That'll Be The Day'. I always get so carried away in David's films that I imagine myself in the plot but it's just wishful thinking. Somehow it doesn't seem to matter how often I see the screen story, I still get jealous, angry, sad and excited. I'll never be anyone special to David Essex in real life so it's just me, him, the cheapest seat in the stalls and my imagination.

You see, I've never actually met David, except in my dreams . . .

A feelgood film it ain't.

The movie's soundtrack can't be beaten, either. 'Stardust' aside, all of Essex's contributions to the set – yes, even the excerpt from the rock opera that is his farewell to public life – are magnificent. Elsewhere, the two-LP soundtrack essentially followed the biggest hits of the decade on display, replacing *That'll Be The Day*'s late-Fifties vista with a trip through the Sixties and then padding out the vinyl action with a few custom-made classics of its own. *That'll Be The Day* prompted fresh brilliance out of former Bonzo Dog Band vocalist Viv Stanshall ('Red Leather Jacket'); *Stardust* roped Dave Edmunds into the brew.

The greatest British producer of the era – even if he did squander most of his talent on Pub-Rock bands – and one of the finest guitarists as well, Edmunds arrived with a clutch of tracks that sounded suspiciously like outtakes from his own latest album, 'Subtle As A Flying Mallet' and instructions to back Essex on a few decidedly Cavernesque rockers.

The musical vista does get confused on screen; songs appear in what appears to be chronological sequence, taking the listener through the Sixties and, presumably, into 1970 – Derek and the Dominoes' 'Layla' plays on MacLaine's reel-to-reel as he prepares himself for his final interview.

A little earlier, during a scratch football match in their castle courtyard, Faith threatens his over-exuberant dog with a yellow card, a penalty that was introduced to the professional game at the World Cup that same summer. But earlier, during the recording of the rock opera, a *Rocky Horror Show* poster can be seen on the studio wall, dating the film (and, in truth, the sheer scale of the operatic conceit) to some time after 1973. And there are moments, as MacLaine's hair grows longer and he learns how to really move with his guitar, when he looks a dead ringer for Marc Bolan.

Such nitpicking, of course, is irrelevant. On vinyl as much as the screen it was Essex who prevailed, his title track not only granting him a fifth successive hit single but also offering a requiem for every rock'n'roller who has ever climbed too high and fallen too hard. Plus it boasts a guitar solo to die for – literally, in Jim MacLaine's case.

October 1974 – Queen: Killer Queen/Flick Of The Wrist (EMI 2229)

Previewing the 'Sheer Heart Attack' LP, 'Killer Queen' was, said Freddie Mercury, 'about a high-class call girl. I'm trying to say that classy people can be whores as well. That's what the song is about, though I'd prefer people to put their interpretation upon it – to read into it what they like, 'Killer Queen' would rise to Number 2, but David Essex would keep them off the top. Who's just a pretty face now?

October 1974 – Sparks: Never Turn Your Back On Mother Earth/Alabamy Right (Island WIP 6211)

Not only is this Ron Mael's most beautiful composition, it's one of the loveliest songs anybody has ever written. It was a song, Ron revealed, that simply appeared to him 'fully formed. I never even had to go to the piano for that one.'

He also knew that there was nothing to compare it to, not in Sparks' universe, nor anybody else's.

Perhaps David Bowie's 'Life On Mars?' could venture close in terms of a gorgeous melody, a mystifying lyric and a peerless performance stepping out of the artist's expected milieu to illustrate abilities that went beyond simple pop writing.

Bob Dylan, too, had shaken up the constituency once or twice in the past, tearing up the form book simply because he could.

But Bowie did it at a time when he had nothing to lose, on the 'Hunky Dory' album that announced his intentions long before he got to deliver on them; and Dylan did it later, in an age when his success was already inviolate. Sparks weren't merely going out on an artistic limb, they were venturing out on a commercial one as well. But 'Never Turn Your Back On Mother Earth' swept imperiously to Number 13 in October 1974 – lower than its predecessors, perhaps, but respectable all the same

October 1974 – Angel: Little Boy Blue/ Tragedy Queen (Cube BUG 51)

Warming up another Andy Scott song that had once been considered for the Sweet's own purposes, Angel's second single with their glamorous producers went no further than the first.

October 1974 – Fancy: Touch Me/I Don't Need Your Love (Antic K11814)

Mike Hurst: 'You could say, I made one terrible mistake with Fancy. As it turns out, I don't really feel that way, but any critic could say I made a cardinal error. I made a commercial record of "Wild Thing" with friends of mine, did that and out of the blue it was in the American Top Twenty.

'So what did I do? I didn't do what every sensible person would do, I didn't go and make another version of "Wild Thing" with "You Really Got Me" or something. I thought, "Jesus, I've got a hit in the States. I've got great musicians here. I'm going to find a fantastic girl singer to put with them and we're going to have a great rock band."

And that's what he did.

With Fenwick and Foster hanging on from the original line-up and drummer Les Binks being prised away from Alvin Stardust's Heartbeats, Fancy set out in search of a new female vocalist. Legend insists they tried out some 200 singers, including Carol Grimes and Curved Air's Sonja Kristina, before finally settling on Annie Cavanaugh, a Londoner who had spent 10 of her 23 years living in Australia.

There she starred in the local cast of the rock musical *Hair* before returning to England to join the show's London chorus. In summer 1972, she moved across to *Jesus Christ Superstar* and joined Fancy just in time to record a new single.

And so the reconstituted Fancy returned to the US Top Twenty with the utterly dissimilar, but really rather good 'Touch Me'. They toured the country as well, making their first ever live appearance at a theological college in Grand Rapids, MI, on 8 November, then marching on for another month to land some extraordinarily encouraging reviews and catch an early glimpse of Patti Smith as she undertook her own debut tour. The two were billed together (with Fancy headlining) at the Whisky A Go Go in Los Angeles.

October 1974 – Bay City Rollers: All Of Me Loves All Of You/The Bump (Bell 1382)
October 1974 – Bay City Rollers: Rollin' (Bell 244)

Traditionally, most teen idols viewed LPs as a place to put their singles once they'd fallen out of the chart and grab some more sales from the diehard fans. Three A-sides, three B-sides, half a dozen don't-break-sweaters, job done.

Not the Rollers. It had taken them four years to get into a position where the world was screaming (literally in some cases) for a long-playing dose of tartan love and 'Rollin'' did not disappoint.

Yes, the singles were here – 'Shang-a-Lang', 'Summerlove Sensation', 'Remember' and even 'Saturday Night', rerecorded from the old flop 45 to prove that idiot chants can live forever. But any song here could have been a single, including the band's own self-compositions, and several others had been. Singer John Kincaid had released a version of 'Jenny Gotta Dance' a few months earlier, while 'Give It To Me Now' was originally recorded by 'Heart Of Stone' hitmaker Tony Kenny during 1973.

'Rollin'' was an inevitable Number 1 and stayed on the chart for 62 weeks. Rollin' indeed! But the moment didn't end there. It was joined in the upper echelons of the chart by 'All Of Me Loves All Of You', a rollicking singalong of a single backed by a song which itself would take on a life of its own shortly, Martin-Coulter's 'The Bump'.

Igniting what was hitherto a somewhat obscure dance move, 'The Bump' was a sensational record and one that deserved a lot

more exposure than a backside on Bell could provide. It got it, too, but only after the Rollers dispensed with the services of songwriters Bill Martin and Phil Coulter in a bid to prove themselves as songwriters (and musicians – they had yet to play on any of their own hits).

The break cost them £20,000 and, according to press reports, was amicable. But still Martin-Coulter took immediate revenge, re-recording 'The Bump' for Christmas release and going head-to-head with the treacherous Tartans.

October 1974 – Michael Des Barres: Leon/ New Moon Tonight (Purple 123)

With the 'Teenybopper Death' scandal still buzzing around his ears, Des Barres had all but abandoned England for a new life in Los Angeles by the time his much-discussed solo career finally got off the ground. Although his first and only solo single was scarcely what anyone had expected to hear from him, Des Barres included.

'I did it in 20 minutes,' he only slightly exaggerates. 'They booked me into the studio, gave me a Philip Goodhand-Tait song and said, "sing this". So I did. I don't even think about that record, I just went in and said, "This is fantastic – now who am I going to be this time? I know, I'm the third Ryan Twin [as in singing siblings Paul and Barry...] Great, let's do that." Apart from that, I don't really remember making it.'

It's very likely nobody remembers buying it, either.

October 1974 – The Sweet: Turn It Down/Someone Else Will (RCA 2480)
October 1974 – Suzi Quatro: The Wild One/Shake My Sugar (RAK 185)
October 1974 – Suzi Quatro: Quatro (RAK 509)

After the electric vitality of its predecessor and the prepossessing energy of her first four singles, Suzi Quatro's second album was a dreadful disappointment, the fault – one assumes – of having been cut so quickly after its predecessor that nobody involved in the process had time to even catch their breath.

Just two Quatro/Tuckey originals made it aboard and one of them, 'Klondyke Kate', was little more than a throwaway. But Chinnichap, too, seem uncharacteristically lacklustre – the

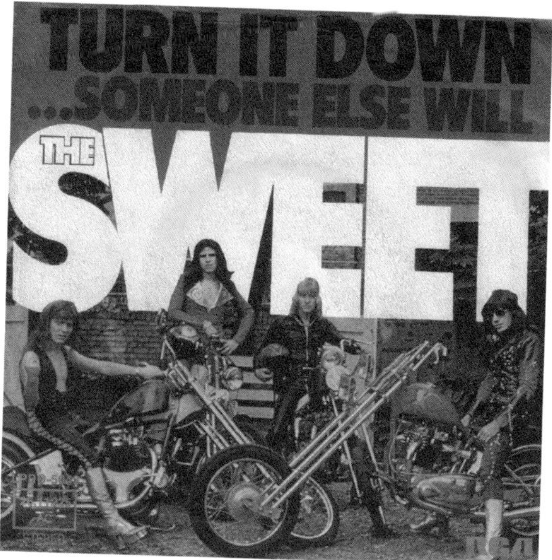

still vital 'Devil Gate Drive' notwithstanding.

Of course there were mitigating circumstances. The Chinnichap duo themselves were in transition at this time, trying to retool a super-successful but hideously hidebound writing formula towards a less glam-entrenched listening audience. And the next few Quatro singles would reflect the then-prevalent belief that 'mature' songs were the way to go – 'mature', in those days, meant not having quite so much fun as they used to.

The Sweet's 'Turn It Down' was the first salvo they would fire, followed just weeks later by

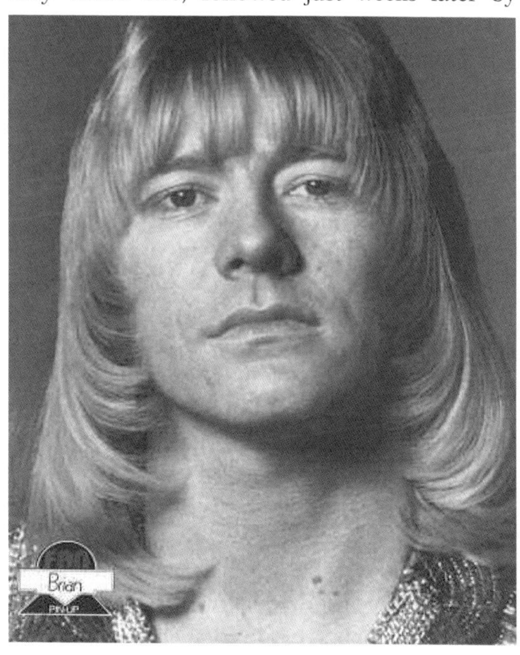

Quatro's 'The Wild One'. Re-recorded from the 'Quatro' album, it became her sixth consecutive UK hit and rose to Number 7. But the Sweet limped to Number 41, their worst performance since the Parlophone days.

'We did wonder about that,' Connolly confessed. 'We'd always assumed there was a solid core of however many thousands of kids who bought our records because they liked us as a band. And suddenly, two singles on the trot, we realised that, without *Top Of The Pops*, we really weren't any bigger than anybody else... We weren't any bigger than Geordie.'

October 1974 – The Kindness of Smokey Strangers

What the Sweet and everybody else did not seem to understand was that Chinnichap didn't care about being bigger than Geordie any longer. Success was not the issue now. It was respect the duo craved more than anything and they thought they'd found a way of obtaining it with the latest additions to the empire, Smokey.

'The criticism of our music was wearing us down,' Chapman confessed. 'The culmination came when I was in the studio with Suzi and we picked up the *New Musical Express*, which contained a review of [her] latest...single by Charles Shaar Murray. It said something like Nicky and I were misrepresenting the artist by making such banal music, that Suzi would be better off without us, that we were both fakes, that we didn't know what we were doing.

'I took it pretty well I guess, but Suzi broke down in tears, so I got angry. We sent a roadie out to buy some pig's brains, some wrapping paper and a card, wrapped it all up with a big bow and wrote on the card something like "Dear Charles, If you are bent on becoming as..." and I thought of all the egotistical words I could, "as I am, then perhaps you could do with some of these".'

The brains sat stinking in their wrapper on Murray's desk all weekend. 'When he got in and opened it up the thing stunk the place out. I think they cut off my subscription the next week. But that's when the critics got to me. I'd had enough, Suzi had had enough, and when I told Nicky about it he'd had enough too. We needed credibility, we were tired of being put down.'

They began to make amends immediately by moving in on a band that had already passed across Mickie Most's radar when they were picked up as Peter Noone's backing band in 1973. They were called Kindness and, while Most didn't sign them, he certainly didn't baulk when he was offered them on a plate.

Lead guitarist Alan Silson fills in the group's earliest days. 'Chris Norman, Terry Uttley and I met at school in Bradford, Yorkshire. As teenagers, Chris and I began meeting up and spending nearly all our spare time learning new songs on our guitars. We asked Terry and a drummer friend called Ron Kelly to join us and formed our first band.'

Over the next few years the group underwent a string of name changes: they were the Yen for a time, then Sphynx and Essence before merging with the Black Cats and becoming the Four Corners and then the Elizabethans.

'By 1968, we had turned professional via a stint at Butlin's holiday camp, Skegness. During the next seven years the band gained much experience playing around the UK, many live radio broadcasts and managed to sign a recording contract with RCA.'

It was RCA who changed the band's name to Kindness and a single, 'Light Of Love' (not the T Rex number)/'Lindy Lou' (RCA 1942 – 'awful song', shudders Silson) followed in early 1970. It did little and the band moved on, eventually signing to Decca.

Three singles followed: 'Let The Good Times Roll'/'Oh Yea' (Decca F13318) in June 1972; 'Oh Julie'/'I Love You Carolina' (Decca F13338) in August 1972 and 'Make It Better'/'Long Lonely Lady' (Decca F13429) in 1973, but with no success.

Ron Kelly left and was replaced by Pete Spencer and, by 1974, 'We had developed our own sound, reflecting close three-part harmonies wrapped up in a guitar rock sound, a sort of mixture between Crosby, Stills and Nash and Creedence Clearwater Revival.'

It was at this time that the band's manager Bill Hurley arranged for Mike Chapman to see Kindness perform at Hatchett's in Piccadilly Circus. But claims that there now ensued a rocky courtship, with Chinnichap hemming and hawing over the band's potential while Hurley refused to take 'no' for an answer, appear to be wide of the mark.

Silson: 'Chinnichap were looking for a new band to sign who were more album-oriented and not so Glam as their other acts. He liked us and a week later he brought Nicky Chinn to see us at a gig in East Grinstead, Sussex. They were both impressed and signed the band on a three-album deal to Chinnichap productions on RAK.'

Chinnichap would compose the band's hits, of course, but Kindness would also be given their songwriting head. Silson reveals that most of the songs for their forthcoming debut album were written during a three-month residency at a club in Blackpool in summer 1974 – around the same time as the group changed their name to Smokey.

Behind the scenes, however, jealousies arose immediately. Brian Connolly added the distracting draw of Smokey to the reasons why the Sweet's last single had not been up to the usual Chinnichap quality; Mud, less prone to condemn, nevertheless wondered whether there would be enough good songs to go around. And over at RAK, where Arrows' second single, 'Toughen Up', had passed by without a whimper, there was a definite sense that they'd been superseded on the list of priorities.

Asking when they would cut a new single, Arrows were astonished to be told that there were still hopes that the now two month-old 'Toughen Up' might suddenly pick up...a surprise invitation onto *Top Of The Pops*, for instance. But the invitation never came and the feeling grew stronger that, if it did, Mickie Most would rather pack Smokey onto the box than Arrows. It would be the work of a moment to record their first single and send the new group skyward, particularly after Smokey entered the studio in October following a three-week tour of Finland.

They used Chinnichap's favourite Audio International and there began work on the record that, or so it was said, would prove once and for all to the snotty rock critics that the dynamic duo were legitimate songwriters. Smokey, they insisted, were destined to become RAK's answer to Bad Company and Led Zeppelin and, between Chinnichap and themselves, they had the songs that would make that so.

October 1974 – Why do the Americans have all the best TV?

With Bowie's 'Diamond Dogs' concert carcass dragging across America, losing money all the way, MainMan moved to recoup some of the money by licensing a one-hour edit of the final Ziggy Stardust show to US network ABC.

Plans to release DA Pennebaker's full movie version as a film in its own right had faltered; Bowie was not interested in reliving his past when his future was still up for grabs – his latest single, a cover of the old soul stomper 'Knock On Wood', was new on the racks and so uncertain was Bowie about its reception that, when *Top Of The Pops* called up to request some film footage, they were told to do what they wanted. The result has to be the oddest 'video' ever attached to a Bowie record, a few minutes of footage following a girl around a London street market interspersed by a few seconds of stills from the 'David Live' LP cover. 'Knock On Wood' climbed to Number 10.

The Hammersmith Odeon footage was broadcast as part of the ABC network's *In Concert* series and in turn became the source for all the bootlegs that subsequently emerged from the show. The ABC edit is readily distinguished from Bowie's own 1983 release of the show via a much superior mix and the inclusion of the special treat that Bowie laid on for the night, the appearance of Ronno's idol Jeff Beck for a punchy 'Jean Genie'. Beck later claimed he'd nixed its use in the later edition because he hated the flares he was wearing that night.

British fans would not get to see the show. The BBC was preparing its own Bowie special, director Alan Yentob's *Cracked Actor* and while moments from the Pennebaker production would be incorporated the concert itself remained unseen.

So, what did we miss?

Hilly Michaels, drummer with the American band Peach and Lee as they toured 'every dive west of the Mississippi River' recalls, 'we'd watch TV in our rooms after shows and always see Bowie, Slade, Edgar [Winter], etc playing live on *Kirshner* or special Bowie moments/concerts... And I remember one broadcast in particular, when Jeff Beck joined Bowie on stage.

'I remember Mick Ronson had on a white

sparkly suit and paid Beck some obvious respect when he walked on and jammed with them. Me and my band sat and stared, glued to the images and sound coming out the TV. I was a Beck freak my whole life, I bought anything Beck played guitar on back then, and I saw him on TV getting up on stage, Mick shaking his hand. Wow!'

October 1974 – Geordie: Ride On Baby/Got To Know (EMI 2226)

Another non-album A-side, but once again it didn't help.

October 1974 – Sally James: Isn't It Good/ Wake Me When It's Over (Philips 6006 418)

The effervescent James bubbled into view in 1973 as the hostess of London Weekend Television's *Saturday Scene*, a morning-long children's show that mixed movies and repeats of other kid's shows with sometimes lengthy linking sequences, interviews with visiting pop stars, musical performances and more.

Considerably more anarchic than anything on 'the other side' at that time and with James' eye for current fashion ensuring a regular audience of dads as well, *Saturday Scene*'s success pushed James – hitherto a little-known actress – firmly into the public eye with regular columns in *Look In* and other publications and even a short-lived recording career.

She was also co-host (with Kid Jensen) of this author's debut television appearances on the Yorkshire TV game show *Pop Quiz* in November/December 1976.

October 1974 – Slik: The Boogiest Band In Town/Hatchet (Polydor 2058 523)

Alternately revered and reviled as the band that offered Midge Ure his first taste of his future superstardom, Slik – or Salvation, as they were originally known – came together in 1970 in Glasgow.

Formed by brothers Jim (guitar) and Kevin McGinlay (vocals), the band initially moved in a metallic direction but shifted towards lighter pop following a 1972 split that left the McGinlays alone. Guitarist/vocalist James Ure, drummer Kenny Hyslop and guitarist Billy McIsaac completed the new-look Salvation and the group devoted the next two years to the Scottish discotheque circuit with the occasional hop up the scale to support some visiting superstar; they opened for the Sweet at Glasgow Apollo in November 1973.

And all the while, the band was becoming more commercial, poppier and poppier until Kevin McGinlay had had enough. His last words, as he walked out in April 1974, were 'If you carry on like this, you'll end up recording Martin-Coulter songs.'

Weeks later, that's exactly what they were doing. Having just broken with the Bay City Rollers, Bill Martin and Phil Coulter were alerted to Salvation by reports of their growing local fame – sold-out nightclubs and the first glimmerings of a screamybop following. They made contact just as the band changed its name to Slik and the members adopted pseudonyms to further the aura of band unity – Ure became Midge (and, a decade later would prompt that immortal *NME* crossword clue 'What is small and irritating about Ultravox?'), Hyslop became Oil Slik, McGinlay became Jim Slik and McIsaac became Lord Slik.

Things moved quickly. Martin-Coulter signed Slik to Polydor and set about recording their debut single, a scarcely autobiographical confection that nevertheless had a kick and a punch that threatened great things.

27 October 1974 – The Basil Brush Show: Sailor

A month after they appeared on *In Concert*, Sailor were back as special guests of everybody's favourite (or otherwise) wisecracking fox. It was a good move, as well. According to Kajanus, 'It was our appearance on *Basil Brush* that cemented our fame. More people stopped me in the street after *Basil Brush* than after *In Concert*!'

ON THE RADIO
20 October 1974 – Sounds On Sunday: Slade
29 October 1974 – Top Gear: Cozy Powell
ON THE BOX
1 October 1974 – Lift Off With Ayshea: David Essex
3 October 1974 – Twiggs: David Essex
4 October 1974 – Russell Harty: David Essex
4 October 1974 – Top Of The Pops: David Essex, Roxy Music, David Bowie

5 October 1974 – Saturday Scene: Sparks
5 October 1974 – Nana Mouskouri Show: Sparks
8 October 1974 – Lift Off With Ayshea: Hello
10 October 1974 – 45: Sparks
11 October 1974 – Russell Harty: Bryan Ferry
11 October 1974 – Top Of The Pops: Barry Blue, Bay City Rollers, Queen, Slade
15 October 1974 – Lift Off With Ayshea: Barry Blue, Bay City Rollers
17 October 1974 – 45: David Essex
17 October 1974 – Twiggs: Bryan Ferry
17 October 1974 – Top Of The Pops: Roxy Music, Slade, David Essex
24 October 1974 – 45: Cockney Rebel
24 October 1974 – Top Of The Pops: Glitter Band, Bay City Rollers, Queen, Sparks
31 October 1974 – Top Of The Pops: Barry Blue, David Essex, Suzi Quatro, Hello, Slade
ON THE SHELVES
October 1974 – Bunk Dogger: Red Light/Whenever I See Your Light (UK 81)
October 1974 – Ayshea: Another Without You Day/Moonbeam (DJM DJS 339)
October 1974 – Paul Da Vinci: If You get Hurt/Just Kiss (Penny Farthing PEN 852)
October 1974 – Kiss: Hotter Than Hell (Casablanca 7007)

November 1974 – The Sweet: Desolation Boulevard (RCA 5080)

The Sweet's third album (although they only counted two), 'Desolation Boulevard' was the latest stage in the band's bid to gain some critical respect, recorded at a time when their commercial impact was beginning to wane. And the possibility that one might have anything in common with the other really didn't seem to have dawned on them.

Sales were low and few of the reviews mustered much enthusiasm for the disc; indeed, complained one, 'The Sweet try so hard to grasp artistic integrity that one cannot help but applaud their every effort. The trouble is, they still look and behave like a man who knows he's wearing an invisible giant chicken outfit and knows that the rest of us know it as well.'

When it was good, and it often was, 'Desolation Boulevard' proved that the Sweet had already made the transition they'd been harping on about for so long; that they had proven their worth in a universe that was not peopled exclusively by teenyboppers and chart fanatics.

But still there was an over-earnestness to their music that couldn't help but raise the listener's hackles and even as you listened to the record it was difficult to escape the knowledge that there was a half-a-side-long drum solo to wade through before the thing was over. Bluntly, the Sweet were trying too hard to prove what they could do rather than just going out there and doing it. And the fact that they were still reliant on Chinnichap for their singles, no matter how poorly they might perform, was not going to diminish that condemnation.

November 1974 – Mr Big: Christmas With Dicken/Time For A Laugh (Epic EPC 2823)

A suitably seasonal offering, namechecking the band's frontman. "Christmas With Dicken' must rank as one of the worst Christmas records ever,' he admits. 'But never mind.'

November 1974 – Sparks: Propaganda (Island ILPS 9312)

'Kimono My House' was still being assimilated into the UK music scene when Sparks set to work on its successor, reconvening with producer Muff Winwood with the express intention of cutting an album to demolish the already-prevalent belief that there was any such thing as a 'typical' Sparks sound.

That they succeeded in this (admittedly perverse) aim is not in question. But just how far they took that ambition can only be gauged from returning your own heart and mind to late 1974 and hearing for the first time 'Never Turn Your Back On Mother Earth.'

It is impossibly brief, clocking in at just two minutes 20. In that span, however, both Russell Mael's vocal and Ron Mael's lyric encompass more emotions than many bands can cram into an entire career – admiration, admonition, adoration and, most of all, regret: 'I'll admit I was unfaithful, but from now I'll be more faithful.'

'The way [the Maels] looked at it,' Trevor White recalls, 'was that the last album had been a success but everyone had heard it, so now we had to do something completely different that

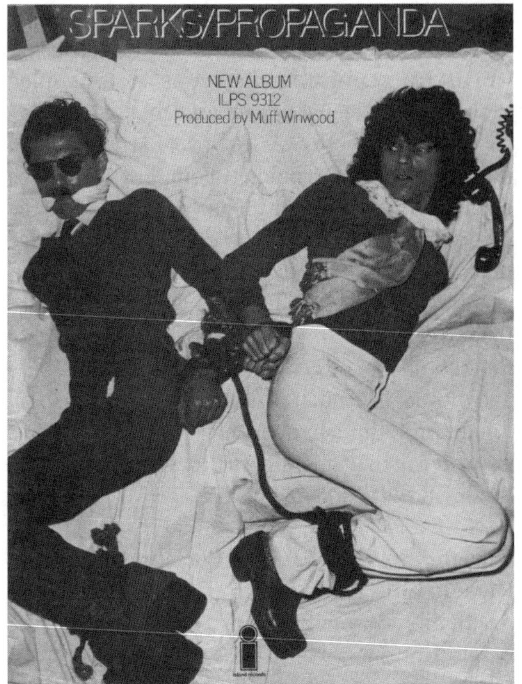

they won't have heard. They felt that they always had to be one step ahead of what people expected from them, so they would just veer off in a new direction whenever they felt like it.'

The tumbling wordplay of the title track, the militaristic mania of 'Reinforcements', the violence of 'Something For The Girl With Everything' and the bitter sentiment of 'Miss The Start, Miss The End' all differed from the reputation that Sparks had already confirmed – and if the brothers could drop a few extra bombshells all the better.

'I remember when I joined,' says White, 'I thought it a bit strange that they should want two guitarists, especially as they already had one as good as Adrian Fisher But I think it had been on their minds for a long time to get rid of him; they were just looking for the right moment.'

That moment came just as 'Propaganda' was completed. First the brothers erased all the guitarist's solos. Then they erased the guitarist.

November 1974 – Queen: Sheer Heart Attack (EMI 3061)

4 November 1974 – ***Bob Harris*****: Queen**

While Queen's sold out UK tour saw them film the in-concert movie *Queen At The Rainbow*, distilling two shows (19-20 November) down to 53 minutes of film, 'Sheer Heart Attack' arrived to push them to Number 2 on the chart with the album that established the sound that would dominate the remainder of their career.

Opening with the guitar concerto 'Brighton Rock', hopping through both their current single and its successor, 'Now I'm Here', 'Sheer Heart Attack' is as much a series of snapshots as it is a collection of songs.

The bulk of side one is schemed as a medley, the songs cross-faded so closely that they played havoc with the album's first CD pressings; side two as a string of vignettes, framed by the epochal 'Lap Of The Gods' and ending with the sound, says Brian May, of the studio exploding into a shower of sonic shards. 'The explosion's meant to break up. It's totally intentional. We said "the explosion will be too big for the studio, so tape saturation will be a part of the sound."'

Queen never did things by halves, and that includes concert films. The opening 'Now I'm Here', stagelit specifically to showcase Freddie's hide-and-seek abilities, reminds us just what a fine line Queen walked between Glam and Rock and how effortlessly they pulled it off. Of course Freddie looks a prize prat in an outfit that is half medieval smock, half Mothercare sale item, but nobody could relish that role like he did.

Plus that voice could do things that no other tonsils on earth were capable of, and as early as second track 'Ogre Battle' he's turning vocal gymnastics at the same time as giving every would-be flamboyant showman of the Seventies an object lesson in how to cut shapes. And slowing it all down for 'White Queen' doesn't tap the energy in the slightest.

Yet there is a humility to the band that is just as genuine as their sometimes preposterous pomposity; introducing a medley of cuts from 'Sheer Heart Attack' and 'Queen II', Mercury sounds genuinely touched as he thanks the audience for sending it 'racing up the charts', at the same time as the band give their own dexterity maximum welly with a blurring run through 'Lap Of The Gods', 'Killer Queen', 'March Of The Black Queen' (the ultimate Queen song, at least until 'Bohemian Rhapsody' came along) and 'Bring Back That Leroy Brown'.

There's a menacing 'Son And Daughter', a

metallic 'Father To Son', a drum solo to remind us that this was the Seventies, another mini-medley that leads into 'Stone Cold Crazy' and, finally, 'Lap Of The Gods' once again, the stage drenched in dry ice, the audience in full voice for the 'woh-oh-oh' refrain and an explosion that almost burns the TV tube out. No matter what Queen went onto achieve, this was the sight and sound of the band when they still needed to work for applause rather than go out knowing they would receive it.

In fact, watching the show, it seems incredible that, just months before the album was released, rumour insisted that Queen were on the point of breaking up. Brian May was even visited by the Mael brothers asking if he wanted to replace Adrian Fisher in Sparks.

'I did like the band,' May reflects. 'I loved "This Town Ain't Big Enough For Both Of Us". Anyway, they came round, the two brothers, and said "Look, it's pretty obvious that Queen are washed up, we'd like to offer you a position in our band, if you want." I said, "I don't think we're quite dead yet."'

Does he have any regrets? 'No, not a lot.'

November 1974 – Slade: Slade In Flame (Polydor 2442126)

Nothing, it seemed, would return Slade to the kind of omnipotence they enjoyed in 1973, but their first feature film, *Slade In Flame*, at least raised itself above the pedestrian ranks of in-concert extravaganzas and knockaround comedies that were the rock star's traditional concession to celluloid.

With a genuinely engaging storyline and musical interludes that were part of the show, *Slade In Flame* also revealed untapped acting abilities, while the accompanying soundtrack saw the band run through motions that effortlessly matched the movie's own storyboard.

Best of the batch were the singles 'Far Far Away' and the forthcoming 'How Does It Feel'. But 'Them Kinda Monkeys Don't Swing' tracked back to the classic sound of balls being broken and the album as a whole had a cohesion that would appear all the more valuable as the next year unfolded. Barely was the movie in theatres than Slade were announcing their intention to relocate to the US; and barely had that decision been taken than it seemed obvious that an era had ended. Slade would still have hits, of course. But they weren't Slade records any longer.

November 1974 – Alvin Stardust: Tell Me Why/ Roadie Roll On (Magnet MAG 19)
November 1974 – Alvin Stardust: Alvin Stardust (Magnet MAG 5004)
16 November 1974 – Lift Off With Ayshea: Alvin Stardust

Alvin was *not* leaving the UK. He made that very clear in late October after rumours flew that he too would be heading abroad to avoid the Labour government's latest tax regime. But everything else *was* changing.

His first balladic single became the first to avoid the Top Ten (it peaked at Number 16), his first TV show of the season saw him eschew black leather for a bright red suit, his Fifties hair had grown out to its natural state of curliness and his second album really wasn't much to write home about, either, as he served up a disc that wasn't *that* dissimilar to Peter Shelley's first album, released the same day.

November 1974 – Stephen: Right On Running Man/Epitaph (Antic K11513)
'Stephen' was actually Stevie Vann, wife of producer Robert 'Mutt' Lange, debuting in the UK after a successful career in South Africa. 'Right On Running Man' was rediscovered following its inclusion on the 'Blitzing The Ballroom: 20 UK Power Glam Incendiaries' compilation (Psychic Circle PCCD 7021).

November 1974 – Showaddywaddy: Hey Mr Christmas/Rock'n'Roll Man (Bell 1387)
Showaddywaddy swaggered into Christmas with a festive single that pinned down all their strongest elements while somehow conspiring to sound unlike anything they'd released before. The result, a wholly modern updating of their precious Fifties sound, was what Showaddywaddy and producer Mike Hurst had been seeking all along and now there'd be no looking back. Or Glamming up, either.

We bid farewell to Showaddywaddy with this Number 13 hit, a glorious seasonal romp that roped in the National Children's' Home Harpenden Choir to offer an extra 'oooh' factor for the mums and grans.

They would march on, of course, not only outliving their old Glam-Rock peers but outselling them as well. Outselling, too, sundry other revivalist rivals – both Darts and Rocky Sharpe and the Replays made a grab for Showaddywaddy's crown in the late Seventies, but both were forced to concede defeat.

It would be 1979 (following their break with producer Mike Hurst) before Showaddywaddy were finally forced to bow out of the Top Twenty when 'Sweet Little Rock'n'Roller' went to Number 15 – and how ironic was it that their demise should coincide precisely with the rise of Shakin' Stevens, another Hurst discovery? While Showaddywaddy scrapped around the lower reaches of the chart for the next two years, Shaky launched into a season of supremacy that established him as Britain's biggest Fifties revivalist since…Showaddywaddy.

November 1974 – Dum: In The Mood/ Watching The Clock (RAK 179)
A not-altogether-convincing Mud alias missed the chart and that despite anticipating by a full year the Glenn Miller revival of early 1976 ('Moonlight Serenade' reached Number 13; Jonathan King/Sound 9418's remake of 'In The Mood' itself made Number 46).

November 1974 – Kenny: The Bump/Forget The Janes, The Jeans, The Might Have Beens (RAK 186)
Although an artist named Kenny had already scored two Bill Martin/Phil Coulter-scripted hits for RAK, 'Heart Of Stone' and 'Give It To Me Now', *Tony* Kenny was an Irish balladeer who had already retired when Mickie Most decided to subpoena his identity for RAK's next superstars.

This Kenny was a band, legend insisted, whom Martin and Coulter discovered rehearsing in a banana warehouse in Enfield, North London. Quite what two such renowned songwriters as Bill and Phil were doing in a North London banana warehouse in the first place is another matter entirely…actually, they'd been tipped off by an agent they knew who caught a band called Chuff opening for the Troggs at Middlesex Poly.

The pair were impressed, and so Chuff – Ross Pringle (vocals), Yan Style (guitar), Chris Redburn (bass), Chris Lacklison (keyboards) and Andy Walton (drums) – received the traditional

RAK offer they could not refuse. 'We'll sign you on one condition...you change your name to Kenny. Two conditions...you record "The Bump". Three conditions...you annihilate the Rollers. Four conditions...you ditch the singer.'

With Rick Driscoll replacing the hapless Pringle, three out of four ain't bad – and they had a good stab at the fourth as well. 'Our image is better, more clean-cut than the Bay City Rollers,' they proclaimed, and it probably was.

They even survived the world being informed that 'The Bump' had been readied and, indeed, released long before anyone at RAK had even heard of Chuff. In fact, Kenny's 'The Bump' was simply the backing track to the Rollers' 'The Bump' (itself the work of session musicians) with new vocals.

But still it was Kenny, not the Rollers, who had the country banging bottoms that winter, Kenny who scored a Number 3 hit and Kenny who would reap the rewards of the rest of Martin/Coulter's future output. At least for the time being.

November 1974 – The Rubettes: Juke Box Jive/When You're Falling In Love (Polydor 2058 529)

Number 3 in time for Christmas, the third Rubettes single saw the band utterly defying all predictions for their future, probably including their own.

Bill Hurd: 'It was a big surprise just how big an impact we made. We went on to have quite a few hits and, with European hits as well, our reputation grew throughout the world. We *were* fortunate to have that bit of luck with the TV break, but we also worked very hard to build on that and over the years our live shows have become very well respected.

'For me, the highlights were the European successes and the enormous popularity we achieved in France! France had always been a totally different and unique market, with mainly French artists in the charts and appearing on TV shows etc. Many big UK artists had failed to make any impression at all, but for whatever reason the French took us to their hearts.

'Without exaggeration, we were as big as the Beatles in France at one time and it was an incredible experience. We had many Number 1 singles in France and our first three went Gold – 500,000 sales in those days!' They probably saved a lot on laundry bills, too, as they turned out on TV in sharp black suits.

November 1974 – Cockney Rebel: Big Big Deal/Bed In The Corner (EMI 2233)

An odd one, this. The long-awaited follow-up to 'Mr Soft', a new Harley composition and recording and the band were already out promoting it (an appearance on *45*) when the release was canned. 'Big Big Deal' would remain unavailable until the CD age.

November 1974 – Roxy Music: Country Life (Island ILPS 9303)

Trailered by the mighty 'All I Want Is You', Roxy Music's fourth album continued down the 'Stranded' road of appearing a lot more adult than it really ought to, a sophisticated walk through literary pastures that nevertheless unleashed some savage emotions. Bryan Ferry himself acknowledged a lack of the earlier spontaneity and excitement, but 'The Thrill Of It All', 'Out Of The Blue' and 'Casanova' all handed the record a stentorian mood that matched perfectly the band's latest live presentation, a brooding stage set which many observers instantly compared to Hitler's Nuremberg Rallies.

It was a powerful, not to mention controversial, offering, but when Roxy Music hit the headlines again, it was not Nazis but nudity which powered the press. As was the band's tradition, 'Country Life' arrived bedecked in a cover depicting a young lady (or in this instance, two) in provocative dress and position. None, however, had been this provocative.

One girl stood topless, her hands covering her nipples but her genitals barely disguised by near-transparent knickers, her only other concession to modesty. The other wore a bra, but her nipples were clearly visible and though she, too, wore underwear the hand which lay on her genitals was clearly not simply covering things up. And that shot, insiders insisted, was the tamest one taken at what was a decidedly steamy photo session.

In Britain, the album cover raised a few eyebrows, but fears that high-street record stores might baulk at carrying so blatantly provocative a sleeve without at least the precaution of a brown paper bag proved unfounded.

In America, however, the outrage was such that, following an initial run tightly shrink-wrapped in green plastic, Atlantic were forced to withdraw the sleeve altogether, replacing the girls (a pair of Valkyrie-esque fans Ferry met while in Germany) with a closer look at the foliage they were standing in front of.

Ferry was furious, but Atlantic had a point. American morals were far more easily outraged than British. The effect on Roxy Music's career, had that sleeve been allowed out unattended, would have been disastrous. Instead, news of the controversy sent demand soaring. 'Country Life' cracked the Top Forty.

A single of 'The Thrill Of It All' was culled from the album around the same time as Warner Brothers forgot that they'd been responsible for the most ignominious moment in Roxy Music's history so far when they dropped the group from their roster and created another single, 'Do the Strand'/'Virginia Plain', within the Back to Back Hits series. Suddenly Roxy Music were hot, and a full American tour was scheduled for 1975.

November 1974 – Eno: Taking Tiger Mountain By Strategy (Island ILPS 9309)

Retaining the same musical shapes as its predecessor, Eno's second solo album emerged another bundle of fractured fairytales, impossible rhythms and implausibly catchy pop scratchings, highlighted by the immense 'Third Uncle' and not even losing the listener when he unleashed the Portsmouth Sinfonia across some of the proceedings.

With lyrics as shattered as any shredder could render them, and lyrical concepts to match, 'Taking Tiger Mountain By Strategy' would have colossal influence on the musicians who were still growing up to be the electro-pop warriors of the early Eighties, and David Bowie was paying attention as well. For now, though, it simply hung in splendid isolation both chartwise and in Eno's own mind. From here on in, the words would not be half as important to him.

The SOUNDS Talk-in
Interview by Steve Peacock
ENO
Tricks
Recipe
Technology

November 1974 – Gary Glitter: Oh Yes! You're Beautiful/Thank You Baby For Myself (Bell 1391)

Another ballad and another future crowd-stirrer, 'Oh Yes! You're Beautiful', reached Number 2, clamped behind Barry White. How were we to know it was Gary's final major hit?

November 1974 – Sensational Alex Harvey Band: Anthem Part 1/Anthem Part 2 (Vertigo 6059 112)

Spread over both sides of the disc, the eight-minute 'Anthem' was culled from 'The Impossible Dream' and came the closest yet to giving the band the Top Forty breakthrough they now demanded. In the event, they'd have to wait a little longer. But they were getting closer.

November 1974 – Mott the Hoople: Live (CBS 69093)
November 1974 – Mott the Hoople: Saturday Gigs/Live Medley (CBS 2754)

Ariel Bender had already departed when the long awaited Mott the Hoople live album arrived, which may be why it didn't seem so exciting. We wanted to hear them with new guitarist Mick Ronson, not the long-gone Bender.

It was an oddly parsimonious set as well. Two shows five months apart were featured (London's Hammersmith Odeon in December 1973; New York's Uris Theater in May 1974) but with just seven songs and one medley was scarcely an extravaganza. The hits 'All The Young Dudes' and 'All The Way From Memphis' were present, but the remainder of the track list wandered between B-side ballads and straightforward rockers, none of which truly captured the dexterity and drama of a full Mott the Hoople concert. (It took three decades, but both shows were finally released in their entirety aboard a thirtieth anniversary remaster).

No matter what one's opinion of 'Live was, one thing was certain. The band that recorded it was dead and buried.

It was photographer Mick Rock who first suggested Ian Hunter consider Mick Ronson as a replacement for the absent Bender. 'So I did. And I think [Tony] Defries figured he could get Ronson out with Mott to plug his second solo album. It started endless complications but we didn't care because the two of us got on great and Mick was right at the top of his game. We thought all the creativity would return; the band were over the moon about it.'

From a fan's point of view, too, Ronson's arrival in Mott the Hoople was regarded as a marriage made in heaven. The guitarist had already confessed to some bewilderment over what was expected of him in the solo shoes which he'd been struggling to fill since he and David Bowie parted ways earlier in the year; admitted, as well, that his best work came as an interpreter of other people's ideas rather than as a vehicle for his own. When Angie Bowie sent a telegram proclaiming his union with Mott the Hoople 'The Wedding of the Year', few argued with her.

But the marriage was not to be a happy one. Hunter was hospitalised following a nervous breakdown which scuppered the band's live plans, bar short tours of Scandinavia and France; and even once they hit the road Ronson was miserable, stuck touring with a group who, Hunter aside, apparently viewed his recruitment, stature and expense account with vitriolic distrust.

'Two limos were turning up, one from Columbia for Mott, one from RCA for Mick. And the others in the band got upset,' Hunter sighed. 'And so, a split developed.'

Ronson's wife, Suzi, agreed, adding, 'Mick couldn't buy a drink without four pairs of eyes watching him.' And the bitterness didn't fade, either – years later, when Overend Watts came to compile the first Mott the Hoople greatest hits album, Ronno was relegated to a sleeve credit no larger than that afforded the session men who'd helped out on everything else.

'It seemed real good for about a week. No, I'm kidding, 10 days,' Ronson told *Circus* magazine. 'It all seemed like everybody was enthusiastic, but after a few days it was a drag really. People would lie in bed or not bother to turn up and nobody would speak to each other. They were together for a long time and then, when they got a little bit of money, they didn't want to pour any of it back into the band. What they wanted at that stage was everything out of the business, but nothing in the business. They didn't want to gamble – to them it was a steady job.

'They're not a band. Just people who play to satisfy their ego. We played together on stage, but offstage, everyone was on his own. And the last tour they did was not done for the pleasures of playing live, making the crowd happy. No, they played to make money for Christmas. They simply needed the money to buy Christmas presents! How could I play with people like that?'

To the public at large, of course, the whole

world was rosy and about to get even rosier. Hunter proclaimed the Scandinavian outing 'one of our best tours ever' and a new album, provisionally titled 'Weekend', was being talked about.

News from the rehearsal rooms contained any number of possible song titles: a Buffin composition titled 'Sunset Summer Nights', Hunter's 'Tell Your Brother', '3,000 Miles From Here', 'Silver Needles' and 'Did You See Them Run?' and others: 'Black Stuff', 'Electronic Robot', even a cover of the old Shadows/Ventures hit 'FBI'.

And their next single was magnificent, Hunter resuscitating the last set of desultory sessions, rewriting 'Saturday Kids' as 'Saturday Gigs' and reworking it around Ronson's explosive guitar solo. An elegiac recounting of Mott the Hoople's entire history, it came close to justifying every hope Mott the Hoople had ever inspired. With Ronson's soaring guitar as perfect as any he had played with Bowie, with Hunter's voice as scathing and saddening as ever, these ingredients alone made all the recent troubles seem worthwhile.

And then you got to the fade-out...

Two years before, wrapping up 'All The Young Dudes' in the studio, Hunter started to ad-lib over the fade, a few lines of exhortation calling the audience to his side. Now he started to do it again, only this time it wasn't a call to arms. It was the last rites.

On the single, all you really hear is a distant chorus singing goodbye. The 'All The Young Dudes' box set, however, creates a collage from a handful of the band's working mixes and alternate takes and Hunter's intentions are revealed. 'Now, don't you ever forget us, we'll never forget you,' he cries. 'We're just going to sleep for a little while. See you again sometime.'

November 1974 – Mud: Lonely This Christmas/ I Can't Stand It (RAK 187)

Entering the chart at Number 4 and inevitably destined to become Mud's second British Number 1, 'Lonely This Christmas' has also become one of the most enduring festive pop hits of the Seventies, a moving, heartfelt ballad which wouldn't have been out of place on one of Elvis Presley's festive collections.

The fact that Les Gray is once again in full Elvis soundalike mode for the song only heightens that impression, which was precisely what songwriters Nicky Chinn and Mike Chapman were intending. 'Nicky and I were only concerned with writing songs that he could sing like Elvis,' Chapman confessed, 'and I took that to its absolute extreme with "Lonely This Christmas".

'It started as a send-up,' Gray explained. 'It was meant to be like one of those old schmaltzy Christmas songs. Then we found out people took it seriously. But that was fine, because it didn't matter if you laughed at it or if it meant something to you as long as it affected you in some way.'

You could even forgive the band for performing it straight. The first few times, anyway. By the end of its chart-topping run, Les had a ventriloquist's dummy to sing to and the roadies were up on stepladders, dropping snow on their employers' heads. Classic.

November 1974 – Rik Kenton: Bungalow Love/ Lay It On You (Island WIP 6214)

An excellent solo offering from the one-time Roxy Music bassist.

November 1974 – Bilbo Baggins: Sha Na Na Na Song/Run With The Devil (Polydor 2058 530)

Another Bickerton/Waddington composition and production, 'Sha Na Na Na Song' debuted the latest Baggins image – white bomber jackets with school-like cloth badges.

November 1974 – Stavely Makepeace: Runaround Sue/There's A Wall Between Us (Deram DM 423)

Stavely Makepeace's final single before Lieutenant Pigeon's live obligations finally forced the band on hiatus was a distinctive cover of Dion's 'Runaround Sue', debuted as usual on *Lift Off* (26 November 1974) alongside appearances from Hello and Alvin Stardust.

It would be four years before Stavely stirred again with a couple more singles during 1977-78: 'Baby Blue Eyes'/'Big Bad Baby Blondie' (Unigram U6312) and 'No Regrets'/'You're Talking Out Of Your Head' – on Chas Chandler's Barn label (2014 118) were outtakes from past sessions. The following year Stavely Makepeace cut their first new 45 in five years, 'Coconut Shuffle'/'Napoleon Brandy' (Barn 001). 'Songs Of Yesterday'/ 'Storm' (Hammer HS 304) followed in 1980; the self-released 'Just Tell Her Fred Said Goodbye'/'Opus 306' (SMA 1502) appeared in 1983.

Woodward and Fletcher continue working together today, creating radio jingles and voice-overs; publishing a joint autobiography, *When Show Business Is No Business* (2000) and, in 2004, seeing the complete Stavely Makepeace catalogue compiled as the CD 'The Scrap Iron Rhythm Revue.'

November 1974 – Marc Bolan and T Rex: Zip Gun Boogie/Space Boss (T Rex MARC 9)

The zip gun boogie was coming on strong, sang Bolan. But not so strong that it could climb above Number 41.

November 1974 – Top Of The Pops Volume 41 (Hallmark SHM 880)

Playing back 'Volume 41' today, it seems impossible so many utterly unmemorable records were considered worthy of attention. Who even vaguely recalls 'Get Your Love Back', 'Down On The Beach Tonight', 'Let's Put It All Together'...who, that is, aside from fans of the Three Degrees, the Drifters and the Stylistics? They bought the wretched things in droves, and one hopes they can still sing along.

It's an album of extremes, as well. It was a Top Of The Pops tradition to stumble when faced with a distinctive vocalist. Rod's rasp, Bryan's

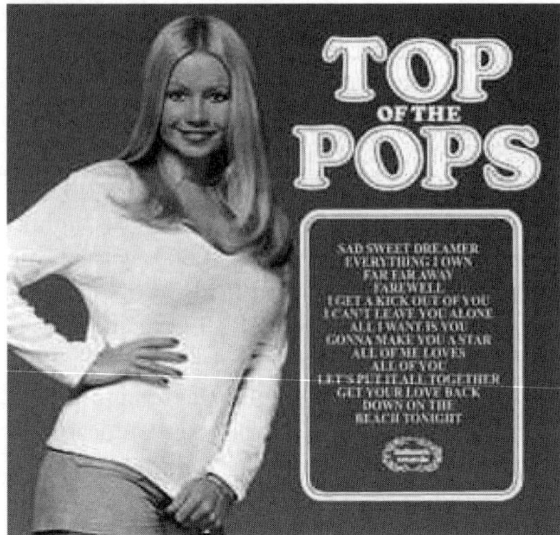

bassiness, Holder's howling, Essex's Essex. What, then, were the chances of each of those artists making it onto one single album – and what are the odds on any of them sounding very lifelike? Well, one out of three isn't bad.

The latest addition to the *Top Of The Pops* team, singer Bert Meagher, was a Bryan Ferry devotee who had long since learned the art of impersonating his idol. A computer operative by day, this was Meagher's vinyl debut and the series never needed worry about Roxy again. The others would not be so lucky.

ON THE BOX

1 November 1974 – Russell Harty: Leo Sayer
5 November 1974 – Lift Off With Ayshea: Slade
7 November 1974 – 45: Mud
7 November 1974 – Top Of The Pops: Roxy Music, Sparks, Queen, Glitter Band, the Rubettes
7 November 1974 – The Geordie Scene: Geordie
14 November 1974 – 45: Ayshea Brough
14 November 1974 – Top Of The Pops: Gary Glitter, Suzi Quatro, David Essex
19 November 1974 – Lift Off With Ayshea: Geordie
21 November 1974 – 45: Geordie
21 November 1974 – Top Of The Pops: The Rubettes, Queen, Alvin Stardust, Hello, David Essex
22 November 1974 – Russell Harty: Gary Glitter
23 November 1974 – The Sound Of Petula: David Essex
26 November 1974 – Lift Off With Ayshea:

Stavely Makepeace, Hello, Alvin Stardust
28 November 1974 – Top Of The Pops: Suzi Quatro, Gary Glitter, David Essex
28 November 1974 – 45: The Sweet
28 November 1974 – Top Of The Pops: David Essex, Gary Glitter, Suzi Quatro
ON THE SHELVES
November 1974: Giggles: Diggle Wiggle/O Wish I Could (EMI 2246)

December 1974 – David Essex: Stardust/Miss Sweetness (CBS 2828)

Essex's new single was released just days after he concluded his first concert tour with a sold out week at London's New Victoria Theatre (2-7 December), with *Melody Maker* having proclaimed him 'Britain's answer to David Cassidy'. But 'Stardust' drew a defiant line in the critical sand with what, thematically, remains one of the most unlikely hits any teen dream ever scored.

Even on 45, the *Stardust* title theme remained a powerful performance. Maybe too powerful. Inextricably bound as it was to the heartbreaking conclusion to the movie and certainly too gloomy to set the Christmas charts afire, 'Stardust' did well to hit Number 7; it would be another nine months before Essex was back at the top with another slice of good-time Cockney mocking, 'Hold Me Close'. Until then, we were left with the memory of Jim MacLaine.

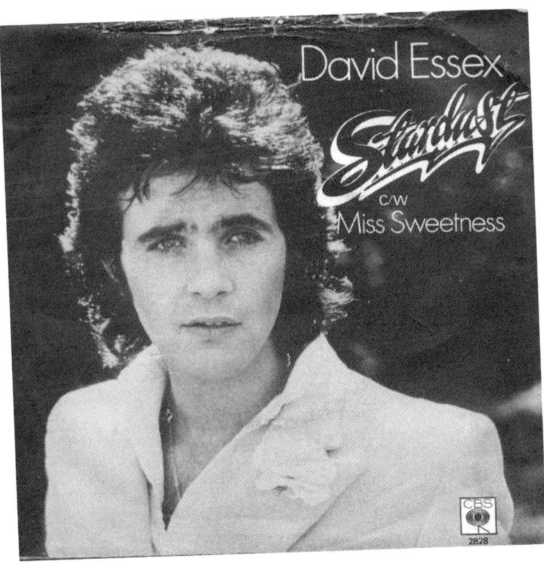

December 1974 – Roy Powell and the Shiver Givers: Rock Ness Monster/King Kong (RCA 2490).

1974 was the year in which the Loch Ness Monster, Scotland's greatest tourist attraction, was 'rediscovered' via a series of newly-taken underwater snapshots and granted a fresh few days in the media sun.

The great beastie also, if the hype can be believed, dropped by the recording studio to add a few words. But it would be another three years before Nessie truly enjoyed her day in the Glam-Rock afterglow as Alex Harvey threw himself into the creation of the spoken-word 'Presents The Loch Ness Monster' LP (K-Tel). He only sings one song on the album and Nessie is conspicuous by her silence. But it's a rewarding listen regardless.

December 1974 – Top Of The Pops Volume 42 (Hallmark SHM 885)

The final word on a tempestuous year comes from the Wombles. 'Wombling Merry Christmas', a Number 2, was the rolling rats' fifth hit in 12 months, and that fact alone is indicative of just what a mess this season was. Carl Douglas was now dancing, not fighting, the Kung Fu craze, and with Elton John's grotesque reggae mangling of 'Lucy In The Sky With Diamonds' also flying high, 'Volume 42' captures Christmas with ruthless inanity. It really was not a good time.

Make the best of things. 'Stardust' is as moody as the movie soundtrack original, while there are marvellous jabs at 'Juke Box Jive' and 'Tell Him' too. A crunch through 'You Ain't Seen Nothin' Yet' reminds us just how 'right' that record sounded at the time and maybe 'Volume 42' is not, in the words of Barry White, your first, your last, your everything. But Gary Glitter wasn't that far off the mark, either. It was *almost* beautiful.

ON THE BOX
3 December 1974 – Lift Off With Ayshea: Gary Glitter
5 December 1974 – 45: Alvin Stardust
5 December 1974 – Top Of The Pops: Alvin Stardust, Hello, Mud, the Rubettes
5 December 1974 – The Geordie Scene: The Sweet
7 December 1974 – Saturday Scene: Alvin Stardust
10 December 1974 – Lift Off With Ayshea: Mr Big
12 December 1974 – 45: Bay City Rollers
12 December 1974 – Top Of The Pops: Gary Glitter, Showaddywaddy, Wizzard
17 December 1974 – Lift Off With Ayshea: Showaddywaddy
19 December 1974 – Top Of The Pops: David Essex, Kenny, Alvin Stardust, Mud
25 December 1974 – 45: Mud, Bay City Rollers, Queen
25 December 1974 – Top Of The Pops: Mud, David Essex, Slade
26 December 1974 – Cilla: David Essex
27 December 1974 – Top Of The Pops: The Rubettes, Alvin Stardust, Sparks, Gary Glitter, Queen, Suzi Quatro, Mud

CHAPTER SIX

1975

Thanks for the Memories

2 January 1975 – Top Of The Pops

By late 1974, the mad rush of glorious new talent (or even non-talent) that had hallmarked the last couple of years of British popdom had finally run out of steam and the first *Top Of The Pops* of the new year had no intention of making you think otherwise.

Oooh, there are some nasties in store here, a latter-day Wizzard proving that even Roy Wood would run out of good ideas eventually – 'Are you ready to rock?' he asks; 'Not with you, sunshine,' we grimly reply – and the super-smarmy Pilot ('January') were the scum at the bottom of the pure pop barrel, however hip it is to dig them today.

We remember that disco (the Tymes) and country (Billy Swan) will always rise to the top when you think you've reached that bottom; and only Kenny ('The Bump'), Status Quo ('Down Down') and Mud ('Lonely This Christmas') remain to remind us of how wonderful things used to be.

Pilot were especially disappointing. Formed by two former Bay City Rollers, their 'Magic' debut at the end of 1974 prompted vast outpourings of excitement from critics in search of the next 10cc. The success of the follow-up and its rapid rise to the top of the chart ('January in February', as some wag put it) seemed set to justify their enthusiasm, even if it was little more than formulaic pop written expressly, it seemed, to fulfil all the criteria of the BBC playlist.

But Pilot faded fast thereafter, crashing after two further minor aural barbiturates, and here's why. Because great pop, whatever its commercial fate, should at least sound like its makers are enjoying themselves and then communicate that excitement to everybody else. Watching the *Top Of The Pops* audience while Pilot play, you know they'd rather be doing anything but twitching to Pilot's po-faced jangle.

The week's featured new release was Philip and Vanessa, celebrating the love of 'Two Sleepy People'. Mercifully it did not chart and that despite being watched by 13 million potential record buyers. But pap like this was to become all too common as 1975 wandered on.

January 1975 – Glitter Band: Goodbye My Love/ Got To Get Ready (Bell 1395)

The diminishing delights of every Glitter Band single since 'Angel Face' were suddenly reversed as the boys came out with this, a sadly sweet anthem for everybody who has ever left their loved one at an airport.

The first fruits of the Band since John Rossall's departure late in 1974, a solo Gerry Shephard composition was both delivered and performed with no more than a hint of glitter, as lead vocalist John Springate recalls. 'It was actually our biggest hit which I was quite pleased about because, up until then, Gerry had sung lead on all the singles and when we were recording it I was "No, I'm singing this". I put my foot down.

'It *was* a change of direction, but the great thing about it was although it was ballad rock, it kept the glitter sound nicely. But it was a totally different style of writing, away from the handclaps and "Hey!" It was really a good song.'

Actually, it was even better than that. 'Goodbye My Love' would have been an astonishing (and astonishingly mature) performance for almost any band, but coming from a group that a lot of folk had already written off as merely fistwaving thud merchants it was spellbinding. 'Goodbye My Love' reached Number 2 behind Pilot's 'January'.

'That was our only real piss-off. We were kept off for two weeks. The second week was the worst. We were in a hotel room in Germany and we were listening to the radio to see if we'd got to Number 1, and we hadn't.'

January 1975 – Sparks: Something For The Girl With Everything/Marry Me (Island WIP 6221)

The second single to be pulled from 'Propaganda' and the maddest track of the lot. Russell Mael's falsetto was at its most maniacally staccato, hurtling incomprehensibly over a rinky-dink accompaniment that in turn was ruthlessly punctured amidships by a guitar that sounded like a vacuum cleaner. And all rounded off with a fast-punning catalogue of somethings for the girl who does, indeed, have everything. 'Careful with that crate, you wouldn't want to dent Sinatra…'

After all that, it halted at Number 17. People hadn't got sick of Sparks already, had they?

January 1975 – Queen: Now I'm Here/Lily Of The Valley (EMI 2256)

A second superlative slice from 'Sheer Heart Attack', highlighted by inventive stereo, a clever promo film and, of course, that ineffable 'something' Queen had discovered which had suddenly transformed them into something very special. Queen, too, would not be bothering the charts again for a while, but that was their own fault – they were too busy making 'Bohemian Rhapsody' and the next time we saw them, at the end of the year, they were unrecognisable.

January 1975 – Arrows: My Last Night With You/Movin' Next Door To You (RAK 189)

Christmas came and Arrows were still waiting for 'Toughen Up' to fulfil Dave Most's prophecy and suddenly be reactivated. Hopes that Chinnichap might take the band under their wing were dashed when Mickie Most made it clear Arrows were his project, but while the

RON MAEL DINKY DIAMOND IAN HAMPTON TREVOR WHITE RUSSELL MAEL

band did go back into the studio with Most to cut some new material nobody believed it was hit material. Apart from one song, an old Jack Scott number called 'What In The World's Come Over You' which Most promptly handed to another recent RAK recruit, Tam White. It became his first and only UK hit.

And then Most turned up 'My Last Night With You', a vaguely Fifties-flavoured creation penned by Roger Ferris, and suddenly Arrows' career was back on track. The single rose to Number 25 and Arrows were on the road, joining up with Suzi Quatro (with whom they'd already toured Germany) and Cozy Powell, for the RAK Rocks Britain package tour. 'Jeff Levine (who is now Nicholas Cage's business partner) became our shadow guitarist for the tour,' recalls Merrill. 'We were a four-piece band on stage. We sounded pretty good.'

January 1975 – Fancy: Wild Thing (Atlantic K51502)

Fancy's debut album could scarcely be described as much-anticipated, but it did fulfil all that was expected of it. The two hit singles (plus 'Wild Thing's B-side, the Pretenders-esque 'Fancy') notwithstanding, it was a solid slice of blues-rock, with Annie Kavanagh effortlessly proving why she got the nod at the auditions. 'What a voice,' Hurst still marvels today. Indeed, 'Wild Thing' was as deserving as most every other hit album of the new year, the difference being it did not come even close to actually being a hit.

January 1975 – Anthony Bygraves: Painted Lady/Love's Starship (Pye 7N 45429)

A little too old to be considered within the same kind of son-of-the-father breath as Ricky Wilde, Max Bygraves' boy cut three singles for Pye, not one of which was as successful as dad's 1973 rendering of 'Deck Of Cards'.

But they were certainly a lot hipper, with 'Painted Lady' – as resurrected by the compilation 'Glitter From The Litter Bin: 20 Junk Shop Glam Rarities From The Seventies' (Castle CMQCD 675) – a solid stab at the Bolan warble, performed at Bygraves' breathiest best. 'Heads to toes-ah, you're a poser,' he lisps at whoever is standing closest. 'Painted Lady' should have been a hit.

January 1975 – Suzi Quatro: Your Mama Won't Like Me/Peter Peter (RAK 191)

Chinnichap were writing Suzi's singles in their sleep by now – or, at least, one hopes they were. There could be no other excuse for continuing to foist so many second-rate rockers on her, and when they heaped brass and funk atop this one it was the final straw. It petered out at Number 31 and Suzi would not see the inside of the chart again until 1977.

January 1975 – Small Wonder: Ordinary Boy/ Ride A Black Sheep (Dawn DNS 1094)
Mike Berry was behind this T Rex pastiche, although complaints that it arrived very late in the day would explain why it was buried away on the B-side (there to be rediscovered by the compilation 'Glitter From The Litter Bin: 20 Junk Shop Glam Rarities From The Seventies' – Castle CMQCD 675). 'Ordinary Boy' was... well, ordinary.

January 1975 – Go Go Thunder: The Race/ Mrs Mann (RCA 2494)
Find the A-side on 'Killed By Glam: 16 UK Junk Shop Glam Rarities From The Seventies' (Moonboot MB 01).

January 1975 – Soho Jets: Hi Heel Tarzan/ Night Flight (Polydor 2058 525)
Grant Stevens and the Jets' debut single is included on 'Killed By Glam: 16 UK Junk Shop Glam Rarities From The Seventies' (Moonboot MB 01).

January 1975 – Sailor: Blue Desert/Blame It On The Soft Spot (Epic 2929)
Sailor's second UK single, says Georg Kajanus, was 'my ultimate portrayal of life at sea from a sailor's point of view, what it's like to be out on the ocean for months at a time and then the euphoria of putting into some exotic harbour town. Although I was never a sailor myself, I lived near the docks in the harbour town of Trondheim as a child, so my imagination was captured by the romance of the sea at an early age.

'I still like "Traffic Jam" and "Blue Desert" as songs today. At the time I wrote them, I remember feeling very passionately about them, even though the inspiration came from two very different emotional sources.'

In the Netherlands, 'Blue Desert' became Sailor's third successive Top Five hit, following 'Traffic Jam' and a Europe-only release, 'Let's Go To Town'. It didn't chart in the UK, but interest in the band was definitely growing.

January 1975 – Dana Gillespie: Really Love That Man/Hold Me Gently (RCA 2489)
A trailer for the forthcoming 'Ain't Gonna Play No Second Fiddle', co-produced with John Porter.

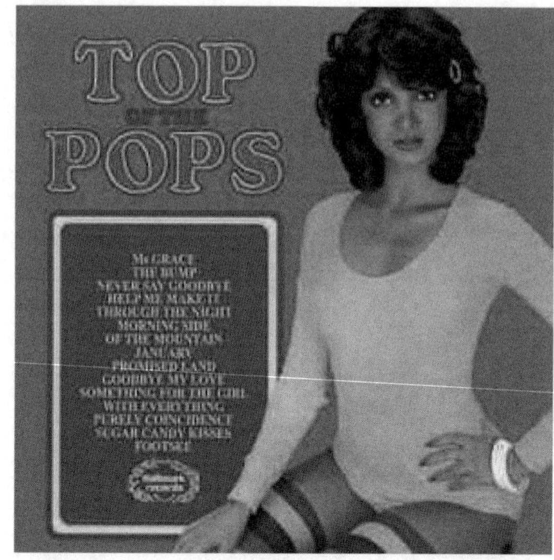

January 1975 – Top Of The Pops Volume 43 (Hallmark SHM 895)
A scattershot blend of breezy soul, revived rock'n'roll, cool R&B and studio-bound professionalism, 'Volume 43' is exactly what you'd expect from a line-up led by Sweet Sensation, Elvis Presley, Wigan's Ovation and Pilot. Almost. The Glitter Band's 'Goodbye My Love' is executed with even more Beach Boys flair than the original and in the midst of it all the joker in the pack. 'Something For The Girl With Everything' is the real treat, though; slower than the original and not so musically manic, it is fronted by a wacked falsetto that knows it's failing miserably and doesn't give a damn. Deconstructive pop at its most wickedly subversive.

ON THE BOX
2 January 1975 – Top Of The Pops: Kenny, Mud
5 January 1975 – Crackerjack: Wizzard
9 January 1975 – Top Of The Pops: David Essex, Kenny, Sparks, Mud
16 January 1975 – Top Of The Pops: Glitter Band, Queen, Wizzard
18 January 1975 – In Concert: David Essex
23 January 1975 – Top Of The Pops: Arrows, Sparks
24 January 1975 – Russell Harty: Angie Bowie
26 January 1974 – Omnibus – David Bowie: Cracked Actor
30 January 1975 – Top Of The Pops: Alvin Stardust, Glitter Band, Queen, Steve Harley and Cockney Rebel

ON THE SHELVES
January 1975 – Oosh Band: Hari Kari On/My Good Woman (Bradley's 7424)
January 1975 – Shabby Tiger: Slow Down/Road Chase (RCA 2492)
January 1975 – Wildfire: Come On Down/When I Know You Love Me (RAK 190)
January 1975 – Sloply Bellywell: If You Wanna Be Happy/Summer Concerto (UK 87)

February 1975 – The Winkies: The Winkies (Chrysalis CHR 1066)
The Winkies' self-titled debut album spent five months awaiting release. For reasons undisclosed to anyone, Chrysalis had decided on a Valentine's Day release date, no matter how impatient or demoralised the band became.

They filled their days gigging, but a band that should have moved onto the theatre circuit behind an album that was still fresh in their minds was instead still playing the same circuit they'd been riding for over a year – pubs, small clubs and the like. Between June and December 1974 the Winkies appeared at the Marquee five times and no matter how historic a venue may be there's such a thing as over-familiarity.

Finally February rolled around; the album was released – and Guy Humphrys promptly quit. And that was the end. Rambow cut a solo single, 'Dem Eyes'/'Solitude's So Precious' (Chrysalis CHS 2065), then returned to the United States where he helped deliver the imminent Punk storm; Desmarais joined the Tyla Gang.

The album was terrific. Imagine if Mott the Hoople had not gone off with Bowie in 1972, but Ariel Bender had joined them regardless ('Davey's Blowtorch'). Imagine if the Stones sacked Jagger and went back to the pubs after 'Goat's Head Soup' ('Red Dog'). Imagine Dylan, if he'd grown up in Dalston but still wrote 'It Takes A Lot To Laugh, It Takes A Train To Cry'.

'The Winkies' is not the album it could have been, nor the one it should have been. But listened back to back with the Heavy Metal Kids' debut (and there's a lot of similarities between the two bands), 'The Winkies' pinpoints the future of British street rock a lot more accurately than any number of other, critically feted punk precedents.

February 1975 – Suzi Quatro: Your Mama Won't Like Me (RAK SRAK 514)
Of course she doesn't. She's not stupid. Or so opined one of the reviews that awaited this album and, to be honest, it wasn't far off the mark. Chinnichap's attempts to adjust to the changing times have already been chronicled, but the divine Miss Q's third album is the least divine of them all.

It finds her midway through the reinvention that transformed the early-Seventies' most convincing rocker chick into the sweetheart of later-decade balladeering, it is probably best remembered today for the lukewarm 'Fever' – a performance so lacklustre that when Cherie Currie turned up for her Runaways audition, later in the year, having been instructed to learn any song she wanted off this LP, she chose the only one her would-be bandmates hadn't bothered learning. Joan Jett and manager Kim Fowley responded by writing 'Cherry Bomb', so something good came out of this mess. But not much else.

Quatro would bounce back, of course, and in terms of influence she remains one of the most significant artists (of either gender) to have emerged from the Glam-Rock era. But her impact lies in what she *was* as opposed to what she did, and once past that still-glorious blast of early singles that's probably just as well.

Or maybe she really was, as the song says, 'A Prisoner Of Your Imagination'.

Suzi Quatro's RAK singles catalogue is compiled, together with a number of outtakes, as 'Suzi Quatro: As, Bs And Rarities' (EMI 7243 8 75953 2 3).

February 1975 – Hello: Game's Up/Do It All Night (Bell 1406)

Having scored one hit raiding the Glitter Band cupboard, Mike Leander suggested that Hello return there to find out if lightning strikes twice. An astonishing John Springate/Gerry Shephard/ Edward Seago original, one of the finest songs in the Band's entire catalogue had yet to be released by its own creators (on the 'Rock'n'Roll Dudes' LP) and that suited producer Mike Leander fine. 'I knew we had to establish Hello in their own right,' he said, 'especially after "Tell Him". And they did a great job.'

Recorded in December 1974, Bob Bradbury recalls, 'It's a great song that always went down well at gigs.' But, while it was a hit in Germany, it did nothing in the UK. Which, said Leander, 'was when I told David [Blaylock, manager] that they needed to get back with Russ Ballard.'

February 1975 – T Rex: Bolan's Zip Gun (T Rex BNLA 7752)

Sadly, more of the same as Bolan served up last time. There are highlights, including the opening 'Light Of Love', but 'Bolan's Zip Gun' is best experienced not through the finished vinyl but via the outtakes and demos that, 21 years later, would make up 'Precious Star – The Alternate Bolan's Zip Gun' (Edsel).

Melodies were enhanced, ideas were expanded and energies exploded. And a 10-minute mangling of 'Token Of My Love', recorded on T Rex's final (1974) American tour, is phenomenal, tearing off the strictures of its studio incarnation and streaking to the firmament. So the boy could still boogie when he wanted to.

February 1975 – Alvin Stardust: Good Love Can Never Die/The Danger Zone (Magnet MAG 21)
February 1975: Alvin's Heartbeats – Chilli Willi Part 1/ Part 2 (Magnet MAG 24)

Understandably mindful of the Glitter Band's success, Magnet dispatched Stardust's backing band, Alvin's Heartbeats, out on their own solo career, with the two-part 'Chilli Willi' as their opening shot.

Sadly, warmed-up Pub Rock shot through with a few distinctly Stardust-shaped guitar licks was not much more appetising than Alvin's latest guise – and, quite frankly, once he'd accepted a booking on the televised working-man's night out that was *The Wheeltappers And Shunters Social Club* (22 February 1975) to push the upcoming 'Good Love Will Never Die' it was all over bar the pouting.

The last Stardust single to be written and produced by Peter Shelley was also the first to truly grasp Shelley's personal musical tastes. 'Pete was quite a country fan and I was directed towards the Glam Rock thing, so we fell between two stools. I had this Glam-Rock image and Peter was writing country songs.'

On this occasion, Shelley won, but Alvin scored another hit, Number 11.

February 1975 – Milk'n'Cookies: Little, Lost And Innocent/Good Friends (Island WIP 6222)

Sparks aside, Milk'n'Cookies really were America's best bet at breaking into the Glitter market, albeit at the more pop orientated end of things. Singer Justin Strauss even had the kind of voice that left a lot of people eyeing him as a potential pretender to a Roller/Kenny-shaped throne. There was just one drawback. Island label head Chris Blackwell hated them.

Sal Maida: 'He didn't want us on the label. The single ['Little, Lost And Innocent'] came out before the LP and it got absolutely destroyed in the *NME*. Apparently Blackwell read that, and it was the first time he'd ever even heard of us! He was like "They're on my label? Who is this?" He didn't even know he had us!'

Worse was to follow. To promote the 45,

Island dispatched the band on a nationwide promotional tour with instructions to look sweet, smile a lot and say lots of nice things. And, for a while, the band did as required. Right up until a Scottish radio host mentioned the Bay City Rollers. Then they stopped looking sweet, stopped smiling and said some positively horrid things about the lovable tartan tops. And that, to all intents and purposes, was the end of Milk'n'Cookies in this country.

With the screams of several thousand indignant Roller girls still ringing in their ears, Milk'n'Cookies returned to London, there to be told that Island had decided against releasing the album and that their contract had been curtailed.

Joseph Fleury, the band's manager, was not downhearted; indeed, he succeeded in landing the band a new contract within days, this time with the Rollers' own record company Bell. Ian North, however, had different ideas.

According to Fleury, he made just one phone call, to Bell's managing director, and suddenly that deal was off. The band returned to New York, re-established themselves on the local circuit and, by the end of 1976, they within a hair's breadth of signing to either Sire or Warner Brothers.

Island immediately changed their tune. Obviously forgetting the days when North would wander around their offices insulting staff and roster alike, they offered the guitarist a solo deal, waving as bait the belated release of the Milk'n'Cookies album. North fell for it and, having dissolved the band, returned to England.

Whereupon Island decided they didn't want him after all. But they did finally release the LP ('Milk'n'Cookies' – Island 9320), before deleting it almost immediately. When finally reissued as a bonus track-stacked CD in 2005, it was instantly seized upon by an entire new generation of Glam archaeologists. But, for those fans who came to it via other, earlier, routes, even posthumous recognition is so much less than Milk'n'Cookies deserved. They should have been enormous.

February 1975 – Slade: How Does It Feel/So Far So Good (Polydor 2058547)
February 1975 – Slade: Slade Talk To 19 Readers (Lyntone 2797)

The second single from the *Slade In Flame* soundtrack was one that Jim Lea first wrote in

1969 and later called 'a much better record than we'd made before and that was all I cared about.'

It was, too, but as a single it suffered from the fact that everyone who wanted it already had the album. And those who didn't were so taken aback by the band's precipitous dive into the realms of gentle balladeering that they mistook it for somebody else entirely.

'How Does It Feel' bottomed out at Number 15 and with Slade's own eyes now firmly on the American prize it was clear that their reign was at an end.

'There were just one way of breaking America in those days, and we all went for it,' manager Chandler later reflected. 'Bolan, the Sweet, Bowie, all of us. And that was, you toured and toured and toured, because it was all very well having a name in the cities, "big in Pittsburgh" or whatever. But you wanted the kids out in farmland to know who you were because they were ones who'd jump in their tractors and drive to the filling station and buy your new eight-track in larger quantities than you could even imagine.

'Bands like Kiss and Aerosmith and all those names we'd barely heard of in England, Foghat and Fleetwood Mac, they were all out there playing the midwest and the south and wherever. They'd go back to the coasts, New York and California, to replenish their batteries and then it would be back to Palookaville or wherever because those were the kids who paid the rent.

'So that's what we all did, even though we

knew it would mean losing our support at home. It wasn't even a financial thing, or just financial. It was pride and accomplishment – break America and you'd conquered the world, and that's what we all wanted to do. We wanted to say we'd conquered the world.'

February 1975 – Steve Harley and Cockney Rebel: Make Me Smile (Come Up And See Me)/Another Journey (EMI 2263)

And suddenly, all was forgiven. Cockney Rebel's original fanclub dreaded to see what Steve Harley would get up to after a few months in the studio with the beardy cohorts he was now surrounded by. But 'Make Me Smile' was superlative, the melodic promise of the old band pushing out from behind the controlled weirdness that once swamped it, married to both a lyric and a liveliness that were utterly irresistible.

Yes he looked a little silly on *Top Of The Pops* messing up the lyric not once but twice…proof, perhaps, that the average pop star cannot play guitar and chew gum at the same time. But still 'Make Me Smile' had no problem whatsoever driving straight to Number 1 – in at Number 33 on 8 February, it was Top Ten the next week and Number 1 after that. And no other record of the month (or even the year) manages to still sound this good today.

February 1975 – Mud: Secrets That You Keep/ Watching The Clock (RAK 194)

Ray Stiles' all-time favourite Mud song was also Mud's most overtly Presley-shaped single yet, and it was great fun watching it joust with Cockney Rebel and Telly Savalas for the right to top the chart. They both succeeded, Mud stopped at Number 3. But at least they still got up there, while the heart-shaped guitar that Rob brought out on television has its own possible claim to fame – check out the logo on Tom Petty's first LP for further details.

'I love that song,' says Stiles. 'Clever words. Nicky and Mike used to get slagged off all the time, people saying it was all cheap stuff, but Mike Chapman is a genius. He didn't play great guitar, he only knew about half a dozen chords but he had a capo and he'd stick it on the neck and write another song.'

But there was an irony to the song title and lyric that even Mud may not have been aware of. Nothing had yet been said openly, but there was a growing feeling that, no less than the Sweet, Mud were growing restless – tiring of being tied to the songwriters' strings and convinced that they were just as powerful an outfit without the Chinnichap touch as with it.

In fact, the band were divided on the subject. 'I was pretty good mates with Mike,' recalls Stiles. 'His girlfriend, my wife, Mike and I, we used to go out for dinner and I really didn't want to leave Chinnichap. I do remember a couple of the guys in our band saying we ought to move on because Mike couldn't possibly want any more success! I think Rob would have gone either way but Les and Dave wanted to move on.'

Money, of course, was involved. Mud's contract with RAK was up for renewal and Mickie Most wasn't offering them very much money to stay. Certainly not as much as another suitor, the newly launched Private Stock label. Whatever RAK's offer was, Private Stock didn't simply double it, they then doubled that, as well. It was hard to turn such riches down.

Mud announced their decision while the single was still on the chart and the secrets that they kept were secrets no more.

February 1975 – Kenny: Fancy Pants/I'm A Winner (RAK 196)

Destined for a Number 4 berth but soundly crushed by the upcoming juggernaut that was the Rollers' 'Bye Bye Baby', Kenny's second single was a neat replay of their first minus the dance but with added danceability. Not so many bruised hips, you see.

February 1975 – Mick Ronson: Billy Porter/ Seven Days (RCA 2482)
February 1975 – Mick Ronson: Play Don't Worry (RCA 0681)

According to Ronson, 'Billy Porter' was written after Lou Reed offered to teach him the art of lyric-writing. He obviously paid attention. The tale of a young man being menaced on the street and calling for the streetwise Billy to come to his aid before discovering he didn't need him after all, 'Billy Porter' leaped out of the previous LP's 'Hey Ma, Get Papa' and with quizzical rhythms and coiled-to-strike percussion should have gone

trampling up the chart. He didn't, so we all flipped the single and wallowed in the sadness of the flip, a mournful Annette Peacock ballad recorded live at Ronson's debut solo show.

Then the album arrived and we could all smile again, beginning the moment where the siren that blares 'Billy Porter' out of earshot merges with the triumphant guitar lick of 'Angel Number Nine'. Ronson had been singing that particular song's praises ever since he was called in to arrange strings on the Pure Prairie League's 1972 album 'Bustin' Out', but his rearrangement left the Prairie in the dust, the vehicle for one of his best ever guitar solos and, a few months earlier, one of the highlights of the final Mott tour.

'Bustin' Out' also provided the album's closer, 'Woman', while another early Ronson collaboration with ex-New Seeker Laurie Heath produced 'This Is For You'. His days with Bowie were reprised by a dip into the 'Pinups' archive, for the unfinished backing track to 'White Light White Heat', but then it was bang up to date with Ian Hunter leaping in for a frantic 'The Girl Can't Help It'.

But perhaps the most telling moment of all came with the title track, a co-write with Bob Sargeant, whose own solo debut, 'First Starring Role', was co-produced by the guitarist. The lyric lets the side down a little, but it still packs a powerful autobiographical punch. Ronson was always an unwilling candidate for solo stardom and 'Play Don't Worry' was, in many ways, his own solution to the pressures of that particular career – 'Don't you think about them, start dreaming again.'

Or you could just form a new band with Ian Hunter.

February 1975 – Be Bop Deluxe: Between The Worlds/Lights (Harvest HAR 5091)

A sneak preview of Be Bop's upcoming second album, recorded by Nelson, Fox and bassist Charlie Tumuhai alone.

February 1975 – Fox: Only You Can/Out Of My Body (GTO 8)

Australian singer Susan Traynor and American producer/songwriter Kenny Young first worked together in the mid-Sixties, when he produced her band, the Charmettes. They moved to the UK together in 1968 and, by 1973, Traynor was fronting the folk band Wooden Horse, cutting a brace of singles for Yorkshire television's York label ('Pick Up The Pieces'/'Wake Me In The Morning' – York SYK 526; and 'Wooden Horses'/'Typewriter And Guitar' – York SYK 543) and two LPs ('Wooden Horse' – York FYK 403 and 'Wooden Horse II' – York FYK 413).

Young, meanwhile was working alongside singer Clodagh Rodgers and a number of the songs Rodgers demoed and recorded would reappear in Young and Traynor's next joint project, Fox.

Image was Fox's strongest suit; Traynor renamed herself Noosha and, adopting a scarved and swathed look reminiscent of Marlene Dietrich, became the band's immediate figurehead even though Young was just as prominent in the band's frontline. Indeed, by the time of Fox's second album, 'Tails Of Illusion', the vocal credits were split almost 50-50.

But it was Noosha who sang lead on the band's opening shot, a spaciously phased sonic seduction that raced to Number 3 and should have inched higher. But Telly Savalas was still out in front of her and so was the Rollers' 'Bye Bye Baby'. There'd be no getting past either of them for a while.

ON THE BOX

6 February 1975 – 45: Alvin Stardust
6 February 1975 – Top Of The Pops: Showaddywaddy, Slade
7 February 1975 – Russell Harty: Slade
13 February 1975 – Top Of The Pops: Alvin Stardust, Arrows, Fox, Queen, Mud, Steve Harley and Cockney Rebel
15 February 1975 – Tiswas: Slade
21 February 1975 – Top Of The Pops: Hello, Steve Harley and Cockney Rebel
22 February 1975 – The Wheeltappers And Shunters Social Club: Alvin Stardust
27 February 1975 – Top Of The Pops: The Rubettes, Showaddywaddy, Mud, Fox, Arrows, Steve Harley and Cockney Rebel

ON THE SHELF
February 1975 – Disco Kid: Rollercoaster/ Guitar'd And Feather'd (RAK 195)
February 1975 – Geordie: Got To Know/Ride On Baby (EMI 2226)

---

1 March 1975 – *Supersonic*
It promised to be the greatest television spectacular pop had ever seen, a non-stop parade of the most visual talent around, while creator Mike Mansfield surveyed it all from his control room and directed the action straight into your living room. 'Cue Gary Glitter, cue the exploding, inflatable octopus, cue televisual madness!'

It was vibrant, it was vital...and it was also two or three years too late. Just imagine how spectacular *Supersonic* might have been had it hit our screens in 1972. But it did its best regardless, with the limited resources that the new year provided it and the pilot episode, screened six months ahead of the first full season, captured the flavour of all that was to come.

Status Quo, Rod Stewart, the Bay City Rollers, Gary Glitter, Alvin Stardust, Maggie Bell and Sunny all turned out to be doused in confetti, scalded by dragons, unhinged by wind machines and anything else that Mad Scientist Mansfield could concoct for the cameras; here was a show that you'd never want to miss.

9 March 1975 – Leo Sayer: live in Boston, USA
Was this the legendary night on his first American tour when Sayer's entire record company and promotions team turned up at the venue dressed as clowns and so shocked the headlining Albert Brooks that 'I just went blank and had a real panic attack'?

Probably not, but the audience is certainly delirious enough that he could be wearing anything, while Sayer turns in a performance that makes complete and utter nonsense of his subsequent reputation as one of rock's most grisly MOR balladeers.

Armed with a band that burns and a 12-song repertoire that hits all the high spots from his two albums to-date ('Silverbird' and 'Just A Boy'), this was Sayer as blues-rocking singer-songwriter, as raucous as you'd like and a billion miles from the schmaltz of the future. 'Tomorrow', with Chris Stainton's keyboards chiming throughout; 'Oh Wot A Life', with guitarist Les Nicol soloing fit to bust; a purposefully knockabout 'One Man Band'...this was all-round great rock'n'roll. By the time they hit 'Long Tall Glasses', when Sayer introduces the song by suggesting 'Let's pretend there's 5,000 people in here,' the audience obeys with maniacal glee.

'The Show Must Go On' closes the set and it's amazing, a duet for banjo and cackle that reminds us just what an incredible single that was when it first hit the airwaves – and that was before you saw Sayer himself. He, too, wore a clown suit for his first TV performances and though he dropped it quickly enough the memory lingers. Especially, one suspects, if you're Albert Brooks.

March 1975 – Shambles: Hello Baby/Held Me Spellbound (RCA 2533)
Yet another punchy sideline for the Mandrake Paddle Steamer pair of Briley and Engels, with Roy Thomas Baker layering his best Glam notions across the A-side, then adding extra rock'n'roll to the flip. 'Hello Baby' would be rediscovered following its inclusion on the 'Blitzing The Ballroom: 20 UK Power Glam Incendiaries' compilation (Psychic Circle PCCD 7021).

March 1975 – The Sweet: Fox On The Run/Miss Demeanour (RCA 2524)
Chinnichap had clearly lost their minds. 'I Wanna Be Committed' was a great song, a mental rocker, the hardest-hitting thing they'd ever put their pens to. But was it really a good choice for the next Sweet single?

Steve Priest seemed to think so. 'It is rather insane, but in the nicest possible way. [It's] about a man who's going round the bend. It's rather a scream and shouldn't offend.'

But RCA weren't so sure, and when the BBC weighed in with their opinion – very nice, boys, but there's no way that we'll play it – that was it. 'I Wanna Be Committed' was canned and the label asked for something else to release.

The problem was they didn't have anything, and when the Sweet called Mike Chapman as he holidayed in America, Brian Connolly recalled,

'Basically, he told us "tough shit". He said they didn't have anything that was suitable for us – well, there were a couple of things he suggested, but we told him what he could do with them, songs we'd turned down in the past or ones they'd obviously written for Suzi.

'See, they were completely tied up with Smokey now, writing their fake west-coast Eagles ballads and while we could probably have taken almost any of them and rearranged it into a Sweet single that wasn't what we wanted to do. We wanted something that was Sweet and if Mike and Nicky couldn't come up with anything then we'd have to see what we could do. And we didn't do badly.'

The label's Australian wing had already taken matters into its own hands, pulling 'Peppermint Twist' off the 'Sweet Fanny Adams' album and scoring a completely unexpected Number 1 with it. But RCA UK were not willing to go that route, and the Sweet would not have permitted it anyway.

'We needed a single,' Priest continues, 'and Chapman said, "Sorry, I'm in LA and I can't be bothered", so we went to the record company with our manager Ed Leffler. And they said, '"You need a single and there's not really one on the album." Then they said, "Go in and do three tracks and remake them into singles instead of obvious album tracks." So I said we should go ahead and do "Fox On The Run". No three to choose from; just go in and do one.'

'There wasn't really any discussion,' Tucker recalled. 'RCA were screaming for a single, so was management, and we were really up against the wall because we hadn't written anything new that would work – and they were right, there really wasn't anything on the LP. Besides, we'd already taken two singles from "Desolation"; it would have been taking the piss to just pull another one. But then we thought about "Fox On The Run". We came up with a rearrangement that worked, cut it down, tightened it up, made the chorus more chorus-y and that was it.'

It took the Sweet three days in early January to completely reroute 'Fox On The Run'; three days to take the one last step they had sometimes never dreamed they'd actually be able to pull off and turn one of their own songs into a viable hit single. 'It was as though a light bulb had been switched on,' said Mick Tucker. 'For the first time, we could see what Sweet should sound like and why we never had in the past. It was amazing.'

RCA certainly thought so. 'Fox On The Run' was accepted without a solitary qualm; the BBC, too, was placated. Days later, 'Fox On The Run' was in the shops, the Sweet were on *Top Of The Pops* and all the disappointments of 1974 were behind them.

The single entered the chart at Number 42, then marched – Number 21, Number 10, Number 5... As the following week's chart came together, it was clear that the only thing standing in the way of the Sweet's first Number 1 since 1973 was the Bay City Rollers, stomping their way through Phil Wainman's production of 'Bye Bye Baby'.

And it dawned on the Sweet that Chinn and Chapman not only weren't essential, they weren't even necessary any longer.

Priest recalls the bitter end of the relationship. 'I remember one Wednesday morning, the phone ringing in my little house in Hayes and hearing Mike Chapman on the other end. "Well, I guess you won't be needing us any more," he said. I thought for about a nanosecond and replied, "It doesn't look much like it, does it?" That was the end of that and I didn't see or hear of him again until 1988.'

March 1975 – Bay City Rollers: Bye Bye Baby/It's For You (Bell 1409)

The Bay City Rollers' first British chart-topper, 'Bye Bye Baby' and their first move away from Bill Martin and Phil Coulter made a bit of a mockery of the boys' insistence that they wanted to write their own songs. Original songwriters don't then turn around covers of old Four Seasons hits, do they?

But Tam Paton later revealed that 'Bye Bye Baby' was the first Rollers hit single ever to feature the Rollers' own instrumental talents; the arrangement was sensational. Part ballad, part rocker and wholly Rollermanic, 'Bye Bye Baby' would do for the spring what 'Summerlove Sensation' did the last time that the sun came out. It made the whole world seem brighter.

March 1975 – Mr Big: I'm A Lucky Man/Josephine (Epic EPC 3087)

Mr Big's final Epic release. Shortly afterwards, a gig at the Speakeasy brought the band to the attention of Stan Tippens, Mott the Hoople's long-serving road manager, who in turn alerted Mott manager Bob Hirschmann. 'Bob then decided that we should start afresh,' Dicken recalls, 'so the image went out the window and we became a rock band again.'

They certainly weren't, in their own opinion, a Glam band. 'In fact,' admits Dicken, 'I was surprised that people thought so. I'm not sure we were anything more than a rocky songy-type band, with a few odd solos to boot – although we *were* described as a punk band in 1975 before punk hit big time. I even think Malcolm McLaren sort of liked us – we got our stage gear from his shop, which was fun. I loved all that tight leather and plastic trousers!'

The band returned to the live circuit, regulars still at the Marquee and the Fulham Greyhound and after a few A&R nibbles raised the temperature a little EMI's Nick Mobbs signed them up. Work began on their debut LP, the John Punter-produced 'Sweet Silence', in June.

March 1975 – Cockney Rebel: The Best Years Of Our Lives (EMI 3068)

'Make Me Smile' was not a fluke. But neither was it a golden dawn. Probably half of 'The Best Years Of Our Lives' is Harley wordplay by numbers as fed through the anonymity of his supremely musicianly band. But when the best years are at the finest, they outweigh all the offcuts... The swaying, lamenting title track, the freakish twitch of 'Back To The Farm', the compulsive 'Mr Soft'-ness of near-namesake 'Mr Raffles', 'Make Me Smile' of course, these were the moments that justified all the self-justifications that Harley had hurled at his detractors all along and, against more odds than he should ever have needed to face, ol' big mouth was still a big name.

Which makes Harley's subsequent decline all the harder to bear. Between the inevitable release of 'Mr Raffles' as the follow up to The Hit and the startling return to form of 'Freedom's Prisoner', a Number 58 in 1979, Harley snatched just two further hits; one of those was quite possibly the most annoying version of George Harrison's

'Here Comes The Sun' that the human mind could sustain. (The other, for the record, was 'Love's A Prima Donna', the title track to his 1976 album.) And nowhere within those sorry years did he even threaten to revisit the peaks he had once scaled, not even if you happen to actually like the ensuing records.

It is for Harley himself to explain what he was thinking; whether he allowed his own self-belief to get the best of him or if he just lost touch with what the music scene was doing and couldn't put his finger on a foothold back to life. Or maybe a combination of the two.

Either way there'd be no coming back, with even his periodic comebacks naught but sad impersonations of the God he once was. Man, that was mean.

March 1975 – The Rubettes: I Can Do It/You've Got The Time (State STAT 1)

Yes they could, and they did, all the way to Number 7 to give the newly-launched State label a wonderful start in life. Powder blue and lemon yellow jackets this time and the loss of Pete Arnesen (to Ian Hunter's band) doesn't seem to have hurt them a bit.

13 March 1975 – Top Of The Pops
20 March 1975 – Top Of The Pops

And this is what we gave up our Thursday evenings for? Like its long-playing namesake, *Top Of The Pops* could only ever reflect what the Great British Public was actually buying in any given week, but even with the benefit of hindsight and aided by lashings of nostalgia some episodes just don't bear replaying.

We get off to a good start with the Rubettes premiering their latest single and very exuberant they are, so many smiles for the camera that even host Noel Edmonds is left in the shade.

Later, 'Fox On The Run' rocks as hard as the determinedly dressed-down Sweet always wanted to (even if Andy Scott looks almost laughably serious for the guitar break) and Pan's People military marching routine (to Elton John's 'Philadelphia Freedom' – not at all coincidentally released alongside David Bowie's stylistic sojourn in that same city) is eye-catching in an odd *Confessions Of A Drum Majorette* kind of way.

This week's Number 4, Noosha and Fox, turn in a performance that makes you wish the band had more than one string to their so-seductive bow (Edmonds reminds us to 'watch out for an album in a month's time') while two places higher Les McKeown offers some tantalising glimpses of Rollerchest beneath his open denim jacket and gently swaying scarf.

But what to do with 1970 Eurovision winner Dana, the roly-poly Tam White, Johnny Mathis, Pete Shelley and his sheepdog and the chart-topping Telly Savalas, deadpanning through David Gates' 'If', while the accompanying video could doubles as the opening scenes to an especially gruesome porn movie. Yeah, come and pour yourself on me, baby.

Fast forward a week. The Rollers have displaced Savalas and Kenny look set to displace them…better hair, cooler T-shirts and patchwork rainbow fancy pants that might match the song title but clash with absolutely everything else in the studio. Even Tony Blackburn is dressed in black and white, while Wigan's Ovation look like they just left some dour northern discotheque. Which was probably the idea.

This is one of the episodes where you get up to make a cup of tea after two songs and don't come back till it's over. Tony Blackburn reminds us that he predicted big things for Guys and Dolls long before they charted (the insensitive lout); the Goodies are good, the Average White Band are average and Pan's People are swathed in dry ice. Lulu isn't. The Moments appear without their Whatnauts ('sounds painful', grins Blackburn) and comedian Mike Reid leaves his humour at home for a version of 'The Ugly Duckling'.

March 1975 – Striking the Bell

By 1975, Bell Records was the single most successful record label the UK industry had ever known. Other, smaller, concerns (RAK and UK) had better hit-to-release ratios; others had higher record sales through the auspices of a single band or two – Parlophone and Apple with the Beatles, for example.

But in terms of a not only piling up the hits but hit artists as well, Bell was peerless: Gary Glitter, the Glitter Band, Hello, Harley Quinne, the Bay City Rollers, Showaddywaddy, Barry Blue – and that was just the British Glam contingent.

Which is why, over in America, former Columbia records chief Clive Davis wanted to buy the company. He was launching his own Arista label, but saw Bell as a source of back catalogue that would give the new company both financial clout and history.

It would be late 1976 before the takeover impacted on the British operation; Showaddywaddy's 'Under The Moon Of Love' (Bell 1495) was the label's last major hit that November. In the US, on the other hand, the changes commenced as soon as legally viable. Overnight, acts that had percolated happily along on the label found themselves cast into the wilderness; and not only the poor sellers as well. Not even the high and mighty were spared.

David Cassidy, for example. Over the past five years in America and much of the rest of the world as well, Cassidy *was* Bell. 'I had become the most successful act in the label's history,' he explains. 'I had the first gold album they ever had, then platinum and had sold 20 million records with them.'

But 'When Clive Davis took over Bell, he was most interested in putting his own signature on things and he wanted to bring in his own artists. The only artists that he kept, that he felt would serve his purposes [were] Barry Manilow and Melissa Manchester. They were already signed and had made records but they had not been released. And at that point, I just kind of realised that my career was over if I stayed there.'

Moving across town to RCA, Cassidy was replaced as Teen Idol in residence by the Bay City Rollers as they prepared for their American breakthrough. And, while there is a degree of irony to be drawn from the fact that Cassidy's first single for his new home should be a Manilow composition ('I Write The Songs'/'Get It Up For Love' – RCA 2571), the boy was to be congratulated for growing up a whole lot more gracefully than his old teenybop rivals.

A double A-side, the new single promptly ran into trouble when the BBC banned one song for sounding too sexually suggestive. But it reached Number 11, five places higher than his last 45, a live cover of the Beatles' 'Please Please Me', while advance reports of his new album at least caused a knowing smirk or two. It was to be called 'The Higher They Climb, The Harder They Fall'.

March 1975 – 10cc: Life Is A Minestrone/ Channel Swimmer (Mercury 6008 010)
March 1975 – 10cc: The Original Soundtrack (Mercury 9102 500)

On 22 February 1975, it was announced that 10cc had signed to Phonogram for the then unprecedented sum of $1 million. According to Ric Dixon, 10cc's co-manager with Harvey Lisburg, 'We decided that if 10cc were to reach their full potential we must change to a truly international record company,' while a spokesman for UK, while expressing disappointment at losing the band, added that 'a million dollars buys a lot of loyalty.'

'There were certain regrets socially,' Lol Creme acknowledged. 'We like Jonathan [King], even though he's a bum and a punk and tight, but we love him because he's one of those very likeable people. But regrets as far as our career went, there were none.' The band's third album, 'The Original Soundtrack', had already been recorded and it appeared a fortnight later with a Number 7 hit single, the fast-punning 'Life Is A Minestrone', trailing in its wake.

Once again, the album was a remarkable

achievement, but as so often happens last year's critical darlings were in line for a good kicking. Opening with the convolutions of 'One Night In Paris' (three parts, eight minutes and only the ghost of a tune behind the deliberately atrocious French accents), the album paired genuine brilliance with brilliant in-jokes – 'The Film Of My Love' was the perfect pastiche of some bad old-time Hollywood musical theme, but the joke does wear thin after a while. Godley's showcase 'Brand New Day' was lovely but just a little too piping and 'Second Sitting For The Last Supper' was compulsively heavy but a wee bit laboured.

There were moments of sublime wonder – slight it may have seemed, but 'Flying Junk' remains a 10cc highlight and 'Blackmail' is brilliant too. And then there's the breathlessly brilliant 'I'm Not In Love'. But few reviews were immediately complimentary, while the handful that could praise the album were also swift to damn it. Too clever, too perfect, too smug, 10cc had effectively reduced rock'n'roll to a science – and no matter how much one marvelled at their brilliance, still a part of one's body cried out for some good old-fashioned boogie. In fact, 10cc themselves would eventually confess that the album was not as good as it could have been; a couple of tracks had not been intended for inclusion, but were thrown on at the last minute because they'd run out of time to record anything else.

But still 'The Original Soundtrack' was to prove the band's most successful album, reaching Number 3 in Britain even before it spawned the single that remains their best-loved and most-feted moment, 'I'm Not In Love'.

March 1975 – John Rossall: I Was Only Dreaming/Every Night And Every Day (Bell 1411)

Glitter Band mainstay John Rossall's departure from the ranks in late 1974 was one of those events that passed most people by – and continued to do so even when he resurfaced with his first solo single.

A less-than-haunting number, it was largely dignified only by the presence of management-mates Jet as his backing band – bassist Martin Gordon recalls producer Mike Leander trying to get Jet's drummer, Chris Townson, to play like the Glitter Band's two, 'and not unsuccessfully'.

Five tracks were recorded at sessions at Mike Leander's favourite haunt, Mayfair Sound studios in South Molton Street; both sides of the current single and its follow-up 'You'll Never Know'/'Don't Believe A Word', plus a remarkable facsimile of the Glitter Band's 'Angel Face'. And that was the closest either Rossall or Jet ever came to a hit single.

March 1975 – Slik: The Boogiest Band In Town/Hatchet (Bell 1414)

A flop on its original release in late 1974, Slik's mentors Martin/Coulter snatched them back from Polydor and brought them to Bell, using the band's performance in the upcoming *Never Too Young To Rock* movie as bait. With it came an image change, *Great Gatsby*-style suits, but again the single was stillborn.

Of course, that wouldn't stop the duo from having Arrows cover it the following year, and they weren't ready to give up on Slik yet either.

March 1975 – Tiger Lily: Ain't Misbehavin'/ Monkey Jive (Gull GULS 12)

It is frequently remarked upon just how little leakage there was between the Glam bands of the first half of the Seventies and the Punk/New Wave movement that replaced it. Even among the artists who could trace their careers back to the earlier age, few had truly bathed themselves in spangles, working their apprenticeships instead in sundry Pub-Rock concerns.

The Hollywood Brats (reborn in the Boys), the ex-Jet remains that became Radio Stars and Peter Perrett's pre-Only Ones outfit England's Glory notwithstanding, the best-remembered crossover is Tiger Lily, a band that would flower in 1976 as Ultravox!, but retain their original tastes by hiring Eno on as producer on their first album.

Dennis Leigh (vocals), Stevie Shears (guitar), Chris St John (bass – brother of Hello's Jeff Allen), Billy Currie (keyboards) and Warren Cann (drums) formed in 1974, and that summer were spotted opening for the Heavy Metal Kids at the Marquee (16 August), when they were described (by *Melody Maker*) as an apocalyptic collision between Bowie and the Velvets.

The chance to slap that sound upon Fats Waller 'Ain't Misbehavin'' arrived when the band was commissioned to write the theme to an upcoming X-rated movie. And while the record itself has little in common with the band's future, it was in many ways directly responsible for it. The money they received from the session was spent on their first synthesiser.

March 1975 – Fancy: She's Riding The Rock Machine Parts 1/2 (Arista 3)
March 1975 – Fancy: Something To Remember (Arista 102)

While their debut album had passed unnoticed, Fancy continued gigging, hitting the Far East and Europe before returning to England and beginning work on a new album, one that all concerned believed would break the band worldwide.

The fledgling Arista picked them up in the UK, RCA grabbed them for America and 'Something To Remember' ('Fancy Turns You On' in the US) erupted across fiery remakes of Stevie Wonder's 'I Was Made To Love Him' and Mose Allison's 'Everybody's Crying Mercy' and leading off with what amounted to Kavanagh's own autobiography, the persuasively funky 'She's Riding The Rock Machine'.

But the music press merely yawned. *Melody Maker* declared *it* 'pretty thin gruel', while the only decent review the single landed was for its

B-side, a reprise of the A-side minus Annie Kavanagh. 'Doubtless lovely and talented, I have nothing against her at all,' the review explained. 'It's just that the band are so good that she gets in the way of my enjoyment.'

Within days of their London showcase at Ronnie Scott's in February. Fancy headed out for their first full British tour, opening for 10cc, a three-week outing that proved Fancy more than capable of matching the headliners.

March 1975 – Barry Blue: You Make Me Happy/Kiss Me, Kiss Your Baby (Bell 1415)

Despite Radio 1 apparently loving it, Blue's sixth Bell single proved a surprising flop. Perhaps they should have flipped it over; 'Kiss Me, Kiss Your Baby' later became a hit for the Brotherhood of Man. In France.

March 1975 – Ian Hunter: Once Bitten Twice Shy/3000 Miles From Here CBS 3194)
March 1975 – Hunter-Ronson Live

''Allo.' After Mott went out singing their goodbyes, there was no other conceivable intro to Ian Hunter's solo debut and, though you have to raise eyebrows at the subject matter, rejecting the affections of a rather well-used groupie girl, Hunter's hubris and Ronson's guitar merged magnificent on a rocker that remains a benchmark in either man's career.

The single was credited to Hunter alone. On the road, however, there was no separating the pair. With Ronno's 'Play Don't Worry' on the shelves alongside his 'Ian Hunter' debut and the live set split between the two records, this was both men's show.

The concert experience was stunning, dynamic versions of the best bits from 'Ian Hunter' including a surprisingly effective 'Boy' and some classic Ronson histrionics through 'The Truth, The Whole Truth...' A rearranged 'Roll Away The Stone' was slowed to funereal pace and awarded a whole new intro and when the tour reached Hammersmith Odeon both Mick Ralphs and Ariel Bender joined the group on stage for it. That was a sight to behold.

'All The Young Dudes', too, lived up to every superlative that has ever been thrown at it, but the real revelations were Ronson's contributions, a sparkling solo-fired 'Angel Number Nine' and a straightforward but still superlative 'Slaughter'. Not, perhaps, the equal of the version preserved on the same team's 1979's 'Welcome To The Club' live album, but a gem nevertheless.

Of course, Hunter-Ronson never fulfilled the extraordinary potential that brought them together in the first place – one, it seemed, wanted to go play with too many other people; the other, regrettably, wanted to go off and write too many lousy songs. But when they were together, in fiery full flight, there were few other double acts to match them. And in 1975 they weren't simply flying, they were scraping the sky.

Spare a thought, then, for the opening act, going out hoping to make an impression every night, in the knowledge that no musical memory was likely to make it past the behemoth at the top of the bill. Jet.

March 1975 – Jet: My River/Quandary (CBS 3143)
March 1975 – Jet: Jet (CBS 86099)

'I completely failed to recognise Ian Hunter one night, while we were still on tour. It was in a sauna and he had naturally left his glasses in his room. After a long conversation at cross-purposes, I asked him what he did for a living.

He was not much amused and I was somewhat cold-shouldered for the rest of the tour.' – Martin Gordon

Jet were finally unveiled as the opening act on labelmate Ian Hunter's first UK tour, with their debut single, O'List's 'My River' and album likewise alongside. The loss of drummer Chris Townson, forced to sit out the tour while he recovered from the leg he broke playing football, was a harsh blow, but with Jim Toomey from Colin Blunstone's band replacing him Jet turned in some dynamite performances, two of which (Bristol and London) have since been released as the live download album 'Some Flotsam'.

The vinyl front was not so encouraging.

Martin Gordon: 'I said at the time that "My River" was really the wrong choice for a single, but was over-ruled by RAM.' His own choice, albeit in retrospect, was 'Whangdepootenawah', a maniacal Townson/Ellison creation that Gordon set to music. 'So you can imagine my surprise, 30 years later, when browsing through the *Devil's Dictionary* by Ambrose Bierce, I found, under W, an entry for "Whangdepootenawah". Not only the words were there, in their entirety, but also the description of the song, furnished to me by one or other plagiarist: "From the Ojibwa tongue – a sudden disaster which strikes hard."

'Bierce's protagonist was named William Bryan – Andy and Chris renamed him Hector Zany. Otherwise the words are identical. I pointed this out to Chris in 2006. "Oh, didn't we tell you at the time? I'm sure we did..." he said, having the grace to sound at least a little sheepish.'

In the duo's favour, nobody else seems to have noticed it either, although that might be because they were too busy comparing the album's artwork with a page from Marvel Comics' *Mr Miracle* strip (*New Musical Express* journalist Charles Shaar Murray was even able to include the actual issue and page number in his review of the album). Rejecting a frankly wonderful Hipgnosis sleeve design, CBS instead turned to in-house graphics artist Roslav Szabo and, according to Gordon, wound up being sued by Marvel.

As for 'Jet' itself...

The band's own choice for a title had been 'Have You Seen Charlotte?', playing on the old joke about actress Rampling ('have you seen...' oh, never mind). That was rejected by CBS and a lot of the band's other notions went out of the window, too, including Gordon's insistence that he should produce. But still they were left with an album that, today, sums up a lot of the madness and magic that the rest of 1975 was so very sadly lacking.

Opening with the wildly panning 'Start Here' before moving on through the Spector-esque snippet of 'Song For Hymn', 'Jet' radiated a near-symphonic air of grandeur and that was long before you reached the album's key notes – the romantic miscommunication of 'Diamonds Are A Girl's Best Friend'; the smirking 'Cover Girl' and the maddeningly catchy doggerel of 'Nothing To Do With Us'.

'Jet' was a magnificent album, but it was too original. The world had been promised the best of everybody, from Roxy to Sparks to T Rex to Queen. They got 'Whangdepootenawah' instead.

March 1975 – The divorce of the year

Citing financial mismanagement and sundry other complaints, David Bowie's departure from MainMan, the company that he and Tony Defries had built, was finally made public, amid a slew of journalistic memories of the company's spendthrift ways.

A film division had been launched and then closed after just three high profile ventures went belly-up.

A magazine was planned and abandoned.

A theatrical department born with considerable brouhaha and a play about Marilyn Monroe, *Fame*, which proceeded to close after just one night. Bowie's disgust may or may not have been registered in the song he recorded just days after that, the bitter denouncement of 'Fame'.

But all that was in the past. MainMan supremo Defries hit back by discovering and launching the young Johnny Cougar, amid the Colonel Tom Parker-shaped insistence that Bowie had merely been his Eddy Arnold; Cougar was the new Elvis Presley.

And past MainMan staffers began their own careers, too. Leee Black Childers moved into management and was soon guiding New York Doll Johnny Thunders' next band, the Heartbreakers. Wayne County was gigging regularly around New York, growing ever more outrageous every time he took the stage; and Cherry Vanilla was about to launch the Rymbo Band, the best American Glam band that you've never heard.

March 1975 – Chicory Tip: Survivor/Move On (Route RT 01)
Brian Shearer and Barry Mayger had both departed by now, leaving Peter Hewson the sole surviving member of the act that had risen so high just three years before. Chicory Tip's final single, the first release on a new, but short-lived, label, was accompanied by a farewell Scandinavian tour and the band called it a day.

Chicory Tip's entire CBS and Route singles catalogue is compiled on 'Chicory Tip: The Singles Collection' (7Ts GLAM CD 29).

March 1975 – Shelby: Motorbike Girl/Cirrus (Route RT 02)
Imagine waking up one day and discovering that your labelmates are Chicory Tip! And that your new record is better than theirs!

22 March 1975 – The Eurovision Song Contest
Had the fates and Mickie Most not been so capricious, Arrows might have been representing the UK in this event. At Most's request, Merrill and Hooker penned 'Wake Up', a song that seemed eminently suitable for glory. However, Most then lost interest (or simply forgot); the song was not even submitted for contention and while the Shadows twanged Britain into second place (behind the Netherlands' Teach In), Arrows could only watch and wonder 'what if?'

March 1975 – Finnius Fogg: Roller Skating Baby/Nowhere Road (Dawn DNS 1105)
These literary-named Glammers would be rediscovered following their A-side's inclusion on the 'Blitzing The Ballroom: 20 UK Power Glam Incendiaries' compilation (Psychic Circle PCCD 7021).

ON THE BOX
6 March 1975 – Top Of The Pops: David Bowie, Bay City Rollers, Kenny, Slade, Showaddywaddy
7 March 1975 – Russell Harty: Steve Harley and Cockney Rebel
13 March 1975 – Top Of The Pops: The Rubettes, the Sweet, Fox, the Bay City Rollers
20 March 1975 – Top Of The Pops: Kenny, Bay City Rollers
22 March 1975 – Tiswas: The Rubettes
27 March 1975 – Top Of The Pops: 10cc, the Rubettes, the Sweet, Bay City Rollers
ON THE SHELVES
March 1975 – Barry Ryan: Do That/Summer's Over (Dawn DNS 1109)
March 1975 – Kiss: Rock And Roll All Night/ Getaway (Casablanca 510)
March 1975 – Kiss: Dressed To Kill (Casablanca 4004)

---

1 April 1975 – Shang-a-Lang
April 1975 – Bay City Rollers: Once Upon A Star (Bell SYBEL 8001)
'Once Upon A Star' inevitably crashed straight to the top of the chart and, like 'Rollin'' before it,, remained on the listings for what seemed like an eternity. The nationwide tour that accompanied it sold out weeks in advance and the tabloids finally twigged that a British act was at last challenging the Americans' stranglehold on local youth affections.

'Roll over Donny, tell David the news, the Bay City Rollers are coming for you, you and YOU!' was one of the more innovative headlines, set in inch thick capitals over a grainy picture of the Bay City Rollers' latest in-concert triumph.

It mattered not that the band were of only average musical ability, nor that barely half the band was even remotely good looking. The fact that the Bay City Rollers had inspired this kind of support without the aid of any but the most blatant pin-up orientated magazines, suggested that the Bay City Rollers were more than a teenage fad, they were the real thing.

And they didn't even have fuzzy hair!

Maisy, a 16 year-old Scottish girl, told *Record Mirror* how she felt about Eric. 'He's my dream come true, my god. I thought it was just a fad, but now I've really grown to love him deeply. My parents think I'm crazy and the teachers at school have lectured me about my failed exams and the way my standard of work has dropped since I became a Bay City Rollers fan. They just cannot begin to understand that Eric is the most important thing to me.'

The Bay City Rollers were not averse to taking advantage of this kind of thing. 'Before I joined the Bay City Rollers I used to have my fair share of birds running after me,' Les once said. 'But it wasn't like it is now.'

Only partially veiled tales of on-the-road debauchery grew up around the band, while their off-stage behaviour, too, was beginning to cause their mentors some very serious concern. Feted as gods, the band tried to act accordingly. Les confessed to a sexual proclivity quite unbecoming in a person of his stature and was then involved in a headline-grabbing manslaughter case after he knocked down and killed a senior citizen on a crosswalk.

Having painted them as angels, the press was fast coming to the conclusion that the Bay City Rollers might, in fact, be demons. It was time, Tam Paton astutely determined, to turn their attentions elsewhere.

It was time to paint America tartan. But, before they went, they had one more gift for their British fans. Their own TV show, half an hour each week for a total of 20 weeks, the brainchild of the brilliant Granada TV/*Lift Off With Ayshea* producer Muriel Young.

Filmed at a rate of two a day in the weeks before the Rollers left, all twenty programmes were much of a muchness: the Rollers would play a clutch of numbers, a couple of guests would turn up to plug their latest single, a dance troupe would hop, skip and gyrate around and 'serious' rock fans would look down their noses at the whole affair, because you'd never get Zeppelin or ELP prostituting themselves like that. Huurruumph.

Add an audience that drowned out every sound beneath the barrage of screams and *Shang-a-Lang* brought madness into every house in the land. And if it was bad for the hosts, imagine how the guests felt.

Weekly, Big Jim Sullivan offered guitar lessons to what must have been the rowdiest set of students he'd ever faced; and weekly, the likes of Gary Glitter (performing 'Love Like You And Me'), the Glitter Band ('Love In The Sun'), the Goodies ('Funky Gibbon'), Alvin Stardust ('Sweet Cheatin' Rita'). Mr Big ('Lucky Man'), Lulu ('Boy Meets Girl'). Showaddywaddy ('Three Steps To Heaven'), the Rubettes ('I Can Do It ') and even Slade ('Thanks For The Memory') were humbled before the sheer weight of Rollermania.

Lieutenant Pigeon were another of the bands invited to guest on the show, performing 'I'll Take You Home Again, Kathleen' and being interviewed about 'an album we had released of diesel-train sounds,' ('Westerns', for the specialist

Argo label, was the first of three collections of train sounds the duo created.)

As Rob Woodward recalls, 'The TV show proved a profound and somewhat daunting experience.' At the end of the day, both Lieutenant Pigeon and the Goodies found themselves 'trapped in the car park by literally thousands of screaming Rollers fans. The Rollers, of course, were smuggled out earlier – and as manifested itself with the great Elvis Presley – a voice should have announced that they had *left the building'!*

And that was always the Rollers' problem. No matter how hard they attempted to demonstrate a musical ability beyond the 'talentless tartan teen totty' tag that haunted them, the Rollers were *never* going to convince anyone that they were serious musicians in control of their own destiny and so *Shang-a-Lang* has sunk into the memory as little more than a 30-minute advert for whatever Rollers record was being shoved down our throats that week.

Watching *Shang-a-Lang* from all these decades' distance, however, you do wonder if maybe history has misjudged the band. At least they looked like they were trying, they sounded like they meant it and, wrapping themselves around some of the biggest hits of the age, they did have a knack for crafty hooks and singalong choruses. And all the hits are here, often in multiple versions, together with a healthy crop of album cuts and all-purpose covers, performed either live to the cameras, or accompanied by some pre-shot footage...the Rollers invent the music video, shock horror.

It does get a little wearing if you try to watch the whole thing in one sitting, but most people probably wouldn't even attempt that. In half-hour snatches, though, with a finger on fast forward for some of the more obnoxious guests, *Shang-a-Lang* is an excellent reminder of both a time and a band whose like we will never see again. (And you still remember all the words to the songs as well, don't you?)

10 April 1975 – Top Of The Pops

One question comes to mind while re-watching this show – two, if you really want to know how Pan's People felt improvising a dance to the Goodies' 'Funky Gibbon'?

(Or three, if you ever wondered how Jamaican reggae chanteuse/Lee Perry protégée Susan Cadogan felt when host Emperor Rosko introduced 'Hurts So Good' as a disco hit?)

And that is, given the unrestrained and even uncontrollable hysteria that greeted the Bay City Rollers every time they stepped out in public and which was now being blasted into our living rooms every week by *Shang-a-Lang, how* did the BBC manage to keep the audience so calm when the boys appeared on *Top Of The Pops?*

Those girls are so lifeless they could be watching Pilot.

April 1975 – Smokey: Pass It Around/ Couldn't Live (RAK 192)

Chinn and Chapman's response to Mud's perfidy was swift and awful. Nobody doubted, after all, that Smokey was destined for great things. But it was only now that Chinnichap decreed *how* great.

Both 'Pass it Around', Smokey's first single, and 'If You Think You Know How To Love Me', earmarked as their second, were strong soft-rockers, considered and lyrical and closer to the Eagles than anything else. And then there was 'Don't Play Your Rock'n'Roll To Me', based around Elvis Presley's 'His Latest Flame', that had hitherto been intended to be Mud's next release. They were in the midst of routining it, in fact, when they announced they would leaving the label. It was immediately passed on to Smokey.

In the meantime, 'Pass It Around' arrived laden with all the laid-back tunefulness that Chinnichap were convinced was in tune with their new-found maturity; and so confident were they that the UK press was offered an extra treat in the form of a four-song promotional EP that proved the super-smooth single was not a fluke. Two further songs, 'Day Dreamin'' and 'Turn Out Your Light', emphasised Smokey's commitment to melody.

Chinnichap turned to face America, too, making plans to relocate there permanently, and regarded Smokey as the band that would give them their first foothold. And when it didn't turn out that way, they changed the spelling of the band's name to Smokie and kept on pushing forward.

Smokie (or Smokey) were not Glam, no matter how far you stretch the boundaries. As Arrows' Alan Merrill put it, 'I see Smokie on a lot of Glam-Rock lists, but their music and look were always like Eagles wannabes. Construction workers with guitars. Nothing camp there at all.'

Andy Scott agreed. 'Mike definitely wanted an Eagles. He wanted to produce a band like the Eagles, I remember him saying it to me.'

Indeed, with the fledgling exception of New World, back at the dawn of the duo's career, it would be have been difficult to have conjured up a less Chinnichap-like band – which may be why Smokie's best-remembered hit remains a song that New World themselves couldn't give away when they cut it, 'Living Next Door To Alice'.

April 1975 – Mud: Oh Boy/Watching The Clock (RAK 201)

After eight UK hit singles, all but two of which stormed the Top Ten, Mud had established themselves as the most successful graduates yet of the Nicky Chinn/Mike Chapman songwriting factory. And now they had gone.

RAK weren't left empty-handed, of course. There was a second Mud album already in the can and Mickie Most was nursing a considerable grudge. Even before they looked at the release schedules, Mud knew that RAK would wreak its revenge. And so they did, pulling a track off 'Mud Rock 2' that was *so* unlike anything the band had released before that the only possible reason for releasing it was spite.

Ray Stiles: 'Back in the days of slogging around in the van, we had two songs we used to sing. One was "Sealed With A Kiss", and the other was "Oh Boy", with all these four-part harmonies. We'd be driving along, and we'd worked out all these Four Freshmen-type harmonies and while we were working on the album we needed a couple of songs to finish it. We said. "Well, we've got this" and Mike said. "Great, we'll do it."' Chapman joined them at the mike for some of the harmonies and a fine performance was slotted onto the album.

'But when we left, RAK started putting out stuff of ours to spite us and "Oh Boy" was really that. When they put out "Oh Boy", we thought "Well, that's really nasty" because it was a great LP track but it's not a single. But then Kenny Everett picked up on it; I remember him saying this is going to be Number 1, and it was. But as far as we were concerned, they put it out for spite. That was their intention and it backfired on them.' (The B-side was lifted directly from the flip of the previous year's Dum single.)

A sombre drumbeat, ensemble vocals, doowop-ish harmonies and even a spoken word section all conspired to create a record that didn't simply soar to Number 1 in May 1975, it displaced the Bay City Rollers in the process. It remained at the top for two weeks, Mud's final chart-topper and one of their most memorable records ever – particularly when they came to replicate the record's super-sultry spoken female vocal on TV.

Usually, Dave Mount would don a blonde wig and then pull every face he could think of. But on *Top Of The Pops*...there were these cleaning women tidying the stage while they played and – well, you can guess the rest.

April 1975 – Ian Hunter: Ian Hunter (CBS 80714)

Ian Hunter's eponymous solo debut, with Mick Ronson an equal partner in all but name, might well be the finest piece of work he ever did.

Divorced from the emotional attachment that most Mott fans feel with that band's output, Hunter's vocals have rarely sounded so sincere, so controlled or so wild as they do here, while the album positively creaks with jewels... The chorale strains of 'It Ain't Easy When You Fall', the thumping swirl of 'I Get So Excited', the instantly immortal 'Once Bitten Twice Shy'. Ronson's 'The Truth, The Whole Truth' showcase. The brief Hunter poem 'Shades Off'. And 'Boy', an eight-minute ballad whose understated orchestral backing and 'word to the wise'-type admonishments drew speculation from every angle.

It was, the era's observers pronounced, Hunter's ode to David Bowie, although Hunter cautioned that 'other record industry figures also come to mind.'

But it's more romantic, and perhaps more accurate, to regard 'Boy' as less a personal requiem than a cultural one. Glam Rock was dying and might even have been dead. A lyric that warned 'the carnival is closed, your streets are lined with ghosts' took on more resonance every day, after all.

Maybe it *was* about Bowie, after all.

April 1975 – Arrows: Broken Down Heart/ I Love Rock'n'Roll (RAK 205)

Penned by Roger Ferris, Arrows' fourth (and fifth – the sides were flipped a few weeks later) single, 'Broken Down Heart' is remembered today for just one reason. Its B-side. Which then became the A-side.

Alan Merrill wrote 'I Love Rock'n'Roll' as 'a knee-jerk reaction to the Rolling Stones' "It's Only Rock'n'Roll",' a vibrant response to that song's apparent dismissal of the art form.

Subsequently described by Mick Jagger as the band's sole concession to Glam Rock (sailor suits and bubbles can have that effect), the title track of the Stones' latest album hit the chart in spring 1974, at a time when Jagger was hanging out in aristocratic circles far beyond the club and pub-goers with whom he'd once socialised.

Merrill continued, 'I almost felt like "It's Only Rock'n'Roll" was an apology to those jet-set princes and princesses that he was hanging around with. That was my interpretation as a young man: it's *only* rock'n'roll and I like it. *Like*. Well, I loved it, so okay – I love rock'n'roll. And then, where do you go with that?

'You have to write a three-chord song with a lick that people remember and it has to build. So I had the chorus, which to me sounded like a hit. And I thought, I'll do something really unusual. I'll write it that this is a song separate from the verse. So the actual chorus is something that's coming out of a jukebox and the two kids in the disco who are flirting are hearing this song that's a hit. It felt like the *Twilight Zone*. A hit within a hit. A fictional hit coming out of the chorus with the kids singing it as their favourite song in the verse of the song.'

With the single in the shops, Arrows made the usual round of TV appearances, including a showing on *45*. Which was where Granada TV producer Muriel Young caught sight of the band and began considering them as suitable hosts for a new teatime pop show, to replace the Bay City Rollers' *Shang-a-Lang*.

Otherwise unsuccessful in Arrows' hands, 'I Love Rock'n'Roll' caught Joan Jett's attention during the Runaways' first UK tour in September 1976, after she saw the band performing it on the ensuing *Arrows* TV show. Three years later, Jett recorded it with Sex Pistols Steve Jones and Paul Cook, and that version flopped.

But a recut in 1981, the title track to Jett's second LP, soared to the top of the American chart and, while a generation wondered what would happen if you did put a dime in a jukebox (they took quarters at least, by that time), 'I Love Rock'n'Roll' became the universally renowned classic we always knew it was.

April 1975 – Gary Glitter: Love Like You And Me/I'll Carry Your Picture Everywhere (Bell 1423)

Insistent and chiming, 'Love Like You And Me' made Number 10, the last genuine classic the Glitter-Leander team would create, although according to Gary Leander's credit was more of a requirement than a reality. 'Most of it was written by myself and Gerry Shephard of the Glitter Band; it was the only Gary Glitter/Glitter Band studio collaboration ever.'

Glitter was desperately seeking change by now and this song produced it, centring around 'a heavy-metal sound [created] by working the guitar and bass into a hard-driving Free-type riff.' Unfortunately, its success was an illusion. 'It went straight into the Top Ten, but that was due to shops over-ordering it on the strength of the record before. It fell sharply the next week, when people weren't actually buying it.'

And why weren't they buying it? 'I think it was the too-wallowy lyrics...'

April 1975 – A Raincoat – I Love You For Your Mind (Not Your Body)/Vote For Me (EMI 2289).

A Raincoat was the brainchild of one Andy Arthurs, a Cheltenham-born student of recording technology. Graduating in 1974, he approached EMI with a solo demo, only to be told (in a smart reversal of Decca's dismissal of the Beatles) that guitar groups were in and solo singers were yesterday's news.

He quickly rounded up a band's worth of friends and A Raincoat cut their debut album the following year. 'Digalongamacs' punned the band's name and their chosen cemetery-based sleeve photograph against the latest album by family entertainer Max Bygraves and was arrived at only after EMI rejected Arthurs' original title, 'Macs By Graves'.

The super-quirky 'I Love You for Your Mind (Not Your Body)', the band's debut single, picked up a little airplay, but it was A Raincoat's final single, 1976's non-LP 'It Came In The Night' (EMI 2393), that caused the biggest splash after Kenneth Anger picked it up for inclusion in his re-edit of the *Rabbit Moon* super short (seven minutes) in 1979. It is credited there, incidentally, to Arthurs alone.

Unfortunately, A Raincoat had long since hung themselves up by then, folding later in 1976. Arthurs next resurfaced, solo at last, on TDS. Two singles bookended a burst of activity during 1978-79, 'I Can Detect You (For 100,000 Miles)' and 'I Feel Flat'; he relocated to Australia in 1991 and is today Discipline Leader of Music and Sound at the Queensland University of Technology in Brisbane.

April 1975 – Tim Dandy: Run Run Run Run Run/Boney Moronie (Penny Farthing PEN 873)

Frenetic fun from the mysterious Mr D, rediscovered following its inclusion on the 'Blitzing The Ballroom: 20 UK Power Glam Incendiaries' compilation (Psychic Circle PCCD 7021).

24 April 1975 – Slade, live at the New Victoria Theatre, London

Four years had passed since Slade broke through, in an age when four years was a virtual eternity and, though they no longer hit Number 1 like they used to, it would be churlish to say they'd lost it completely. Their fourteenth straight hit single, 'How Does It Feel', had just spun off their movie debut, *Slade In Flame*; their fifteenth, 'Thanks For The Memory', was poised for release. And the roar that accompanies their arrival on stage, to power through a dynamite 'Them Kinda Monkeys Can't Swing', proves that the faithful had never lost their devotion.

Listening back to the BBC recording of this show reveals that it is at least 18 months too late to truly recreate the magic that Slade audiences once took for granted. But, as they pound through 'The Bangin' Man', 'Gudbuy T'Jane', 'Far Far Away', 'Everyday', 'Mama Weer All Crazee Now' and a well-chosen clutch of recent album cuts, you can still feel the glitter flying, the satin flapping and the electricity arcing from stage to stalls. Though a lot of hits were left unplayed, memories of Slade as perhaps *the* primo live band of the first half of the Seventies come hurtling back.

April 1975 – Glitter Band: The Tears I Cried/ Until Tomorrow (Bell 1416)
April 1975 – Glitter Band: Rock'n'Roll Dudes (Bell 253)

The departure of John Rossall was a blow from which the Glitter Band would never recover, although nobody realised that at the time. As John Springate recalls, 'The general idea was, John wanted to go out and do his own thing. But it did create a little bit of instability in the group, because up until then he'd been the leader – after he left, it became democratic and democratic groups don't really work. You always need somebody there to say "Right, this is what we're going to do", but nobody wanted to make any decisions because nobody wanted to be the leader.'

Perhaps the first sign of this new indecision was the group's willingness to allow Mike Leander to choose the name of their latest LP.

Because...was this the worst album title anyone had ever conceived?

Maybe not...there are probably more sick-inducing terms than this out there somewhere. But at a time when the only people who used the term 'dude' were the cartoon cast of Tony Benyon's Lone Groover strip in the *NME* and almost 20 years before *Wayne's World* gave it at least a hint of ironic value, calling yourself a 'rock'n'roll dude' was a little like going to the youth club with a bunch of your friends and seeing your dad, dressed up like Gary Glitter, dancing the kung fu.

Plus, it opened the door for the *NME*, again, to rechristen it 'Rock'n'Roll Duds'.

Peel away the embarrassment, though, and 'Rock'n'Roll Dudes' is quite the dandy highwayman, opening with the crystalline clatter of 'For Always And For Ever', marching on through 'Goodbye My Love' and topping everything off with 'Game's Up' – Hello's latest single and a great Glam stomper as well.

Shame, then, about 'The Tears I Cried', a soggy Gerry Shephard ballad that might well have been the weakest cut on the record. It reached Number 8 and nobody can say whether a different record might have done a bit better. But on an album that glittered with gems, from 'I Can't Stop' and 'Sweet Baby Blue' to 'Bring Her

Back' and on to 'Do You Remember', 'The Tears I Cried' could make you weep.

April 1975 – Bilbo Baggins: Hold Me/Dance To The Band (Polydor 2058 575)

With the band's destiny transferring now to producer Miki Dallon, all the promotional guns came out for this one, with Bilbo Baggins seemingly ubiquitous for a few months.

Deep breath – a Luxembourg Hit Pick, appearances on *Saturday Scene*, *45* and, of course, *Shang-a-Lang*. They toured with the Rubettes and 'Hold Me' sat on the Radio Forth chart for months on end.

But Bilbo Baggins' fortunes were destined never to improve. 'Back Home'/'What's Going On' (Polydor 2058 575) missed again in early 1976; 'It's A Shame'/'Please Sir' (Polydor 2058 707) stiffed later in the year and by the time the band got round to releasing their final single, 1978's 'I Can Feel Mad'/'Dole Q Blues' (Lightning LIG 521), did anyone even remember them?

Nevertheless, the band does have one place in Glam folklore for the inadvertent role they played in one of manager Paton's greatest hoaxes. In March 1976, with the elder Longmuir about to be squeezed out of the Rollers, Paton flew Irish teenager Ian Mitchell to Edinburgh to become his replacement. Mitchell, however, didn't know this.

'I was told one of Bilbo Baggins was leaving and they wanted me to replace him, so that's what I thought it was. But Tam had other ideas, which I literally knew nothing about until the night before. I was just hanging out with the Bay City Rollers, jamming and stuff and that night there was a Radio Luxembourg DJ, Peter Powell, around. Suddenly he turned to Tam and said, "Can I congratulate him now?" Tam said "I guess so", so Peter asked how I felt about joining the Bay City Rollers.

'I looked at Tam and he just nodded, and I was like – what? I wasn't even asked, it was just "Okay, you're in." I do wonder what they'd have done if I'd turned round and said "piss off".'

April 1975 – Sensational Alex Harvey Band: Tomorrow Belongs To Me (Vertigo 9102 003)

SAHB's first and, surprisingly, only LP Top Ten entry was, ironically, their least satisfying release yet, weighed down by too much nearly-prog bombast ('Give My Compliments To The Chef', 'Shark's Teeth') and scarcely ever looking towards the idiosyncrasies that had hitherto been Harvey's hobby.

'The Tale Of The Giant Stone Eater' comes the closest, but its eccentricity feels laboured and un-thought-out, and it was left to the shorter rockers to push tomorrow closer to Alex's grasp – the psychosis of 'Action Strasse', the rawness of 'Snakebite', and the immortal title track, lifted from *Cabaret* and stripped of the political overtones that rendered it so moving there, but heartfelt and haunting regardless.

Because after three years as the most theatrical band in the land, tomorrow did indeed belong to them.

April 1975 – Mal Grey and Flight 56: Look Out For Love/Ballroom Queen (Arista

'Killed By Glam: 16 UK Junk Shop Glam Rarities From The Seventies' (Moonboot MB 01) includes this solitary single by the former Wild Angels frontman.

April 1975 – Thunderthighs: Stand Up And Cheer/I'm Free (EMI 2276)

Intended as a trailer for a forthcoming Thunderthighs album, but lost when the LP was scrapped.

Karen Friedman passed away in 1991.

April 1975 – Top Of The Pops Volume 44 (Hallmark SHM 900)

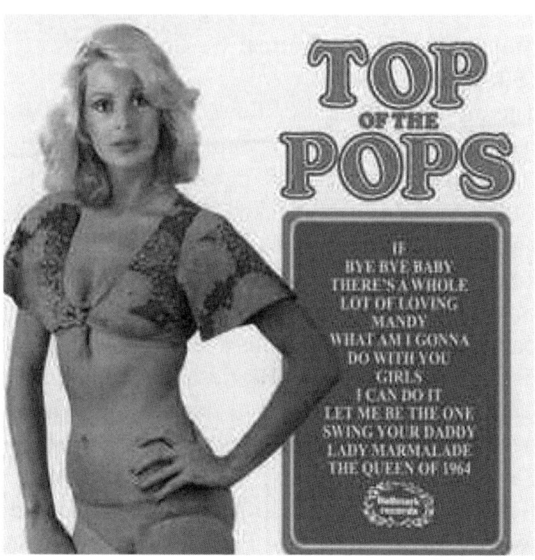

'Bye Bye Baby'... 'Fancy Pants'... 'I Can Do It'... A lot of this album feels like barrels being painfully scraped, but this triptych glows with a fanatical joy that is only going to grow brighter. In the real world, Guys And Dolls' 'There's A Whole Lotta Loving' was so profoundly saccharin that you get a cold shower just thinking about it. Here, it's positively delirious.

ON THE BOX
1 April 1975 – Shang-a-Lang: Bay City Rollers
3 April 1975 – Top Of The Pops: Glitter Band, Kenny, the Sweet, Bay City Rollers
4 April 1975 – Russell Harty: Cockney Rebel
8 April 1975 – Shang-a-Lang: Bay City Rollers
10 April 1975 – Top Of The Pops: The Sweet, 10cc, Bay City Rollers
11 April 1975 – Old Grey Whistle Test: Mick Ronson
17 April 1975 – Top Of The Pops: Glitter Band, Bay City Rollers
22 April 1975 – Shang-a-Lang: Bay City Rollers, the Goodies
24 April – Top Of The Pops: 10cc, Gary Glitter, Bay City Rollers
29 April 1975 – Shang-a-Lang: Bay City Rollers
ON THE SHELVES
April 1975 – Chuckles: Music Goes Round/Together Forever (Bell 1413)
April 1975 – Sugar Candy: Mummy I Want To Go To The Discotheque/You Only You (EMI 2285)

May 1975 – The Rubettes: We Can Do It (State 001)

The album that finally allowed the Rubettes to demonstrate the sheer depth of both their musicianship and their songwriting abilities. Of course it's still firmly locked in the Fifties (and, with songs as great as 'At The High School Hop Tonight' and 'Juke Box Jive', why not?), but Showaddywaddy's pre-eminence had pushed the band to expand its horizons a lot more than they might have. Thus the Beatlesque 'Something's Coming Over Me', armed by one of those heartbroken guitars that dictated the course of Seventies rock balladry; thus 'It's Just Make Believe', to merge harmony with whispered word, to foreshadow the Bay City Rollers' later 'Dedication'. And 'Beggarman', which makes Tom Waits sound sober.

Not that such variety did the band much good. The hits still drew the kids in, but the Rubettes' audience ended there. Except in France. 'We were never a big-selling album band,' admits Bill Hurd. 'But "We Can Do It" went gold there.'

May 1975 – Flame: Teenager In Love/Hear The Band Play (Sonet 4008)

Flame were among the heroes resurrected on 'Velvet Tinmine – 20 Junk Shop Glam Ravers' (RPM 251) in 2003, although their contribution to that set, 'Big Wheel Turning', arrived as the last embers of their career were finally blinking out, in 1977 (EMI 2669). For two years before, that the band had blazed with lisping camp Glam glory, not least of all on this cover of the old Dion chest-beater.

May 1975 – Sailor: Sailor/Open Up The Door (Epic EPC 3184)

Considering just how mature the band's musical themes might appear today, Epic had no

Kaum eine andere britische Band sahnte in diesem Jahr auf dem deutschen Plattenmarkt so ab wie Sailor. Und bislang waren die vier Musiker Georg Kajanus, Phil Pickett, Grant Serpell und Henry Marsh Lieblingskinder sowohl des Publikums wie auch der meisten Rockkritiker – eines der vielen Phänomene, denen man bei Sailor auf Schritt und Tritt begegnet.

Mitverantwortlich für den großen Erfolg der Gruppe ist sicherlich die Tatsache, daß sie enorm „camp" wirkt, daß sie es also durch eine absichtliche und gewitzte Überbetonung althergebrachter Stilformen geschafft hat, eben diese Formen wieder zu aktualisieren. Georg Kajanus, der die Seemannsmasche ausarbeitete und die Band zwischen Segelschulschiff „Gorch Fock", Krabbencocktail und „pimps and prostitutes" (Strichjungen und Nutten) ansiedelte, mußte indes schwer kämpfen, um sein durchschlagendes Konzept an den Mann zubringen: Mit seiner Plattenfirma stritt er in zähen Verhandlungen, ehe er grünes Licht bekam. Heute, nach guten LP-Verkäufen vor allem auf dem deutschen Markt und den drei Riesenhits „A Glass Of Champagne", „Girls, Girls, Girls" und „Stiletto Heels", steht die Firma einmütig hinter Sailor: Erfolg schafft Anhänger und Freunde.

Man muß sich allerdings fragen, wieso Gruppen wie Sailor eigentlich mehr als nur ein paar tausend Platten verkaufen. Denn ähnlich wie auch die Rollers oder Sweet lockten Sailor während ihrer jüngsten Deutschlandtournee zum Beispiel nur etwa zwölfhundert Zuschauer in die [illegible] also blieben die Plattenkäufer? Zufallsgäste wiederum hatten sich auch nicht versammelt: Die 1200 Mann hinter der Band, sangen die Texte zum Teil mit, egal ob sie nun acht Jahre jung oder fünfzig Jahre alt waren – Ungereimtes, wohin man blickt.

Georg Kajanus versteht diese Sache selbst nicht, meint aber, diese Bandbreite der Publikumswirksamkeit sei erfreulich und beabsichtigt. Von Zielgruppen, wie sie doch von jeder Art Wirtschaftsunternehmen (und was anderes ist eine Popgruppe?) anvisiert werden, mag er nichts hören: „Wir verstehen uns einzig als Unterhalter, und wenn wir so viele verschiedene Leute ansprechen, ist das einfach fantastisch."

Unterhalter

In der Tat sind Sailor die perfektesten Entertainer, die wohlweislich zwischen Show und Privatleben einen dicken Strich ziehen; wie der Gitarrist von Kiss auch noch horrorbemalt ins Bett zu gehen, ist bei Sailor nicht drin. Dem leicht verruchten Image der offiziellen Sailor-Jungs steht das stinknormale, britisch-seriöse Gehabe abseits der Bühne gegenüber: Grant Serpell fragt die Promo-Dame Dominica nicht [illegible] sondern erklärt ihr in Oxford-Englisch, daß die Band und die Plattenfirma einen Vertrag eingegangen seien, den es halt nach besten Kräften beiderseits zu erfüllen gelte. Wie wahr!

Die Ausgebufften

Vielleicht hängt die ganze Sache mit der Reife und der Ausgebufftheit der Bandmitglieder zusammen. Georg (30), Henry (28), Grant (34) und Phil (30) gehören zu einer Altersklasse, der man Ende der sechziger Jahre nicht über den Weg traute; trotzdem wurden sie – unter anderem – Teeny-Stars. Ein weiterer Hauptgrund dafür: Sailor produziert laut Georg „contrived music", ausgearbeitete, durchkonzeptionierte Musik ohne Improvisation, aus festen Bestandteilen zusammengesetzt." Und Georg als wichtigster Ideenlieferant ist intelligent genug zu wissen, was publikumswirksam ist und was nicht. Ich bin fast sicher, daß er schon bei der Produktion von „Girls, Girls, Girls" die neue Single „Stiletto Heels" gleich mitkomponiert hat, weil der adäquate Nachzieher eines Hits meist ebenso [illegible]

compunction at aiming Sailor towards the same singles-buying public as every other group of the age; an indication, perhaps, of just how deeply the twin chimera of modern political correctness and Health and Safety have eroded a once-vibrant national culture. The seamy side of life does not go away if you sweep it under the carpet; it just becomes more real when it is finally revealed.

Kajanus certainly never considered how a younger audience might construe his work. 'I didn't set out to be controversial. To my mind, I was merely illustrating my own observations of human nature. Of course, having been raised in Norway and France – countries that have a more relaxed attitude towards sexual matters than the Anglo-Saxon world – meant that I never really thought that my songs were specifically "adult" material and thus could be considered unsuitable for younger people.'

At the same time, however, Epic did demand one concession to 'public decency'. '"Sailor" was unusual in that it utilised a rawer vocabulary than most of the other songs. I had to remove the word "ass" from the lyrics, and change "get your ass into town" to "get your*self* into town", before they would release it as a single in the UK!'

'Sailor' reached Number 2 in the Netherlands.

May 1975 – Cockney Rebel: Mr Raffles/ Sebastian (live) (EMI 2299)

Slipping off 'The Best Years Of Our Lives' for a rush to Number 13, 'Mr Raffles' had another treat in store as you flipped it for a live 'Sebastian', and found Harley's masterpiece sounding as great in the new band's hands as it ever did in the past – and maybe even stronger, as musicianship finally triumphed over madness. The synthesiser intro was a nice touch as well.

May 1975 – Slade: Thanks For The Memory/ Raining (Polydor 2058585)

The bubble had burst. The generation that grew up Glam was leaving school, and childlike things, behind. The charts were choking on disco and reggae, novelty songs were the order of the day, and novelty remakes of novelty songs were beginning to creep in as well – how else to explain Yin and Yan's 'If'?

America was rock's last frontier, so that's where Slade had moved.

Ultimately, of course, it wouldn't work out for them, and they'd eventually return home with their tails so far between their legs that their next-but-one album would pointedly ask 'Whatever Happened To Slade?'

Chas Chandler: 'For some reason, and I never understood this and I don't think the boys did either, we got it into our heads that in order to sell records in America we had to sound American. Fair enough. Why that then translated into ballads and slow rock songs, I don't know because when we were over there we heard just as much rock, really hard rock as well, heavy stuff that was doing well and wasn't that different to what we were doing before.

'But we had this idea and we stuck to it, and it wasn't just us. Marc and Nicky and Mike came to the same decision, and I think what it showed was, our naivety for a start, but also how out of touch the record companies were, that they would take a band that was huge everywhere else in the world, or a songwriting team, and say "you're doing it wrong", and try to turn them all into an English version of whatever lightweight rockers were selling well that week.

'When what we all should have done is what people like Brownsville Station and Flash Cadillac were doing, these American bands who were taking Nicky and Mike's songs and Gary and Mike's songs, and Roy's songs and the list goes on, Barry Blue songs, and having big American hits with them, because it turned out that that was what American kids wanted from us, not the ballads. They were great songs, some of my favourite songs date from that period. But they weren't necessarily great Slade songs.'

Right now, that was a realisation that was still waiting to dawn. With Noddy a vision in polka-dotted red and yellow, 'Thanks For The Memory' rode in on a catchy keyboard hook line, a neatly bellowed chorus, and a sly tip of the hat to David Bowie. Three years ago, his 'wham bam, thank you ma'am' was one of the foundation stones of Glam. Now Slade were saying goodbye with it. Thanks for the ball.

'Thanks For The Memory' made it to Number 7. Sometimes, a great song is all you really need.

POSTSCRIPT: The band would bounce back. The late Seventies were hard but a storming performance at the 1980 Reading Festival pushed them back into contention and 1983-84 brought a fresh rash of major hit singles – 'My Oh My', 'Runaway' and 'All Join Hands', together with a Top Twenty reissue of 'Merry Xmas Everybody'. At last the band made headway in the US too, and Slade continued having hits until 1991.

Noddy Holder and Jim Lea subsequently left the band; Slade continue touring, however, with Don Powell and Dave Hill still leading the charge.

May 1975 – Jet: Nothing To Do With Us/Brian Damage (CBS 3317)

A highlight of both the live show and the album, 'Nothing To Do With Us' was one of Jet's most joyfully frenetic numbers; one that even composer Martin Gordon concedes needed to have its lyrics 'shoehorned into the existing musical structure. Well, I was still learning, you see.

'As Charles Shaar Murray rightly noted, "it doesn't seem to be about very much in

particular", and indeed it wasn't. But – unlike management's choice for Jet's last single – what it also wasn't was about losing a river, so I call that a kind of draw, at least conceptually speaking.' The single slipped away and so, eventually, did Jet. Townson was back from his broken leg, but now O'List was 'let go', to be replaced by Iain Macleod, an unknown from Southend.

Intending to rehearse for their second album, Jet took up residence in a converted church in Bruton, Somerset, and were still demoing when they learned that both CBS and RAM had dropped them (material from this period would later appear on Jet's 'Nothing To Do With Us: A Golden Treasury' anthology). Jet's final session, a demo for Island Records, saw them record four songs. Two, 'Antlers' and 'Don't Cry Joe', are also on the anthology; two others, 'Dirty Pictures', and 'Sail Away' became the first single by Ellison and Gordon's next band, Radio Stars.

POSTSCRIPT: Radio Stars survived through the Punk era, scoring a Top Forty hit with 'Nervous Wreck' and releasing two LPs before breaking up in 1979. Various reunions of Radio Stars, John's Children and Jet still occur today, while Martin

Gordon now conducts a suitably eclectic and brilliant solo career under his own name.

Davy O'List also launched a solo career.

Peter Oxendale teamed with Gerry Shephard and Pete Phipps of the Glitter Band in a new group, Oxendale-Shephard. Their LP 'Put Your Money Where Your Mouth Is' (Nemperor 36063) was released in 1979.

Chris Townson passed away on 10 February 2008.

May 1975 – The Rymbo Band

In early spring 1975, Cherry Vanilla flew from New York to Tulsa, OK, to meet with Patrick Henderson, pianist with Leon Russell's band, to talk about setting her poetry to music.

Within a week, she had a full set of material, ranging from 'Groupie Lament' (a 'tender, touching ballad') to 'Disco Rymbo', a term that may or may not have been teasing the then-omniscient Patti Smith's favourite poet (Vanilla insisted it was 'a tongue-in-cheek reference to rimming'), but would be put out there for everyone else to consider when she announced she would call her group the Rymbo Band.

'Madison Avenue', a thumping walk down the street of the same name; the pretty 'Only In Her Hair', and the sassy 'Little Red Rooster', dedicated to David Bowie's unfulfilled promise to produce her first album, all fell into place. There was a reggae number, and another song called 'Pull It Off'.

Now all she needed to do, Vanilla recalls, 'was to learn how to sing them. And get a band together to play them.'

Mick Ronson to the rescue.

Coming off the road following the Ian Hunter tour, Ronson settled (as did Hunter) in New York, and immediately threw himself into the city's burgeoning live circuit. Tapes are constantly cropping up of him taking the stage with one artist or another over the next two years (he returned to the UK in 1977), while he was also working, albeit unwillingly, towards a third solo album. Five songs recorded at the Sundragon Studios towards the end of the year are the closest he came to this, but he was by no means inactive in the meantime.

He was there when Tony Defries launched Johnny Cougar, stopping by the studio to layer trademark guitar over the youngster's first album.

He was there when Bob Dylan started dropping by the Greenwich Village folk clubs to piece together his next band. ('Ian Hunter was *so* jealous', Ronson laughed a decade later.)

And he was there when Vanilla called him up, to ask for help in putting a band together. Ronson, too, was working with Patrick Henderson at the time, tentatively assisting a New Haven-based singer named Michael Bolton (yes, *that* Michael Bolton); together, they began planning what they could do for Cherry – including piecing together a hot group to back her.

Drummer Hilly Michaels: 'I was in New Haven visiting Michael Bolton when Patrick pulled me aside to tell me about Cherry, this other project he was working on in the city and that Ronno was in the band. He asked me if I'd be interested in joining, auditioning I guess for her with Ronno.'

Avid Bowie/Ronson fan that he was, Michaels accepted. Bassist Gary Ferraro and guitarist Billy Elworthy followed and then it was back to New York, 'and this huge dark loft with Mick Ronson – stencilled flight cases lying around.

'Cherry appeared and said hello, Patrick introduced us and explained, "We have ten songs, all different styles, so let's just plough through them all." Cherry was a bit timid at the mike, but Patrick led us all through ten songs in a row. Fantastic melodies, grooves, we all just melted together in this bizarre wall of sound. Gary Ferraro and I locked together like we'd been playing together for years, almost telepathic. It was amazing. 'But, where's Ronno? "Well, errr, ummm, Mick couldn't be here tonight..."'

The band was hired on the spot, and locked into rehearsals both in New York and out in the Berkshires of Massachusetts, where friends of friends had offered Vanilla a debut show, away from prying city eyes. The Rymbo Band would play their first ever concert at what Cherry describes as 'a little biker bar in the middle of nowhere,' the Square Rigger in West Stockbridge, Massachusetts.

In the midst of all this, with that first show now looming, Cherry was called away to attend the Springfield Rock Festival in Springfield, Missouri, with Angie Bowie and Leee Black Childers. There, they were to confer their blessing on a local band, the presciently named Queen City Punks – proto-punk trash merchants of the highest degree, who opened for the New York Dolls when that band played their city. (The other support act that evening was Lynyrd Skynyrd.)

'It was a quick trip,' recalls Cherry, 'because my first gig with the band [was coming up] and I need to rehearse. I flew down that day and back the next.' But it was here that she heard her lyrics being performed live for the first time, as she handed her poem 'Ziggy Stardust' to the Queen City Punks and they worked an arrangement into their set. And it moved into illustrious company; Queen City Punks drummer Tom Whitlock later moved to Los Angeles where, alongside soundtrack work with Giorgio Moroder and a slew of other songwriting feats, he later won an Academy Award (Oscar) for the song 'Take My Breath Away'.

Back to West Stockbridge, then, and that first show was rough. 'At this point, I still had a lot of poetry and comedy in the act and the boys in the band all wore matching outfits, which they hated – black tank tops and white cotton knickers adorned with a print of red roses and male models' faces; and I insisted they deliver some lines I'd written for them, which they also hated. They wanted to be known only for their musical prowess, while I was still developing mine and was relying on the comedy to camouflage the fact that I wasn't exactly hitting every note.'

But playing almost every night for a fortnight broke the tension and relieved the nerves and, by early June, Cherry Vanilla and the Rymbo Band were ready to take Manhattan.

May 1975 – 10cc: I'm Not In Love/Good News (Mercury 6008 014)

'The title is the first thing that happened,' Eric Stewart explained. 'My wife used to say to me, "Why don't you say I love you more often?" And I talked to Graham [Gouldman] about this, and we came up with the title "I'm Not In Love", but here are all the reasons why I *am* very much in love. And it was also quite quirky and very 10cc to switch something on its head.'

The band's first attempt at the song went nowhere. 'It was a completely different feel,' says Gouldman. 'It was like a bossa nova, but it didn't work at all. Fortunately, the song stayed with us; we knew the song was good, and then Kevin [Godley] came up with a different beat and Lol [Creme] came up with the idea of the choirs. And that was it.'

The revised 'I'm Not In Love' famously required in the region of 256 vocal overdubs to complete. Less famously, it also demanded a guest appearance from Kathy Warren, the receptionist at Strawberry.

'They were trying to work out what to put in the middle eight, and a telephone call came through for Eric,' Warren recalled. 'So I went to the studio door and just opened it quietly and whispered, "Eric, there's a phone call for you". And they all said, "That's it!" The line they asked me to say was, "Be quiet, big boys don't cry".'

The band themselves believed 'I'm Not In Love' was a risky release. 'We decided to put it out, thinking it would either be a hit, or a resounding flop,' Lol Creme admitted, with Gouldman adding, 'Phonogram said that as well.' In fact, the second single from 'The Original Soundtrack' became 10cc's second British Number 1, a Number 2 smash in America and has also spawned a wealth of cover versions, not one of which can touch the original. Petula

Clark's, in fact, remains 'probably the worst cover' Gouldman has ever heard of any song.

May 1975 – Fox: Imagine Me Imagine You/If I Point At The Moon (GTO GT 21)
May 1975 – Fox: Fox (GTO GTLP 001)

Having seduced us all with the steamy 'Only You Can', Fox followed through with the similarly spellbinding 'Imagine Me Imagine You', and maybe they should have sensed that something was amiss when it stumbled at Number 15. Or maybe we should have because, turning to the accompanying LP, it became swiftly apparent that the best of Fox spun at 45, and the rest was nowhere near as special.

On single, Fox were a sultry wash of post-coital balladry, ultra-phased effects and Noosha's exotically accented whoosh. And her opening purr through 'Love Letters' matched those standards with ease. But deeper into the disc and what the lyric sheet mapped out as a mysterious world of patient tigers, silent jugglers and Pisces babies was revealed on vinyl to be a lot of bad poetry, awkwardly slapped across a musical lushness that deserved far better. And that includes their next single, 'He's Got Magic'/'Love Ship' (GTO GT37).

May 1975 – Arthur Brown: We've Got To Get Out Of This Place/Here I Am (Gull GULS 13)

The God of Hell Fire makes an unexpected comeback, synthi-glamming up the old Animals hit, and attracting the attention of 45 viewers everywhere with the latest addition to the well-heeled wardrobe. Gold wellington boots!

Sadly, the remainder of the accompanying album, 'Dance', led off in some very different directions, but just for three minutes Brown burned again.

May 1975 – Be Bop Deluxe: Futurama (Harvest SHSP 4045)

Overlooking the fact that Be Bop Deluxe were without doubt the most overrated band ever to drag itself out of the Glam-Rock era by pretending to be something else entirely; forgetting, too, that Bill Nelson was the Rock Intellectual With Cheekbones upon whom David Byrne based his entire subsequent career, 'Futurama' captures the band at precisely the right moment in their history.

Blessed with a shattering Roy Thomas Baker production, the band was on the cusp of a most delicious dilemma. Pop stars or pop art? Decisions, decisions. 'Jean Cocteau' went the latter route, of course, a Technical Drawing class set to music. But 'Sister Seagull', 'Maid In Heaven' and 'Love With The Madman' scream 'See me, feel me, luurrrrvve me!' with abandon, and the audience would clap and sing its soul out. We know which direction they want the band to go in and, for a few fleeting moments, Bill Nelson knew it as well.

May 1975 – Kenny: Baby I Love You OK/The Sound Of Super K (RAK 207)

Kenny's third single reached Number 12.

May 1975 – The end of the Osmonds

The sales had been dipping for a while now. The solo Donny had not seen the Top Twenty since November 1974; Jimmy since six months before that. Marie had mustered just one hit on her own, the unfortunate 'Paper Roses' (unfortunate if you have difficulties with the letter 'R', anyway) and the full clan's last hit, 'Having A Party' in March, scarcely made the Top Thirty.

Things did pick up a little once the family

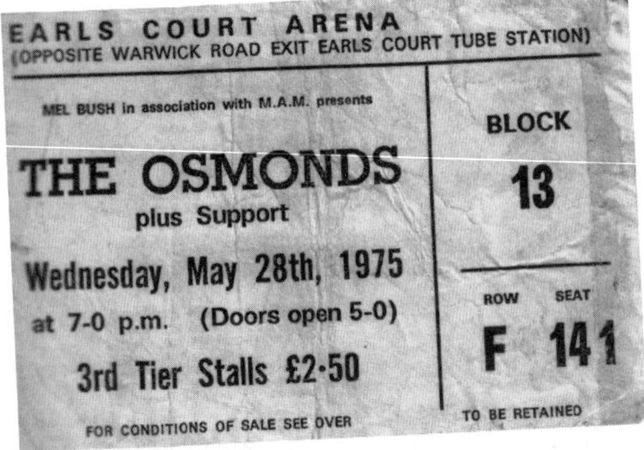

arrived in Britain again. The brothers' 'The Proud One' was destined for Number 5, while Donny and Marie's latest would peak at Number 18. But maybe they should have thought twice before recording a song called 'Make The World Go Away' because, suddenly it looked as though it had.

Still it was business as usual at Earl's Court, as the requisite 18,000 weenies descended to scream and shriek at more or less precisely the same act that they'd been screaming and shrieking at the last time the Osmonds played. And the time before that. And that may be why the fame began to melt. Their audience had changed a lot over the last three years; 12 or 13 in the first flush of puppy love, they were now 15 or 16. They'd grown, they'd developed, they'd matured. Would it have been so difficult for the Osmonds to do the same?

Meanwhile, they took their decline out on their support band. Hello were booked as the opening act for the entire World Tour. Unfortunately, Bob Bradbury remembers, 'The first gig in Paris we blew them off stage – the audience went wild. We were put on the first plane home.'

May 1975 – Hello: Bend Me Shape Me/ We Gotta Go (Bell 1424)

The loss of the Osmonds tour might also have accounted for the loss of what could have been another hit. Although, in truth, 'Bend Me Shape Me' was an awkward choice for a single, an old American Breed/Amen Corner song that always felt a lot more annoying than it probably intended.

Bob Bradbury: 'It was our manager, David Blaylock's idea. I didn't want to record this track. Amen Corner's version was great and there was no way to beat it. However, people loved it.' Another German hit, it was also one of Hello's two contributions to *Side By Side* ('Game's Up' was the other.)

May 1975 – Top Of The Pops Volume 45 (Hallmark SHM 905)

Collectors, lured by an enthusiastic *Mojo* article, know this as the volume that features a version of Kraftwerk's 'Autobahn'. But 'Volume 45' is also dignified by a superbly arranged cover of 'Oh Boy', while one could also marvel at the version of Minnie Riperton's 'Lovin' You', which strives so hard to match the crystal-shattering purity of the original that it seems churlish to flinch when the notes go astray.

A PAN FAN WAS REALLY TAKEN

STUDENT Keith Jackson was cleared of a shoplifting charge yesterday — after blaming TV dancing girls Pan's People for distracting him.

Keith, aged 18, had been watching the glamorous girls on a TV set in a supermarket before he wandered through the check-out without paying for two rolls of tape.

The dancers proved so much of a distraction that he could not remember putting the tape, worth 55p, into his pocket, he said.

Keith told Makerfield magistrates' court, Wigan: "Pan's People have a particular attraction for me.

"I don't recollect putting the tape in my pocket."

Keith, of Culcheth Avenue, Abram, near Wigan, denied stealing from the Asda supermarket at Golborne.

Dismissing the case, magistrate James Cheetham told him: "Let this be a lesson to you."

May 1975 – Pan's People: He's Got Magic/ Sooner Or Later (Epic EPC 3339)

The troupe's second single, not as powerful as its predecessor but still a deserving effort.

ON THE BOX

1 May 1975 – Top Of The Pops: Glitter Band, Mud
6 May 1975 – Shang-a-Lang: Bay City Rollers
8 May 1975 – Top Of The Pops: Slade, Gary Glitter, Mud
13 May 1975 – Shang-a-Lang: Bay City Rollers
15 May 1975 – Top Of The Pops: Ian Hunter, Fox, Showaddywaddy
17 May 1975 – 45: Gary Glitter
20 May 1975 – Shang-a-Lang: Bay City Rollers

22 May 1975 – 45: Hello
22 May 1975 – Top Of The Pops: Slade
29 May 1975 – Top Of The Pops: 10cc, Kenny, Fox
30 May 1975 – Old Grey Whistle Test: Sensational Alex Harvey Band
ON THE SHELVES
May 1975 – Mountain Child: Maybe I'm In Love/Ragged Trousers (EMI 2300)
May 1975 – Tiger Tim: Stargirl/Yes I Will (GTO 22)

June 1975 – Gary Glitter: Doing Alright With The Boys/Good For No Good (Bell 1429)

'Doing Alright With The Boys' hit Number 6 and barely deserved to do that. Little more than an insubstantial rewrite of 'Leader Of The Gang', Glitter himself described it as an attempt to 'play it safe and get back with the Gang', and its swift rise up the chart was matched only by its speedy descent. Gary would continue to glitter, of course, but the old magic was terminally tarnished.

June 1975 – Mud: Moonshine Sally/Bye Bye Johnny (RAK 208)
June 1975 – Mud: Mud Rock Volume 2 (RAK 513)

'Mud Rock Volume 2' was released in the shadow of 'Oh Boy' and readily motored to Number 6, another non-stop party set that wrapped up some fabulous moods – the summer sun and swaying palm trees of 'Hula Love', the balls-out rock'n'roll of 'Let's Have A Party' and 'One Night'; a production-heavy take on Cliff Richard's 'Living Doll'; and 'Oh Boy', of course.

Meanwhile, there was the business of their next hit single and, with Mud having departed for pastures new, that meant a quick dart into the Chinnichap archive to pull out one of the first recordings the group made with the songwriters some three years earlier.

'Moonshine Sally' was the thematic twi[n] 'Wig-Wam Bam', the Sweet's latest hi[t] time it was recorded, and musicall[y] dissimilar. Which is why it [...] favour of 'Crazy'.

Now, however it was ou[t] proved a fabulous follow-up t[o]

Boy'. Indeed, after so many Elvis impersonations it was a joy to hear Mud returning to Glam-Rock basics. 'Moonshine Sally' reached Number 10, but it still had one final trick to play on Mud.

Having agreed to continue promoting their RAK Records, although they were no longer with the label, the band adhered to the usual Musicians Union rules and taped a new version of the song to mine along to a few days before their next *Top Of The Pops*.

Drummer Dave Mount missed the date; the band were filming their part in the movie *Never Too Young To Rock* at the time and Mount was needed on set. A roadie filled in for him and when the show rolled around he spent the broadcast with his nose buried in the copy of *The Beano*. Rules were rules: Mount didn't play on the tape, therefore he couldn't pretend to play on the telly, either.

[...]pera: Diana Demon [...]now
had elapsed since Virginia [...]ky Gardiner cut the first [...] The Immortal Show, a hiatus [...] the need to record two further [...]pera albums for their German label. The second of these, 'Sagittary', was

delivered at Christmas 1974, and early in the new year Scott and Gardiner returned to TW Studios (where that LP was recorded) to begin demoing the new material.

Written by Scott, with lyrics by Colin MacFarlane, *The Immortal Show* now comprised
...ongs, interspersed with a number of
Mo...s and interludes: 'Footsteps On The
Brave...ce Of Decadence', 'From 1984 To The
'Nearly...
'Instellar...rld', 'Dear Computer Penfriend',
Complex B...man', 'The First Federation',
Mind Has Go...n', 'Revolution On Alpha
Earth' and 'Lo... Cosmos', 'Where Your
It was not a ...trol', 'The Stories Of
– Scott singles ...
Perfect Woman', 'V...'.
and 'Dance Of Deca...red creation
Glam. But the execu... now 'Nearly
theatrics that were ... Gone'
project unquestionably lau...bly
heart of the music and cultu...

With Scott now modelling new costuming by Bowie's sometimes-designer Natasha Kornilov, simultaneously form-huggingly severe and softly diaphanous, vibrantly sexual and dramatically abrupt, and *The Immortal Show* already alive in the photography of Terry O'Neill, Diana Demon was ready to take the next step.

In mid-June, Scott, Gardiner, drummer Gerry Conway and bass player Bruce Lynch joined producer Visconti in his Good Earth Studios, to cut five further demos; new versions of 'Paradise Patrol', 'Where your Mind Has Gone' and 'Dear Computer Penfriend', plus 'Space Pilgrims' and 'Alpha Centaur 1'.

However, RCA – to whom Visconti's Good Earth Productions placed much of their work – passed on the project and, with further Beggars Opera projects now looming, *The Immortal Show* was shelved.

Gardiner, Scott and Visconti would remain in one another orbit; in 1976, Gardiner was ...uited to David Bowie's band for the Visconti-...ed 'Low' LP, and when Bowie and Iggy

Pop (plus Gardiner) toured the UK and US in March 1977 Scott was appointed tour astrologer.

June 1975 – Soho Jets: Denim Goddess/Smile (Polydor 2058 598)
Not as deliriously delightful as the jungle gym of their debut, but a mighty Glam-rocker all the same.

June 1975 – Sleaze: Sleaze (white label)
Amid all the treasures to have surfaced in the annals of Junk Shop Glam, Glitter from the Litterbin, the Velvet Tinmine, call it what you will, here's one that not only got away it's creators insist that it will continue to do so. Which is a shame, because it's a bloody good record.

Former members of the North Tawton, Devon-based band Slaby Witness, vocalist Tim Smith and bassist Andy Bennie formed Sleaze upon arrival at Torquay's South Devon Tech in autumn 1974. Rhythm guitarist Buzz Chanter was a close friend of Bennie's; lead guitarist Stuart Guest was a blues musician whose conditions for joining included the right to perform Jimi Hendrix's 'Red House' during the band's otherwise Smith-composed live performances. (Smith left the stage for the duration).

Quickly becoming renowned for performing two-hour live shows, Sleaze played around a dozen concerts in the Torquay area – colleges, pubs, hotels and the Tech's Christmas 1974 party at Tiffany's supporting George Melly.

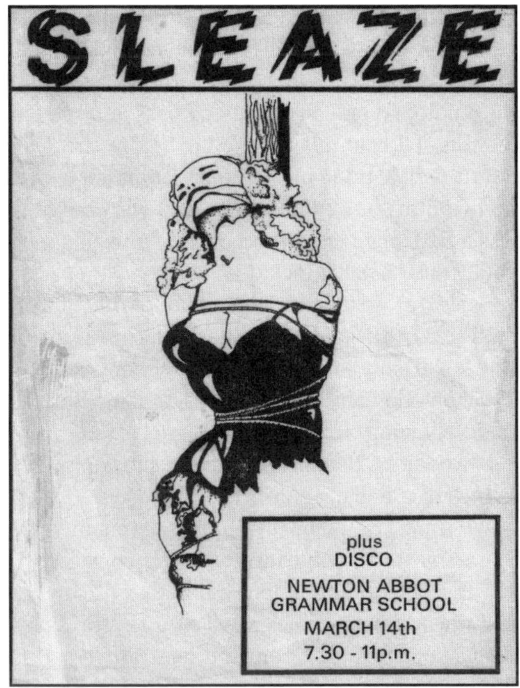

Sleaze's final act was to record a limited edition (50 copies) LP, to be distributed amongst friends and family in a plain white sleeve.

'We did the Sleaze album in June 1975, just before the end of the college year,' recalls Bennie. 'It was the first time any of us had ever been into the studio; I'd only been playing bass about eight months, I'd been playing guitar before that. We did the whole thing in two hours, completely live, no overdubs or anything. The guy who mixed it was a BBC engineer, he did a really amazing job.' Total cost – £38.88, including VAT.

'Sleaze' was patently a child of its time – protracted revisions of the dark, daring glam of Bowie's 'Diamond Dogs' and Cockney Rebel's 'Psychomodo' can be numbered among Sleaze's sonic contemporaries; a full-length LP numbers just five tracks. But 'Sleaze' is also a shockingly far-sighted disc, and not only because one song, 'Listen Don't Think', would be revived by the renamed TV Smith's next band, the Adverts, as 'Newboys'.

Elsewhere, the interplay between rhythm and melody puts one in mind of an extravagant Television ('Signals', from the band's live set, is 'Marquee Moon' two years early), while Smith's self-confessedly 'stream of consciousness...like the worst elements of Glam' lyrics pack a decadent edge that would not come into fashion for another five years or more. 'Hollywood', in particular, remains an astonishingly overwhelming song, both lyrically and musically, while 'Dum De Dum' resurfaced (once) in Smith's 21st-century live set.

Unfortunately, the band's days were numbered. With the end of the school year a few weeks later, Sleaze broke up.

POSTSCRIPT: Smith formed the Adverts, one of the key acts in the first Punk generation; Andy Bennie moved to Leicester where he joined the Wendy Tunes (who later became Last Touch and cut a couple of singles for the aptly named Zilch label). He and Smith later reunited in Cheap; Smith now performs solo.

Chanter and drummer Dave Heath formed Driving Force with future Members guitarist Nigel Bennett before Chanter and Bennie reunited in Last Touch. Guest moved to Los Angeles.

June 1975 – Tiger: I Am An Animal/Stop That Machine (UA UP 35848)

Co-written by Michael Baron, ex-the Liverpool Glam band Worth, Tiger's debut single was rediscovered following its inclusion on the 'Blitzing The Ballroom: 20 UK Power Glam Incendiaries' compilation (Psychic Circle PCCD 7021).

June 1975 – Be Bop Deluxe: Maid In Heaven/ Lights (Harvest HAR 5098)

The most astonishing track on a remarkable album, 'Maid In Heaven' was surely poised to hand Be Bop Deluxe their first proper hit single. In fact it failed, and they'd have to wait six months for 'Ships In The Night'. But Be Bop Deluxe were at the top of their game before their Glam sense was subverted by art sensibility and the next album, 1976's 'Axe Victim', would confirm that.

June 1975 – The Rubettes: Foe-Dee-O-Dee/ With You (State 007)

The title may have better suited a Worsens record than the Rubettes, but 'Foe-Dee-O-Dee' rose to Number 15.

June 1975 – Alvin Stardust: Sweet Cheatin' Rita/Come On (Magnet MAG 32)

Paired now with songwriters Geoff Stephens and Roger Greenaway, 'Sweet Cheatin' Rita' was 'going halfway again between Glam and country', the singer recalls. Alvin's final hit until his early-Eighties revival made a lowly Number 37.

June 1975 – Mick Ronson in New York

A friendship developed, Mick Ronson and Hilly Michaels. 'I spent a lot of time writing and playing drums with and for Mick,' the drummer recalls. 'We used to bash out (guitar and drums) songs either we had written together or ones Mick wrote or liked from another writer. We wrote and recorded six or seven tunes together, including one called "Paris" – as in "I met you in Paris, under the Eiffel Tower" – that was really great.'

Occasionally they would even host auditions, but few progressed beyond long jam sessions with whoever happened to be passing.

Meanwhile, a fresh collaboration of a very different kind was brewing. Fresh from the release of his 'The Higher They Climb, The Harder They Fall' album, David Cassidy remained adamant that he would never tour again. He was not, however, averse to a spot of jamming and, one night at a New York club, he

22 May 1975 – 45: Hello
22 May 1975 – Top Of The Pops: Slade
29 May 1975 – Top Of The Pops: 10cc, Kenny, Fox
30 May 1975 – Old Grey Whistle Test: Sensational Alex Harvey Band
ON THE SHELVES
May 1975 – Mountain Child: Maybe I'm In Love/Ragged Trousers (EMI 2300)
May 1975 – Tiger Tim: Stargirl/Yes I Will (GTO 22)

June 1975 – Gary Glitter: Doing Alright With The Boys/Good For No Good (Bell 1429)
'Doing Alright With The Boys' hit Number 6 and barely deserved to do that. Little more than an insubstantial rewrite of 'Leader Of The Gang', Glitter himself described it as an attempt to 'play it safe and get back with the Gang', and its swift rise up the chart was matched only by its speedy descent. Gary would continue to glitter, of course, but the old magic was terminally tarnished.

June 1975 – Mud: Moonshine Sally/Bye Bye Johnny (RAK 208)
June 1975 – Mud: Mud Rock Volume 2 (RAK 513)
'Mud Rock Volume 2' was released in the shadow of 'Oh Boy' and readily motored to Number 6, another non-stop party set that wrapped up some fabulous moods – the summer sun and swaying palm trees of 'Hula Love', the balls-out rock'n'roll of 'Let's Have A Party' and 'One Night'; a production-heavy take on Cliff Richard's 'Living Doll'; and 'Oh Boy', of course.

Meanwhile, there was the business of their next hit single and, with Mud having departed for pastures new, that meant a quick dart into the Chinnichap archive to pull out one of the first recordings the group made with the songwriters some three years earlier.

'Moonshine Sally' was the thematic twin of 'Wig-Wam Bam', the Sweet's latest hit at the time it was recorded, and musically was not that dissimilar. Which is why it was shelved in favour of 'Crazy'.

Now, however it was out and it readily proved a fabulous follow-up to the mighty 'Oh Boy'. Indeed, after so many Elvis impersonations it was a joy to hear Mud returning to Glam-Rock basics. 'Moonshine Sally' reached Number 10, but it still had one final trick to play on Mud.

Having agreed to continue promoting their RAK Records, although they were no longer with the label, the band adhered to the usual Musicians Union rules and taped a new version of the song to mine along to a few days before their next *Top Of The Pops*.

Drummer Dave Mount missed the date; the band were filming their part in the movie *Never Too Young To Rock* at the time and Mount was needed on set. A roadie filled in for him and when the show rolled around he spent the broadcast with his nose buried in the copy of *The Beano*. Rules were rules: Mount didn't play on the tape, therefore he couldn't pretend to play on the telly, either.

June 1975 – Beggars Opera: Diana Demon and The Immortal Show
More than a year had elapsed since Virginia Scott and Ricky Gardiner cut the first recordings for *The Immortal Show*, a hiatus caused by the need to record two further Beggars Opera albums for their German label, Jupiter. The second of these, 'Sagittary', was

delivered at Christmas 1974, and early in the new year Scott and Gardiner returned to TW Studios (where that LP was recorded) to begin demoing the new material.

Written by Scott, with lyrics by Colin MacFarlane, *The Immortal Show* now comprised 13 songs, interspersed with a number of overtures and interludes: 'Footsteps On The Moon', 'Dance Of Decadence', 'From 1984 To The Brave New World', 'Dear Computer Penfriend', 'Nearly Perfect Woman', 'The First Federation', 'Instellar Business Man', 'Revolution On Alpha Complex B', 'Angels Of The Cosmos', 'Where Your Mind Has Gone', 'Paradise Patrol', 'The Stories Of Earth' and 'Love Camp On Venus'.

It was not a wholly Glam-flavoured creation – Scott singles out just three tracks, 'Nearly Perfect Woman', 'Where Your Mind Has Gone' and 'Dance Of Decadence' as incontrovertibly Glam. But the execution of the set, and the theatrics that were now building around the project unquestionably launched it deep into the heart of the music and culture.

With Scott now modelling new costuming by Bowie's sometimes-designer Natasha Kornilov, simultaneously form-huggingly severe and softly diaphanous, vibrantly sexual and dramatically abrupt, and *The Immortal Show* already alive in the photography of Terry O'Neill, Diana Demon was ready to take the next step.

In mid-June, Scott, Gardiner, drummer Gerry Conway and bass player Bruce Lynch joined producer Visconti in his Good Earth Studios, to cut five further demos; new versions of 'Paradise Patrol', 'Where your Mind Has Gone' and 'Dear Computer Penfriend', plus 'Space Pilgrims' and 'Alpha Centaur 1'.

However, RCA – to whom Visconti's Good Earth Productions placed much of their work – passed on the project and, with further Beggars Opera projects now looming, *The Immortal Show* was shelved.

Gardiner, Scott and Visconti would remain in one another orbit; in 1976, Gardiner was recruited to David Bowie's band for the Visconti-produced 'Low' LP, and when Bowie and Iggy

Pop (plus Gardiner) toured the UK and US in March 1977 Scott was appointed tour astrologer.

June 1975 – Soho Jets: Denim Goddess/Smile (Polydor 2058 598)
Not as deliriously delightful as the jungle gym of their debut, but a mighty Glam-rocker all the same.

June 1975 – Sleaze: Sleaze (white label)
Amid all the treasures to have surfaced in the annals of Junk Shop Glam, Glitter from the Litterbin, the Velvet Tinmine, call it what you will, here's one that not only got away it's creators insist that it will continue to do so. Which is a shame, because it's a bloody good record.

Former members of the North Tawton, Devon-based band Slaby Witness, vocalist Tim Smith and bassist Andy Bennie formed Sleaze upon arrival at Torquay's South Devon Tech in autumn 1974. Rhythm guitarist Buzz Chanter was a close friend of Bennie's; lead guitarist Stuart Guest was a blues musician whose conditions for joining included the right to perform Jimi Hendrix's 'Red House' during the band's otherwise Smith-composed live performances. (Smith left the stage for the duration).

Quickly becoming renowned for performing two-hour live shows, Sleaze played around a dozen concerts in the Torquay area – colleges, pubs, hotels and the Tech's Christmas 1974 party at Tiffany's supporting George Melly.

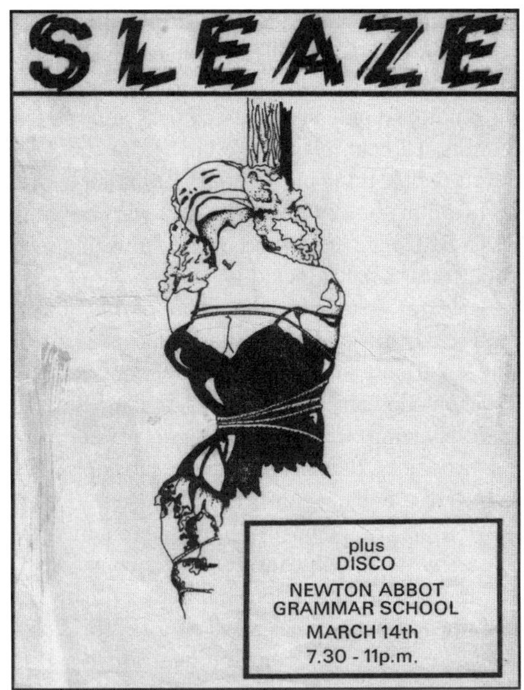

Sleaze's final act was to record a limited edition (50 copies) LP, to be distributed amongst friends and family in a plain white sleeve.

'We did the Sleaze album in June 1975, just before the end of the college year,' recalls Bennie. 'It was the first time any of us had ever been into the studio; I'd only been playing bass about eight months, I'd been playing guitar before that. We did the whole thing in two hours, completely live, no overdubs or anything. The guy who mixed it was a BBC engineer, he did a really amazing job.' Total cost – £38.88, including VAT.

'Sleaze' was patently a child of its time – protracted revisions of the dark, daring glam of Bowie's 'Diamond Dogs' and Cockney Rebel's 'Psychomodo' can be numbered among Sleaze's sonic contemporaries; a full-length LP numbers just five tracks. But 'Sleaze' is also a shockingly far-sighted disc, and not only because one song, 'Listen Don't Think', would be revived by the renamed TV Smith's next band, the Adverts, as 'Newboys'.

Elsewhere, the interplay between rhythm and melody puts one in mind of an extravagant Television ('Signals', from the band's live set, is 'Marquee Moon' two years early), while Smith's self-confessedly 'stream of consciousness...like the worst elements of Glam' lyrics pack a decadent edge that would not come into fashion for another five years or more. 'Hollywood', in particular, remains an astonishingly overwhelming song, both lyrically and musically, while 'Dum De Dum' resurfaced (once) in Smith's 21st-century live set.

Unfortunately, the band's days were numbered. With the end of the school year a few weeks later, Sleaze broke up.

POSTSCRIPT: Smith formed the Adverts, one of the key acts in the first Punk generation; Andy Bennie moved to Leicester where he joined the Wendy Tunes (who later became Last Touch and cut a couple of singles for the aptly named Zilch label). He and Smith later reunited in Cheap; Smith now performs solo.

Chanter and drummer Dave Heath formed Driving Force with future Members guitarist Nigel Bennett before Chanter and Bennie reunited in Last Touch. Guest moved to Los Angeles.

June 1975 – Tiger: I Am An Animal/Stop That Machine (UA UP 35848)

Co-written by Michael Baron, ex-the Liverpool Glam band Worth, Tiger's debut single was rediscovered following its inclusion on the 'Blitzing The Ballroom: 20 UK Power Glam Incendiaries' compilation (Psychic Circle PCCD 7021).

June 1975 – Be Bop Deluxe: Maid In Heaven/ Lights (Harvest HAR 5098)

The most astonishing track on a remarkable album, 'Maid In Heaven' was surely poised to hand Be Bop Deluxe their first proper hit single. In fact it failed, and they'd have to wait six months for 'Ships In The Night'. But Be Bop Deluxe were at the top of their game before their Glam sense was subverted by art sensibility and the next album, 1976's 'Axe Victim', would confirm that.

June 1975 – The Rubettes: Foe-Dee-O-Dee/ With You (State 007)

The title may have better suited a Worsens record than the Rubettes, but 'Foe-Dee-O-Dee' rose to Number 15.

June 1975 – Alvin Stardust: Sweet Cheatin' Rita/Come On (Magnet MAG 32)

Paired now with songwriters Geoff Stephens and Roger Greenaway, 'Sweet Cheatin' Rita' was 'going halfway again between Glam and country', the singer recalls. Alvin's final hit until his early-Eighties revival made a lowly Number 37.

June 1975 – Mick Ronson in New York

A friendship developed, Mick Ronson and Hilly Michaels. 'I spent a lot of time writing and playing drums with and for Mick,' the drummer recalls. 'We used to bash out (guitar and drums) songs either we had written together or ones Mick wrote or liked from another writer. We wrote and recorded six or seven tunes together, including one called "Paris" – as in "I met you in Paris, under the Eiffel Tower" – that was really great.'

Occasionally they would even host auditions, but few progressed beyond long jam sessions with whoever happened to be passing.

Meanwhile, a fresh collaboration of a very different kind was brewing. Fresh from the release of his 'The Higher They Climb, The Harder They Fall' album, David Cassidy remained adamant that he would never tour again. He was not, however, averse to a spot of jamming and, one night at a New York club, he was doing just that when Ronson walked in.

Cassidy recalls: 'I got up and started playing at 2am in a club. Playing blues. Mick came up to me afterwards and I think he was pleasantly surprised at what I could do, how I could play. We began to talk and hang out, and the next thing I knew we actually talked about doing a band together. We rented a rehearsal hall and started playing together, we hung out and wrote a little bit.'

Hilly Michaels continues: 'I remember David Cassidy came over a few times looking very paranoid and depressed and tried to convince Mick that they should team up. I was extremely excited at the possibilities of that happening and kept asking Mick, "Are you and David going to do this?" But then the media caught wind of the meetings, there was a huge article in a teen magazine and Mick was completely put off by the whole idea.

'As usual, Mick wanted nothing to do with instant, predictable, commercial music/success. That also trickled down into his songwriting/chord changes when we'd write together, "Nah, it's too predictable, that chord. Let's use this chord change instead." Booing!'

Cassidy's proximity to Ronno also scuppered another project. 'Bowie wanted to produce me at the time, and we met in New York. Then I sort of said, "You know I've been hanging out with Mick," and I think that put him off. I didn't know what their dynamic was, what their relationship was, and I didn't want to pursue it.'

But the partnership did not perish unheard. The following year, Ronson would stop by as Cassidy worked towards his next album at the Caribou Ranch in Colorado, and can be heard on its title track, 'Getting It In The Street'.

'He was one of the most unusual guitar-players I ever worked with,' Cassidy recalled. 'There was nothing conventional about what he did, which was so interesting. I think he was very flattered that I wanted him to play but I think he was worried that the fan base that he had established with that *avant garde*, underground, Velvet Underground kind of world was going to elude him if he went too mainstream, from being David Bowie's sideman to David Cassidy's sideman. I think he thought it and I don't think he was wrong. But we had great fun together.'

June 1975 – The [Heavy Metal] Kids: Blue Eyed Boys/You Got Me Rollin' (Atlantic K10613)

An early taste of the slowly gestating second Heavy Metal Kids LP, confusingly released under an abbreviated new name after somebody decided that the band's name was putting people off. After all, not everyone has read William Burroughs, so if you're calling yourself the Heavy Metal somethings you'd better play Heavy Metal.

With their homeland steadfastly ignoring them, the Kids set out to conquer America; 'a few weeks with ZZ Top,' recalls Keith Boyce. 'They were a really great band, and lovely guys. We also did a week of gigs with the Chambers Brothers, another amazing band and also great guys. Others we played with were Bob Seger, Flo and Eddie, Freddie King and the Average White Band, all great bands and fun to be with.

'We were playing to really big audiences most nights and were going down great, so it was a really good time for us. I'd already toured the States [with Long John Baldry in 1972] but for the rest of the band it was their first time there, so it was great seeing them all open-eyed as it was so different there from Europe.

'Everything seemed to be open 24 hours a day, TV was on all night, the bars stayed open late, people were really friendly. I had my 21st birthday on that tour, and that was really something. I couldn't have thought of a better place to be at the time.'

But even with the name-change, and despite a burgeoning reputation for hotel-wrecking hellraising (they were banned from at least three national chains), America as a whole refused to pay any attention. The band returned to Britain and 'Blue Eyed Boys' was ignored as well.

ON THE RADIO
19 June 1975 – Top Gear: Jet
ON THE BOX
3 June 1975 – Shang-a-Lang: Bay City Rollers
5 June 1975 – 45: Showaddywaddy
5 June 1975 – Top Of The Pops: Steve Harley and Cockney Rebel,
7 June 1975 – Russell Harty: Angie Bowie
10 June 1975 – Shang-a-Lang: Bay City Rollers
12 June 1975 – Top Of The Pops: 10cc, Kenny, Gary Glitter

17 June 1975 – Shang-a-Lang: Bay City Rollers
19 June 1975 – 45: Arthur Brown
19 June 1975 – Top Of The Pops: Steve Harley and Cockney Rebel, Mud
24 June 1975 – Shang-a-Lang: Bay City Rollers
26 June 1975 – Top Of The Pops: Kenny, Gary Glitter, the Rubettes, 10cc

---

July 1975 – The Tubes: The Tubes (A&M AMLH 64534)

Another American stab at Glam, shot through with the same bitter cynicism all Stateside performers now seemed to wear when they felt like dressing up. In this case, the Tubes were a hopelessly surreal outfit better suited to the hard-rock circuit than anything else but dignified in their antics by two phenomenal songs, the maniacal game show of 'What Do You Want From Life', and 'White Punks On Dope' – the final word in Glam theatrics married to the first word in punky snottiness.

In scant years to come, every joke ever levelled at California's attempts to conduct a Punk Rock scene were drawn from the lyrics of the song, but the all-pervading memory of both Tubes and their mini-hit was when they performed 'White Punks' on the *Old Grey Whistle Test* in November 1977. With frontman Fee Waybill in shock wig and monstrous platforms, staggering and flailing around the stage, and seven shades of craziness erupting all around him, one thought proved inescapable.

Four years earlier, the Tubes could have been enormous.

July 1975 – Tartan Horde: Bay City Rollers We Love You/Rollers Theme (UA UP 35891)

Foiled in his first attempt to document the teenybop phenomenon with Michael Des Barres, Brinsley Schwarz's Nick Lowe pieces together a heartfelt ode to the Bay City Rollers. He was aided and abetted by Dave Edmunds, but not (despite the picture sleeve's insistence) an unknown drummer named Chris Miller – revealed a year later as the Damned's Rat Scabies, and later still revealed to have had nothing to do with the record. He turned up at the photoshoot for the cover and they let him stay.

A second Horde single, 'Rollers Show', would follow in the new year; unfortunately (or not), an accompanying LP was abandoned.

July 1975 – Various Artists: Never Too Young To Rock (GTO GTLP 004)
July 1975 – Various Artists: Original Rocking Hits From the film Side By Side (Pickwick SHM 902)

Mud, Slik, Hello, the Glitter Band, the Rubettes, Scott Fitzgerald, Bob Kerr's Whoopee band and the Silver Band. The stars were out for *Never Too Young To Rock,* a distinctly low-budget but high-excitement movie that told the tale of life in a post-Orwellian world in which the outlawing of pop music is being enforced by Dennis out of *Please Sir!*.

Piloting a converted ice-cream van around the streets, his Group Detector machine alert for offenders, one can only imagine what he'll do if he catches any.

Wonder no more. What he's really doing is seeking fellow outlaws to help him put on a concert, and he finds them. The Rubettes are seen performing 'Tonight' on the back of a lorry; Mud have a food fight in a café run by Sheila Steafel; Noddy Holder dresses up like David Bowie, the Whoopee Band make whoopee. And so on.

'It was a good experience for us,' recalls Rubette Bill Hurd. 'Hard work with lots of early mornings and long days, but enjoyable. We only had musical appearances in the film, not acting roles and, with the plot being a bit thin really, maybe that wasn't such a bad thing. Being honest, we certainly didn't think it was a masterpiece by any means, but it is a fun movie and has become a collectors piece with Seventies music buffs etc!'

In fact, if *Never Too Young To Rock* had been shot 15 years earlier with Cliff Richard and the Shadows it would be acclaimed a pop classic today. Instead, it's all but forgotten, a fate that befell GTO Films' *Side By Side*.

Here, Terry-Thomas and Billy Boyle are rival club owners, battling it out for supremacy by staging a battle of the bands. With Barry Humphreys brilliant as Boyle's booking agent, Hello, Fox, Stephanie De Sykes and Twogether (who perform the title song) are enlisted for the conflict...with hilarious results.

July 1975 – The Sweet: Action/Sweet FA (RCA 2578)

Following up the massive success of Fox On The Run', the Sweet's second entirely self-composed hit, 'Action', was a defiant hard-rocker that made no attempt to disguise the bitterness of the lyric, lashing out at everybody who had tried to snatch a piece of Sweet's acclaim. And, in case that was all too subtle for the listener, the mid-section chiming of a cash register underlines the song's message with unmistakable brutality.

In interviews the band rattled off the song's intended targets with songwriters Chinn and Chapman very close to the top. How ironic it was to sit back and watch the Sweet being proclaimed as rock superstars in America, at the same time as their erstwhile mentors were trying to break a new band, Smokie, over there, and barely being given the time of day?

Smokie's latest single, 'If You Think You Know How to Love Me' reached the dizzying heights of Number 96 in the US; the Sweet, on the other hand, had just come off a Top Five hit with 'The Ballroom Blitz' and were now expecting similar glories from 'Fox On The Run'.

But Chinnichap weren't alone in incurring Sweet's wrath. Queen, too, were ripe for a kicking as Brian Connolly explained a decade later.

'We knew Queen were listening to us, picking the records apart, seeing how we did things. They were a great band, don't get me wrong, and they had some great ideas. But a little acknowledgement would have been nice. If one of them had just turned around once and said, "We really dig what the Sweet did on...whatever record" it wouldn't have been so bad.

'Instead they just sat back and let everyone tell them what clever little bastards they were, coming up with all this stuff on their own, and we were sitting back saying "Hang on..." There's half a dozen Queen songs at least that are direct lifts from Sweet records, but did anybody ever call them on it?'

Talking to *Classic Rock* magazine in the early 2000s, Scott agreed. 'I remember having a wry smile when I met Brian May in Los Angeles. "Bohemian Rhapsody" was out and there were definite similarities. I told Brian that I liked the last part of that one, that it was

very reminiscent of "Action". But that's okay. You beg, steal and borrow.'

'Action' peaked at a relatively lowly Number 15, but the Sweet didn't care. They were turning their backs on singles, they insisted, and diving head first into the world of 'real music'. So when it became apparent that this was their final major hit at least until 1978's 'Love Is Like Oxygen' brought a breath of surprisingly fresh air back to their career...well, hopefully they weren't too disappointed.

July 1975 – Cherry Vanilla and the Rymbo Band Their tentative beginnings behind them, the Rymbo Band were now regulars at Trudi Heller's, a Greenwich Village cabaret/nightclub on 9th and Avenue of the Americas.

'That band of ours *rocked,*' enthuses Hilly Michaels. 'Damn, we were hot. Cherry had never fronted a band before but she pulled it off with sheer balls. Sometimes she would sing and jump from a verse to a chorus (no bridge part), stuff like that. But we were always on our toes, and ready for those Cherry bombs. The best times of my life... Cherry Vanilla World.'

Plus 'It was a quick wake up call to the underground art scene. Wayne County would always be there, as would Monty Rock, Lou Reed and people I was never properly introduced to and could only imagine now, sitting there week after week for months listening to us.'

Costuming blossomed. Suzi Ronson cut and styled the musicians' hair; Cherry and her make-up girl would then apply the cosmetics...so much that, by the end of the set, it would be running down the players' faces, and so much that even the watching Mick Ronson was impressed. Bright red with laughter, he reckoned he'd never worn that much, even with Bowie.

'I was shocked senseless but loved it,' Michaels continues. 'Cherry would come out looking very vampy, scantily-clad and sparkly after the one warm-up song we had, and then she read poetry and sang her song list, acting out x-rated cabaret-style shows, and, all the while, laughing, singing and smiling, the audience egging her on screaming and hooting, standing on their chairs going berserk.

'At one point in the show, a projector would turn on and Bowie and the Spiders footage would play all over our bodies and the back wall. It was heaven, total Glam madness with a kick-ass, smokin' band. We were outrageous.'

On stage and off. One day, Cherry became New York headline news when, having gathered a coterie of newsmen on the sidewalk outside Trudi Heller's, she pulled down her pants and planted her bottom into a block of wet pink cement. She signed her name, then watched as her ass was hoisted up to hang above the club's front entrance, Grauman's Chinese Theatre-style.

But neither Bowie nor Ronson ever got around to delivering on the promised production work, and while the band did survive Patrick Henderson's departure (he was replaced by Kasim Sulton; Michael Kamen also sat in on a few occasions), the second generation of the Rymbo Band petered out just as, elsewhere on the New York scene, new moods were petering in. By the end of the year, Vanilla had a fresh band, the Staten Island Boys, and her former band-mates were moving on.

Michaels, however, speaks for them all when he declares, 'I can truly say I never played with a more ferocious-sounding band in all my days playing drum.' Which, in a career that includes stints with Sparks, Dan Hartman, Hunter-Ronson, Ellen Foley and Phil Rambow, plus his own vibrant solo project, is saying something.

POSTSCRIPT: Vanilla relocated to London in 1977, recording two RCA LPs before returning to the US. Performing sporadically since then, she published her autobiography in 2010.

July 1975 – Bay City Rollers: Give A Little Love/ She'll Be Crying Over You (Bell 1425)

No matter that they already owned it on the band's last album, where it was certainly one of the wetter songs in earshot, the fans went out and bought 'Give A Little Love' again in such vast quantities that, having entered the chart at Number 7, it then hogged the top spot for the next three weeks. Until Captain Tobias Wilcock flew in, that is, and shipped us all off to Barbados.

The film clip supplied to accompany the song's *Top Of The Pops* airings, incidentally, found the Rollers distributing a little love and largesse at a children's hospital. One little girl promptly burst into tears. ('But nurse! I wanted Status Quo!')

July 1975 – Geordie: Goodbye Love/She's A Lady (EMI 2314)

Geordie's final EMI single, issued a full year before third album 'Save The World' (EMI EMC 3134), passed unnoticed by almost everyone. But Bon Scott never forgot them. Scots-born, he was still living in the UK when he first encountered Geordie when his own band, Fraternity, opened a show for them.

AC/DC guitarist Angus Young recalled, 'The first night, [Bon] went to check out Geordie because all he could hear was this yelling and screaming coming from the stage. Bon looked up, and he saw this guy – Brian – on the floor, legs going all over the place.' The singer had been stricken with appendicitis, but Scott thought it was part of the show. 'Bon was on the table yelling "More! more!" He thought it was all part of the act.'

Following Scott's death in 1980, Johnson was recruited to AC/DC and has remained on board ever since.

POSTSCRIPT: Geordie continued recording into the early Eighties. Geordie's EMI singles catalogue, plus a solo Brian Johnson single from 1976, is compiled as 'Geordie: The Singles Collection' (7Ts GLAM CD 7).

July 1975 – T Rex: New York City/Chrome Sitar (T Rex MARC 10)

Three years after 'Bang A Gong' (the retitled 'Get It On') gave Bolan his first and last US hit single, his American label, Reprise, finally gave up hoping that he might finally break his duck. Bolan quickly moved across town to Casablanca, where he could only hope there'd be room to park his platforms in the home of the all-conquering Kiss. There wasn't and, after just one album, the 'Light Of Love' compilation, and one final tour which included several dates with his

bemasked and made-up labelmates, Bolan finally stopped worrying about America – which meant his British fans were able to stop worrying about him.

June Child, Bolan's now ex-wife, watched the transformation gratefully. 'He only used to do things he liked. He would never construct records for the market, and when he tried deliberately to write songs for America they lacked his intuitive thing and he then became desperate. He made some awful records that were so empty and lacked all his wonderful warmth and feeling.' Now it all came flooding back.

He rode out the February 1975 departure of long-time percussionist Mickey Finn with no visible ill-effects, and began regaining his shape and enthusiasm. A new band grew up around Bolan – original T Rex bassist Steve Currie and girlfriend Gloria Jones were joined in the line-up by keyboard player Dino Dines and drummer Davy Lutton (Paul Fenton and Tony Newman also recorded with him) and, in July 1975, Bolan reunited with Flo and Eddie for 'New York City', a frivolous piece of nonsense about women with frogs in their hand and a singalong knockabout which bore all the hallmarks of vintage T Rex, while still managing to sound fresh.

'It sounds terrible,' Mark Volman admits, 'but every major hit single he had revolves around us. We said that to Marc, every day of the week. There never was a time when we didn't remind him that we had hit records before him and, if he hadn't brought us in, he'd never have had a hit of his own. We always brought that down on him and it just made him laugh.'

But he also appeared to agree with them because 'New York City' saw T Rex storm back into the Top Twenty for the first time in over a year when it reached Number 15.

July 1975 – Sensational Alex Harvey Band: Delilah/Soul In Chains (Vertigo ALEX 1)

Taken from the band's forthcoming live album, a stage-stealing rendition of the old Tom Jones murder ballad 'Delilah' finally catapulted SAHB. into the British Top Thirty. And, six months past his fortieth birthday, Alex Harvey finally rolled out on *Top Of The Pops* to ham his way through the song that would rise to Number 7.

July 1975 – Ian Hunter: Who Do You Love?/ Boy (CBS 3486)

Slinky, with just the hint of old Bo Diddley circulating the rhythm, but a shock flop.

July 1975 – Warwick: Let's Get The Party Going/How Does It Feel (RAK 251)

A Chinnichap production without the Chap. Nicky Chinn produced this with Peter Coleman, and the duo didn't even compose it – that was left to Warwick Rose, who had once played with Chapman in the band Tangerine Peel. 'Let's Get The Party Going' resurfaced aboard 'Velvet Tinmine – 20 Junk Shop Glam Ravers' (RPM 251) in 2003.

July 1975 – Bubbles: This Is Where The Hurdie Gurdie Heebie Geebie Greenie Meenie Man Came In/Zapn'Cat (Decca F13583)

Produced by Decca house producer Nick Tauber, and commanding high prices on the collectors market even before it was included on 'Killed By Glam: 16 UK Junk Shop Glam Rarities From The Seventies' (Moonboot MB 01), 'This Is Where...' is arguably the record that ignited the entire Junk Shop Glam boom in the first place. The very idea that a record this maddeningly infectious, singalong and silly could be lying neglected in a charity shop near you is really too much to bear.

July 1975 – Eno: The Lion Sleeps Tonight/ I'll Come Running (Island WIP 6233)

From the master of the avant garde, proof that most of the people who call him that 'avant garde a clue' what they're on about. Recorded alongside 'Seven Deadly Finns' in late 1973, and again packing superlative backing from the Winkies, Eno's second solo single was a more or less straight faced cover of the old Tokens novelty hit, most interesting for what it doesn't incorporate – namely, anything that detracts from the song itself.

July 1975 – David Essex: Rolling Stone/ Coconut Ice (CBS 3425)

A Number 5, no sweat.

July 1975 – Sparks: Get In The Swing/Profile (Island WIP 6236)

United with producer Tony Visconti, the Maels' third UK album was to be the one that finally exhausted their audience. Breaking completely with the 'established' Sparks sound, absurdly convoluted though that already was, they now hatched an album that bordered on the avant-garde, at least in terms of its audience appreciation, and served notice with 'Get In the Swing', a rollicking singalong based around a one-sided conversation with God. And God wasn't saying much.

'Get In The Swing' reached Number 27, largely on the strength of the sight of Russell's knees knobbling around on *Top Of The Pops* set. He looked as though he was having fun, too. His non-sibling bandmates, on the other hand, merely looked bewildered.

ON THE BOX
1 July 1975 – Shang-a-Lang: Bay City Rollers
3 July 1975 – Top Of The Pops: T Rex, David Essex, Bryan Ferry, Alvin Stardust, Mud, the Rubettes, 10cc
8 July 1975 – Shang-a-Lang: Bay City Rollers
10 July 1975 – Top Of The Pops: The Rubettes, the Sweet, Bay City Rollers

Get in the swing!

Ron and Russell were tired. They called it jet lag. They had flown from Los Angeles and not many hours after arrival were at TOTP. So they had little time to get in the swing of British life and routine after their six months or more absence.

They told us whereas singles were important for them here, in the States, albums meant more. They found this rather strange but for the moment had to go along with such a situation.

Hence their eagerness in flying over and performing on TOTP, for TOTP is a singles show and countless shops order discs of anyone who appears on the programme.

Their single Get In The Swing is the first public demonstration on disc of work with their new producer, Tony Visconti. Tony is husband of Mary Hopkin, the Welsh girl who had hits with Those Were The Days, Goodbye, Temma Harbour, Knock Knock Who's There and Think About Your Children. He has produced many hits for Marc Bolan and David Bowie.

They feel a new musical era is dawning for them and see a gradual change in their work. However to TOTP and about the show and television in general they had this to say, "TV has its own technique and it can make facial expressions very important (they should know that!). TV is very subtle and movement in a short space of time has to be very good.

"On a programme like TOTP you do just one number and that's very unlike a show where you can work up atmosphere to your main number. TV means doing it straight away and still communicating.

"It's an exciting medium though. In the studio like tonight there might be thirty young people yet millions are actually seeing everything."

Sparks were rather uncertain how long they would be in Britain prior to their Autumn tour. This tour is very important to them for they hope their absence has not seen a falling-off of their support. Last yeat it was a great and successful tour. They hope everyone will quickly get in the swing when the tour commences!

13 July 1975 – 45: Fox
15 July 1975 – Shang-a-Lang: Bay City Rollers
17 July 1975 – Top Of The Pops: SAHB, T Rex, David Essex, Bay City Rollers
19 July 1975 – Old Grey Whistle Test: Be Bop Deluxe
22 July 1975 – Shang-a-Lang: Bay City Rollers
24 July 1975 – Top Of The Pops: The Sweet, Sparks, the Bay City Rollers, the Rubettes
26 July 1975 – 45: T Rex
29 July 1975 – Shang-a-Lang: Bay City Rollers
31 July 1975 – Top Of The Pops: Kenny, T Rex, SAHB, Sparks, Bay City Rollers

---

August 1975 – Mott: Monte Carlo/Shout It All Out (CBS 3528)

With Ian Hunter's solo debut having proved such a superlative gift, all eyes now turned to his former bandmates, to see what they might come up with. Sadly, it wasn't much.

With unknowns Nigel Benjamin and Ray Majors replacing the errant Hunter-Ronson, the newly abbreviated band name was reduced to little more than rentarock plodding with even Overend Watts, purveyor of 'Born Late 58' on 'The Hoople', unable to come up with a mainline attraction.

Live, on the other hand, they remained a joy to behold. Whether pounding through new material or their Hoople heritage, Mott were marvellous; 'By Tonight – Live 1975-76' (Angel Air SJPCD 289) offers up highlights from shows in both the UK (Aylesbury, Leeds) and the US, and it's just a shame they didn't release it at the time.

August 1975 – Chris Spedding: Motorbikin'/ Working For The Union (RAK 210)
August 1975 – Chris Spedding: Chris Spedding (RAK SRAK 519)

'Motorbikin" sounds like its maker looked – tight, mean and taking no trash from no-one, a leather-clad, quiff-topped rocker who had nothing to do with Showaddywaddy or Mud but recaptured the mood of a bygone age regardless. The first and only guitar-hero pin-up of the Punk era, a full year before even Punk's progenitors had heard of the term, Spedding glowered his way to Number 14 and then kicked a killer album into play as well, ditching the bike for a car with fins but otherwise picking up exactly where the single left off.

August 1975 – Hello: New York Groove/Little Miss Mystery (Bell 1438)

Just as Mike Leander had predicted, it took a reunion with Russ Ballard to break Hello out of the rut. Demoed in June and recorded in July, his 'New York Groove' catapulted the band into the Top Ten in both Britain (Number 9) and Germany (Number 7) and launched Hello into a period of staggering visibility.

No matter that the riff sounded remarkably similar to Hamilton Bohannon's recent 'Disco Stomp' hit. The single reached the Top Ten, Bob Bradbury's big eyes gazed soulfully out from every surface and over in America Kiss guitarist Ace Frehley was taking careful notes. Two years later, 'New York Groove' would become his first solo hit single.

Bob Bradbury: 'Russ wrote "New York Groove" and offered it to us – what a great idea! When we were recording it we felt it had a Bo Diddley feel to it; at the time we never thought about "Disco Stomp".'

RAM, the management company that they shared with Gary Glitter and the Glitter Band, were completely behind the band, and 'working with Mike Leander was an amazing experience.

He came up with some great and unusual ideas, such as harmonies and the "stomps" in "New York Groove". He worked very hard for us.'

With so much support, a swift follow-up should have been a given. Instead it would be the new year before the band's next single, Ballard's 'Star Studded Sham'/'Jenny Dream' (Bell 1470) brought them another German Top Twenty hit on the heels of a sell-out tour with Smokie. 'We were too busy touring I guess,' shrugs Bradbury, 'doing PAs and TV shows. Relations with Bell Records were great, we gigged with Slik, we were great mates.'

A Christmas single, 'Christmas Day In The Workhouse', was mooted but abandoned. 'We decided to do two comedy songs under a totally different name as a laugh for a Christmas release,' Bradbury explains. 'They never got released as everyone thought it was very silly; we weren't going to tell anyone who we were.'

Hello's now much-anticipated debut album, meanwhile, seemed the victim of an interminable wait, sessions 'scattered over a period of a few months, starting in February 1975. We played most of the tracks live in the studio with very little overdubs, mostly using the first takes,' as the band recorded when they got the opportunity.

'Keeps Us Off The Streets' was finally released in May 1976, wrapped in a mock denim cover that looked great on the racks, and was stunning from beginning to end. But Hello's career petered out from there, at least so far as UK audiences were concerned.

Bradbury: 'I guess that in 1975-76 we naturally took on a change in sound and image because we were reaching our late teens/early twenties and were growing up. We were kids when we started, it was a natural progression for things to change.'

'Love Stealer'/'Out Of Our Heads' (Bell 1482) was their final single for Bell before the label was absorbed into Arista; two final UK singles appeared on that label in 1977 and the band turned their attentions exclusively to Germany.

POSTSCRIPT: Hello's full UK singles catalogue is compiled on 'Hello: The Glam Singles Collection' (7Ts GLAM CD 5), while 'Keeps Us Off The Streets' was reissued with a selection of bonus demos and outtakes in 2007 (7Ts GLAM CD 30).

Several post-Hello rarities, including a solo cut by Jeff Allan and Keith Marshall's production of the Teasers, were included on former manager David Blaylock's Biff label's compilation LP 'The Great Glam Rock Explosion' (Biff BIFF 3) in 1986.

August 1975 – Mud: One Night/Shake Rattle And Roll/See You Later Alligator (RAK 213)

Another album cut, this Elvis cover became Mud's final RAK single before the new regime moved into view and hit a lowly Number 32.

August 1975 – Alvin Stardust: Rock With Alvin (Magnet 5007)

August 1975 – Alvin Stardust: Move It/Be Smart Be Safe (Magnet MAG 39)

The hits stopped, but Stardust had already made plans for the future. And no, it wasn't his involvement in the traffic safety campaign that inspired his latest B-side.

He had already dropped the leather and the scowl, while his last two singles had revealed a sensitive side to the once-demonic performer. A recreation of Cliff Richard's first hit, 'Move It' was a little tougher, but with his audience now including as many parents as children he turned his attention towards the rock'n'roll revival circuit and remained a successful live draw well into the early Eighties.

Stardust then engineered a quite remarkable comeback, signing to the Stiff Records label and returning to the chart with 'Pretend'. It reached Number 4 in 1981. Three years later, Mike Batt's 'I Feel Like Buddy Holly' returned him to the UK Top Ten, to be followed by 'I Won't Run Away' and the festive 'So Near To Christmas'.

The following year, he celebrated when 'Got A Little Heartache' breached the Top Sixty. It was to prove his final hit as he moved instead into theatre and acting, starring in the first two seasons of *Holby City* and proving a hit in a revival of *Godspell* before returning to music and proving himself eminently capable of appearing on both Glam and rock'n'roll revival bills.

2010 saw him reliving his most glorious years with a killer cover of Arrows' 'I Love Rock'n'Roll'.

August 1975 – Kenny: Julie Ann/Dancin' Feet (RAK 214)

For a band whose hitmaking career extends to no more than 12 minutes' worth of music, Kenny managed to squeeze an awful lot out of it. 'Julie Ann' hooted and hollered its way to Number 10 and, if RAK had their wits about them, an album would have followed immediately.

As it was, it would be the new year before 'The Sound Of Super K' (RAK SRAK 518) reached the streets and, while later ears would decree it a slab of latter-day Glam genius, with a sensibility at least on a par with the Mud and Rubettes, at the time...who cared?

By the time Kenny made their breakthrough, both the pop and glam veins they were mining were running dry, while songwriters Bill Martin and Phil Coulter were still reeling from their dismissal from the Bay City Rollers camp. And when they did regain their equilibrium, it was to turn their affections to Slik. Indeed, Kenny's status as a kind of noble no-man's-land between those two giants is only reinforced by the two best cuts they ever got their hands on, 'The Bump', which had already seen service on a Rollers B-side, and 'Forever And Ever', which would become Slik's debut hit.

For the remainder of their career, Kenny slipped blithely between punchy glam pop and dreamy teen ballads, and a few high-tempo dancefloor crashers. They broke with both RAK and Martin/Coulter after their fifth single together, 'It's So Nice (To Have You Home)'/'Happiness Melissa' (RAK 225), proved to be nothing more than a dry-run for the New Seekers' next hit; but although they marched on into 1977, Kenny called it a day following the release of their second (Germany-only) album, 'Ricochet'. Perhaps (and hopefully) remembering the pirating of 'The Bump', the Bay City Rollers would subsequently take that same title for their own final LP.

Kenny's entire UK singles catalogue, together with cuts from 'The Sound of Super K' has since been compiled as 'Kenny: The Singles Collection Plus...' (7Ts GLAM CD 3).

August 1975 – Glitter Band: Love In The Sun/ I Can Hear Music (Bell 1437)

A cunning Beach Boys pastiche co-written by Gerry Shephard and John Springate rose to Number 15 at the height of the hottest summer in years.

August 1975 – Barry Blue: If I Show You I Can Dance/Rosetta Stone (Bell 1452)

Blue's final Bell single before he moved to the Private Stock label was another miss, a fate that befell subsequent releases. A return to straight songwriting and production beckoned, with Blue enjoying immediate success at the helm of the British disco band Heatwave – themselves renowned for band member Rod Temperton's part in the Michael Jackson story; he wrote 'Thriller'.

Other Blue projects include early-Eighties hits by Toto Coelo ('I Eat Cannibals'), Bananarama and Cheryl Lynn. He also returned to the chart in 1989 under the pseudonym Cry Sisco! ('Afro Dizzi Act').

Blue's entire 1973-77 singles catalogue is compiled on 'Barry Blue: The Singles Collection' (7Ts GLAM CD14).

ON THE BOX
5 August 1975 – Shang-a-Lang: Bay City Rollers
7 August 1975 – Top Of The Pops: Glitter band
12 August 1975 – Shang-a-Lang: Bay City Rollers
14 August 1975 – Top Of The Pops: Suzi Quatro, Sparks, David Bowie
19 August 1975 – Shang-a-Lang: Bay City Rollers
21 August 1975 – 45: Leo Sayer
21 August 1975 – Top Of The Pops: Leo Sayer, Glitter Band
25 August 1975 – Shang-a-Lang: Bay City Rollers
28 August 1975 – 45: Showaddywaddy
28 August 1975 – Top Of The Pops: Chris Spedding, Kenny
ON THE SHELVES
August 1975 – A Raincoat: Nostalgia '75/ excerpts from LP (EMI 2331)

September 1975 – David Essex: Hold Me Close/ Good Ol' Rock And Roll (live) (CBS 3572)
September 1975 – David Essex: All The Fun Of The Fair (CBS 69160)

David Essex's third album was a conceptual affair, dedicated to the roustabout life that he had already mined so convincingly through *That'll Be The Day,* but which exquisitely matched the cheerful Cockney chappie persona that he couldn't have shaken if he'd wanted to.

Which he didn't.

Of course, there are two sides to the story and, for every raucous rocker on the Essex rollercoaster, there was a tunnel of love to dream through, too. 'Hold Me Close' – which became his second Number 1 – was ridiculously jaunty, and the aitches he dropped every time he sang the title could have stocked an unabridged dictionary. Thirty years later, Essex revealed that this most unaffectedly heart-warming of performances was banged out on the very last day of the sessions with record-label bigwigs waiting in reception anxious to hear the finished LP. 'Two vocal takes, a quick half-hour mix and bosh! It turned out to be one of my biggest records.'

The accompanying tour, meanwhile, would be preserved on Essex's next album, a double live affair, sensibly titled 'On Tour'.

September 1975 – Bay City Rollers US tour

The Bay City Rollers hit America in autumn 1975 and found the PR men already priming the publicity pump. On 20 September, the band made their American debut on Howard Cosell's *Saturday Night Variety Show* performing their next single, 'Saturday Night', and their hitless past was forgotten overnight.

Rollermania followed the band across the ocean, and 'Saturday Night' stormed all the way to Number 1. 'Money Honey', a Faulkner/Wood composition that made Number 3 in Britain, followed it to Number 9 in the new year, while 'Rock'n'Roll Love Letter', an album based around the Bay City Rollers' latest British release, 'Wouldn't You Like It?', made Number 20.

Suddenly the whole thing was starting again, and this time, it was the Bay City Rollers who were calling the shots. A cracking cover of Tim Moore's 'Rock'n'Roll Love Letter' was the only non-original on the album. But as the Bay City Rollers' stock rose in America, so it started to dip in their homeland. British fans felt they had been deserted by the Bay City Rollers. Wasn't their love strong enough to keep the boys at home?

From a period of maximum visibility, the band were apparent now only in the pages of

those newspapers who had bothered briefing their Stateside correspondents to cover some aspect of the outing, and they, too, grew progressively thinner on the ground as the band's absence stretched longer and longer.

September 1975 – Sensational Alex Harvey Band – Live (Vertigo 6360 122)

The ideal primer for the ultimate live band, one killer cut from each of their albums plus a hit single ('Delilah') to make sure we're all paying attention. Career-best versions of 'Framed', 'Faith Healer' and 'Tomahawk Kid' topped the show, with 'Vambo' making an appearance in a wildly extended, improvised form and 'Give My Compliments To The Chef' adding its own wild energies.

September 1975 – Diary of a Pop Tart

Former David Bowie/MainMan publicist Cherry Vanilla 'spills all' in the September edition of *Penthouse* magazine. No names, though…

September 1975 – Arrows: Hard Hearted/My World Is Turning On Love (RAK 218)

While Arrows toured the UK with Showaddywaddy, RAK unleashed yet another Roger Ferris A-side. The single missed, but the TV series had now been confirmed. *Arrows* would debut in March 1976, the same time as RAK released the band's final single, 'Once Upon A Time'/'The Boogiest Band In Town' – a song that writers Bill Martin and Phil Coulter had already tried out with Slik. The same duo would also handle the band's debut album, 'First Hit', although Merrill has few happy memories of it. 'It was not really representative of the band. I felt like a session singer, doing as I was asked.'

Worse was to come. Against Most's wishes, but wanting to maximise their television profile, Arrows signed a new management deal with the MAM agency. Most responded by all but blacklisting the band. No matter that they were on television every week for the next 14, with a second series arriving later in the year. RAK would not release another Arrows record.

Meanwhile, with guitarist Terry Taylor added to the line-up, and Bill Wyman, Dallas Taylor and Ian McLagan stepping in among the guests, Arrows cut another album's worth of material, much of which (including demos and alternate takes of some earlier material) later appeared as the CD 'Tawny Tracks' (Geltoob Records).

The band broke up in 1977.

POSTSCRIPT: Merrill subsequently formed several new bands and worked as a sideman with Rick Derringer and Meatloaf among others. He also launched a solo career that continues to this day. Hooker moved into management; Hilly Michaels, drummer with Cherry Vanilla's Rymbo Band, was among his earliest successes.

Arrows' full UK singles catalogue, plus selected unreleased cuts, is compiled as 'Arrows As, Bs And Rarities' (EMI 7243 8 75998 2 6).

September 1975 – Mud: L'L'Lucy/My Love Is Your Love (Private Stock PVT 41)

Mud's first post-RAK/Chinnichap hit suggested that it would be business as delightfully usual, a Number 10 cut with producer Phil Wainman using all the old tricks.

Yes, *that* Phil Wainman. 'You can imagine how Chinn and Chapman reacted to that,' Les Gray cackled a decade later. 'They were not amused. No sir.'

September 1975 – Sparks: Looks Looks Looks/ Pineapple (Island WIP 6249)
Another sneak peek into the upcoming 'Indiscreet', 'Looks Looks Looks' invoked the sound of the big bands of the Thirties with accompaniment supplied by former members of the old Ted Heath Band. 'It was great to walk into the studio and see all these grey-haired guys who hadn't seen each other for years, with their Harman cup mutes and a big double bass and this guy with an old F-hole guitar,' Visconti recalls. 'None of the band played on it, not even Ron, because we hired an old piano player to do all that Count Basie type of stuff.'

Visconti wrote the song's arrangement, listening first to his own collection of period music 'and the way you have to write for saxophones.' The backing vocals, performed by Russell, Visconti and his then-wife Mary Hopkin, were based on old Frank Sinatra records. As a recording, it was an absolute triumph and a stylistic highlight of the ensuing album. But it made a peculiar choice for a single, as its performance proved. It bottomed out at Number 26, Sparks' final British hit for four years.

September 1975 – Roxy Music: Love Is The Drug/Sultanesque (Island WIP 6248)
The consummate rock-disco record, 'Love Is The Drug' would remain the most successful song of its type for another three years until the Rolling Stones' 'Miss You'.

A Number 2 UK hit and Roxy Music's long-awaited US breakthrough – it reached Number 30 in early 1976 – 'Love Is The Drug' followed in the footsteps of David Bowie's 'Fame' but with one profound difference. Bowie needed to completely dismantle his own sound and attitude to make his disco record. Roxy Music simply strengthened theirs, creating a dramatic art-funk fusion from ingredients that had been littering their arsenal for years.

As taut as it is tight, as sordid as it is sensual, pulsating on an unself-consciously visceral bass line, 'Love Is The Drug' not only predicts the Euro-dance rhythms David Bowie would be employing on the new year's 'Station To Station' but also much of the post-punk electrofunk of the late Seventies. Ironic, then, that its ascent up the chart was halted by a chart-topping reissue of Bowie's 'Space Oddity'.

Meanwhile, period pub regulars still cower from the memory of its jukebox-jamming B-side, 'Sultanesque', a droning instrumental Ferry composed directly onto tape using a Farfisa organ fed through an effects box. With Eddie Jobson (who later professed to 'hate' the song) adding synthesiser and bass, 'Sultanesque', too, cast its shadow over Bowie as he linked up with Eno for 'Low'.

September 1975 – Flame: Checkin' On You/ Isn't It Nice (Live Wire SON 4010)
The follow-up to 'Teenager In Love'.

September 1975 – Glitter Band: Alone Again/ Watch The Show (Bell 1462)
A first chart flop for the Glittermen.

ON THE BOX
4 September 1975 – Supersonic: Suzi Quatro, David Essex, Alvin Stardust
4 September 1975 – Top Of The Pops: Glitter Band, Showaddywaddy
11 September 1975 – Supersonic: Chris Spedding
11 September 1975 – Top Of The Pops: David Essex
18 September 1975 – Supersonic: Bay City Rollers
18 September 1975 – Top Of The Pops: Mud
20 September 1975 – The London Weekend Show: Arthur Brown

25 September 1975 – Supersonic: Hello, Smokie, Sparks, Alvin Stardust
25 September 1975 – Top Of The Pops: Sparks, Showaddywaddy, Alvin Stardust, David Essex
ON THE SHELVES
September 1975 – Kiss: Alive (Casablanca 2008)
September 1975 – Rocky Horror Show: Science Fiction Double Feature/Time Warp (Ode 66305)

October 1975 – Roxy Music: Siren (Island 9344)

Roxy's 1975 American tour was swiftly followed by visits to Australia and Japan. There would be a break to record the next album, and then the whole routine would begin again, this time in Europe. It is no wonder that when that album, 'Siren', did appear, for the first time in Roxy Music's recorded career the sound appeared to be getting tired. It probably was.

October 1975 – Sparks: Indiscreet (Island ILPS 9345)

Trevor White: 'The places Ron and Russell seemed most at home were in places like Paris, trolling up and down the Champs Elysées, that was really where they were at. Or even in England, they were really into the English way of life. They used to get up in the morning, have a cup of tea, then look up an Egon Ronay restaurant to have lunch in. That whole upper-class, sophisticated decadence thing that they tried to put over on the records, that's what they were really like. That's what Sparks was all about.' And that's what 'Indiscreet' created.

'Russell and Ron,' producer Tony Visconti continued, 'wanted to make a completely left-field, bizarre, album. With all due respect to Muff Winwood, he's very straightahead and down the line: "Let's double-track this, put harmonies there, mix it and get it out." He's very singles-oriented, and he helped immeasurably in the beginning. But they still had all these weird ideas in mind and were looking for someone like me to help them put them across.

'There were a lot of bizarre things on that album, a lot of tangents from the mainline way of recording.' Over a decade later, Visconti was still impressed. 'It's one of my favourite albums. Totally uncommercial, but so creative. We did everything under the sun and I learned a lot.' And besides, 'there was nothing on it that was remotely like "This Town Ain't Big Enough".' Which meant, that in the Maels' vision of the future, there was no need for the kind of musicians who could play that song.

Sparks toured Europe through the end of 1975, then split. The Maels were returning to America to work, concentrating solely on that market and using session men as and when required. In a widely quoted remark which today, he puts down to 'a case of stomach flu or something', Ron informed the media. 'We'd got sick of England. The weather was disgusting, the food was terrible and we got tired of the provincial atmosphere. What at first seemed quaint later got really annoying.'

'Actually, the weather's still disgusting,' he smiled, looking out of his hotel window almost two decades later. 'But the food's got much better.'

Relocating to New York, the Maels' first stop was Mick Ronson's house, where they talked seriously about forming a whole new Sparks with Ronno and drummer Hilly Michaels. 'We originally thought of Ronson as a producer,' Ron says, 'but then we recorded some demos with him and Hilly, and they were so good that we asked him to join Sparks.' Ronson declined.

Three songs were demoed with Mick Ronson, 'I Wanna Be Like Everybody Else', 'Big Boy' and 'Everybody's Stupid', recorded on a tiny mono cassette recorder in one corner of the room. Later, after guitarist Jeffrey Salem had been added to the band, the Maels would play him that cassette and ask him to 'play like that'. 'It must have been awful for Jeffrey,' recalled manager Joseph Fleury.

With Michaels remaining on board, Sparks recorded 'Big Beat' in 1976, then broke the band up and have effectively remained a sibling double-act ever since and bouncing back to glory with repetitive regularity.

The late Seventies brought a period of disco success as great as any they enjoyed earlier in the decade, and was followed by the subjugation of the US on the crest of the early-Eighties new wave. Recent years even brought a string of born-yet-again UK hits, together with wild critical acclaim for the albums 'Lil' Beethoven', 'Hello Young Lovers' and 'Exotic Creatures Of The Deep'.

Drummer Michaels, too, was destined for success. Following stints with Dan ('Instant Replay') Hartman, the Hunter-Ronson Band, Ellen Foley and the Bionic Gold Orchestra (accompanying Phil Rambow on a Phil Spector tribute album), he scored a string of worldwide hits as a solo artist, under the managerial aegis of former Arrow Jake Hooker.

'Kimono My House'/'Propaganda' guitarist Adrian Fisher died on 31 March 2000.

Bandmate drummer Dinky Diamond died on 10 September 2004.

October 1975 – The Sadistic Mika Band in England

Japan's Sadistic Mika Band had been in action since 1972, although the first UK audiences knew of them was when Harvest released their eponymous debut album in June 1974 (Harvest SHSP 4029).

Lining up as Mika Fukui (vocals), her husband Kazuhiko Kato (guitar), drummer Hiro Tsunoda and lead guitarist Masayoshi Takanaka, the Sadistic Mika Band's first single, 'Cycling Boogie', was a Japanese hit in 1973. Bassist Ray Ohara joined shortly after, together with new drummer Yukihiro Takahashi and the band turned their attentions westward.

Cursed though it was to be the butt of countless 'can yellow men sing the whites?' jokes from the press of the day, Japanese Glam Rock was already a mythic beast, developed from Bolan and Bowie's experiences in the Far East earlier in the decade. 'Kazuhiko Kato had dyed red hair in 1972, like Bowie,' Alan Merrill recalls. 'They did wear glitter. Stack heels, makeup.' Early on in their career, the Sadistic Mika Band were as Glam as could be but had already moved restlessly on by the time the UK got to hear them, as Mika readily explained.

'We always tried to make a different [music] on each album. If you eat Chinese food or Japanese food all the time you are going to tire of eating the same food. So we changed our style just like you change clothes.'

Still 'Sadistic Mika Band' did not disappoint and neither would two further albums, released at six-monthly intervals. Both produced by Chris Thomas, the first time a Japanese rock band had ever worked with a foreign producer, 'Black Ship' (Harvest SHSP 4043) set sail in April 1974. 'Hot! Menu' (Harvest SHSP 4049) was storebound as the band made their UK debut as support on the latest Roxy Music tour.

The Sadistic Mika Band's Glam credentials rest largely on their theatrical skills; eschewing traditional Japanese musical forms, the band nevertheless dressed the part, particularly singer Mika Fukui. But there was also a questing eclecticism that allowed their music to be listened to in the same breath as Roxy Music, Bowie or Cockney Rebel and, although the Japanese lyrics weren't always easy to sing along with, the melodies were memorable.

The Roxy tour was a success; so was the band's appearance on the *Old Grey Whistle Test* (7 October 1974). Japanese audiences would soon receive the sensational 'Live In London' (EMI DTP 72185), a Kato-produced document of the band's shows in Manchester and London. In interviews, the band talked of their next album, 'a straight rock'n'roll album,' said Kato, 'just like the Velvet Underground.'

It never happened. Soon after their return home, Kato and Mika divorced (she then married

Chris Thomas) and both left the band. The remainder continued on as the Sadistics for a couple of albums, but it wasn't the same. The group broke up and everyone launched a variety of solo activities.

The Sadistic Mika Band reunited on several occasions during the Nineties and 2000s, albeit with a new vocalist; Kato committed suicide on 17 October 2009.

October 1975 – Jobriath: Creatures Of The Street (Elektra K42163)

A glorious mash of ambition and insanity, a rock opera layered with real operatics 'Creatures Of The Street' is a soundtrack for every great movie that needed music to match, seen through a prism of loneliness and tears. Peopled by fallen stars and forgotten heroines, icicle icons and tragic auteurs, there is surely a touch of autobiography here as Jobriath came to terms with the knowledge that the media generally considered him a joke, and his own record company only put up with him in the hope he'd recoup their investment.

He didn't and he was dropped soon after. He would not record again.

Jobriath died on 3 August 1983.

October 1975 – The Rubettes: Little Darling'/ Little Miss Goodie Two Shoes (State STAT 13)

A lowly Number 30 was as far as this one climbed, and it was clear the Rubettes were approaching their sell-by date. Or so it was said; in fact, they would continue having hits into 1977, when 'Baby I Know' gave them one final Top Tenner, but the band had changed much in the intervening years.

1976's countrified 'Under One Roof' marked the change; there's an intriguing clip of the now casually dressed band performing it on *Supersonic* (8 November 1976), pausing for the near-end break and being greeted by what sounds suspiciously like cat-calls, some boos and, just maybe, a loud cry of 'fuck you'.

The band was breaking apart, however, with Bill Hurd the next to exit. 'We had been together, on the road etc, for quite some time and I honestly felt we had lost our way a little and some members of the band had different ideas about the direction we should follow. I'd also got married, we'd just had a son and I really wanted to take some time out at home.'

Hurd would go on to record a few tracks with Rubettes producers Bickerton and Waddington, including the single 'Fools And Lovers'. He resurfaced in 1979 in Suzi Quatro's band, recording and touring alongside her into the early Eighties. The Rubettes, meanwhile, continued going into the late decade, first as a four-piece and finally a trio. Several reunions followed, with Hurd's own current incarnation of the band releasing the album '21st Century Rock'n'Roll' in 2010 (Angel Air SJPCD 343).

October 1975 – Tubthumper: Kick Out The Jams/Kahoutec (Alaska ALA 18)

While it is best known for being invoked within DJ Kenny Everett's *World's Worst Records* marathon (and the accompanying LP), 'Kick Out The Jams' was actually a nifty instrumental that melded football terrace chanting with the opening invocation to the MC5 track of the same title. Don Reedman, the future genius behind 'Hooked On Classics', was responsible claims Bob Stanley, liner-noting 'Velvet Tinmine – 20 Junk Shop Glam Ravers' (RPM 251) in 2003.

October 1975 – Scarface: Dance To The Band/ Tootsie Roll Baby (DJM DJS 616)

The B-side made it onto 'Killed By Glam: 16 UK Junk Shop Glam Rarities From The Seventies' (Moonboot MB 01).

October 1975 – The [Heavy Metal] Kids: Ain't Nothin' But A Houseparty/You Got Me Rollin' (Atlantic K10671)

Keith Boyce: 'The old Show Stoppers song. Our manager Rikki suggested it to us. We really liked it as it's a great song, and we were all really into soul music. We thought it would be a hit but it didn't make it. Always a real powerhouse stage favourite, though.'

October 1975 – David Bowie: Space Oddity/ Changes/Velvet Goldmine (RCA 2593)

A breath of clean air in between the twin monstrosities of Bowie's Plastic Soul diversion, 'Young Americans', and whatever the old fraud was planning next this reissue of his first ever hit arrived with unexpected bounty on the B-side.

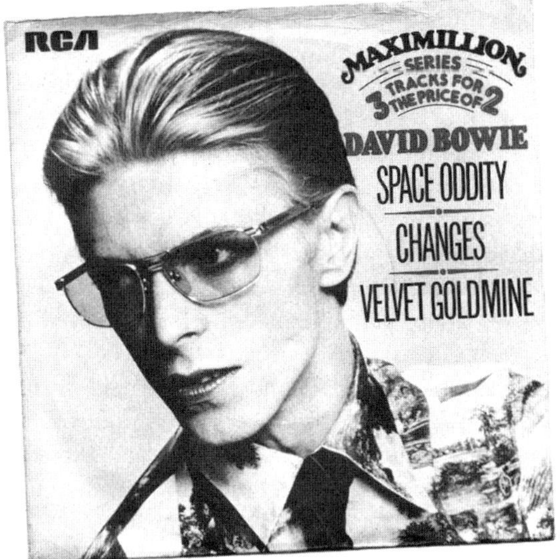

'Three tracks for the price of two' declares the picture sleeve, but for collectors it was one that was worth the cost of many. 'Space Oddity' and 'Changes' were old hat, of course, which didn't prevent the A-side from giving Bowie his first ever British chart-topper. But 'Velvet Goldmine' was a 'Ziggy Stardust' out-take (mislabelled here as a 'Hunky Dory' offcut) that was at least as strong as most of that album, and Bowie was apparently livid when he learned that it had been released from the vault.

He was unhappy, too, when the title was borrowed for Todd Haynes' 1998 movie of the Glam-Rock era, all the more so since it was purportedly based upon Bowie's relations with Lou Reed and Iggy Pop. But there was little he could do about it, any more than Jayne (formerly Wayne) County could do anything after her story was fictionalised for John Cameron Mitchell's *Hedwig And The Angry Inch* in 2001.

Or any more than Pan's People could do after elements of their *Top Of The Pops* routine for 'Space Oddity' was borrowed for virtually every video Bowie and Kate Bush made in the early Eighties.

POSTSCRIPT: With the exception of Bryan Ferry, David Bowie is the single most successful artist to have emerged from the Glam-Rock era, at least in terms of persistence and influence. Not content with blueprinting so much of what would become the post-Bolan Glam ethos, two further LPs in 1977, 'Low' and 'Heroes', are widely regarded as the touchpaper that lit the post-punk electronic boom, with that movement's own most visible figurehead, Gary Numan, little more than a self-confessed Bowie clone.

Three years later, 'Scary Monsters (And Super Creeps)' would further define those currents by breaking the New Romantic movement into the mainstream – and with it British rock's most profound acknowledgement yet of the importance of Glam Rock, both visually and (synths notwithstanding) musically. Duran Duran, Depeche Mode, Spandau Ballet, Soft Cell and more were all formed by the kids who'd been buying Glam in their early teens and the influence shone through much of what they now created.

Bowie, for his part, dropped his own quest to be constantly innovative after that; albums like 'Let's Dance' (1983), 'Tonight' (1984) and 'Never Let Me Down' (1987) were tiresome at best; his Tin Machine rock project was little more than grinding and the early-Nineties' 'Black Tie White Noise' must rate among the worst albums any so-called top-line act has ever inflicted upon his listeners. Since 'Tonight', anyway.

But he regained his muse in the mid Nineties and while the five albums that led him into the current century could never be described as electrifying, they were at least honest, the sound of an artist who had finally come to terms with both his reputation and everything that reputation meant to his public. For the first time in almost 20 years it was no longer a bit embarrassing to describe yourself as a David Bowie fan.

Unfortunately a heart attack in mid 2004 slowed Bowie to a virtual halt; at the time of writing, six years have elapsed without any new music.

October 1975 – Gary Glitter: GG (Bell 257)
The subtly-altered Rolls Royce logo on the cover suggested luxury, class and motor-vating smoothness. The vinyl within was less alluring, as Gary turned out an album that was high on gloss but low on anything else. 'Papa Oom Mow Mow', that most unappetising of recent singles, was the main attraction; a ghastly 'Baby I Love Your Way' was the pit of despair, and most of what lurked in-between was simply bland and

disposable. Glitter's own disillusion with his career, and maybe his musical output too, is fairly well-known today. At the time, we could only ask 'What is he thinking?'

October 1975 – Sailor: Trouble (Epic 69192)
Sailor's second album was recorded at CBS Studios in Whitfield Street, London, and Kajanus recalls, 'it was more or less within the same framework thematically as our debut, with the addition of a big and punchy American production sound, thanks to the producers, Jeffrey Lesser and Rupert Holmes.'

Although the first album went gold in the Netherlands, Kajanus also remembers being 'gently encouraged to write something a bit more commercial and audience-friendly for this second album. Hence, "Glass Of Champagne" – one of those ditties that popped out of my head and took no more than 20 minutes to write – and "Girls Girls Girls", which I slaved over for weeks.'

October 1975 – T Rex Disco Party: Dreamy Lady/Do You Wanna Dance/Dock Of The Bay (T Rex MARC 11)
The billing was ominous enough, which may explain why this not-bad ballad faltered at Number 30.

30 October 1975 – Renaldo and Ronno
If we judge such things by image alone, Mick Ronson is probably the most unlikely ever member of a Bob Dylan band. But dressed down in the denim in which he was personally most comfortable, and mixed in with a veritable circus of other players (Bobby Neuwirth, Roger McGuinn, Rob Stoner, Ronee Blakley, Scarlet Rivera, Joan Baez and so on and so forth), he looked happier than he had in a long time.

Tapes of the shows that followed bear that out. Dylan's Rolling Thunder tour kicked off in Plymouth, MA, on 30 October 1975 and would play through until the following May and, though you can't always pick out Ronson's contributions to Dylan's performance, when you can they're unmistakeable.

Bootlegs of the entire evening's proceedings feature him taking a solo spot too, to perform a Roscoe West number which he surely picked with a wry smile on his face; it was called 'Is There Life On Mars?' He also plays a memorable role in the ensuing *Renaldo And Clara* movie, playing a security guard who refuses to allow the passing Ronnie Hawkins backstage.

Hawkins, probably three times Ronson's size, naturally disagrees, but they go back and forth for a few minutes before Hawkins announces that he's going backstage and he doesn't care *who* this pasty jobsworth is. 'You could be David Bowie's guitar-picker for all I care.'

'Life On Mars?' was one of the numbers Ronson took with him into Sundragon Studios in December 1975, during Rolling Thunder's winter break, as he worked towards that possible third album. That set was never completed (the session was included as bonus tracks on the 1997 reissue of 'Play Don't Worry'); he returned to the Dylan tour and then resumed his meanderings through the musical underground.

Sparks thought they'd snared him for a time; he jammed with John Cale and the New York Dolls. Back in London, he produced albums by Dead Fingers Talk and the Rich Kids, then reunited with Ian Hunter for both the leviathan 'You're Never Alone With A Schizophrenic' and the debut album by singer Ellen Foley – a set that picked up a couple of songs, 'Night Out' and 'Young Lust', by another player Ronson almost formed a band with, ex-Winkie Phil Rambow.

One session marks the culmination of that particular partnership. Four songs, including 'Young Lust' and 'Fallen', were recorded at Wessex Studios in spring 1978 with producer Chris Thomas for a projected Rambow solo album – only for Chrysalis' Doug Darcy to listen to the first completed track, 'Fallen', and write it off as 'just a thrash'. As Rambow recalls, 'he let the whole thing dissolve.'

Ronno went back to New York and, while Rambow would re-record 'Fallen' with guitarist Hugh Burns cchoing Ronno's parts note for note, it was never going to be the same. Today, Rambow looks back on 'Fallen' and calls it 'the best thing I ever recorded. It captures the essence of what I was trying to do. Ah well, the memories are forever.'

POSTSCRIPT: Following the 'You're Never Alone With A Schizophrenic' album and tour, Ronson resumed his wanderings, producing albums for Kiss That and Morrissey and reuniting with Hunter for 'YUI Orta' He died on 29 April 1993. His third solo album 'Heaven And Hull' was released posthumously.

October 1975 – Top Of The Pops Volume 48 (Hallmark SHM 920)
After a run of less-than-essential offerings, 'Volume 48' got back to doing what the series does best, reinventing songs rather than simply mirroring them. A delightfully whimsical version of 'Space Oddity' ranks among the series' finest Bowie covers, while 'Hold Me Close' is played as much for fun as for fidelity – the original's Cockney chirp is exaggerated to almost hilarious proportions.

There's a glorious rush through Mud's 'L-L-Lucy' to remind us just how far that band had moved since they left Chinnichap and, to crown everything, a version of 'Don't Play Your Rock'n'Roll To Me' that pinpoints just how desperately Chris Norman wished he was Rod Stewart.

ON THE BOX
1 October 1975 – *Twiggy*: **David Essex**
2 October 1975 – *Supersonic*: **Marc Bolan, David Essex, Mud**
2 October 1975 – *Top Of The Pops*: **Mud, David Essex**
9 October 1975 – *Supersonic*: **Arthur Brown, Leo Sayer, Roxy Music**
9 October 1975 – *Top Of The Pops*: **Sparks, Hello, David Essex**
15 October 1975 – *Lift Off With Ayshea*: **Barry Blue, Bay City Rollers**
16 October 1975 – *Supersonic*: **David Essex, Marc Bolan, the Sweet, Bay City Rollers**
16 October 1975 – *Top Of The Pops*: **Mud, David Bowie, David Essex**
17 October 1975 – *Russell Harty*: **Alice Cooper**
23 October 1975 – *Supersonic*: **Gary Glitter, Roxy Music**
23 October 1975 – *Top Of The Pops*: **T Rex, Roxy Music**
30 October 1975 – *Supersonic*: **Wizzard, Mud**
30 October 1975 – *Top Of The Pops*: **Hello, David Bowie**
ON THE SHELVES
October 1975 – Ayshea: Don't Wait Till Tomorrow/Moonbeam (DJM 612)
October 1975 – Fox: Strange Ships/Little Brown Box (GTO GT 41)
October 1975 – Mott: I Can Show You How It Is/By Tonight (CBS 3741)

October 1975 – Patches: Look Alive/Don't Give Me A Hard Time (Bradley 7526)
October 1975 – Villain: Photograph/You Should Know Me By Now (Bell 1457)
October 1975 – Mud: Greatest Hits (RAK 6755)

November 1975 – The Sweet: Strung Up (RCA 0001)
Anxious for a new album but too busy to actually create one, the Sweet bowed to RCA's demands and dug into the vault to see what could be salvaged. They emerged with one of their most fascinating documents yet, and a double album too!

Recorded at the December 1973 Rainbow show, a full disc's worth of live cuts bear out what Andy Scott said about it being one of the band's best ever gigs...there was room, sadly, only for highlights of the show, but they were dynamic.

The studio cuts were less instantly alluring, concentrating in the main on the band's self-composed B-sides, a few recent singles ('The Six Teens', 'Fox On The Run' and 'Action'), and a couple of songs laid down during the sessions for 'Desolation Boulevard'. In modern terms, it's the kind of compilation that would form the basis for a tremendous box set; at the time, however, it spoke more of the uncertainty with which the band's record label, if not the band themselves, viewed the future. And, tellingly, it sank like a stone.

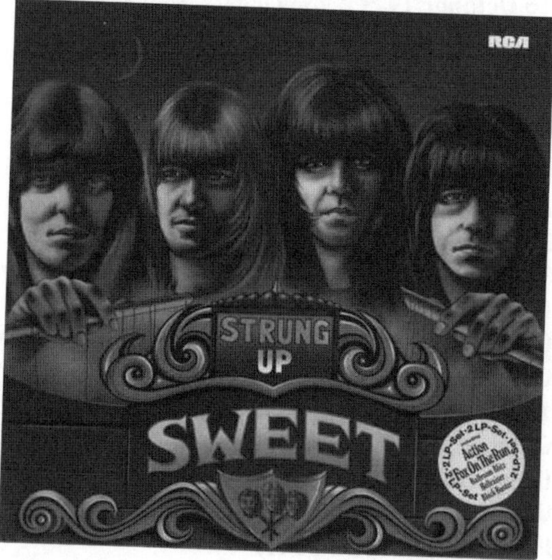

November 1975 – Bay City Rollers: Money Honey/Maryanne (Bell 1461)
The Rollers go metal! The band's first self-composed hit reached Number 3, a distinctly Sweet-influenced rocker that was neither the best, nor the most memorable, of the Rollers' biggest hits. But it was the most unexpected.

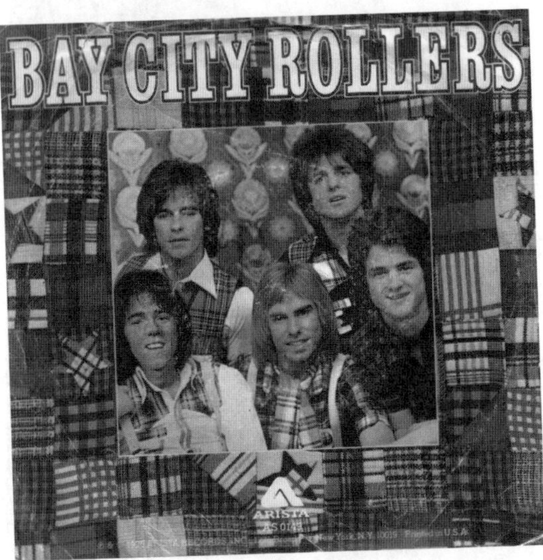

November 1975 – Slade: In For A Penny/Can You Just Imagine (Polydor 2058663)
Though it only reached Number 11, 'In For A Penny' was simultaneously one of Slade's most timeless hits, a truly magnificent piece of balladry; and their most time-specific as well. Actress Sandra Dickinson, who'd already tapped into one cultural obsession with her memorable performance as Marilyn Monroe in the touring production of *Legend* (both Elton John and 10cc had recently eulogised the icon in song) was now starring in a TV commercial, the punchline of which was a squeaked 'Gee, they got a band!'

Soon, everybody was saying it, including Noddy, who throws it into 'In For A Penny' right before the guitar break kicks in. And though Slade would have one more UK hit ('Let's Call It Quits' in the New Year) this was a far better way to go out.

November 1975 – David Essex: If I Could/ Funfair (CBS 3776)
A Number 13 in time for Christmas, the almost painfully sentimental 'If I Could' effectively brought the curtain down on David Essex's days

as a true teenage idol as he shifted towards full family entertainment.

He achieved it with style to spare. His reading of 'Oh! What A Circus' from *Evita* proved him the only viable (and still the only worthwhile) contender for the Che Guevara role in the Argentinean soap cycle, and subsequent singing actor roles in *Silver Dream Machine* and *Mutiny On The Bounty* established him as one of Britain's best loved all-round performers.

But his 1994 version of Buddy Holly's 'True Love Ways', performed with actress Catherine Zeta Jones, proved that such an accolade doesn't necessarily foreshadow a descent into full-blooded mawkishness any more than a 1989 Shep Pettibone revision of 'Rock On', or a late-2000s revival of his *All The Fun Of The Fair* concept proved that he'd run out of ideas for new songs.

November 1975 – Mr Big: Sweet Silence (EMI EMC 3101)
November 1975 – Mr Big: Wonderful Creation/ Enjoy It (EMI 2372)

'Sweet Silence' was recorded at Rockfield Studios in Wales. Dicken: 'I recall the sessions with fondness. It was a great time in my life. For the first time, we were being allowed to be ourselves and play and record the music we wanted to, which was a lovely freedom for the whole band. In the past, we were always surrounded by pessimistic people – "You're too old, you're too ugly" – and this was our chance to prove we could do it. In the end it was a nice album.'

There would be some early misgivings, a belief that somehow the music lost a lot of its power in the journey from studio to the cutting room. But Dicken says 'I grew to love it, and there's no denying that it did the trick for us.'

The single didn't sell, but still Mr Big closed 1975 by going out on perhaps the biggest tour of the year, opening for Queen as they toured their 'A Night At The Opera' album and, of course, the 'Bohemian Rhapsody' single.

It was, says Dicken, 'a great eye-opener for us as a band, thrown right into the deep end as we were with not that much experience of the bigger gigs. Freddie [Mercury] was such a nice guy to me, helping me a lot, as did Brian May, encouraging me along the way. They were on the verge of greatness as a band, and we were privileged to experience it close hand, travelling together in one coach. One evening in particular, I recall all of us, both bands, sitting watching *Top Of The Pops* as Queen hit the Number 1 spot with 'Bohemian Rhapsody'. That was cool.

'We all learned a lot from them. A lot of trivial stuff went on in hotels etc. TVs out the window and stuff, and a drugs raid just before we hit the motorway. But, all in all, I think we managed to come out of that tour a much better, more equipped band.'

A little over a year later, Mr Big would have their own massive hit as 'Romeo' rose to Number 4 in February 1977; 'Feel Like Calling Home' followed (Number 35), while the band released two further albums before breaking up in 1979.

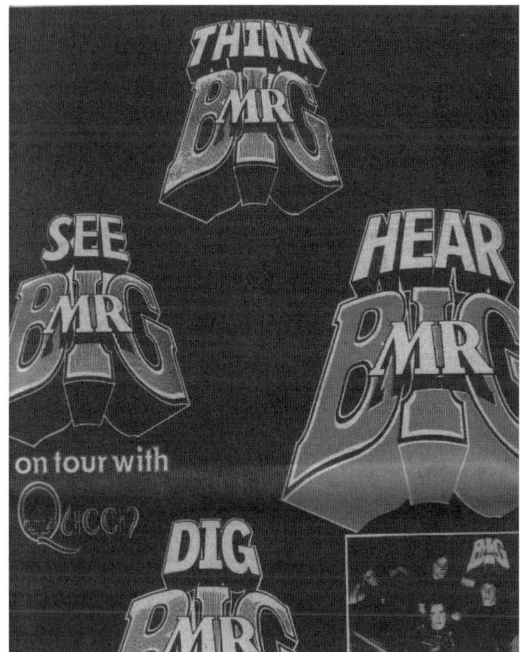

November 1975 – Mud: Show Me You're A Woman/Don't You Know? (Private Stock PVT 45)

A lesser song but a big hit, a ballad that reached Number 8 and confirmed 1975 as the most successful year not only in Mud's history, but almost any band. Between RAK ram-raiding the archive and Private Stock putting out new material, Mud had no less than seven singles on the chart this year, the first band to manage that since the Beatles in 1964.

November 1975 – T Rex: Christmas Bop/ Telegram Sam/Metal Guru (T Rex MARC 12)
It's hard to say whether or not this would have been a hit – certainly it continued Bolan's musical rehabilitation, and three years earlier there's no doubt it would have been enormous. But the question became academic when the release was cancelled.

Six months later, however, the sublime 'I Love To Boogie' returned Bolan to glory at the same time as torpedoing a lot of those knockers who accused him of simply rewriting old rock'n'rollers for the best Bolan boogies. And a year after that, hosting his own weekly TV show for Granada TV, he was almost back to his best, pumping out the 'Dandy In The Underworld' album as though he had been following up 'The Slider' his entire career long, and celebrating summer with 'Celebrate Summer', a single that married classic Glam to modern Punk, and still sounds fresh today.

He was back. And then he was gone.

Returning home from a club in the early hours of the morning of 16 September 1977, the car in which Bolan was a passenger crashed into a tree on Barnes Common, in south-west London. Bolan was killed outright, girlfriend (and the mother of his two year-old son Rolan) Gloria Jones was critically injured. Journalists arriving at the scene were quick to notice the headline, from that week's issue of *New Musical Express* which flapped on the ground beside the wrecked vehicle. An interview with Pete Townshend, it implored, 'Hope I get old before I die.' Bolan died two weeks shy of his thirtieth birthday.

POSTSCRIPT: Steve Peregrin Took died on 27 October 1980

Steve Currie died on 28 April 1981

June Child (Bolan) died on 31 August 1994

Tony Secunda (manager) died on 12 February 1995

Chelita Salvatori (Secunda) died on 7 March 2000

Micky Finn died on 11 January 2003

Dino Dines died 28 on January 2004

November 1975 – The Jumping Bean Bag (approximate date)
David Dixon, Richard Bentine and Kenny Brown were among the cast filming writer Robin Chapman's *The Jumping Bean Bag*, an instalment in BBC 1's *Play For Today* series, detailing the travails of a public school-based Glam band called Slag Bag.

They dream of playing the Hammersmith Odeon in drag, 'big false eyelashes and crazy Greek metallic hair.'

They dream of being as big as the Bay City Rollers.

They dream.

The hour-long play was screened on 17 February 1976.

November 1975 – Sailor: Glass Of Champagne/Panama (Epic 3770)
Sailor's first hit came about, says Georg Kajanus, as a result of four fundamental changes. 'First, we acquired first class professional management by EMKA, Steve O'Rourke's company, who was the manager of Pink Floyd. Our personal manager within the company was Robert Wace, who had previously managed the Kinks. Along with CBS, Robert also encouraged me to "go home and write a hit."

'Second, because the group had management, CBS started to spend serious money on marketing and promoting Sailor.

'Third, because we'd achieved four Top Five hits and a gold album in Holland, CBS regarded Sailor as a more viable concern

'And finally, we all knew that – as a catchy

celebration song – "Glass Of Champagne" was a sure-fire hit single, so everyone pushed very hard to make it so.'

'Glass Of Champagne' made Number 2 in the New Year, but that was only because *nothing* could get past 'Bohemian Rhapsody'.

The band soared again with their follow-up single, 'Girls Girls Girls' – although this time, Kajanus confesses, '"Girls Girls Girls" was always a bit of an embarrassment to me because it had a similar feel to trad jazz, which I've never liked. Why I wrote the song, I can't say. I guess the "girl" part drove me to complete it. Unlike "Champagne", I was surprised by the success of "Girls Girls Girls" which has now become a standard in Europe.'

The Sailor project was definitely nearing its end, however. The founding concept of the *Red Light Revue* was simply too specific to spawn an endless supply of albums and Kajanus admits, 'I was coming to the end of my inspiration with the whole Sailor concept.' A third album, 'Third Step', would emerge, and 'there are some songs on the album that I still like, such as "Quay Hotel", "Dancing" and "Cool Breeze".'

But audiences, too, picked up on the dimming of the day. Two singles, 'Stiletto Heels' and the Tex-Mex flavoured 'One Drink Too Many', were hits around Europe but the excitement had gone.

POSTSCRIPT: Sailor continued recording into 1980, but with ever-decreasing returns. However, the reformed band is a major concert draw today, while Sailor's entire back catalogue has returned to the shelves, together with several live albums and the anthology 'Buried Treasure – 1975-2005' (Angel Air SJPCD249).

Meanwhile, Kajanus has returned to the original *Red Light Revue*, reworking it into '*Sailor*, a hard-edged musical in development for stage and screen, with many of my original Sailor songs as well as new material.'

November 1975 – Barry Blue and Lynsey de Paul: Happy Christmas To You From Me/Stick To You (Jet 762)

Over a year had elapsed since either de Paul or Blue last sniffed a solo hit (de Paul had most recently scored with the theme to television's *No Honestly*), which might explain why nobody even noticed this sickly duet.

November 1975 – Spiders from Mars: Black Man White Man/National Poll (Pye 45549)
November 1975 – Spiders from Mars: Spiders From Mars (Pye 18479)

The Spiders from Mars were David Bowie's backing band throughout his years of greatest worth – guitarist Mick Ronson, bassist Trevor Bolder and drummer Woody Woodmansey. Subtract Ronson, however, and fill in the gaps with singer Pete McDonald and guitarist Dave Black who either write or co-write the bulk of the songs, and the Spiders' first Bowie-less excursion is suddenly not such an appetising proposition.

Hard rock with the rougher edges chipped away, a dry run for Bolder's future in Uriah Heep (or Woodmansey's next band, the swiftly sunk U-Boat), 'Spiders From Mars' is not a bad album. It's the name that's the problem, and the sense that someone is dancing on our memories of a group that once was very special indeed. And for that they were rightfully damned.

November 1975 – The [Heavy Metal] Kids: Anvil Chorus (Atlantic K50143)

The Kids wound down 1975 on tour with Alice Cooper – they'd already played some shows together in the US and the two bands had a healthy love for another. Keith Boyce recalls, 'Alice was doing the Welcome To My Nightmare show and it really was special. I think we watched the show every night for weeks, and never got tired of it. Likewise, Alice would watch our show from the wings most nights. By now, Alice was a solo act and I think he could see that we were very much a band, a gang much as the original Alice Cooper were. I think Alice dug that.' Indeed, on more than one occasion, Cooper sung the Kids' praises to the press.

Unfortunately, the press wasn't listening, and 'Anvil Chorus' didn't change their minds.

Both guitarist Waller and producer Dave Dee had absented themselves by now, while the last year of touring had allowed the band precious little time in which to write new songs – there would be nothing here as captivating as their debut LP. And the abbreviated name was still bothering the band. 'Now our own fans don't know who we are,' growled Holton.

There were some highlights, however. Keith Boyce recalls producer Andy Johns recruiting 'this Ukrainian couple to come down to put backing vocals on the song "The Big Fire". They were a really old straight married couple and they didn't know what to make of us. They did a great job though. Also for "On The Street" and "You Got Me Rollin'" we had Madeline Bell and the Chanter sisters come and do backing vocals. They were great and really fun to be in the studio with. 'Alongside the lazy 'Situation's Out

Of Control' and the lost single 'Blue Eyed Boy', those tracks all dignify the disc.

Further line-up changes shook the band. Danny Peyronel departed in late 1975, to be replaced by John Sinclair from the Jackie Lynton Band – Peyronel himself then resurfaced in UFO, in time for their 'No Heavy Petting' album.

Cosmo departed, to be succeeded by Barry Paul. And Holton himself was sacked, amid a tidal wave of drug-tinged accusations. He was always a drinker, but drugs brought a new, and troubling, influence into play. Friends blamed the American tour, where the very nature of the venues where the Kids were booked lent themselves to such introductions – but whatever the cause the rest of the group couldn't deal with it.

Holton remained in the cold for three months, returning to the band around the same time as producer Mickie Most began showing an interest in them. Atlantic Records promptly sold the group's contract onto him – the Heavy Metal Kids, they warned, were 'unmanageable'. But Most did not seem to care and history, it seemed, was about to agree with him.

Boyce: 'Atlantic had spent a lot of dough on us. I think we were in the hole to them for a quarter of a million dollars or more. Anyway, they wouldn't give us any more money, so Rikki Farr managed to get us out of the deal and onto RAK, who were bankrolled by EMI, so we were back in the lolly again. Or, at least, Rikki was.'

Most's first move was to get working on a new album; 'Kitsch', the now re-renamed Heavy Metal Kids' third album, was recorded in France in spring 1976 as part of Most's tax arrangements.

'We actually recorded it in this hotel in the countryside somewhere outside Paris,' recalls Boyce. 'We moved in there and set up all the gear up in the basement and had the RAK mobile truck outside. So it was a bit like the Stones doing "Exile On Main Street", the difference being is that the hotel was open to regular guests, so there were all these normal straight people staying there while we were making all this noise and staying up all hours!

'After we left there, Mickie disappeared with the tapes into the studios for months on end, overdubbing orchestras and choirs and stuff and not letting us hear any of what he was doing.

Meanwhile, Holton's taste for the rock'n'roll life was getting increasingly out of control. Finally, he was fired, 'and we spent months looking for a new singer, only to give up after trying about 300. So we got Gary back in the band after he swore he'd mend his ways, and finally "Kitsch" was released about a year after we started it. We then carried on. I finally left the band to join Bram Tchaikovsky in late 1978, and shortly after this the band split.'

In the years that followed, Holton continued to record sporadically, most frequently with Casino Steele of punk power-poppers the Boys. He was briefly a member of the Damned, depping for vocalist Dave Vanian on a tour of Scotland, and was one of the leading contenders to replace the late Bon Scott in AC/DC.

But a return to his original career in acting paid far greater dividends, as he landed roles in the movies *Music Machine*, *Quadrophenia*, *Breaking Glass* and *Bloody Kids* before finally grasping stardom in 1983 as wide boy Wayne in British TV's *Auf Wiedersehen, Pet*. He returned to the stage, appearing alongside Paul Jones and Kiki Dee in the London cast of *Pump Boys And Dinettes*; he starred in a big-budget lager commercial and was just completing the much-anticipated second series of *Auf Wiedersehen, Pet* when he died from a drug overdose on 25 October 1985.

His final recording, just two weeks before his death, was alongside Glen Matlock, James Stevenson and the Winkies' Phil Rambow, on a Rambow-Matlock composition called 'Big Tears'. It should have been enormous. It remains unreleased.

POSTSCRIPT: Ronnie Thomas, Keith Boyce and Danny Peyronel, together with the group's mid-Seventies manager Dave Dee, reformed the Kids in 2002 and released a new album 'Hit The Right Button' the following year.

Dave Dee passed away on 9 January 2009.

November 1975 – Slik: Forever And Ever/Again My Love (Bell 1464)

When Slik re-emerged in December 1975, Fifties-style baseball outfits had replaced the suits and keyboard player Billy McIsaac was furiously defending them.

'It's an image that we feel close to. We hope that [it] helps the music. Everybody has an image, whether they like it or not, [and] it's really not on for people to slag it because it has been created quite naturally.'

Where, on all the baseball diamonds of mid-Seventies Glasgow?

'We're not a joke band.'

The pseudonyms, too, had been abandoned, but some things remained the same; the group were now performing a song Martin-Coulter had already recorded as an album track with Kenny, the sombre (but so impressive) 'Forever And Ever'. At the same time, however, the duo inaugurated a publicity campaign that blasted Slik into every teenage consciousness in the land.

A string of high-profile TV appearances (including the New Year's Day edition of *Top Of The Pops)* was organised, and while the pop press was courted with Rollers-esque ferocity the mainstream media was deluged with reports of the growing chaos that attended the band's every live performance.

The campaign paid off. Within weeks of the single's release, readers of *The Sun* had voted Slik the best new band of the year, 'Forever And Ever' was top of the UK chart and George Tremlett was preparing a book-length biography. Even the band's most cynical detractors were forced to admit, Slik looked likely to be around for a long time to come.

Unfortunately, it was not to be.

In April 1976, Bell released the band's next single, the dirge-like 'Requiem'. Just weeks later, however, on 20 May, Ure was seriously injured in a car accident. Slik's forthcoming UK tour was cancelled and the loss of television exposure saw 'Requiem' grind to a halt at a lowly Number 24. The band's eponymous debut album, a three-way split between well-chosen covers, the band's own material and some of their mentors' best work ever, spent just one week at the lower end of the British chart and, by the time Ure returned to action, every last drop of momentum was lost. Even a *Top Of The Pops* appearance for the single 'The Kid's A Punk', could not restore it.

Slik played just one further concert, supporting Hello in Berlin, then returned to their hometown. It wasn't only their own career which had changed irrevocably – the musical landscape itself had been utterly reshaped during Ure's absence as Punk swept in to consume the nation's attention. Little more than a year after they topped the chart, Slik were already regarded as a relic of a long-distant past.

Attempting to regain at least some kind of footing, the band changed their name to PVC2 and cut a single for the local Zoom label. The subterfuge fooled no-one, however, and Slik shattered in late 1977.

POSTSCRIPT: Ure later turned up in ex-Sex Pistols Glen Matlock's Rich Kids before establishing himself first as frontman for Ultravox, then as a successful solo artist. His erstwhile bandmates, meanwhile, became the Zones and recorded the seriously under-rated 'Under Pressure' for Arista.

November 1975 – Gary Glitter: Papa Oom Mow Mow/She Cat Alley Cat (Bell 1451)

Gary's next single, November 1975's 'Papa Oom Mow Mow' was a lousy song even before he decided to cover it, and accordingly stalled at an unthinkable Number 38. But even worse was to follow as March 1976's contrarily brilliant 'You Belong To Me' under-performed to criminal standards, scratching to Number 40.

But it was also true that the actual record in no way captured the true majesty of the song. For the full impact, hunt out a tape of Glitter's first farewell concert at the New Victoria Theatre in London. Filmed by Mike Mansfield and televised that same month, the guitar riff lasts forever and Glitter himself has never sounded so sincere.

But maybe his audience didn't want Gary Glitter to be sincere. They wanted him to be physical, vulgar, crude and raw.

'My success is because I entertain,' he once told the *New Musical Express*. 'The kids want to see a show because they're not just interested in the music. I'm trying to recreate the enthusiasm of the Fifties, and I'm being successful at it. I've done it by introducing new rock'n'roll songs. Reviving old ones never works. I think that factor has helped me tremendously.'

By turning his back on that factor he signed his own death warrant, and it was only later that Gary revealed he'd only retired to sell concert tickets.

Sporadic live reappearances, of course, ensured that Gary was seldom far from the public eye, but in his 1991 autobiography, *The Leader*, he spoke openly of the financial and psychological pressures which first helped force him into retirement, then drew him out again. Hounded into bankruptcy by the voracious sharks at the Inland Revenue, bruised and battered by his sudden decline, drinking heavily: 'The self-destruct button was firmly pushed.'

Spiralling between brief highs (taking the lead, Frank N Furter role in a New Zealand production of the *Rocky Horror Show*, and a scoring pair of minor British hits with 'It Takes All Night Long' and 'A Little Boogie Woogie In The Back Of My Mind'), and devastating lows, Gary Glitter finally reached the end of his tether in early 1980.

Homeless, he was staying with his ex-wife, Ann, and ostensibly enjoying a barbecue party. 'I was drinking quite heavily. I went upstairs to the room I was using. I had some sleeping tablets there, Mandrax, and I started to take them one after another. I don't know what happened next, but I've been told that Ann had wondered where I'd gone and got worried, then found me upstairs unconscious, and called an ambulance when she saw the empty pill bottle. I woke up in Wandsworth Hospital after I'd had my stomach pumped out.'

Slowly he began piecing his life back together, throwing himself headlong into the only thing he really understood – entertaining. His hits had served him in good stead in the past, and they were still selling healthily. Without stooping as low as the cabaret party, Gary realised what his mistake had been – 'progressing' as an artist, trying to move with the times. The kids wanted the hits, and it was his job, his duty, to give them to them.

A tentative return to the live circuit saw him embraced immediately by the new generation of Punk Rockers. It was 1980, true, and the fiery roar of Punk itself had long since been extinguished. But still the audiences hurled lungfuls of phlegm as a sign of appreciation and Gary accepted the honour. 'I walk out there as Gary Glitter,' he smiled before a packed Lyceum show in 1981, 'but I walk off as Sidney Spittoon.'

Putting five years worth of personal tragedies and musical disasters behind him, Gary Glitter was on the road to recovery, returning to the public glare as a grotesque parody even of the parody he once set out to be. For a new generation raised on the scratchy old singles they found in big sister's closet, it was suddenly possible to see just what all the fuss had been about in the first place.

'It's scary, man, it's almost like Hitler, everybody has their arms raised yelling "Hey!". Everybody in the whole place is yelling "Hey!"' (*New Musical Express*, 1974)

'With the most disparate audience imaginable, completely united in one common cause, the chants sounded like the Nuremberg Rallies, the singalongs like the Welsh Male Voice Choir.' (*ZigZag*, 1984)

It was the comeback to end all comebacks. Only Tina Turner did it better, and she had help from sundry famous admirers. Gary did the whole thing on his own – well, with a few thousand loyal fans for support.

In 1981, he returned to the studio and recorded a new single, a dance medley of all his greatest hits, 'All That Glitters'. By 1984, he was playing upwards of 80 gigs a year, mainly around the college and club circuit, but was rewarded with a return to the chart with the contagious 'Dance Me Up'. By 1986, he was even back at the Number 1 slot on *Top Of The Pops*, when he joined Doctor and the Medics on stage for a performance of their Glitter-esque reworking of 'Spirit In The Sky'. Soon after, the Justified Ancients of Mu Mu changed their name to the Timelords and released 'Doctorin' The Tardis', a tribute to television's *Dr Who* set to Gary's own 'Rock And Roll' rhythm (with a hint of 'Blockbuster!' thrown in for good measure). That, too, topped the chart.

His tours became increasingly more elaborate. Perhaps he would never return to the days of $20,000 wardrobe budgets, but the show went on regardless. A 1988 live video, *Gary Glitter's Gangshow*, may have been low on effects but was high on adrenalin, and simply busting at the seams with hits. He revitalised his first monster smash with four new versions, recorded with Frankie Goes To Hollywood Svengali Trevor Horn. 'Rock And Roll Parts 3 to 6' were spread across both sides of 7' and 12' singles and, though they add little to the majesty of the original recording, even technology could not destroy the sublime purity of that hammerhead beat.

He even survived the revelations of a teenage former lover who went to the tabloids with the news that the grand old man of rock was bald. People had accused him of wearing a wig for years; in 1994, he allowed himself to be photographed without it and joked that his head was now as shiny as his stage clothes. Nothing could phase him; nothing, it seemed, could stop him.

That same year, Gary Glitter was one of the star turns at the official World Cup concert in Chicago, broadcast live to 46 countries. He stole the show. At Christmas 1996, he played a sold-out, delirious, Wembley, and his acclaimed performance as the Modfather in the Who's *Quadrophenia* reminds us that you really are never too old to rock. A new single, Glitter-ising 'The House Of The Rising Sun' kicked ass. And then it all came crumbling down as Glitter's sexual life became the stuff first of rumour, and then legal action, and today he is *persona non grata* even within nostalgia circles.

But even that doesn't change what he accomplished. Gary was always the unlikeliest of pop stars and, at his peak, his strongest point was always his knowledge of why he was where he was. It wasn't ego, it wasn't artistic fulfilment. Even at the outset, his live show was a battering ram at the twin gates of Taste and Decency, his imminent descent into grotesque buffoonery prevented only by the sheer absurdity of the whole occasion. He transcended simple tackiness and got away with it to the extent that, even when he quit the stage and let the Glitter Band take charge for a couple of numbers, the magic remained.

No gesture was too hammy. Whether he was thrusting his pelvis forward and demanding, 'Do you wanna touch me there?' or shedding real tears, overcome at the intensity of his reception, turning on the house lights to see how beautiful the audience really were, or throwing roses to the crowd at the end of the show, he was Super-Pop personified.

November 1975 – 10cc: Art For Art's Sake/ Get It While You Can (Mercury 6080 017)

October 1975, saw Justin Hayward and John Lodge take a break from the Moody Blues and chart with 'Blue Guitar', a song that featured 10cc as both producers and accompanying musicians. The following month, 10cc re-emerged in their own right with 'Art For Art's Sake', their seventh British Top Ten entry and an uncharacteristically unmemorable one.

'Art For Art's Sake' had not been 10cc's own choice for a single; indeed, Lol Creme acknowledged, '[Phonogram] wanted a single out in America to coincide with the [latest] tour, and to follow up "I'm Not In Love" as quickly as possible, because there'd been too long a delay already. They thought "Art For Art's Sake" was a good idea, so they released it there, then Phonogram in England released it here. We just went along with it, thinking we'd give them the opportunity to make that sort of decision, and in fact they were wrong in America. It didn't happen there but it did happen here. [But] if it had been up to us I doubt we'd have put it out.'

It was not the band's greatest ever record. Unfortunately, however, it proved an all too accurate introduction to the new album, the new year's 'How Dare You'.

The four writers in the band had always naturally gravitated into two distinct schools of thought (Godley/Creme and Gouldman/Stewart). Across 'How Dare You', however, the once healthy friction between the pairs was becoming uncomfortable. The band were evidently struggling for ideas and, while a handful of tracks (notably the psychotic 'I Wanna Rule The World', the pleading 'Don't Hang Up' and the sweet 'I'm Mandy Fly Me', another hit single) did bear repeated listening, the collection as a whole showed 10cc to be suffering from an acute dearth of inspiration.

'There were two main writing partnerships in 10cc,' explains Kevin Godley. 'Godley and Creme were into experimentation. Gouldman and Stewart were into writing classic songs. It wasn't quite that black and white but, fundamentally, these two approaches formed the backbone of our work. Any other hybrids were an attempt to mix it up a little but kind of felt more like diversions in democracy than serious songwriting.

'That said, my outings with Mr G were always enjoyable and challenging. "Iceberg" [another 'How Dare You'highlight] is one of my favourites; it originally began, as I recall, with a proposed monologue that went something like: "Hey baby I want to get down on all fours and shit in your handbag" or words to that effect. Part of my personal brief, when working with Graham back then, was trying to fuck him up.'

Unfortunately, there was not enough fucking-up on 'How Dare You'. 'Some of our lyrics sound a little dumb now,' Godley reflects. 'Like we would sing about anything so long as it sounded "different". I think we sometimes got too in-jokey, too lightweight and too deep into Americana. Lyrically we lost a little soul along the way. It's subtle and we disguised it really well, but I can hear it happening. It's not that we ran out of things to say, we just ran out of things worth saying.'

Band relations soured. Gouldman recalls 'a conversation with Lol in the front office of the studio. We'd just recorded "I'm Mandy Fly Me"; Eric and I were really pleased with it; we thought it was just really good. But Lol was, sort of, mewing about it, y'know, like, "Is this the direction we should be going in? Was it interesting enough? And, was it music? And was is this?" And, I thought, "What're you talking about?" For me, the seeds of doubt were planted then; that this was leading to some inevitability; that the end was nigh.'

Reviews were hostile, and further damage

was done when Eric Stewart, enraged by a scathing review in the *New Musical Express*, wrote an indignant letter to the editor that was duly published in all its apparent spoiled-brat glory. As another magazine, *Street Life*, remarked, 'It was predictable that [*NME*] would allow the reviewer equal space to reply and so make Stewart's impassioned outburst look rather silly. The *NME* always has the last word.'

The band never recovered. In October, under the banner headline, 'We're Not In Love', *National Rock Star* reported that Godley and Creme had left the band to work on the Gizmo, a guitar attachment they'd been playing with since the Hotlegs days, but which was now ready to go into production. It never took off as they dreamed, but did spawn 'Consequences', the first ever product demonstration disc to consume six sides of a concept album.

Looking back from the late 2000s, shortly after he and Godley reunited as the duo GG06, Gouldman was asked whether he would have changed anything about 10cc's mercurial lifespan. 'Yes, I would have spent more time trying to persuade Kevin and Lol not to leave the band. I hate waste and that was waste. I'm not saying we could have gone on as long as U2

or the Rolling Stones, but as we got older we'd have become more rational. We would have morphed and changed, but it seems like we could…we should have had a sham marriage but we had a divorce.

'"How Dare You" was where it was starting to come apart. Kevin and I have talked a lot about it and why it happened and what was going on, and we both…we should have said, "Go and do the Gizmo, do the thing, do whatever you want and, when you're ready, come back." We could have waited, Eric and I could have gone on and done things together or separately, we had a million things to do. We should have waited.

'But I think we were under pressure; we'd got into that cycle of writing/recording/touring and somehow it didn't seem…if you're not with us you're against us, whereas we should have said go ahead and come back when you're ready. That was an incredible few years that we had and…up until that last album I think our light burned very brightly.'

Godley agrees – up to a point. 'I'm rather proud of what we did and I think it's a shame we're not included, very often, in the roll call of influential Seventies artists. My memories of the music are supremely fond ones. My memories of the working relationships are a little less rose-tinted.'

POSTSCRIPT: Stewart and Gouldman continued as 10cc into the early Eighties, scoring one final Number 1 in 1978, 'Dreadlock Holiday'. Godley and Creme, too, worked on as a duo into the late Eighties. A brief reunion of the original quartet took place around the 1992 'Meanwhile' album. Today Gouldman still tours as 10cc; he and Godley also record together as GG06.

November 1975 – Sensational Alex Harvey Band: Gamblin' Bar Room Blues/Shake That Thing (Vertigo ALEX 2)

Assuming that the 'Delilah' lightning might strike twice, 'Gamblin' Bar Room Blues' was another cover but, sadly, a less exciting one. The single barely scraped the Top Twenty and that despite SAHB delivering some captivatingly vaudevillian TV performances to promote it.

Elsewhere, however, the band had little cause for complaint. In December, they played a triumphant Christmas party-like show at the New Victoria Theatre, while the new year brought not one but two new albums, the odds and sods collection 'Penthouse Tapes', and the supersonic 'SAHB Stories'. Another hit single, 'Boston Tea Party', followed, but just months later Harvey quit.

'I don't wanna be a rock'n'roll star,' he told *National Rock Star* magazine. He continued: 'I'm not saying I haven't had a good time. I'm not knocking it. I can still get a terrific buzz out of performing with guys who really know how to play. But I don't wanna crash through walls on stage any more.'

Vambo was gone, then, and the poor mug who was 'Framed'. So was Adolf Hitler, a parody routine that Harvey first developed during SAHB's earliest concerts, but which reached its zenith when the group toured Germany in early 1976. 'We did it in Hamburg. It was great!'

The death of his manager in an air crash had also affected Harvey deeply, but he stressed that wasn't why he was leaving SAHB. 'I'll always be with them. They're my boys. Maybe I'll be doing other things, but I'll always be involved.'

Unfortunately, health problems considerably narrowed his options, and with Harvey spending much of the next year in hospital only one his proposed solo projects, a spoken-word album about the Loch Ness Monster, came to fruition. He returned to SAHB in August 1977, but Harvey had lost one of his more reliable songwriting partners in Hugh McKenna and Zal Cleminson later remarked that Harvey actually caused more harm than good upon his return.

The new-look group debuted at a Belgian festival, followed by a well-received headline performance at the Reading Festival. But the album which they spent much of September recording, 'Rock Drill', was at best a pale imitation of the original SAHB.

'I think he came out of hospital too early,' Chris Glen said later. 'And during the weeks that followed, he was expected to do too much. It just came to the point where he felt he couldn't do it any more.' The failure of a new single, 'Mrs Blackhouse', was followed by the delayed release of the album itself and only compounded Harvey's renewed disillusion. In October, during rehearsals for a BBC *Sight And Sound In Concert* broadcast, the singer walked out of the band for the last time. 'Rock Drill' eventually appeared in March 1978, and sank like a stone.

Harvey became something of a musical itinerant over the next two years, playing with a succession of musicians, and occasionally even alone, most notably at the Rock Against Racism festival at Alexandra Palace in spring 1979, where he performed a stellar version of Bob Marley's 'Small Axe'.

Shortly after, Harvey began work on his first solo album for precisely ten years, 'The Mafia Stole My Guitar', in October 1979; six months later, a single of the Marley song closed Harvey's recording career.

On 4 February 1981, having just completed a four-week tour of Europe, Harvey suffered a fatal heart attack, while waiting for a ferry home from Zeebrugge. As journalist Pete Frame later put it, 'Rock lost one of its greatest characters'. Harvey's final album, 'Soldier On The Wall', was released a year later.

The Sensational Alex Harvey Band was a unique combination, their music the product of a chemistry that even the band members themselves could not guarantee to produce every time. That they succeeded in doing it as much as they did was an achievement of miraculous proportions, and while one can regard the less than satisfactory CD treatment of their back catalogue with considerable distaste, the fact that it still sells strongly is a sure sign that the magic has not been forgotten.

Indeed, the Sensational Alex Harvey Band has actually reformed, establishing itself as a surprisingly viable attraction on the UK club circuit. Through their efforts, a whole new generation of fans has discovered the sensational Alex. For them, and for his many 'original' fans, Alex Harvey will never really die.

Vambo still rules.

November 1975 – Bearded Lady: Rock Star/ Country Lady (Youngblood YB 1076)

'Somebody 'ere is a keen listener to Steve "Wordbender" Harley', declared reviewer Caroline Coon, but that didn't stop her proclaiming 'Rock Star' A HIT. But that was not to be.

'We were,' says frontman Johnny Warman,

'young, brash, and so confident, bordering on arrogant, and we thought we were the best band in the world. We were rubbing shoulders with Thin Lizzy, Phil Lynott really liked us. We dressed up very flashy and we were a great live band – especially at the Marquee where we achieved residency status. We supported the Heavy Metal Kids and Gary Holton was another star who loved our band.'

On three separate occasions, Bearded Lady came close to signing with Mickie Most's RAK label – and, on three separate occasions, the deal fell through because 'our management were asking for stupid advances which Mickie was not going to pay.'

The group went, in the end, to the less celebrated Youngblood label, where producer Miki Dallon spent a day in the studio with them before confessing that their original demo was better than anything he was able to wring out of the proceedings.

'We worked so hard at our craft and, especially at this time, I wrote like a man possessed,' Warman recalls. 'I personally pushed the guys to be the best we possibly could' – and 'Rock Star' suggests he succeeded.

The song was reprised in 2003 on the 'Velvet Tinmine' compilation, and Warman reflects: 'Some of our early recordings are so punky both in attitude and content. We were playing very fast rhythms, as well as classy pop songs and ballads. Maybe we were the Godfathers of Punk?' Maybe. But it didn't really help.

The Young Blood deal was instigated through publisher Barry Anthony, who put the band in touch with Miki Dallon and Youngblood International. As Warman recalls, 'We felt elated when we got our first deal, as going through the recording and production process all takes time and the people we met were all extremely complimentary about the band s material and the musicianship.'

Sadly, it didn't take long for disillusion to step in. Bassist Chris Peel remembers the band's drummer, Paul Martin, taping the whole conversation 'and later playing it back several times to his great amusement,' and once the single was out, the label seemed to lose interest.

The album that the band had been promised never came together, despite them recording new songs as often as they could, and when a new deal did seem to be imminent it dissolved just as quickly. "We were approached by Warner Brothers A&R man Larry Yaskiel,' Warman recalls, 'and he said that we were going to be the "New Humble Pie!" But once again [a deal] failed to materialise.'

Drummer Martin departed, to be replaced by Clive Brooks, but Bearded Lady broke up soon after. 'It just got to be not so enjoyable any more,' says Peel. 'We had stopped playing live and were rehearsing and auditioning for drummers. I think we had difficulty agreeing on a drummer. The difficulty was, prior to that we hadn't just been a band, but mates from similar backgrounds who, as well as playing together, could relate to each other and go out and party together. So getting a great drummer alone didn't seem enough. I needed to do it for the enjoyment.'

POSTSCRIPT: Warman launched a solo career following Bearded Lady's demise and scored a minor hit with 'Screaming Jets', featuring distinctive backing vocals from Peter Gabriel. Bearded Lady's entire recorded canon is compiled on the 'Bearded Lady – The Rise And Fall' (Angel Air SJPCD 153); the same label has also reissued Warman's solo output.

November 1975 – Fancy: Music Maker/ Bluebird (Arista 32)

Sometimes, the world makes no sense whatsoever. Fancy had everything, but second single 'I Was Made To Love Him'/'Tour Song' (Arista 15) followed 'Rock Machine' into oblivion. By the time a third, 'Music Maker', followed suit, Fancy had already broken up following a brilliant appearance at the Montreux Festival.

Anne Kavanagh remained in Britain, singing sessions before returning to Australia. Fenwick and Foster, too, went back to session work, while Binks eventually turned up in Judas Priest.

November 1975: Andy Scott – Lady Starlight/ Where D'ya Go (RCA 2929)

A first solo release for the Sweet guitarist, blessed with a chord sequence that recalled 'Hunky Dory'-era David Bowie, released at a time when the entire band was searching for fresh challenges. They'd already had their first self-composed hit. What other miracles could they pull out of the hat?

While Brian Connolly talked of the group making a movie ('but not a typical pop film'), bandmates Scott, Tucker and Priest toyed with forming a breakaway power trio, to exist alongside the Sweet and rejoicing beneath the drug-tinged name of STP...their initials, of course.

Connolly himself later recalled spending time 'planning an album of ballads and jazz standards, along the lines of what Bryan Ferry had been doing, but showing off everything that I could do with my voice, proving that I wasn't just a rocker.' Sadly, none of these projects ever amounted to anything.

ON THE RADIO
1 November 1975 – In Concert: Heavy Metal Kids
ON THE BOX
5 November 1975 – Top Of The Pops: Gary Glitter, the Rubettes, Roxy Music, David Bowie
11 November 1975 – Musical Time Machine: Bay City Rollers
13 November 1975 – Top Of The Pops: Hello, David Bowie
14 November 1975 – Supersonic: Bay City Rollers, Cockney Rebel
15 November 1975 – The London Weekend Show: Doctors of Madness
20 November 1975 – Top Of The Pops: Slade, Queen, Bay City Rollers
21 November 1975 – Supersonic: Slade, Leo Sayer, Gary Glitter
27 November 1975 – Top Of The Pops: Mud, SAHB
28 November 1975 – Russell Harty: David Bowie
28 November 1975 – Supersonic: Mud, Sailor, Showaddywaddy, Alvin Stardust
ON THE SHELVES
November 1975 – The Rubettes: The Rubettes (State 004)

December 1975 – Bay City Rollers: Wouldn't You Like It? (Bell SYBEL 8002)

The 'classic' Rollers' final release before the elder Longmuir brother, 26-year-old Alan, was replaced by 17 year-old Ian Mitchell in April 1976. But the hysteria was already dying down; 'Wouldn't You Like It?' peaked no higher than Number 3; its successor, 'Dedication', would halt at Number 4 and Rollermania was over. Ian Mitchell would be gone within a year, his successor Pat McGlynn even sooner. Les McKeown would depart and the Rollers' last few albums passed by without anybody really even noticing.

The group finally broke up in 1980 and, while sundry reunions have ensured that the Rollers have rolled on ever since, today it seems hard to believe that their reign lasted little more than a couple of years on either side of the Atlantic.

Manager Tam Paton led a troubled life following the band's demise, embroiled for a string of legal and sexual controversies. He died on 8 April 2009.

December 1975 – Chris Spedding and Suzi Quatro

Recording his next single, 'Jump In My Car', on the RAK Mobile in France, Spedding admitted: 'Suzi discovered the song for me in Australia. I'll have to buy her a drink if this is a hit.' It wasn't.

December 1975 – Mud: Use Your Imagination (Private Stock PVLP 1003)

There was a very popular saying that smirked around the industry for a good couple of years, that what Mud do this week, Showaddywaddy do next week. And sometimes, it was hard to disagree.

One day Ray Stiles was thumbing through his record collection when he came across an old Curtis Lee single, 'Under The Moon Of Love'. He played it for Rob Davies, and told him 'We should do this'; the band were in the studio working on their latest LP, there was a sax player on hand, a trio of backing vocalists and, watching proceedings, Showaddywaddy singer Dave Bartram.

A year later, Showaddywaddy not only recorded the same song with much the same arrangement; they even used the same sax player. The difference was they released theirs as a single and went to Number 1. Mud's cut was stuck at Number 33 aboard a surprisingly under-performing album.

POSTSCRIPT: Mud continued recording until the end of the decade. Ray Stiles joined the Hollies in the mid Eighties and until recently still performed 'Tiger Feet' during their live set.

Les Gray passed away on 21 February 2004

Dave Mount passed away on 2 December 2006

December 1975 – The Sweet: Lies In Your Eyes/Cockroach (RCA 2641)

Poised for release the moment the Christmas holidays were over, the Sweet's latest single was their farewell to the past.

'I remember when 'Lies In Your Eyes' came out, telling the others that we were basically telling Britain to fuck off,' Brian Connolly recalled. 'Everything we did from then on was geared completely towards America. We didn't care about the UK any more, we didn't care about *Top Of The Pops*, Tony Blackburn and *Melody Maker*. If we could have upped sticks and emigrated, become American citizens and wiped out the past five years, just been a brand new band making the music we were making, we would have. We were that determined. Later on, people said we burned a lot of bridges when we went to the States, but we burned them ourselves. We knew exactly what we were doing.'

They were saying goodbye.

POSTSCRIPT: The Sweet continued recording until the early Eighties, but shed Brian Connolly several LPs before the end. Both Andy Scott and Steve Priest continue touring and occasionally recording as the Sweet today.

Brian Connolly passed away 9 February 1997.

Mick Tucker passed away 14 February 2002.

December 1975 – Frenzy: Poser/Things You Do (DJM 633)

Clydebank-based Frenzy had apparently been around for several years before being signed to DJM at the tail end of Glam... too late for this, and way too late for its follow up. 'Lady Of Spain' was canned, and if and when Frenzy ever resurfaced, they were not, as stated in the liner notes to 'Blitzing The Ballroom: 20 UK Power Glam Incendiaries' compilation (Psychic Circle PCCD 7021), Marco Pirroni's punk outfit the Models.

17 December 1975 – Twiggy: Doctors of Madness

They'd been sighted on *The London Weekend Show* already, but this was the Doctors' nationwide TV debut, sharing the stage with the redoubtable Twiggy (with whom the band shared management), and dropping jaws everywhere as the blue-haired Kid Strange took the mike alongside her to perform the band's 'Perfect Past'. Dropping jaws because even Glam had never seen anything like it.

The Doctors of Madness emerged at a time when Glam and its manifold roots were literally withering on the vine. Bowie and Bolan had blown it, Sweet and Slade were far, far away. Chinnichap had gone American. Sparks and Cockney Rebel had burned their best-made bridges, Roxy Music were about to implode.

Punk was round the corner, of course, but nobody knew that at the time. Instead, the rock intelligentsia was either waiting for the next ELP album, Genesis to announce Peter Gabriel's replacement, or for Pub Rock to catch on with more than a handful of beery malcontents.

What it wasn't waiting for was what it got – a band Twiggy's former manager Justin de Villeneuve was describing as 'a reflection in the Seventies of the decadence of Berlin in the Thirties'. No indeedy.

de Villeneuve's partner in the Doctors' practice was former Pink Floyd/Tyrannosaurus Rex guru Bryan Morrison, and his confidence knew no bounds either. 'This band are going to be the biggest for ten years,' he said, and the Doctors of Madness – the objects of such untrammelled admiration – were not about to argue with him. Strange himself was curiously convincing when he explained that John Lennon and Bob Dylan alone were equal to him in the songwriting stakes, and even more so when he berated them both for deserting him. 'They've really let me down,' he complained. 'And now I'm on my own. It's lonely at the top.'

Especially when you have blue hair. 'When I first dyed my hair I went to see my parents, and my mother just looked at me and said, "Okay dear, you can take the wig off now."'

As Richard Harding, Strange first came to public attention as a member of the delightfully named Great White Idiot, a band whose solitary live show – at the 100 Club in London – coincided with what the audience thought was the venue's soul night. When it turned out to be anything but, the crowd rioted, the venue was stormed by the local police and Great White Idiot shattered just as the record-company bigwigs they'd invited along showed up.

Not to be put off, Harding promptly threw himself into another band, comprising several former Idiots – Peter Hewes (drums), Martin Martin (keyboards), Eddie Macaro (guitar), Geoffrey Hickman (violin) and a bassist who apparently believed he could write songs as well as the group's lead singer.

Harding tolerated him for a while, but the hapless bandmate was finally sacked and Colin Bentley recruited in his place. Then, with Martin and Macaro following the bassist out of the door, the remaining quartet rented a rehearsal room at a nearby pub, the Cabbage Patch and, in Bentley's words, 'Sat around plotting these absurd ideas, this really outrageous image that we wanted to create to match the type of songs Richard was writing.

'We are concerned with a kind of cinematographic style, where images come in and out,' Harding confirmed, 'not making much sense on a rational level, more on a sensory one. Our music, our show, has got this cold, sleazy feeling to it, of those old street corners. We are much more nasty than Alice Cooper, very sleazy, underground and outrageous.'

But how outrageous can you be with names like Colin, Richard, Geoffrey and Peter? A drunken, stoned, evening ended with the rechristening of all four: Stoner (nothing more, nothing less), Kid Strange, Urban Blitz and Pete DiLemma. Then, with the assistance of Mrs Stoner, the grotesque make-up was created 'to add something to our personalities'. 'We are,' Strange announced, 'one of the few bands who get booed before we play a note. Not many others can get that reaction.' Stoner, resplendent in full zombied skeleton drag, told the *NME*, 'the make-up I wear puts the shits up people.'

So far so good, and it soon got better. A talent scout for Bryan Morrison heard the band rehearsing while he was out walking his dog one evening. He alerted Morrison; Morrison brought in de Villeneuve and the Doctors were launched onto an unsuspecting nation just in time for Christmas, special guests on *Twiggy*.

Rumours began flying immediately – record companies were allegedly offering up to £100,000 for the band's signature; NBC television were flying over from America to make a documentary on the band; they were going to steal the show at the Great British Music Festival. In the end, they signed to Polydor for considerably less money than that, the NBC documentary turned out to be a less than glowing report on 'how to hype a band in Britain' and the festival gig ended when the band's PA broke down. Still there was a buzz about the Doctors, and one that was only going to get bigger.

A nationwide tour opening for Be Bop Deluxe in early 1976 earned the group a modicum of respect, if only for their dogged resistance to the total animosity of the dour headliners' audience. They were, indeed, getting booed before they played a single note, and when Be Bop Deluxe were forced to reschedule one show for a few weeks later the new support band reported back that they'd been met by the most hostile audience they'd ever faced in their lives – until they told them 'It's okay, we're not the Doctors of Madness.'

The Doctors would release three albums, beginning with March 1976's 'Late Night Movies, All Night Brainstorms', following with the year-end 'Figments Of Emancipation' and, finally, 1978's 'Sons Of Survival'. All three were scorned by the press and public; all three have contrarily weathered the succeeding years a lot better than acts who were lionised in their stead.

But it is the first two, bookending the year in which the British music scene would be irrevocably altered by the birth of Punk, that both presage that imminent future, and sign off on the now-distant past. Or, as *All Music Guide* put it, 'as Punk began squeezing out of Glam-Rock's urethra [sic], this was the sound which drowned out the screams.'

The Doctors of Madness may not have been around for the birth of Glam. But they were unquestionably responsible for ensuring it died a dignified death. Without them, it might never have gone away.

POSTSCRIPT: Strange launched a solo career, and moved also into art and writing. Stoner joined ex-Sleaze frontman TV Smith's Explorers.

December 1975 – Roxy Music: Both Ends Burning/For Your Pleasure (live) (Island WIP 6262)

'Love Is The Drug' was followed into the British chart (Number 25) by 'Both Ends Burning', the first time Roxy Music had culled two singles from the same album. Any murmurs of discontent from the band's audience, however, were stilled, the moment the records were flipped over. 'Both Ends Burning' was backed by an intense live rendering of 'For Your Pleasure', a taster for the proposed live album scheduled for the following year.

Roxy Music toured incessantly in the aftermath of 'Siren'. In the space of less than six months, two American tours were crammed in, together with a British outing that culminated with two sold-out nights at the gigantic Wembley Empire Pool, and a European tour, while riding a live show for the ages.

Highlighting all five albums, with the 'Siren' material far outshining its lacklustre studio counterpart, it culminated not only with a selection of tried and trusted past favourites, but also with a handful of solo projects, Mackay's 'Wild Weekend', Manzanera's 'Diamond Head' (from the album of the same name) and two Ferry efforts, 'The In Crowd' and 'A Hard Rain's A-Gonna Fall'.

'It was great fun being able to play those numbers,' Manzanera remembers. 'But remembering that it was a Roxy Music show, I think then things started to get a little bit out of hand so it had to be brought back a little.'

This was the first time any solo material was included in the band's live show. Indeed, aside from a handful of British shows the previous autumn, when he nervously appeared alongside a 55-piece orchestra, it was the first opportunity Ferry himself had received to test his solo material in front of a live audience. He had previously restricted himself to television appearances only.

The solidarity these interludes seemingly suggested, however, did not disguise the fact that Roxy Music was slowly falling apart. The individual members were at loggerheads, often over quite insignificant matters, but that was not the point. Petty squabbles have a nasty habit of exploding into major eruptions and, as the summer of 1976 approached and Roxy Music finally came off the road, it was announced that the group was to disband.

'Viva! Roxy Music', recorded at various venues over the past three years, would be their farewell and, as if to compound the disappointment, an accompanying single of 'Do The Strand', coupled with a new Mackay composition, 'War Brides', was scheduled but never appeared.

Mackay did not let his song go to waste, though. He delivered it instead to the *Rock Follies* TV series which he was co-writing with Howard Schuman for UK broadcast that same summer. Originally issued as the B-side of the show's first spin-off single, what fun we had imagining Bryan Ferry declare 'I'll be a boogie-woogie war bride.'

POSTSCRIPT: Following Roxy's 1976 split, Manzanera formed a new band (briefly featuring Eno) called 801. Roxy Music then reformed in 1979 for three new LPs before breaking up again in the early Eighties. Manzanera and Mackay formed a new band, the Explorers; Ferry continued as a solo artist. The group regrouped again in 2001 for live work; hopes for a reunion LP have yet to materialise, although Ferry's 2010 album 'Olympia' featured contributions from Mackay, Manzanera and Eno.

Ferry continued as a solo artist on either side of the earlier reunion, although it is debatable whether any of his releases can be said to truly fulfil the promise with which he started; rather, like the post-Glam Bowie, Ferry's career should be measured in terms of persistence rather than consistency.

The late-Seventies 'In Your Mind' was distinguished by one song alone, the rambunctious 'This Is Tomorrow'; the mid-Eighties' 'Boys And Girls' mingles lightweight soundscapes with a handful of genuinely seductive opuses; and 1995's 'Mamouna' boasted his first reunion with Eno, yet still couldn't cut it.

But even with that in mind, it is sometimes worth remembering just how far ahead of the pack Bryan Ferry's career has consistently been. Taking a quickly-discarded leaf out of Eno's book (he covered the same song on the Winkies tour), Ferry's solo version of the Velvet Underground's 'What Goes On' in 1978 did something nobody had done before, and took Lou Reed's best-known band onto the British chart.

And Ferry's appearance at 1985's Live Aid concert was generally regarded as the only truly genuine performance of the entire bloated festival and the only one which remembered that, at the end of the day, it's only rock'n'roll.

Because, for all his musical (and sartorial) sins, Bryan Ferry remains the only man who can make 'Will You Love Me Tomorrow' sound like a threat or the Esso Blue tune sound like a dirge. The sexiest dancer on earth, he is also quite possibly the coolest man alive.

December 1975 – Glitter Band: People Like You And People Like Me/Makes You Blind (Bell 1471)
December 1975 – Glitter Band: Listen To The Band (Bell 259)

An impressive return to the chart, the Number 5 hit 'People Like You And People Like Me' was, to put it bluntly, boring. Or, as John Springate says, insipid. 'As songs go, it was great, we were getting great airplay, but it was just so insipid. The making of that record was hard work as well. We did three different versions of it – we knew it was a hit, but where to put it? Was it country or rock or what? Then the Bee Gees' "Jive Talkin'" came out, and we thought "That's it, that's where we should base it," so I did this mock Curtis Mayfield type of voice which made it a little bit weak...well, it *was* weak. But it put it in the right area.'

The album, on the other hand, left the single in the dust.

'We were really so proud of "Listen To The Band". It was our "Pet Sounds", if you like, but this is the funny thing. The first album sold over a quarter of a million and it took seven days to make. "Listen To The Band", an infinitely better album, took three months and it sold 40,000.'

The Glitter Band tried to adjust, but no subsequent single would make the chart – 'Don't Make Promises' came closest in mid-1976, while a label switch to CBS and no less than two name changes (plus a reversion to their first) also failed to make a dent.

First came the G Band, and a new LP, 'Paris Match' – 'which I loathed,' condemns Springate. 'I never listen to that album, I hated it. Mike [Leander] was getting onto this disco vibe, and it was dreadful. The version of "Sympathy For The Devil" is fucking awful. It's funny because Mike did a four-minute version of it which was great, he condensed it right down. But the full-length one is just awful.

'We tried to make it go forward, calling it the G Band and shaking off the glitter, but it wasn't going to happen.' A return to the Glitter Band name brought the EP 'She Was Alright' (c/w 'I Really Didn't Love Her At All'/'Almost American/'Love Street' – CBS S5223) in June 1977; before finally Springate's 'Gotta Get A Message Back To You' (c/w 'Move On Up' – Epic SEPC 5665) was released under the name Air Traffic Control in late 1977. 'Everybody loved it, and the idea was to send it to the BBC and see if they'd play it as a new band. They didn't. And that's when we knew that it wasn't going any further.'

Finances, too, were parlous, with management now demanding that the musicians bring their instruments into the office so they could be sold on. Springate explains: 'After five years of touring we were staying in four-star hotels, trying to copy Gary – "If he can do that so can we" – but forgetting that there was only one of him. We were going out for £1,000 a night, which was the going rate at that time, and about £600 of that would be spent on hotels and getting drunk so the profit margin was getting reduced.'

But, singing a song that so many of the bands of the age know well, they were also 'screwed royally' over song publishing, a fact Springate only truly appreciated when he compared the statements he received from RAM with those from Southern Music, to whom two of his Glitter Band songs ('Shout It Out' on 'Hey' and 'Sweet Baby Blue' from "Rock'n'Roll Dudes") were assigned. 'I could never understand why I made more money from those two songs with Southern than I ever did with RAM.'

It was because he'd signed a contract (as had his bandmates) that actually stated that the group were not permitted to inspect the company's books.

POSTSCRIPT: The Glitter Band never officially broke up; rather, they drifted apart, but they kept in touch and would periodically resurface.

1979 saw Shephard, Phipps and ex-Sparks/Jet keyboard player Peter Oxendale combine as Oxendale and Shephard for the LP 'Put Your Money Where Your Mouth Is' (Nemperor 36063); the Glitter Band reconvened the following year for live work and a couple of 45s.

A mid-Eighties revival saw the band play

several shows alongside the sensational Sexagisma, and proved so successful that, at one point late in the decade there was no less than three Glitter Bands on the circuit, one led by John Rossall and Harvey Ellison, one by Gerry Shephard and Tony Leonard and one by Phipps.

Legal action halted Rossall's activities (he and Ellison now perform as the Glitter Band featuring John Rossall), while Leonard's unit retired following Gerry Shephard's death (6 May 2003). A new incarnation, fronted by Springate and Phipps, continues to gig today.

December 1975 – Top Of The Pops Volume 49 (Hallmark SHM 925)

Another of the albums that has been revered by kitsch history for one signal achievement – in this case, the delivery of a 'Bohemian Rhapsody' that was recorded in about a twentieth of the time that Queen devoted to it – Top Of The Pops bows out of 1975 with 'Money Honey', 'Art For Art's Sake' ('money for God's sake') and 'In For A Penny', all suggesting that as Glam Rock came to an end all people cared about was where the next cheque was coming from.

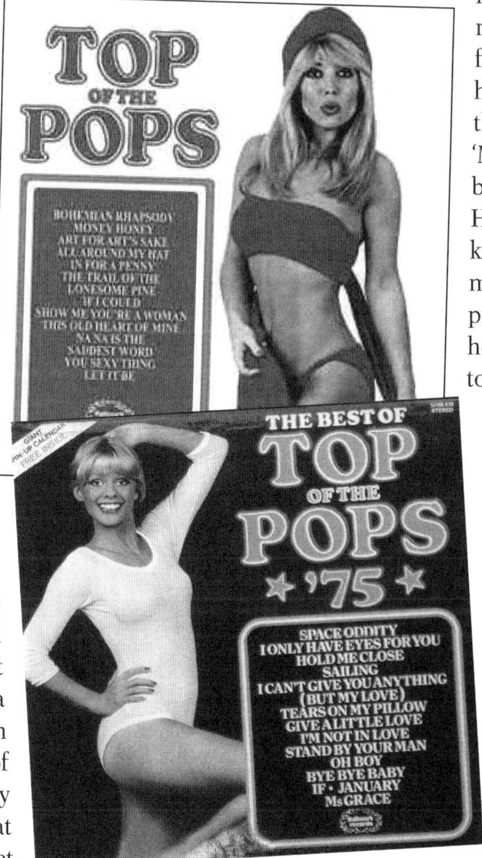

And maybe they did. Five years had passed since 'Ride A White Swan' birthed a musical movement that would consume a generation; five years which likewise birthed a host of talents who still matter today – and an army more that don't. And, if it did all get taken over by record label bean-counters, rentasong composers and factory-line productivity that is the fate of every musical movement that means enough to sell some records.

Glam Rock sold a lot of records. But it also sparked a lot of dreams, and it changed a lot of lifestyles as well. Arguably, none of the political liberations Punk Rock held so dear would have been possible without Glam to ease them into view, and for all the later movement's disregard for the so-called cheap pop that preceded it Glam's influence would be writ large.

It was not the music, after all, that was being rejected. It was the industry that milked the music for all it was worth, made million-sellers from another pretty face, put a catchy chorus over a meaningful lyric, that placed virtuoso sessionmen over the band members' raw ability…and which had hung onto the status quo so long that it had forgotten what it was like to be starving. Punk would make it starve.

In early 1976, one of Alan Merrill's neighbours was a woman named Cheryl. She worked for Malcolm McLaren, who happened to have a new band that he was trying to launch. 'Malcolm wanted Cheryl to bring me around to the shop. He knew about Arrows. He knew we had some hits and a media profile. He wanted to pick my brains, to know about how to put a pop group together.'

Merrill resisted McLaren's manoeuvrings for as long as he could. But in April, he agreed to take up McLaren's invitation and to see his Sex Pistols at the El Paradise strip club in Soho.

Accompanied by his bandmates, Merrill made his way into the venue, paused while photographer Kate Simon fired off a handful of shots, then relaxed at the bar with McLaren buzzing around him, watching Johnny Rotten berate the crowd for 'being stupid enough to stay through this shit', for being 'ugly stupid fuckers' and hissing insult after insult at the tiny audience.

It was, Merrill mused to himself, 'a negative

masochist bizarre cabaret. I didn't think it a serious project, just a dark joke. You know the concept, bad is good. Garbage is valuable. An antiworld. Just like in the *Superman* comics that I read as a child, where it was called the Bizarro World.'

Once the Pistols finally filed off the tiny stage, McLaren asked, 'What did you think? Did you like it?'

'Are you serious?' replied the pop star, and he ran through all of the Sex Pistols' failings. But McLaren didn't bat an eyelid. 'You're wrong. What you've just seen is the destruction of your lot.'

He waved a hand airily. 'Arrows, Mud, Sweet, Bolan, all of you. By this time next year, the entire face of the music scene will have changed.'

Then he grinned such a mad grin that Merrill swore he would never forget it. 'It was like the Joker in the *Batman* comics. Or Dr Sardonicus.' Because, when he recalled that conversation less than six months later, he knew that McLaren was correct.

It was time, as Slade's last Top Twenty single for eight years had just declared, to finally say goodbye. Or, as they put it, 'let's call it quits.'

ON THE BOX

4 December 1975 – Supersonic: David Essex, Sensational Alex Harvey Band

4 December 1975 – Top Of The Pops: 10cc, Slade, Bay City Rollers, Sailor, Queen

6 December 1975 – Basil Brush Show: Kenny

11 December 1975 – Supersonic: Bay City Rollers, Andy Scott, Mud, Glitter Band

11 December 1975 – Top Of The Pops: Sailor, Mud, Queen

12 December 1975 – Russell Harty: Alvin Stardust

18 December 1975 – Supersonic: Sailor, Roxy Music

18 December 1975 – Top Of The Pops: David Essex, David Bowie, Queen, 10cc

19 December 1975 – Russell Harty: Elton John and Bernie Taupin

20 December 1975 – Tiswas: The Rubettes

23 December 1975 – Top Of The Pops: Steve Harley and Cockney Rebel, the Sweet, Mud, David Bowie, Bay City Rollers, Queen

25 December 1975 – Queen Christmas Concert

25 December 1975 – Supersonic: Slade, Marc Bolan, Roxy Music, the Sweet, David Essex, Mud, Bay City Rollers

25 December 1975 – Shang-a-Lang Christmas Special: Bay City Rollers, Gilbert O'Sullivan, Showaddywaddy

25 December 1975 – Top Of The Pops: Bay City Rollers, Mud, 10cc, David Essex,

EPILOGUE

I had two Glam Rock summers. The first, the one I shared with everybody else of the era, lasted from the end of 1970 to the early part of 1976 and threw up what remains some of the greatest music that the UK has ever been responsible for.

The second, which was somewhat shorter and a lot less visible, encompassed a year or so in the middle of the Eighties and began, as all good stories begin, on the dark and stormy night when *Melody Maker*, the weekly newspaper for which I was then writing, packed me off to Croydon to review a Specimen gig.

It wasn't an assignment I particularly relished, but I grabbed my bus pass and set off into the night. But the sights I saw that evening remain with me today. For, after a decade of growing increasingly disgruntled with the state and nature of live music in London, I finally found a band I could love. And a quarter of a century later, that emotion remains as strong as ever. That band was called Sexagisma, and this is their story.

Although history prefers to condemn it as a stagnant, static wasteland, British rock through the mid Eighties was actually even worse than that. On the one hand, the dying snorts of the New Romantic movement were echoing through the tentative stabs at Industrial electronics of Depeche Mode and Duran; on the other, the dour-faced denizens of Indie Rock were beginning to flex their first flabby muscles.

Sourpuss pretensions were the order of the day. Precocious talent laboured beneath attention grabbing *noms de guerre* like We've Got a Fuzzbox and We're Gonna Use It, Half Man Half Biscuit and Turkey Bones and the Wild Dogs; mundane normality lay camouflaged beneath layers of normal mundanity – Bogshed, the Three Johns, the Sound. There was no fun any more, no pizzazz, no glamour, just the relentless hum of the Jesus and Mary Chain, and the *bête noire* dementia of sunglasses after dark.

And then there was Sexagisma. Ratty and tatty, oozing a subterranean sleazeball brilliance which hadn't been sighted in over a decade, Sexagisma were a Glam band with a spangle-strangled vengeance, erupting out of nowhere to splash sequins on

SEXAGISMA live!

SPECIMEN/SEXAGISMA

The Underground, Croydon

IF it's true that the mid-1980s are really the Seventies in some weird disguise (and I won't dispute *that!*), then Sexagisma are going to be very big indeed.

They might look like Jobriath, but their sound is pure Spiders From Mars, right the way down to the Mick Ronson lookalike on guitar. They even play "Cracked Actor" and "Jean Genie", for Chrissakes; the first straightforward runthrough of what was never more than an above average heavy metal song, the other part of an irreverant medley that encompassed "Blockbuster" and "School's Out" before turning to its original theme.

Yes, Sexagisma are a Glam band, and proud of it. Ratty and tatty and oozing a subterranean sleaze-ball brilliance which far surpassed the sub-Glitter posturings of other bands who tread these paths. Sexagisma, you see, actually have the songs to match the image, and that without once lapsing into turgid revivalism. If there's any real criticisms to level it's that the androgynous dancing boy who pops up now and again to leer provocatively at the audience spends too much time doing that, and not enough actually contributing to the proceedings. Sort him out and Sexagisma could be perfect.

DAVE THOMAS

your dreams and remember a day when all bands looked this good.

'Good old fashioned Glam-chaos,' laughs singer Vaughan Funnell. 'Or the Sweet Pistols from Mars.'

In April 1985, their first live review misnamed them Sexagesima but hit the rest of the nails on the head, championing the south Londoners like there was no tomorrow. A slew of ecstatic reviews in the other weeklies followed, a management contract promised the earth, an imminent record deal hung in the air. It was all, the band bemusedly confessed, a very long way from a pizza parlour in chintzy South Kensington.

Funnell formed the original Sexagisma in late 1981 with Phil Lecrombe (guitar), Richard Cooper (keyboards, sax), Adam Jeerey (bass) and Steve Paice (drums – soon replaced by Steve Wren). Devoted from the outset to realigning their juvenile Glam-Rock dreams for a decade that neither rocked nor glammed, they played their first show at the Ship in Plumstead in May 1982, cut two sets of demos and, before the year's end, had landed one of them, 'Freak's Graveyard', on the 'Sing As We Go' compilation of synth and DIY bands.

China Moon, the Spoons, Left at the Lights and more joined them on board, and none appear to have gone onto anything. Which was not the case with Sexagisma. Soon after the album's release, Wren departed on the course that would lead him to Then Jerico. Lecrombe followed him out, and frontman Funnell was back to square one.

He killed time with a handful of solo shows, 'leather-clad and made up like a slut'...including one supporting reggae heroes Clint Eastwood and General Saint, 'clip-clopping onto the stage like some leather whore in jackboots, very, very, drunk.

'There was a small group of friends and gismanauts there to see me, but the rest were all Rastafarians. Oh dear. And being so drunk, the first thing I did was put the microphone next to my rear end and, amid all the feedback, proceeded to pass wind. I then returned the mike to its stand and said, "I'm sorry about that, it was a bum note." They hated me.'

A new Sexagisma began to coalesce in early 1983 after Funnell was introduced to drummer Mark Carter. With Richard Cooper hanging on from the band, bassist Jem Soar and ex-Praxis guitarist Jerry Moore completed the line-up, although Funnell admits, 'it was hard trying to find people who wanted to be in a band like mine, as they all seemed to want to be in Bauhaus.' Moore, then, was perfect – Praxis were a Bauhaus clone.

'Reborn, we had moved on a bit from pubs and started to play colleges...Thames Poly, Goldsmith's, Wandsworth.' Their repertoire, too, had snowballed, to slide effortlessly between Funnell's startlingly authentic originals ('Good Morning George', 'Betcha Can't Dance To This One, Baby') and a host of staggering covers – 'Virginia Plain', 'Do You Wanna Touch Me?', 'Hang On To Yourself' and a positively devilish medley that swung from Bowie's slowed-down ''David Live'-style 'The Jean Genie' into its doppelganger 'Blockbuster!' and on to a frenzied 'School's Out'.

A new demo preserved two further originals, 'Monster Fun' and, reprised from one of the earlier tapes, 'Silverize', and with that to attract further work Sexagisma found themselves opening for the Alarm, Icicle Works and, best of all, the Glitter Band, themselves recently reformed in the wake of Gary Glitter's latest comeback.

Sexagisma had already started to find their own audience; they were now finding a context as well.

Musically, Sexagisma were immaculate. Drawing their inspiration from a genre which was long since dead and buried could easily have backfired on the band, might have seen them labelled mere revivalists, and condemned them unheard on the strength of the tag. Yet songs like 'Monster Fun', 'Gargoyles' and 'Glitter Devils' owed none of their impact to a celebration of years gone by, even as they made it patently obvious where the band's heart lay.

Plus, they weren't all blurred lamé trousers and codpieces. 'Good Morning George' was an idiot mantra aimed at everybody who made sure they wore their socks on the right feet every morning, and 'Betcha Can't Dance To This One, Baby' was exactly what it should have been, mutant disco with discordant tempos and a vested interest in clearing the dancefloor.

Moore quit, but was quickly replaced by Mark Carter's cousin Vince, a near dead ringer for Mick Ronson and a fluid and remarkable guitarist. There was just one further refinement to make.

One day in late 1983, Funnell was passing by a local newsagent 'when I saw an advert in the window for pirate Bowie videos, one being *The 1980 Floorshow* which was still quite scarce in those days. I went to see the guy, got chatting, told him about my band and he came to see us. He became the most important new member of the band.'

A flamboyant exhibitionist, a dancer with an eagle eye for outrage, costume and theatrical effect, it was the arrival of Andy Rogene that finally took Sexagisma in the direction Funnell had always imagined – an ocular feast that not only incorporated dress and make-up but would rush towards even grander visual extremes.

Another demo, 'To Believe Him Is Lethal' and a fabulous studio version of the 'Jean Genie Medley' preceded the final line-up change, as Cooper quit and one of Vince Carter's cousins, Mick Cronin, moved in. A manager arrived, and we return to the aforementioned pizza parlour in chintzy South Kensington.

Funnell: 'One day, our manager announced "I have got us a gig in Kensington." Wow! we thought. Our first proper London gig…at the Café Emile.'

'So there were we in a Pizza Hut sort of place. There were guys with their girlfriends, people who were getting something to eat on their way home from work. The restaurant was probably expecting a jazz band, and out we came on in blue Lurex with Steve Zodiac shoulder pads and silver fucking boots. Vince turned his amp up full pelt and, with an enormous screech of feedback and a drum roll, we tore into "Monster Fun".

'All the plates on the tables were vibrating, and I was fighting to fend off some Arabic guy who wasn't sure what sex I was – as if it even mattered, because I looked like one of the Ugly Sisters.' They were never asked to return.

Roxy reincarnate, the Spiders of your dreams, Sexagisma dressed like the Sweet on a methadone comedown. They sounded like Bowie being butchered by the Stooges. And they looked like six guys re-enacting the Last Passion of Christ in a Paris bordello, midway through your deep-dish cheese and anchovy. In fact, Sexagisma were *so* good that Rogene's parents didn't even know where he went every evening.

'For eight months, every time we had a gig, I'd tell my parents I was going to a fancy-dress party,' admitted the boy whose idea of a wholesome performance was to don a silver Afro, then try to escape his G-string. 'Finally I confessed to them, and showed them a couple of photographs. They weren't amused.'

A new ally arrived; Dave Fanning, a fan who passed a copy of the most recent demo along to Specimen, Goth band supreme and the powers behind the Batcave. 'They liked it and gave us a gig, 21 September 1984. We were a bit apprehensive as it really would be the first time we were to play in front of a proper London club audience; even though the Batcave had gone past its glory days, it was still quite a big deal to us.

'But we went down really well; Jon Klein took a liking to us, especially with the Bowie thing and all, and Specimen took us under their wing. We started to support them at gigs outside the Batcave – Upstairs at Eric's in Bournemouth, December 1984, will always stay with me as one of my favourite gigs as it all seemed to go so well.

'We were also still gigging on our own turf, supporting the Glitter Band again, Mari Wilson and Specimen at the Clarendon Hotel that Christmas. Being Christmas, we decided to do something terrible involving a full-sized crucifix, Andy as a glittering boy Christ and a rubber phallus. In hindsight, I am so glad that we were rushed onto stage and never did what we intended as we may have ruined Jesus' birthday party and procured eternal damnation to boot. But I don't know what the Clarendon must have thought when they found two boards nailed together in the shape of a cross in the changing room.'

1985 saw things continue to blossom. A tour with Specimen introduced a second dancer, Linda Rowell, to the package. Those first glowing press reviews appeared; there were shows at the Marquee and Dingwalls, and the Tunnel Club in Greenwich, where they opened for the Glitter Band by attacking Rogene with a carving knife. The blood was just a stage prop, but it didn't look like that from the front row.

An on-stage electrocution two weeks earlier was equally colourful; next time around, Carter (a bit-part actor fresh from Tobe Hooper's *Space Vampires*) insisted, they were going to torch the lad for an encore. And when someone suggested that it was all a bit Alice Cooper, Funnell was down their throat in a second. 'You could look at it like that, but there again most of the people who come to see us are too young to remember him. What we're doing, for them, is a completely new thing. It's not as if we're simply lifting Alice's ideas wholesale, anyway. The only real comparison is that we both use the image of violence to complement the music.'

By mid-summer, Sexagisma were poised on the brink of imminent stardom, sequestered in Alaska Studios laying down their debut single. The freakishly autobiographical 'Glitter Devils', an insistent call-and-response stomp rocker, powered by haunting keyboards and Pythonesque Gumby backing vocals, was to be first off the block, with the Munster-baiting 'Monster Fun' lined up for the B-side.

Leaving the studio for the san(ct)ity of the subway at the end of the rough mix session, it was impossible not to grin; the songs were just so damnably, joyously, catchy. 'Who's a Glitter Devils? We are Glitter Devils! Who's a Glitter Devil? Not you, but I.'

The assault lined up on every imaginable front. A British tour was in the works, keeping the band on the road for three months until Christmas. Their own West End dance club was a distinct possibility, a home from home for the disaffected millions who still worshipped old Marc Bolan. There was even the dream, or maybe a threat, to book the massive Hammersmith Odeon, then come on in tartan trousers and mime to Bay City Rollers records.

Unfortunately, however, a persuasive new manager had also appeared; and, presumably seeing something there that the rest of the band was oblivious to, he began pushing for changes. He recruited trained choreographers to replace the glorious chaos of the band's earlier attempts.

He canned the notion of releasing 'Glitter Devils' independently and spoke of holding out for a 'real' record deal. He even nixed the Hammersmith Odeon idea. And so the band lurched from one lost brainwave to the next misused opportunity until finally, in February 1986, Sexagisma played their last show at Goldsmith's College. All that remained was the memory – a few years of fun, a few months of hope, and a few minutes of magnificent music on tape.

Funnell shrugs off his disappointment. 'It probably wasn't the right time to be doing what we did,' he admits. 'But no-one else was doing it, so we thought we'd have a go. Someone has to take chances, you know.'

Spoken like a true Glam Rock hero. Spoken like a Glitter Devil.

APPENDIX ONE

Glam on the Box, 1976

Music television is notoriously a few months behind contemporary tastes, and the mid Seventies were no exception. The following is a necessarily selective guide to what was on, although for most of us only one show truly mattered – Granada TV's teatime Arrows!

1 January 1976	Top Of The Pops: Slik, Queen
3 January 1976	Supersonic: The Rubettes
4 January 1976	London Weekend Show: Be Bop Deluxe
8 January 1976	Top Of The Pops: Sailor, Queen
10 January 1976	Supersonic: Smokie, Slik, Kenny
13 January 1976	Old Grey Whistle Test: Be Bop Deluxe
15 January 1976	Top Of The Pops: 10cc, Roxy Music, Queen
17 January 1976	Supersonic: The Sweet
22 January 1976	Top Of The Pops: Sailor, Slik, Queen
24 January 1976	Supersonic: Bilbo Baggins, Be Bop Deluxe
29 January 1976	Top Of The Pops: The Sweet
31 January 1976	Supersonic: Sailor, Chris Spedding, Fancy, Slik
2 February 1976	Parkinson: Elton John
3 February 1976	Pebble Mill At One: Queen
5 February 1976	Top Of The Pops: Slik, Slade, Be Bop Deluxe
7 February 1976	Supersonic: The Sweet, Mr Big, Steve Harley and Cockney Rebel
7 February 1976	Tiswas: Jim Lea and Dave Hill, Glitter Band
12 February 1976	Top Of The Pops: Slik
14 February 1976	Supersonic; Slade, Hello
17 February 1976	Play For Today: The Jumping Bean Bag
19 February 1976	Top Of The Pops: Slade, Glitter Band
21 February 1976	Supersonic: T Rex
24 February 1976	Rock Follies
2 March 1976	Arrows: Peter Noone, Jesse Green, Glyder
2 March 1976	Rock Follies
4 March 1976	Top Of The Pops: Glitter Band

6 March 1976	Supersonic: Slade
9 March 1976	Arrows: Slade, Bilbo Baggins
9 March 1976	Rock Follies
11 March 1976	Top Of The Pops: T Rex
13 March 1976	Supersonic: Sensational Alex Harvey Band, the Rubettes, Gary Glitter
16 March 1976	Rock Follies
18 March 1976	Top Of The Pops: David Essex, Be Bop Deluxe
19 March 1976	Russell Harty: Gary Glitter
20 March 1976	Supersonic: Glitter Band, Kenny
23 March 1976	Arrows: Paul Nicholas, Dana
23 March 1976	Rock Follies
25 March 1976	Top Of The Pops: 10cc
27 March 1976	Supersonic: Marc Bolan, Sailor
30 March 1976	Arrows: Hello, Scottie
30 March 1976	Rock Follies
1 April 1976	Top Of The Pops: Sailor, Fox
8 April 1976	Top Of The Pops: 10cc, Bay City Rollers
13 April 1976	Arrows: Randy Edelman, the Drifters
15 April 1976	Top Of The Pops: Fox, Sailor
16 April 1976	Russell Harty: Bay City Rollers
20 April 1976	Arrows: Alan Warren, Frank Jennings Syndicate, Butterflies
22 April 1976	Top Of The Pops: Bay City Rollers, the Rubettes
27 April 1976	Arrows: Flintlock, Sheer Elegance, Louisa Jane White
29 April 1976	Top Of The Pops: Slik
4 May 1976	Arrows: Gilbert O'Sullivan, Showaddywaddy
6 May 1976	Top Of The Pops: Mud, Fox
11 May 1976	Arrows: Bilbo Baggins, the Rubettes
13 May 1976	Top Of The Pops; Slik
18 May 1976	Arrows: Lynsey de Paul, Alvin Stardust
20 May 1976	Top Of The Pops: Showaddywaddy, Mud
25 May 1976	Arrows: Kathy Jones, Stevenson's Rocket
27 May 1976	Top Of The Pops: Heavy Metal Kids, David Bowie
3 June 1976	Top Of The Pops: Glitter Band, Mud
8 June 1976	Arrows: Geraldine, Slik
10 June 1976	Top Of The Pops: Sensational Alex Harvey Band, Slik, Bryan Ferry
12 June 1976	Tiswas: Slik
15 June 1976	Arrows: Buster, Lieutenant Pigeon
17 June 1976	Top Of The Pops: T Rex, Mud
22 June 1976	Arrows: Glitter Band, Wurzels
24 June 1976	Top Of The Pops: Bryan Ferry, SAHB
1 July 1976	Top Of The Pops: Hello, T Rex
8 July 1976	Top Of The Pops: Sensational Alex Harvey Band
13 July 1976	Rollin' Bolan: T Rex
22 July 1976	Top Of The Pops: Steve Harley, Sensational Alex Harvey Band
31 July 1976	Rollercoaster: Bay City Rollers
5 August 1976	Top Of The Pops: Slik, Steve Harley
19 August 1976	Top Of The Pops: Bryan Ferry, Steve Harley

21 August 1976	So It Goes: Be Bop Deluxe
21 August 1976	So It Goes: Kiss
2 September 1976	Top Of The Pops: Bryan Ferry
9 September 1976	Top Of The Pops: Bay City Rollers
13 September 1976	Supersonic: Be Bop Deluxe, Alvin Stardust
23 September 1976	Top Of The Pops: Bay City Rollers
28 September 1976	Arrows: Paul Nicholas, Real Thing
4 October 1976	Supersonic: Sailor, David Essex
5 October 1976	Arrows: Bay City Rollers, Dana
7 October 1976	Top Of The Pops: T Rex
11 October 1976	Supersonic; Marc Bolan, Mud, Slik
12 October 1976	Arrows: Jonathan King, Billy Ocean
14 October 1976	Top Of The Pops: David Essex
16 October 1976	Basil Brush Show: Mud
19 October 1976	Arrows: Showaddywaddy, J Vincent Edwards
21 October 1976	Top Of The Pops: Steve Harley
23 October 1976	Basil Brush Show: David Essex
25 October 1976	Supersonic: Smokie
26 October 1976	Arrows: Child, Gilbert O'Sullivan, Wurzels
30 October 1976	Tiswas: The Rubettes
1 November 1976	Supersonic: Showaddywaddy
2 November 1976	Arrows: Sunshine, T Rex
4 November 1976	Top Of The Pops: Showaddywaddy
8 November 1976	Supersonic: The Rubettes, Steve Harley and Cockney Rebel
9 November 1976	Arrows: Billy Ocean, Arbre, Keely Ford
15 November 1976	Supersonic: Glitter Band
16 November 1976	Old Grey Whistle Test: Be Bop Deluxe
16 November 1976	Arrows: Glitter Band, Red Hurley, Chris Neal
18 November 1976	Top Of The Pops: Mud, Showaddywaddy
22 November 1976	Supersonic: Mud, Bay City Rollers
23 November 1976	Arrows: Billy J Kramer, Paul Nicholas, Kettle
25 November 1976	Top Of The Pops: Be Bop Deluxe
27 November 1976	Tiswas: Showaddywaddy
30 November 1976	Arrows: Jonathan King
2 December 1976	Top Of The Pops: Mud, Showaddywaddy
7 December 1976	Arrows: Gene Pitney, Ginger
9 December 1976	Top Of The Pops: Showaddywaddy
13 December 1976	Supersonic: Chris Spedding, the Rubettes
14 December 1976	Arrows: John Christie, Wurzels, Robin Sarstedt
16 December 1976	Top Of The Pops: Mud, 10cc, Showaddywaddy
18 December 1976	Saturday Scene: Marc Bolan
21 December 1976	Arrows: Rollers, Slik
25 December 1976	Supersonic: Marc Bolan, Gary Glitter
25 December 1976	Top Of The Pops: Slik, Queen
26 December 1976	Top Of The Pops: Showaddywaddy, Sailor

Disco

British TV's penchant for wiping shows once they were broadcast has had innumerable unfortunate consequences. But, for Glam fans at any rate, salvation was at hand in the form of Disco, a monthly German pop show best described as that country's answer to Top Of The Pops and, thankfully, one that was as fascinated by Glam Rock as the UK. For many bands, fans and collectors, Disco performances remain the only generally available footage of too many great records; even more ironically, the BBC frequently licensed Top Of The Pops performances for use on Disco – and that's the only reason why they have survived.

The following list includes original Disco studio footage only.

Note: due to the differing release dates between Germany and the UK, artists and song titles are provided; *Disco* appearances were often several months, and even hits, behind the 'corresponding' British performances. So if you've ever wondered why Alvin Stardust wore red on *Disco* for 'You You You', whereas Britain didn't see that colour scheme until the following single, that's why.

8 May 1971	Hotlegs: 'Desperate Dan'
11 September 1971	The Sweet: 'Co-Co'
11 December 1971	Slade: 'Coz I Luv You'
15 January 1972	T Rex: 'Jeepster'
27 May 1972	Chicory Tip: 'What's Your Name?'
14 October 1972	Gary Glitter: 'Rock And Roll'
11 November 1972	Blackfoot Sue: 'Standing In The Road'
9 December 1972	Slade: 'Mama Weer All Crazee Now'
28 April 1973	Alice Cooper: 'Hello Hurray'
23 June 1973	The Sweet: 'Blockbuster!', 'Hell Raiser'
21 July 1973	Alice Cooper: 'No More Mr Nice Guy'

25 August 1973	10cc: 'Rubber Bullets', Wizzard: 'See My Baby Jive', Suzi Quatro: 'Can The Can'
27 October 1973	The Sweet: 'The Ballroom Blitz'
24 November 1973	Barry Blue: 'Dancin' (On A Saturday Night)', Suzi Quatro: '48 Crash'
22 November 1973	Slade: 'My Friend Stan'
2 February 1974	Gary Glitter: 'I Love You Love Me Love', Suzi Quatro: 'Daytona Demon'
2 March 1974	Mott the Hoople: 'Roll Away The Stone', Sweet: 'Teenage Rampage', Alvin Stardust 'My Coo Ca Choo', Barry Blue 'Do You Wanna Dance'
13 April 1974	Suzi Quatro: 'Devil Gate Drive', Marc Bolan: 'Teenage Dream'
11 May 1974	Mud: 'Tiger Feet', Alvin Stardust: 'Jealous Mind'
8 June 1974	Leo Sayer: 'The Show Must Go On'
3 August 1974	The Sweet: 'The Six Teens', Rubettes: 'Sugar Baby Love'
31 August 1974	Mud: 'The Cat Crept In', Gary Glitter: 'Always Yours'
28 September 1974	Sparks: 'This Town Ain't Big Enough For Both Of Us', Suzi Quatro: 'Too Big'
26 October 1974	Mud: 'Rocket', Slade: 'Bangin' Man'
23 November 1974	The Sweet: 'Turn It Down', Alvin Stardust: 'You You You', the Rubettes: 'Tonight'
1 February 1975	Slade: 'Far Far Away'
1 March 1975	David Essex: 'Gonna Make You A Star', Rubettes: 'Juke Box Jive'
26 April 1975	The Sweet: 'Fox On The Run', Fox – 'Only You Can'
24 May 1975	The Rubettes: 'I Can Do It'
5 July 1975	Kenny: 'Fancy Pants'
2 August 1975	Mud: 'Oh Boy', Bay City Rollers: 'Bye Bye Baby'
13 September 1975	The Sweet: 'Action', Rubettes: 'Foe-Dee-O-Dee'
8 November 1975	Bay City Rollers: 'Give A Little Love'
6 December 1975	Hello: 'New York Groove'
3 January 1976	Kenny: 'Julie Anne'
31 January 1976	Mud: 'L'L'Lucy', Showaddywaddy: 'Heartbeat'
28 February 1976	Bay City Rollers: 'Money Honey', Rubettes: 'Little Darling'
27 March 1976	Sailor: 'Glass Of Champagne'
22 May 1976	Slik: 'Forever And Ever'
19 June 1976	Kenny: 'Hot Lips'
17 July 1976	The Rubettes: 'You're The Reason Why'
9 October 1976	Hello: 'Love Stealer'
4 December 1976	Suzi Quatro: 'Tear Me Apart', Sailor: 'Stiletto Heels'

APPENDIX THREE

UK Glam Chart-Toppers

GLAM ROCK NUMBER 1 SINGLES 1971-1976

20 March 1971	T Rex: 'Hot Love' (6 weeks)
24 July 1971	T Rex: 'Get It On' (4)
13 November 1971	Slade: 'Coz I Luv You' (4)
5 February 1972	T Rex: 'Telegram Sam' (2)
19 February 1972	Chicory Tip: 'Son Of My Father' (3)
20 May 1972	T Rex: 'Metal Guru' (4)
1 July 1972	Slade' 'Take Me Bak 'Ome' (1)
12 August 1972	Alice Cooper: 'School's Out' (3)
9 September 1972	Slade: 'Mama Weer All Crazee Now' (3)
14 October 1972	Lieutenant Pigeon: 'Mouldy Old Dough' (4)
27 January 1973	The Sweet: 'Blockbuster!' (5)
3 March 1973	Slade: 'Cum On Feel The Noize' (4)
19 May 1973	Wizzard: 'See My Baby Jive' (4)
16 June 1973	Suzi Quatro: 'Can The Can' (3)
23 June 1973	10cc: 'Rubber Bullets' (1)
30 June 1973	Slade: 'Skweeze Me Pleeze Me' (3)
28 July 1973	Gary Glitter: 'I'm The Leader Of The Gang (I Am)' (4)
22 September 1973	Wizzard: 'Angel Fingers' (1)
17 November 1973	Gary Glitter: 'I Love You Love Me Love' (4)
15 December 1973	Slade: 'Merry Xmas Everybody' (5)
26 January 1974	Mud: 'Tiger Feet' (4)
23 February 1974	Suzi Quatro: 'Devil Gate Drive' (2)
9 March 1974	Alvin Stardust: 'Jealous Mind' (1)
18 May 1974	The Rubettes: 'Sugar Baby Love' (4)
22 June 1974	Gary Glitter: 'Always Yours' (1)
16 November 1974	David Essex: 'Gonna Make You A Star' (3)
21 December 1974	Mud: 'Lonely This Christmas' (4)
22 February 1975	Steve Harley and Cockney Rebel: 'Make Me Smile (Come Up And See Me)' (2)
22 March 1975	The Bay City Rollers: 'Bye Bye Baby' (6)
3 May 1975	Mud: 'Oh Boy' (2)
28 June 1975	10cc: 'I'm Not In Love' (2)

19 July 1975	The Bay City Rollers: 'Give A Little Love' (3)
4 October 1975	David Essex: 'Hold Me Close' (3)
8 November 1975	David Bowie: 'Space Oddity' (2)
29 November 1975	Queen: 'Bohemian Rhapsody' (9)
14 February 1976	Slik: 'Forever And Ever' (1)
4 December 1976	Showaddywaddy: 'Under The Moon Of Love' (3)

ALBUMS

7 August 1971	Various Artists: 'Hot Hits Volume 6' (1)
21 August 1971	Various Artists: 'Top Of The Pops Volume 18' (3)
27 November 1971	Various Artists: 'Top Of The Pops Volume 20' (1)
18 December 1971	T Rex: 'Electric Warrior' (6)
5 February 1972	T Rex: 'Electric Warrior' (2)
6 May 1972	Tyrannosaurus Rex: 'Prophets, Seers And Sages The Angels Of The Ages'/'My People Were Fair And Had Sky In Their Hair But Now They're Content To Wear Stars On Their Brows' (1)
20 May 1972	T Rex – 'Bolan Boogie' (3)
13 January 1973	Slade – 'Slayed?' (1)
27 January 1973	Slade – 'Slayed?' (2)
24 March 1973	Alice Cooper – 'Billion Dollar Babies' (1)
5 May 1973	David Bowie: 'Aladdin Sane' (5)
30 June 1973	Original Soundtrack: 'That'll Be The Day' (7)
6 October 1973	Slade: 'Sladest' (3)
3 November 1973	David Bowie: 'Pinups' (5)
8 December 1973	Roxy Music: 'Stranded' (1)
19 January 1974	Slade: 'Sladest' (1)
2 March 1974	Slade: 'Old New Borrowed And Blue' (1)
8 June 1974	David Bowie: 'Diamond Dogs' (4)
12 October 1974	Bay City Rollers: 'Rollin'' (1)
26 October 1974	Bay City Rollers: 'Rollin'' (1)
9 November 1974	Bay City Rollers: 'Rollin'' (2)
3 May 1975	Bay City Rollers: 'Once Upon A Star' (3)
27 December 1975	Queen: 'A Night At The Opera' (2)
17 January 1976	Queen: 'A Night At The Opera' (2)

APPENDIX FOUR

The Greatest Glam Show on Earth

On 6 March 2010, DJ Dan Reed and I co-hosted WXPN Philadelphia's Highs In The Seventies, a four-hour Saturday afternoon show devoted in its entirely that week to Glam Rock. The play list that follows was also the soundtrack that accompanied me writing this book. See what you think...

Mott the Hoople – American Pie (live)
Gary Glitter – Rock And Roll (Part 1)
The Sweet – Blockbuster
Cockney Rebel – Judy Teen
T Rex – Metal Guru
Eno – Seven Deadly Finns
Slade – Coz I Luv You
David Essex – Rock On
Elton John – Madman Across The Water (Mick Ronson version)
Geordie – All Because Of You
Suzi Quatro – Can The Can

BEFORE THEY WERE GLAM BLOCK
Paul Raven – Alone In The Night
David Bowie – Penny Lane
T Rex – Elemental Child

THE JUNK SHOP BLOCK
Sleaze – Hollywood
Grudge – I'm Gonna Smash Your Face In
Sexagisma – Glitter Devils
The Top Of The Poppers – The Jean Genie
Alice Cooper – King Of The Silver Screen

ALAN MERRILL INTERVIEW
Arrows – I Love Rock'n'Roll ('Tawny Tracks' version)
Arrows – A Touch Too Much

THE BOWIE BLOCK
David Bowie – Rebel Rebel
Dana Gillespie – Andy Warhol
Lulu – The Man Who Sold The World
David Bowie – Moonage Daydream

The Glitter Band – Angel Face
Slik – Forever And Ever
Roxy Music – Virginia Plain
The Bay City Rollers – Summerlove Sensation
Hello – New York Groove
Kiss – Christine Sixteen
T Rex – Raw Ramp
Cockney Rebel – Sebastian

FUTURE GLAM!
Carter The Unstoppable Sex Machine – Glam Rock Cops
Marc Almond – The Idol

Mud – Tiger Feet
Alvin Stardust – My Coo Ca Choo
The Sweet – Ballroom Blitz
Lou Reed – Hangin' Round
David Essex – Stardust
Sweet – Wig-Wam Bam
Brett Smiley – Va Va Va Voom
Slade – Mama Weer All Crazee Now
Bay City Rollers – Saturday Night
Mott the Hoople – Saturday Gigs

ACKNOWLEDGEMENTS

Back when I was 13 or 14, while the rest of my schoolfriends built models, played cricket or threw the dining-room chairs at one another, my hobby was to compile encyclopaedias of music. Page upon page of handwritten scrawl, pieced together from whichever source I could find, biographies, discographies, TV appearances, gigs, I noted them all and diligently built up what I thought was a major piece of research work – but which my headmaster, the indomitable Warthead, described an absolute waste of time, ink and purloined school exercises books. This is what that waste grew into.

Sadly, the original writings were lost long ago, and that's probably just as well. I doubt whether I could have read my scrawl and, even if I could, I wouldn't have liked the way it read.

But I have delved back into some of my other writings in the course of this book, ranging from the inevitable childhood diaries and scrapbooks to over thirty years worth of magazines (*Melody Maker, Record Collector, ZigZag, Mojo, Q, Goldmine, Alternative Press* etc)...

... fanzines (*TV Times – No Relation, British Punk Collector, Live! Music Review* etc)...

... websites (allmusic.com, davethompsonbooks.com, bigo.com, and others too defunct to mention)...

... liner notes for a variety of CD and LP reissues and compilations...

... and some of my past books as well (see bibliography for details)...

... to reread, revise and occasionally contradict the opinions and thoughts that most of my record collection is based upon. Occasionally I left them all but unchanged, sometimes I tore them to shreds. But they're all here in spirit, if not in fact, five years of life that I have spent the last 30 years writing about.

An army of my teenage idols also sat down to aid me in my quest, and for the interviews and stories that give this book so much of its colour, I'd like to thank:

Alan Lee Shaw, Alan Merrill (Arrows), Alan Silson (Smokey), Alvin Stardust, Andrew Loog Oldham (creator – Grunt Futtock, manager – Brett Smiley), Andy Bennie (Sleaze), Andy Ellison (John's Children, Jet), Andy Scott (Sweet), Angie Bowie, Ariel Bender aka Luther Grosvenor (Mott the Hoople), Bill Hurd (Rubettes), Bob Bradbury (Hello), Bob Grace (music publisher – Chrysalis Music/David Bowie), Brett Smiley, Brian Engel (Starbuck, True Adventure, Shambles – interview by Mark Johnston), Buzz Chanter (Sleaze), Cherry Vanilla (*Pork*, poet, performer, press officer – David Bowie/MainMan), Chris Peel (Bearded Lady), Chris Spedding, Colin 'Stoner' Bentley (Doctors of Madness), Dale 'Buffin' Griffin (Mott the Hoople), Dana Gillespie, Danny Adler (Smooth Loser), David Allen (Carmen), David Blaylock (manager – Hello), David Cassidy (additional interviews by Amy Hanson, Ken Sharp), David Courtney (producer/co-writer – Leo Sayer), Davy O'List (Roxy Music, Jet), Fred Sherriff (Bearded Lady), Georg Kajanus (Sailor), Graham Gouldman (Strawberry Studios, 10cc), Harley Feinstein (Sparks), Hilly Michaels (Cherry Vanilla Band, Mick Ronson Band, Sparks), Howard Kaylan (Flo and Eddie, T Rex), Ian Hampton (Jook, Sparks), Ian Kimmet (Jook – interview by Mark Johnston), Ian Mitchell (Bay City Rollers), Iggy Pop (the Stooges), Jamie Turner (manager – Jet), Jeff 'Dicken' Pain (Mr Big), Jerry Brandt (manager – Jobriath), John Fiddler (Medicine Head), John Hewlett (John's Children; manager – Jook, Sparks), John Springate (Glitter Band), Johnny Warman (Bearded Lady), Keith Boyce (Heavy Metal Kids), Kenneth Pitt (manager – David Bowie, Alan Lee Shaw), Kevin Godley (Strawberry Studios, Hotlegs, 10cc), Larry Dupont (road manager/photographer – Sparks), Laurice Marshall (Paul St John, Grudge, Spiv), Lawrence Myers (Gem Management), Leee Black Childers (*Pork*, press officer – David Bowie/MainMan), Lou Reed, Lulu, Mark Volman (Flo and Eddie, T Rex), Martin Briley (Starbuck, True Adventure, Shambles – interview by Mark Johnston), Martin Gordon (Sparks, Jet), Michael Chapman (session – Elton John), Michael Des Barres (Silverhead), Mike Hurst (producer – Marc Bolan, New World, Showaddywaddy, Fancy), Mo Foster (bassist – Fancy), Neal Smith (Alice Cooper), Nigel Fletcher (Stavely Makepeace, Lieutenant Pigeon), Overend Watts (Mott the Hoople), Peter Frampton (Grunt Futtock), Peter Noone, Phil Manzanera (Roxy Music), Phil Rambow (the Winkies), Ray Stiles (Mud), Richard 'Kid' Strange (Doctors of Madness), Rob Woodward (Stavely Makepeace, Lieutenant Pigeon), Rod 'Bell' Latter (Alan Lee Shaw), Roger Wootton (Comus), Ron Mael (Sparks), Russell Mael (Sparks), Sal Maida (Roxy Music, Milk'n'Cookies, Sparks), Scott Richardson (co-writer – Mick Ronson), Shel Talmy (producer – David Bowie), Steve Priest (Sweet), Suzi Quatro, Tony Defries (manager – David Bowie, MainMan), Tony Visconti (producer – T Rex, David Bowie, Carmen), Tony Zanetta (*Pork*, Vice president – MainMan), Trevor White (Jook, Sparks, Jet), TV Smith (Sleaze), Virginia Scott (Beggars Opera), Wayne County (*Pork*).

Also, fond memories of sitting down with the following:
Brian Connolly (Sweet), Chas Chandler (manager – Slade), Chris Townson (John's Children, Jook, Jet), Cozy Powell, Gerry Shephard (Glitter Band), Gus Dudgeon (producer – Elton John, David Bowie), Guy Stevens (producer – Mott the Hoople, the Winkies), Johnny Thunders (New York Dolls), Joseph Fleury (manager – Milk'n' Cookies, Sparks), Les Gray (Mud), Malcolm McLaren (owner – Let It Rock, manager – New York Dolls), Mick Ronson (David Bowie, Mott the Hoople, Ian Hunter), Mick Tucker (Sweet), Mickie Most (RAK Records), Mickey Finn (T Rex), Mike Leander (producer – Gary Glitter, Glitter Band, Hello etc), Ron Asheton (the Stooges), Tony Secunda (manager – T Rex).

And finally, family, friends and relations without whom...
Amy Hanson, Jo-Ann Greene, Jen W, Mike Sharman, Vaughan Funnell and Sexagisma, Dan Reed and WXPN (plus Ann and Max), Dave & Sue, Gaye and Tim, Linda and Larry, Andrew and Esther, Karen and Todd, Deb and Roger, Oliver, Trevor and Captain Tobias Wilcox, Jenny and James, Betsy and Steve, Thompsons, Lowes and the Nyack Hansons, Glass Onyon PR, David Harness, Siobhan Cronin, all at Cherry Red.

RESOURCES & BIBLIOGRAPHY

RESOURCES:

With so many websites dedicated to so many bands, it's fruitless to try and list them all – half will probably have disappeared before you get your computer turned on, and there'll be a whole bunch more that have replaced them. But here's a few hardy Internet veterans that you should definitely spend some time with.

http://purepop1uk.blogspot.com/
Ex-Barracuda Robin Wills' painstaking examination of the Junk Shop Everything the Seventies left behind. For Glam and all points north and south, there is no finer resource.

http://www.bigozine2.com/
For when you need to find details of that Recording of Indeterminate Origin in a hurry or just want to relax with some of the most provocative rock and current affairs writing around. Anybody fondly remembering *Street Life* (the UK answer to *Rolling Stone*, but about a squidillion times more interesting) will immediately recognise the Big O's brief.

http://www.45cat.com/
The ultimate discographical resource. Maybe not every UK single of the Seventies is here, but a lot of them are – and if you know of any more, then you can add them yourself.

http://www.angelfire.com/vt2/70sinvasion/
All period culture is here. For better or for worse...

http://784533.co.uk
Another brilliant musical blog. David Nelson's quest to find yesterday's Junk, and then point you in its direction. Mission statement – 'For the person who, armed with a spare £100, would spend it not on a single rarity, but on 50 or 100 obscure and cheap records they hadn't heard before.'

http://missingepisodes.proboards.com/
The television researcher's dream...or maybe nightmare. What do you mean, they wiped that *Top Of The Pops*? My ex-girlfriend's sister was in the audience for that.

http://www.marmalade-skies.co.uk
A decade long (1965-1975) calendar of British psychedelia as it morphed into so many other things. Peruse its pages and there's more Comus than Kenny, but it's a great era to spend the evening in.

http://www.allmusic.com
A one-stop rock, pop and everything else encyclopaedia, constantly expanding and updating and probably the most exhaustive general musical resource on the web.

http://www.davethompsonbooks.com

BIBLIOGRAPHY:

Ambrose, Joe – *Gimme Danger: The Story Of Iggy Pop* (Omnibus 2004)
Angell, Callie – *Andy Warhol Screen Tests: The Films Of Andy Warhol Catalogue Raisonné* Vols 1/2 (Abrams)
Antonia, Nina – *The Prettiest Star – Whatever Happened To Brett Smiley?* (SAF 2006)
Auslander, Philip – *Performing Glam Rock: Gender and Theatricality in Popular Music* (University of Michigan Press 2006)
Bangs, Lester – *Psychotic Reactions And Carburettor Dung* (William Heinemann 1988)
Blacknell, Steve – *The Story Of Top Of The Pops* (Patrick Stephens Ltd 1985)
Bockris, Victor – *Transformer: The Lou Reed Story* (Simon & Schuster 1995)
Bolan, Marc – *The Warlock Of Love* (Lupus, 1969)
Bowie, Angela with Patrick Carr – *Backstage Passes* (Orion, 1992)
Bowie, Angie – *Free Spirit* (Mushroom 1981)
Bracewell, Michael – *Re-make/Re-model: Art, Pop, Fashion And The Making Of Roxy Music, 1953-1972: The Band That Invented An Era* (Faber & Faber 2008)
Bruce, Michael with Billy James – *No More Mr Nice Guy: The Inside Story Of The Alice Cooper Group* (SAF 1996)
Buckley, David – *Strange Fascination: David Bowie* (Virgin 1999)
Cann, Kevin – *David Bowie: A Chronology* (Fireside 1983)
Cato, Philip – *Crash Course For The Ravers: A Glam Odyssey* (ST Publishing 1997)
Cohn, Nik – *Awopbopaloobopalopbamboom* (Weidenfeld & Nicolson 1969)
County, Jayne – *Man Enough To Be A Woman* (Serpent's Tail 1995)
Defries, Tony and Thompson, Dave – *Gods And Gangsters: The Autobiography Of Tony Defries* (unpublished/uncompleted 2007)
Devine, Campbell – *Mott The Hoople And Ian Hunter: All The Young Dudes – The Biography* (Cherry Red 1998)
Downing, David – *Future Rock* (Panther 1976)
Edwards, Henry and Tony Zanetta – *Stardust: The Life And Times Of David Bowie* (Michael Joseph 1986)
Essex, David – *A Charmed Life – The Autobiography Of David Essex* (Orion 2003)
Farren, Mick – *The Black Leather Jacket* (Plexus 1985)
Fletcher, Nigel and Woodward, Rob – *When Show Business is No Business* (Ranwell Press 2000)
Frame, Pete – *Rock Family Trees* (Omnibus Books, various editions)
Garner, Ken – *In Session Tonight* (BBC Books, 1992);
Glitter, Gary with Lloyd Bradley – *Leader: The Autobiography Of Gary Glitter* (Ebury Press 1991)
Greene, Jonathan – *Days in The Life: Voices From The English Underground 1961-1971* (William Heinemann 1989)
Guinness Book Of British Hit Singles… Albums (Guinness World Records, various editions)

Harry, Bill – *Arrows* (Everest 1976)
Hodkinson, Mark – *Queen: The Early Years* (Omnibus 1995)
Holder, Noddy – *Who's Crazee Now? My Autobiography* (Ebury Press 1999)
Hoskyns, Barney – *Glam! Bowie, Bolan And The Glitter Rock Revolution* (Pocket Books 1998)
Hunter, Ian – *Diary Of A Rock'n'Roll Star* (Star Books 1973)
Jasper, Tony – *The Top 20 Book* (Blandford Books, various editions).
Kent, Nick – *Apathy For The Devil: A Seventies Memoir* (Faber & Faber 2010)
Kent, Nick – *The Dark Stuff* (Penguin 1994)
Marshall, Bertie – *Berlin Bromley* (SAF 2006)
Matheu, Robert and Bowe, Brian J (eds) – *Creem: America's Only Rock'n'Roll Magazine* (Collins 2007)
McKeown, Les and Lynne Elliot – *Shang-A-Lang: The Curse Of The Bay City Rollers* (Mainstream 2006)
McLenehan, Cliff – *Marc Bolan 1947-1977* (Zinc Alloy 1999)
McNeil, Legs and McCain, Gillian – *Please Kill Me: The Uncensored Oral History Of Punk* (Grove Press 2006)
Melly, George – *Revolt Into Style: The Pop Arts In Britain* (Penguin 1970)
Murray, Charles Shaar – *Shots From The Hip* (Penguin 1991)
New Musical Express 1973 Annual (Fleetway 1973)
New Musical Express 1974 Hot Rock Guide (Fleetway 1974)
New Musical Express Greatest Hits: The Very Best of NME (IPC 1974)
Nilsson, Per – *The Wild One: The True Story of Iggy Pop* (Omnibus 1988)
Novick, Jeremy and Middles, Mick – *Wham Bam Thank You Glam: A Celebration Of The 70s* (Aurum Press 1998)
Paytress, Mark – *Bolan: The Rise And Fall Of A 20th Century Superstar* (Omnibus 2002)
Paytress, Mark and Pafford, Steve – *Bowie Style* (Omnibus 2000)
Pegg, Nicholas – *The Complete David Bowie* (Reynolds & Hearn 2004)
Pitt, Kenneth – *The Pitt Report* (Design 1983)
Pop Today – A Disc Special (Hamlyn 1974)
Pop, Iggy – *I Need More: The Stooges & Other Stories* (2.13.61 1997)
Quatro, Suzi – *Unzipped* (Hodder & Stoughton 2007)
Rigby, Jonathan – *Both Ends Burning* (Reynolds & Hearn 2008)
Rock File Vols 1-5 (New English Library 1973)
Rock, Mick – *Blood & Glitter* (Vision On 2001)
Rock, Mick – *Raw Power: Iggy And The Stooges* (Omnibus 2005)
Rock, Mick & Bowie, David – *Moonage Daydream: The Life And Times Of Ziggy Stardust* (Universe 2005)
Rolling Stone Cover To Cover (Bondi Digital Publishing 2008)
Rowett, Alan – *The Rubettes Story* (Alan Williams Entertainment Ltd 1994)
Sewall-Ruskin, Yvonne – *High On Rebellion: Inside The Underground At Max's Kansas City* (Thunder's Mouth Press, 1998)
Simmons, Sylvie – *Too Weird For Ziggy* (Grove Press, 2004)
Strong, Martin – *The Great Rock…* and *Psychedelic Discography* (Canongate Books, various editions)
Thomson, Elizabeth and Gutman, David (eds) – *The Bowie Companion* (MacMillan 1993)
Tobler, John and Grundy, Stuart – *The Record Producers* (BBC Books 1982)
Tremlett, George – *10cc* (Futura 1976)
Tremlett, George – *Alvin Stardust* (Futura 1976)
Tremlett, George – *David Bowie* (Futura 1974)
Tremlett, George – *David Essex* (Futura 1974)

Tremlett, George – *Gary Glitter* (Futura 1974)
Tremlett, George – *Marc Bolan* (Futura 1975)
Tremlett, George – *Queen* (Futura 1976)
Tremlett, George – *Slade* (Futura 1975)
Tremlett, George – *Slik* (Futura 1976)
Tremlett, George – *The Osmonds* (Futura 1974)
Trynka, Paul – *Iggy Pop – Open Up And Bleed* (Sphere 2008)
Vanilla, Cherry – *Lick Me: How I Became Cherry Vanilla* (Chicago Review Press 2010)
Visconti, Tony – *Bowie, Bolan And The Brooklyn Boy* (Harper Collins 2007)
Welch, Chris and Simon Napier-Bell – *Marc Bolan: Born To Boogie* (Eel Pie 1982)
Whitburn, Joel – *Top Pop Singles… Albums* (Record Research, various editions)

Also by Dave Thompson

Beyond The Velvet Underground (Omnibus 1989)
Blockbuster! The True Story Of The Sweet (Cherry Red Books 2010)
Children Of The Revolution – Gum Into Glam 1967-1976 (self-published 1985)
David Bowie: Moonage Daydream (Plexus 1987)
Glam Rock: 20th Century Rock & Roll (Collectors Guide Publishing 2000)
Growing Up With John's Children (Babylon Books 1988)
Joan Jett: An Unauthorised Biography (Backbeat Books – due 2011)
Hallo Spaceboy – The Rebirth Of David Bowie (ECW 2007)
Ignatius Pope – The Iggy Pop Story (unpublished manuscript, 1978)
Moonage Daydream (Plexus Books 1987)
Sparks: No 1 Songs In Heaven (Cherry Red Books, 2009)
To Major Tom: Letters To David Bowie (Sanctuary Books 2002)
Your Pretty Face Is Going To Hell: The Dangerous Glitter Of David Bowie, Iggy Pop And Lou Reed (Backbeat Books 2009)

Plus individual issues of the following publications:

Alternative Press, Circus, Classic Rock, Creem, Cream, Daily Express, Daily Mirror, Disc & Music Echo, Disco 45, Goldmine, Guardian, Interview, Jackie, International Times, LA Times, Live! Music Review, Let It Rock, Look In, Melody Maker, Mojo, Music Now!, Music Scene, Music Star, National Rock Star, New Musical Express, New York Times, Observer, Popswop, Q, Record Collector, Record Mirror, Rolling Stone, Sounds, Spin, Street Life, Sounds, The Sun, Superstar, Uncut, Vox, The Word, ZigZag.

Other must-read titles availabl

You're Wondering Now – The Specials from Conception to Reunion
Paul Williams

Celebration Day – A Led Zeppelin Encyclopedia
Malcolm Dome and Jerry Ewing

All The Young Dudes: Mott The Hoople & Ian Hunter
Campbell Devine

Good Times Bad Times - The Rolling Stones 1960-69
Terry Rawlings and Keith Badman

The Rolling Stones: Complete Recording Sessions 1962-2002
Martin Elliott

Embryo – A Pink Floyd Chronology 1966-1971
Nick Hodges and Ian Priston

Those Were The Days – The Beatles' Apple Organization
Stefan Grenados

The Legendary Joe Meek - The Telstar Man
John Repsch

Truth... Rod Steward, Ron Wood And The Jeff Beck Group
Dave Thompson

Our Music Is Red – With Purple Flashes: The Story Of The Creation
Sean Egan

Quite Naturally – The Small Faces
Keith Badman and Terry Rawlings

Irish Folk, Trad And Blues: A Secret History
Colin Harper and Trevor Hodgett

Number One Songs In Heaven – The Sparks Story
Dave Thompson

A Plugged In State Of Mind – The History Of Electronic Music
Dave Henderson

Random Precision - Recording The Music Of Syd Barrett 1965-1974
David Parker

Bittersweet: The Clifford T Ward Story
David Cartwright

Fucked By Rock (Revised and Expanded)
Mark Manning

PWL: From The Factory Floor
Phil Harding

Goodnight Jim Bob – On The Road With Carter USM
Jim Bob

Tamla Motown – The Stories Behind The Singles
Terry Wilson

Blockbuster! – The True Story of The Sweet
Dave Thompson

rom Cherry Red Books:

Independence Days – The Story Of UK Independent Record Labels
Alex Ogg

Indie Hits 1980-1989
Barry Lazell

No More Heroes: A Complete History Of UK Punk From 1976 To 1980
Alex Ogg

Rockdetector: A To Zs of '80s Rock/ Black Metal/Death Metal/Doom, Gothic & Stoner Metal/Power Metal
Garry Sharpe-Young

Rockdetector: Black Sabbath – Never Say Die
Garry Sharpe-Young

Rockdetector: Ozzy Osbourne
Garry Sharpe-Young

The Motörhead Collector's Guide
Mick Stevenson

Prophets And Sages: The 101 Greatest Progressive Rock Albums
Mark Powell

The Day The Country Died: A History Of Anarcho Punk 1980 To 1984
Ian Glasper

Burning Britain – A History Of UK Punk 1980 To 1984
Ian Glasper

Trapped In A Scene – UK Hardcore 1985-89
Ian Glasper

The Secret Life Of A Teenage Punk Rocker: The Andy Blade Chronicles
Andy Blade

Best Seat In The House – A Cock Sparrer Story
Steve Bruce

Death To Trad Rock – The Post-Punk Fanzine Scene 1982-87
John Robb

Johnny Thunders – In Cold Blood
Nina Antonia

Deathrow: The Chronicles Of Psychobilly
Alan Wilson

Hells Bent On Rockin: A History Of Psychobilly
Craig Brackenbridge

Music To Die For – The International Guide To Goth, Goth Metal, Horror Punk, Psychobilly Etc
Mick Mercer

Please visit:
www.cherryredbooks.co.uk
for further information and mail order.

The 7Ts and Big Break Records catalogues are available at all good record stores, or directly from *www.cherryred.co.uk*

GLAMCD1	GLITTER BAND, THE	BELL SINGLES COLLECTION
GLAMCD2	SHOWADDYWADDY	SHOWADDYWADDY
GLAMCD3	KENNY	SINGLES COLLECTION
GLAMCD4	SHOWADDYWADDY	STEP TWO
GLAMCD5	HELLO	GLAM ROCK SINGLES COLLECTION
GLAMCD6	LIEUTENANT PIGEON	THE BEST OF...
GLAMCD7	GEORDIE	SINGLES COLLECTION
GLAMCD8	GLITTERBAND, THE	HEY
GLAMCD9	SHOWADDYWADDY	THE BELL SINGLES 1974-76
GLAMCD10	SHOWADDYWADDY	TROCADERO
GLAMCD11	ARROWS	SINGLES COLLECTION
GLAMCD12	SHOWADDYWADDY	THE ARISTA SINGLES VOL. 1
GLAMCD13	SHOWADDYWADDY	RED STAR
GLAMCD14	BARRY BLUE	SINGLES COLLECTION
GLAMCD15	SHOWADDYWADDY	CREPES AND DREPES
GLAMCD16	SHOWADDYWADDY	BRIGHT LIGHTS
GLAMCD17	SHOWADDYWADDY	ARISTA SINGLES VOL. 2
GLAMCD18	MUNGO JERRY	THE POLYDOR YEARS
GLAMCD19	MUD	USE YOUR IMAGINATION
GLAMCD20	SHOWADDYWADDY	GOOD TIMES
GLAMCD21	SHOWADDYWADDY	LIVING LEGENDS
GLAMCD22	MUD	IT'S BETTER THAN WORKING
GLAMCD23	MUD	OFF THE RAK:SINGLES 1975-79
GLAMCD24	GLITTER BAND, THE	ROCK N ROLL DUDES
GLAMCD25	10 CC	10 CC
GLAMCD26	10 CC	SHEET MUSIC
GLAMCD27	10 CC	UK RECORDS SINGLES COLLECTION
GLAMCD28	SLIK	SLIK
GLAMCD29	CHICORY TIP	SINGLES COLLECTION
GLAMCD30	HELLO	KEEPS US OFF THE STREETS
GLAMCD31	HELLO	HELLO AGAIN
GLAMCD32	DRIFTERS	NOW / LOVE GAMES
GLAMCD33	DRIFTERS	THERE GOES MY FIRST LOVE
GLAMCD34	DRIFTERS	EVERY NITE'S A SATURDAY NIGHT
GLAMCD35	BAY CITY ROLLERS	IT'S A GAME
GLAMCD36	SMOKEY	PASS IT ROUND
GLAMCD37	SMOKEY	CHANGING ALL THE TIME
GLAMCD38	SMOKIE	MIDNIGHT CAFE
GLAMCD39	SMOKIE	BRIGHT LIGHTS & BACK ALLEYS
GLAMCD40	SMOKIE	MONTREAUX ALBUM
GLAMCD41	SMOKIE	THE OTHER SIDE OF THE ROAD
GLAMCD42	SMOKIE	SOLID GROUND
GLAMCD43	SMOKIE	STRANGERS IN PARADISE
GLAMCD44	DEAD END KIDS	BREAKOUT
GLAMCD45	BAY CITY ROLLERS	STRANGERS IN THE WIND
GLAMCD46	GEORDIE	HOPE YOU LIKE IT
GLAMCD47	BAY CITY ROLLERS	ELEVATOR
GLAMCD48	GEORDIE	DON'T BE FOOLED BY THE NAME

GLAMCD49	BAY CITY ROLLERS	VOXX
GLAMCD50	BAY CITY ROLLERS	RICOCHET
GLAMCD51	GEORDIE	SAVE THE WORLD
GLAMCD52	10 CC	MEANWHILE
GLAMCD53	10 CC	LOOK HEAR?
GLAMCD54	10 CC	FOOD FOR THOUGHT
GLAMCD55	10 CC	LIVE AND LET LIVE
GLAMCD56	SHOWADDYWADDY	JUMP, BOOGIE AND JIVE
GLAMCD57	OSMONDS, THE	OSMONDS / HOMEMADE
GLAMCD58	OSMONDS, THE	PHASE III / LIVE
GLAMCD59	OSMONDS, THE	CRAZY HORSES / THE PLAN
GLAMCD60	OSMONDS, THE	LOVE ME FOR A REASON/I'M STILL
GLAMCD61	DONNY OSMOND	TO YOU WITH LOVE, DONNY
GLAMCD62	DONNY OSMOND	A PORTRAIT OF DONNY/TOO YOUNG
GLAMCD63	DONNY OSMOND	ALONE TOGETHER / A TIME FOR US
GLAMCD64	DONNY OSMOND	DONNY / DISCO TRAIN
GLAMCD65	DONNY & MARIE (OSMOND)	IM LEAVING IT ALL UP TO YOU...
GLAMCD66	DONNY & MARIE (OSMOND)	DEEP PURPLE/NEW SEASON
GLAMCD67	DONNY & MARIE (OSMOND)	WINNING COMBINATION/GOIN'..
GLAMCD68	SUZI QUATRO	MAIN ATTRACTION
GLAMCD69	ALVIN STARDUST	THE UNTOUCHABLE
GLAMCD70	ALVIN STARDUST	ALVIN STARDUST
GLAMCD71	ALVIN STARDUST	ROCK WITH ALVIN
GLAMCD72	SAILOR	SAILOR & TROUBLE
GLAMCD73	OSMONDS, THE	BRAINSTORM / STEPPIN' OUT
GLAMCD74	TERRY JACKS	SEASONS IN THE SUN
GLAMCD75	MARIE OSMOND	PAPER ROSES/IN MY LITTLE...
GLAMCD76	MARIE OSMOND	WHO'S SORRY NOW/ THIS IS THE..
GLAMCD77	LITTLE JIMMY OSMOND	KILLER JOE / LITTLE ARROWS
GLAMCD78	MUD	ROCK ON / AS YOU LIKE IT
GLAMCDD79	BROTHERHOOD OF MAN	GOOD THINGS HAPPENING / LOVE..
GLAMCDD80	BROTHERHOOD OF MAN	OH BOY! / IMAGES
GLAMCD81	GUYS 'N' DOLLS	GUYS 'N' DOLLS
GLAMCDD82	HOT CHOCOLATE	CICERO PARK
GLAMCD83	HOT CHOCOLATE	HOT CHOCOLATE
GLAMCDD84	NOLAN SISTERS	NOLAN SISTERS / MAKING WAVES
GLAMCD85	HOT CHOCOLATE	MAN TO MAN
GLAMCD86	HOT CHOCOLATE	EVERY 1'S A WINNER
GLAMCDD87	RACEY	SMASH AND GRAB
GLAMCD88	SAILOR	THE THIRD STEP / CHECKPOINT
GLAMCD89	SAILOR	HIDEAWAY
GLAMCD90	DAVID SOUL	DAVID SOUL
GLAMCD91	DAVID SOUL	PLAYING TO AN AUDIENCE OF ONE
GLAMCDD92	NEW SEEKERS	TOGETHER AGAIN / ANTHEM
GLAMCDD93	BILLY OCEAN	BILLY OCEAN / CITY LIMIT
GLAMCD94	DAWN	CANDIDA / DAWN FEATURING..
GLAMCD95	BONNIE TYLER	THE WORLD STARTS TONIGHT
GLAMCD96	BONNIE TYLER	NATURAL FORCE
GLAMCDD97	DOOLEYS	THE DOOLEYS / THE CHOOSEN FEW
GLAMCDD98	DANA	HAVE A NICE DAY / LOVE SONGS
GLAMCDD99	MIDDLE OF THE ROAD	CHIRPY CHIRPY CHEEP CHEEP / AC

GLAMCDD100	NOLAN SISTERS	20 GIANT HITS PLUS THE TARGET
GLAMCD101	MARMALADE	THE ONLY LIGHT ON MY HORIZON N
GLAMCD102	BONNIE TYLER	DIAMOND CUT
GLAMCD103	BONNIE TYLER	GOODBYE TO THE ISLAND
GLAMCD104	RUBETTES, THE	WEAR IT'S AT
GLAMCD105	SWEET, THE	CUT ABOVE THE REST
GLAMCD106	SWEET, THE	WATERS EDGE
GLAMCD107	SWEET, THE	IDENTITY CRISIS
GLAMCD108	GEORGE MCCRAE	THE SINGLES 1974-76
GLAMCDD109	PAPERLACE	AND OTHER BITS OF MATERIAL/
GLAMCD110	NOLANS	PORTRAIT
GLAMCD111	MATCHBOX	MATCHBOX
GLAMCD112	MATCHBOX	MIDNIGHT DYNAMOS
GLAMCDD114	HEATWAVE	THE G.T.O. SINGLES COLLECTION
GLAM CD 115	DAVID ESSEX	IMPERIAL WIZARD
GLAM CD 116	DAVID ESSEX	HOT LOVE

CDBBR0001	GLORIA GAYNOR	NEVER CAN SAY GOODBYE
CDBBR0002	THREE DEGREES, THE	THE THREE DEGREES
CDBBR0003	GLORIA GAYNOR	EXPERIENCE
CDBBR0004	GLADYS KNIGHT & THE PIPS	ABOUT LOVE
CDBBR0005	ODYSSEY	ODYSSEY/NATIVE NEW YORKER
CDBBR0006	EVELYN CHAMPAGNE KING	GET LOOSE
CDBBR0007	BROOKLYN DREAMS	BROOKLYN DREAMS
CDBBR0008	TAVARES	NEW DIRECTIONS
CDBBR0009	DENIECE WILLIAMS	SONG BIRD
CDBBR0010	HEATWAVE	CURRENT
CDBBR0011	THREE DEGREES, THE	NEW DIMENSIONS
CDBBR0012	JUNE POINTER	BABY SISTER
CDBBR0013	HAROLD MELVIN & THE BLUE NOTES	BLACK & BLUE
CDBBR0014	EARTH WIND AND FIRE	FACES
CDBBR0015	EVELYN CHAMPAGNE KING	SMOOTH TALK
CDBBR0016	A TASTE OF HONEY	A TASTE OF HONEY
CDBBR0017	DENIECE WILLIAMS	WHEN LOVE COMES CALLING
CDBBR0018	HAROLD MELVIN & THE BLUE NOTES	I MISS YOU
CDBBR0019	A TASTE OF HONEY	ANOTHER TASTE
CDBBR0020	THREE DEGREES, THE	INTERNATIONAL (TAKE GOOD CARE OF YOURSELF)
CDBBR0021	HEATWAVE	HOT PROPERTY
CDBBR0022	POINTER SISTERS	SPECIAL THINGS
CDBBR0023	BILLY OCEAN	NIGHTS (FEEL LIKE GETTING DOWN
CDBBR0024	HEATWAVE	CANDLES
CDBBR0025	POINTER SISTERS	SO EXCITED
CDBBR0026	BROOKLYN DREAMS	SLEEPLESS NIGHTS

For further details please visit:
www.cherryred.co.uk/7ts and www.cherryred.co.uk/bbr

7T's
THE HOME OF
QUALITY '70s
REISSUES
PACKED WITH
BIG NAMES
HIT SINGLES
LOST CLASSICS
BONUS TRACKS
RARITIES
AND CD FIRSTS

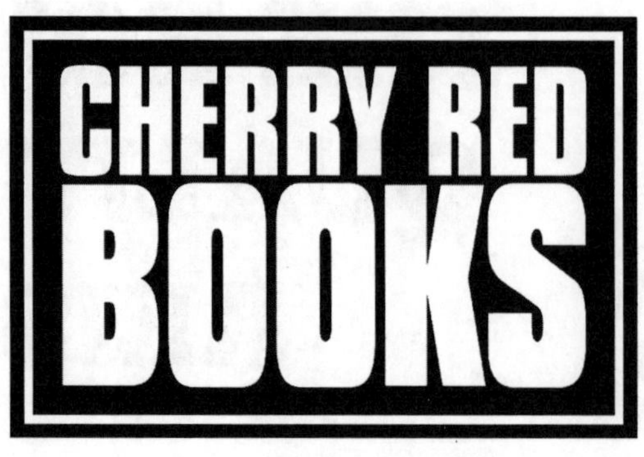
CHERRY RED
BOOKS